THE SOLDIER'S COMPREHENSIVE STUDY MANUAL

Over 6,000 Questions & Answers
Over 50 Subject Areas

6th Edition

SOLDIER BOARDS

PROMOTION BOARDS

SERGEANT MORALES BOARD

SERGEANT AUDIE MURPHY BOARD

compiled by:
d. w. creech

See us at:
http://bandabooks.com

The Soldier's Comprehensive Study Manual

ISSN 1064-1319

ISBN 0-89826-060-4

SIXTH EDITION
FIRST PRINTING

This book is not an official publication of the Department of Defense or the Department of the Army, nor does its publication in any way imply its endorsement by these agencies.

PRINTING HISTORY:

1st Edition = 1989
2nd Edition = 1990
3rd Edition = 1991
4th Edition = 1992
5th Edition = 1994
6th Edition = 1996

Printed in the United States of America.

NOTE: If you bought this book without a cover then it has been sold illegally. Please contact Bagwell & Associates at:

329 North Dogwood Road
Powell, TN 37849

Dedicated to

THE SOLDIER

In continuing memory of John Andrew Creech

Special thanks to Lynda - for tolerating my affair with the word processor and for making this book possible.

Many thanks also to *Bagwell & Associates* for helping to make this book a reality.

PREFACE

This is a COMPREHENSIVE study manual and, as such, will accommodate the needs of a full spectrum of readers - from the private E-1 to the officer; from the mildly curious to the soldier who thirsts for knowledge. It doesn't matter whether you are studying to make "the MAN" on guard duty, studying for selection into the Sergeant Morales Club, or actually asking the questions - this study manual has most, if not all, of what you need.

It is not the intention of this study manual to provide an alternative to Field Manuals and relevant Army publications. Information is constantly being revised and incorporated into an increasingly sophisticated, rapidly changing Army. Even as you read this paragraph information is becoming obsolete and publications are being updated.

Although you have my personal assurance that this study manual is one of the most current, thoroughly researched sources of military information available, readers are strongly advised that all information of a technical or specialized nature be researched in the appropriate, up-dated publications.

My sincere hope is that this study manual will help you to "BE ALL YOU CAN BE!!"

ABOUT THE 6th EDITION

In the two years since the last edition of this study manual many changes have been made to Army regulations, field manuals, and related publications. You will find, for your convenience, that in this edition new or changed material will appear as double-underlined text, while obsolete material will appear as ~~strike-through~~ text. The following subjects covered in this study manual have had significant changes: M203 Grenade Launcher, Grenades (with the addition of the MK-19 Grenade Machine Gun), Light Anti-tank Weapons (with the addition of the M136 AT-4), NBC, and Maintenance Procedures. Of course, the Pre-Board Review and Study Template sections have been updated accordingly.

ACKNOWLEDGEMENTS

This study manual was compiled through the exhaustive research of Technical Manuals, Field Manuals, Pamphlets, and a diversity of other US Army publications. A list of references is provided in the rear of this manual. If any acknowledgements have been inadvertently omitted, I would appreciate receiving full information so that proper credit may be given in future editions. As for myself, I accept credit only for the research and time-consuming compilation of the material contained herein.

STUDY GUIDE
TABLE OF CONTENTS

STUDY GUIDE
TABLE OF CONTENTS

STUDY GUIDE
TABLE OF CONTENTS

TOPIC	LOCATION

APPENDIX

BOARD PROCEDURES

---

board n. 1. A long, flat slab of sawed lumber; plank. 7. A table at which official meetings are held; council table. 8. An organized body of administrators or investigators.

The mere mention of the word "BOARD" is enough to strike fear in the hearts of many soldiers. Stress, in the form of intense anxiety, is a common reaction. If given a choice most soldiers would avoid BOARDS like they would avoid the plague. The fact is, however, that if you intend to stay in the Army for more than a day BOARDS **will not** be a choice - **BOARDS ARE A REALITY!** They are necessary for both advancement and recognition and in today's smaller, more competitive Army you can bet that BOARDS will be a major discriminator in retaining and advancing the most qualified soldiers. The soldiers that recognize this fact early in their careers will be the ones that are justly promoted and/or recognized for achievement. They will be the ones that are properly prepared to face the challenges of today's Army.

The above definition of "board" (provided by the American Heritage Dictionary) tells us that a BOARD is basically an organized body of investigators. Who these "investigators" are is largely dependent on what type of board it is, but for our purposes they normally consist of the senior NCOs of the command - soldiers that have been in your place many times in their careers. What are they investigating? Again, this is dependent on what type of board it is but you can be assured that most boards will be looking for two things:

(1) Appearance; and

(2) Knowledge (and your ability to verbally express this knowledge).

Keep in mind that the board members understand what you are going through. They are not there to hassle or intimidate you but to see how well you have prepared yourself.

When most soldiers think of the Board it is in reference to the Promotion Board - either for promotion to Sergeant or to Staff Sergeant. However, Boards come in a variety of "flavors." Some units require Boarding for promotion to the rank of Specialist. There are retention Boards and unit or higher level Soldier of the Month/Quarter/Year Boards. In addition, there are an assortment of honors and awards that require Boards to select the most competent or qualified individuals. Finally, there are the Sergeant Morales Board in Europe and the Sergeant Audie Murphy Board stateside. Selection into either or both of these organizations represents the pinnacle of NCO achievement.

Q. What is the key to a successful Board appearance?

A. **PREPARATION**

I've had people ask me if I ever get nervous before or during a Board. The answer is an emphatic "**Yes**, I most certainly do," - and so does everyone else. If they say they don't then they are probably not being honest with themselves. Nervousness, anxiety, call it what you will - these conditions are a natural reaction to stressful situations. Sure, some people get more nervous than others, but that is due to a number of factors. The solution is a matter of understanding stress and seeking ways to control it.

First of all, what is stress? Put simply, stress is a physical or psychological response to a demand that is placed on it. Normally, the greater the demand (or perceived demand) the more intense the response. Everyone responds to stress in different ways. Listed below are some common responses:

- tension headache
- hostility
- high blood pressure
- fatigue
- irritability
- muscle tension

- profuse sweating or sweaty palms
- loss of concentration
- upset stomach
- anxiety (uneasiness/apprehension)
- sleep problems
- withdrawal
- backaches
- shortness of breath

So, how do you get rid of the stress? You don't. It'll always be there but you can lessen the effects of stress by being **adequately prepared**. This means starting weeks or even months before a BOARD and keeping yourself on a regular program of repetitious study. Waiting until the night before to "cram" for a BOARD will only serve to compound the stress and will almost always assure disappointing results.

Many physiological stressors are self-imposed. It is important to maintain a proper diet, avoid consumption of alcohol, and get plenty of rest. Be aware that some personality characteristics only serve to exacerbate stress. Examples include:

- perfectionism
- unrealistic self-expectations
- excessive need for achievement, belonging, or power
- inflexibility
- loss of perspective

If one or more of these characteristics describe your personality then be aware that you may be particularly vulnerable.

Some of the tools provided in this Study Manual are designed to help you maximize your study time. Use them, they worked for me.

BOARD PREPARATION POINTERS:

1. PROPER UNIFORM. There's an old saying that goes something like this, "You only have one chance to make a good first impression!" This is so true and it is a natural reaction for people to judge others based on first impressions. If your first impression is a bad one then you're likely to find yourself fighting an uphill battle for the remainder of the board. Face it, you don't need the additional stress. Take adequate time to insure that you are in proper uniform. Use the following checklist:

< > The uniform should be clean, pressed and correctly fitted. The trousers of the uniform should reach the top of the instep and be cut on a diagonal line to reach a point approximately midway between the top of the heel and the top of the standard shoe in the back (may have a slight break in the front). Skirts not more than one inch above, or two inches below the middle of the knee. Remove all loose threads.

< > Insure that shoes do not have worn heels and that they are highly shined. Use edge dressing on the edges of shoes and soles, unless prohibited by local SOP.

< > Insure that collar insignia are positioned correctly and are highly polished. Insure name plate is correctly placed. If in doubt, refer to AR 670-1.

< > Have all required patches and chevrons sewn properly on the uniform. Although not required, machine-sewn patches and chevrons present a more professional appearance than hand-sewn ones.

< > All authorized decorations, tabs and badges will be worn. Insure they are worn correctly. Be able to describe them without looking.

BOARD PROCEDURES

< > Be clean shaven and have a fresh haircut. Mustaches are not recommended but if you have one, insure that it is trimmed IAW AR 670-1. Females should be neatly coiffured and excessive cosmetics should not be used.

< > Remember that although not required for enlisted personnel, the all-polyester uniform presents a better appearance than the issue polyester-wool blend uniform.

< > Make sure you are wearing identification tags and that you have your ID Card in your possession.

< > Ensure that your gig line is straight and that your brass belt buckle is highly polished as these items may be checked.

< > All pockets are buttoned.

< > Fingernails clean and trimmed to within 1/8". No wearing of distasteful jewelry.

< > Do not wear sunglasses - even if they are prescription.

2. REPORTING. Normally there will be from three to six members on a board. The senior member of the board, the President, is the person you report to. He/She will normally be seated in the center of the board members. When reporting, enter and proceed by the most direct route to a distance of approximately three feet from the front edge of the table in front of the President of the Board. Halt at the position of attention and give the proper hand salute. While saluting, report in the following manner: "<Sir><Ma'am><SGM>, Private Jones reports." Hold your salute until you have finished reporting and the President returns your salute. At this time you may be asked to execute a combination of facing movements so that the Board members can view your uniform appearance, posture, hair, etc, from different angles as well as your ability to make these movements correctly. You should be prepared for this, as executing a simple facing movement incorrectly may cost you points (practice the ABOUT FACE movement as it tends to give people the most trouble). If you are asked to take one step to the rear, make sure that you start with your LEFT foot!

NOTE: If you take the time to practice these movements before a Board, be sure to do it with the shoes you will be wearing during the Board. You'll be surprised at the difference between executing an ABOUT FACE movement with boots, and executing the same movement with dress shoes.

3. SITTING POSITION. After reporting and the President has returned your salute, he/she may direct you to be seated. At this point most Boards are interested in finding out what you know, not how well you can sit at attention. So relax, take up a comfortable but professional sitting position, and get ready to show them what you know.

4. ANSWERING QUESTIONS. When answering a question, or giving an opinion, direct your answer to the member of the board who asked the question. As an example, SFC Smith, a member of the board, asks the question, "What does the color blue on a map represent?". Your reply would be "Sergeant, the color blue on the map represents water features." Always address the person who asked the question (by Sir or Ma'am if he/she is an Officer or by SGT/SGM if he/she is an NCO) and give your answer. Be enthusiastic when giving your answer or opinions and use eye to eye contact. It is important for you to remember that you will

not be rated on your answers alone, but also on how well you present them. Speech and voice control, vocabulary, attitude and enthusiasm will enhance your appearance and thus add points. Don't jeopardize yourself by giving answers you do not know to be correct. An incorrect answer may be worse than an honest "SGM, I do not know the answer to that question" or "1SG, I cannot recall the answer to that question". If you feel your voice starting to waiver because of nervousness, raising your voice will sometimes help to steady it. If you do not understand a question, ask the board member to repeat it or rephrase it. Don't mumble or begin a reply with "Uh....","I think...", or "I believe...". This indicates indecisiveness and could cost you points. Never say "I'm sorry" if you don't know the answer. Lastly, avoid "talking" with your hands (try to keep them resting comfortably on your upper legs), and don't look at the ceiling or make other noticeable gestures.

5. EXITING. When you are dismissed by the President of the Board, assume the position of attention at approximately the same location in which you reported and give the hand salute. After your salute is returned exit by the most direct route.

6. OTHER POINTERS.

a. Don't display mannerisms such as rolling your eyes, sighing, or making extreme hand gestures. Don't shuffle your feet or cross your legs.

b. It is helpful and impressive to repeat the question as part of your answer. For example, "SGM, the lifesaving steps are..."

c. When asked your opinion, be sure it is your opinion. Board members do not penalize you for an opinion they don't agree with. They only want to evaluate your knowledge, your speaking ability, and your ability to intelligently present an opinion; however, make sure your response is a sound and logical one.

d. It is a good practice to be keeping abreast of current local and world events. If you don't do this on a regular basis then you should at least begin reading the newspaper about one week in advance of your Board appearance so that you will have a knowledgeable grasp of what is happening in the world around you. Pay particular attention to headline news on the day of your Board but keep in mind that you may be asked to give the details leading up to a particular event. Furthermore, listen to the TV or Radio for any late-breaking news flashes and check to see if any important historical events took place on the same day as your Board.

e. Check your 201 file and DA Form 2A and 2-1. Make sure that they are up-to-date. Check your promotion point worksheet (if applicable) to ensure that it is correct.

f. You may be asked to tell the board members about yourself, your military career, plans, ambitions, etc. Know what you are going to say in advance but don't make it sound rehearsed.

7. MISCELLANEOUS. Before appearing before a Board you should receive a memorandum listing the board members, subject areas to be covered, the uniform, location, time, and any other special instructions regarding the Board. Listed below are a sampling of the subject areas you may be required to know. Use it as a checklist in preparing yourself for the board.

< > Duties and Responsibilities of NCO's
< > Leadership
< > Counseling
< > Flags & Guidons
< > Drill & Ceremonies
< > NCOERs

BOARD PROCEDURES

< > Current Events
< > Military Justice (UCMJ)
< > First Aid
< > Physical Training
< > Guard Duty
< > Maintenance Procedures
< > Code of Conduct
< > Military Customs and Courtesy
< > NBC
< > History of your Unit/Division
* < > Selected STP 21-1 Tasks (Common Tasks)
< > Army Promotion System
< > Map Reading and Land Navigation
** < > Military Programs
< > Chain of Command
< > M16A1/A2 Rifle and your personal weapon (if different)
< > Intelligence
< > Vehicle/aircraft recognition
< > Wear of ID tags
< > Field Sanitation
< > ~~SDT~~/CTT/ITEP
< > Physical Security
< > Wear of the Uniform
< > Unit/Division Standards
< > Weight Control

* ..... To include the following:
- communications
- grenades
- light anti-armor weapons
- M18A1 claymore mine
- M203 grenade launcher
- M60 machinegun
- Law of Land Warfare

** .... To include the following:
- Quality of Life Program (QOLP)
- Army Community Services (ACS)
- Army Emergency Relief (AER)
- ADAPCP
- American Red Cross (ARC)
- Army Safety Program
- Equal Opportunity (EO)

..... Use GTA 17-2-13 Armored Vehicle Recognition cards and GTA 44-2-10 Aircraft Recognition cards. Also, FM 44-30 & FM 1-402

.... Make sure you are wearing them!

REMEMBER....

"In the end, it is not the board members who determine the outcome of a board, it is the members that appear before the board."

GOOD LUCK !!!!

CHAIN OF COMMAND
AR 600-20

Q. What Army regulation defines Army command policies to include the "Chain of Command", it's purpose and how it can best be used to accomplish the overall mission of the Army?
A. AR 600-20, "Army Command Policy".

Q. What additional purpose does AR 600-20 serve?
A. It provides guidance covering military discipline and conduct, precedence of rank, and the military Equal Opportunity (EO) Program.

NOTE: For questions regarding the Army Equal Opportunity program, refer to section 34, "Military Programs."

Q. What is meant by the term "Chain of Command"?
A. It is the succession of commanders, superior to subordinate, through which command is exercised. It is the most important organizational technique in use in the Army today.

Q. What are the three formal channels of communication in the Army?
A. The Chain of Command, the NCO Support Channel, and Staff and Technical Channels.

Q. Describe the structure of the NCO Support Channel.
A. It begins with the commander's CSM and ends with the section, squad, or team leader.

Q. How does the chain of command support the NCO support channel?
A. By legally punishing those who challenge a sergeant's authority.

Q. Who is the only person who performs as both a member of the Chain of Command and the NCO Support Channel?
A. The section, squad, or team leader.

Q. What is "command"?
A. The authority a person in the military service lawfully exercises over subordinates by virtue of rank and assignment or position.

Q. Who is the only civilian authorized to exercise command in the military?
A. The President of the United States.

Q. What are the key elements of command?
A. Authority and responsibility.

Q. How does a commander exercise command?
A. Through subordinate commanders.

Q. What is "military rank"?
A. The relative position or degree of precedence granted military personnel marking their station in military life. It confers eligibility to exercise command or authority in the military within the limits of prescribed law.

Q. Rank in the military is divided into what classes and grades?
A. General Officer -- BG through General, including General of the Army (GA).
Field Officers -- Major through Colonel
Company Officers -- Second Lieutenant through Captain
Warrant Officers - WO1 through CW4, and Master Warrant (CW5).
Cadets -- Cadet, Senior Advanced (ROTC) to Cadet, US Military Academy

CHAIN OF COMMAND
AR 600-20

Candidates -- Warrant Officer Candidate to Officer Candidate (OCS)
Senior Noncommissioned Officers -- SFC through CSM, including SMA
Junior Noncommissioned Officers and Specialist -- SPC, CPL, SGT, SSG
Privates -- PV1 through PFC

Q. Rank is generally held by virtue of _________ or ________ in the Army.
A. Office or grade.

Q. What is the difference between pay grade and rank?
A. The pay grade is an abbreviated numerical device with useful applications in pay management, personnel accounting, automated data organization, and other administrative fields. However, the **pay grade alone should not be used as a form of address or title in place of the proper title of address or grade of rank**. When military personnel are addressed or referred to, orally or in writing, the grade of rank will normally be used.

Q. What is the exception to the last sentence in the above question?
A. Chaplains; all chaplains are addressed as Chaplain, regardless of military grade or professional title.

Q. Describe the precedence of rank between members of the Army and other Services serving with the Army.
A. Members of other Services serving with the Army have equal status with Army members of equivalent grade of rank (see "Comparative Ranks", appendix C).

Q. The abbreviation SP4 for Specialist changed to SPC effective with the implementation of what system?
A. SIDPERS-3 (Standard Installation Division Personnel System-3).

Q. What is the difference between MANAGEMENT and LEADERSHIP?
A. Management has an INDIRECT influence on subordinates while leadership has a DIRECT influence on subordinates.

Q. What is the Sergeant Major of the Army?
A. The senior Sergeant Major grade of rank. It designates the senior enlisted position of the Army.

Q. What is a Command Sergeant Major?
A. This is the position title designating the senior noncommissioned officer of the command at battalion or higher levels.

Q. What is the difference between a Specialist grade and a noncommissioned officer?
A. A Specialist is a selected individual (enlisted) appointed to discharge duties requiring a high degree of skill. Normally, their duties do not require exercising enlisted command of troops, which is an NCO's responsibility.

Q. What is an "ADC-S"? "ADC-M"?
A. Asst Division Commander for Support; ADC for Maneuver.

Q. Which of the above is the ranking ADC?
A. Generally, the ADC-M.

CHAIN OF COMMAND
AR 600-20

When most people refer to the "Chain of Command", they are actually talking about two separate channels of communication lumped together. Not only is there the "Chain of Command", but also the "NCO Support Channel". It is important to keep in mind that these are two distinct and separate channels having the same goal of mission accomplishment but operating in slightly different ways. Local channels of communication will generally be set up as indicated in the example below. Depending on your assignment, variations may exist. A sample Chain of Command/NCO Support Channel for a typical unit is included as an example.

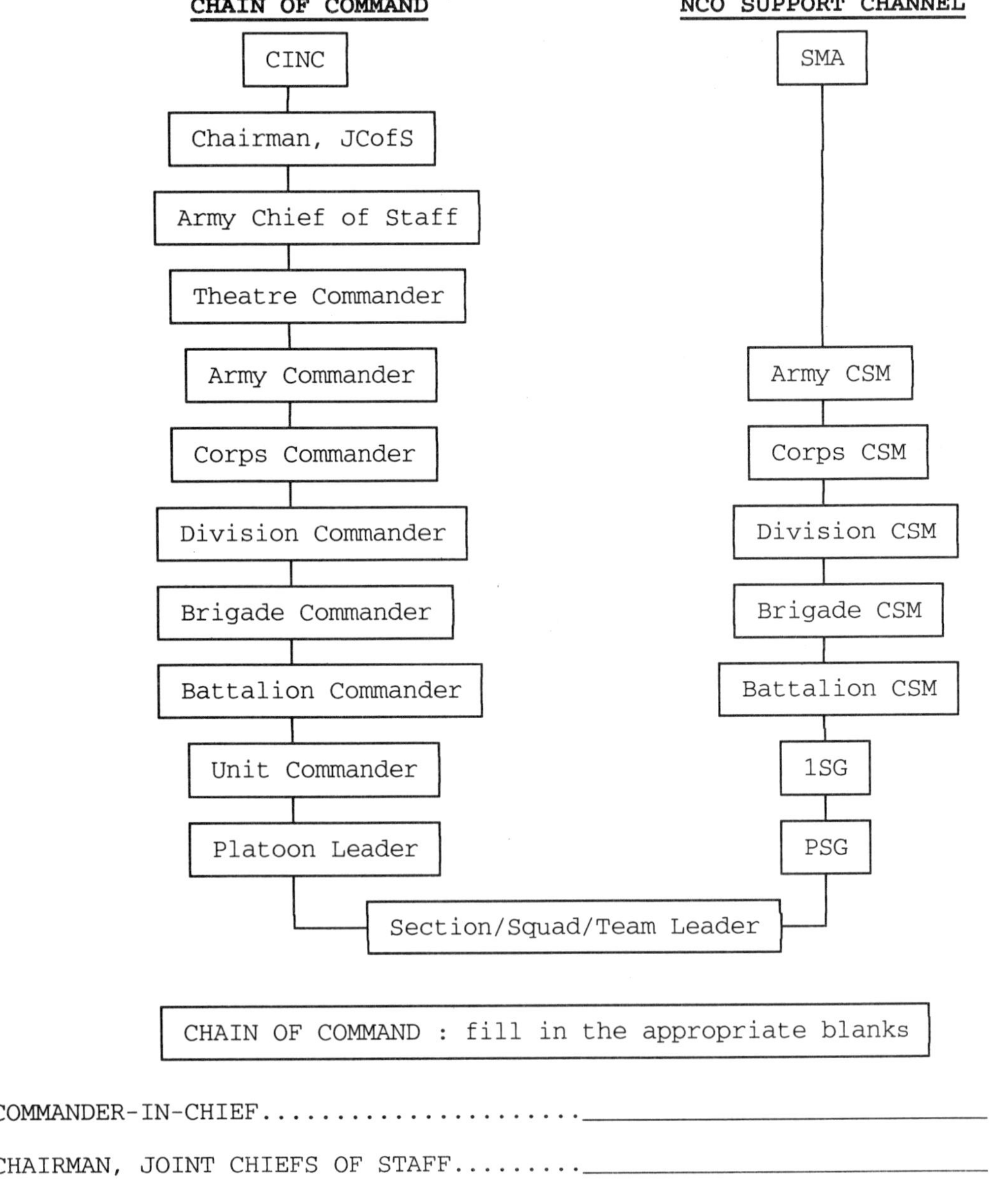

CHAIN OF COMMAND : fill in the appropriate blanks

COMMANDER-IN-CHIEF....................._______________

CHAIRMAN, JOINT CHIEFS OF STAFF........._______________

CHAIN OF COMMAND
AR 600-20

ARMY CHIEF OF STAFF.................... ____________________

THEATRE COMMANDER...................... ____________________

CORPS COMMANDER........................ ____________________

DIVISION COMMANDER..................... ____________________

BRIGADE COMMANDER...................... ____________________

BATTALION COMMANDER.................... ____________________

COMPANY/TROOP COMMANDER................ ____________________

PLATOON LEADER......................... ____________________

SECTION/SQUAD/TEAM LEADER .... ____________________

NCO SUPPORT CHANNEL

SERGEANT MAJOR OF THE ARMY............. ____________________

THEATRE CSM............................ ____________________

CORPS CSM.............................. ____________________

DIVISION CSM........................... ____________________

BRIGADE CSM............................ ____________________

BATTALION CSM.......................... ____________________

COMPANY 1SG............................ ____________________

PLATOON SGT............................ ____________________

SECTION/SQUAD/TEAM LEADER .... ____________________

MISCELLANEOUS

VICE-PRESIDENT .... ____________________

SECRETARY OF DEFENSE................... ____________________

SECRETARY OF THE ARMY.................. ____________________

SECRETARY OF STATE .... ____________________

SECRETARY OF TREASURY .... ____________________

SECRETARY OF LABOR .... ____________________

CHAIN OF COMMAND
AR 600-20

SPEAKER OF THE HOUSE ....______________________________

SENATE MAJORITY LEADER ....______________________________

CHIEF JUSTICE, SUPREME COURT ....______________________________

ADC-M (yours)..........................______________________________

ADC-S (yours)..........................______________________________

COMMUNITY COMMANDER....................______________________________

PRIME MINISTER, GREAT BRITAIN ....______________________________

PRESIDENT, USSR ....______________________________
(previously "General Secretary")

______________________________ ....______________________________

______________________________ ....______________________________

______________________________ ....______________________________

UNITED STATES ARMY HISTORY

Q. When was the US Army created and by what?
A. June 14, 1775; it was created by the Second Continental Congress.

Q. Who was the first Commander in Chief of the Continental Army and when?
A. George Washington on July 3, 1775.

Q. When and where did the Army receive its first real training and by whom?
A. During the winter of 1778 at Valley Forge by the former Prussian officer, Baron Friedrich von Steuben.

Q. When and with what event did the United States emerge as a world power?
A. In 1898, with the outbreak of the Spanish-American War.

Q. When and by what means was the Medal of Honor established?
A. 12 July 1862, by a congressional act.

Q. By what act and when was the Department of the Army established?
A. The National Security Act of 1947 created the Department of the Army which was previously known as the War Department.

Q. What famous General was relieved of his command during the Korean War?
A. General of the Army Douglas MacArthur.

Q. What is the official Army song? When was it dedicated? Who composed the music and when? And what was this song originally known as?
A. "The Army Goes Rolling Along"; it was dedicated on Veterans Day by the Secretary of the Army, November 11, 1956 (however, it was not officially announced until December 12, 1957); it was composed by Lt (later BG) Edmund L. Gruber in 1908; originally known as the "Caisson Song".

Q. Name the Army's newest branch.
A. Aviation.

Q. In 1926 Congress changed the name of the Air Service to what?
A. The Army Air Corp.

Q. What agency was created on August 10, 1949?
A. The Department of Defense.

Q. By what generic name were the earliest American military organizations called?
A. Militia.

Q. What are the words on the official seal of the Army?
A. "This we'll Defend".

Q. The signing of what peace treaty ended the War of 1812?
A. The Treaty of Ghent.

Q. The signing of what treaty ended the Mexican War?
A. The Treaty of Guadelupe Hidalgo.

Q. How long did the Mexican siege of the Alamo last?
A. 13 days.

Q. What did an Executive Order signed by President Eisenhower promulgate?
A. The Code of Conduct for members of the United States Armed Forces.

UNITED STATES ARMY HISTORY

Q. What legislation provided the National Guard with Federal funds, prescribed twice-a-month drills and annual training, and patterned the National Guard's organization and equipment after that of the Regular Army?
A. The Militia Act of 1903.

Q. What Army branch began as a section of the Signal Corps?
A. Aviation.

Q. How long did it take the Army to build the Panama Canal?
A. 8 yrs.

Q. On what date was the Army Flag dedicated?
A. June 14, 1956 (the 181st anniversary of the US Army).

Q. Name the flag hoisted by General George Washington in January of 1776 at Cambridge, Massachusetts as the standard of the Continental Army.
A. The Grand Union Flag.

Q. What is "DA"?
A. The Department of the Army.

Q. To what groups does the term "Total Army" refer?
A. The Active Army, the Army Reserve Components (USAR and ARNG) and the Army's Civilian Workforce.

Q. Name the city where Roosevelt, Churchill, and the combined chiefs of staff met to plan future WWII strategy.
A. Casablanca.

Q. When was the Uniform Code of Military Justice enacted?
A. May, 1950.

Q. What did the Hoover Committee recommend renaming the National Military Establishment?
A. The Department of Defense.

Q. Name the plane that dropped the first atomic bomb.
A. The "Enola Gay".

Q. The outbreak of the Korean War caused what to be extended until 1959?
A. The draft.

Q. What was the password used by the Army on D-Day, June 6, 1944?
A. "Mickey Mouse".

Q. For what action was the Army's first battle streamer awarded?
A. The battle of Fort Ticonderoga on May 10, 1775.

Q. On August 16, 1903 the first ________ took office.
A. Chief of Staff of the Army.

Q. What information was contained on the first dog tags used by the Army?
A. Name, rank and unit.

Q. When initially authorized, the Medal of Honor could only be awarded to whom?
A. NCO's and privates.

Q. What colors are the Army's battle streamers from the Civil War?
A. Blue and Gray.

UNITED STATES ARMY HISTORY

Q. Who within the Army built the Panama Canal?
A. The Corps of Engineers.

Q. What is May 12, 1945 called?
A. VE Day (Germany surrendered).

Q. On what date did North Korea invade South Korea?
A. June 25, 1950.

Q. How many Allied powers occupied Germany after WWII? Who were they?
A. Four; United States, France, Soviet Union, Great Britain.

Q. When the US Army Flag is displayed in a stationary position, the streamer embroidered with what words should be in the center facing forward and completely identifiable?
A. "Yorktown 1781".

Q. What was the name of the only female servicewoman killed as a result of enemy action in Vietnam?
A. 1st Lt Sharon A. Lane of the Army Nurse Corps.

Q. When did the Air Force separate from the Army?
A. September, 1947.

Q. Where did Roosevelt, Churchill and Chiang Kai Shek meet to pledge continuation of the war against Japan until unconditional surrender?
A. Cairo, Egypt.

Q. What social reform in the Army was precipitated by the Korean War?
A. Racial integration.

Q. When was the infantry branch established?
A. June 14, 1775, with the creation of the US Army.

Q. What was the coalition of Germany, Italy and Japan, which lasted from 1936-1945, called?
A. The Axis.

Q. What was the name of the daily newspaper for US Armed Forces in WWII?
A. "The Stars and Stripes".

Q. When did the Grenada operation commence?
A. October 25, 1983.

Q. Of the eight major wars since the Revolution, five were fought under a Congressional Declaration of War. Name the three which were not.
A. Civil War, Korean War, Vietnam War.

Q. Name the group which recommended the addition of large numbers of helicopters to Army divisions.
A. The Howze Board.

Q. What does the term "CARS" refer to?
A. Combat Arms Regimental System.

Q. What was "Operation Downfall"?
A. It was the WWII plan for the invasion of Japan. It was never executed due to the Japanese surrender.

UNITED STATES ARMY HISTORY

Q. During WWII, a small flag with one or more blue stars on it placed in the front window represented what?
A. Family members serving their country.

Q. During WWII, a small flag with one or more gold stars on it placed in the front window represented what?
A. Family members killed serving their country.

Q. Name the single horse that survived the Battle of Little Big Horn and for the rest of his days appeared saddled, but riderless, in all 7th Cavalry parades.
A. Comanche.

Q. In what war was the helicopter first used on any scale?
A. Korean War.

Q. In which US war did the greatest number of American casualties occur?
A. Civil War.

Q. What was the German term used to describe a rapid, violent, overwhelming attack?
A. "Blitzkrieg".

Q. What was the greatest single mass troop operation in Army history?
A. The Meuse-Argonne Offensive of WWI, where more than 1,200,000 Americans advanced on a 90-mile front.

Q. Pershing considered it an American victory, yet the Meuse-Argonne resulted in how many American casualties?
A. 120,000 (1 out of every 10 men died).

Q. What division was the rear guard unit for X Corps' evacuation at Hungnam in December of 1950?
A. The 3rd Infantry Division.

Q. During the Korean War, what was "Task Force Dog"?
A. A task force of the 3rd Infantry Division, which fought inland to assist X Corps during it's evacuation to Hungnam.

Q. What is the common name of the last major German offensive of WWII, which occurred in December 1944/January 1945?
A. The Battle of the Bulge.

Q. What map reference was used as the line of demarcation during the Korean War?
A. The 38th parallel.

Q. From what port city in North Korea did X Corps conduct its withdrawal in December of 1950?
A. Hungnam.

Q. What was the full scale assault conducted by the enemy on all major South Vietnamese cities in early 1968 called?
A. The Tet Offensive.

Q. Name the weapon for which General Matthew Ridgeway reinstituted training for combat soldiers during the Korean War.
A. The bayonet.

UNITED STATES ARMY HISTORY

Q. What geographic feature was the line of demarcation between North and South Vietnam?
A. The 17th Parallel.

Q. In September 1944, the US Army's first penetration of the German border occurred at what point?
A. Remagen.

Q. What was the defensive line that guarded the heartland of Germany in WWII called?
A. The Siegfried Line.

Q. Name the longest war in US history.
A. The Vietnam War.

Q. What was the name of the largest battle of the Pacific Theatre in WWII?
A. Okinawa.

Q. What was the name given to the area that divided North and South Vietnam along the 17th parallel?
A. The DMZ (Demilitarized Zone)

Q. The US Army landed on two of the five invasion beaches of Normandy. Name them.
A. Utah and Omaha beaches.

Q. What was called the "Great War"?
A. WWI.

Q. Name the decisive AEF Offensive that was a prelude to victory in WWI.
A. The Meuse-Argonne Offensive.

Q. What was the name of the first major WWI victory won by the US Army under its own command?
A. The St Mihiel Offensive.

Q. What were the Japanese code words that confirmed the attack on Pearl Harbor?
A. "Climb Mount Niitake".

Q. What was the famous Japanese assault cry signaling victory or death?
A. "Banzai".

Q. The Meuse-Argonne in WWI was nicknamed the __________ because of the huge number of casualties suffered there.
A. "Meat grinder".

Q. What was the name of the devices used by the Chinese communists in Korea to enable convoy movement at night?
A. Retractable bridges.

Q. What was the Allied code name for the US Army in WWII?
A. "Destiny".

Q. Who was code-named "Duckpin" during WWII?
A. General Dwight D. Eisenhower.

Q. Who was the most popular WWII pin-up girl?
A. Betty Grable.

UNITED STATES ARMY HISTORY

Q. Who was Iva D'Auquino?
A. "Tokyo Rose".

Q. Who could properly be called "The Father of US Army Helicopter Operations"?
A. Major-General Harry W.O. Kinnard.

Q. When did "The Star Spangled Banner" officially become the National Anthem by law?
A. March 3, 1931, title 36, US Code 170.

Q. Who wrote our first manual by which ceremonies were conducted in America? What was this book called?
A. Baron Frederick von Stuben; "The Blue Book".

Q. Where did the word "Cavalry" originate? What does it mean?
A. In France; it is the French word for "horse".

Q. Who was the first General to lead the American Army?
A. General George Washington.

Q. Who is the Father of American Rangers?
A. Maj Robert Rogers, 1756.

Q. What famous set of "rules" were written by Maj. Robert Rogers during the French and Indian Wars and can still be applied to the US Army today?
A. "Robert Rogers' Famous Ranging Rules" (known as Rogers' Rules).

Q. On what date did the Japanese attack Pearl Harbor?
A. December 7, 1941.

Q. When was the first atomic bomb dropped on Japan? On what city was this bomb dropped?
A. August 6, 1945; Hiroshima.

Q. When and where was the second atomic bomb dropped on Japan?
A. August 9, 1945 on Nagasaki.

Q. Who was president during the Korean Conflict?
A. Harry S. Truman.

Q. Who was "Uncle Sam"?
A. Samuel Wilson, a government meat inspector during the War of 1812.

Q. What peninsula did the US and its Allies make an assault on 6 June 1944?
A. Normandy.

Q. Who was the first Command Sergeant Major of the US Army?
A. CSM William O. Woolridge.

Q. What was D-Day?
A. 6 June 1944, France was liberated when the US and its Allies stormed Normandy beach.

Q. What was the TET Offensive?
A. Major Communist offensive of 1968 in Vietnam.

Q. What is the Army motto?
A. This we'll defend.

UNITED STATES ARMY HISTORY

Q. The first field manual was commonly known as the "Blue Book". What was its actual title?
A. "The Regulations for the Order and Discipline to the Troops of the United States".

Q. When was the Constitution of the United States written?
A. 1787 (ratified in 1789).

CODE OF CONDUCT & SERE/LAW OF LAND WARFARE & GENEVA CONVENTION
AR 350-30/FM 27-2/FM 27-10

CODE OF CONDUCT

Q. What does "SERE" stand for?
A. Survival, Evasion, Resistance, and Escape.

Q. What AR covers the Code of Conduct and SERE?
A. AR 350-30.

Q. Who authorized the Publishing of the Code of Conduct in 1955?
A. President Dwight D. Eisenhower, Executive Order 10631.

Q. What is the Code of Conduct and what is it's purpose?
A. It is a set of rules that outline the basic responsibilities and obligations of all members of the Armed Forces of the United States during times of conflict. It is designed to give the U.S. Soldier strength and guidance should they fall into the hands of the enemy.

Q. The Code of Conduct has how many articles?
A. Six.

Q. What are the six Articles of the Code of Conduct?
A. 1. I am an American, fighting in the forces which guard my country and our way of life. I am prepared to give my life in their defense.

2. I will never surrender of my own free will. If in command, I will never surrender the members of my command while they still have the means to resist.

3. If I am captured, I will continue to resist by all means available. I will make every effort to escape and aid others to escape. I will accept neither parole nor special favors from the enemy.

4. If I become a prisoner of war, I will keep faith with my fellow prisoners. I will give no information or take part in any action which might be harmful to my comrades. If I am senior, I will take command. If not, I will obey the lawful orders of those appointed over me and will back them up in every way.

5. When questioned, should I become a prisoner of war, I am required to give only my name, rank, service number and date of birth. I will evade answering further questions to the utmost of my ability. I will make no oral or written statement disloyal to my country and its allies or harmful to their cause.

6. I will never forget that I am an American, fighting for freedom, responsible for my actions, and dedicated to the principles which made my country free. I will trust in my God and in the United States of America.

Q. When is the best time to escape?
A. As soon as possible (most likely, this is when you will be closest to your own lines).

Q. What is the main purpose of the Geneva Conference?
A. It provides rules that prisoners of war must be treated humanely.

Specifically forbidden are violence to life and person, cruel treatment and torture, outrages on personal dignity; in particular, humiliating and degrading treatment.

Q. Can a person worship as he pleases under the Geneva Conference Rules?
A. Yes.

Q. What information are you authorized to give under these rules?
A. Name, rank, service number (SSN), and date of birth.

Q. What should prisoners be searched for?
A. Hidden weapons and documents of intelligence value.

Q. Prisoners should be separated into what groups?
A. Officers, NCOs, enlisted personnel, civilians and females.

Q. An individual can be sure that while he is a POW the US Government will do what?
A. Make every possible effort to secure his release.

Q. According to the Geneva Convention, the detaining power can require POWs to perform labor in what situations or conditions?
A. If it is neither military in character or purpose and provided the POWs are not endangered by combat.

Q. A good way to remember what you should do if you capture a prisoner is to use the 5-"S" Rule. What are the 5 S's?
A. Search, segregate, silence, speed, and safeguard.

Q. Why is it important to properly handle POWs and speed them to the rear?
A. They may possess valuable intelligence information which interrogators can obtain from them.

Q. Why is it important to silence POWs?
A. It prevents them from planning resistance or escape and tends to keep them under control.

Q. Why should prisoners be segregated into groups?
A. So leaders cannot organize escapes and cannot remind the men to be security minded.

Q. Safeguarding POWs means what?
A. Making sure that no one is allowed to abuse them. Making sure that they are properly guarded to prevent escape, and making sure that they arrive safely at the POW processing point.

LAW OF LAND WARFARE

Q. What Field Manuals deal with The Law of Land Warfare and contain information concerning the Geneva Convention?
A. FM 27-2 and FM 27-10.

Q. The law of war is derived from what two principle sources?
A. (1) Lawmaking Treaties (or Conventions), such as the Hague and Geneva Conventions.

(2) Custom - Customary or unwritten law is firmly established by the custom of nations and well defined by recognized authorities on international law.

Q. What convention dealt specifically with the treatment of prisoners of war?
A. Geneva Convention of 12 August 1949.

Q. When did the 1949 Geneva Conventions for the Protection of War Victims come into force for this country?
A. When they were ratified on 2 February 1956.

Q. The law of war consists of four categories. What are they?
A. (1) Forbidden targets, tactics, and techniques: applies to fighting between you and the enemy.
(2) Enemy captives and detainees: deals with the laws that govern when a prisoner is taken or someone is detained.
(3) Civilians and private property: deals with your responsibilities with regard to the civilian population in the war zone.
(4) Prevention and reporting of unlawful acts and orders: applies to your responsibilities when criminal acts have been committed or ordered.

Q. What are the six "DON'Ts" of the first category of the law of war (forbidden targets, tactics, and techniques)?
A. (1) DON'T attack noncombatants.
(2) DON'T shoot at a parachute unless it holds a combatant.
(3) DON'T shoot at the Red Cross or hide behind medical service symbols.
(4) DON'T cause destruction beyond the requirement of your mission.
(5) DON'T attack protected property.
(6) DON'T use poison or alter your weapons to increase enemy suffering.

Q. How do you define "noncombatants"?
A. All persons participating in military operations or activities are considered combatants. ALL OTHERS ARE NONCOMBATANTS. Noncombatants include civilians, medical personnel, chaplains, and other persons captured or detained.

Q. Is an enemy soldier who is captured, sick, or wounded or one who surrenders considered a combatant?
A. No.

Q. Will you be subject to punishment under the UCMJ if you fire upon an enemy soldier who is parachuting from a burning or disabled aircraft?
A. Yes, individuals parachuting from a burning or disabled aircraft are considered helpless until they reach the ground. Firing on them while they are in the air is a violation of the law of war and punishable under the terms of the Uniform Code of Military Justice.

Q. Concerning the above question, when is a soldier that has parachuted from a burning aircraft considered a combatant?
A. When they use their weapons or do not surrender upon landing.

Q. Under the law of land warfare, can you fire on paratroopers while they are still in the air?
A. Yes, they are jumping from an airplane to fight. They are combatants and therefore targets.

Q. How are medical personnel and facilities usually marked?
A. With a red cross on a white background.

CODE OF CONDUCT & SERE/LAW OF LAND WARFARE & GENEVA CONVENTION AR 350-30/FM 27-2/FM 27-10

Q. Some countries, such as Moslem countries and Israel, use different distinctive emblems to designate their medical service personnel and facilities. Describe these emblems.
A. Moslem countries: Red Crescent on white background
Israel: the Red Shield of David on a white background

Q. When can you mark your position or yourself with a medical service emblem?
A. ONLY if you have been designated to perform only medical duties.

Q. What should you do if you enter an enemy village and are engaged by sniper fire?
A. Use only that firepower necessary to neutralize the sniper.

Q. Under the law of land warfare, what is considered "protected property"?
A. Buildings dedicated to cultural or humanitarian purposes. Examples are buildings dedicated to religion, art, science, or charitable purposes; historical monuments; hospitals and places where the sick and wounded are collected and cared for; and schools and orphanages for children.

Q. When is a church or other religious building not considered protected property?
A. When it is being used by the enemy for military operations or purposes. This applies to all other buildings normally considered to be protected property.

Q. What six things should you keep in mind regarding the second category of the law of war (enemy captives and detainees)?
A.
- Let enemy soldiers surrender.
- Treat all captives and detainees humanely.
- Don't use coercion in questioning captives and detainees.
- Provide medical care for sick and wounded captives.
- Safeguard captives from the dangers of combat.
- Don't take personal property from captives.

Q. What is the most important guide to remember when handling enemy captives and detainees?
A. Treat them as you would like to be treated if captured.

Q. What should be remembered about enemy soldiers that surrender or are captured?
A. They are a valuable source of information.

Q. What is the only information an enemy soldier is required to give?
A. Name, rank, service (serial) number, and date of birth.

Q. What has combat experience proven about information obtained from captives?
A. Useful information has been gained from captives who have been treated humanely, while information gained through torture or coercion is unreliable.

Q. Are sick and wounded enemy captives entitled to the same medical care as friendly sick and wounded?
A. Yes.

Q. Can your captors require you, a prisoner of war, to perform labor?
A. Only if the labor is nonmilitary related and not humiliating, dangerous, or unhealthy.

CODE OF CONDUCT & SERE/LAW OF LAND WARFARE & GENEVA CONVENTION
AR 350-30/FM 27-2/FM 27-10

Q. Can you force captives to dig foxholes or build bunkers?
A. Only if it is for their own protection. They cannot be required to work in support of the war effort.

Q. Under the law of war, can you use captives to help you carry your ammunition or heavy gear?
A. No.

Q. What items may a captive be searched for?
A. Only items of military or intelligence value, such as weapons, maps, or military documents.

Q. According to the law of land warfare, what items can you not take from a captive?
A. Protective items such as gas masks, mosquito nets, or items of clothing such as parkas; or personal items of no military value such as jewelry, photos, or medals.

Q. What must be given to a captive for items that are taken from him?
A. A receipt.

Q. What three things must you remember regarding the third category of the law of war (civilians and private property)?
A. - Don't violate civilians' rights in war zones.
- Ensure the safety of civilians.
- Don't burn or steal civilian property.

Q. What will most likely be the effect of needlessly ravaging private property and terrorizing civilians?
A. You will strengthen the enemy's will to fight and you may end up fighting both the enemy armed forces and civilians.

Q. When is it lawful to move or resettle civilians?
A. If it is urgently required for military reasons such as clearing a combat zone or if civilians are in danger due to immediate military activities.

Q. How should you treat civilian refugees when the military situation necessitates moving or evacuating them?
A. As you would want your family treated under similar circumstances.

Q. What type of actions will make civilians more likely to fight you or to support the enemy forces?
A. Stealing private property, the needless destruction of private property, or terrorizing them.

Q. If you see that an unlawful act is about to be committed what are some of the things you can do to prevent it?
A. - Ask to have the order clarified.
- Use moral arguments.
- Threaten to report the act.
- State your personal disagreement.
- Ask the senior individual to intervene as a means of preventing the crime.
- Refuse to obey an order to commit a criminal act.

Q. In the event the crime directly and immediately endangers your life or the life of another person, you may use the amount of force necessary to prevent

it. When is the use of deadly force justified?
A. Only to protect life and only under conditions of extreme necessity as a last resort, when lesser means have failed.

Q. If you violate any of the laws of war because you were ordered to, can you still be punished under the UCMJ?
A. Yes, orders are not a defense for violating the laws of war.

Q. What can be said about obeying orders issued by your leaders?
A. You are responsible for promptly obeying all legal orders; you are obligated to disobey an order to commit a crime.

Q. What should you do if you witness a violation of the law of war or are ordered to violate any of the laws of war?
A. Report the crime immediately through your chain of command. If the crime involves your immediate superiors, report to their superior.

Q. In addition to the chain of command, who may violations of the law of war be reported to?
A. The Inspector General, Provost Marshall, chaplain, or judge advocate.

Q. Although combat is different from everyday life, common sense still applies. Law and order and humane treatment in combat will do what four things?
A. - Increase unit discipline and security.
- Win support for the mission.
- Maintain dignity, honor, and conscience.
- Win the battle and the peace.

Q. What are considered to be lawful weapons and ammunition under the law of war?
A. Weapons and ammunition that is issued to you and has not been poisoned or altered to cause unnecessary injury or suffering to the enemy.

Q. Describe some illegal tactics that may be used on the battlefield.
A. - Using enemy marked vehicles or uniforms during combat.
- Booby trapping dead or wounded personnel.
- Faking surrender and then continuing to fight.
- Using medical service symbols to protect combat soldiers and other legitimate military targets.
- Using captives or civilians as shields or screens from enemy fire.
- Using captives or civilians to plant or remove mines or booby traps.
- Taking hostages; using hostages to stop hostile acts.

Q. List five items you should provide for a captured enemy soldier.
A. - adequate clothing
- adequate food
- shelter
- medical care
- protection from violence or abuse
- protection from dangers of combat

Q. What is the special protection that should be afforded female captives and detainees?
A. Protection from sexual abuse.

Q. What are the "Soldier's Rules" in regards to conducting combat operations in accordance with the law of war?

CODE OF CONDUCT & SERE/LAW OF LAND WARFARE & GENEVA CONVENTION
AR 350-30/FM 27-2/FM 27-10

A. 1. Fight only enemy combatants.
   2. Safeguard enemies who surrender.
   3. Do not kill or torture enemy prisoners.
   4. Care for the wounded, whether friend or foe.
   5. Do not attack medical personnel, facilities, or equipment.
   6. Destroy no more than the mission requires.
   7. Treat all civilians humanely.
   8. Respect private property and possessions. Do not steal.
   9. Identify the rights and duties of prisoners of war (PW).
   10. Report all violations of the law of war.

GUARD DUTY
FM 22-6

Q. What Field Manual covers Guard Duty?
A. FM 22-6

Q. What are the two types of guard duty?
A. Interior guard and exterior guard.

Q. What is an "interior guard"?
A. Guard force detailed by commanders of military installations to protect property and enforce specific military regulations.

Q. The interior guard force of an installation is composed of two elements that can be classified according to their purpose. What are these two elements?
A. Main guard - consists of a combination of patrols and fixed guard posts.
Special guard - guards detailed when it is impractical to use members of the main guard to guard property or an area (ie to protect parks, trains, boats, aircraft, etc).

Q. What is considered an "exterior guard"?
A. Guards detailed outside a military installation, guards in a combat area, guards in hostile or unfriendly territory, and guards (located anywhere) whose duties and responsibilities are different from those set down for interior guards (ie lookouts, listening posts, outposts, specifically designated patrols, and other guards outside the limits of a military installation). Exterior guard is not as formal and restricted as interior guard.

Q. A guard on post is governed by two types of orders. What are they?
A. General orders and special orders.

Q. What is the difference between general orders and special orders?
A. General orders outline the fundamental responsibilities of a guard while special orders instruct the guard in the actual performance of duty while on a particular post.

Q. What are the three General Orders?
A. Number 1: I will guard everything within the limits of my post and quit my post only when properly relieved.
Number 2: I will obey my special orders and perform all my duties in a military manner.
Number 3: I will report violations of my special orders, emergencies, and anything not covered in my instructions to the Commander of the Relief.

Q. Briefly explain the meaning of each of the three General Orders.
A. Number 1: I am responsible for everything that occurs within the confines of my post while I am on duty and I will not abandon my post unless I have obtained specific permission from the proper authorities to do so.
Number 2: I will familiarize myself with the special orders for my assigned post prior to being posted and will obey, execute, and enforce all special orders pertaining to my post in a military manner.
Number 3: I will immediately report all violations of my special orders to the commander of the relief and will apprehend the offender if necessary. I will also report immediately any emergencies that may occur on or near my post and when in doubt as to what action to take for any circumstance, I will contact the commander of the relief for instructions or assistance.

Q. Who is responsible for insuring that all guards understand their special instructions (orders) prior to being posted?

GUARD DUTY
FM 22-6

A. The Commander of the Relief (COR).

Q. Are all persons, regardless of rank, required to respect members of the guard in the performance of their duties?
A. Yes.

Q. Only authorized persons can give guards orders or instructions. Who is considered an "authorized person"?
A. Post Commanding Officer, Field Officer of the Day (FOD), Staff Duty Officer (SDO), Commander of the Guard (COG), Sergeant of the Guard (SOG), or Commander of the Relief (COR). Any special instructions from any other source should be issued through the guard's chain of command.

Q. When are you <u>not</u> required to render the hand salute upon recognition of an officer while on post?
A. If you are on a post that requires challenging or if you are engaged in a specific duty, the performance of which prevents saluting. Guards will display all other military courtesy and respect while in conversation with an officer.

Q. Should a guard talking to an officer interrupt the conversation to salute another officer?
A. No; however, if the officer salutes a senior, the guard should also salute.

Q. What is meant by "countersign"?
A. The combination of a secret challenge and its reply, or password (ie "Today's countersign is NUTS-WINE." The challenge is "NUTS" and the appropriate reply, or password, is "WINE").

Q. What is meant by "challenge"?
A. Any process carried out by one unit or person with the objective of ascertaining the friendly or hostile character or identity of another. It is the first part of the countersign and requires an appropriate reply.

Q. What is meant by "password"?
A. A secret word or distinctive sound used to reply to a challenge. The second word or part of the countersign.

NOTE: The term "sign and countersign" are often used to denote "challenge and password," the latter usage being the more precise since the term "countersign" by definition includes both the challenge and the password.

Q. What is the punishment for any person who discloses the parole word or countersign to any person not entitled to receive it during time of war?
A. Death or such other punishment as a court-martial may direct (Article 101, UCMJ).

Q. When a guard asks "WHO IS THERE?", confusing or misleading answers are not acceptable. Is the reply "Friend" or "Friendly Patrol" considered misleading?
A. No. This is the usual answer of an inspecting officer or patrol when they do not wish to reveal their official capacity.

Q. What is meant by "mutual identification"?
A. The person challenged should not give the password if he fails to recognize the challenge; and the challenger (guard) will use only the challenge and never the password (except as prescribed in the use of the parole word).

Q. Explain how an unauthorized person can gain access to a post when mutual

identification is not adhered to.
A. (1) An unidentified person approaches a post and calls "friendly party", or "friend", but does not come into view.
(2) Surprised or flustered, the guard commands "HALT!" and then gives the challenge, "BOSTON". The enemy simply fades away and goes to the next outpost.
(3) At the second outpost the enemy will, when halted, call out "BOSTON", hoping to confuse the guard and get him to say the password, "BEANS".
(4) Again, the enemy slips away, armed with both the challenge and the password, ready to approach a third outpost where he may be passed through the lines.

Q. How is the challenge and password given?
A. In a low tone to prevent them from being overheard by others.

Q. What is a "parole word"?
A. A secret word imparted only to those persons entitled to inspect the guard and to commanders and members of the guard.

Q. How is the parole word used?
A. When an inspecting officer gives a guard the parole word, the guard gives the inspector both parts (the challenge and the password) of the countersign. The guard does not use the password at any other time. If a guard challenges an individual and the reply is the parole word instead of the password, he should know that he is being inspected by an authorized person and replies with the appropriate password.

Q. What is the proper procedure for challenging a single individual while on guard duty?
A. (1) If you see any person on or near your post during the time for challenging, position yourself so that you can control the situation. If possible, you should be positioned out of sight.
(2) When the person is approximately 30 steps from your position, or at sufficient distance to allow you time to react, assume the correct challenge position (port arms unless inappropriate for the situation) and command "HALT!" When the person has halted, ask, "WHO IS (OR GOES) THERE?" If necessary, you may then advance toward the person to put yourself in a better position.
(3) When you are in the best position to pass or apprehend the person, you may do one or more of the following:

- require the person to advance toward you by commanding, "ADVANCE TO BE RECOGNIZED";
- have the person remain in position;
- have the person advance to a particular place, face toward the light, or take any position necessary to determine whether the person should be passed, denied, or turned over to the COR.

(4) If you advance the person to be recognized, make sure that you command "HALT" again when the person has approached sufficiently for you to recognize them or to give the challenge.
(5) After you have satisfied yourself beyond a reasonable doubt that the individual challenged is who he represents himself to be and that he has a right to pass, you should say, "ADVANCE, SERGEANT SMITH" or "ADVANCE, FRIEND", or whatever name or title is represented.

Q. How does the process for challenging a single group differ from that of challenging a single individual?
A. (1) You should permit only one member of a group to approach you for identification. After halting the group and receiving an answer that indicates the group is authorized to pass, say, "ADVANCE ONE TO BE RECOGNIZED".

(2) After you have satisfied yourself beyond a reasonable doubt that the individual challenged is who he represents himself to be and that he has a right to pass, you should say, "ADVANCE, ANOTHER ONE (or REMAINDER) AND BE RECOGNIZED" or "ADVANCE, FRIENDS" or whatever title is represented. Have the first individual verify each member of the group as they pass through to prevent unauthorized entry of persons that may infiltrate a group.

Q. How do you challenge persons that are in a vehicle?
A. Proceed as if they were on foot. If necessary, have one or all of the passengers dismount.

Q. What is considered the best means of identification when doubt exists?
A. A visual check of an individual's ID card.

Q. If you are not satisfied beyond a reasonable doubt that the individual challenged is who they represent themselves to be (ie suspect fake ID), what should you do?
A. Ask only questions a friendly person would be likely to know. It further doubt exists, contact supervisor.

Q. What is the correct procedure for challenging two or more separate persons or groups that approach your position from different directions at the same time?
A. They are halted in turn and remain halted until advanced by you. The senior individual or group is advanced first.

Q. What should you do if you, or any other person in the military service, finds an irresponsible guard on post (ie sleeping)?
A. It is your duty to notify the commander of the guard or other noncommissioned officer of the guard and stay on the post until a qualified guard is posted.

Q. Who is the only person a guard should surrender his weapon to?
A. The person from whom he lawfully receives orders while on post (normally the COR).

Q. Who is responsible for establishing special orders for guard posts?
A. The Post Commander.

Q. Special orders differ for various posts depending upon the nature of the area being guarded and are based on what two considerations?
A. Realism and clarity.

Q. Where are copies of special orders posted?
A. They should be continuously and conspicuously posted in the guardhouse for reference. Copies are normally also posted on a fixed guard post and roving patrols may be required to carry a copy with them while on duty.

Q. When a guard is asked by an inspecting officer, "What are your orders?", what would be the appropriate response?
A. "Sir, my orders are of two classes, general and special. My general orders are: Number One - I will guard everything within the limits of my post and quit my post only when properly relieved. Number Two - ...." and continues to recite the general orders until stopped by the officer or until all of the general orders have been recited. You should be able to answer any questions pertaining to the special orders for your assigned post.

GUARD DUTY
FM 22-6

Q. What are the two main qualifications for performing guard duty?
A. (1) Guards must have completed range firing (qualification or familiarization) or training with the weapon they use on guard duty.
(2) Guards must know the three general orders.

Q. What is a fixed post or patrol "reserve"?
A. Guard duty personnel not on post at any given time. They normally remain in the guard shack or designated location and should be large enough to meet any local emergency, threat condition, or alert.

Q. Who supervises the enlisted members of the guard, assigns them to reliefs, and is responsible to the commander of the guard or assumes the responsibilities of the commander of the guard if one has not been detailed?
A. The Sergeant of the Guard (SOG).

Q. An extra member of the guard who is used when needed to replace a guard or perform duties prescribed by local directives is known as what?
A. The supernumerary.

Q. Who is responsible for the instruction, discipline, and performance of the guard as well as security of weapons and ammunition (may be an officer or senior NCO)?
A. The Commander of the Guard (COG).

Q. Who is responsible for assigning posts to guard members and ensuring that guards are posted on time?
A. The Commander of the Relief (COR).

Q. Who inspects the guard (formal guard mount)?
A. The Officer of the Day (SDO) or the COG/SOG when an OD is not appointed.

Q. What is the Army's policy toward the use of deadly force?
A. The use of deadly force is justified only to protect life and/or to prevent sabotage and only under conditions of extreme necessity as a last resort, when lesser means have failed. You should attempt to verbally warn the offender, then if necessary (and if innocent bystanders will not be harmed) fire a warning shot. As a last resort, shoot to disable and not to kill.

PHYSICAL SECURITY
FM 19-30/AR 190-13

Q. What FM covers Physical Security and what AR deals with the Army Physical Security Program?
A. FM 19-30; AR 190-13.

Q. What is the purpose of physical security?
A. To identify, reduce, eliminate, or neutralize conditions favorable to criminal activity; or, in other words, to make access so difficult that an intruder will hesitate to attempt penetration, or to provide for his apprehension should he be successful.

Q. Physical security is the responsibility of whom?
A. The Commander; he/she must insure that appropriate physical security measures are taken to minimize the loss of supplies, equipment, and material through threats, natural or human.

Q. The commander normally exercises appropriate security measures through whom?
A. The Provost Marshal and/or the Physical Security Officer.

Q. What are considered physical security measures?
A. Physical systems or devices used to protect security interests.

Q. List some physical systems or devices included in physical security measures.
A.
- security forces
- military working dogs
- physical barriers
- badging systems
- secure containers
- electronic IDS
- security lighting
- access control devices
- CCTV
- locking devices

Q. The Physical Security Program supports what other program in the protection of military operations and activities against hostile intelligence exploitation?
A. OPSEC

Q. List some subjects that are pertinent to physical security training.
A.
- NBC training
- map reading & land navigation
- marksmanship
- patrolling
- OPSEC
- unarmed defense
- physical fitness
- use of force
- squad tactics
- guard duty

Q. The degree of protection desired on any installation depends primarily on an analysis of what two factors?
A. Criticality and vulnerability.

Q. What is meant by protection or security "in-depth"?
A. A series of security measures are employed so that they complement and supplement each other; as a result, an accumulated delay time for the intruder is built into the system.

Q. What is considered a "security threat"?
A. Acts or conditions that may result in the compromise of information; loss of life; damage, loss, or destruction of property; or disruption of the mission of the installation or facility.

Q. Security threats are classified into two categories. Name these categories

and give some examples of each.
A. (1) Natural threats: floods, storms, earthquakes, winds, snow and ice, fires, fog.
(2) Human threats: pilferage, sabotage, espionage, attacks on key persons, carelessness, human intelligence (HUMINT) threat.

Q. Of the two categories of security threats, which is not normally preventable by physical security measures?
A. Natural threats.

Q. If natural threats are not normally preventable through the use of physical security measures, why should we be concerned about it?
A. Because they may reduce the effectiveness of existing security measures by such occurrences as:

- collapsed perimeter fences
- inoperable protective lighting
- damaged patrol vehicles
- poor visibility

Q. Security personnel cannot effectively accomplish their mission without the active interest and support of whom?
A. Everyone on the installation.

Q. Such interest and support (see above question) can only be secured through what means?
A. An effective security education program.

Q. What are the objectives of the physical security education program?
A. To acquaint all personnel with the reasons for security measures and to insure their cooperation.

Q. What security measures contribute to the effectiveness of a good personnel movement control system?
A. Access lists, personal recognition, security identification, cards and badges, and personnel escorts.

Q. What is considered to be the standard identification media for military personnel?
A. The DD Form 2A (Military ID Card).

Q. What is a "duress code"?
A. A simple word or phrase used during normal conversation that alerts other security personnel that an authorized person has been forced to vouch for an unauthorized individual. It requires preplanning to insure appropriate response and is changed frequently to minimize compromise.

Q. Explain the "two-man rule".
A. At least two authorized persons, each capable of detecting incorrect or unauthorized procedures with respect to the task being performed and who are familiar with applicable safety and security requirements, will be present during any operation that affords access to sensitive weapons. It is designed to prohibit access to sensitive weapons by a lone individual.

Q. How is the term "restricted area" defined?
A. Any area, access to which is subject to special restrictions or controls for reasons of security or safeguarding of property or material.

PHYSICAL SECURITY
FM 19-30/AR 190-13

Q. What are the four designations of restricted areas?
A. Restricted Area, Controlled Area, Limited Area, and Exclusion Area.

Q. In which of the above restricted areas would you expect to find the greatest degree of security?
A. An Exclusion Area.

Q. According to the Internal Security Act of 1950, is the use of deadly force authorized in a restricted area?
A. Yes.

Q. What are the three levels of security classifications and what cover sheets are used for each?
A. Confidential......DA Label 22.....Blue
Secret............DA Label 23.....Red
Top Secret........DA Label 24.....Yellow

Q. How often are you required to read security regulations (SOPs, etc)?
A. Twice per year.

Q. What is the most secure means of transmitting classified information?
A. By messenger.

Q. What is the highest classification of material that may be discussed over the phone?
A. Unclassified.

Q. What is the physical security requirement for POVs?
A. All privately owned/visitor operated motor vehicles on the installation should be registered with the Provost Marshal or the installation physical security officer.

Q. What are protective barriers primarily used for?
A. To define the physical limits of an installation, activity, or area and to restrict, channel, or impede access.

Q. What are the two primary benefits of protective barriers to a physical security posture?
A. (1) They create a psychological consideration for anyone thinking of unauthorized entry.
(2) They have a direct impact on the number of security posts needed and on the frequency of use for each post.

Q. Protective barriers are divided into what two major categories?
A. Structural and natural.

Q. What four types of fencing are authorized for the protection of restricted areas?
A. Chain-link, barbed wire, barbed tape, and concertina.

Q. Which of the above types of fencing will generally be used for protection of permanent limited and exclusion areas?
A. Chain-link fencing.

Q. What are the minimum requirements for a chain-link fence?
A. Must be constructed of 9-gauge or heavier wire galvanized with mesh openings not to exceed 2 inches per side, and a twisted and barbed selvage at the top

and bottom. It must be 7-feet in height (excluding top guard) and must be taut and securely fastened to rigid metal or reinforced concrete posts set in concrete.

Q. Standard barbed wire is twisted, double-strand, ______-gauge wire, with four-point barbs spaced an equal distance apart.
A. 12

Q. Describe standard concertina barbed wire.
A. It is a commercially manufactured wire coil of high-strength-steel barbed wire, clipped together at intervals to form a cylinder. Opened, it is 50 feet long and 3 feet in diameter.

Q. What is a "top guard"?
A. An overhang of barbed wire or barbed tape along the top of a fence, facing outward and upward at approximately a 45-degree angle.

Q. Describe a "tanglefoot wire" obstacle.
A. Barbed wire or tape that is supported on short metal or wood pickets spaced at irregular intervals of 3 to 10 feet, and at heights between 6 and 12 inches. The wire or tape is frequently crisscrossed to provide a more effective obstacle.

Q. If a building less than two stories high forms part of the perimeter, what must be used along the outside coping to deny access to the roof?
A. A top guard.

Q. Masonry walls, when used as perimeter barriers, must have a minimum height of _______ feet and must have a barbed wire top guard. If the height of the wall is 8 feet, what can be substituted for the top guard?
A. 7; broken glass, set on edge and cemented to the top surface.

Q. Warning signs for a limited area must be positioned on or outside the limited area physical barrier and should be at intervals of no more than ______ feet.
A. 100

Q. Signs setting forth the conditions of entry to an installation or area should be plainly posted at all principal entrances and should be legible under normal conditions at a distance not less than ____ feet from the point of entry.
A. 50

Q. How is protective lighting an essential element of an integrated physical security program?
A. It provides a means of continuing, during hours of darkness or limited visibility, a degree of protection approaching that maintained during daylight hours.

Q. The type of lighting system to be used depends on the overall security requirements of the installation concerned. What are the four general types of lighting units used for protective lighting systems?
A. Continuous, standby, movable, and emergency.

Q. Basically, for an item to be secure, an intrusion detection system must focus upon detecting unauthorized individuals at what three points?
A. The entry point (gate, door, fence, etc), the area (building, etc), and at a

specific object (vault, file, safe, etc).

Q. What are some basic principles upon which a viable intruder detection system operates?
A. - breaking an electrical circuit
- interrupting a light beam
- detecting sound
- detecting vibration
- detecting motion
- detecting a change in capacitance due to penetration of an electrostatic field

Q. J-SIIDS is the functional intruder detection system used in most arms rooms. What does "J-SIIDS" stand for?
A. Joint Service Interior Intrusion Detection System.

Q. J-SIIDS has been certified for use in what areas?
A. - finance offices
- post exchanges
- class VI stores
- narcotics storage areas
- accountable property storage areas
- high value item storage areas
- CID evidence rooms
- conventional weapons storage areas
- billets and offices
- aircraft hangers
- nonconventional weapons and chemical weapons storage areas

Q. J-SIIDS is <u>not</u> certified for use in what areas?
A. - sensitive weapons storage areas (REDEYE, DRAGON, LAW, and STINGER)
- nuclear fuel storage areas
- nuclear reactor facilities
- computer centers
- classified storage areas
- areas where cryptographic devices are stored, used or maintained
- ammunition and explosives storage and manufacturing areas
- radioactive isotope storage areas
- communication centers

Q. What is "FIDS"?
A. The Facility Intrusion Detection System; a joint service project intended to provide DOD with a system to detect intrusions into, theft and pilferage from, or espionage/sabotage activities against all types of facilities worldwide.

Q. What does "BISS" stand for?
A. Base Installation Security System; a product of the Air Force and is a standard for DOD.

Q. What is "REMBASS"?
A. Remotely Monitored Battlefield Sensor System; used primarily in tactical situations in remote areas and acts as a squad or platoon early warning system.

Q. What is considered to be the most accepted and widely used security device of the basic safeguards in protecting installations and activities, personnel, classified material, and government and personal property?
A. The lock.

Q. Regardless of the quality or cost, a lock should only be considered a ______ ________, and not a positive bar to entry.
A. Delay device.

PHYSICAL SECURITY
FM 19-30/AR 190-13

Q. Who is responsible for the installation and maintenance of locks, latches, padlocks, or other locking devices on doors, cabinets, vaults, and similar built-in items that are an integral part of a building or structure?
A. The Army Corps of Engineers.

Q. The degree of protection afforded by any well-constructed vault, safe, or filing cabinet may be measured in terms of the resistance of the locking mechanism to picking, manipulation, or drilling. Name seven types of locking devices in use today.
A. Key locks, conventional combination locks, manipulation-resistant combination locks, other combination locks, re-locking devices, interchangeable cores, and cipher locks.

Q. How do you determine the number of possible combinations on a combination padlock?
A. Raise the total number of reference points on the dial to a power equal to the number of tumblers (for example, A lock has 40 numbers on the dial and a three-number combination. The three-number combination indicates that there are three tumblers in the lock. Therefore, the number of combinations possible is 40 raised to the third power, or 64,000).

Q. How can an inexperienced locksmith find the combination to a padlock (with 64,000 possible combinations) in less than an hour?
A. On inexpensive combination padlocks there is usually a serial number stamped on the back. These serial numbers can be checked in a code book (available from locksmith supply houses) and the combination of any such lock obtained.

Q. What words should be imprinted on all master and higher level control keys?
A. "US Government - DO NOT REPRODUCE".

Q. Key boxes must be constructed of at least ____-gauge steel.
A. 20

Q. What is AE Form 2670 used for?
A. The issue and turn-in of keys.

Q. What form lists individuals who have access to a particular security container or safe (access roster)?
A. DA Form 727.

Q. What is DA Form 672 used for?
A. It is a security record which is usually kept posted on or near a safe or other secure container. It is used by personnel unlocking or checking classified or controlled storage areas.

Q. What is considered to be the commander's most effective and useful tool in a comprehensive integrated physical security program?
A. The installation security force (guard force).

Q. Most of the qualities desired of security personnel are developed through training and become instinctive through experience. What are some of the desirable qualities of security force personnel?
A. Alertness, sound judgment, confidence, physical fitness, tactfulness, self-control, loyalty to job, responsibility, trustworthiness, reliability, security clearance, and good mental attitude.

Q. A breach of physical security is, in most instances, a crime; and the scene

of the breach must be treated as such. The first principle, then, is to do what to the scene of the crime?
A. Refrain from disturbing it and afford necessary protection to keep it undisturbed until investigating personnel arrive.

Q. What is probably the most common and annoying hazard with which security personnel are concerned?
A. Pilferage.

Q. What are the two types of pilferers?
A. (1) Casual pilferer - one who steals primarily because he is unable to resist the temptation of an unexpected opportunity and has little fear of detection.
(2) Systematic pilferer - one who steals according to preconceived plans.

Q. What is meant by "sabotage"?
A. Any act which maliciously destroys property or disrupts the operation or mission of an installation or facility for any reason.

Q. What are the five methods of sabotage?
A. Fire, explosive devices, mechanical devices, chemical, and psychological.

Q. What is meant by "espionage"?
A. The act of spying on a country - of secretly or under false pretenses, searching out information, or making observations with the intention of relaying the information or observation to another country.

Q. What organizations are primarily responsible for investigating subversive activities and for counter-espionage operations?
A. US Army Military Intelligence and the FBI.

Q. What is the primary objective of physical security personnel with respect to espionage?
A. To render it ineffective, or at least to make it more difficult by applying protective measures.

Q. A bomb is a device capable of producing damage to material and injury or death to personnel when detonated or ignited and can be classified into two categories. What are they?
A. Explosive and incendiary.

Q. Terrorists act to spread fear primarily for what three reasons?
A. (1) Retaliation - for a variety of political and/or organizational reasons.
(2) Destruction of property - a message, warning, or sign of things to come.
(3) Taking of hostages as bargaining tools for various goals.

Q. What is the final result (and the desired result) of all terrorist acts?
A. They receive widespread news media exposure.

Q. Every terrorist incident can be categorized into what three phases?
A. Initial response, negotiation, and assault.

Q. Who is the Crime Prevention Officer in your unit?
A. The Company Commander.

Q. It is recommended that all unit members mark clearly their name and SSN on

all personal property valued at $_____ or higher.
A. $50.00

Q. What is DA Form 4986 used for?
A. It is the Personal Property Record, commonly referred to as the "high value item sheets" or "high dollar item sheets" and is a list by name, brand/model, serial number, and value of all personal property in excess of $50.00 in value.

FIRST AID
FM 21-11

Q. What FM covers "First Aid for Soldiers"?
A. FM 21-11

Q. What is meant by "first aid"?
A. The emergency care given to the sick or injured before medical treatment can be administered by medical personnel.

Q. What three tasks are considered to be the *basics* of first aid?
A. (1) Check for BREATHING.
(2) Check for BLEEDING.
(3) Check for SHOCK.

Q. What is the first thing you should do if you come upon a sick or injured soldier?
A. Properly evaluate the casualty as to the nature and extent of the injuries.

Q. What are the eight steps in properly evaluating a casualty?
A. (1) Check the casualty for responsiveness.
(2) Check for breathing.
(3) Check for pulse.
(4) Check for bleeding.
(5) Check for shock.
(6) Check for fractures.
(7) Check for burns.
(8) Check for possible head injury.

NOTE: Complete each step in sequence. Proceed to the next step only after you have taken care of the preceding steps (i.e., check for shock only after you have determined that the casualty is breathing, has a pulse, and all wounds have been bandaged).

Q. During step 3 above you determine that a casualty **does not** have a pulse. What should you do?
A. Immediately seek medically trained personnel.

NOTE: CPR should be performed only by qualified personnel.

Q. What are the two vital body functions?
A. Respiration and blood circulation.

Q. What fingers should be used when checking for pulse?
A. The tips of the first two fingers (never use the thumb because you may confuse your pulse beat with that of the casualty).

Q. Name four common points for checking pulse.
A. (1) The side of the neck (carotid).
(2) Groin (femoral).
(3) Wrist (radial).
(4) Ankle (posterial tibial).

Q. FM 21-11 talks about four <u>adverse conditions</u> that affect life. What are they?
A. Lack of oxygen, bleeding, shock, and infection.

Q. What are the three *basic measures* (life-saving steps) of first aid?
A. (1) Open the airway and restore breathing.

(2) Stop the bleeding and protect the wound.
(3) Check and treat for shock.

Q. What is "CPR"?
A. Cardiopulmonary Resuscitation - a combination of rescue breathing and chest compressions.

NOTE: Change 2 to FM 21-11, dtd 4 DEC 91, removed all reference to CPR as a "first aid" measure for soldiers. CPR is a medical procedure that should only be performed by properly trained and qualified personnel.

Q. What is the single most common cause of an airway obstruction?
A. The tongue. In most cases, the airway can be cleared by simply extending the neck. This action pulls the tongue away from the air passage in the throat.

Q. What are the two prescribed methods for opening an airway?
A. The jaw thrust or head tilt/chin lift methods.

Q. If a casualty is suspected of having a neck/spinal injury or severe head trauma, which of the above methods should be used?
A. The jaw thrust technique because in most cases it can be accomplished without extending the neck.

Q. While maintaining an open airway the rescuer should check for breathing by observing the casualty's chest and performing what three actions within 3 to 5 seconds?
A. (1) LOOK for the chest to rise and fall.
(2) LISTEN for air escaping during exhalation by placing your ear near the casualty's mouth.
(3) FEEL for the flow of air on your cheek.

Q. What are the two prescribed methods of rescue breathing?
A. Mouth-to-mouth and mouth-to-nose resuscitation.

Q. What is the preferred method of rescue breathing?
A. Mouth-to-mouth resuscitation.

Q. When would you use the mouth-to-nose method in lieu of the mouth-to-mouth method of artificial respiration?
A. When the casualty has a severe jaw fracture or mouth wound or jaws that are tightly closed by spasms.

Q. If you suspect the casualty has a neck injury and you are using the jaw thrust technique (with both hands on either side of the casualty's jaw), how do you "pinch" the nostrils closed for rescue breathing?
A. Close the nostrils by placing your cheek tightly against them.

Q. What are the steps in performing artificial respiration?
A. (1) Open the airway.
(2) Take a deep breath and place your mouth (in an airtight seal) around the casualty's mouth.
(3) Blow two full breaths into the casualty's mouth. Watch the casualty's chest out of the corner of your eye to determine if sufficient air is getting to the casualty's lungs.
(4) After giving two breaths which cause the chest to rise, attempt to locate a pulse on the casualty. Allow 5 to 10 seconds to determine if there is

a pulse. If no pulse, immediately seek medically trained personnel for assistance. If pulse is found, continue rescue breathing at the rate of one breath every five seconds (approximately 12 breaths per minute) until casualty begins breathing on their own.

Q. While administering rescue breathing, how often should you pause to check the pulse?
A. About once every 12 breaths (once per minute). Rechecks can be accomplished in 3 to 5 seconds.

Q. How long should rescue breathing be continued?
A. Until the casualty starts to breath on his own, until relieved by another person, or until too tired to continue.

Q. What are the two prescribed methods for opening an airway obstruction on a conscious casualty?
A. Abdominal thrust and chest thrust.

Q. How many times should the abdominal or chest thrust be repeated?
A. Until the obstruction is expelled or until the casualty becomes unconscious.

Q. When should the chest thrust be used in lieu of the abdominal thrust?
A. When the casualty has an abdominal wound, when the casualty is pregnant, or when the casualty is so large that you cannot wrap your arms around the abdomen.

Q. What is the procedure for opening the obstructed airway of an unconscious casualty?
A. (1) Open the airway and attempt rescue breathing.
(2) If unable to ventilate the casualty, perform 6 to 10 manual (abdominal or chest) thrusts.
(3) Perform finger sweep and attempt to dislodge foreign body.
(4) Repeat procedure until the object is cleared from the obstructed airway.

Q. What should you keep in mind about all open (or penetrating) wounds that you find on a casualty?
A. There may be more than one wound. Check for points of entry and exit and treat accordingly.

Q. What are the five prescribed methods (in order of precedence) for controlling bleeding?
A. Field dressing, manual pressure, elevation, pressure dressing, and tourniquet.

NOTE: Digital pressure (also called "pressure point") is an alternate method of controlling bleeding and is covered in appendix E of FM 21-11.

Q. How many pressure points are there to control bleeding?
A. 11

Q. When treating a casualty with an open wound, whose field dressing should be used?
A. The casualty's field dressing.

Q. How should the tails be tied on a field dressing?
A. In a non-slip knot over the outer edge of the dressing. It should be tied firmly enough to prevent the dressing from slipping but without causing a

tourniquet-like effect.

Q. In attempting to control bleeding, how long should manual pressure be applied before resorting to a pressure dressing?
A. 5 to 10 minutes.

Q. Should you elevate a fractured or suspected fractured limb?
A. Yes, but only after it has been properly splinted.

Q. How should the ends of an improvised dressing be tied on a pressure dressing?
A. In a non-slip knot, directly over the wound site.

Q. A soldier whose arm or leg has been completely amputated may not be bleeding when first discovered. Why is this and what should you do for this injury?
A. The absence of bleeding is due to the body's normal defenses (contraction of blood vessels) as a result of the amputation, but after a period of time bleeding will start as the blood vessels relax; apply a tourniquet anyway and bandage and dress the stump.

Q. Who should loosen a tourniquet once it is applied?
A. Only medical personnel.

Q. Why should <u>you</u> never loosen or release a tourniquet once it has been applied?
A. Because it could enhance the probability of shock.

Q. Where are the only places that a tourniquet can be used?
A. On the arm(s) or leg(s).

Q. How should a tourniquet be placed on an injured limb?
A. Between the wound and the body trunk (or between the wound and the heart), preferably 2 to 4 inches from the edge of the wound site.

Q. What should be done with any severed (amputated) limbs or body parts?
A. They should be transported with, but out of sight of, the casualty.

Q. What should you do after applying a tourniquet to a casualty?
A. Mark the casualty's head with a "T" to indicate that a tourniquet has been applied. If necessary, use the casualty's blood to make this mark.

Q. Shock may be caused by severe or minor trauma to the body. It is usually the result of one or more of what seven conditions?
A.
- significant loss of blood
- heart failure
- dehydration
- severe and painful blows to the body
- severe burns of the body
- severe wound infections
- severe allergic reactions to drugs, foods, insect stings, and snakebites.

Q. What are the signs/symptoms of shock?
A.
- sweaty but cool skin (clammy skin)
- paleness of the skin
- restlessness, nervousness
- thirst
- loss of blood (bleeding)

- confusion (or loss of awareness)
- faster-than-normal breathing rate
- blotchy or bluish skin (especially around the mouth and lips)
- nausea and/or vomiting

Q. In the field, how do the procedures to treat shock compare with the procedures that would be performed to prevent shock?
A. They are identical.

Q. What are the seven steps in treating/preventing shock?
A. (1) Move the casualty to cover, if cover is available and the situation permits.
(2) Position the casualty on their back.
(3) Elevate the casualty's feet higher than the level of their heart.
(4) Loosen constricting clothing (at the neck, waist, boots, or wherever it may be binding).
(5) Prevent chilling or overheating.
(6) Calm the casualty.
(7) Seek medical aid.

Q. When would you NOT elevate the legs when treating/preventing shock?
A. When the casualty has an unsplinted broken leg, head injury, or abdominal injury.

Q. In the case of an abdominal injury, how should the legs be positioned?
A. Place the knees in an upright (flexed) position.

Q. You are treating a casualty for shock due to a severe leg wound (for which you applied a tourniquet). It is cold. To prevent chilling and maintain body temperature should you cover the casualty?
A. Yes, but leave the tourniquet exposed if possible.

Q. What is the best way to "calm" a casualty?
A. By being authoritative (taking charge of the situation) and by showing self-confidence. Assure the casualty that you are there to help them.

Q. When treating/preventing shock, should you give a casualty anything to eat or drink?
A. No

Q. What action should you take if you must leave the casualty or if the casualty becomes unconscious?
A. Turn the head to the side to prevent choking should they vomit.

Q. What are some of the signs/symptoms of a severe head injury?
A.
- current or recent unconsciousness
- nausea or vomiting
- convulsions or twitches
- slurred speech
- confusion
- sleepiness (drowsiness)
- loss of memory
- clear or bloody fluid leaking from nose or ears
- staggering in walking
- dizziness
- a change in pulse rate
- breathing problems
- eye problems (unequal pupils)
- paralysis
- headache
- black eyes
- bleeding from scalp/head area
- deformity of the head

NOTE: Anyone with a severe head injury should be treated as a suspected neck/spinal injury.

Q. When treating a severe head injury that has an object protruding from the scalp, should you attempt to remove the object?
A. No. Improvise bulky dressings from the cleanest material available and place these dressings around the protruding object for support after applying the field dressing.

Q. Should you give a casualty with a head injury anything to eat or drink?
A. No

Q. Should a pressure dressing ever be used to stop the flow of blood from a severe head injury?
A. No. Only a field dressing should be used. DO NOT place unnecessary pressure on the wound or attempt to push any brain matter back into the head.

Q. What are some indications of a spinal cord injury?
A. Lack of responses to stimuli, stomach distention (enlargement), or penile erection.

Q. What is a brain "concussion"?
A. An injury to the brain that involves a temporary loss of some or all of the brain's ability to function.

Q. Convulsions (seizures/involuntary jerking) may occur after a mild head injury.
What first aid measures should be taken for a casualty with convulsions?
A. PROTECT THE CASUALTY FROM HURTING THEMSELF!!
- ease casualty to the ground
- support head and neck
- maintain open airway
- call for assistance
- treat the casualty's wounds and evacuate immediately

Q. Briefly define the following terms: abrasion, contusion, laceration, avulsion.
A. - abrasion: a scrape of the skin.
- contusion: injury without a break in the skin (usually causes swelling); bruise.
- laceration: cuts or breaks in the skin.
- avulsion: a rip in the skin (torn away tissue).

Q. You are treating a casualty for a severe facial injury. You clear the airway with your fingers, removing blood, mucus, pieces of broken teeth and bits of flesh. What should you do with any pieces of ear, nose, detached teeth, etc., that you find?
A. Place them on a field dressing and send them along with the casualty to the medical facility. Detached teeth should be kept damp.

Q. What is the procedure for treating a laceration of the eyeball?
A. Cover the injury with a <u>loose</u> sterile dressing. When one eyeball is injured, you should immobilize <u>both</u> eyes. Because the eyes move together, covering both will lessen the chances of further damage to the injured eye.

Q. Under what circumstance would you NOT cover both eyes when an eyeball injury has occurred?
A. In hazardous surroundings so that the casualty may see.

FIRST AID
FM 21-11

Q. What is the first aid measure for chemical burns to the eyes?
A. Flush with large amounts of water for 5 to 20 minutes (5-10 minutes for acids; 20 minutes for alkalis), or as long as necessary to flush out the chemical. Apply a bandage over the eyes and evacuate.

Q. What are some things that can be done to treat a nose bleed?
A. The bleeding may be controlled by placing an ice pack over the nose, pinching the nostrils together, or placing torn gauze (rolled) between the upper teeth and lip.

Q. How do you treat a chest wound?
A. When the casualty exhales, seal the wound and make it airtight by covering it with plastic, cellophane, foil, the casualty's poncho, or similar material (the inside of the field dressing packet or an MRE packet will work). Secure in place with a pressure dressing. Apply manual pressure for 5 to 10 minutes to help control the bleeding.

Q. What is "tension pneumothorax"?
A. A life-threatening condition that results when air enters the chest cavity and cannot escape (such as with a pressure dressing applied). If breathing worsens after placing the dressing, quickly lift or remove (allowing the trapped air to escape), and replace. Continually monitor a casualty with a chest wound for this condition.

Q. When treating a casualty with an abdominal wound, why are the legs placed in an upright (flexed) position?
A. The knees-up position helps relieve pain, assists in the treatment of shock, prevents further exposure of the bowel (intestines) or abdominal organs, and helps relieve abdominal pressure by allowing the abdominal muscles to relax.

Q. What are the first aid measures for an abdominal wound?
A. - Remove the casualty's clothing to expose the wound but do not attempt to remove clothing that is stuck to the wound.
- Apply a field dressing to the wound and loosely secure with a nonslip knot at the casualty's side. The dressing should be tied firmly enough to prevent slipping without applying pressure to the wound site.

Q. What should be done with any organs that may be protruding from the wound or lying nearby on the ground?
A. DO NOT attempt to push protruding organs back inside the body; with a clean, dry dressing or with the cleanest material available, gently pick up any organs that may be on the ground and place them on top of the casualty's abdomen (adjacent to the wound). Do the same with protruding organs. Apply a field dressing or dressings as necessary to protect them and control contamination.

Q. Before administering the proper first aid for burn injuries you must be able to recognize the type of burn to be treated. What are the four types of burns?
A. (1) Thermal burns: caused by fire, hot objects, hot liquids and gases, or by nuclear blast or fire ball.
(2) Electrical burns: caused by electrical wires, current, or lightning.
(3) Chemical burns: caused by contact with wet or dry chemicals or white phosphorous (WP).
(4) Laser burns.

Q. What are the four first aid measures for treating burns?
A. (1) Eliminate the source of the burn.

(2) Expose the burn.
(3) Apply a field dressing to the burn.
(4) Seek medical attention.

Q. What is the first aid treatment for white phosphorous that strikes the skin?
A. Smother with water, a wet cloth, or wet mud. Keep covered with a wet material to exclude air which will prevent the particles from burning.

Q. Should you apply grease or ointments to burns before applying a field dressing?
A. No

Q. What is a "fracture"?
A. A break in the bone.

Q. What are the two kinds of fractures?
A. (1) Closed fracture: a broken bone that does not break the overlying skin.
(2) Open fracture: A break in the bone with a corresponding break in the overlying skin. The bone may protrude through the skin or, as in the case of an open fracture produced by a missile, a bullet or shell fragment may go through the flesh and break the bone.

Q. Briefly define the following medical terms: dislocation, sprain.
A. - dislocation: when a joint, such as a shoulder, knee, or ankle, is not in its proper position.
- sprain: when the connecting tissues of the joints have been torn.

NOTE: Both dislocations and sprains are treated as closed fractures.

Q. What are some of the signs/symptoms of a fracture?
A. - deformity
- tenderness
- swelling
- pain
- inability to move the injured part
- protruding bone
- bleeding
- discolored skin at the injured site

Q. What is the *Basic Splinting Principle*?
A. *Immobilize the joints above and below any fracture.*

Q. Why should fractures be immobilized?
A. To prevent the sharp edges of the bone from moving and causing further damage to tissue, muscles, blood vessels, and nerves.

Q. What are some examples of improvised splinting materials?
A. Wooden boards, tree branches, poles, rolled newspapers or magazines. Basically, anything that is relatively straight and long enough to reach beyond the joints above and below the fractured site.

Q. What is an "anatomical splint"?
A. Using an uninjured part of the body as a splint for an injured limb when no other splinting material is available (i.e., splint fractured arm to the chest wall or a fractured leg to the uninjured leg).

Q. Should you attempt to straighten or reposition a fractured limb?
A. NO. Splint the fracture(s) in the position found.

Q. What is the first and last thing you should do when splinting a fracture?
A. Check the circulation below the sight of the injury.

FIRST AID
FM 21-11

Q. One reason to recheck the circulation below the sight of the injury after applying a splint is to ensure that the bandages holding the splint have not been tied too tightly. How tight should the bandages be?
A. A "finger-tip check" can be made by inserting the tip of the finger between the wrapped tails and the skin. If you cannot insert the tip of your finger, it is too tight.

Q. What is a cravat bandage used for?
A. To maintain a sterile dressing that does not have tail bandages attached. It can also be used to tie slings and as a swathe to help secure splinted limbs to the body.

Q. How and where are knots tied when splinting a fracture?
A. In nonslip knots tied on the side of the splint AWAY from the casualty.

Q. How many ties should be used to secure a splint?
A. As many as necessary to securely hold splinting materials in place. Generally, four ties are used - two above the sight of the fracture and two below.

Q. What are the three types of heat injuries?
A. Heat cramps, heat exhaustion, and heatstroke (sunstroke).

Q. Heat cramps are caused by an imbalance of chemicals (called electrolytes) in the body as a result of excessive sweating. What are the signs/symptoms of heat cramps?
A. - muscle cramps in the extremities (arms and legs)
- muscle cramps of the abdomen
- heavy (excessive) sweating (wet skin)
- thirst

Q. What are the first aid measures for heat cramps?
A. - move the casualty to a cool or shady area (or improvised shade)
- loosen clothing (if not in chemical environment)
- have casualty slowly drink at least one canteen full of cold water
- seek medical aid if cramps continue

Q. Should salt tablets be used in the prevention or treatment of heat injuries?
A. No. Usually, eating field rations or liberal salting of the garrison diet will provide enough salt to replace what is lost through sweating in hot weather.

NOTE: DO NOT use salt solution in first aid procedures for heat injuries.

Q. The body, which depends on water to help cool itself, can lose more than ____ quart(s) of water per hour through sweat.
A. One.

Q. Heat exhaustion is caused by loss of water through sweating without adequate fluid replacement. What are the signs/symptoms of heat exhaustion?
A. - Symptoms that occur often:
-- heavy (excessive) sweating with pale, moist, cool skin
-- headache
-- weakness
-- dizziness
-- loss of appetite

- Symptoms that occur <u>sometimes</u>:
    - -- heat cramps
    - -- nausea - with or without vomiting
    - -- urge to defecate
    - -- chills (gooseflesh)
    - -- rapid breathing
    - -- tingling of hands and/or feet
    - -- confusion

Q. What are the first aid measures for heat exhaustion?
A. - move the casualty to a cool or shady area (or improvised shade)
- loosen or remove clothing and boots (unless in a chemical environment)
- pour water on the casualty and fan them (unless in chemical environment)
- have casualty slowly drink at least one canteen full of cold water
- elevate the legs
- if possible, the casualty should not participate in strenuous activity for the remainder of the day
- monitor the casualty until the symptoms are gone, or medical aid arrives

Q. Heatstroke (sometimes called "sunstroke") is caused by the failure of the body's cooling mechanisms. What are the signs/symptoms of heatstroke?
A. - casualty's skin is red (flushed), hot, and dry to the touch
- weakness
- dizziness
- confusion
- headaches
- seizures
- nausea (stomach pains)
- respiration and pulse may be rapid and weak

Q. What are the first aid measures for heatstroke?
A. COOL CASUALTY IMMEDIATELY BY:
- moving to a cool or shaded area (or improvised shade)
- loosening or removing clothing (except when in a chemical environment)
- spray or pour water on casualty; fanning to permit a coolant effect of evaporation
- massaging casualty's extremities and skin which increases the blood flow to those body areas, thus aiding the cooling process
- elevating the legs
- having casualty slowly drink at least one canteen full of cold water if conscious

Q. What is the first aid procedure for heat related injuries caused by wearing individual protective equipment?
A. Move the casualty to a clean (shady) area and give water to drink.

Q. Name the cold weather injuries.
A. Chilblain, immersion syndrome (immersion foot/trench foot), frostbite, snow blindness, dehydration, and hypothermia.

Q. What are NAPP tablets?
A. Nerve Agent Pyridostigmine Pretreatment tablets - a blister pack of nerve agent pretreatment tablets, one taken every eight hours. Must be taken prior to possible exposure to nerve agents. The purpose of the tablets is to make the effects of the MARK I, Nerve Agent Antidote Kit, more effective.

Q. What are the eight MILD symptoms of nerve agent poisoning?

A. - unexplained runny nose
- unexplained sudden headache
- sudden drooling
- difficulty seeing (blurred vision)
- tightness in chest or difficulty in breathing
- localized sweating and twitching (as a result of small amount of nerve agent on skin)
- stomach cramps
- nausea

Q. What are the nine SEVERE symptoms of nerve agent poisoning?
A. - strange or confused behavior
- wheezing, difficulty in breathing, and coughing
- severely pinpointed pupils
- red eyes with tearing (if agent gets into the eyes)
- vomiting
- severe muscular twitching and general weakness
- loss of bladder/bowel control
- convulsions
- unconsciousness
- stoppage of breathing

Q. Where is the injection site for the Mark I, Nerve Agent Antidote Kit?
A. Normally the outer thigh muscle. It is important that the injections be given into a large muscle area. If the individual is thinly built, then the injections must be administered into the upper outer quarter (quadrant) of the buttocks.

Q. There is a nerve that crosses the buttocks, so it is important to inject only into the upper outer quadrant to avoid hitting it. What could happen if you accidentally hit this nerve?
A. Hitting the nerve can cause paralysis.

Q. What is contained in the Mark I, Nerve Agent Antidote Kit?
A. One atropine autoinjector and one pralidoxime chloride (2 PAM CL) autoinjector.

Q. Which autoinjector is used first?
A. The small one (atropine).

Q. What action "arms" the needle of the autoinjectors?
A. Pulling the injector out of the clip.

Q. What causes the needle to inject into the thigh muscle?
A. Firm pressure automatically triggers the coiled spring mechanism. This plunges the needle through the clothing into the muscle and automatically injects the contents into the muscle tissue.

Q. How long should the autoinjectors be held in place once activated?
A. At least 10 seconds.

Q. How many sets of the nerve agent antidote are you authorized to administer to yourself?
A. Three.

Q. After injecting yourself with the nerve agent antidote, what do you do with the expended autoinjectors?

A. Push the needle of each injector (one at a time) through one of the pocket flaps of your protective overgarment. Bend each needle down to form a hook which will hold them in place.

Q. Why is it important to attach expended autoinjectors to your pocket flaps?
A. So medical personnel can determine how much antidote has been given and the proper follow-up treatment can be provided, if necessary.

Q. If within 5 to 10 minutes after administering the first set of injections, your heart begins to beat rapidly and your mouth becomes very dry, what should you do?
A. DO NOT give yourself another set of injections. You have already received enough antidote to overcome the dangerous effects of the nerve agent.

Q. What might happen if you give yourself another set of injections when they are not needed?
A. You may create a nerve agent antidote overdose, which could cause incapacitation.

Q. What should you do while waiting the 5 to 10 minutes between sets of injections?
A. Decontaminate your skin, if necessary, and put on remaining protective clothing.

Q. A soldier exhibiting SEVERE signs/symptoms of nerve agent poisoning will not be able to care for himself and must therefore be given buddy aid as quickly as possible. How does buddy aid differ from self aid with respect to nerve agent poisoning?
A. You may be required to mask the casualty and you must administer all three sets of injectors.

Q. What are the first aid measures for treating blister agent poisoning?
A. - Use uncontaminated water to flush the eyes. Use the M258A1 decon kit to decontaminate the skin (except where blisters have already formed).
- If blisters form, cover them loosely with a field dressing and secure

NOTE: Blisters from blister agent poisoning are actually burns. DO NOT attempt to decon the skin where blisters have formed. If you receive blisters over a wide area of the body, you are considered seriously burned.

Q. What are the first aid measures for blood agent poisoning?
A. Other than masking immediately, there are no first aid measures. SEEK MEDICAL ATTENTION IMMEDIATELY!

NOTE: For more in-depth information regarding chemical agents and their effects refer to Chapter 16 of this study manual, NBC.

Q. What is meant by the term "psychological first aid"?
A. It is nothing more than assisting people with emotional distress whether it results from physical injury, disease, or excessive stress.

Q. What are the goals of psychological first aid?
A. (1) Be supportive; assist the soldier in dealing with his stress reaction.
(2) Prevent, and if necessary control, behavior harmful to him and to others.
(3) Return the soldier to duty as soon as possible after dealing with the stress reaction.

FIRST AID
FM 21-11

Q. Name four principles to remember when administering psychological first aid.
A. - respect everyone's right to have his own feelings
- accept emotional disability as being just as real as physical disability
- realize that every physically injured person has some emotional reaction to the fact that he is injured
- realize that there is more strength in most distressed soldiers than appears at first glance

Q. What is "battle fatigue"?
A. A temporary emotional disorder or inability to function, experienced by a previously normal soldier as a reaction to the overwhelming or cumulative stress of combat.

Q. What is the best "cure" for battle fatigue?
A. Reassurance, rest, physical replenishment, and activities which restore confidence.

Q. What are "CSRs"?
A. Combat Stress Reactions - include drug and alcohol abuse, committing atrocities against enemy prisoners and noncombatants, looting, desertion, and self-inflicted wounds.

Q. Transportation of the sick and wounded is normally the responsibility of whom?
A. Medical personnel who have been provided special training and equipment for doing so.

Q. There may be some instances when a manual carry is essential to saving a casualty's life. Although manual carries are accomplished by one or two bearers, the two-man carries are used whenever possible. The distance a casualty can be carried depends on what four factors?
A. (1) Strength and endurance of the bearer(s).
(2) Weight of the casualty.
(3) Nature of the casualty's injuries.
(4) Obstacles encountered during transport.

Q. What are the nine one-man carries?
A. - fireman's carry
- support carry
- arms carry
- saddleback carry
- pack-strap carry
- pistol-belt carry
- pistol-belt drag
- neck drag
- cradle drop drag

Q. What are the five two-man carries?
A. - two-man support carry
- two-man arms carry
- two-man fore-and-aft carry
- two-hand seat carry
- four-hand seat carry

FIELD HYGIENE AND SANITATION
FM 21-10

Q. What FM covers "Field Hygiene and Sanitation"?
A. FM 21-10

Q. What is the purpose of FM 21-10?
A. To assist individual soldiers, unit commanders, leaders and field sanitation teams in preventing disease and environmental injuries.

Q. What is "hygiene"?
A. The self-employment of practices which will keep one healthy.

Q. What is "sanitation"?
A. The effective use of measures which will create and maintain healthful environmental conditions.

Q. What is meant by "military sanitation"?
A. Includes the practice of both environmental sanitation and personal hygiene, particularly within the framework of situations and experiences associated with Army life.

Q. How do you define "communicable diseases"?
A. Those illnesses that can be transmitted from man to man, from animal to man, and from insect to man. They are often called "contagious" or "infectious" diseases.

Q. What are the five communicable disease groups classified by the Army?
A. Respiratory, intestinal, insect-borne, venereal, and miscellaneous.

Q. Which of the five communicable disease groups accounts for the highest incidence of disease in the Army?
A. Respiratory infections.

Q. What is the principle source of the organism which causes intestinal disease?
A. The feces of man.

Q. Intestinal diseases usually are caused by the contamination of food and water with germs from human feces or urine. For this reason they are often called what?
A. "Filth Diseases".

Q. What is the chain of disease transmission?
A. Reservoir (source) --> vehicle (means of transmission) --> susceptible person.

Q. What are the three basic control measures for communicable diseases?
A. Control the source, stop the transmission, and protect the susceptible person.

Q. What are the five Fs of field sanitation?
A. Feces, flies, fingers, food, and fluids.

Q. One of the methods of controlling respiratory disease is by the avoidance of overcrowding. How many feet apart should cots be placed?
A. At least 5 feet; if less than 5 feet they should be positioned head-to-foot.

Q. What does "DNBI" stand for?

FIELD HYGIENE AND SANITATION
FM 21-10

A. Diseases and NonBattle Injuries.

Q. What are PMMs?
A. Preventive Medicine Measures - simple, commonsense actions that any soldier can perform and every leader must know in order to reduce time loss due to DNBI.

Q. FM 21-10 covers eight categories of medical threats. What are they?
A. - heat
- cold
- arthropods and other animals
- food/waterborne diseases
- the unfit soldier
- noise
- toxic chemicals - nonNBC
- nonbattle injury

Q. Which of the above categories is considered to be the most lethal of all?
A. Heat.

Q. Failure to apply the principles of PMM can result in mission failure. What are the three principles of PMM?
A. (1) Soldiers perform individual principles of PMM.
(2) Chain of command plans for and enforces PMM.
(3) Field sanitation teams train soldiers in PMM and advise the commander on implementation of unit level PMM.

Q. What are the individual PMMs for heat injuries?
A. - Drink plenty of water.
- Use work/rest cycles.
- Eat all meals (to replace salt).
- Recognize the risk of MOPP/body armor/armored vehicles.
- Modify your uniform.

Q. Water discipline is especially important in hot weather. What steps of water discipline should you follow?
A. (1) Drink small quantities frequently.
(2) Drink water even if you are not thirsty.
(3) Refill your canteen at every opportunity (preferably with cool water, which is absorbed faster than cold water).
(4) Prevent water waste.
(5) Protect water sources by good sanitary practices.

Q. If your urine is dark yellow, what is this an indication of?
A. You are not drinking enough water (thirst is not a good indication of dehydration).

Q. The quantity of water required for soldiers varies with the season of the year, the geographical area, and the tactical situation. What is a good "general" guide for planning water requirements?
A. 3-6 gallons per individual per day (15 gallons or more if improvised shower facilities are available).

Q. What are the six sources of water?
A. Surface, ground, rain, ice, snow, and sea water.

Q. What five factors should be considered when selecting a water source?
A. (1) The military situation.
(2) The quantity of water needed.
(3) The accessibility of the source.
(4) The general quality of the source.

(5) The type of purification equipment available for use.

Q. Water taken from any of the six sources mentioned above must be treated before use, as all sources of water in the field are considered ________.
A. Contaminated.

Q. When should salt tablets or salt solutions be taken to replace salt?
A. **Only** when directed by medical personnel.

Q. Part of a leader's PMM for heat injuries is to obtain and use "heat condition". Heat Condition information is used to determine required water intake and work/rest cycles and may be reported in what two ways?
A. By category (I, II, III, IV, or V) and/or by Wet Bulb Globe Temperature (WBGT) Index.

Q. What is the Wet Bulb Globe Temperature (WBGT) Index used for?
A. The WBGT Index is a single numeral by which air temperature, air movement, relative humidity, and radiant heat can be expressed as favorable or unfavorable for certain types of activities.

Q. MOPP gear or body armor adds at least _____ degrees F to the WBGT index.
A. 10 degrees.

Q. At what heat condition category should physical training and strenuous activity be suspended?
A. Category V (WBGT Index of 90 degrees and above).

Q. When using the "WORK/REST" column on the heat condition chart, "REST" means minimal physical activity and should be accomplished in the shade if possible. What are some examples of minimal physical activities that may be performed during "REST" cycles?
A. Training by lecture or demonstration, minor maintenance procedures on vehicles or weapons, personal hygiene activities - such as skin and foot care.

Q. Some soldiers are inherently at higher risk of heat injury than others and should be promptly identified. What are some examples?
A.
- Soldiers with previous heatstroke/severe heat exhaustion injuries.
- Soldiers with diseases/injuries, especially fevers, vomiting/diarrhea, heat rash/sunburn.
- Soldiers that recently (within 24 hours) consumed alcohol.
- Overweight/unfit soldiers.
- Soldiers over 40 years of age.
- Fatigued soldiers.
- Soldiers on medication, especially for high blood pressure, colds, or diarrhea.
- Soldiers with lack of previous experience in a hot environment (not acclimated).

NOTE: Heavy meals and hot foods put unnecessary stress on the body. Hot meals add heat which must be eliminated. Heavy meals direct blood flow to the digestive tract. Eat light meals during the hottest portion of the day.

Q. What are the individual PMMs for cold injuries?
A.
- Wear uniform properly.
- Keep your body warm.
- Protect your feet, hands, face, ears, and eyes.
- Protect your buddy.

FIELD HYGIENE AND SANITATION
FM 21-10

Q. Why should the use of tobacco products be avoided in extremely cold weather?
A. It decreases blood flow to the skin, placing you at greater risk of a cold weather injury.

Q. What should be used by leaders to approximate the equivalent temperature of the cooling power of wind on exposed flesh, thereby reducing the probability of cold weather injuries to soldiers?
A. Leaders should use a Windchill Factor Chart (GTA 8-5-40) to determine the appropriate windchill index and ensure that soldiers understand the intrinsic danger involved.

Q. Any movement of air has the same effect as wind - running, riding in open vehicles, or helicopter downwash and should be taken into consideration. Wind speeds greater than _____ mph, however, have little additional effect on windchill.
A. 40

Q. Leaders should identify soldiers with conditions that place them at high risk of cold injuries. What are some examples of these conditions?
A.
- Previous cold weather injuries.
- Fatigue.
- Recent consumption of alcohol.
- Significant injuries.
- Poor nutrition.
- Use of medications which cause drowsiness.
- Little previous experience in cold weather (not acclimated).
- Immobilized or subject to greatly reduced activity.
- Frequent or recent use of tobacco products.

Q. When using insect repellent, where should it be placed and how often should it be applied?
A. Use on all exposed skin (face, ears, neck, arms, hands), where clothing fits tightly (upper back, buttocks, knees), and all openings of the uniform (collar, cuffs, shirt front, waistband, boot tops); reapply coat immediately if you get wet, every 2 hours if you get sweaty, or every 4 hours regardless.

Q. After-shave lotion, cologne, and/or perfume soaps should not be used in a field environment for what reason?
A. They attract biting or stinging insects.

Q. What is the proper procedure for "fumigating" a bednet or small tent?
A. Use an aerosol insect spray inside the bednet after it is tucked (or in your tent if it can be sealed). Spray for only 1 or 2 seconds. Allow at least 10 minutes for aerosol to disperse before occupying the bednet or tent.

Q. In the field it is a good practice to do what to clothing, shoes/boots, and bedding before using them?
A. Shake out and inspect them.

Q. Leaders should not permit soldiers to eat in sleeping/work areas for what primary reason?
A. Food (crumbs/wrappers from "pogey bait", in particular) attracts a variety of undesirable insects and arthropods.

Q. Why should freshly killed snakes be handled with a long tool or stick?
A. Snakes can inflict fatal bites by reflex action after death.

FIELD HYGIENE AND SANITATION
FM 21-10

Q. What is meant by "potable" water?
A. Water that is safely drinkable.

Q. What is the objective of water treatment?
A. To produce potable water.

Q. Good water discipline involves filling your canteen with treated water at every chance. When treated water is not available, you must disinfect the water in your canteen using one of five approved methods. What are they?
A. Iodine tablets, chlorine (calcium hypochlorite) ampules, tincture of iodine, household/common bleach, or boiling.

Q. Which of the above methods for disinfecting water is the preferred method?
A. Iodine tablets for individual canteens of water; calcium hypochlorite (chlorine) for disinfecting large quantities of water such as a Lyster bags or water buffaloes.

Q. Iodine tablets used to purify individual water supplies should be what color?
A. Steel-gray (do not use if they are discolored, stuck together, or crumbled).

Q. Describe how water may be disinfected using each of the above methods.
A. (1) Iodine tablets (preferred method):
- Fill canteen with the cleanest water available.
- Use one tablet for clear water, or two for cold or cloudy water (double amounts for 2-qt canteen).
- Place cap on canteen, wait 5 minutes, then shake. Loosen the cap and tip the canteen over to allow leakage of treated water around threads. Tighten the cap and wait an additional 25 minutes before drinking.

(2) Chlorine amputate (calcium hypochlorite):
- Fill canteen with the cleanest water available.
- Mix one ampule of chlorine with one-half canteen cup of water. Stir the mixture with a clean device until contents are dissolved.
- Pour one-half plastic canteen capful or one NBC canteen capful of the above solution into your canteen of water.
- Place the cap on your canteen and shake. Slightly loosen the cap and tip the canteen over to allow leakage around the threads. Tighten cap and wait 30 minutes before drinking.

(3) Tincture of Iodine:
- Fill canteen with cleanest water available.
- Add 5 drops of 2% Tincture of Iodine per canteen/quart. If water is cold or cloudy, add 10 drops.
- Mix thoroughly by shaking canteen. Slightly loosen the cap and tip the canteen over to allow leakage around the threads. Tighten cap and wait 30 minutes before drinking.
- NOTE: Very cloudy or cold water may require prolonged contact time. Let stand several hours or overnight if possible.

(4) Household/common bleach:
- Fill canteen with cleanest water available.
- Read label on bleach bottle to determine amount of available chlorine. Liquid chlorine laundry bleach usually has 4 to 6 percent available chlorine.
- Add drops to canteen based on following chart:

available chlorine	**clear water**	**cold/cloudy water**
1%	10	20
4-6%	2	4
7-10%	1	2

- Place cap on canteen and shake. Slightly loosen the cap and tip canteen over to allow leakage around threads. Tighten cap and wait 30 minutes before drinking.

Q. What is Calcium Hypochlorite?
A. A chlorine compound that releases 70% of its weight as chlorine when dissolved in water. Common forms: HTH, perchloron.

Q. What is meant by "chlorine demand" and "chlorine residual"?
A. Chlorine demand is the amount of chlorine necessary to destroy organisms in the water; chlorine residual is the remaining chlorine (above the chlorine demand) that serves as a continuing disinfectant.

Q. At the point of consumption, water obtained from an **approved water distribution point** should have at least _____ ppm chlorine residual.
A. 1 ppm

Q. When the unit must obtain water from a raw water supply, or from another source such as a stream or pond, the finished product should have a ____ ppm chlorine residual after 30 minutes.
A. 5 ppm

NOTE: Under certain conditions the local medical authority may direct a higher residual of 10 ppm.

Q. How is the level of chlorine in treated water determined?
A. By use of a color comparator (included with chlorination kits).

Q. There are two different types of chlorination kits in use. Describe them.
A. (1) Orthotolidine chlorination kit: contains three plastic tubes (comparators), three vials of orthotolidine tablets, and calcium hypochlorite ampules. Each plastic tube has a band of different shade of yellow around it. The lightest shade of yellow indicates 1 ppm; the medium shade, 5 ppm; and the darkest shade, 10 ppm.
(2) New DPD chlorination kit: contains a color comparator with color comparisons for measuring 1, 1.5, 2, 3, 5, and 10 ppm chlorine residual; DPD tablet packages; and calcium hypochlorite ampules.

Q. How long should water be boiled when chlorine and iodine are not available?
A. Boiling water at a rolling boil for 5 to 10 minutes kills most organisms that are known to cause intestinal diseases.

NOTE: In an emergency, even boiling water for 15 seconds will help. Boiled water must be protected from recontamination since there is no residual protection.

Q. What are some common water-borne diseases of man?
A. Hepatitis, typhoid and paratyphoid fever, dysentery, cholera, and common diarrhea.

Q. What is dysentery?
A. A medical term applied to a number of intestinal disorders characterized by stomach pain and diarrhea. It is attributed to poor sanitary conditions.

FIELD HYGIENE AND SANITATION
FM 21-10

Q. Who is responsible for establishing standards for water quality, inspecting water points or sources, and approving water for consumption?
A. The Army Medical Department.

Q. Who is responsible for selecting sources of water and for establishing water points?
A. The Army Corps of Engineers.

Q. Who is responsible for setting up and operating bulk water treatment equipment and distributing treated water?
A. The Army Quartermaster Corps.

Q. Who is responsible for ensuring that the unit has an adequate supply of safe drinking water?
A. The Unit Commander.

Q. Why should foods or beverages that have been prepared or stored in galvanized containers not be eaten?
A. Galvanized containers have been coated with zinc to prevent rust. Therefore, eating foods or drinking beverages that have been prepared or stored in galvanized containers may result in heavy-metal (zinc) poisoning.

Q. Using a dirty mess kit will almost always result in what medical condition?
A. Diarrhea.

Q. You should get into the habit of immediately burying your waste. What is the primary reason for this?
A. To prevent flies from spreading germs from your waste to your food.

Q. Whenever possible, you should take a full bath at least how often in a field environment?
A. Once every week (if showers and baths are not available, use a washcloth daily to wash genital areas, armpits, feet, and other areas where you may sweat or that become wet).

Q. To keep skin dry you should use talcum powder in areas where wetness is a problem. What may be used as a substitute for talcum powder?
A. Cornstarch.

Q. What is considered to be the most frequent medical problem females face in the field?
A. Urinary tract infections (caused by not drinking enough fluids and holding urine due to the lack of privacy in field latrines).

Q. One of the field medical threats is noise. What are the two types of noise?
A. (1) Impact noise - very loud, short bursts of noise such as small arms fire, cannon, or gun fire.
(2) Continuous noise - loud, steady noise such as wheeled/track vehicles, aircraft, and other equipment operation.

Q. From a tactical standpoint, why is hearing conservation so important?
A. Soldiers with impaired hearing cannot hear important combat noise such as snapping twigs, metal to metal, and approaching vehicles resulting in the unit position being overrun or destroyed.

Q. What are some of the immediate effects of noise on the unprotected soldier?

FIELD HYGIENE AND SANITATION
FM 21-10

A. Ringing in the ears; temporary loss of some hearing that lasts for minutes or hours; or pain/broken eardrums.

Q. There are four properties or characteristics of noise which determine whether a given noise is likely to be hazardous to workers' hearing. What are they?
A. Frequency, intensity, nature of the noise, and exposure duration.

Q. What are the four categories of toxic chemical NON-NBC threats?
A. (1) Carbon monoxide - from gasoline engines and fuel space heaters.
(2) Hydrogen chloride - from rocket system exhaust.
(3) Bore/gun gases - such as lead, carbon monoxide, and other gases from ammo propellant.
(4) Solvents, greases, and oils - from vehicle maintenance and repair.

Q. Enforcing sleep discipline is important in protecting against the temporary effects of sleep loss on alertness, mood, and task performance. When feasible, work/rest shifts should be set to give everyone how many hours of sleep per 24 hours?
A. 6-9

Q. During "continuous operations," set shifts and rotate jobs to allow everyone at least _____ hours of uninterrupted sleep per 24-hour period.
A. 3-4

Q. During brief (up to 48 hours) sustained operations when shifts are impossible, what should leaders do in regards to sleep discipline?
A. Rotate jobs so all individuals catnap as safely and comfortably as possible.

NOTE: The mission, unit readiness, and individual security must come first, but never miss a chance to give someone in the unit time to sleep.

Q. What precaution should be taken for vehicles moving in, near, or around suspected bivouac areas?
A. Use ground guides to prevent accidentally running over sleeping soldiers.

Q. What is an "FST"?
A. Field Sanitation Team.

Q. What FM covers the roles and responsibilities of the Unit Field Sanitation Team (FST)?
A. FM 21-10-1

Q. What is the primary role of the Field Sanitation Team?
A. To aid the unit commander in protecting the health of the command by advising and assisting him in the many duties essential to reducing DNBI.

Q. What are the two basic duties of the FST?
A. (1) Basic sanitation and protection.
(2) Arthropod and rodent control.

Q. Food contained in insulated containers (ie, Mermites) should be kept at _____ degrees F or above for hot foods and _____ degrees F or below for cold foods.
A. 140; 45.

Q. Any temperature between 46 degrees F and 139 degrees F is in the **DANGER**

ZONE. Food products may have to be in the danger zone during some periods of preparation. What is considered to be the maximum **cumulative** time that potentially hazardous foods (ham, meats, potato/egg salads, fish, poultry) can be in the danger zone and not be a health hazard?
A. 3 hours.

Q. A mess kit laundry (wash line) should contain how many cans? What is contained in each can and how many personnel will such a wash line support?
A. 4; (1) Scrap can: for food waste.
(2) Wash can: hot soapy water (120-150 degrees F) for scrubbing mess kit; use long handle brush.
(3) Rinse: clear boiling water.
(4) Disinfect: clear boiling water - immerse mess kit for at least 10 seconds, shake off excess water and allow to air dry.

NOTE: Each hot water setup of four cans will support 80 personnel.

Q. What is used in the mess kit laundry cans to keep the water hot (or boiling)?
A. Immersion heaters (displaces approximately 12 gallons of water).

Q. If immersion heaters are unavailable or not in use, what should be done? With this setup, how many personnel will it support?
A. When it is not possible or practical to heat the water, a chlorine solution is used in the fourth container. Utensils are washed in the soapy water; rinsed in the third can of clear water; then are immersed in the fourth container of sanitizing solution for at least 30 seconds. Use Food Service Disinfectant (follow directions on label); or 3 MRE spoonsful of calcium hypochlorite powder for every 10 gallons of water; or 1 canteen cup of 5% liquid chlorine bleach in 32 gallons of water. This method is usually sufficient for servicing 100 soldiers.

Q. When should water containers be inspected?
A. Quarterly in garrison when not being used; prior to deployment; and before filling at water distribution points.

Q. Personnel detailed to fill water trailers should do so where?
A. At approved water points.

Q. What is a Lyster bag?
A. A 36-gallon fabric bag in which water can be chlorinated and held for later use.

Q. The Lyster bag is issued to units on what basis?
A. 1 bag per 100 persons.

Q. After the initial chlorine demand is satisfied, 1 additional ampule of calcium hypochlorite will raise the residual approximately how much in 36 gallons of water?
A. 2 ppm

Q. What are the four types of field waste?
A. Garbage, rubbish, liquid kitchen or bathing waste, and human waste.

Q. What is the difference between garbage and rubbish?
A. Garbage is considered to be the solid or semi-solid waste resulting from the preparation, cooking, and serving of food. Rubbish normally refers to refuse

or trash not associated with the preparation, cooking, or serving of food.

Q. What is a "cat-hole"?
A. A field expedient human waste hole used primarily when on the move. It is dug approximately 12 inches wide, 6-12 inches deep and covered up when finished.

Q. A camp or bivouac area without proper waste disposal methods soon becomes an ideal breading area for flies, rats, and other vermin and may result in diseases such as dysentery, typhoid, and cholera among soldiers. What are the recommended methods of disposing of field waste?
A. (1) Garbage/rubbish disposal:
- burial: less than one week.
- incineration: longer than one week.

(2) Liquid kitchen or bathing waste disposal:
- grease trap
- soakage trenches
- soakage pits
- evaporation beds

(3) Human waste disposal:
- cat-hole latrine: for marches
- straddle trench latrine: for 1-3 day bivouac sites
- deep pit latrine for temporary camps
- burn-out latrine or pail latrine: when ground is too hard or the water table is too high (soil is very wet)
- soakage pits for urinals at temporary camps:
  -- trough urinal
  -- pipe urinal
  -- urinoil
- chemical toilets (porta-potties): when local, state, or host nation laws prevent construction of standard field latrines.

Q. How far should field latrines be located from food operations and sources of water?
A. At least 100 yards from food operations - downwind and on down slope if possible; and at least 100 feet down slope of any unit ground water sources.

Q. Usually latrines are built at least _____ yards from the border of the unit area but within reasonable distance for easy access.
A. 30

Q. What percentage requirements should be used when constructing straddle trench and deep pit latrines?
A. Enough for 4% of males and 6% of females.

Q. What three things must you consider when determining the TYPE of latrine(s) to be constructed?
A. The length of stay, the water level, and the soil conditions.

Q. What two things, in order of precedence, must be considered when determining the LOCATION within the camp area for construction of latrines?
A. (1) Protection from food preparation areas and water sources.
(2) Accessibility to the users.

Q. What are the dimensions of a straddle trench latrine?
A. 1 foot wide by 4 feet long by 2(1/2) feet deep (additional trenches constructed parallel to one another and at least 2 feet apart).

Q. When digging a straddle trench latrine, what do you do with the dirt?

FIELD HYGIENE AND SANITATION
FM 21-10

A. Pile it at one end of the trench. Provide a shovel so that each soldier can promptly cover his excreta.

Q. One straddle trench will accommodate how many soldiers?
A. Two.

Q. Knowing the percentage requirements and accommodation of a straddle trench latrine, how many trenches should be provided per 100 males? 100 females?
A. 2; 3.

Q. When should latrines and garbage pits be closed?
A. When filled to within 1 foot of the ground surface.

Q. What is the proper procedure for closing a latrine or garbage pit?
A. (1) Spray with residual insecticide.
(2) Pack dirt in successive 3-inch layers until mounded 1 foot above ground level. Spray again with residual insecticide.
(3) Post a sign with the date and the words "closed latrine" or "closed garbage pit" (except in combat).

Q. Liquid and solid wastes produced under field conditions may amount to ____ lbs per person per day.
A. 100 lbs

Q. What should be the dimensions of a deep pit latrine?
A. 2 feet wide and either 3(1/2) or 7(1/2) feet long, depending upon the size of the latrine box. The depth of the pit depends on the estimated length of time the latrine will be used. As a guide, a depth of 1 foot is allowed for each week of estimated use, plus 1 foot of depth for dirt cover. Generally, it is not desirable to dig the pit more than 6 feet deep because of the danger of the walls caving in.

Q. When using a burn-out latrine, what is the desired mixture of gasoline to diesel oil?
A. 1 qt gasoline to 4 qts diesel oil.

Q. What should be done with any ashes obtained from a burn-out latrine?
A. The ashes should be buried.

Q. A urinoil is a 55-gallon drum designed to receive and trap urine and to dispose of it into a soakage pit. What is the purpose of the oil in a urinoil?
A. The oil acts as an effective seal against odors and against fly entrance (urine immediately sinks through the oil to the bottom of the drum).

Q. How far should garbage be buried from any natural source of water?
A. At least 100 feet.

Q. What are the dimensions of a garbage pit?
A. 4 feet square and 4 feet deep.

Q. How far should a garbage burial area be from the field kitchen?
A. A **reasonable distance** to minimize problems with flies, odor, and appearance.

Q. Field incinerators for garbage create an odor nuisance and for this reason should be located at least how far from and downwind of camp sites?
A. 50 yards.

FIELD HYGIENE AND SANITATION
FM 21-10

Q. What are the dimensions of a soakage pit?
A. Same as a garbage pit (4x4x4), only filled with sand and gravel.

Q. Liquid kitchen wastes accumulate at the rate of ____ to ____ gallons per man per day.
A. 1 to 5

Q. A standard soakage pit will accommodate how much liquid waste per day?
A. 200 gallons (in porous soil).

Q. Name five diseases commonly carried by mosquitoes.
A. Malaria, yellow fever, dengue fever, encephalitis (sleeping sickness), and filariasis (elephantiasis).

Q. What are some commonly used control measures for mosquitoes?
A. Screens, residual sprays such as Malathion, insecticides such as pyrethrum, individual issue insect repellents such as DEET, and in some cases, chemoprophylactic medication.

Q. What medication is taken by individuals entering a known malaria area?
A. Chloroquine-Primaquine (C-P) tablets; take one tablet one day prior to entering the area and upon returning take one tablet per week for 8 weeks.

Q. Name three diseases commonly carried by flies.
A. Cholera, typhoid fever, and dysentery.

Q. Name some diseases commonly carried by rodents.
A. Plague and salmonella.

Q. Why is it so important that **ALL** members of a team or unit practice good personal hygiene?
A. Because one careless member of the team can cause disease that may incapacitate the entire unit.

Q. Should mud be used as a field expedient camouflage for exposed skin?
A. Only as a last resort since mud contains bacteria, some of which is harmful, and may cause disease or infection.

MAP READING AND LAND NAVIGATION
FM 21-26

Q. What FM covers "MAP READING AND LAND NAVIGATION"?
A. FM 21-26

Q. What is a "map"?
A. A map is a graphic representation of a portion of the earth's surface drawn to scale, as seen from above.

Q. The art and science of expressing the known physical features of the earth graphically by maps and charts is known as what?
A. Cartography

Q. What organization provides mapping, charting, and geodesy support to the armed forces and all other national security operations?
A. The Defense Mapping Agency (DMA).

Q. In the division, who is responsible for map requisitions and distribution?
A. Division Support Command (DISCOM), G2 section.

Q. If a military map is no longer needed, what must be done to it?
A. It must be turned in to the proper authority. If a map is in danger of being captured, it must be destroyed. MAPS ARE DOCUMENTS THAT MUST NOT FALL INTO UNAUTHORIZED HANDS.

Q. Military maps are categorized by what two things?
A. Scale and Type.

Q. What is meant by the "scale" of a map?
A. The scale is expressed as a fraction and gives the ratio of map distance to ground distance.

Q. DMA maps are classified by scale into what three categories?
A. Small scale --------- 1:1,000,000 and smaller
   Medium scale -------- 1:75,000 to 1:1,000,000
   Large scale --------- 1:75,000 and larger

NOTE: The terms "small scale", "medium scale", and "large scale" may be confusing when read in conjunction with the numbers. However, if the number is viewed as a fraction, it is apparent that 1/600,000 is "smaller" than 1/75,000. The larger the number after the colon (:), the smaller the scale.

Q. What is the standard "small scale" map and what is it used for?
A. 1:1,000,000; it is used for general planning and for strategical studies.

Q. What is the standard "medium scale" map and what is it used for?
A. 1:250,000; it is used for planning operations, including the movement and concentration of troops and supplies.

Q. What is the standard "large scale" map and what is it used for?
A. 1:50,000; it is used to meet the tactical, administrative, and logistical needs of field units.

Q. What are some examples of different TYPES of maps?
A. TOPOGRAPHIC, planimetric, photomap, Joint Operations Graphics (JOG), photomosaic, terrain model, military city, and special.

Q. Joint Operations Graphics, or JOGS, are normally based on what size military

topographic maps?
A. 1:250,000

Q. JOGS are produced in what two formats? What is the major difference?
A. JOG (Air) and JOG (Ground); both formats emphasize airlanding facilities (shown in purple), but the air version has additional symbols to identify aids and obstructions to air navigation. Also, elevations and contours are given in feet on the JOG (Air) format and meters on the JOG (Ground) format.

Q. What are some examples of "special" military maps?
A. Maps designed specifically to show one of more of the following:

- drainage characteristics
- climate
- coasts and landing beaches
- urban areas
- electric power
- fuels
- water resources
- natural construction materials

Q. A map can be compared to any piece of equipment, in that before it is placed in operation the user must read the instructions. These instructions are placed around the outer edge of the map and are known as ____________ ____________.
A. Marginal information.

Q. List some items of information that may be contained in the margin of a military map.
A. Sheet Name, Sheet Number, Series Name, Scale, Series Number, Edition Number, Index to Boundaries, Adjoining Sheets Diagram, Elevation Guide, Declination Diagram, Bar Scales, Contour Interval Note, Vertical Datum, Horizontal Datum, Grid Reference Box, Special Note, Legend.

Q. Where does a map get its name and where is the "sheet name" located?
A. A map is named after the most prominent cultural or geographical feature. Whenever possible, the name of the largest city on the map is used. The sheet name is found in bold print at the center of the top and in the lower left area of the map margin.

Q. Where is the sheet number found on a military map?
A. In bold print in both the upper right and lower left areas of the margin, and in the center box of the adjoining sheets diagram.

Q. What three pieces of information are located in both the upper right and lower left margins?
A. Edition, Series, and Sheet Numbers.

Q. Certain maps require a note indicating the security classification. Where would this information be located?
A. In the upper and lower margins.

Q. What does "DMATC" located in the margin next to Edition Number stand for?
A. Defense Mapping Agency Topographic Center.

Q. Topographic map symbols are positioned in such a manner that the ________ of the symbol remains in its true location.
A. Center.

Q. What are exceptions to the above rule?
A. Exceptions would be, for example, features adjacent to major roads (if the width of the road has been exaggerated then the feature is moved from its true

position to preserve its relation to the road).

Q. The size of a map symbol shows the approximate size of an object in comparison to surrounding objects. However, they are enlarged ____ to ____ times so that they can be seen under dim light.
A. 6 to 10.

Q. Identify the colors used to facilitate the identification of features on a military map.
A. Black - indicates cultural (man-made) features ~~such as buildings and roads~~ other than roads.
Blue - identifies hydrography or water features such as lakes, swamps, rivers, and drainage.
Brown - identifies all relief features and elevation, such as contours on older edition maps, and cultivated land on red-light readable maps.
Green - identifies vegetation with military significance, such as woods, orchards, and vineyards.
Red - classifies cultural features, such as populated areas, main roads, and boundaries, on older maps.
Red-Brown - the colors red and brown are combined to identify cultural features, all relief features, non-surveyed spot elevations, and elevation such as contour lines on red-light readable maps.

NOTE: Occasionally other colors may be used to show specific information. As a rule, these are indicated in the marginal information.

Q. The rings around the earth parallel to the equator are known as what?
A. Parallels of Latitude, or simply Parallels.

Q. A second set of rings around the globe at right angles to lines of latitude and passing through the poles are known as what?
A. Meridians of Longitude, or simply Meridians.

Q. One meridian is designated as the Prime Meridian. What is its location?
A. It passes through the old Greenwich (gren'-ich) Observatory in London, England. It was agreed upon by international treaty in 1884 as the line on which global time zones are based.

NOTE: The Prime Meridian is also known as the Greenwich Meridian, thus time here is referred to as Greenwich Mean Time (GMT) or Universal Time.

Q. Where is the International Date Line located?
A. On the other side of the globe, opposite the Prime Meridian at 180° West or East.

Q. Geographic coordinates are expressed in angular measurement. How is each circle (parallel or meridian) divided?
A. Into 360 degrees; each degree into 60 minutes ('); and each minute into 60 seconds (").

Q. Starting with 0 degrees at the equator, the parallels of latitude are numbered to ______ degrees both north and south.
A. 90

Q. Starting with 0 degrees at the Prime Meridian, the meridians of longitude are numbered to ______ degrees both east and west.
A. 180

MAP READING AND LAND NAVIGATION
FM 21-26

Q. At any point on the earth, the ground distance covered by one degree of latitude is about ____ miles, and one second is equal to about _____ feet.
A. 69; 100

Q. The ground distance covered by one degree of longitude at the equator is about ____ miles, and one second is equal to about _____ feet.
A. 69; 100

NOTE: Longitudinal ground distance decreases as one moves north or south of the equator, until it becomes zero at the poles.

Q. The four lines (borders) that enclose the body of the map are known as ______ ______ and are actually lines of latitude and longitude.
A. Neatlines.

Q. What is meant by the "military grid reference system"?
A. A network of squares formed by north-south, east-west lines on a military map.

Q. On what two grid systems are the military grid reference system (MGRS) based on and when are they used?
A. Universal Transverse Mercator (UTM) - designed to cover that part of the world between 84° N Lat and 80° S Lat.
Universal Polar Stereographic (UPS) - used to represent the polar regions.

Q. UTM grid zones are numbered from west to east, 1 through 60, starting at the 180 deg meridian. Grid Zones are further designated by letters, from south to north. What letters are used?
A. C thru X (I and O omitted because they may easily be confused with the numerals 1 and 0).

Q. What letters are used to represent a UPS grid?
A. A, B, Y, and Z.

Q. What is the approximate width of one grid zone?
A. One grid zone = 6 degrees wide x 69 miles = 414 miles.

Q. A UTM grid zone is further divided into 100,000-meter squares that are identified by the combination of two alphabetical letters. The first letter is the _________ designation; the second letter is the ________ designation. What is this combination of letters known as?
A. column; row; 100,000-meter square identifier.

Q. What is the distance between grid lines on a military map?
A. 1,000 meters (1 km).

Q. What graphic training aid contains four types of coordinate scales and is used by the soldier in plotting coordinates?
A. GTA 5-2-12

Q. What is the principle for reading grid coordinates on military maps?
A. Read RIGHT and UP.

Q. It is a military requirement that the ___________________ be included in any point designation.
A. 100,000-meter square identifier.

MAP READING AND LAND NAVIGATION
FM 21-26

Q. How many digits are required to locate a point to within 1000 meters?
A. 4

Q. How many digits are required to locate a point to within 100 meters?
A. 6

Q. How many digits are required to locate a point to within 10 meters?
A. 8

Q. How many digits would be required to locate a point to within 1 meter?
A. 10

Q. Normally, grid coordinates are determined to the nearest ______ meters for reporting locations.
A. 100

Q. The location of targets and other point locations for fire support are determined to the nearest ____ meters.
A. 10

Q. What items of information are contained in the Grid Reference Box?
A. Grid Zone Designation; 100,000-meter square identifier; instructions on how to use the grid.

Q. What special precaution should be taken when transmitting map coordinates over the radio during combat?
A. Encrypt the coordinates using authorized numerical codes so that the enemy cannot determine your location should the message be intercepted.

Q. What does a scale of 1:50,000 mean on a military map?
A. The scale 1:50,000 is actually a ratio that can be written as a fraction, known as the representative fraction (RF) - it is independent of any unit of measure. For example, an RF of 1/50,000 means that one unit of measure on the map is equal to 50,000 units of the same measure on the ground.

Q. What three things should you remember when measuring distance on a map?
A. (1) Measure center of mass to center of mass.
(2) Use the correct graphic scale.
(3) Use the same side of the road, or river, etc, when measuring curved-line distance.

Q. What is the Graphic (Bar) Scale on a map used for?
A. To convert distances on the map to actual ground distance.

Q. The graphic scale is divided into two parts. What are they?
A. Primary Scale and Extension Scale.

Q. One method of determining distance is by pace count. What six conditions must be considered when adjusting pace count?
A. Slopes, winds, surfaces, elements, clothing, and visibility.

Q. What is meant by "direction"? What is the most common military method of expressing direction?
A. An imaginary straight line on the map or ground; the azimuth.

Q. What is an "azimuth"?

MAP READING AND LAND NAVIGATION
FM 21-26

A. A horizontal angle measured in a clockwise manner from a north base line.

Q. Name three common units of angular measure used by military personnel to express direction.
A. Degree (360 deg in circle); Mil (6400 mils in circle); Grad (400 grads in circle).

Q. Which unit of measure is used mainly in artillery, tank, and mortar gunnery?
A. Mils

Q. Which unit of measure is found on some foreign maps?
A. Grads

Q. What is meant by "base line"?
A. The starting point or point of reference from which a unit of measure is taken.

Q. How many "base lines" are there on a military map and what are they?
A. 3; true north, magnetic north, and grid north.

Q. What are the two most commonly used base lines?
A. Grid and magnetic.

Q. Describe the three north's on a military map.
A. True North - a line from any point on the earth's surface to the north pole. True north is usually represented by a line with a star at the apex.

Magnetic North - the direction to the north magnetic pole, as indicated by the north-seeking needle of a magnetic instrument. Magnetic north is usually symbolized by a line ending with a half-arrowhead.

Grid North - the north that is established by using the vertical grid lines on the map. Grid north is symbolized by the letters "GN" or the letter "y" at the apex.

Q. All lines of (longitude/latitude) are considered true north lines.
A. Longitude.

Q. What is a "back azimuth" and how is it obtained?
A. A back azimuth is the opposite direction of an azimuth. To obtain a back azimuth from an azimuth: if the azimuth is less than 180 deg - add 180 deg; if more than 180 deg - subtract 180 deg.

Q. What is the back azimuth of 180 degrees?
A. May be stated as either 0 degrees or 360 degrees.

Q. What is the back azimuth of 270 degrees?
A. 90 degrees.

Q. What is the back azimuth of 20 degrees?
A. 200 degrees.

Q. When using a protractor, the inner scale is graduated in _________ while the outer scale is graduated in ________.
A. Degrees; mils.

Q. What is meant by "declination"? How many declinations are there?
A. Declination is the angular difference between true north and either magnetic or grid north; 2 - magnetic declination and grid declination.

MAP READING AND LAND NAVIGATION
FM 21-26

Q. What is the "declination diagram" and where is it located?
A. It is located in the lower central portion of the margin and shows the angular relationship between true north, grid north, and magnetic north.

NOTE: On medium-scale maps, the declination information is shown by a note in the map margin.

Q. What is the Grid-Magnetic (G-M) Angle used for and where is it found?
A. It is used for converting from grid north to magnetic north and vice-versa; it is found in the declination diagram.

Q. What is meant by "grid convergence"?
A. Similar to the G-M Angle, only it is the difference between true north and grid north (or the centerline of the map sheet).

Q. What is the reason for the difference between grid north and magnetic north?
A. The angular difference is caused by the attraction of the earth's magnetic field (Northern Canada) on all compasses. Since the location of this field does not correspond exactly with the grid-north lines on the maps, a conversion from magnetic to grid or vice-versa is needed.

Q. What are the rules for converting from a grid to a magnetic azimuth?
A. (1) Easterly G-M Angle (mag north lies to the east of GN in the declination diagram)
   a. conversion from grid to magnetic: sub G-M angle.
   b. conversion from magnetic to grid: add G-M angle.

(2) Westerly G-M Angle (mag north lies to the west of GN in the declination diagram)
   a. conversion from grid to magnetic: add G-M angle.
   b. conversion from magnetic to grid: sub G-M angle.

MEMORY AID: Remember that for an easterly G-M angle, a change from "G"eneral to "M"ajor is a subtraction (in rank), while a change from "M"ajor to "G"eneral is an addition. A westerly G-M angle is just the opposite.

Q. What is the best way to convert between grid and magnetic north if you can't remember the "rule" or formula?
A. On newer military maps you can use the "notes" section of the declination diagram. This tells you exactly how to convert between the two.

Q. What is meant by "intersection"?
A. Intersection is the location of an unknown point by successively occupying at least two (preferably three) known positions on the ground and then map sighting on the unknown locations.

Q. What are the steps for intersection using a map and compass?
A. (1) Orient the map using the compass.
(2) Locate and mark your position on the map.
(3) Determine the magnetic azimuth to the unknown position using the compass.
(4) Convert the magnetic azimuth to a grid azimuth.
(5) Plot the grid azimuth on the map.
(6) Move to a second known point or have a second known point (observer) complete steps 1-5.
(7) The location of the unknown position is where the lines cross

(intersect) on the map.

Q. What is meant by "resection"?
A. Resection is the method of locating one's position on a map by determining the grid azimuth to at least two well-defined locations that can be pinpointed on the map. For greater accuracy, the desired method of resection would be to use three well-defined locations.

Q. What are the steps for resection using a map and compass?
A. (1) Orient the map using the compass.
(2) Identify two or three known distant locations on the ground and mark them on the map.
(3) Measure the magnetic azimuth to the known positions from your location using a compass.
(4) Convert the magnetic azimuths to grid azimuths.
(5) Convert the grid azimuths to back azimuths and, using a protractor, scale the back azimuths on the map from the known positions back toward your unknown position.
(6) The intersection of your lines is your location.

Q. What method of intersection/resection is used when a compass is not available?
A. The straightedge method - orient the map using terrain association. Place a straightedge (ruler) on the map with one end on your location (pivot point) for intersection or on a known point for resection. Look over the top of the straightedge and rotate it until it is aligned with you and the desired location. Draw a line along the straightedge. Repeat using other locations. The point where the lines intersect (for intersection) or resect (for resection) is the desired coordinate.

Q. What is meant by a "modified resection"?
A. Modified resection is the method of locating one's position on the map when one is located on a linear feature on the ground, such as a road, canal, stream, etc. Only one azimuth is required since the linear object can be substituted for the second azimuth (you already know its location and direction!).

Q. What is a "polar plot" and what three elements must be present when using polar coordinates?
A. A polar plot is a method of locating or plotting an unknown position from a known point by giving a direction and a distance along that direction line.
(1) present known location on the map
(2) azimuth (grid or magnetic)
(3) distance (normally in yards or meters)

Q. What is meant by "dead reckoning" navigation?
A. The use of polar plot navigation; begins with the determination of a polar coordinate on a map and ends with the act of finding it on the ground.

Q. What is an "overlay"?
A. An overlay is a clear sheet of plastic (acetate) or transparent paper on which information is plotted to the same scale as the map it is to be used on.

Q. One use of an overlay is to clarify information that is difficult to explain in writing. What is this kind of overlay called?
A. An Annex Overlay.

MAP READING AND LAND NAVIGATION
FM 21-26

Q. Aerial photography most commonly used by military personnel may be divided into two major types. What are they?
A. Vertical and oblique.

Q. What are the four most commonly used types of film in aerial photography?
A. (1) Panchromatic - black & white; most commonly used.
(2) Infrared - black & white film sensitive to infrared waves; used to detect artificial camouflage and to take photographs at night if there is a source of infrared radiation.
(3) Color - limited because of the time required for processing and the need for clear, sunny weather.
(4) Camouflage Detection - special type that records natural vegetation in a reddish color; artificial camouflage materials appear bluish or purplish.

Q. What are the four types of compasses described in FM 21-26?
A. Lensatic, artillery, wrist/pocket, and protractor.

Q. What is considered to be the most common and simplest instrument for measuring direction?
A. The lensatic compass.

Q. What should be noted when using a protractor on a map to determine direction?
A. Only grid azimuths are obtained.

Q. What are the three major parts of the lensatic compass?
A. Cover, base, and lens.

Q. Where does the arrow on a lensatic compass always point (when open)?
A. Magnetic north.

Q. There are two scales on a lensatic compass; the outer scale, normally in _______ (color) denotes ________ and the inner scale, normally in ______ denotes __________.
A. Black - mils; red - degrees.

Q. The bezel ring on the base of a lensatic compass is a ratchet device that clicks when turned. It contains ______ clicks when rotated fully; each click is equal to ____ degrees. What is its primary purpose?
A. 120; 3; for use at night (if you need to make a 30 degree turn, rotate the bezel ring 10 "clicks" in the desired direction).

Q. The lens, or rear sight, also serves as a lock and clamps the dial when closed for its protection. How far MUST the rear sight be opened to allow the dial to float freely?
A. More than 45 degrees.

Q. When opened, the straightedge on the left side of the compass has a coordinate scale. What is this scale on the newer compasses?
A. 1:50,000.

NOTE: Some older compasses will have a scale of 1:25,000. This scale can be used with a 1:50,000 scale map, but the values read must be halved.

Q. Metal objects and electrical sources can affect the performance of a compass. It is recommended that you maintain the following safe distances to ensure proper functioning.

A. - high-tension power lines.................. 55 meters
- field gun, truck, or tank................. 18 meters
- telegraph or telephone wires/barbed wire... 10 meters
- machine gun.............................. 2 meters
- steel helmet or rifle..................... .5 meter

Q. A compass should be checked periodically on a known line of direction. A compass with more than ______ degrees variation should not be used.
A. 3

Q. What are the two approved techniques for holding the compass when sighting?
A. Centerhold and Compass-to-cheek.

Q. Which of the two above techniques will result in a greater degree of accuracy?
A. Compass-to-cheek.

Q. Name three field expedient methods for determining the four cardinal directions.
A. Shadow-Tip method, Watch method, and Star method.

Q. Explain the Shadow-Tip method of determining direction.
A. Step 1: Place a stick or branch into the ground at a level spot where a distinctive shadow will be cast. Mark the shadow tip with a stone, twig, or other means.
Step 2: Wait 10 to 15 minutes until the shadow tip moves a few inches. Mark the new position of the shadow tip in the same way as the first.
Step 3: Draw a straight line through the two marks to obtain an approximate east-west line.
Step 4: Place your left foot on the first mark and your right foot on (or in line with) the second mark. North will be to your front, south to your rear, west on your left side, and east on your right side.

Q. What is a simple rule to remember if you are uncertain which mark is east and which is west?
A. The sun always rises in the east and sets in the west, the shadow will move in the opposite direction - so the first shadow-tip mark is <u>always</u> in the west direction, <u>anywhere</u> on earth (except as noted below).

NOTE: The shadow-tip system is not intended for use in polar regions (above 60 degrees Latitude in either hemisphere).

Q. How do you use the shadow-tip method as a shadow clock to find the <u>approximate</u> time of day?
A. Once you have drawn the east-west line, draw another line perpendicular to it (forming the north-south line). Move the stick to the intersection of the east-west line and the north-south line, and set it vertically in the ground. The west part of the east-west line indicates 0600 hours, and the east part is 1800 hours, <u>anywhere</u> on earth, because the basic rule always applies. The north-south line becomes the noon line and the stick shadow becomes the hour hand in the shadow clock.

NOTE: Remember that the shadow clock is not a timepiece in the ordinary sense. It makes every day 12 unequal hours long, and always reads 0600 hours at sunrise and 1800 hours at sunset. It is closest to conventional clock time at midday. However, it does provide a satisfactory means of telling time in the absence of properly set watches.

Q. Explain the Watch method of determining direction.
A. In north temperate zones, the hour hand is pointed toward the sun. A south line can be found midway between the hour hand and 1200 hours.
In south temperate zones, the 1200-hour dial is pointed toward the sun, and halfway between 1200 hours and the hour hand will be a north line.

Q. Less than ______ of approximately 5,000 stars visible to the eye are used by navigators. The stars seen as we look up at the sky at night are not evenly scattered across the whole sky. Instead they are in groups called ____________.
A. 60; constellations.

Q. Due to the rotation of the earth, the stars seem to travel in a circle through the course of the night. But there is one star that is in almost exactly the same place in the sky all night long every night. What is this star?
A. The North Star, also known as the Polar Star or Polaris.

Q. Where can the North Star be found?
A. It is the last star in the handle of the <u>little</u> dipper.

NOTE: The North Star can only be seen in the northern hemisphere so it cannot serve as a guide south of the equator. Additionally, above 70 deg N Lat it is too high in the sky to be useful.

Q. What constellation is used as a guide south of the equator?
A. The Southern Cross.

Q. What does "GPS" stand for? Explain it and the advantages of its use.
A. Global Positioning System; it is a highly accurate, space-based, radio-positioning navigation system that uses satellite signal triangulation to determine latitude, longitude, and altitude of the individual user. In addition to position information, which can also be expressed in military grid coordinates, precise steering information and time to next destination can be given by entering the desired checkpoint into the GPS computer. The GPS is being fielded in hand-held, manpack, vehicular, aircraft, and watercraft configurations. It can be operated in all weather, day or night, anywhere in the world; it can also be used during NBC warfare. The GPS does not have inherent drift like the Inertial Navigation System (INS) and the receiver will automatically update its position.

Q. What is meant by the "datum plane"?
A. The reference point from which all measurement in elevation are taken (normally mean sea level, the point halfway between high tide and low tide).

Q. What is "elevation"?
A. The vertical distance above or below the datum plane.

Q. What is "relief"?
A. The representation of the shapes of hills, valleys, streams, or landforms on the earth's surface.

Q. What are the five methods of depicting relief?
A. Layer tinting, form lines, shaded relief, hachures, and contour lines.

MAP READING AND LAND NAVIGATION
FM 21-26

Q. Which of the above methods is the most common on standard topographic maps?
A. Contour lines.

Q. What are "contour lines"?
A. Imaginary straight lines on the ground that connect points of equal elevation.

Q. What are the three types of contour lines?
A. Index - heavy lines; normally every fifth contour line is an index contour. Normally numbered at some point with the elevation of points along that line.
Intermediate - the lighter contour lines falling between index contours.
Supplementary - resemble dashes; show sudden changes in elevation of at least one-half the contour interval.

Q. What is meant by "contour interval"?
A. The vertical distance between contour lines.

Q. Where can you find out what the contour interval is on the map you are using?
A. In the contour interval note located in the lower central portion of the map.

Q. What is usually the contour interval on 1:50,000 scale maps?
A. 20 meters

Q. How do you determine the elevation of a hilltop?
A. Add one-half the contour interval to the value of the highest contour line before the hilltop.

Q. How do you determine the elevation of a depression?
A. Subtract one-half the contour interval from the value of the lowest contour line before the depression.

Q. What, in addition to contour lines, are used to indicate points of known elevations on the map? Which is considered to be more accurate?
A. Bench marks and spot elevations; bench marks.

Q. What is a "bench mark" and how is it symbolized on the map?
A. A point of known location and elevation along a line of survey that is either permanently or semi-permanently marked. Monumented bench marks are symbolized by a black "X" and the letters "BM" next to it. The number (ie X BM 214), indicates the elevation of the center of the "X". Non-monumented bench marks are simply indicated by a black "X" on the map and the corresponding elevation.

Q. What are "spot elevations" and how are they symbolized on the map?
A. Points of known location and elevation that are usually located at road junctions and on hilltops and other prominent terrain features. They are symbolized by a brown "X". If the elevation is shown in black numerals it has been checked for accuracy; if it is in brown, it has not been checked.

Q. What are "hachures"?
A. Short broken lines used to show relief. They are used extensively on small-scale maps to show mountain ranges, plateaus, and mountain peaks.

Q. Identify the following types of slopes:
(1) Contour lines evenly spaced and wide apart.

(2) Contour lines evenly spaced, but close together.
(3) Contour lines closely spaced at the top and widely spaced at the bottom.
(4) Contour lines widely spaced at the top and closely spaced at the bottom.
A. (1) gentle slope
(2) steep slope
(3) concave slope
(4) convex slope

Q. The speed at which personnel and equipment can move up or down a hill is affected by the slope of the ground and the limitations of the equipment. Because of this, a more exact way of describing a slope is necessary. Name three commonly used methods for describing slope angle.
A. (1) Percent: ratio of vertical distance to horizontal distance.
(ie, VD=210-m and HD=3,000-m ==> slope = .07 x 100 = 7%)
(2) Degrees: angle formed by the ratio of VD to HD.
(ie, VD=210-m and HD=3,000-m ==> angle = tan (VD/HD) = 57.3*(.07) = 4°)
(3) Gradient: relationship of horizontal and vertical distance expressed as a fraction with a numerator of one.
(ie, VD=210-m HD=3,000-m ==> gradient = 1/14.3 (or in other words, 1-meter rise for every 14.3-meters of horizontal distance))

* 57.3 is a tangential constant that is reasonable accurate for slope angles less than 20°.

Q. All terrain features are derived from a complex landmass known as a mountain or ridgeline. What is a "ridgeline"?
A. A line of high ground, usually with changes in elevation along its top and low ground on all sides, from which a total of 10 natural or man-made terrain features are classified.

Q. What are the five MAJOR terrain features?
A. Hill, ridge, valley, saddle, depression.

Q. What are the three MINOR terrain features?
A. Draw, spur, and cliff.

Q. What are the two SUPPLEMENTAL terrain features?
A. Cut and fill.

NOTE: The previous edition of FM 21-26 listed the terrain features as five major, two minor, and three supplemental. Note the above changes.

Q. Identify the following terrain features:
(1) A vertical or near vertical feature; it is an abrupt change of the land.
(2) Short, continuous sloping line of higher ground, normally jutting out from the side of a ridge; often formed by two roughly parallel streams cutting draws down the side of a ridge.
(3) If you are here, the ground slopes down in all directions.
(4) A sloping line of high ground; normally, there is low ground in three directions and high ground in one direction.
(5) An area of low ground surrounded by high ground in all directions.
(6) If you are here, the ground slopes upward in three directions and downward in the other direction; there is essentially no level ground and therefore, little or no maneuver room within its confines.
(7) A man-made feature resulting from cutting through high ground, usually to form a level bed for a road or railroad track.
(8)If you are here, there is high ground in two opposite directions and lower

ground in the other two directions.
(9) A man-made feature resulting from filling a low area, usually to form a level bed for a road or railroad track.
(10) If you are standing here, there is high ground in two opposite directions and a gradual inclination in the other two directions and often has a course of running water through it.

A. (1) cliff
(2) spur
(3) hill
(4) ridge
(5) depression
(6) draw
(7) cut
(8) saddle
(9) fill
(10) valley

Q. Contour lines tend to parallel a stream before crossing it, forming a "U" or "V" shape. Which way is upstream?
A. The closed end of the contour line (U or V) always points upstream.

Q. In contrast to contour lines crossing a stream or river, contour lines forming a ridge or spur have a "U" shape with the closed end of the "U" pointing toward (higher/lower) ground.
A. Lower (or away from higher ground).

Q. A recommended technique for identifying specific terrain features and then locating them on the map is to make use of five of their characteristics. What are these characteristics and what word is used to help remember them?
A. (S)hape
(O)rientation
(S)ize
(E)levation
(S)lope

Q. What is a map profile? What is the primary use of profiles?
A. A method used to change the "overhead" view of a portion of a map to a "side" or cross-section view, giving the user an accurate depiction of elevations at specific points. The primary purpose of a profile view is to determine if line of sight is available from one specific point to another on the map (ie, determine dead spaces, defilade positions, potential weapon emplacements, etc).

Q. What is the best way to orient a map without a compass?
A. By aligning the features on the map with the same features on the ground (terrain association).

Q. What are the elements of a good terrain analysis and what mnemonics are used to aid in remembering them?
A. OCOKA and METT-T:

(O)bservation and fields of fire	(M)ission
(C)over and concealment	(E)nemy
(O)bstacles	(T)errain and weather
(K)ey terrain	(T)roops
(A)venues of approach	(T)ime available

NOTE: METT-TS is often used instead of METT-T, with the last letter (S) representing Safety.

Q. One key to success in tactical missions is the ability to move undetected to the objective. What are the four steps to land navigation?
A. (1) Know where you are.
   (2) Plan the route.
   (3) Stay on the route.
   (4) Recognize the objective.

Q. What are "steering marks"?
A. Landmarks selected during actual navigation that are on or near the highest points you can see along the azimuth line you are following. They are uniquely shaped trees, rocks, hilltops, posts, towers, buildings - anything that can be easily identified.

Q. If you cannot see a good steering mark along the azimuth line you are following what can you do?
A. Use a back azimuth to some feature behind you until a good steering mark appears in front of you.

Q. What are "handrails" to navigation?
A. Linear features like roads or highways, railroads, power transmission lines, ridgelines, or streams that run roughly parallel to your direction of travel and act as a "handrail" to guide the way.

Q. What is a "catching feature" used for?
A. It is a prominent feature located near a point where your route changes direction or separates from a handrail and is designed to "catch" your attention to the change. Catching features can also be used as a boundary to tell you when you have gone too far.

Q. What is "orienteering" and what are the most common forms?
A. Orienteering is a competitive form of land navigation; route, line, cross-country, and score orienteering.

Q. In military symbols (not topographic symbols), what colors are often used and what are their meanings?
A. Blue or Black------------- friendly forces
   Red----------------------- enemy forces
   Green--------------------- engineering obstacles both friendly and enemy
   Yellow-------------------- contaminated areas both friendly and enemy

Q. When colors are not available, how are symbols for enemy forces indicated?
A. By double lines.

Q. How will proposed or future locations of forces be represented on a map or overlay?
A. By a broken line.

Q. How are friendly positions indicated on a map without color?
A. As single lines.

Q. A cliff is often indicated by a "ticked" contour line. The "ticks" always point in which direction?
A. Toward lower ground.

Q. What are two commonly used methods for keeping track of a pace count?

A. Put pebbles in pocket or tie knots in a string or rope.

Q. The best route to an objective will do what three things?
A. - favor the best tactical advantage
- meet the mission requirement on time
- result in the fewest casualties possible

Q. What four units of measure are most commonly used on military maps and can be found in the Graphic (Bar) Scales?
A. Statute miles, nautical miles, yards, and meters.

M16A1 AND M16A2 RIFLE MARKSMANSHIP
FM 23-9

Q. What Army publication covers the M16A1/A2 rifles and the fundamentals of rifle marksmanship?
A. FM 23-9

Q. Describe the M16A1 Rifle.
A. It is a 5.56-mm, magazine-fed, gas-operated, shoulder-fired weapon capable of firing in either the semiautomatic or automatic modes through the use of a selector lever (SAFE, SEMI, and AUTO).

Q. Describe the M16A2 Rifle.
A. It is a 5.56-mm, magazine-fed, gas-operated, shoulder-fired weapon capable of firing in either the automatic three-round burst or semiautomatic single-shot modes (SAFE, SEMI, and BURST).

Q. Describe the proper procedure for CLEARING the M16 Rifle.
A. (1) Attempt to place the selector lever on SAFE. If the selector lever will not go on SAFE, pull the charging handle to the rear and place the selector lever on safe.
(2) Remove the magazine, if there is one, from the magazine well.
(3) Lock the bolt to the rear by pulling the charging handle to the rear while pressing the lower portion of the bolt catch; allow the bolt to move forward until it engages the bolt catch. Return the charging handle to the forward position.
(4) Visually inspect the chamber and receiver areas for ammunition.
(5) With the selector lever still on SAFE, allow the bolt to go forward by pressing the upper portion of the bolt catch.

NOTE: When on a range clearing procedures will differ slightly. When the last round is fired the bolt will automatically lock in the rear position. Simply place the weapon on SAFE, drop the magazine from the magazine well, and wait to be "rodded" from the range (or for additional instructions).

Q. What are the firing weights of the M16A1 and M16A2 Rifle with 20- and 30-round magazines?
A.

	M16A1	M16A2
20-round mag	7.6 lbs	8.5 lbs
30-round mag	7.9 lbs	8.8 lbs

Q. It follows then, from the above question, that the difference in firing weight between the M16A1 and M16A2 rifles is what?
A. Approx 1 pound (15 oz).

Q. What bayonets are used with the two rifles?
A. M16A1 - M7 Bayonet; M16A2 - M9 Bayonet.

Q. What is the overall length of the M16A1 rifle with flash suppressor?
A. 39 inches

Q. What is the overall length of the M16A2 rifle with compensator?
A. 39(5/8) inches

Q. Which has a longer barrel, the M16A1 or the M16A2?
A. The barrel lengths are the same (does not include suppressor/compensator).

Q. What types of ammunition are used in the M16 rifle?
A. Ball, tracer, blank, dummy, and plastic.

M16A1 AND M16A2 RIFLE MARKSMANSHIP
FM 23-9

Q. What is the recommended basic load for the M16 rifle (30-round magazine)?
A. 210 rounds (one mag in weapon and six in ammo pouches).

Q. Describe the differences in the following operational characteristics of the two weapons.

	M16A1	M16A2
A. rifling	RH, 1/12 twist	RH, 1/7 twist
muzzle velocity	3,250 fps	3,100 fps
cyclic rate of fire	700-800 rpm	same (theoretically)

NOTE: RH, 1/12 twist means that the rifling twists clockwise one complete revolution in 12 inches. It can be seen that M16A2 rifling is tighter, allowing greater stability of the heavier A2 rounds.

Q. Describe the differences in the maximum effective rates of fire of the two weapons.

	M16A1	M16A2
A. semiautomatic	45-65 rpm	45 rpm
automatic	150-200 rpm	90 rpm (3-rnd burst)
sustained	12-15 rpm	same

Q. What are the maximum ranges of the two weapons?
A. M16A1 - 2,653 meters; M16A2 - 3,600 meters.

NOTE: Some references give maximum range of M16A2 as 3,534 meters. In this instance the maximum range has been rounded off. In all instances, the maximum range would depend on a variety of factors and is never absolute.

Q. What are the maximum effective ranges of the M16A1/A2 rifles?
A. M16A1 - 460 meters; M16A2 - 550 meters (point target), 800 meters (area target).

Q. Name some of the basic differences between the two rifles.
A. The M16A2 is 5/8" longer; the A1 has a flash suppressor - the A2 a compensator; the barrel on the A2 has a larger outside diameter; A2 handguards are interchangeable; A2 has brass deflector molded into receiver; sight system is different; A2 fires on 3-round burst; A2 is more accurate at longer distances and recommended ammunition is different.

Q. What is the purpose of the compensator on the M16A2?
A. Helps keep the muzzle down during firing.

Q. What was the major advantage of the M16A1 over the M16?
A. The addition of the forward assist.

Q. What are the eight steps in the cycle of functioning of the M16 rifle?
A. Feeding, chambering, locking, firing, unlocking, extracting, ejecting, and cocking.

Q. While operating the M16A2 in the BURST fire mode, you inadvertently release the trigger interrupting the three-round cycle and producing only two shots. What will happen when the trigger is pulled to the rear again?
A. Only one shot will be fired (this is not a malfunction, the weapon is merely completing the interrupted three-round cycle).

Q. What is meant by the "stoppage" of a weapon?
A. The failure to complete the cycle of functioning of a weapon.

M16A1 AND M16A2 RIFLE MARKSMANSHIP
FM 23-9

Q. What is meant by "immediate action"?
A. The unhesitating application of a probable remedy to reduce a stoppage without investigating the cause.

Q. What is the proper procedure for applying immediate action?
A. Gently slap upward on the magazine to ensure that it is fully seated, and the magazine follower is not jammed. Pull the charging handle fully to the rear and check the chamber (observe for the ejection of a live or expended cartridge). Release the charging handle (do not ride it forward). Strike the forward assist assembly to ensure bolt closure. Try to fire the rifle.

Q. What word is commonly used to remember the procedure for applying immediate action?
A. SPORTS;
- (S)lap upward on the magazine;
- (P)ull the charging handle to the rear;
- (O)bserve the chamber;
- (R)elease the charging handle;
- (T)ap the forward assist;
- (S)hoot.

Q. How many times should immediate action be applied to a weapon?
A. Only once, if the rifle still fails to fire, inspect it to determine the cause of the stoppage or malfunction and take appropriate remedial action.

Q. What is meant by "remedial action"?
A. The continuing effort, through inspection, to return a weapon to operation.

Q. What is considered a "malfunction"?
A. A procedural or mechanical failure of the rifle, magazine, or ammunition.

Q. What are the three primary categories of malfunctions?
A. (1) Failure to feed, chamber, or lock.
(2) Failure to fire cartridge.
(3) Failure to extract and eject.

Q. Explain which weapon the following ammunition may be used in.
A. M193 Ball........................A1 only....no identifying marks
M196 Tracer......................A1 or A2...red or orange tip
M199 Dummy......................A1 or A2...grooved cartridge
M200 Blank.......................A1 or A2...violet tip
M855 Ball........................A2 only....green tip
M856 Tracer......................A2 only....red tip
M862 PPA.........................A1 or A2...light blue plastic

Q. How is M862 Plastic Practice Ammunition (PPA, also known as Short-Range Training Ammunition (SRTA)), used with the M16 rifle?
A. With the special M2 bolt, which converts the rifle from gas-operated to blowback-operated. The SRTA can be used in an unmodified rifle; however, the rifle will only function in the single-shot mode.

Q. When firing M200 Blanks from the M16 rifle, what device must be used to ensure the proper functioning of the weapon?
A. The M15A2 Blank Firing Attachment (BFA). It is designed to keep sufficient gas in the barrel of the weapon to allow semiautomatic, automatic, or burst firing.

M16A1 AND M16A2 RIFLE MARKSMANSHIP
FM 23-9

Q. When it is necessary to store ammunition in the open, it must be raised on dunnage at least ______ inches from the ground and protected with a cover, leaving enough space for air circulation.
A. 6

Q. If destruction of the individual rifle must be performed to prevent enemy use, the rifle must be damaged so it cannot be restored to a usable condition. What are the four preferred means of destruction of M16 rifles?
A. Mechanical, burning, demolition, and disposal.

Q. Expedient destruction requires that key operational parts be separated from the rifle or damaged beyond repair. What is the destruction priority for the parts of the weapon?
A. FIRST: bolt carrier group.
SECOND: upper receiver group.
THIRD: lower receiver group.

Q. What are the four basic fundamentals of rifle marksmanship?
A. Steady position, Aiming, Breath Control, and Trigger Squeeze.

Q. What are the two basic firing positions?
A. Individual supported and prone unsupported.

Q. Name five other firing positions (considered advanced firing positions)?
A. Kneeling unsupported, kneeling supported, standing unsupported, standing supported, lying flat on back (supine).

Q. What firing positions would best be used while defending against an air attack?
A. Standing supported (with bi-pod), and supine.

Q. What is the purpose of battlesight zeroing?
A. To align the fire control system (sights) with the rifle barrel, allowing a round to strike the point of aim of a target 300 meters down range (M16A2) or 250 meters down range (M16A1).

Q. What is the underlying concept behind battlesight zero (ie Why 300 meters?)?
A. Battlesight zero is the sight setting for a weapon that provides the highest hit probability for most combat targets with minimum adjustment to the aiming point. This has been determined by field testing to be at a range of 300 meters for the M16A2.

Q. What are the parts of the "fire control system" on the M16A2?
A. Front sight, rear sight apertures (2), rear windage knob, elevation knob.

Q. What is the larger aperture, marked 0-2, on the M16A2 used for?
A. For engaging moving targets and for engaging targets in limited visibility.

Q. What is the unmarked aperture used for?
A. Normal firing situations, zeroing, and with the elevation knob for target distances up to 800 meters.

Q. What is the proper procedure for firing the M16 while wearing the protective mask?
A. The weapon should be rotated (canted) only as far as necessary to properly see through and line up the sights. The center tip of the front sight post should remain on the ideal aiming point.

M16A1 AND M16A2 RIFLE MARKSMANSHIP
FM 23-9

Q. List some training aids/devices used to sustain/practice basic marksmanship skills.
A. M15A1 Aiming Card, Riddle Sighting Device, M16 Sighting Device, Target-Box Exercise, Ball-and-Dummy Exercise, Dime (Washer) Exercise, Weaponeer, and MACS.

Q. What does "MACS" stand for?
A. Multipurpose Arcade Combat Simulator.

Q. Explain the "Elevation and Windage Rule".
A. The elevation and windage rule states that one click of elevation or windage moves the strike of the bullet a specific distance at a specific range. At a range of 25 meters, one click of windage moves the strike of the bullet .33 cm (right or left), and one click of elevation on the front sight moves the strike of the bullet .83 cm (up or down). NOTE: This rule applies to the M16A2 only.

Q. Each "click" of elevation on the elevation knob changes the point of impact how much at 100 meters?
A. 1.1 inch (3.3 inches at 300 meters, etc).

Q. Explain how to place the initial sight setting on the M16A2 rifle for 25 meters.
A. Adjust the front sight post up or down until the base of the sight post is flush with the sight post well. Turn the rear windage knob until the index mark on the 0-2 sight is aligned with the rear sight base index. Turn the elevation knob all the way down and then up, one click past the 8/3 mark (8/3 + 1).

Q. Which sight aperture is used for zeroing?
A. The small sight aperture.

Q. Why must the elevation knob be set to (8/3 + 1) on an M16A2 when zeroing on a 25-meter range?
A. The objective of battlesight zeroing is to adjust the sights in such a way that a round fired from the weapon will strike the point of aim of a target 300 meters down range. When a round is fired from a weapon that is battlesight zeroed it will strike a 25-meter target slightly below line of sight, crossing line of sight at about 50 meters, continuing to a maximum height at about 200 meters and then dropping again through the line of sight (point of aim) at 300 meters. Since you are not actually shooting at a target 300 meters away (only simulated due to a reduction in size) you must compensate by making an adjustment of one click "up". Recall that each "click" in elevation on the elevation knob raises the strike of the round 1.1 inch at 100 meters (or approx 3/8 inch at 25 meters). Therefore, this adjustment will cause you to strike your point of aim at 25 meters.

Q. After zeroing on a 25 meter target you move on to a Known Distance (KD) Qualification Range. You will be firing at targets out to 300 meters. What adjustments, if any, do you need to make to your M16A2?
A. Move the elevation knob back to 8/3.

Q. If you must zero on a field fire range with 300-meter feedback targets, what should the elevation knob be set to?
A. 8/3 (since you are actually firing at a target 300 meters away, the one click of adjustment is not necessary).

Q. What does the "8/3" stand for, anyway?

M16A1 AND M16A2 RIFLE MARKSMANSHIP
FM 23-9

A. The "3" in 8/3 represents 300 meters when the elevation knob is turned all the way down. If you turn the elevation knob all the way up (back to 8/3), the "8" represents 800 meters (Sound familiar? Maximum effective range against area target).

Q. Your weapon is battlesight zeroed and you engage a target that you estimate to be 400 meters down range. The normal "instinct" is to aim high but if you know the M16A2 like you should you will do what instead?
A. Adjust the elevation knob from "3" to "4" and aim center-mass.

Q. Explain how to set an M16A1 to mechanical zero.
A. Adjust the front sight post up or down until the base of the sight post is flush with the sight post well. Then adjust the front sight post 11 clicks in the "UP" direction (marked on weapon). This moves the post down into the well 11 clicks. Turn the rear windage drum until the rear sights are all the way to the left side. Then turn the windage drum back (right) 17 clicks so the rear sight is approximately centered.

Q. Which sight aperture is used for zeroing on an M16A1?
A. The "L" sight ("L"ong range).

Q. What are the standards for zeroing an M16A2 rifle?
A. Using 18 rounds or less, fire five out of six rounds in two consecutive shot groups within a 4-cm circle.

Q. An angle of fire that covers 4 cm at 25 meters covers _______ inches at 300 meters.
A. 19"

Q. When firing for qualification, what is an considered an "alibi"?
A. A malfunction of the rifle or ammunition, which is not associated with firer error.

Q. What are the qualification standards for a Record Fire (RF) range (pop-up targets)?
A. Expert........36 - 40
Sharpshooter..30 - 35
Marksman......23 - 29
Unqualified...22 - below

Q. What are the qualification standards for the Known Distance Alternate Course (KDAC) or the scaled 25-meter Alternate Course (AC)?
A. Expert........38 - 40
Sharpshooter..33 - 37
Marksman......26 - 32
Unqualified...25 - below

Q. What does "RETS" stand for and what is a "RETS Range"?
A. Remote Electronic Targeting System; a record fire range with electronically controlled, moving targets and/or pop-up targets.

Q. What firing positions and targets are used on a KD alternate course?
A. - prone supported position, 300 yards, E-type silhouette, 20 rounds, 60 seconds
- prone unsupported, 200 yards, E-type silhouette, 10 rounds, 60 seconds
- prone unsupported, 100 yards, F-type silhouette, 10 rounds, 60 seconds

M16A1 AND M16A2 RIFLE MARKSMANSHIP
FM 23-9

Q. What are "E-type" and "F-type" silhouettes?
A. E-type......full silhouette
F-type......shoulder silhouette

Q. What firing positions and targets are used on a Record Fire (RF) range?
A. Two F-type silhouettes are placed at 50 meters with subsequent targets placed at 50 meter intervals out to 300 meters. Only E-type silhouettes are used beyond 100 meters. Targets are randomly raised, timed targets. 20 shots fired from the prone unsupported position and 20 shots from the supported fighting position (foxhole).

Q. What targets are represented on the scaled 25-meter alternate course?
A. 50- and 100-meter F-type silhouettes; 150-, 200-, 250-, and 300-meter E-type silhouettes. 10 targets total. 4 rounds in each target - 20 from prone supported position (120 seconds); 20 from prone unsupported position (120 seconds).

Q. When the M16A2 (w/magazine)is properly field stripped, how many parts are there (not including bi-pod)?
A. 14

Q. Are the M16A1 and M16A2 zeroing targets the same?
A. No, they are different.

Q. The M16A2 zero target is a network of squares superimposed on an E-type silhouette. Each "square" in the grid is 1-cm across. One click of adjustment on the front sight post will move the strike of the round _______ square(s) up or down on the zero target. Additionally, how many clicks of windage are required to move the strike of the round one square left or right on the zero target?
A. One; three.

Q. What does "LFX" stand for?
A. Live Fire Exercise

Q. The front sight post of the M16A1/A2 can be used to estimate range. In this way, the front sight post will be the same width as a man-size target when the target is located at a distance of ______ meters.
A. 175 (similarly, a man-size target will be half the width of the front sight post at 350 meters).

Q. Can .22-caliber rimfire ammunition be fired from the M16 rifle?
A. Yes, with the M261 Rimfire Adapter (RFA).

Q. What caliber bore does the M16 have?
A. .223

Q. What is an "LLLSS"?
A. Low-Light Level Sight System

Q. What do the following acronyms stand for: BRM, ARM, MILES, MOUT, POI, PPA, KD, AC, PRI, TASC, PMI.
A. BRM - Basic Rifle Marksmanship
ARM - Advanced Rifle Marksmanship
MILES - Multiple Integrated Laser Engagement System
MOUT - Military Operations on Urbanized Terrain
POI - Program Of Instruction

M16A1 AND M16A2 RIFLE MARKSMANSHIP
FM 23-9

PPA - Plastic Practice Ammunition
KD - Known Distance
AC - Alternate Course
PRI - Preliminary Rifle Instruction
TASC - Training and Audiovisual Support Center
PMI - Preliminary Marksmanship Instruction

Q. What is a "chamber plug"?
A. A range safety device that is a small plastic plug designed to fit into the chamber of the M16. A handle extends out the ejection port so safety personnel can see at a glance that the rifle is cleared of ammunition.

Q. What is a "cookoff"?
A. A round that fires as a result of a hot chamber without the trigger being pulled. It can occur at any time until the weapon has cooled.

NOTE: Firing 140 rounds (4(1/2) 30-rnd magazines), rapidly and continuously from the M16A1, will raise the temperature of the barrel to the COOKOFF POINT. At this temperature, any live round remaining in the chamber for any reason may cook off (detonate) in as short a period as 10 seconds.

Q. What is "cross dominance"?
A. A soldier with a dominant hand and a dominant eye that are not the same; for example, a right-handed firer with a dominant left eye.

Q. Will the M16 fire without the cam pin installed in the bolt group?
A. Yes, but it will explode.

Q. How much chamber pressure is generated with the firing of each round in the M16A2?
A. 52,000 psi

Q. Proper maintenance of the M16A2 rifle includes what five steps?
A. Clear, disassemble, Inspect, Clean & lubricate, Assemble.

Q. What does "CLP" stand for and how does it work?
A. Cleaner, Lubricant, and Preservative;
(1) it contains solvents to dissolve firing residue and carbon,
(2) it lays down a layer of Teflon as it dries to provide lubrication,
(3) it prevents rust from forming.

Q. What does "LAW" stand for and when is it used?
A. Lubricating oil, Arctic Weapons; at temperatures below 0 degrees F.

Q. Explain the proper procedure for performing a function check on an M16A2 rifle.
A. (1) Place the selector lever on SAFE. If the selector lever will not go on SAFE, pull the charging handle to the rear and release. Place the selector lever on SAFE. Pull the trigger to the rear. The hammer should not fall.

(2) Place the selector lever on SEMI. Pull the trigger to the rear and hold. The hammer should fall. While holding the trigger to the rear, pull the charging handle to the rear and release. Release the trigger and pull it to the rear again. The hammer should fall.

(3) Place the selector lever on BURST. Pull the charging handle to the rear and release. Pull the trigger to the rear and hold. The hammer should fall. While holding the trigger to the rear, pull the charging handle to the rear three times and release. Release the trigger and pull it to the rear again.

The hammer should fall.

Q. Tracer ammunition is used to help hit targets during hours of darkness or low light levels. When using tracers, what is the recommended method of mixing with ball ammunition?
A. - top three tracer: to help you get on target
- every 5th or 6th round tracer: to help you stay on target
- bottom four tracer: to let you know when to change magazines.

NOTE: Tracer ammunition is not as effective as regular ball ammunition against most targets.

Q. When inspecting ammunition, what deficiencies should you look for?
A. - seriously corroded ammunition
- dented cartridges
- cartridges with loose bullets
- cartridges with the bullet pushed in (short rounds)

Q. The first consideration when handling any weapon is to do what?
A. CLEAR IT!

Q. Blank ammunition should not be fired toward personnel within _____ feet or less from the muzzle, because fragments from a closure wad or particles of unburned propellant might inflict injury within that range.
A. 20

Q. What is the purpose of the "flash suppressor" on the M16/M16A1 model rifles?
A. Reduces the amount of flash from the muzzle when the weapon is fired.

Q. What is contained in the front sight post on weapons equipped with LLLSS?
A. A small glass vial of radioactive Tritium H 3.

M203 GRENADE LAUNCHER
FM 23-31

Q. What FM covers the use of the M203 Grenade Launcher?
A. FM 23-31

Q. What is the description of the M203 Grenade Launcher?
A. It is a lightweight, single-shot, breech-loaded, pump action (sliding barrel), shoulder-fired weapon that attaches to the M16A1 or M16A2 rifle.

Q. What is the length of the M203 Grenade Launcher (rifle and launcher assembly)?
A. M16A1 with flash suppressor - 39 inches
M16A2 with compensator - 39(5/8) inches

Q. What is the length of the M203 barrel assembly?
A. 12 inches

Q. What is the maximum range of the M203 Grenade Launcher?
A. 400 meters

Q. What is the maximum effective range of the M203?
A. Point target - 150 meters
Area target - 300 meters

Q. What is the rate of fire for the M203 grenade launcher?
A. 5 to 7 rounds per minute.

Q. What is considered to be the minimum combat load for the M203?
A. 36 HE rounds.

Q. What is the weight of the M203 (not including rifle)?
A. unloaded - 3.0 lbs
Loaded - 3.5 lbs

Q. What is the weight of the M203 (including rifle)?
A. M16A1 with 30-rd magazine - 11.0 lbs
M16A2 with 30-rd magazine - 11.8 lbs

Q. How many "lands" are there in an M203 barrel?
A. 6

Q. What is meant by a "land"?
A. It is the raised portion between a grooved surface. Looking through the barrel, the lands are the smooth portions of the barrel between grooves.

Q. What is considered the minimum "safe" range of the M203?
A. Training - 165 meters
Combat - 31 meters

Q. What sized projectile is fired from the M203?
A. 40-mm (weighs 8 oz (0.5 lb) and is 3.9 inches long).

NOTE: It is extremely important that the correct 40-mm ammunition be used. Never use high-velocity 40-mm ammunition designated for other 40-mm weapons such as the MK19 - these rounds are longer than used in the M203 and may explode.

Q. At what range does the M203 projectile arm itself?
A. Between ~~10 and 30 meters~~ 14 and 38 meters (varies depending on type of round

used).

Q. What is the chamber pressure on the M203?
A. 35,000 psi in the high-pressure chamber and 3,000 psi in the low-pressure chamber.

Q. What is the muzzle velocity of the M203?
A. 250 fps.

Q. What direction does the projectile rotate upon exiting the barrel? How fast is it rotating and what is the reason for this?
A. The grenade has a right-hand spin which serves the dual purpose of stabilizing the grenade during flight and also applies enough rotational force to arm the fuze. The grenade spins at approx 37,000 rpm.

Q. What are the major components of the M203 Grenade Launcher?
A. Handguard, quadrant sight assembly, receiver assembly, barrel assembly, leaf sight assembly, trigger guard, and safety.

Q. What is the difference between the leaf and quadrant sights of the M203?
A. - leaf sight: scaled in 50 meter increments for targets from 50-250 meters; with a "1" at 100 meters and a "2" at 200 meters. It mounts on top of the M16A2 aft of the front sight post and can be flipped up (perpendicular to the barrel) or down (parallel to the barrel). It can be adjusted for windage and elevation.
- quadrant sight: marked in 25 meter increments for targets from 50-400 meters. It attaches to the left side of the rifle's carrying handle.

Q. What are the parts of the leaf sight assembly?
A. Sight base, sight mount and sight, elevation adjustment screw and scale, windage screw and scale.

Q. What is useful for adjusting the elevation adjustment screw?
A. The rim of a 40-mm cartridge case.

Q. Name the parts of the M203 quadrant sight.
A. Clamp, sight arm and range quadrant, front sight post, and rear sight aperture.

Q. What portion of the quadrant sight is used to make minor adjustments in elevation when zeroing the launcher?
A. Front sight post.

Q. What adjustment to the front sight post needs to be made in order to move the impact of a projectile 5 meters (in elevation) at a range of 200 meters?
A. Turn the elevation adjustment screw one full turn right (to decrease elevation) or left (to increase elevation).

Q. What portion of the quadrant sight is used to make minor adjustments in deflection (windage) when zeroing the launcher?
A. Rear sight aperture.

Q. What adjustment to the rear sight aperture needs to be made in order to move the impact of a projectile 1 ½ meters (left or right) at a range of 200 meters?
A. Press the rear sight aperture retainer and move the rear sight aperture one notch away from the barrel (to move left) or toward the barrel (to move right).

Q. The quadrant sight assembly has a built-in front sight post. What serves as

the front sight for the leaf sight assembly?
A. The front sight post of the M16-series rifle.

Q. Why is the 50-meter mark on the leaf sight blade marked in red?
A. To emphasize that this range must not to be used in zeroing procedures. Zeroing is extremely dangerous at 50 meters or less due to fragmentation.

Q. What feature allows the M203 to be fired while the firer is wearing gloves or mittens?
A. The rear portion of the trigger guard can be depressed and rotated downward and away from the magazine well of the rifle.

Q. Where is the M203 safety located?
A. Inside the trigger guard, just in front of the trigger.

Q. In order for the launcher to fire, the safety must be (forward/rearward)?
A. Forward.

Q. What are the steps for CLEARING the M203 grenade launcher?
A. - Push in the release button, and pull the barrel forward;
- Watch to see if a round extracts;
- Place the safety on SAFE;
- Inspect the breech to ensure a round is not present;
- Pull the barrel to the rear until it clicks (this cocks the weapon);
- Place the safety on FIRE.

Q. What are the steps in LOADING the M203 grenade launcher?
A. - Depress the barrel latch and slide the barrel forward;
- Place the weapon on SAFE;
- Insert clean, dry, undented cartridge into the chamber;
- Slide the barrel rearward until it locks with an audible click.

Q. What are the steps in UNLOADING the M203 grenade launcher?
A. - Depress the barrel latch and slide the barrel forward (the cartridge case or round should automatically eject);
- Place the weapon on SAFE;
- Slide the barrel rearward, locking it to the breech.

Q. While UNLOADING the M203 grenade launcher, if the cartridge case or round does not automatically eject, what should you do?
A. Tap the round with a cleaning rod through the end of the barrel.

NOTE: Avoid detonation of an unfired round by either catching the unfired round or holding the weapon close to the ground to reduce the distance the round will fall.

Q. Loading a round into the chamber and pulling the trigger initiates the various parts of the weapon functioning in a cycle. What are the steps in the CYCLE OF FUNCTIONING of the M203?
A. (1) Unloading - depressing the barrel latch and sliding the barrel forward.
(2) Cocking - movement of the barrel forward then backward to cock the weapon.
(3) Extracting (occurs at the same time as cocking) - spring-loaded extractor keeps cartridge case or round seated until the barrel clears the cartridge case.
(4) Ejecting
(5) Loading - grenadier inserts round into the breech end of the barrel.
(6) Chambering - Cartridge seats against the breech as the barrel assembly

slides rearward.

(7) Locking - cocking lever engages barrel assembly so it cannot move forward.

(8) Firing - spring-driven firing pin is forced against the cartridge primer when trigger is pulled.

Q. What is a "hangfire"?
A. A delay in the propellant charge igniting (this may range between a split second and 30 seconds).

Q. What could cause a hangfire?
A. An ammunition defect, faulty firing mechanism or the presence of grit, sand, frost, ice, or excess oil or grease.

NOTE: Any failure to fire must be considered a hangfire until that possibility is eliminated.

Q. What is a "misfire"?
A. A complete failure of the weapon to fire.

Q. What action should be taken in the event of a "misfire" of the M203?
A. Keep the muzzle on target. Clear all personnel from the area (at least 80 meters). Wait 30 seconds to eliminate the possibility of a hangfire before opening the barrel assembly to remove the round. Attempt to determine the cause of the hangfire/misfire before reloading weapon.

Q. What types of ammunition are used in the M203 Grenade Launcher?
A. High-explosive, illuminating, signaling, CS, and training ammunition. Specifically:

M406 - high explosive (HE)
M433 - high-explosive dual purpose (HEDP)
M781 - practice
M583A1 - star parachute (white)
M661 - star parachute (green)
M662 - star parachute (red)
M585 - white star cluster
M713 - ground marker (red)
M715 - ground marker (green)
M716 - ground marker (yellow)
M651 - tactical CS round

Q. What is the arming range for HE and HEDP grenades?
A. Between 14 and 27 meters.

Q. What is considered to be the casualty radius for HE and HEDP rounds?
A. 5 meters.

Q. The star parachute round is designed to lower at what rate of descent?
A. 7 feet per second.

Q. The star parachute round is designed to burn for approximately how long?
A. 40 seconds.

Q. Which grenade can easily be identified at night by a raised letter at its apex (letter denoting color)?
A. Star parachute rounds.

Q. Which grenade can be identified at night by a raised "W" on the attached

plastic ogive and raised dots at the apex?
A. White star cluster.

Q. What is the approximate burn time for white star clusters?
A. 7 seconds (during freefall).

Q. What is the approximate arming radius for the ground marker round?
A. Between 15 and 45 meters.

Q. Which round produces a yellow or orange signature on impact?
A. M781 practice round.

Q. What is the danger radius of practice grenades?
A. 20 meters.

Q. What is the danger of firing 40-mm rounds into snow?
A. The rounds may not hit hard enough to detonate. If an undetonated round is stepped on or driven over, it may explode.

Q. HE and HEDP rounds come boxed in "bandoleers" or belts. How many grenades are contained in each bandoleer?
A. 12

Q. What score must be attained to qualify with the M203?
A. At least 60 out of 90 points, with each target hit being worth 10 points.

NOTE: The M79 grenade launcher is a single-shot, break-open, breech-loading, shoulder-fired weapon and is discussed in appendix A of FM 23-34 but will not be covered in this study guide.

MACHINEGUN, 7.62-mm, M60
FM 23-67

Q. What FM covers the 7.62-mm, M60 machine-gun?
A. FM 23-67

Q. Describe the M60 machine-gun.
A. The M60 is an air-cooled, belt-fed, gas operated machine-gun capable of firing in the fully automatic mode. It can be used on a bi-pod, a tripod, or a vehicular mount. It is loaded, fired, unloaded, and cleared from the open bolt position and ammunition is fed by a metallic split-link belt.

Q. What is the "open bolt" position on the M60?
A. The bolt is in the rearward or cocked position.

Q. When field stripping the M60, what position should the bolt be in?
A. The forward or closed position.

NOTE: To prevent possible bodily injury and weapon damage, personnel should not stand the weapon on its barrel assembly when disassembling the weapon.

Q. What two positions can the selector lever be placed in on the M60 machine-gun?
A. "S" (for SAFE) or "F" (for FIRE).

Q. What are the five types of ammunition used with the M60?
A. - 7.62-mm Ball (M80)
- Armor Piercing (M61)....black tip
- Tracer (M62)...........red or orange tip
- Dummy (M63)
- Blank (M82)

Q. What is the recommended combat mix for M60 Ball and Tracer ammunition?
A. 4:1

Q. How is ammunition for the M60 packaged?
A. In 100-round bandoleers each weighing approximately 6.5 lbs.

Q. What is the maximum range of the M60?
A. 3,725 meters.

Q. What is the maximum effective range of the M60?
A. - Moving point target, bi-pod..................200 meters
- Stationary point target, bi-pod or tripod....600 meters
- Area target, bi-pod.........................800 meters
- Area target, tripod........................1100 meters

NOTE: Maximum effective range during night fire is limited to tracer burnout range of approximately 900 meters.

Q. The rear sight on the M60 is adjustable out to what range?
A. It is graduated from 300 to 1100 meters.

Q. What is the length of the M60 machine-gun?
A. 43.5 inches.

Q. What is an M60D?
A. The "Delta" model M60 is designed primarily for aircraft-door mounts or vehicular mounts.

MACHINEGUN, 7.62-mm, M60
FM 23-67

Q. What is the weight of the M60 machine-gun?
A. Approximately 23 lbs (M60D weighs 25 lbs).

Q. What is issued with each M60 in order to extend the life of the barrel, retain accuracy, and allow for continuous firing over long periods of time?
A. Two barrel assemblies.

Q. What are the following rates of fire for the M60 machine-gun and what is the recommended barrel change time for each?
A. - sustained fire..100 rounds per minute.........every 10 minutes
- rapid fire......200 rounds per minute..........every 2 minutes
- cyclic fire.....550 rounds per minute..........every minute

Q. What is the muzzle velocity of the M60?
A. ~~3800 fps~~. 2800 fps. (Ch 1, TM).

Q. Describe the rifling of the M60 machine-gun.
A. RH, 1/12 twist.

Q. How many "lands" are there in an M60 barrel?
A. 4

Q. What is meant by a "land"?
A. It is the raised portion between a grooved surface. Looking through a barrel, the lands are the smooth portions of the barrel between grooves.

Q. What is the M122?
A. The tripod mount with traversing and elevating (T&E) mechanism.

Q. What is the approximate weight of the M122 assembly?
A. 15 lbs.

Q. What is the height of the M122 T&E mechanism?
A. 14 inches.

Q. What is the maximum extent of grazing fire obtainable over level or uniformly sloping terrain?
A. 600 meters.

Q. What are the maximum elevation/declination ranges of the M60 when mounted on the M122 tripod mount?
A. - max elevation, tripod controlled..........+200 mils.......+11 degrees
- max elevation, tripod free................+445 mils.......+25 degrees
- max declination, tripod controlled........-200 mils.......-11 degrees
- max declination, tripod free..............-445 mils.......-25 degrees

Q. What is the maximum traverse of the M60 machine-gun when mounted on the M122 tripod mount?
A. - controlled by traversing handwheel.........100 mils........6 degrees
- controlled by traversing bar...............875 mils........50 degrees
- free.....................................6400 mils.......360 degrees

Q. One click on the elevating wheel of the traversing and elevating mechanism is equivalent to what (in mils)?
A. 1 mil.

MACHINEGUN, 7.62-mm, M60
FM 23-67

Q. The traversing bar scale on the M122 is marked in ______mil increments.
A. 5

Q. When the bolt of the M60 is pulled to the rear by the cocking handle, how is it returned to the forward position?
A. Manually.

Q. What are the two types of disassembly of the M60 machine-gun?
A. (1) General: removing and replacing the eight major groups.
(2) Detailed: removing and replacing the parts of those major groups.

Q. What are the eight major groups of the M60?
A. (1) Barrel Group
(2) Trigger-mechanism group
(3) Stock group
(4) Forearm assembly group
(5) Cover, feed tray, and hanger group
(6) Buffer and operating-rod group
(7) Bolt group
(8) Receiver group

Q. The M60 machine-gun functions automatically as long as ammunition is fed into it and the trigger is held to the rear. Each time a round fires, the parts of the gun function in sequence. Many of the actions occur at the same time and are separated only for instructional purposes. This "sequence of functioning" is known as what?
A. The CYCLE OF FUNCTIONING.

Q. What are the eight separate steps to the complete "cycle of functioning" of the M60 machine-gun?
A. (1) Feeding: a round is positioned in the feed-tray groove.
(2) Chambering: a round is stripped from the belt and placed in the chamber.
(3) Locking: the bolt is locked inside the barrel socket.
(4) Firing: the firing pin strikes and fires the primer, which fires the cartridge.
(5) Unlocking: the bolt is unlocked from the barrel socket.
(6) Extracting: the empty cartridge case is pulled from the chamber.
(7) Ejecting: the empty cartridge case is thrown from the receiver.
(8) Cocking: the sear pin engages the sear notch on the operating rod (unless the trigger is still pulled to the rear, in which case it will continue to feed, chamber, etc...).

Q. How do you properly load the M60?
A. (1) Pull the cocking lever fully to the rear.
(2) Put the selector lever on "S".
(3) Raise the cover.
(4) Place the ammunition open-side-down on the feed tray.
(5) Close the cover and latch it in place.
(6) Move the selector lever to "F" and squeeze the trigger.

Q. What is the procedure for CLEARing the M60 machine-gun?
A. (1) Attempt to place the selector lever on "S". If it will not go on "S", pull the cocking handle fully to the rear, locking the bolt open. Place the selector lever on "S" and return the cocking handle forward.
(2) Turn your head to the side and while doing so, lift the feed tray cover and feel for any remaining rounds on the feed tray. If present, remove them.
(3) Lift the feed tray and observe the chamber area for the presence of chambered rounds.
(4) Drop the feed tray and close the feed tray cover.
(5) Pull the cocking handle rearward until it engages the bolt carrier mechanism.

(6) Place the selector lever on "F".
(7) While holding the cocking handle, squeeze the trigger and manually ride the bolt carrier mechanism forward.

Q. Why should you turn your head in step #2 above?
A. For safety. If the cover is opened on a hot cartridge (hot barrel), an open-cover cookoff could occur and result in serious injury or death.

Q. What caution should you note whenever opening or closing the feed tray cover?
A. Insure that the bolt assembly is pulled rearward (open-bolt position).

Q. Describe the proper procedure for performing a function check on the M60.
A. (1) CLEAR the weapon as described above (only stop at step #5).
(2) While holding the cocking handle, ensure that the weapon is still on "S" and attempt to squeeze the trigger. The bolt should not move forward.
(3) Continue to hold the cocking handle and place the selector lever on "F". Pull the trigger and ride the bolt forward slowly.

NOTE: If the bolt moves forward with the selector safety on "S", the weapon must be turned in for maintenance.

Q. What are the two most common malfunctions of the M60 machine-gun?
A. Sluggish operation and uncontrolled fire/runaway gun.

Q. Uncontrolled fire is when the weapon continues to fire after the trigger is released. This is usually caused by what?
A. The gunner not pulling and holding the trigger all the way to the rear or a worn sear pin.

Q. What immediate action is taken for "uncontrolled fire"?
A. (1) Continue to hold weapon on target or down range and break the ammunition belt by twisting quickly in either direction. Or let machine-gun continue to fire if near the end of the link belt.
(2) Pull cocking handle all the way back and hold it. Place safety to "S" and remove the link belt.
(3) Properly CLEAR the weapon (NEVER reload a runaway machine-gun until it has been repaired).
(4) Notify organizational maintenance for repairs.

Q. Unlike "uncontrolled fire," a misfire results when the weapon ceases firing prematurely. In the event of a misfire, you must perform IMMEDIATE ACTION within ________ seconds.
A. 10

NOTE: If a cover is opened on a hot cartridge (hot barrel), an open-cover cookoff could occur and result in serious injury or death. Any time this is suspected, DO NOT perform immediate action. Evacuate the area for 15 minutes and then perform remedial action.

Q. What immediate action is taken for a "misfire"?
A. (1) Pull cocking handle rearward;
(2) Check ejection port;
(3) If a round or cartridge case is ejected, push cocking handle forward and fire again;
(4) If nothing is ejected and the barrel is hot enough to cause a cookoff, lock the bolt to the rear and wait at least 15 minutes;

(5) Repeat steps 1 through 3.

Q. When could you expect the barrel of an M60 to be hot enough to cause a cookoff (see step 4 above)?
A. If 200 or more rounds have been fired within 2 minutes.

NOTE: The climate temperature in different regions will make a difference as to what constitutes a "hot gun." A weapon and ammunition that have been exposed to direct sunlight in hot climates can cause a cookoff with as few as 50 rounds fired.

Q. If immediate action for a misfire fails to remove a cartridge case, what must you do?
A. Perform REMEDIAL ACTION.

Q. What are the remedial action steps for a misfire (if immediate action fails to work)?
A. (1) Keep weapon on target (down range/impact area). Clear weapon when barrel is cool (after minimum 15 minute wait);
(2) Cocking handle should already be locked rearward; however, if it is not then do so;
(3) If a round is not ejected place the safety to "S";
(4) Open cover, remove ammunition link belt and raise feed tray;
(5) Inspect receiver, chamber, extractor, and ammunition;
(6) If a round is in the chamber, lower the feed tray and close cover;
(7) Push cocking handle forward.
(8) Place safety to "F".
(9) Attempt to fire - if a round is fired and ejected, reload and continue to fire; if weapon does not fire or eject, clear and unload the weapon, and notify organizational maintenance for repair.

Q. What is considered the "basic load" for the M60 machine-gun?
A. The BASIC LOAD is designated by the Commander but is generally from 600 - 900 rounds distributed as follows:
- gunner carries three 100-round bandoleers (one attached to weapon)
- asst gunner(if assigned or designated) carries three 100-round bandoleers (also carries spare barrel and bi-pod assembly)
- ammunition bearer (when present) carries three 100-round bandoleers.

Q. What should the gunner/asst gunner use to safely change the barrel of the M60?
A. Heat protective mittens ~~(asbestos mittens).~~ Barrel may also be safely changed by holding the bipod legs.

Q. What is carried in the carrying case of the M60 besides the spare barrel?
A.
- 1 ea combination tool
- 1 ea handle assembly
- 1 ea swab holder section
- 5 ea cleaning rod sections
- 1 ea heat protective mitten
- 1 ea bore cleaning brush
- 1 ea chamber cleaning brush
- 1 ea receiver cleaning brush
- 1 ea ruptured cartridge extractor

Q. When is the M60 considered "safe"?

MACHINEGUN, 7.62-mm, M60
FM 23-67

A. ONLY when the bolt is in the closed-bolt position.

Q. What are the three firing positions which may be used when firing the M60 in the assault (maneuver) mode?
A. Hip fire, shoulder fire, and underarm fire.

Q. When firing the M60 from one of the assault positions (see above question), how is the gunner able to place effective fire on the enemy without aligning the sights?
A. By observing the tracers and the impact of rounds in the target area.

Q. Which assault firing position is used to get a heavy volume of fire in the target area when rapid movement is not necessary?
A. The hip firing position.

Q. The shoulder firing position is used to hit specific points in the target area when rapid movement is not necessary. The gunner should pause and fire a burst as which foot strikes the ground?
A. The left foot.

Q. Which firing position is used when closing with the enemy and when a heavy volume of fire and rapid movement are necessary?
A. The underarm firing position.

Q. In a defensive situation it is important to make a range card for the M60. What are the essential elements of a range card?
A. (1) A known reference point.
(2) The direction and distance from the reference point to the machine-gun.
(3) The machine-gun position.
(4) The primary sector of fire with left and right limits.
(5) Secondary sector of fire.
(6) The magnetic azimuth of the Final Protective Line (FPL).
(7) Locations of all dead space.
(8) Reference points (target numbers) within the sector of fire.
(9) Magnetic north.
(10) Unit and date.

NOTE: A detailed legend or data section should accompany the range card.

Q. Name two field expedient methods for "laying" the M60 machinegun on preselected targets in designated sectors of fire.
A. - The notched stake or tree crotch (fork) method; and
- The notched log or board method.

Q. How many range cards should be prepared for each fighting position?
A. Two, one for the machine gun position and one for the platoon headquarters.

Q. What is meant by "dead space"?
A. A section or sections of an FPL where an individual drops below the line of sight.

Q. When planning a range card, sectors should not exceed what angle?
A. 875 mils (50°) - this is the maximum traverse of a tripod-mounted M60 machinegun.

Q. Are bolts and/or barrels interchangeable between weapons?
A. No. Each barrel and bolt assembly should be tagged during cleaning with the

serial number of the receiver (gun) and should remain together as initially assigned. Interchanging barrels may result in injury or death.

Q. What is meant by the terms "search" and "traverse"?
A. Search - movement of the muzzle of the weapon up or down to distribute fire in depth across the target area.
Traverse - movement of the muzzle of the weapon to the left or right to distribute fire laterally across a target area.

Q. An area target should be engaged using ______- to ______-round bursts.
A. 6; 9

Q. When pulling the trigger on the M60, what is a good rule-of-thumb for determining a six-round burst?
A. Say to yourself, "Fire a burst of six", and then release the trigger.

GRENADES/MK-19 GRENADE MACHINE GUN
FM 23-30/FM 23-27

GRENADES

Q. What FM covers the use of grenades and pyrotechnic signals?
A. FM 23-30

Q. All hand grenades share three characteristics. What are they?
A. (1) Relatively short range in comparison to other infantry weapons.
(2) Small effective casualty radius.
(3) Incorporate a delay element to permit safe throwing.

Q. What are the three main components of the hand grenade?
A. (1) Body: contains the filler and, in some grenades, provides fragmentation.
(2) Filler: the chemical or explosive substance in the grenade body which gives the grenade its characteristics and determines its use.
(3) Fuse assembly: the heart of the grenade which causes it to function by means of a chain reaction of pyrotechnic, mechanical, or electrical actions.

Q. Explain the mechanical function of a hand grenade.
A. The mechanical function of different types of hand grenades may vary depending on the type of fuse employed, however, the following sequence is characteristic of most hand grenades:

- The safety pin is removed from the fuse by pulling the pull ring (pressure must be maintained on the safety lever to prevent the sequence from continuing).
- Once pressure on the safety lever is released, the striker will be forced to rotate on its axis by the striker spring, throwing the safety lever off.
- The striker detonates the primer.
- The primer explodes, igniting the delay element.
- The delay element burns for the prescribed amount of time, and then it activates either the detonator or igniter.
- The detonator or igniter acts either to explode or burn the filler substance.

Q. What is the purpose of a safety clip? Do all grenades have them?
A. The safety clip prevents the safety lever from springing loose even if the safety pin assembly is accidentally removed; all hand grenades do not have them but they are available through supply channels and are adaptable to the M26- and M67-series, the MK2, and the M69 practice grenades.

Q. Under the product improvement program that added an attached safety clip feature, the M26 and M26A1 hand grenades were reclassified as the ______ grenade.
A. M61

Q. What are the two types of fuses used in current U.S. hand grenades and what is the difference between them?
A. (1) Detonating: explode within the grenade body to initiate the main explosion of the filler.
(2) Igniting: designed to burn at high temperatures which causes the chemical filler to ignite.

GRENADES/MK-19 GRENADE MACHINE GUN
FM 23-30/FM 23-27

Q. Give the grenade type and delay element time for the following **detonating** fuses.

A.

Fuse	**Grenade Type**	**Delay Element Time**
M204A1/M204A2	M61	4 - 5 seconds
M206A2	MK3A2 M15	4 - 5 seconds
M213	M67	4 - 5 seconds
C12 integral	M25-series	1.4 - 3 seconds

Q. Give the grenade type and delay element time for the following **igniting** fuses.

Fuse	**Grenade Type**	**Delay Element Time**
M201A1	AN-M8HC AN-M14 TH3 M18	1.5 - 2 seconds
M228	M69	4 - 5 seconds

Q. What is the purpose of the M228 fuse?
A. It is used with the M69 practice hand grenade to replicate the fuse delay of the M67 fragmentation hand grenade.

Q. What is meant by "milking" a grenade? Is this a desirable practice?
A. If pressure on the safety lever is relaxed after the safety clip and safety pin have been removed, it is possible that the striker can rotate and strike the primer while the thrower is still holding the grenade; obviously, this is not a desirable practice and throwers should be instructed to maintain enough pressure on the safety lever so that the striker cannot rotate.

Q. Depending on the characteristics of a particular hand grenade, it can be used to accomplish one or more of what five tasks?
A. (1) Disable or kill personnel
(2) Signal
(3) Screen (provide concealment)
(4) Destroy equipment and start fires
(5) Control riots or disable individuals without causing serious injury.

Q. To disable or kill personnel you must use what types of grenades (cite specific examples)?
A. Preferred - fragmentation: M61, M67.
Alternate - offensive (concussion): MK3A2.

Q. What grenades are used to signal personnel?
A. - M18 colored smoke
- AN-M8 HC white smoke
- M34 WP Smoke

NOTE: The M34 WP smoke grenade replaces the M15 white phosphorous grenade.

Q. What grenades are used to screen or provide concealment?
A. Preferred - AN-M8 HC white smoke
Alternate - M18 colored smoke
M34 WP Smoke

Q. What grenades are used to destroy equipment and start fires?
A. AN-M14 TH3 incendiary and ~~M15 white phosphorous~~ M34 WP.

GRENADES/MK-19 GRENADE MACHINE GUN
FM 23-30/FM 23-27

Q. What grenades are used primarily to control riots or to disable personnel without causing serious injury?
A. - ABC-M25A2 CS (baseball-shaped; persistent agent)
- ABC-M7A2/A3 CS (canister-shaped)

Q. Identify the following grenades from the given description.
A. (1) Fragmentation hand grenade; olive-drab oblong sheet-metal body with a single yellow band at the top; nomenclature and lot number markings in yellow; filler is 5.5 ounces of Composition B; fragments produced by serrated wire coil; weight is 16 ounces.

(2) Emits a dense cloud of white smoke for 105 to 150 seconds; canister-shaped light green body with black markings and a white top; filler is 19 ounces of Type C smoke mixture; weight is 24 ounces.

(3) Riot control; canister-shaped gray body with a red band and red markings; filler is CS; weight is 15.5 ounces.

(4) Fragmentation hand grenade; olive-drab steel-sphere body with a single yellow band at the top; nomenclature and lot number markings in yellow; filler is 6.5 ounces of Composition B; weight is 14 ounces.

(5) Light green ~~Light gray~~ canister-shaped gray body with one yellow band and red markings ~~yellow markings~~; filler is 15 ounces of white phosphorous; weight is 31 ounces.

(6) Riot control; baseball-shaped gray body with a red band and red markings; filler is CS; weight is 8 ounces.

(7) Offensive hand grenade; canister-shaped black body with yellow markings around its middle; filler is 8 ounces of TNT; weight is 15.6 ounces.

(8) Incendiary hand grenade; canister-shaped gray body with purple markings and a single purple band (may also be light red with black markings); filler is 26.5 ounces of thermate; weight is 32 ounces.

(9) Practice hand grenade; baseball-shaped light blue steel body with white markings; emits a small puff of white smoke and a loud popping noise; weight is 14 ounces.

(10) Cylindrical-shaped olive drab body; emits colored smoke for signaling or screening; filler is 11.5 ounces of colored smoke mixture; weight is 19 ounces.

A. (1) M61 fragmentation
(2) AN-M8 HC white smoke
(3) ABC-M7A2/ABC-M7A3 CS
(4) M67 fragmentation
(5) ~~M15~~ M34 WP Smoke
(6) ABC-M25A2 riot control CS
(7) MK3A2 offensive
(8) AN-M14 TH3 incendiary
(9) M69 practice hand grenade
(10) M18 colored smoke

Q. Fragmentation and concussion grenades generally explode how soon after the safety lever is released?
A. 4 to 5 seconds.

Q. What is a "Willie Pete"?
A. This is the common nickname for a white phosphorous grenade. The ~~M15~~ M34 white phosphorous hand grenade will burn for 60 seconds at temperatures exceeding 5,000 degrees Fahrenheit.

Q. How can you tell the color of smoke that will be delivered by an M18 colored smoke hand grenade?
A. Either by the top of the canister, which will be the same color as the smoke, or by reading the indicated color on the face of the canister.

Q. The M18 colored smoke hand grenade is available in what smoke colors?
A. Red, yellow, green, and violet.

GRENADES/MK-19 GRENADE MACHINE GUN
FM 23-30/FM 23-27

Q. What color is the top of the AN-M8 HC smoke grenade?
A. White

Q. Of the two riot control grenades, the ABC-M25A2 CS and the ABC-M7A2/A3 CS, which is a bursting-type grenade that can cause injury up to 5 meters away?
A. The ABC-M25A2 CS.

Q. What grenade is considered the best all-around choice for combat? What is its killing radius? What is the effective casualty-producing radius?
A. The fragmentation hand grenade; 5 meters; 15 meters.

NOTE: Although the killing radius is 5 meters and the casualty-producing radius is 15 meters, fragments can disperse as far away as 230 meters.

Q. Which grenade is considered poor against targets in the open, but very effective against targets in confined spaces, such as rooms, bunkers, or caves?
A. The MK3A2 concussion hand grenade (has only a 2-meter effective casualty radius against targets in the open).

Q. Which grenade is considered perhaps the most versatile hand grenade and why?
A. The ~~M15~~ M34 white phosphorous (WP) hand grenade; it can be used for signaling, screening, incendiary missions, or for producing casualties.

Q. The fillers of the M25-series riot control hand grenades are mixed with what for increased dissemination efficiency?
A. Silica aerogel.

Q. What filler is used in the AN-M14 TH3 incendiary hand grenades?
A. 26.5 oz of thermate (TH3) mixture.

Q. Describe the incendiary effects of the AN-M14 TH3 hand grenade.
A. A portion of the thermate mixture is converted to molten iron, which burns at 4,000 degrees Fahrenheit. It will fuse together the metallic parts of any object that it contacts. Thermate is an improved version of thermite, the incendiary agent used in hand grenades during WWII. The thermate filler of the AN-M14 hand grenade burns for 40 seconds and can burn through a 1/2-inch homogeneous steel plate. It produces its own oxygen and will burn under water.

NOTE: Avoid looking directly at the incendiary grenade as it burns. The intensity of the light is potentially hazardous to the retina.

Q. The M25-series of riot control hand grenades have an arming sleeve which serves the same purpose as the safety lever on other grenades. When throwing these grenades, how is the arming sleeve held in place?
A. By applying constant pressure with the thumb of the throwing hand.

Q. The ~~M15~~ M34 white phosphorous hand grenade has a bursting radius of ___ meters.
A. 17

Q. What is the first aid procedure for WP particles that become embedded in your skin?
A. If particles are embedded in the skin, immerse the wound in water or pack with wet cloths to halt combustion, then pick out or squeeze out the WP. The particles will re-ignite spontaneously if allowed to dry. If available, apply copper sulfate solution to halt combustion of the WP particles, which permits

them to be removed without igniting. Treat burns in the same way as ordinary burns (see FM 21-11).

Q. What is the warning regarding damaged AN-M8 HC grenades?
A. Exposure of the filler to moisture and air could result in a chemical reaction that will ignite the grenade.

Q. Give a specific example why the AN-M8 HC white smoke grenade should not be used in closed-in areas unless soldiers are wearing protective masks.
A. The AN-M8 HC hand grenade produces harmful hydrochloric fumes that irritate the eyes, throat, and lungs.

Q. What six things should you look for when inspecting grenades for defects?
A. (1) Ensure fuse is not unscrewed from the body of the grenade.
(2) Ensure safety clip is in the correct position; if no safety clip is present, attach one.
(3) Check the safety pin for bends and security.
(4) Check safety lever for breaks.
(5) Check safety ring for cracks.
(6) Check for dirt; wipe off dirt if necessary.

Q. Bending the ends of the safety pin back flush against the fuse body to prevent accidental pulling of the safety pin is not recommended for what two reasons?
A. This makes removal of the pin difficult and repeated working of the safety pin in this manner will cause the pin to break, creating a hazardous condition.

Q. What is the prescribed manner for carrying hand grenades?
A. Attached to the ammunition pouch using the carrying straps, which are designed for this purpose.

Q. How should you NEVER carry a hand grenade?
A. By its pull ring or by attaching it to equipment by its safety pin or safety lever. Also, under no circumstances will a grenade be carried in a uniform pocket. Extra hand grenades should be carried inside the rucksack or in a utility bag.

Q. When properly positioned on the ammo pouch, where should the grenade safety lever be?
A. Against the side of the ammo pouch (with the pull ring in the downward position and the carrying strap wrapped around the neck of the fuse).

Q. Maximum safety and throwing comfort as well as control are obtained when the hand grenade is held how?
A. Cradled in the throwing hand with the safety lever placed between the first and second joints of the thumb.

Q. For right-handed personnel, the grenade is held upright in order to position the pull ring where it can be easily removed by the index finger of the free hand. How does this differ from the way left-handed personnel would hold the grenade?
A. For left-handed personnel the grenade is held INVERTED with the fingers and thumb of the throwing hand positioned in the same manner as right-handed personnel.

Q. When throwing hand grenades it is important not to remain exposed for more than how many seconds?

GRENADES/MK-19 GRENADE MACHINE GUN
FM 23-30/FM 23-27

A. ~~2 seconds~~ 5 seconds.

Q. A technique that can be employed with time-delay-fused grenades (such as the M67) is the cookoff. Explain what this is and the advantages of using it.
A. To "cookoff" a grenade, you release the safety lever and hold the grenade for a count of two (approx two seconds). When the grenade is thrown, enemy personnel will not have time to pick it up and throw it back. If it is thrown high into the air, it can explode over the target (airburst).

Q. What is the most important factor in determining the basic load for hand grenades?
A. Unit mission.

Q. What are the five EMPLOYMENT RULES that should be remembered prior to the use of hand grenades?
A. (1) Leaders should identify soldiers who should not throw or carry grenades in combat.
(2) Know where all friendly soldiers are.
(3) Use the buddy team system.
(4) Ensure the projected arc of the fragmentation or an offensive hand grenade is clear of obstacles.
(5) Evacuate positions into which a fragmentation or offensive hand grenade is thrown, if possible. If this is not feasible, then use the grenade sump.

Q. What is the preferred course of action if an enemy grenade lands in your position or near you?
A. Since Soviet grenades use fuses with only a 3- to 4-second delay there will be very little time to react. The preferred course of action is to immediately roll out of your fighting position or throw yourself flat on the ground.

Q. Some characteristics and vulnerabilities of Soviet armor must be understood in order to kill or disable the enemy armored vehicle or its crew. Name three vulnerabilities common to most threat vehicles.
A. Fuel cells, ammunition storage areas, and power trains.

Q. How many stations are there on a Hand Grenade Qualification Course?
A. 7

Q. What are the hand grenade qualification levels?
A. Passed 7/7 .... Expert
Passed 6/7 .... First Class
Passed 5/7 .... Second Class
Passed 4/7 or less .... Unqualified

Q. What is the effective engagement radius for troops in the open when using hand grenades? Troops with overhead cover? Troops dug in without overhead cover?
A. - Troops in the open .... within 5 meters of center
- Troops with overhead cover .... inside the enclosure
- Troops dug in without overhead cover .... inside the position

GRENADES/MK-19 GRENADE MACHINE GUN
FM 23-30/FM 23-27

MK-19 GRENADE MACHINE GUN

Q. What FM cover the MK (Mark) 19 grenade machine gun?
A. FM 23-27

Q. What size grenade (projectile) is fired from the MK-19?
A. 40-mm

Q. Describe the MK-19.
A. The MK-19 is an air-cooled, blowback operated, belt-fed machine gun that is fed by a disintegrating metallic-link belt and fires 40-mm grenade cartridges.

Q. Is the barrel of the MK-19 designed to be changed during continuous operation to prevent overheating?
A. No, the barrel is designed not to overheat, even during prolonged firing.

Q. Describe the sight system of the MK-19.
A. The MK-19 has a blade-type front sight attached to the top cover assembly and a leaf-type rear sight (with an adjustable range plate) mounted on a spring dovetail base. The rear sight range plate is incremented in 100-meter intervals from 300 to 1500 meters. Range changes are made using either the slide release or the elevation wheel. The rear sight is also adjustable for windage.

Q. When making range changes using the slide release or the elevation wheel (see above question), which is used for making fine adjustments in elevation? Major adjustments?
A. Elevation wheel; slide release.

Q. One click in rear sight windage equals how much change?
A. 1 mil.

Q. The MK-19 supports the soldier in both the offense and defense by giving the unit a heavy volume of close, accurate, and continuous fire. There are seven other applications stated in FM 23-27. Name some of them.
A. (1) Protect motor movements, assembly areas, and supply trains in bivouac.
(2) Defend against hovering rotary aircraft.
(3) Destroy lightly armored vehicles.
(4) Fire on suspected enemy positions.
(5) Provide high volumes of fire into an engagement area.
(6) Cover obstacles.
(7) Provide indirect fires from defilade positions.

Q. What is an MK (Mark) 64?
A. The gun cradle for the MK-19.

Q. What is the weight of the MK-19 weapon system?
A. MK-19............... 75.6 lbs
MK-64................ 21 lbs
M3 Tripod........... 44 lbs

System weight.......140.6 lbs

Q. What mounts are available for the MK-19?
A. M3 tripod

GRENADES/MK-19 GRENADE MACHINE GUN
FM 23-30/FM 23-27

M4 pedestal
M66 ring
HMMWV weapon platform
M113 APC commander's cupola

Q. What type ammunition is fired from the MK-19?
A. M430 (HEDP), M383 (HE), M918 (TP), and M922 (dummy).

Q. What is the length of the MK-19?
A. 43.1 inches

Q. Describe the following operational characteristics of the MK-19: maximum range, maximum effective range, rates of fire, and muzzle velocity.
A. Maximum range.................... 2,212 meters
Maximum effective range.......... 1,500 meters (point target)
2,212 meters (area target)
Rates of fire:
sustained.................... 40 rds/min
rapid........................ 60 rds/min
cyclic....................... 325-375 rds/min

Muzzle velocity.................. 790 ft/sec

Q. What is the planned operating load for the MK-19?
A. 400 rounds for the HMMWV; all others as prescribed by local commanders.

Q. What are the angle-of-fire capabilities of the MK-19?
A. The MK-19 is capable of automatic fire at any angle between 0 and 70 degrees in elevation (based on the mounting arrangements).

Q. What is the average recoil force of the MK-19?
A. 500 lbs.

Q. What are the six steps in the MK-19 cycle of operation?
A. Charging, extracting (delinking), cocking, firing, blowback, and automatic feeding.

Q. A malfunction is a failure of the weapon to function properly. What are the two most common malfunctions of the MK-19?
A. Sluggish action and runaway gun.

Q. What is the immediate action for a runaway gun?
A. Consider the amount of ammunition left and the type of MK-19 mount used when finding the best way to stop the weapon:
(1) If ammunition is not low and the MK-19 is used in the free gun mode, keep rounds on target until all the rounds from the belt have been fired;
(2) If the MK-19 is mounted on either the M3 tripod or on a vehicle with the T&E mechanism attached, hold the grip with one hand while at the same time pressing the charger handle locks and lowering one of the charger handles - this action will interrupt the cycle of operation.

Q. When taking immediate action for a runaway gun, should you ever attempt to break the ammunition belt?
A. No, not for the MK-19.

Q. What is immediate action in the case of a stoppage?
A. Recharge the weapon and attempt to fire again.

GRENADES/MK-19 GRENADE MACHINE GUN
FM 23-30/FM 23-27

Q. In the event that immediate action (see above question) is not effective, what remedial actions should be taken to correct a stoppage?
A. (1) Unload and clear the MK-19;
(2) Inspect the weapon and ammunition to find the cause of the stoppage.

Q. Only the commander can direct the destruction of the MK-19. What are some approved methods of destruction?
A. Destruction by mechanical means, burning, gunfire, demolition or disposal.

Q. What is the best way to destroy ammunition?
A. Fire it.

ANTIPERSONNEL MINE, M18A1, CLAYMORE
FM 23-23

Q. What FM covers the use of the M18A1 Claymore mine?
A. FM 23-23

Q. Describe the M18A1 Antipersonnel (Claymore) mine.
A. It is a curved, rectangular-shaped weapon with an olive drab, molded case of fiberglass-filled polystyrene (plastic). In the front portion of the case is a fragmentation face containing steel spheres embedded in a plastic matrix. The back portion of the case behind the matrix contains a layer of explosive.

Q. The first thing you should do before employing an M18A1 Claymore mine is to account for all accessories in the bandoleer. List the components of the M18A1 you should find when conducting such an inventory.
A. - bandoleer (M7)
- antipersonnel mine (M18A1)
- test set (M40)
- firing device (M57)
- electrical blasting cap (M4)
- spool of firing wire
- insulation tape

Q. One M40 test set is included with how many Claymores?
A. With each case of six.

Q. How can you quickly identify a bandoleer that has an M40 test set included in it?
A. The bandoleer will have an identification tag with the words "THIS FIELD PACK CONTAINS M40 ELECTRICAL TEST SET".

Q. Where will you find the instructions for the employment of the M18A1 Claymore mine?
A. Under the flap of the bandoleer.

Q. What are the four steps of a complete circuit test of the M18A1 Claymore mine?
A. - **Initial test at firing point:**
   (1) M57 firing device connected to the M40 test set. When the handle of the firing device is squeezed, a flashing light indicates that the firing device and the test set are functioning properly.
   (2) M57 firing device connected to the M40 test set and the M40 test set connected to the connector of the firing wire (ensure that blasting cap is placed under a sandbag, behind a tree, or in a hole in the ground). Light should flash when handle of firing device is squeezed.
- **Final test at firing point** (after installation of Claymore):
   (3) Repeat step # 1.
   (4) Repeat step # 2.

Q. What should you keep with you at all times while setting up the Claymore mine?
A. The M57 firing device (to prevent accidental firing by another individual).

Q. When performing step #2 of the circuit test, why should you ensure that the blasting cap is placed under a sandbag, behind a tree, or in a hole in the ground?
A. To protect you in case the blasting cap detonates prematurely.

ANTIPERSONNEL MINE, M18A1, CLAYMORE
FM 23-23

Q. When aiming the mine you should push the legs how far into the ground, with the mine facing in the desired direction?
A. 1/3 of the way.

NOTE: In windy areas or when the legs cannot be pressed into the ground, spread the legs as far as they will go (about 180°) so that the legs are to the front and rear of the mine and the mine will not tip over.

Q. How should the mine be positioned?
A. So that the face of the mine marked "FRONT TOWARD ENEMY" and the arrows on top of the mine point in the direction of the enemy.

Q. What are the two sights used on the mine to aim it?
A. The knife-edge and the slit-type peep sights.

Q. When aiming the mine using either of the two sights provided, you should position your eye how far to the rear of the sight?
A. 6 inches.

Q. When using the knife-edge sight, where should your aiming point be?
A. At ground level, approximately 50 meters (150 feet) in front of the mine.

Q. When using the slit-type peep sight, where should your aiming point be?
A. 8 feet above the ground and approximately 50 meters (150 feet) in front of the mine.

Q. After installing the mine you should secure the firing wire about how far to the rear of the mine? Why is this necessary?
A. 1 meter; so that the mine will not become inadvertently misaligned if the firing wire is disturbed.

Q. What do you do after securing the shipping plug priming adapter with blasting cap into the detonator well?
A. Recheck the aim of the mine. Camouflage the mine and, if possible, bury the firing wire and move back to the firing position.

Q. What type of explosive is used in the M18A1 Claymore mine?
A. 1.5 lbs Composition C4 (plastic explosive).

Q. The firing position for the Claymore mine should be a foxhole or covered position at least how far to the rear or the side of the emplaced mine?
A. 16 meters.

Q. After the final circuit test, when the mine is ready for detonation, what should you remember to do?
A. Remove the M40 test set and connect the firing wire directly to the M57 firing device. Ensure that the firing bail is in the SAFE position until ready for use.

Q. When conducting the final circuit test on the Claymore you should ensure that friendly troops within _____ meters to the front and sides and _____ meters to the rear of the mine are under cover.
A. 250; 100.

Q. The M18A1 Claymore mine is most effective when employed against targets at what range in front of it?
A. 20 to 30 meters.

ANTIPERSONNEL MINE, M18A1, CLAYMORE
FM 23-23

Q. When staking the firing wire at the firing point and at the mine installation point, you should take care that the stakes do not stick up more than _______ above the ground.
A. 1 foot.

Q. What are the steps in successfully employing the M18A1 Claymore mine?
A. (1) inventory
(2) conduct initial circuit test
(3) set up, aim, and arm the mine
(4) conduct final circuit test
(5) fire mine

Q. When recovering an M18A1 Claymore mine, what should you do after separating the shipping plug primer adapter and the blasting cap?
A. Reverse the shipping plug and screw the plug end of the adapter into the detonator well. Insert the blasting cap back into the firing wire spool.

Q. What are the casualty effects of the M18A1 Claymore mine?
A. When detonated, the M18A1 mine will deliver spherical steel fragments over a 60 degree fan-shaped pattern that is 2 meters high and 50 meters wide at a range of about 50 meters. These fragments are moderately effective up to a range of 100 meters and can travel up to 250 meters forward of the mine.

Q. What is considered the danger area of backblast and secondary missiles?
A. Within an area 16 meters to the rear and sides of the mine.

Q. How much does the Claymore mine weigh?
A. 3.5 lbs.

Q. The M4 electric blasting cap is connected to a spool of wire that is _____ feet long.
A. 100

LIGHT ANTIARMOR WEAPONS
FM 23-25

Q. What FM covers the use, care, and disposition of light antiarmor weapons?
A. FM 23-25

Q. Which two types of light antiarmor weapons are specifically covered in FM 23-25?
A. The M72-series LAW and the M136 AT4.

Q. What FM covers the use of the 66-mm, M72-series LAW?
A. ~~FM 23-33~~ Superseded by FM 23-25, "Light Antiarmor Weapons".

Q. What is a LAW?
A. The LAW is a lightweight, self-contained antiarmor weapon consisting of a rocket packed in a launcher. It is man-portable and may be fired from either shoulder. The launcher, which consists of two tubes, one inside the other, serves as a watertight packing container for the rocket and houses a percussion-type firing mechanism that activates the rocket.

Q. What kind of projectile is fired from the LAW?
A. A 66-mm high explosive antitank (HEAT), percussion-ignited, fin-stabilized, fixed-munition rocket.

Q. How many spring-loaded fins are attached to the M72 LAW?
A. 6

Q. Exhaust gas temperatures exiting the launcher may reach what temperature?
A. 1,400°F.

Q. What is the primary difference between the M72A1 and the M72A2/A3 LAW?
A. The M72A2 and M72A3 have a greater armor penetrating capability.

Q. What are the following characteristics of the M72A2 and M72A3 LAW (launcher)?
A. length .... ~~20"~~
closed .... 24.8"
fully extended ..... 34.67"
weight .... ~~2.2 lb~~
complete M72A2 ..... 5.1 lbs
complete M72A3 ..... 5.5 lbs

Q. What are the following characteristics of the M72A2 and M72A3 LAW (rocket)?
A. length .... 20"
weight .... 2.2 lbs
muzzle velocity .... 475 fps
minimum range .... 10 meters
maximum range .... 1000 meters
maximum effective range
stationary target .. 200 meters
moving target ...... 165 meters

Q. Engaging targets beyond the maximum effective ranges given above will result in a less than ____% chance of hitting the target.
A. 50%

Q. What is the M72-series weapon designed to be employed against?
A. Primary - light antiarmor
Secondary - gun emplacements, pillboxes, buildings, or light vehicles.

LIGHT ANTIARMOR WEAPONS
FM 23-25

Q. What are the warhead penetrative capabilities of the M72A2/A3 LAW?
A. Will penetrate 300-mm of rolled homogenous steel armor.

Q. Describe the front sight of the M72A2 and M72A3 LAW.
A. A leaf sight with an embossed vertical range line showing ranges from 50 to 350 meters in 25-meter increments. It has an illuminant (promethium) range marker at the 100- and 150-meter marks to aid the gunner in engaging targets under low light level conditions. Two curved stadia lines are etched on the sight, but these are no longer used for range estimation. Lead indicators are located on either side of the stadia lines to aid in the engagement of moving targets.

NOTE: Do not touch the 100- and 150-meter range marks as they are mildly radioactive.

Q. Describe the rear sight of the M72A2 or M72A3 LAW.
A. Consists of a steel bracket with a rubber boot and plastic peep sight which automatically adjusts to changes in temperature.

Q. What is considered correct eye placement when aiming the M72-series LAW?
A. The firing eye should be as close to the rear sight as is comfortable.

Q. What is the first step in preparing the LAW for use?
A. Inspect its overall condition.

Q. When visually inspecting the LAW, what things should you look for?
A.
- check the body for dents, cracks, or bulges
- check the rubber boots covering the trigger bar and barrel detent for tears or punctures
- ensure that the arming handle is present and on SAFE and that the pull pin is in place
- ensure that the statement "W/COUPLER" is on the data plate. If these words are not on the data plate, do not use the launcher.

Q. What is meant by the statement "W/COUPLER" on the data plate (see above question)?
A. This indicates that the launcher has been modified for safety. The coupler prevents the inner and outer tubes from separating and possibly causing premature detonation.

Q. The trigger arming handle has only two positions. What are they?
A. SAFE and ARM.

Q. What are the steps in preparing the M72A2 or M72A3 LAW for firing?
A. (1) Remove the pull pin and rotate the rear cover downward. The front cover and adjustable sling assembly should fall free. Do not discard the sling assembly until the rocket is fired.

(2) Extend the launcher by grasping the rear sight cover with the firing hand and the launcher tube forward of the barrel detent with the non-firing hand. The muzzle of the launcher should be pointed downrange at all times. It is recommended that both hands be placed on top of the LAW when extending it.

(3) Sharply pull the launcher to the extended position by moving the hands in the opposite directions.

(4) To insure that the launcher is fully extended and locked, reverse the motion of the hands and attempt to collapse the launcher.

(5) Place the launcher on the shoulder. Do this by raising the launcher

slightly above shoulder level and rotating your body under it (remember to keep the muzzle pointed downrange).

(6) Check the backblast area.
(7) Pull the trigger arming handle to the ARM position.
(8) Aim the launcher and depress the trigger bar firmly.

Q. If the trigger arming handle will not remain in the ARM position, what is likely the cause?
A. The launcher is not fully extended.

Q. What are the steps in restoring the M72A2 or M72A3 LAW to carrying configuration?
A. (1) Return the trigger arming handle to SAFE position.
(2) Remove from shoulder.
(3) Depress barrel detent and guide front and rear sights into position while collapsing launcher tube.
(4) Close rear cover and replace cover pull pin.
(5) Replace sling assembly.

Q. How should the cover pull pin be inserted?
A. From right to left with the short end through the cover closing lug and the long end through the round lock, which protrudes through the rear cover.

Q. For carrying, the launcher should be slung over either shoulder with the muzzle or forward end pointed in what direction?
A. Down

Q. Describe the functioning (firing process) of the LAW.
A. NOTE: The launcher must be extended before it can be fired.
(1) The trigger is depressed and the firing pin strikes the primer.
(2) The primer ignites the black powder in the flash tube.
(3) Ignition of black powder in flash tube ignites propellant in the rocket motor.

Q. Once the launcher has been prepared for firing and returned to the carry position, it is no longer __________.
A. Watertight.

Q. What is the first step in applying immediate action (misfire procedures) on an M72A2 and M72A3 LAW?
A. Immediately re-squeeze the trigger.

Q. What are the immediate action steps for the LAW while in combat?
A. (1) After a failure to fire, immediately re-squeeze the trigger;
(2) If the launcher still fails to fire, place the trigger arming handle on SAFE;
(3) Partly collapse the launcher, then extend it to cock again;
(4) Place it on your shoulder, check the backblast area again, then arm, aim, and fire;
(5) If the LAW still fails to fire, squeeze the trigger again and return the trigger arming handle to SAFE. Collapse the launcher, set it aside, and try another one. As soon as you can, dispose of the misfired LAW in accordance with SOP.

NOTE: Do not leave an intact LAW on the battlefield. The enemy can and will use it against you.

LIGHT ANTIARMOR WEAPONS
FM 23-25

Q. What are the immediate action steps for the LAW while in training?
A. (1) After a failure to fire, immediately re-squeeze the trigger;
(2) If the launcher still fails to fire, keep the launcher on your shoulder, announce "MISFIRE," and wait 10 seconds. Place the trigger arming handle on SAFE;
(3) Move the launcher from your shoulder and wait one minute;
(4) Extend the launcher to cock it again, check the backblast area, place the launcher back on your shoulder, pull the arming handle to the ARM position, aim, and squeeze the trigger bar;
(5) If the launcher again fails to fire, wait 10 seconds before returning the trigger arming handle to the SAFE position;
(6) Keep the launcher trained on the target area for at least one minute; **DO NOT** collapse the launcher;
(7) Move the launcher to a safe area and dispose of it IAW unit SOP.

Q. How is the M72A2 and M72A3 LAW modified for training purposes?
A. With the M190 sub-caliber launching insert and ~~33-mm~~ 35-mm, M73 sub-caliber rockets. The smaller and lighter training rocket simulates the 66-mm rocket's smoke and flight trajectory but with less noise and backblast.

Q. Why should you avoid frontal shots at enemy tanks?
A. The tank's armor is thickest up front so the LAW is less likely to penetrate at this point.

Q. What are the four prescribed combat expedient disposal methods for the LAW or the AT4?
A. Live (unexpended) round: Demolition, burning, or firing.
Expended: Mechanical (LAW only), demolition, or burning.

Q. Mechanical means should never be used to destroy LIVE (unexpended) antiarmor weapons or expended M136 AT4s, but may be employed to destroy the residue from an expended M72-series LAW. What are some examples of mechanical destruction of an expended M72?
A. Driving over it with a tracked vehicle or striking it with a pick, ax, or other object, so long as you make it unusable.

Q. How should the lead markers be used on the LAW when engaging moving targets?
A. First estimate the target's speed as either slow (5 mph or less) or fast (above 5 mph). For slow-moving targets, or those moving in an oblique direction, locate the proper range mark on the vertical range line, locate the lead cross which is horizontal to the range mark, place the lead cross on center mass of the target, and fire. For fast-moving targets, use the same procedure as for slow targets except that the lead cross is placed on the front leading edge of the target.

Q. What is the backblast "danger zone" for the LAW?
A. The area to the rear of the weapon covered by a 60-degree fan (30 degrees on either side of the center-line), and 15 meters deep (extends to 40 meters to include caution zone).

Q. What FM covers the use of the M136 (AT-4) Launcher and Cartridge?
A. FM 23-25, "Light Antiarmor Weapons".

Q. What size/type projectile is fired from the AT-4?
A. 84-mm; HEAT.

LIGHT ANTIARMOR WEAPONS
FM 23-25

Q. Describe the M136 (AT-4) Launcher and Cartridge.
A. The AT-4 is a lightweight, self-contained anti-armor weapon. It consists of a free-flight, fin-stabilized cartridge packed in a one-piece, disposable, fiberglass-wrapped tube (launcher).

Q. The AT-4 is fired from the ________ (right/left) shoulder only.
A. Right.

Q. How are both the M72 and the M136 AT-4 issued?
A. As a round of ammunition (rather than an individual weapon) and in addition to a soldier's assigned weapon(s) and the unit's organic antiarmor weapons.

Q. What serves as a watertight packing container for transportation and storage of the AT-4?
A. The launcher itself.

Q. What is the AT-4 designed to be employed against?
A. Primary - Armored Personnel Carriers (APCs);
Secondary - bunkers and field fortifications.

Q. What is the overall weight of the AT-4?
A. Approximately 15 lbs.

Q. What is the length of the AT-4?
A. 40 inches.

Q. What is the approximate muzzle velocity of the AT-4's 84-mm HEAT round?
A. 950 fps.

Q. What are the following range characteristics of the AT-4?
A. - maximum range......................2,100 meters
- maximum effective range............ 300 meters
- minimum arming range............... 10 meters
- minimum target engagement range..... ~~30 meters~~
combat .... 10 meters
training .... 30 meters

Q. What is the approximate length and weight of the AT-4 rocket?
A. length .... 18"
weight .... 4 lbs

Q. What are the warhead penetrative capabilities of the AT-4 shaped-charge rocket?
A. Penetrates more than 14 inches (35.6 cm) of armor.

Q. How is the M136 AT4 modified for training purposes?
A. The AT4 may be completely inert for field handling/training purposes (known as a Field Handling Trainer, or FHT) or may be modified to fire the M287 9-mm tracer bullet.

Q. Does the AT-4 require extending to fire like the M72-series weapon?
A. No.

Q. The AT-4 will not fire unless what three safeties have ALL been disengaged?
A. (1) Transport safety pin - pull outward, then release.
(2) Cocking Lever - push the lever forward and down with the right thumb.
(3) Forward Safety - must be held down while simultaneously pushing the

trigger.

Q. What is the purpose of the "fire-through muzzle cover"?
A. It keeps out moisture and prevents foreign objects from entering the muzzle.

Q. The front and rear sights of the AT-4 were designed to resemble those of what weapon, making its use easier?
A. The M16-series rifle.

Q. Describe the front and rear sights of the AT-4.
A. - Front-sight: consists of a sight blade, center post, and left and right lead posts.
- Rear-sight: consists of a sight blade, range adjustment knob, range scale, 2-mm peephole, and 7-mm peephole.

Q. What is the 2-mm peephole on the rear sight used for? The 7-mm peephole?
A. Normal light conditions; limited visibility.

Q. How do you open the front sight cover?
A. Press down on it and slide it backward until the sight pops up.

Q. How do you open the rear sight cover?
A. Press down on it and slide it forward until the sight pops up.

Q. Can nightsights such as the AN/PVS-4 be used with the M72-series and M136 AT-4 weapons?
A. Yes, with the appropriate mounting brackets.

Q. How is the range scale on the rear sight indexed?
A. From 100 to 500 meters in 50-meter increments.

Q. There is an audible click at each _____-meter increment to aid the firer during limited visibility.
A. 50

Q. When properly positioned for firing, the rear sight of the AT-4 should be how far from your eyes?
A. Between 2 ½ and 3 inches (this is not only for correct sight alignment but to prevent possible injury from the weapon's recoil).

Q. The AT-4 is battle-sighted at what range?
A. 200 meters.

Q. The rear sight may be damaged if the range indicator is not reset on ______ meters before closing the sight cover.
A. 200

Q. The "venturi" on the aft end of the weapon performs two functions. What are they?
A. (1) Protects the weapon from damage if dropped.
(2) Directs the flow of the backblast.

Q. Since the AT-4 is completely sealed, inspection of the weapon is limited to what?
A. The external components.

Q. What things should you look for when inspecting the overall condition of the

launcher?
A. - The rear seal is in place and undamaged.
- The transport safety pin is in place and fully inserted. The lanyard is attached. The lanyard should already be wrapped around the launcher clockwise and the transport safety pin inserted in the retainer hole counterclockwise.
- The cocking lever is present and in the SAFE position and folded down.
- The fire-through muzzle cover is in place and undamaged.
- The launcher has the correct color-coded band (black color-coded band with a yellow band inside indicates a live (non-training) HE antiarmor round).
- The sights function properly.
- The forward safety does not move when depressed.
- The red trigger button is not missing, broken or damaged.
- The launcher body has no cracks, dents, or bulges.
- The shoulder stop is not broken or damaged, and that it unsnaps and folds down.
- The carrying sling is not frayed and is attached firmly to the launch tube.

Q. What should you do if, during your inspection, you find that the fire-through muzzle cover is ruptured or torn?
A. Cut it out to insure that there are no foreign objects inside the launcher tube. Remove any that you find by turning the tube muzzle downward and gently shaking the launcher. Remember that if the cover is not intact, the weapon is no longer watertight.

Q. What is the rear seal made of?
A. Brown ~~Plexiglas~~ acrylic plastic.

Q. What are the steps in preparing the AT-4 for immediate firing?
A. (1) Remove the launcher from the carrying position and cradle it in the left arm. Keep the launcher pointed down range.
(2) With your right hand, pull and release the transport safety pin (if not attached to a lanyard, keep in a safe place since it must be reinserted if the launcher is not fired).
(3) Unsnap, unfold, and hold the shoulder stop with your right hand.
(4) Place the launcher on the right shoulder.
(5) Release the sights with your left hand, then stabilize the launcher by grasping the sling near the launcher's muzzle, also with the left hand.
(6) Set the rear sight for the correct range to the target.
(7) Check the backblast area.
(8) Cock the launcher. Unfold the cocking lever with your right hand. Place your thumb under it and, with the support of your fingers in front of the firing mechanism, push it forward, rotate it downward and to the right, and let it slide backward.
(9) Insure that the shoulder stop is pulled back snugly against the right shoulder.
(10) Use the index and middle fingers on your right hand to hold the forward safety down and to the left while you fire.

Q. What are the misfire procedures for the AT-4 during combat?
A. (1) Release the forward safety;
(2) Remove your right hand from the firing mechanism and cock the weapon again;
(3) Try to fire again. If the launcher still does not fire, maintain the same firing position and return the cocking lever to the SAFE (uncocked)

position;

(4) Move the launcher from your shoulder, keeping the launcher pointed toward the enemy. Reinsert the transport safety pin;

(5) Place the launcher on the ground, pointed toward the enemy, and use another launcher. Dispose of the misfired launcher IAW unit SOP.

Q. What are the misfire procedures for the AT-4 during training?
A. (1) Shout "MISFIRE" as soon as the launcher fails to fire, while maintaining the original sight picture;

(2) Release the forward safety;

(3) Recock the launcher by immediately removing the right hand from the firing mechanism and pushing the cocking lever forward with the heel of the right hand until the lever locks with a loud clicking noise;

(4) Press the forward safety all the way down and try to fire again. If the launcher still fails to fire, release the forward safety and move the cocking lever to the SAFE (unlocked) position. Move the launcher from your shoulder, keeping the weapon pointed toward the target;

(5) Reinsert the transport safety pin, wait two minutes, then carefully lay the launcher on the ground, muzzle toward the target. Notify range safety.

NOTE: Since performing immediate action on the AT-4 takes so little time, there is no need to recheck the backblast area between steps 3 and 4 above.

Q. In the event of a misfire, and if immediate action steps do not solve the problem, what should be done to identify the weapon as a misfired launcher?
A. Combat - break off the sights.

Training - do not damage the field handling trainer (FHT); instead, leave the sights up to so identify it.

Q. What are the steps in restoring the AT-4 to a carrying configuration?
A. (1) Release the forward safety;

(2) Push forward and up on the cocking lever, and let it spring back into the SAFE (uncocked) position;

(3) Move the launcher from your shoulder, ensuring the muzzle is pointed in the direction of fire;

(4) Replace the transport safety pin until it is fully seated in the retainer hole;

(5) To avoid breaking off the rear sight, remember to reset the range indicator to the 200-meter setting before closing the rear sight cover;

(6) Lay down the sights and close their covers;

(7) Snap the shoulder stop into the closed position;

(8) Sling the launcher over either shoulder and move to another location.

Q. What should be used by the soldier to decontaminate the M72 or the M136 AT-4 of V-G-H agents?
A. The M258A1 Personal Decontamination Kit or DKIE (XM280) individual decon packets.

Q. What are the different firing positions for light antiarmor weapons?
A. Standing, kneeling, sitting, and prone.

Q. Which is the least stable of all firing positions?
A. Prone.

Q. When firing the AT-4 from the prone position you must maintain an angle of not less than _____ degrees to the line of fire or injury from backblast may result.

A. 90

Q. When engaging moving targets with the AT-4, fast-moving targets are those estimated to be moving faster than ______ mph.
A. 10

Q. The area immediately to the rear of an AT-4 position must not have walls, large trees, or any other obstructions within ____ meters or the backblast may be deflected onto the firer.
A. 5

Q. What is the backblast "danger zone" for the AT-4?
A. The area to the rear of the weapon covered by a 90-degree fan (45 degrees on either side of the center-line), and ~~60 meters~~ 100 meters deep.

NOTE: When operating temperatures fall below freezing, all backblast areas and safety zones double.

Q. When firing the AT-4 from a covered fighting position (foxhole), what safety considerations must be observed?
A. The rear of the launcher must extend beyond the back wall of the position, no overhead cover may extend into the backblast area, and there must be at least 18 inches clearance around the weapon.

Q. What are the minimum target engagements ranges for the AT-4?
A. Same as the LAW:
combat .... 10 meters
training ..... 30 meters

NBC
FM 3-3, 3-3-1, 3-4, 3-5, 3-7, 3-100

GENERAL

Q. What does "NBC" stand for?
A. Nuclear, Biological, and Chemical.

Q. What does "CBR" stand for?
A. Chemical, Biological, and Radiological. Although the abbreviation "CBR" is still occasionally used, "NBC" is considered to be the modern usage.

Q. What are the three fundamentals of NBC defense?
A. Contamination avoidance, protection, and decontamination.

Q. What are the five Army Field Manuals that explain the fundamentals of NBC defense?
A. FM 3-3....Chemical and Biological Contamination Avoidance
FM 3-3-1..Nuclear Contamination Avoidance
FM 3-4....NBC Protection
FM 3-5....NBC Decontamination
FM 3-7....NBC Handbook

Q. In what FM will you find a general overview of these fundamentals (see above question)?
A. FM 3-100..NBC Operations

Q. What Army regulation covers "Nuclear, Biological and Chemical Defense and Chemical Warfare".
A. AR 350-41

Q. What is considered to be the best defense against the enemy use of nuclear, biological and/or chemical weapons?
A. Contamination avoidance.

Q. There are four steps to contamination avoidance. What are they?
A. - Implement passive defensive measures
- Warn and report NBC attacks
- Locate, identify, track, and predict NBC hazards
- Limit exposure to NBC hazards

Q. What are some good examples of passive defensive measures that reduce the chances of a unit being targeted?
A. - Good communications procedures (OPSEC)
- Light discipline
- Good camouflage
- Remain mobile

Q. What are some good examples of passive defensive measures that reduce the effectiveness of an attack?
A. - Provide Warning
- Dispersion
- Hardening of positions and equipment
- Effective use of overhead cover
- Cover supplies and equipment
- Prevent spread of contamination (CB)
- Prevent spread of fallout (nuclear)

- Limit exposure

Q. How does camouflage, cover, and concealment play an important role in NBC defense?
A. It hinders the enemy's target acquisition capabilities.

Q. Contamination avoidance is a process that begins with an initial assessment of the NBC threat and the IPB. What is an "IPB"?
A. Intelligence Preparation of the Battlefield.

Q. What five functions (as a minimum) are included in the IPB?
A. - Evaluation of the battlefield
- Terrain analysis
- Weather analysis
- Threat evaluation
- Threat integration

Q. The minimum nuclear or CB threat status is set at what level?
A. Division or separate brigade level (as determined by a continuously updated IPB process).

Q. For planning purposes, nuclear and CB threat levels are assigned serial numbers representative of the threat. How many threat levels are there and what degree of threat is represented by each?
A. 4;
- Serial 0 (no threat)
- Serial 1 (low threat)
- Serial 2 (medium threat)
- Serial 3 (high threat)

Q. NBC hazards can be classified into two types. What are they?
A. (1) Immediate hazards - produce casualties immediately after the attack. Includes the blast, thermal, and initial radiation effects of a nuclear explosion; vapor and liquid effects of chemical agents; and the effects of live biological agents or toxins.
(2) Residual hazards - include radiological contamination and induced radiation from a nuclear explosion and the delayed effects from biological or chemical agents. Also include liquid contamination; vapor hazards from persistent liquid chemical agents; and particles that remain on clothing, equipment, or terrain.

Q. NBC protection is divided into what two broad areas?
A. (1) Individual - involves those measures each soldier must take to survive and continue the mission.
(2) Collective - provides a contamination-free working environment for selected personnel, and it allows soldiers relief from continuous wear of MOPP gear.

Q. What is current US policy regarding the use of nuclear, chemical, and biological assets?
A. Biological....No use.
Chemical......No first use.
Nuclear.......Last resort (will use first only if necessary).

NOTE: Herbicides and riot control agents are not classified as military chemicals. Although their uses are covered by different policies than those that apply to chemical warfare, they do have military applications. Current policy regarding herbicides is that they will not be used in war, unless they are first used against us and the President directs their use in retaliation. In war, the US has renounced the first use of riot control agents except in defensive military modes. Advance Presidential approval is required.

Q. Who has the authority to order the use of nuclear weapons?
A. Only the President of the United States.

Q. What forms do NBC contaminants come in?
A. Solids, liquids, and gases.

Q. What are the ~~four~~ five contamination hazards?
A. (1) Transfer - anything that touches a surface covered with liquid or solid contamination will tend to pick up the contamination, thus transferring the contamination from one place to another.
(2) Spread - touching a surface covered with liquid chemical agent can spread contamination on the same surface, thereby, increasing the size of the contaminated area.
(3) Vapor - includes any contamination you breathe, no matter what form it takes - dust in the air, atomized liquids (aerosols), or true gases.
(4) Desorption - liquid chemical contamination is quickly absorbed into most surfaces. Once absorbed, it begins to desorb or outgas; that is, low levels of vapor pass out of the contaminated surface into the air and remain as a contamination hazard.
(5) Radiation - the penetrating energy of radiation given off by radioactive dust or dirt, most of which appears as fallout.

Q. To preclude the absorption of chemical agents into metal surfaces, fielded Army equipment is painted with a hardened, polyurethane paint, known as "CARC". What does "CARC" stand for?
A. Chemical Agent Resistant Coating - resists absorption and makes decon methods easier and more effective; minimizes desorption as a hazard.

Q. Describe the procedures for marking a contaminated area.
A. When possible use an M274 NBC Contamination Marking Set (contains triangular color-coded signs) and place the markers away from the contamination. Markers should be placed on the edge of a contaminated area with additional markers at roads, trails, and other likely points of entry.

Q. When emplacing NBC markers, how far apart should they be?
A. Adjacent signs should be within sight of each other - normally 25-100 meters apart depending on terrain.

Q. What are the dimensions of an NBC marker?
A. 11 ½ inches on the top by 8 inches on either side.

Q. What are the three classifications of NBC markers? Describe them.
A. Chemical: Red letters "GAS" on a yellow background.
Biological: Red letters "BIO" on a blue background.
Radiological: Black letters "ATOM" on a white background.

Q. For biological contamination and for persistent or nonpersistent agents, what other information is required to be entered on the appropriate NBC marker?
A. Type of agent (if known), date and time of detection.

Q. Warsaw Pact countries have contamination markers that are rectangular in shape. Describe the background, lettering, and other markings.

NBC
FM 3-3, 3-3-1, 3-4, 3-5, 3-7, 3-100

A. The background is generally red with black lettering for all types of contamination. A rectangle (box) on the left side of the sign contains the contamination symbol (Nuclear - PB; Biological - b; Chemical - OB). An arrow (dotted line on sign) indicates the direction of the contaminated area. A set of these lines indicates a decontaminated path through the area. A number to the right of the lines indicates the width of the decontaminated path. At the bottom, "4EPE3" followed by a number indicates the distance across the contaminated area. If "4EPE3" is crossed out and replaced by "O6bE3A" (DETOUR), then the area cannot be decontaminated.

Q. What does "NBCWRS" stand for and explain its purpose.
A. The Nuclear, Biological, and Chemical Warning and Reporting System; it is a rapid means of warning units of an actual or predicted NBC hazard.

Q. How many NBC Reports are there and what is the purpose of each?
A. Six;
- NBC 1 - Observer's Initial Report.
- NBC 2 - Evaluated Data Report.
- NBC 3 - Warning of Predicted Contamination and hazard areas.
- NBC 4 - Monitoring and Survey Report.
- NBC 5 - Actual Contaminated Areas Report.
- NBC 6 - Detailed Information on Chemical/Biological Attack Report.

NOTE: Only the first five NBC reports are used in support of radiological defense.

Q. Which of the NBC reports is the most widely used?
A. NBC 1

Q. An <u>initial</u> NBC 1 report should be sent with what communications priority?
A. FLASH.

Q. <u>Subsequent</u> NBC 1 reports should be sent with what communications priority?
A. IMMEDIATE.

Q. NBC 1 reports are normally compiled at the unit level by the NBC defense team and sent to the next higher headquarters. Initial observer reports below the unit level should use what format?
A. Spot or SALUTE report.

Q. A Unit NBC Defense Team is normally comprised of what individuals?
A. Unit chemical NCO (54B20) or an NCO that has been school trained at an area NBC defense two-week school, an officer (OIC), and an enlisted soldier (SPC or above - see NOTE below) who has attended the same two-week school.

NOTE: FM 3-3 specifies SPC or above for enlisted NBC Defense Team member; while FM 3-3-1 specifies CPL or above.

Q. NBC 1 reports are not attack notifications - they simply pass data. What format should an attack notification have?
A. The form of a SALUTE, Spot, or Situation Report (SITREP).

Q. Which NBC report is based on one or more NBC 1 Reports?
A. An NBC 2 Report.

Q. What is the lowest level at which NBC 2 Reports are normally prepared?
A. Division

NBC
FM 3-3, 3-3-1, 3-4, 3-5, 3-7, 3-100

Q. Who normally receives an NBC 3 Report?
A. All units that may be affected by the hazard.

Q. What Army Graphic Training Aid serves as a quick reference for the NBC Warning and Reporting System and includes details on the six NBC Reports, CHEMWARN and ~~NUCWARN~~ STRIKWARN formats, and Chemical Downwind Messages?
A. GTA 3-6-3 (normally carried in the protective mask carry case).

Q. What are the four **principles** of decon?
A. (1) Speed: decontaminate as soon as possible.
(2) Need: decontaminate only what is necessary to continue the mission.
(3) Limit: decontaminate as far forward as possible (limit spread).
(4) Priority: decontaminate the most important things first and the least important things last.

Q. Which of the above principles is considered to be the most important?
A. Decontaminate as soon as possible.

Q. NBC decontamination is expressed in terms of ***levels*** and ***techniques***. There are three basic levels which can be further subdivided into a total of seven techniques. First, what are the ***three basic levels*** of decontamination?
A. (1) Immediate - purpose is to minimize casualties, save lives, and limit the spread of contamination. Carried out by individuals immediately after becoming contaminated.
(2) Operational - purpose is to sustain operations, reduce the contact hazard and limit the spread of contamination to eliminate the necessity or reduce the duration of wearing MOPP gear.
(3) Thorough - purpose is to reduce or eliminate the need for individual protective clothing.

Q. What seven decon **techniques** are used to support the three levels of decon?
A. **IMMEDIATE**
(1) Skin Decon
(2) Personal Wipedown
(3) Operator's Spraydown
OPERATIONAL
(4) MOPP Gear Exchange
(5) Vehicle Washdown
THOROUGH
(6) Detailed Equipment/Aircraft Decon (DED/DAD)
(7) Detailed Troop Decon (DTD)

Q. When should IMMEDIATE decon techniques be initiated?
A. (1) Skin decon - immediately upon actual or suspected contamination.
(2) Personal wipedown - within 15 minutes of contamination.
(3) Operator's spraydown - within 15 minutes after personal wipedown.

NOTE: Skin decon should be initiated within 1 minute, at most, of becoming contaminated because some toxic chemical agents, especially nerve agents, are rapidly absorbed by the skin and can kill in minutes.

Q. Skin decon is a basic soldier survival skill and is used to remove or neutralize contamination on exposed skin. What should be used to accomplish skin decon?
A. Chemical agents - The M291 or M258A1 skin decon kits
Biological agents - hot soapy water or 0.5% bleach solution

NBC
FM 3-3, 3-3-1, 3-4, 3-5, 3-7, 3-100

Radiological agents - no immediate skin decon is required.

Q. What can you do for skin decon (chemical contamination) if you do not have an M258A1 or M291 skin decon kit?
A. Chemical contamination may be pinch-blotted from the skin with a cloth and the area flushed with soap and water (or hot water). Pinch-blotting is better than rubbing because it limits the spread of contamination.

Q. You have been attacked by a chemical agent. You immediately close your eyes, stop breathing, mask, and give the alarm. Your next step is skin decon (preferably within 1 minute of being attacked). What should you do just prior to skin decon?
A. Seek overhead shelter or use your poncho to protect against further contamination while performing skin decon.

Q. Personal wipedown is used to remove or neutralize contamination on the hood, mask, gloves, and personal weapon. What should be used to accomplish personal wipedown?
A. Chemical agents - The M280 (Decontaminating Kit, Individual Equipment) was designed for this purpose but is on hold pending replacement by the M295 (Decontaminating Kit, Personal Equipment). The M291 or M258A1 should be used.
Biological agents - soap and water or, if unavailable, the M258A1.
Radiological agents - brush the dust off equipment and wash exposed areas of skin. Use M258A1 if soap and water are not available. Pay particular attention to hair and fingernails. Avoid breathing the dust you shake off by wearing a piece of cloth over your face.

Q. Operator spraydown is used to remove or neutralize contamination on the surfaces of the equipment that operators must frequently touch to perform their mission. What should be used to accomplish operator spraydown?
A. Chemical agents - DS-2, using M11 or M13 device.
Biological agents - bleach solution is preferred; hot, soapy water is an alternate method; DS-2 or STB may be used as a last resort.
Radiological agents - brush or scrape dust from equipment and flush with water.

Q. What are the four portals of entry that toxic agents may use when entering the body?
A. Nose, eyes, mouth, and skin.

Q. What is "MOPP"?
A. Mission Oriented Protective Posture; a flexible system of protection against chemical and biological agents.

Q. The MOPP suit protective overgarment is known as what? Describe it.
A. Battle Dress Overgarment (BDO). It is a two-piece suit in a camouflage pattern. The material consists of an outer layer of nylon-cotton and an inner layer of charcoal-impregnated polyurethane foam. It comes sealed in a vapor-barrier bag that protects against rain, moisture, and sunlight. The BDO protects the wearer against contact with chemical agent vapors, aerosols, and droplets of liquids; live biological agents; toxins; and radioactive alpha and beta particles. The BDO is water repellent and should be worn as an outer garment. The BDO is not designed to be decontaminated or reimpregnated for reuse and should, therefore, be discarded when unserviceable or contaminated.

NOTE: The green chemical-protective overgarment (CPOG) will continue to be used until stocks are depleted. ~~Material is same as camouflage pattern BDO.~~

NBC
FM 3-3, 3-3-1, 3-4, 3-5, 3-7, 3-100

Q. When the BDO is removed from the package and donned, how long will it retain its protective qualities?
A. 14 days, so long as it remains serviceable and uncontaminated.

Q. Once the BDO is contaminated with a liquid chemical agent, how long will it provide protection?
A. About ~~6 hours~~ 24 hours.

Q. Once the CPOG is contaminated with a liquid chemical agent, how long will it provide protection?
A. About 6 hours.

NOTE: The actual length of time it takes for a chemical agent to penetrate the protective clothing depends on the condition of the MOPP gear and the amount of agent on the gear.

Q. Name three ways the BDO can become unserviceable.
A. If ripped, torn, or soaked with petroleum products.

Q. Can the BDO be worn directly over underwear?
A. Yes, but this should only be done when worn in high temperatures or when engaged in heavy work.

Q. What is the standard time allowed for a soldier (at MOPP level 0) to achieve MOPP levels 1 through 4 in sequence?
A. 8 minutes.

Q. Each chemical-protective glove consists of an outer, impermeable, black, butyl-rubber glove for protection and an inner white cotton glove. What is the purpose of the inner glove?
A. Perspiration absorption.

Q. What are the authorized overboots for wear with the MOPP suit?
A. The traditional black butyl-rubber overboots with either the single or double heel flap, or the recently approved Green Vinyl Overboot (GVO). The GVO is more readily recognized as the traditional green wet-weather boots.

Q. What is the most important piece of individual protective equipment for the protection against chemical or biological attack?
A. The protective mask.

Q. Protective masks are available in what ~~three~~ categories?
A. (1) M17-series: issued to every soldier.
(2) M24/25-series: issued to aircraft and tank crewmembers, respectively.
(3) M40: designed to replace the M17-series protective mask.
(4) M42: designed to replace the M24/25-series protective mask.
(5) Special purpose masks.

Q. When properly fitted and worn, the protective mask will protect the wearer against what?
A. Field concentrations of all known chemical and biological agents in vapor or aerosol form.

Q. The protective mask will not protect against what two types of gases?
A. Ammonia vapors or carbon monoxide.

NOTE: When the air has a low oxygen content, such as in tunnels or caves, or when the air has a high level of smoke mixtures, the mask will not protect the wearer (it is not a respirator).

Q. What must you do to your protective mask prior to washing it (if it is to be immersed)?
A. Remove the filters.

Q. There is a preservative built into the rubber portions of the protective mask facepiece. This preservative will be a white or rust-colored waxy film and will continue to "bleed" off as long as it is good. This is normal and does not indicate that the mask is dirty. What is this "film" called?
A. Bloom.

NOTE: If bloom accumulates or gets crumbly, it needs to be removed.

Q. What is the standard time allowed for the donning of the M17-series protective mask?
A. 9 seconds, plus an additional 6 seconds for the hood; total time - 15 seconds (mask must be cleared and sealed within first 9 seconds).

Q. What is the standard time allowed for the donning of the M24-series protective mask? The M25-series protective mask?
A. M24 - 10 seconds to remove the flight helmet and 9 seconds to put on, clear and seal the mask for a total of **19 seconds.**
M25 - 6 seconds to remove the CVC helmet, 9 seconds to put on, clear and seal the mask, plus an additional 6 seconds for the hood. Total = **21 seconds.**

Q. What is the standard time allowed for the donning of the M40-series protective mask? The M42-series protective mask?
A. M40 - 9 seconds to put on, clear and seal the mask. This is the only portion that is timed. The hood should then be "donned so that it lies smoothly on the head."
M42 - 6 seconds to remove the CVC helmet plus 9 seconds to put on, clear and seal the mask, for a total of 15 seconds. Donning of the hood is not timed.

NOTE: For aviators using the M42-series protective mask, 10 seconds should be allowed for the removal of the flight helmet instead of 6. Total time should then be 19 seconds, as with the M24.

Q. What is the major advantage of the M17A1 and M17A2 protective masks over the M17 protective mask?
A. You can drink water while masked.

Q. Do the M24/25 protective masks have provisions for drinking water?
A. No.

Q. Prior to drinking from a canteen while masked, you should blow into the drink tube. What is the reason for this?
A. Contrary to popular belief, this is not to "pressurize" the canteen but merely to check for leaks. If you do not feel positive pressure while blowing into the drink tube, then there is a leak and you should not attempt to drink.

NOTE: While drinking from a canteen, you will periodically need to blow into it to reestablish positive pressure or to prevent the canteen from collapsing (particularly in the case of the 2-qt canteen).

NBC
FM 3-3, 3-3-1, 3-4, 3-5, 3-7, 3-100

Q. When fitting the protective mask, in what sequence should the straps be tightened to ensure a good seal?
A. Top, bottom, then sides.

Q. What is the last step in donning the protective mask?
A. Snap the mask carrier closed.

Q. There are ~~two~~ three approved methods for wearing the protective mask carrier. What are they?
A. The shoulder carry method, the ~~hip~~ leg carry, and the pistol belt carry.

Q. How many levels of MOPP are there? Describe them.
A. Five;
MOPP 0 - Mask carried; MOPP gear readily available.
MOPP 1 - Protective overgarment worn.
MOPP 2 - Add protective overboots.
MOPP 3 - Add mask/hood.
MOPP 4 - Add protective gloves.

Q. Is "MASK ONLY" a MOPP level?
A. No.

Q. When can soldiers operate in a "mask only" posture?
A. When exposed to vapor hazards but protected from transfer hazards such as direct skin exposure to liquid or solid contamination (ie, tanks, some vans, and buildings).

NOTE: When in MASK ONLY posture, all exposed skin must be covered with ordinary clothing.

Q. MOPP is a tool for leaders to use and should be based on what four considerations?
A. Threat, temperature, work rate, and mission.

Q. As MOPP level increases, ___________ also increases but _________ decreases.
A. Protection; performance (efficiency).

Q. Mission and performance degradation are unavoidable while wearing MOPP gear. Name five other areas that are unavoidably degraded while in MOPP?
A. (1) Fine motor skills - wearing protective gloves reduces ability to grasp tools and manipulate controls.
(2) Gross motor skills - wearing MOPP gear slows a soldier's overland movement.
(3) Visual skills - mask reduces visual acuity.
(4) Hearing skills - hood reduces hearing level.
(5) Stamina - wearing MOPP causes heat and mental stress.

Q. What two tools can be effectively used to reduce the level of mission degradation with the wear of MOPP gear?
A. Acclimation and training.

Q. What command level is responsible for ***directing*** minimum MOPP levels and ***recommending*** the higher MOPP levels appropriate to the threat?
A. Corps and higher.

Q. Considerable flexibility within each MOPP level allows variations based on the situation. With this in mind, Commanders may allow soldiers to leave the

NBC
FM 3-3, 3-3-1, 3-4, 3-5, 3-7, 3-100

MOPP overgarment jacket open (unzipped) during hot weather (to allow for greater ventilation) for which MOPP levels?
A. MOPP 1 thru 3.

Q. At the commander's discretion, can the hood be left open or rolled at MOPP 3?
A. Yes.

Q. Soldiers in MOPP 4 may lose how much water per hour through perspiration?
A. One quart or more.

Q. By what means can soldiers be identified while wearing MOPP 4?
A. Use tape showing the soldier's name and rank placed on the protective mask carrier and overgarment pocket.

Q. What does "MGX" stand for?
A. MOPP Gear Exchange.

Q. What are the three types of procedures for MOPP gear exchange?
A. Buddy team, triple buddy, and individual.

NOTE: MOPP gear exchange can be described for the Battle Dress Overgarment (BDO) and the Chemical Protective Undergarment (CPU). The procedures are roughly the same and only the BDO will be discussed here.

Q. When would the "triple buddy" system be used for MPX (see above question)?
A. This method is used by soldiers equipped with the tankers or aviators masks. A third soldier is needed to hold the filter canister and hose to prevent the transference of contamination to the soldier undergoing the procedure.

Q. When would the individual procedure be used for MPX?
A. Only in extreme emergencies, when no one can assist, since there is a high risk of transferring contamination from the overgarment to skin or undergarments.

Q. Explain the ~~eight~~ nine steps of MOPP Gear Exchange.
A. Pair into "buddy teams". Perform Step 1 simultaneously or in succession. Perform Steps 2-8 before alternating;

(1) Decon gear.
(2) Prepare for decon.
(3) Decon hood.
(4) Remove overgarment/overshoes.
(5) Remove gloves.
(6) Put on new overgarment.
(7) Put on new overboots and gloves.
(8) Secure hood.
(9) Secure gear.

Q. Who is normally responsible for supervising and conducting MPX?
A. The squad or platoon.

Q. What is the approximate amount of time that should be allotted for MGX?
A. 45 minutes.

Q. The company is resupplied with MOPP gear and decontaminants from its battalion, who overstocks MOPP gear by ____% of its personnel strength to ensure a complete range of sizes.

A. 5%

Q. What special equipment is normally used for Vehicle Washdown?
A. The M12A1 Power Driven Decon Apparatus (PDDA) or the M17 Lightweight Decon System (LDS).

Q. Detailed Troop Decon (DTD) is the process of decontaminating individual fighting equipment to negligible risk levels. How many stations does DTD have and what are they?
A. 8;
(1) Individual gear decon.
(2) Overboot and hood decon.
(3) Overgarment removal.
(4) Overboots and gloves removal.
(5) Monitor.
(6) Mask removal.
(7) Mask Decon Point.
(8) Reissue point.

NOTE: It is easy to confuse MPX with DTD. Remember, however, that MPX is an OPERATIONAL level while DTD is a THOROUGH decontamination level.

Q. Detailed Equipment Decon (DED) is the process of removing or neutralizing contamination on interior and exterior surfaces of unit equipment to negligible risk levels to allow MOPP level reduction for extended periods. How many DED stations are there and what are they?
A. 5 stations for CB contamination; 4 for radiological contamination (use all stations except station 2, DS2 application).
(1) Initial wash.
(2) DS2 application.
(3) Wait/interior decon.
(4) Rinse.
(5) Check.

Q. The term "negligible risk" is used in the above two questions. What levels of contamination are considered "negligible risk"?
A. Chemical/Biological - those levels that will cause mild incapacitation in no more than 5% of unprotected soldiers who operate for 12 continuous hours within 1 meter of the contaminated surface.
Radiological - measurements of 0.33 cGy or less. This level will cause no more than 2.5% mild incapacitation to unprotected soldiers.

NUCLEAR

Q. What are the **four** principle effects of any nuclear explosion?
A. Thermal radiation, nuclear radiation, blast, and EMP.

Q. What is the cause of most of the material destruction accompanying a nuclear explosion?
A. The blast (accounts for approximately 50% of the burst energy).

Q. Thermal radiation, which accounts for approximately 35% of the burst energy of a nuclear explosion, has two dangerous components. What are they?
A. Heat and light.

NBC
FM 3-3, 3-3-1, 3-4, 3-5, 3-7, 3-100

Q. Direct burns produced by the flash of thermal radiation from the fireball are referred to as what?
A. "Flash burns."

Q. Indirect burns produced as the result of fires started by the flash of thermal radiation are referred to as what?
A. "Flame burns."

Q. Nuclear radiation from a blast can be further divided into two major types. What are they?
A. Initial radiation (approx 4% of the burst energy)
Residual radiation (approx 10% of the burst energy)

Q. What is "EMP"?
A. Electromagnetic Pulse - represents approximately 1% of the total energy produced by a nuclear burst and can destroy or cause serious damage to electronic equipment through current surges.

Q. Nuclear weapons cause casualties and material damage through one or more of the effects mentioned above. The degree of hazard from each of these effects depends on several factors, either singularly or in combination. Name some of these factors.
A.
- Type of weapon (explosive yield).
- Height of the burst.
- Distance from detonation.
- Hardness of the target.
- Meteorological conditions.
- Terrain.
- Vulnerability of the target.

Q. What is the primary difference between initial and residual nuclear radiation?
A. Initial radiation is that radiation emitted within the first minute after detonation.

Q. Initial nuclear radiation consists primarily of what?
A. Neutrons and gamma rays.

Q. Neutrons and gamma rays travel at what speed?
A. The speed of light (approx 186,000 miles per second).

Q. What is the major problem in protecting against the effects of initial nuclear radiation?
A. An individual may have received a lethal or incapacitating dose of radiation before he can take any protective action (this is why it is so important to **immediately** drop to the ground if you see a bright flash of light - brighter than the sun).

Q. What is "TREE"?
A. Transient Radiation Effects on Electronics - has similar effects to EMP, except that TREE is caused by gamma and neutron (initial) radiation. Gamma radiation causes temporary ionization of electronic components, which can lead to permanent damage to other components. Fast neutrons can also cause permanent damage by emplacing (or dislodging) atoms in crystals.

Q. Residual nuclear radiation consists primarily of what?
A. Alpha, beta, and gamma radiation in the form of fallout, neutron-induced

gamma activity (NIGA), and rainout.

Q. Of alpha, beta, and gamma radiation, which represents the greatest hazard?
A. Gamma rays (because of their range and penetrating power). Neither alpha nor beta radiation are considered tactically significant.

Q. Explain the difference between alpha and beta particles.
A. Alpha particles have a range of only about ~~10 cm~~ 4 cm in open air (from contaminated objects) and cannot penetrate one to two sheets of ordinary paper. Also, alpha particles cannot penetrate the first layer of human skin but present an internal hazard and thus will cause harm if ingested.

Beta particles, on the other hand, have a range of approximately ~~10-15 meters~~ 20 feet in open air, from the source. Beta has the ability to penetrate 1/16 inch of aluminum and may penetrate the first few layers of skin. The primary hazard from this radiation is through prolonged skin exposure resulting in beta burns, which may be similar to first- or second-degree sunburn, or may cause extensive internal damage, similar to alpha, if inhaled.

Q. What are "gamma rays" and what are their effects on the body?
A. Electromagnetic radiation similar to X-rays that penetrate and interact with the human body and cause damage to tissues and the blood-forming cells.

Q. What term is used to describe the center of a nuclear explosion?
A. Ground zero.

Q. What is meant by "fallout"?
A. Fallout is a radiological contamination hazard that occurs when dirt and debris from the earth are drawn up into the fireball of a nuclear explosion, vaporized, combined with radioactive material, and condensed to particles (radioactive debris) that are transported downwind as a cloud and gradually falls back to earth.

Q. What are the indications of the arrival of fallout and its associated hazards?
A. The settling of dust-like particles (unless monitoring shows no radiation). Also, any precipitation following a nuclear attack.

Q. What is meant by "rainout"?
A. The removal of radioactive particles from a nuclear cloud by precipitation. Occurs when the nuclear cloud is within a rain cloud.

Q. What is meant by "washout"?
A. The removal of radioactive particles from a nuclear cloud by precipitation. Occurs when the nuclear cloud is below a rain cloud.

NOTE: Both rainout and washout are forms of fallout.

Q. Residual radiation from fallout comes from what three basic sources?
A. - Unused fissionable material (primarily alpha radiation)
- Fission products (primarily beta radiation)
- Neutron-induced activity (gamma and beta radiation)

Q. What is meant by "induced radiation"?
A. Radiation that occurs around ground zero due to an extremely high dose of initial neutron radiation. Many of the neutrons penetrate the soil up to a depth of one-half meter. This type of radiation remains as a militarily significant hazard for 2 to 5 days after the blast.

NBC
FM 3-3, 3-3-1, 3-4, 3-5, 3-7, 3-100

Q. What is meant by the "7-10" rule?
A. It is a rule-of-thumb for estimating radiological persistency (future radiation levels). The rate of radioactive decay is proportional over time. The 7-10 rule means that for every 7 multiples of time from the burst, the radiation intensity will decrease by a factor of 10 (ie; If, 2 hours after the burst, your reading is 100 cGyph.....then 14 hours after the burst you can expect a reading of about 10 cGy).

Q. What are the three types of nuclear bursts?
A. Air, surface, and subsurface.

Q. Which of the above bursts would be used for maximum radiation effect?
A. Air burst.

NOTE: Commanders who wish to prevent residual radiological hazards would choose a height of detonation that prevents the fireball from coming into contact with the earth's surface.

Q. Of the three types of nuclear bursts, which will produce significant amounts of fallout?
A. Surface burst.

Q. Of the three types of nuclear bursts, which would be characterized by a spherical cloud with no mushroom shape?
A. A high airburst.

NOTE: A low airburst would be characterized by a mushroom-type cloud and may or may not have a stem; a surface burst will always have a stem.

Q. There are three stages in the development of nuclear clouds. What are they?
A. Fireball, burst cloud, and stabilized cloud.

Q. What is ~~"NUCWARN"~~ "STRIKWARN"?
A. Notification of a friendly nuclear strike.

Q. Explain the precaution zones of a ~~NUCWARN~~ STRIKWARN.
A. A ~~NUCWARN~~ STRIKWARN can be visualized graphically by picturing three concentric circles, centered on ground zero, with the innermost circle labeled "ZONE 1" and the outermost, "ZONE 3". The outermost edge of Zone 1 represents the Minimum Safe Distance (MSD 1); the outermost edge of Zone 2 - MSD 2, and so on. Listed below are the precautions for each zone:

Zone 1 - Everyone should be evacuated.
Zone 2 - Everyone should take maximum precautions but need not evacuate the zone.
Zone 3 - Everyone should take at least minimum precautions.

Q. For Zone 2 (see above question), what precautions would be considered appropriate for this area?
A. Personnel should be "buttoned-up" in tanks or sheltered in foxholes with overhead protection.

Q. For Zone 3 above, what precautions would be considered appropriate?
A. Personnel should be prone on open ground with all skin areas covered and with an overall thermal protection at least equal to that provided by a two-layer uniform.

NBC
FM 3-3, 3-3-1, 3-4, 3-5, 3-7, 3-100

Q. What is the lowest level that will receive a STRIKWARN message?
A. Battalion.

Q. STRIKWARN messages should normally be encoded. When may such a message be sent "in the clear"?
A. If the issuing commander determines that safety warnings override security requirements.

Q. A STRIKWARN message sent in the clear should never, under any circumstances, be sent earlier than ______ minutes before the attack.
A. 60 (However, lines Delta and Foxtrot of the STRIKWARN should **never** be sent as clear text).

Q. What is meant by the term "hardening"?
A. Includes all of the things you do to make yourself more resistant to enemy strikes.

Q. What steps should be taken to prepare for an impending nuclear attack (ie, ~~NUCWARN~~ STRIKWARN)?
A. Harden positions and personnel (if possible, dig-in), secure loose equipment, and bury or similarly protect communications and other electronic equipment

Q. What are some individual steps that can be taken to minimize injury during a nuclear attack?
A. Keep clothes loosely fitted, wear headgear at all times, apply sunscreen, insert hearing protection.

Q. The indicators of a nuclear attack are unmistakable. What is normally the first indication that a nuclear explosion has occurred? Name three other indicators of a nuclear explosion.
A. A flash of intense light (brighter than the sun) and heat; enormous explosion, high winds, and mushroom-shaped cloud.

Q. What should you do if you are in the open and see a brilliant flash you recognize as a nuclear explosion?
A. (1) Immediately drop to the ground facedown, with head toward blast if possible. A log, large rock, or any depression in the earth's surface provides some protection.
(2) Close eyes.
(3) Protect exposed skin from heat and debris by putting hands and arms under or near the body and keeping the helmet on.
(4) Remain facedown until both the initial and return blast waves have passed and debris stops falling.
(5) Stay calm, check for injury, check weapons and equipment for damage, and prepare to continue the mission.

Q. What actions should be taken after a nuclear strike?
A. Assess the situation, put out fires before they can spread, assist casualties, secure and organize equipment/check weapons systems, improve or reinforce fighting positions/shelters, and prepare for possible fallout.

Q. Should the M17-series protective mask be worn for an anticipated nuclear strike?
A. No. The heat from the explosion could cause the protective mask to melt to your skin. It is not designed for radiological protection but, when worn properly (after the explosion), provides added alpha and beta dust inhalation

protection. An alternative to wearing the mask is the use of a handkerchief or other material that will provide dust protection.

Q. What equipment is available for monitoring radiological contamination?
A. IM-93/UD Dosimeter - it is a tubular device, about the size of a fountain pen, which allows the user to read the accumulated gamma total dose simply by looking through the lens while pointing the instrument toward the sun or another bright-light source.

IM-174B/PD Radiacmeter - standard ion-chamber gamma survey meter.

AN/PDR-27 Radiac Set - contains a low-range dose-rate Geiger-Mueller type instrument and is used for measuring food, personnel, and equipment.

AN/VDR-2 - used to locate and measure radioactivity in the form of gamma rays and beta particles. It displays dose rates and total accumulated dose resulting from fallout.

DT 236 - a "watch-like" device worn on the wrist and issued to soldiers. It is designed to measure the accumulated neutron and gamma dose rate.

CP696/PDR75 - computer indicator and radiacmeter used to "read" the accumulated dose rate from DT236 dosimeters.

Q. What instrument is designed to replace the IM-174 and the AN/PDR-27 as the standard radiac instrument?
A. The AN/VDR-2.

Q. What does "radiac" mean?
A. Originally an acronym derived from Radioactivity, Detection, Identification, And Computation. The term now is used as a modifier rather than a noun and relates to various types of radiological measuring instruments or equipment.

Q. What range does the scale on the IM-93/UD dosimeter have?
A. 0 to 600 rads (measures cumulative gamma radiation dose).

Q. It is mandatory that the IM-93/UD dosimeter be recharged when the total dose reads more than what? What is used to "recharge" the dosimeter?
A. 500 rads (however, it should be recharged after each use); the PP-1578A/PD is used to recharge the IM-93.

Q. What functions will the AN/PDR-27 perform?
A.
- register battery condition
- detect/measure gamma radiation
- detect presence of beta radiation

Q. The AN/PDR-27 measures gamma radiation in what units?
A. Milli-rads/hour.

Q. The "turn-back-dose-rate" is defined as what?
A. The dose rate at which you must return to your starting point regardless of whether or not you have completed the survey.

Q. Can the IM-93 be used to determine the turn-back-dose-rate?
A. Yes.

Q. What is the vocal alarm for the arrival of radiological contamination in a unit area?
A. "FALLOUT"

Q. What is a centigray?
A. A unit of absorbed dose of radiation. A centigray is the same as a "rad"

and is abbreviated cGy (cGyph = centigrays per hour).

Q. A radiological monitor operating a radiacmeter at a unit command post should sound the alarm "FALLOUT" when the radiacmeter records an increase in dose rate to what?
A. 1 cGyph or higher.

Q. What are the two **types** of area monitoring?
A. Periodic and continuous.

Q. When should periodic monitoring be used?
A. - After the first use of nuclear weapons in theater; or
- When a unit is out of contact with higher headquarters; or
- When ordered by higher headquarters; or
- When the unit stops continuous monitoring.

Q. How often should a reading be made (with an IM174 or AN/VDR-2 radiacmeter) during periodic monitoring?
A. At least once each hour.

Q. When should continuous monitoring be initiated?
A. - When a nuclear detonation is observed, heard, or reported in the area of operations; or
- When an NBC 3 nuclear report is received and the unit is in the predicted area of contamination; or
- When a dose rate of 1 cGyph is recorded during periodic monitoring; or
- When ordered by the unit commander.

Q. Once continuous monitoring is initiated, when does a unit return to periodic monitoring?
A. When the unshielded dose rate falls below 1 cGyph or when ordered to do so.

Q. In addition to the two types of monitoring there are two **techniques**. What are the two techniques?
A. Direct and indirect.

Q. Of the two monitoring techniques (see above question), which is considered the simplest and most precise method?
A. Direct.

Q. Which of the monitoring techniques is preferred when operating in a contaminated area?
A. Indirect.

Q. Describe the procedure for DIRECT monitoring.
A. Stand with the radiacmeter held waist high, or 1 meter off the ground, and rotating your body 360 degrees. The highest reading recorded is the dose rate.

Q. Readings taken in the open should be at least how far from buildings or other large structures or objects that may shield out a portion of the radiation?
A. 10 meters

Q. When the INDIRECT technique is used, most of the readings are taken inside the vehicle or shelter. However, at least one reading is necessary to determine the correlation factor. Both the inside and outside readings must be taken within ________ minutes of each other.

A. 3

Q. All units in a contaminated area must submit certain monitoring reports automatically. These provide the minimum essential information for warning, hazard evaluation, and survey planning. There are three automatic reports. What are they?
A. Initial, Peak, and Special reports.

Q. When should an INITIAL report be made?
A. After noting a dose rate of 1 or more cGyph outside (unshielded).

Q. How is peak radiation determined?
A. Dose rates should be recorded at 15-minute intervals while fallout is arriving. The dose rate steadily rises until it reaches a peak and then it decreases. In some cases the dose rate may fluctuate for a short period before beginning a constant decrease. Once a constant decrease is noted, a peak report should be sent.

Q. What are the two types of radiation surveys?
A. Aerial and ground.

Q. Which of the above surveys is more accurate?
A. Ground.

Q. What are the advantages of an aerial survey?
A. They are faster, more flexible, expose personnel to lower doses, and require fewer personnel and equipment to perform.

Q. What is required in order to correctly calculate ground dose rates from aerial dose rates taken in an aircraft during a survey?
A. An air-ground correlation factor (AGCF).

Q. What information would you expect to find on an "ATOM" (radiological) contamination marker?
A. - The dose rate (in rads or centigrays per hour).
- Date and time of the dose reading (local or zulu time).
- Date and time of the detonation that produced the contamination.

Q. What dose rate requires that a radiological contamination marker be emplaced?
A. 1 or more cGyph at a height of 1 meter.

Q. First aid treatment of nuclear casualties is limited to whom?
A. Soldiers wounded by blast or thermal (heat/light) burns. First aid cannot help radiation casualties.

Q. How would you remove radioactive particles from your body and clothing?
A. Brush or shake clothing and wash the body with hot, soapy water. Pay particular attention to body creases, openings, hands, nails, and hairy portions of the body. Shower if possible.

Q. What is meant by the "yield" of a nuclear weapon?
A. The energy released in the detonation of the nuclear weapon. It is measured in terms of the kilotons or megatons of TNT required to produce the same energy release. Yields are categorized as follows:

Very low.......less than 1 kiloton (kt)
Low............1 to 10 kt

Medium.........10 kt to 50 kt
High...........50 kt to 500 kt
Very high......over 500 kt

BIOLOGICAL

Q. What is meant by "biological warfare"?
A. The intentional use, by an enemy, of germs or toxins to cause death and disease among personnel, animals, plants, or - more rarely - to deteriorate material.

Q. Biological agents can be placed into two ~~classes~~ broad categories. What are they?
A. ~~Germs~~ Pathogens and toxins.

Q. What is the difference between a ~~germ~~ pathogen and a toxin?
A. ~~Germs~~ Pathogens (commonly referred to as simply "germs") are living microorganisms (viruses, bacteria, rickettsiae, etc). Toxins are poisonous (toxic) wastes produced by microorganisms (or by some plants and animals). In the case of toxins, it is not the microorganism that harms man but the by-products themselves.

NOTE: Toxins may also be manufactured in a lab and can be dispersed in much the same manner as chemicals.

Q. How are pathogens delivered?
A. Either directly by aerosol or indirectly through vectors.

Q. What is meant by the term "aerosol" with respect to biological agents?
A. Tiny particles containing biological agents which are dispersed in the air and transported by air currents.

Q. What are the two primary aerosol dissemination techniques?
A. Bursting type munitions (ie, artillery) and spray tanks/generators.

Q. What is a "vector"?
A. An insect used to disseminate biological agents (fleas, ticks, mosquitoes, etc).

Q. There are two basic types of toxins. What are they?
A. Neurotoxins - disrupt nerve impulses
Cytotoxins - destroy cells by disrupting cell respiration and metabolism

NOTE: Fungal toxins, referred to as "mycotoxins" fall under the heading of cytotoxins.

Q. Are toxins <more> or <less> potent than nerve agents.
A. More

Q. The Soviet Union views the use of biological agents in much the same way we do (that is, no use). Why, then, should we be so concerned about the biological warfare threat from the Soviets?
A. Because the Soviet Union and its allies view toxins as chemical - not biological - agents; which greatly increases the likelihood that toxins may be used against us.

NBC

FM 3-3, 3-3-1, 3-4, 3-5, 3-7, 3-100

Q. What is the predominant argument against the use of biological warfare?
A. ~~Germs~~ Pathogens, in particular, are alive and therefore are neither reliable nor predictable.

Q. The body possesses several defenses against biological agents. What are they?
A. Physical barriers (skin), natural immunity, and acquired immunity (chemoprophylaxis).

Q. What are the most effective protective measures against biological agents?
A. Up-to-date immunizations, good field sanitation and personal hygiene, a properly fitted and readily available protective mask, and good physical condition.

Q. Name ~~three~~ four indicators of a possible biological attack.
A. (1) Artillery shells with less powerful explosions than HE rounds.
(2) Aerial bombs that pop rather than explode.
(3) Mist or fog sprayed from low flying aircraft.
(4) Ground generators spraying a fog or mist.

Q. Name two conditions which indicate a high probability that a biological attack has occurred.
A. (1) Mysterious illness - large numbers of soldiers reporting to sick call.
(2) Large numbers of insects or unusual insects.

Q. What detection equipment is available for detecting the presence of biological agents?
A. No currently fielded means of detecting biological agents exist.

Q. What is meant by "persistency" in reference to biological agents?
A. Refers to the duration of effectiveness of the agent (varies greatly between agents).

Q. The ability of biological agents to survive in the atmosphere as an aerosol (persistency) is influenced by what factors?
A. Sunlight (ultra violet rays), weather, terrain, method of dissemination, and type of agent.

Q. What is the preferred decontaminate for biological contamination?
A. Hot, soapy water. An alternate decontaminant is a 0.5% sodium hypochlorite (household bleach) solution. (DS2 or STB is also effective against most known biological contamination, but because of their caustic nature are not preferred).

Q. What is meant by a "window of vulnerability"?
A. This "window" represents the best time, based on weather, for the enemy to employ biological agents (or chemical/radiological agents, for that matter).

CHEMICAL

Q. By what six means may chemical or biological agents be delivered?
A. Mines, artillery, rockets, bombs, aircraft spray, and covert/sabotage.

Q. Chemical agents are classified by the U.S. into three categories. What are

they?
A. Persistent, nonpersistent, and dusty.

Q. Threat forces classify chemical agents according to their effect on the body. What are the six major types of chemical agents classified by threat forces?
A. Nerve, blood, blister, choking, psychochemical, and irritants.

Q. What is meant by "persistency"?
A. The length of time that a hazard remains.

Q. Contamination should be considered nonpersistent if it remains for how long?
A. Less than 10 minutes.

Q. What ~~seven~~ eight factors affect persistency of chemical agents?
A. (1) Type of contamination.
(2) Concentration and droplet size.
(3) Temperature.
(4) Wind speed.
(5) Sunlight.
(6) Humidity and rain.
(7) Composition of the contaminated surface.
(8) Type of soil and terrain.

Q. Name ~~three~~ four indicators of a possible chemical attack.
A. Same as indicators of possible biological attack:
(1) Artillery shells that explode less powerfully than HE rounds.
(2) Aircraft or rocket-delivered bombs or containers of bomblets that pop rather than explode.
(3) Low flying aircraft that spray a mist or fog.
(4) Ground generators spraying a fog or mist.

Q. Name three conditions that indicate a high probability that a chemical attack has occurred.
A. (1) A sounding chemical-agent alarm.
(2) A positive reading through chemical-agent detection means.
(3) Symptoms of chemical-agent poisoning in soldiers.

Q. Name five tactical advantages for the use of chemical agents?
A. (1) Cause casualties.
(2) Degrade performance.
(3) Slow maneuver.
(4) Restrict terrain.
(5) Disrupt support.

Q. How should an individual enter an area suspected of chemical or biological contamination?
A. Upwind and fully protected.

Q. Describe riot control agents.
A. Compounds that produce only a temporarily irritating or incapacitating effect when used in field concentrations.

Q. What are the three types of riot control agents?
A. Tearing (crying), sneezing, and vomiting agents.

Q. Which of the above riot control agents is the most frequently used?

NBC
FM 3-3, 3-3-1, 3-4, 3-5, 3-7, 3-100

A. Tearing agents, the most common of which is CS - a white solid that causes a blinding flow of tears and involuntary closing of the eyes. In greater concentrations, it irritates moist skin and the respiratory tract.

Q. What is the vocal alarm for any chemical or biological hazard or attack?
A. "GAS"!!

Q. What should be the actions of everyone hearing the alarm "GAS"?
A. Immediately mask, repeat the alarm, and take cover or other necessary precautions.

Q. Name three suggested nonvocal signals for a chemical attack.
A. (1) Rapid and continuous beating together of any two metal objects to produce a loud noise.
(2) A succession of short blasts on a vehicle horn or other suitable device.
(3) An intermittent warbling siren sound.

Q. What is the visual signal for a chemical attack?
A. The standard visual signal is done by extending both arms horizontally to the sides with fists closed and facing up, and rapidly moving the fists to the head and back to the horizontal. Unit SOPs may also designate colored smoke or flares as visual signals.

Q. What is "CHEMWARN"?
A. Notification of a friendly chemical strike.

Q. The format for a CHEMWARN message resembles which NBC report?
A. NBC 3

Q. What two hazard areas exist for a chemical attack?
A. The attack area and the downwind hazard area.

Q. What is a "CDM"?
A. Chemical Downwind Message - contains all the weather information needed to calculate a chemical downwind hazard.

Q. How often is a CDM issued?
A. Every six hours and is valid for three consecutive two-hour periods.

Q. What is normally the lowest level that prepares a CDM?
A. Division (separate brigades may be required to prepare a CDM when operating independently).

Q. What is "miosis"?
A. Excessive contraction of the pupils of the eyes (pinpointing) caused by exposure to minute quantities of chemical (nerve) agents. This condition is often accompanied by pain and headache and severely degrades visual acuity.

Q. The effectiveness of a chemical agent employed against friendly troops in a tactical situation is dependent on what five factors?
A. Individual activity, protective equipment, environment, persistency of agent, and level of training.

Q. What is an "IDK"? An "SDK"?
A. Individual Decon Kit; Skin Decon Kit (many of these terms, IDK or SDK, are used interchangeably when referring to decon kits).

NBC
FM 3-3, 3-3-1, 3-4, 3-5, 3-7, 3-100

Q. What decontamination equipment is available for chemical agents?
A. M258A1 - Individual Decontamination Kit; comes in a hard plastic case containing three sets of foil-packaged decontaminating wipes (each set containing one Decon 1 and one Decon 2 wipe packet). The Decon wipe 1 works better against G-type nerve agents but can burn skin. Decon wipe 2 works better against VX-type nerve agents and blister agents. It is not as caustic to skin and helps to neutralize some of the caustic compounds in wipe 1. Each soldier carries a kit in his or her mask carrier (unless an M291 has been issued).

M291 - Individual Decontamination Kit; designed as a replacement for the M258A1. The M258A1 IDK will be used until depleted or expired. Soldiers issued M291 IDKs should store them in the right cargo pocket of the BDU trousers or BDO trousers. Basis of issue is two M291s (12 packages) per soldier.

ABC-M11 - Portable Decontaminating Apparatus; a steel container with an aluminum spray-head assembly and a nitrogen-gas cylinder that provides pressure. It resembles a fire extinguisher (but should **never** be used as one) and is filled with 1(1/3) quarts of DS2, which is sufficient for covering 135 square feet. It is used primarily for decontaminating small areas, such as the steering wheel or other equipment that soldiers must touch. Effective spray range is 6-8 feet.

M13 - Portable Decontaminating Apparatus; about the size of a 5-gallon gas can, it comes prefilled with 14 liters of DS2 decon agent. Decon capability is 1,200 square feet and is normally used to decontaminate vehicles and crew-served weapons larger than .50 caliber.

M12A1 - Power Driven Decontaminating Apparatus (PDDA); a 500-gal tank and pump unit (TPU) used to mix and spray decontaminating agent slurries and solutions, and hot, soapy water rinses during field decon operations. Also may be used for showering personnel in the field.

M17 - Lightweight Decon System (LDS); portable pump and water heating unit for producing hot water and steam. The system incorporates a 1,580-gal collapsible water tank, two wand assemblies, connecting hoses, and a shower rail. Also used during vehicle operational and thorough decon operations.

Q. What is a "Frank Device"?
A. A field-expedient pressurized 5-gallon gas can filled with DS-2 and fixed with a hose and spray wand.

Q. Which wipe packet in the M258A1 kit has an identifying tab on top so you can feel it in the dark?
A. Decon wipe 1.

Q. What is the difference between an M258A1 and an M58A1?
A. The M258A1 Decontamination Kit has an olive drab case and wipe packets and is used by the soldier to decontaminate the skin; the M58A1 Training Aid Decontamination Kit has a black case with blue wipe packets and is used for training purposes only.

Q. What is the major difference between the M258A1 and M291 IDKs?
A. The M258A1 uses a moist towelette with a decon solution, whereas the M291 uses a powder. NOTE: The powder in the M291 is a black substance resembling charcoal.

Q. Where will you find instructions for the use of the M258A1/M291 Decontaminating Kits?
A. On the outside of the kit itself, on the individual wipe packets, in the Soldier's Manual of Common Tasks (STP-21-1-SMCT), and in the Soldier's Manual

(STP 3-54B10).

Q. The stocks and handgrips of individual weapons tend to absorb chemical agents and may present a vapor hazard for days. For this reason, individual equipment such as gloves, hood and mask, helmet, and weapon should be decontaminated using what?
A. M291 or M258A1 IDKs. The M280 DKIE (Decon Kit, Individual Equipment), which was designed for this very purpose is on hold pending replacement by the M295 (Decon Kit, Personal Equipment).

Q. When using the wipe packets of the M258A1 to decontaminate the mask what difference, if any, should be made in procedure?
A. Reverse the order of the decon wipes. This technique is just as effective but does not leave a powdery film on the outserts (lenses) that is difficult to see through.

Q. What is "DS2"?
A. Decontaminating Solution #2. It is available in 1(1/3) quart cans (two authorized per M11) and in 5-gallon pails (two authorized per company-sized element) for filling portable decontaminating apparatuses.

Q. What is used to expel the contents (DS2) of an M11?
A. Nitrogen cylinders (two authorized per can of DS2). One cylinder will normally expel the contents; however, two may be required in cold weather.

NOTE: Four nitrogen cylinders and two 1(1/3) quart cans of DS2 should be carried with each M11.

Q. When should the M11 be filled with DS2?
A. As soon as you are directed to go into any level of MOPP.

Q. DS2 is no longer effective below what temperature?
A. -15 degrees F.

Q. What is "STB"?
A. SuperTropical Bleach. It is available in bulk containers and is mixed to produce a decontaminating solution. It is effective against Lewisite, V and G agents, and biological agents.

Q. What will happen if DS2 and STB are accidentally mixed?
A. Spontaneous combustion.

NOTE: DS2 will also spontaneously combust with HTH (Calcium Hypochlorite), a chlorine compound used in treating water and as an expedient chemical decontaminating solution.

Q. What is the minimum surface contact time for DS2 and STB?
A. 30 minutes.

Q. Equipment decon is most effective when done within _____ minutes after being contaminated. Longer periods of time will result in more of the chemical agent being absorbed into the material and will be little affected by decon.
A. 15 minutes.

Q. What detection equipment is available for chemical agents?
A. ABC-M8 VGH Chemical Agent Detector Paper - consists of a book of 25 sheets of perforated, chemically treated, dye impregnated paper that turns either dark

green, yellow or red upon contact with liquid VGH agents.

M9 Chemical Agent Detector Paper - consists of a 7-oz dispenser containing a 30-foot roll of 2" wide detector paper and a resealable plastic storage bag. It has an adhesive backing for attaching to equipment and clothing and it is used to detect the presence of liquid chemical agents. The paper indicates the presence of liquid V, G, H, and L agents by turning a red or reddish color.

M256/M256A1 Chemical Agent Detector Kit - provides a squad-level ability to identify field concentrations of nerve-, blister-, and blood-agent vapors. It consists of 12 individually packaged samplers/detectors, a set of instruction cards, and a packet of ABC-M8 VGH chemical agent detector papers. A new improved kit is capable of detecting T2 mycotoxin.

M8 Automatic Chemical Agent Alarm (ACAA) - portable, electrochemical, point-sampling chemical agent alarm that can either be hand-carried, backpacked, or vehicle mounted. It consists of the M43 detector unit and the M42 alarm unit. It detects low concentrations of toxic nerve, blood, and choking agent vapors or inhalable aerosols and automatically signals the presence of agent in the air.

Remote Sensing Chemical Agent Alarm (RSCAAL), XM21 - a passive infrared spectroradiometer that uses an onboard microprocessor to detect and identify agent clouds. It operates by viewing a background scene (sky, terrain, buildings, etc) and the airpath along its line of sight. A properly emplaced XM21 will detect significant G, HD, and L munitions events and resulting clouds at ranges of 5 km with a greater than 85% probability of detection.

Chemical Agent Monitor (CAM) - a portable, point-sampling vapor monitor used to search out "clean" areas, to search and locate contamination on personnel, equipment, buildings and terrain, structures, aircraft and land vehicles, and to monitor the effectiveness of decontamination. It responds to nerve and blister agent vapors down to the lowest concentrations that could affect personnel over short periods.

M272 Water Testing Kit, Chemical Agents - a lightweight, portable kit that will detect and identify harmful amounts of chemical warfare agents when present in raw and treated water. The kit will detect cyanide, mustard, lewisite, and nerve agents.

FOX, XM93, NBC Reconnaissance System (NBCRS) - six-wheel, amphibious armored cargo and tactical transport vehicle powered by a 320 hp V8 diesel engine. Its maximum speed is 65 mph with a cruising range of 500 miles. It weighs 18.7 tons combat loaded and 16.9 tons without the crew and ammunition. It is equipped with a collective protection system which keeps the crew's working area free from contamination.

Q. What is the most widely used method of detecting liquid chemical agents?
A. M9 Chemical Agent Detector Paper.

Q. Will M9 Chemical Agent Detector Paper detect chemical agent vapors?
A. No.

Q. The CAM is designed to register minute concentrations of nerve and blister agent vapors within what period of time?
A. Within one minute.

Q. The CAM has an LED readout with vertical bars to indicate the concentration of nerve or blister agent vapors. Describe the protection requirements for the various bar levels.
A. 1 bar .... masking not required
2-3 bars .... 30 minutes unmasking in 24 hours if operationally essential
4-6 bars .... Remain in protective posture and note changing display and

	amount of agent
6-8 bars	Do not unmask

Q. What is the difference between the M8 and the M8A1 Chemical Agent Alarms?
A. The M8A1 will only detect nerve agents and does not require reservicing during continuous operations.

Q. Unless circumstances do not permit, the ACAA should be placed no more than _______ meters upwind from the farthest upwind position of the unit.
A. 150

Q. The M43 detector units (of the ACAA) should never be placed more than _______ meters from the M42 alarm unit.
A. 400

Q. Optimum spacing between detectors reduces the risk that a chemical agent cloud will drift between detectors without sounding the alarm. What is this "optimum" spacing?
A. 300 meters

Q. When emplacing the chemical alarms, the wire connecting the alarm and detector must be protected from indirect fire (by burying, etc), and should be checked periodically for continuity to ensure that it has not been broken or cut. How often should the wire be checked?
A. At least once every four to six hours.

Q. What is meant by VGH agents? L-agents?
A. V- and G-type agents are nerve agents; H- and L-type agents are blister agents.

Q. Where can you find a color comparison bar chart for use with the M8 detector paper? What are the colors and what do they represent?
A. Inside the front cover; dark green - V (nerve), yellow - G (nerve), and red -H (blister).

Q. What is the proper method for using M8 detector paper?
A. Blot the paper on the suspected contaminated surface. Do not rub the paper against a suspected surface because false positive (red) streaks are produced.

Q. What kind of light source should be used when reading the results of ABC-M8 or M9 chemical agent detector paper or the M256 detector kit?
A. A white-light source (do not attempt to use red lens).

Q. When attaching M9 Chemical Agent Detector Paper to clothing, where should it be placed?
A. On opposite sides of the body. If you are right-handed, place a strip of M9 paper around your right upper arm, left wrist, and right ankle. If you are left-handed, place the M9 paper around your left upper arm, right wrist, and left ankle.

Q. When using M9 Detector Paper, what indications should cause you to suspect the presence of chemical agents?
A. Whenever pink, red, reddish brown, or purple color(s) appear on the paper.

Q. What actions should be taken when the above indications appear on M9 paper worn by personnel or attached to vehicles?
A. Soldiers must take protective action to keep from becoming grossly

contaminated; then confirm with the M256 kit or CAM.

Q. What may cause false readings in M8 chemical detector paper?
A. Exposure to high temperatures, DS2, or petroleum products.

Q. What may cause false readings in M9 chemical detector paper?
A. High temperatures, brake fluid, aircraft cleaning compound, DS2, petroleum products, insect repellent, camo stick (sand color), defoliant, antifreeze.

Q. What can cause false readings with the M256 detector kit?
A. High temperatures, DS2, and petroleum products.

Q. Tests with the M256 take approximately how long?
A. 20-25 minutes (may take longer in cold temperatures).

Q. What are some of the limitations of the M8 Chemical Agent Alarm?
A. It cannot detect blister agents; it will become inoperable if tilted more than 45 degrees; smoke can set it off; and a winterization kit is necessary for alarm operations below 20 degrees F.

Q. What is the "warm-up" time for the chemical agent alarm after installing the winterization kit?
A. 50 minutes.

Q. The M43 detector unit must be serviced at what intervals for continuous operations?
A. Every 12 hours.

Q. What is the most readily noticeable symptom of the presence of a nerve agent?
A. Severely pinpointed pupils (miosis).

Q. What are the first aid measures for nerve-agent poisoning?
A. Use of the Mark I Nerve Agent Antidote Kit (NAAK, MkI).

NOTE: Refer to section 7, First Aid, for a complete description of the use of the NAAK and mild and severe symptoms of nerve agent poisoning.

Q. The NAAK is subject to freezing at about the same temperature as water. What should you do with the NAAK when the temperature dips below 40 degrees F?
A. Remove the kit from the carrier and store it in the shirt pocket. Keep it as close to body temperature as possible. This precludes the danger of severe muscle spasm and/or shock from injecting an extremely cold liquid into a muscle.

Q. What are the first aid measures for blister agents?
A. Decontaminate skin with M258A1/M291 kit. Flush eyes with cleanest water available. Treat blisters as burns. Seek medical attention.

NOTE: The contents of the M258A1 kit are caustic. Do not allow the solution to enter breaks in the skin caused by the formation of blisters.

Q. What are the first aid measures for blood agents?
A. There is no self-aid or buddy-aid treatment for blood-agent symptoms. Victims should immediately seek medical attention (amyl nitrate is no longer prescribed).

NBC
FM 3-3, 3-3-1, 3-4, 3-5, 3-7, 3-100

Q. Describe proper unmasking procedures with and without the M256 Kit.
A. With M256: Procedure takes approximately 15 minutes. After all tests with the kit, including a check for liquid contamination, have been performed and the results are negative, the senior person should select one or two soldiers to start the unmasking procedures. If possible, move to a shady place. Bright, direct sunlight can cause pupils in the eyes to constrict, giving a false symptom. The selected soldiers unmask for 5 minutes, reseal, and clear their masks. Observe for 10 minutes. If no symptoms appear, it is safe to give the all-clear signal and unmask.
Without M256: Procedure takes approximately 35 minutes. Find a shady area. Use M8 paper to check the area for possible liquid contamination. When a reasonable amount of time has passed after the attack, the senior person should select one or two soldiers. The selected soldiers take a deep breath and break the mask seals, keeping their eyes wide open, for about 15 seconds. They then clear and reseal their masks. Observe them for 10 minutes. If no symptoms develop, they again break the seals and take two or three breaths, clear, and reseal their masks. Again observe them for 10 minutes. If no symptoms appear, the selected soldiers unmask for 5 minutes and then remask. If no symptoms appear in 10 minutes after remasking, everyone can unmask.

Q. In peacetime, what is the **replacement interval** for the filter elements in your protective mask?
A. Tropic climates: every 2 months.
Temperate climates: every 12 months.
Arctic climates: every 24 months.

Q. If chemical or biological warfare is a threat, what should be the replacement interval for the filters?
A. Every 30 days (replace immediately following any blood-agent attack).

Q. What gases will decay filters more rapidly than other gases?
A. Blood agents (specifically, Hydrogen Cyanide (AC) and Cyanogen Chloride (CK)).

Q. What is the **inspection interval** for the protective mask?
A. - Every time the mask is used; or
- Every 6 months during peacetime; or
- Weekly during combat.

Q. What two types of filter elements are used in the M17-series protective mask?
A. M13/M13A1 (black connectors) - TRADOC training activities only.
M13A2 (green connectors) - protect against all known CB and riot control agents.

Q. What type of filter element is used in the M-24/25 series protective masks?
A. The canister-shaped M10A1 filter that connects to the protective mask via a hose.

Q. What type of filter element is used in the M-40 series protective masks?
A. A "tuna can" canister that screws onto the left or right side of the facepiece to allow use by left-handed or right-handed soldiers.

Q. What type of filter element is used in the M-42 series protective masks?
A. Same canister as M-40, only it attaches to the end of a hose. The canister may be secured in a canister carrier and worn independently of the mask carrier, or the hose may be attached to a vehicle or aircraft GPFU (Gas-

Particulate Filter Unit).

Q. What is another big difference between the M-40 and M-42 protective masks?
A. The M-42 has a microphone for use in high-noise environments (ie, aircraft).

Q. The M-40/42 protective masks have outserts to protect the eyelenses from scratches and other damage. These outserts come in two shades. What are they?
A. Clear and neutral gray.

Q. What should be done to the M-40/42 protective masks if storing them for longer than 30 days?
A. Use the supplied faceform (designed to hold the facepiece in proper shape).

Q. Most of the protective masks come complete with a waterproof bag for use when required by climate and mission. Name two precautions that should be followed regarding the waterproof bag.
A. - Do not allow food to come into contact with the bag because of possible toxic effects.
- Remove the mask from the bag when not absolutely necessary, because storage of the mask in the bag can degrade the protective capability of the facepiece.

Q. What does "CPE" stand for?
A. Chemical Protective Equipment.

Q. What are the four types of CPE?
A. Ventilated-facepiece, overpressure, hybrid, and total systems.

Q. How should the protective mask be cleared during extremely cold weather conditions?
A. By exhaling steadily and slowly (exhaling a large amount of air, as is done in warm weather, will frost the cold eye lenses - impairing vision).

Q. What does "CARC" stand for?
A. Chemical Agent Resistant Coating - a polyurethane base paint that resists the absorption of chemical agents.

Q. What does "CANE" stand for? "NCE"?
A. Combined Arms in the Nuclear/chemical Environment; Nuclear-Chemical Environment.

Q. What does "SCPE" stand for?
A. Simplified Collective-Protection Equipment (pronounced "skippy").

Q. What does "ANBACIS" stand for? What is it?
A. Automated Nuclear, Biological, and Chemical Information System; a software information system which supports the chemical staff officer and NCOs as well as chemical units (squad to brigade) with the communications, recordkeeping, and calculations of NBC warning and reports, tactical decision aids, and databases essential to accomplish their tasks. It can receive any number of NBC 1 Reports and create the correct number of NBC 2 Reports. It will then convert the NBC 2 Reports to NBC 3 Reports utilizing the correct weather information previously received electronically from the staff weather officer.

Q. Identify the following chemical agents by symbol.
A. HD - Distilled Mustard (blister agent)
GA - Tabun (nerve agent)
CL - Chlorine (choking agent)
VX - (nerve agent)

NBC
FM 3-3, 3-3-1, 3-4, 3-5, 3-7, 3-100

AC - Hydrogen Cyanide (blood agent)
MD - Methyldichloroarsine (blister)
CX - Phosgene Oxime (blister agent)
CK - Cyanogen Chloride (blood agent)
HL - Mustard-Lewisite (blister agent)
DA - Diphenylchloroarsine (vomiting agent)
PD - Phenyldichloroarsine (blister agent)
ED - Ethyldichloroarsine (blister agent)
DC - Diphenylcyanoarsine (vomiting agent)
CG - Phosgene (choking agent)
GD - Soman (nerve agent)
CN - Chloroacetophenone (tear agent)
HN - Nitrogen Mustard (blister agent)
CS - O-chlorobenzalmalononitrile (tear agent)
SA - Arsine (blood agent)
GB - Sarin (nerve agent)
DM - Adamsite (vomiting agent)
DP - Diphosgene (choking agent)
L - Lewisite (blister agent)

Q. G-series nerve agents (GA, GB, GD, and GF) are normally classified as ____________ (persistent/nonpersistent) agents.
A. Nonpersistant.

COMMUNICATIONS
FM 24-1/FM 24-18

Q. As a soldier there are several means of communication open to you. Name five of them.
A. Radio, visual, sound, wire, and messenger.

Q. Which of the above means of communications is considered the least secure?
A. Radio.

Q. Which of the above means of communication is considered to be the most secure?
A. Messenger.

Q. What are the limiting factors when using the most secure form of communication?
A. Delivery by messenger requires more delivery time and is limited by weather, terrain, and enemy location.

Q. Most infantry radios are ___________ modulated.
A. Frequency (FM).

Q. List five factors that affect the range of radio equipment.
A. Weather, terrain, antenna, power, and location.

Q. What are some examples of visual signals.
A. Arm-and-hand signals, pyrotechnics, smoke, flashing lights, panel markers, and aircraft maneuvers.

Q. What is the disadvantage of relying too heavily on visual signals?
A. Poor visibility (such as at night) can restrict their use.

Q. What is the major disadvantage of sound signals?
A. Battle noise will reduce their effective use.

Q. What does "CEOI" stand for?
A. Communications-Electronics Operating Instructions.

Q. What does "SOI" stand for?
A. Signal Operating Instructions.

Q. What is the first thing that you do before sending a radio message?
A. Listen to see that the net is clear.

Q. When communicating via radio transmissions, what thought should you keep foremost in your mind?
A. Always assume that the enemy is listening.

Q. What does "MIJI" stand for?
A. Meaconing, Intrusion, Jamming, and Interference.

Q. Where should you look to find the format for transmitting a MIJI report?
A. The SOI.

Q. If you encounter jamming or interference on your radio net, you should transmit a MIJI report within how many minutes of the incident?
A. 10 minutes.

Q. What is a "proword"?

COMMUNICATIONS
FM 24-1/FM 24-18

A. PROcedural WORDs which have a distinct meaning and are used to shorten transmissions and avoid confusion.

Q. What proword should be used to indicate that an error has been made in transmission?
A. "CORRECTION"

Q. What proword is used to request a distant station to respond to challenge?
A. "AUTHENTICATE"

Q. What proword is used by a distant operator to tell you to repeat your last transmission? What should be the appropriate response?
A. "SAY AGAIN"; "I SAY AGAIN, ..."

Q. What proword is used to indicate the end of a transmission to you and that no further answer is required?
A. "OUT"

Q. What proword do you use to indicate the end of a transmission and that you are awaiting a response?
A. "OVER"

Q. What proword is used to ask for a signal strength and readability report (In other words, "How do you read me?")?
A. "RADIO CHECK" ("COMMO CHECK" is commonly used).

Q. What proword is used to indicate that you have received the distant operator's last transmission satisfactorily, and loud and clear?
A. "ROGER"

Q. What proword is used to cease transmission on the net immediately?
A. "SILENCE" (repeated three or more times).

Q. What proword is used to indicate that you must pause for a few seconds? For longer than a few seconds?
A. "WAIT"; "WAIT-OUT"

Q. Which proword means "I have received your message, understand it, and will comply"?
A. "WILCO"

Q. Should the prowords "ROGER" and "WILCO" ever be used together?
A. No, the meaning of "ROGER" is included in that of "WILCO"?

Q. What proword is used to indicate a temporary break in transmission to prevent the enemy from homing in on your location?
A. "BREAK"

Q. What proword is used to indicate that you will spell the next word phonetically?
A. "I SPELL"

Q. Pronounce each letter of the alphabet phonetically.
A. A - ALPHA (AL-FAH)
B - BRAVO (BRAH-VOH)
C - CHARLIE (CHAR-LEE)
D - DELTA (DELL-TAH)
N - NOVEMBER (NOV-EM-BER)
O - OSCAR (OSS-CAH)
P - PAPA (PAH-PAH)
Q - QUEBEC (KEY-BECK)

COMMUNICATIONS
FM 24-1/FM 24-18

E - ECHO (ECK-OH)
F - FOXTROT (FOKS-TROT)
G - GOLF (GOLF)
H - HOTEL (HOH-TELL)
I - INDIA (IN-DEE-AH)
J - JULIET (JEW-LEE-ETT)
K - KILO (KEY-LOH)
L - LIMA (LEE-MAH)
M - MIKE (MIKE)
R - ROMEO (ROW-ME-OH)
S - SIERRA (SEE-AIR-RAH)
T - TANGO (TANG-GO)
U - UNIFORM (YOU-NEE-FORM)
V - VICTOR (VIK-TAH)
W - WHISKEY (WISS-KEY)
X - XRAY (ECKS-RAY)
Y - YANKEE (YANG-KEY)
Z - ZULU (ZOO-LOO)

Q. Pronounce the numbers 0-9 phonetically.
A. 0 - (ZEE-RO)
1 - (WUN)
2 - (TOO)
3 - (TREE)
4 - (FOW-ER)
5 - (FIFE)
6 - (SIX)
7 - (SEV-EN)
8 - (AIT)
9 - (NIN-ER)

Q. What do the letters "AN" and "PRC" stand for?
A. "Army/Navy" and "Portable Radio Communicator".

Q. What are the eight operational steps in using the AN/PRC-77?
A. (1) Install the battery.
(2) Select the appropriate antenna and tighten it down.
(3) Connect the handset.
(4) Select the frequency band.
(5) Turn the function switch to "ON".
(6) Turn the volume control knob about half a turn.
(7) Depress the push-to-talk (PTT) switch on the handset and release it to listen.
(8) Adjust the volume control to the desired level.

Q. What is the approximate range of the AN/PRC-77?
A. 5 to 8 kilometers.

Q. How much does the AN/PRC-77 weigh?
A. Approximately 25 lbs.

Q. What is the frequency range of the AN/PRC-77?
A. 30.00 to 75.95 MHz;
- low band: 30.00 - 52.95 MHz
- high band: 53.00 - 75.95 MHz

Q. How many channels does the "PRC-77" have?
A. 920

Q. What is the transmitter output power of the "PRC-77"?
A. 1.5 to 4.0 kilowatts.

Q. What is the power source for the "PRC-77"?
A. One BA-4386 Magnesium Battery; life: approx 60 hours.

Q. What radio consists of a family of VHF-FM combat net radios designed to provide the primary means of command and control (voice and digital data) for combat, combat support, and combat service support units?
A. The SINCGARS radio.

Q. What does "SINCGARS" stand for?

COMMUNICATIONS
FM 24-1/FM 24-18

A. SINgle Channel Ground/Airborne Radio System.

Q. What does "ECCM" stand for?
A. Electronic Counter Countermeasures.

Q. What function gives the SINCGARS radio its unique ECCM (anti-jamming) capability?
A. Frequency hopping.

Q. Briefly explain the SINCGARS frequency hopping operation.
A. Frequency Hopping (FH) is accomplished by using a digital frequency synthesizer coupled to a microprocessor and a random sequence generator. The process of frequency hopping requires a sequence of variables which allow the receiver-transmitter (RT) to pseudo-randomly change frequencies at the rate of approximately 100 "hops" per second. The variables determine the group of frequencies that the RT will hop on, the frequency hop starting point, and the hopping sequence.

Q. For most conditions there are four variables (see above question) required for proper frequency hopping operation. What are they?
A. (1) HOPSET (Hopping Set): the group of frequencies within the range 30.00 to 87.975 on which the radio will hop.
(2) Net Identification: the part of the HOPSET which identifies a specific net and designates the frequency within the HOPSET on which the radio will start hopping.
(3) Transmission Security Key (TSEC): digital code that controls the hopping sequence.
(4) FH Sync Time: consists of the mission day, hour, minutes, and seconds and is used to determine the different random hopping sequences for each message.

NOTE: In order for a radio to operate in a net with other radios, each of the RTs must contain the same variables.

Q. What is the numerical range for a HOPSET?
A. 000 to 999.

Q. The FH Sync Time for all radios in a net must be within +/- _____ seconds for normal operation.
A. 4

Q. What device is used to enter HOPSET and TSEC information into the SINCGARS RT?
A. An MX-10579 ECCM fill device.

Q. The basic SINCGARS radio was designed on a modular basis that can be arranged in various manpack and vehicle configurations. The AN/PRC-119A is the manpack configuration and is designed to replace what radios?
A. The AN/PRC-77 and AN/PRC-25 radios.

Q. The SINCGARS RT can scan how many single channel presets for traffic?
A. 8

Q. What is the purpose of the "CUE" frequency?
A. It allows a single channel (SC) user to contact a frequency hopping net.

Q. How many power settings does the SINCGARS have and what are the ranges?

COMMUNICATIONS
FM 24-1/FM 24-18

A. 4;
Low: 200-m to 400-m
Medium: 400-m to 5-km
High: 5-km to 10-km
PA (Power Amplifier): 10-km to 40-km

NOTE: Use minimum power required to communicate effectively.

Q. The SINCGARS radio has a "whisper" function. What is the purpose of this?
A. Allows the user to talk softly during transmission and still be received with maximum volume at the distant station.

Q. If a microphone is accidentally keyed causing a "hot mike" situation, how can the rest of the net break away and resume normal operations?
A. By keying the microphone twice.

Q. SINCGARS SC and FH transmissions can be further encrypted for secure communications using what device?
A. KY-57

Q. What preparations to the radio are necessary prior to fording?
A. None, the radio is designed to be water tight.

Q. What is the approximate battery life on the manpack SINCGARS radio?
A. 18 to 20 hours.

Q. What is the SINCGARS operating voltage?
A. Manpack: 13.5 volts with Lithium battery
Vehicular: 27.5 volts from vehicle battery system

Q. How many operating frequencies does the SINCGARS have and what is the channel spacing?
A. 2,320; 25 kHz.

Q. How many channels can be loaded and selected using the CHAN (channel) switch on the SINCGARS?
A. Up to eight SC and six FH channels.

Q. The SINCGARS radio in the manpack configuration uses a lithium battery containing pressurized sulfur dioxide gas. What is the recommended type of fire extinguisher to be used in the event of a fire?
A. Flood the equipment with water or use a carbon dioxide extinguisher. DO NOT use a Halon-type fire extinguisher on a lithium battery fire. In the event that lithium metal becomes involved in the fire, the use of a graphite-based class D fire extinguisher, such as Lith-X or Met-L-X, is recommended.

Q. RF energy is present near the antenna during transmission. For this reason, how much distance should be maintained between vehicles and personnel during transmission?
A. At least 30 inches.

NOTE: High voltage exists at Connector J1 on vehicular mounting adapter. Be sure J1 is covered or capped when not in use to avoid personnel injury.

Q. What is meant by the term "transceiver"?
A. A transmitter and receiver combination.

Q. What is a "SUT"?
A. Small Unit Transceiver.

COMMUNICATIONS
FM 24-1/FM 24-18

Q. What is an AN/PRC-68?
A. A type of squad radio small unit transceiver.

Q. What are the AN/PRT-4 and the AN/PRR-9?
A. A type of squad radio. They should be used together. The AN/PRT-4 is the transmitter and the AN/PRR-9 is the receiver (worn on the helmet).

Q. What is "WD-1"?
A. Communications field wire.

Q. What is "DR-8"?
A. A spool that holds 400 meters of field wire. It is reusable and should be taken up if the situation permits.

Q. What is a "TA-1"?
A. A handheld transmitter/receiver unit that has both a visual and an audible signal.

Q. What type batteries does the TA-1 use?
A. The TA-1 does not require batteries for operation.

Q. What is the approximate range of the TA-1?
A. 6.4 kilometers using WD-1.

Q. What is a "TA-312/PT"?
A. A two-wire, battery operated, portable field telephone.

Q. What does the "TA" and "PT" stand for in TA-312/PT?
A. Telephone Apparatus; Portable Telephone.

Q. What is the power source for the TA-312/PT?
A. Two BA-30 batteries (one up, one down) or an externally applied 3-volt DC source.

Q. When no external power supply is available for the TA-312/PT, how should the INT-EXT switch and the circuit selector switch be positioned?
A. Place INT-EXT switch to "INT" for internal and the circuit selector switch to "LB" for local battery.

Q. How does one signal the distant operator when using the TA-312/PT?
A. By turning the handcrank rapidly several turns.

Q. What is an H-60/PT?
A. The detachable handset for the TA-312/PT.

Q. How much insulation should be stripped from the two wire-ends of WD-1 before inserting them into the posts of the TA-312/PT?
A. One inch.

Q. What is the approximate range of the TA-312/PT?
A. 38 kilometers using WD-1.

Q. What is "ICD"?
A. Imitative Communications Deception.

Q. What is the best defense against ICD?

COMMUNICATIONS
FM 24-1/FM 24-18

A. Authentication.

Q. Which is the highest classification of information which may be discussed over non-secure communications media?
A. Unclassified information.

Q. Methods of denying the enemy intelligence information through good communications security includes what two steps?
A. (1) DO NOT DISCUSS classified information over the telephone or in radio transmissions.
(2) USE CEOI (SOI) ITEMS to encrypt information of intelligence value.

Q. When should you request a station to authenticate?
A. - When making an initial communication.
- When you suspect ICD.
- When transmitting operating instructions which effect the military situation.

Q. What is "COMSEC"? "OPSEC"?
A. Communications Security; Operations Security.

PHYSICAL FITNESS TRAINING
FM 21-20

Q. What Army publications cover the Army Physical Fitness Program?
A. AR 350-15 and FM 21-20.

Q. Physical fitness is but one factor of total fitness. Name some of the other factors of total fitness mentioned in FM 21-20?
A. Weight control, diet and nutrition, stress management, dental health, and spiritual and ethical fitness, as well as the avoidance of hypertension, substance abuse and tobacco use.

Q. Who is responsible for ensuring that soldiers maintain the highest level of physical fitness in accordance with FM 21-20 and AR 350-15?
A. Commanders and supervisors.

Q. There are many things one must consider when developing an effective physical fitness program. How many "considerations" are there and what are they?
A. 5; components of fitness, principles of exercise, phases of fitness, types of programs, and evaluation.

Q. Physical fitness is composed of factors (components) that allow soldiers to function effectively in physical and mental work, training, and recreation and still have energy to handle emergencies. What are the five COMPONENTS of fitness?
A. (1) Muscular strength: greatest amount of force a muscle or muscle group can exert in a single effort.
(2) Muscular endurance: ability of a muscle or muscle group to perform repeated movements with moderate resistance for extended periods of time.
(3) Cardiorespiratory endurance: efficiency with which the body delivers nutrients and oxygen needed for muscular activity and transports waste products from the cells.
(4) Flexibility: ability to move the joints through an entire (normal) range of motion.
(5) Body composition: the amount of body fat a soldier has in comparison to his total body mass.

Q. What are the seven PRINCIPLES of exercise?
A. (1) Regularity
(2) Progression: gradual increase in intensity of exercises.
(3) Overload: exercise must exceed normal demands to provide training effect.
(4) Balance: include activities that develop all components of fitness.
(5) Specificity: gear training to specific improvement desired.
(6) Variety: varying exercise reduces boredom and increases motivation.
(7) Recovery: hard days of training should be followed by easy days to permit recovery.

Q. What is the primary objective of a physical training program?
A. To enhance soldiers' abilities to meet the physical demands of war.

Q. What is an "MFT"?
A. A Master Fitness Trainer, a soldier who has completed either the four-week active-component, two-week reserve-component, or the U.S. Military Academy's MFT course.

Q. The acronym "FITT" makes it easier to remember the key factors in a training program. What do the letters stand for?

PHYSICAL FITNESS TRAINING
FM 21-20

A. Frequency, Intensity, Time, and Type.

Q. What is the Army's policy concerning the length and duration of exercise periods?
A. They should be of sufficient intensity, frequency, and duration so as to produce a training effect (AR 350-15). See questions related to training heart rate (THR) for specifics on determining whether or not a training effect is being produced.

Q. AR 350-15 specifies that vigorous physical fitness training will be conducted _______ to _______ times per week.
A. Three to five.

Q. How many minutes of continuous intense exercise is needed in order to improve cardiorespiratory endurance?
A. At least 20 to 30.

Q. A normal daily exercise routine should consist of three periods. What are they?
A. Warm-up, conditioning, and cool-down.

Q. How does "warming up" help to prevent injuries and maximize performance during physical training?
A. The warm-up increases the body's internal temperature and heart rate. The chance of getting injured decreases when the heart, muscles, ligaments, and tendons are properly prepared for exertion.

Q. An adequate warm-up period should include some running in place, or slow jogging, stretching, and calisthenics and should last for how long?
A. Five to seven minutes.

Q. For warm-up and injury prevention, stretches should be held for how long?
A. 10 to 15 seconds.

Q. How should stretches for flexibility training be done?
A. So that there is slight discomfort but no pain.

Q. What is the purpose for "cooling down" after an exercise period, regardless of the type of workout?
A. The cool-down serves to gradually slow the heart rate and helps prevent pooling of the blood in the legs and feet. Also, stretching during the cool-down period results in optimum improvement in flexibility.

NOTE: During exercise the blood moves faster than usual through the one-way valves of the veins and back to the heart by the squeezing action of moving muscles. If exercise suddenly stops (improper or inadequate cool-down), this extra squeezing action also stops, resulting in the "pooling" of blood in the extremities. This, in turn, results in insufficient oxygen delivery to the heart and to the brain, causing dizziness, fainting, or possible heart attack.

Q. Stretches conducted during the cool-down period should be held for how long?
A. 30 to 60 seconds.

Q. How long should the cool-down period last?
A. Soldiers should walk or stretch until their heart rates return to less than 100 beats per minute (BPM) and heavy sweating stops. Under normal conditions, five to seven minutes is considered a sufficient period of time for cool-down.

PHYSICAL FITNESS TRAINING
FM 21-20

Q. What are the three PHASES of fitness conditioning?
A. Preparatory, Conditioning, and Maintenance.

Q. As an active duty soldier, what "phase" of fitness should you be in?
A. Maintenance (maintaining) phase.

Q. In the maintenance phase of fitness, a ______-minute workout **at the right intensity**, three times a week will maintain almost any appropriate level of physical fitness.
A. 45 to 60 (including warm-up and cool-down).

Q. What are the three TYPES of Army fitness programs?
A. Individual, special, and unit.

Q. What is meant by the "individual" type of fitness programs?
A. Soldiers assigned to duty positions that offer little opportunity to participate in collective unit PT programs must accept individual responsibility for maintaining their own physical fitness.

Q. At least three groups of soldiers may require special fitness training programs. Who are they?
A. (1) Those who fail the APFT and do not have medical profiles.
(2) Those who are overweight/overfat according to AR 600-9.
(3) Those who have either permanent or temporary medical profiles.

Q. What is the "CVSP" and who is required to participate?
A. The CardioVascular Screening Program. Soldiers who reached age 40 before 1 January 1989 must be cleared through the CVSP before taking a record APFT. There is no requirement for clearance in the CVSP for soldiers who reach(ed) age 40 on or after 1 January 1989.

Q. What is a soldier with a medical profile required to do during unit PT?
A. As much of the regular fitness program as they can, along with substitute activities (alternate exercises) provided by the MFT.

Q. What does "APFT" stand for?
A. Army Physical Fitness Test (often called "APRT", Army Physical Readiness Test).

Q. Who is evaluated during an APFT?
A. All soldiers, regardless of age, in all three events.

Q. How often is the APFT administered?
A. Four times per year - twice per year (once every six months) for record, and twice for diagnostic purposes (minimum of 4 months must separate record tests).

Q. What are APFT standards based on?
A. Age and physiological differences between men and women.

Q. What is the basic training (IET) standard for passing the APFT?
A. An overall score of not less than 160, and not less than 50 points in any event.

Q. What is the Army standard (including AIT) for passing the APFT?
A. A minimum of 60 points per event and 180 points overall.

PHYSICAL FITNESS TRAINING
FM 21-20

NOTE: The unit's "standards" may exceed Army minimums. By regulation (AR 350-15), the unit's standards can be established by the unit commander, based on mission requirements.

Q. What is meant by CR fitness?
A. CardioRespiratory fitness (cardiorespiratory endurance), the efficiency of one's body to use oxygen in the production of energy.

Q. What is considered to be the most widely accepted single indicator of one's CR fitness level?
A. Aerobic capacity or VO_2max (this value represents an individual's maximum oxygen uptake).

Q. It is possible to determine a soldier's CR fitness level and get an accurate estimate of aerobic capacity by calculating VO_2max. What is the formula for this?
A. From Appendix F-1, FM 21-20

Males:

$$VO_2max = 99.7 - [3.35 \times (\text{2-mile-run time in decimal form})]$$

Females:

$$VO_2max = 72.9 - [1.77 \times (\text{2-mile-run time in decimal form})]$$

NOTE: Table F-1 in FM 21-20 should be used to determine how your VO_2max translates into fitness ratings.

Q. Many factors can negatively affect one's ability to perform well aerobically. Name some of them.
A.
- Age
- Anemia
- Carbon monoxide from tobacco smoke or pollution
- High altitude (reduced oxygen pressure)
- Illness (heart disease)
- Obesity
- Sedentary life-style

Q. Approximately ____% of a person's aerobic potential is determined genetically.
A. 80%

Q. What does "THR" stand for and what is its purpose?
A. Training Heart Rate. The training heart rate is an excellent tool for determining the appropriate intensity of training for each individual and represents the rate at which a soldier needs to exercise to receive a training effect.

Q. There are two methods for determining training heart rate (THR). What are they? Which method is simplest to use and which is more accurate?
A. Simplest method: percent maximum heart rate (% MHR).
Most accurate method: percent heart rate reserve (% HRR).

Q. Describe how training heart rate (THR) is determined using the % MHR method.
A. Step 1: Maximum heart rate (MHR) is determined by subtracting your age from 220 (a constant).

Step 2: Multiply a percentage of intensity* by the MHR.

* % intensity for this method should be based on the following:
70% - relatively poor shape
80% - well-trained; relatively good shape
90% - excellent shape

Example: well-trained 20-year old --> MHR = 220 - 20 = 200 bpm
(80% MHR = .8 x MHR = .8 x 200 = 160 bpm)

Q. Describe how training heart rate (THR) is determined using the % HRR method.
A. Step 1: Determine MHR (same as above --> 220 - age).
Step 2: Determine the resting heart rate (RHR) in beats per minute (bpm) by counting the pulse for 30 seconds and multiplying by two.
Step 3: Determine the heart rate reserve (HRR) by subtracting the resting heart rate (RHR) from the maximum heart rate (MHR) in step 1.
Step 4: Use the following formula for calculating THR:
THR = [(% intensity) x HRR] + RHR

* % intensity for this method differs slightly from the % MHR method and should be based on the following:
50% - extremely poor condition
60% - healthy, sedentary individual
70% - well-trained; reasonably good shape
>85% - excellent shape

Example: well-trained 20-year old with a resting heart rate (RHR) of
69 bpm --> MHR = 220-20 = 200 bpm
RHR = 69 bpm (given)
HRR = MHR - RHR = 200 - 69 = 131 bpm
THR = (.7 x 131) + 69 = 91.7 + 69 = 160.7 (compare to calculation using % MHR in above question)

Q. Intensity is probably the single most important factor for improving performance. The intensity of exercise for CR development must be strenuous enough to elevate the heart rate to between ____ and ____ percent of the HRR.
A. 60; 90.

Q. Levels above what percentage of the HRR are considered to be dangerous?
A. 90%

Q. Most CR workouts should be conducted with the heart rate between ____ to ____ percent HRR to attain, or maintain, an adequate level of fitness.
A. 70; 75.

Q. What is the optimum time during an exercise period to begin monitoring the heart rate?
A. After 5 minutes of aerobic exercise. The body will usually reach a "steady state" condition after five minutes of exercise and the heart rate will have leveled off. At this time, and immediately after exercising, the heart rate should be monitored.

Q. What is the suggested method of checking for the THR during or immediately following exercise?
A. Place the tip of the third finger lightly over the carotid artery of the neck (located to the left or right sides of the Adam's apple) or inside the wrist just below the base of the thumb (radial artery). Count the pulse for 10

seconds and multiply by 6 to obtain the heart rate for one minute.

Q. What are some examples of aerobic (CR) exercises?
A. - Primary:

running/jogging	rope skipping
swimming	walking (vigorous)
bicycling	aerobic dancing
cross-country skiing	rowing
road marching	stair climbing

- Secondary: racquetball (singles)
  basketball (full court)
  handball (singles)
  tennis (singles)

Q. What is the Army standard for the duration of aerobic and running activities?
A. 20 to 30 minutes at THR.

Q. To provide maximum benefit to soldiers, the commander should divide the unit into ability groups. The number of groups depends on the size of the unit but, generally speaking, a company broken down into ____ ability groups, each with a leader assigned, sets the stage for effective training.
A. 4 to 6.

Q. Without knowing individual training heart rates, what is the best way to assign soldiers to ability groups?
A. Make a list, in order, of the unit's most recent APFT 2-mile-run times.

Q. Road marches are an excellent way to improve and maintain fitness in the field and in garrison. They are classified into two types. What are these classifications?
A. Administrative and tactical.

Q. What are the four TYPES of road marches?
A. Day, limited visibility, forced, and shuttle.

Q. What is the difference between a "day" road march and a "limited visibility" road march?
A. Limited visibility road marches move more slowly and are in tighter formations. Because of this, soldiers may not exercise hard enough to obtain a conditioning effect. One of the advantages of such a march is protection of the soldiers from the heat of the day.

Q. What are the advantages and disadvantages of a "forced" road march?
A. Forced marches move soldiers over long distances in shorter periods of time and are excellent conditioners since they require more than the normal effort in speed and exertion. However, they often leave soldiers too fatigued to do other required training tasks at the end of the march.

Q. What is a "shuttle" march?
A. Road marches that alternate riding and marching.

Q. What should soldiers do during a road march rest halt?
A. Lie down and elevate the feet. If time permits, they should massage their feet, apply powder, and change socks. Relieve swelling feet by slightly loosening the laces across the arches.

PHYSICAL FITNESS TRAINING
FM 21-20

Q. What are the two components of muscular fitness?
A. Muscular strength and muscular endurance.

Q. The human body has over 400 voluntary muscles that move the skeleton. Each muscle can perform three types of contractions. What are they?
A. (1) Isometric: also called a static contraction, occurs when a muscle exerts a force (contracts) but does not shorten or lengthen. Force is produced with no change in the angle of the joint (ie, pushing or pulling against an immovable object). This contraction strengthens the muscles at only one point in the range of motion.
(2) Isotonic: causes a joint to move through the full range of motion against a constant resistance (ie, pushups, sit-ups, and lifting weights).
(3) Isokinetic: causes the angle of the joint to change at a constant rate, with the load or resistance changing at different joint angles to counter the varying forces produced by the muscle(s) at different angles (ie, variable-resistance weight machines or isokinetic machines).

Q. Which of the above three types of muscular contractions is normally emphasized more than the other two?
A. Isotonic.

Q. Theoretically, which exercise places a maximum work load on the muscle throughout the entire range of motion, fostering rapid strength gains?
A. Isokinetic.

Q. Isotonic and isokinetic contractions have two specific phases. What are they?
A. - Concentric or positive phase: muscle contracts or shortens.
- Eccentric or negative phase: muscle elongates or returns to its normal length.

Q. Muscles can control more weight in which of the two phases mentioned above?
A. The eccentric phase. Thus, greater strength gains can be obtained using "negatives" since the muscles are able to handle more of an overload eccentrically.

Q. Which of the seven principles of exercise is the basis for muscular training?
A. Overload (when a muscle is overloaded, it adapts by becoming stronger).

Q. What is meant by "muscle failure"?
A. That point in an exercise when a soldier is unable to perform another correct repetition in a set.

Q. What is an "RM" and what is a 10-RM exercise?
A. Repetition Maximum; a 1-RM represents the maximum weight a person can lift correctly one time. A 10-RM is the maximum weight a person can lift correctly 10 times.

Q. The minimum resistance needed to obtain strength gains is____% of the 1-RM.
A. 50%

Q. In order to achieve enough overload, most programs are designed to require sets with____to____percent of the 1-RM.
A. 70 to 80.

Q. In terms of strict repetitions, what RM resistance is ideal for gaining

muscular strength? Muscular endurance?
A. Muscular strength: 3-7 RM completed in sets (high weight, low repetitions)
NOTE: greatest improvements seem to come from about the 6-RM range.
Muscular endurance: 12+ RM completed in sets (low weight, higher repetitions)

Q. What is the ideal RM resistance for both muscular strength and endurance gains?
A. 8-12 RM

Q. Normal recovery between sets should be how long?
A. 30 to 180 seconds.

Q. Soldiers must use the proper breathing technique to prevent headache, dizziness, or blackouts. The breathing pattern should be constant during exercise; soldiers should **never** hold their breath while trying to lift weights. You should _________ (inhale/exhale) during the shortening (concentric) phase and ________ during the lengthening (eccentric) phase.
A. Exhale; inhale.

Q. The recovery period between workouts of the same muscle group should be at least ___ hours. However, strength losses begin after ____ hours.
A. 48; 96.

Q. Soldiers can maintain their strength by working out how often?
A. One to two times per week.

Q. Listed below are the major muscle groups. Where is each located?
A.
- Trapezius: muscles of the upper back that extend from the neck to the shoulders.
- Deltoids: shoulder muscles.
- Pectoralis major: large chest muscle.
- Biceps: muscle at the front of the upper arm.
- External obliques: muscles at the sides of the midsection and waist.
- Rectus abdominis: muscles of the front midsection (abdominal muscles).
- Quadriceps: a group of four main muscles at the front and sides of the upper leg.
- Rhomboids: upper back muscle.
- Triceps: muscle at the back of the upper arm.
- Latissimus dorsi: large back muscles that extend from the lower spine to the armpits.
- Spinal erector: lower back muscle.
- Gluteus: buttocks muscle.
- Hamstring: muscle at the back of the upper leg.
- Gastrocnemius: calf muscle at the back of the lower leg.

Q. What are "anaerobic" exercises?
A. Exercises performed at an intensity that starves the muscles of oxygen - short "bursts" of energy that exceeds the body's ability to adequately supply oxygen to muscle tissue and remove cellular waste (lactic acid). Examples include relays and sprints.

Q. Name the 15 partner-resisted exercises covered in FM 21-20 and state the major muscle group strengthened.
A.
- split-squat.............................. quadriceps and gluteals
- Single-leg squat.......................... quadriceps and gluteals
- leg extension............................. quadriceps

- leg curl.................................. hamstrings
- heel raise (bent over).................... gastrocnemius and soleus
- toe raise................................. tibialis anterior
- push-up................................... pectoralis major/triceps
- seated row................................ latissimus dorsi/biceps
- overhead press............................ deltoid and triceps
- pull-down................................. latissimus dorsi
- shrug..................................... upper trapezius
- triceps extension......................... triceps
- biceps curl............................... biceps
- abdominal curl............................ rectus abdominous
- abdominal crunch.......................... int/ext obliques

Q. Flexibility refers to the range of movement of a joint or series of joints and their associated muscles and is best developed through stretching exercises. What are the four general categories of stretching exercises?
A. Static, passive, proprioceptive neuromuscular facilitation (PNF), and ballistic (dynamic).

Q. What is the difference between static and dynamic or ballistic stretching?
A. Ballistic stretching involves movements such as bouncing or bobbing to attain a greater range of motion and stretch. Static stretching involves the gradual lengthening of muscles and tendons as a body part moves around a joint.

Q. Of static and ballistic stretching techniques, which should not be used by individuals or units?
A. Ballistic (this method often forces a muscle to stretch too far and may result in an injury).

Q. What is meant by passive stretching?
A. Stretching that involves the use of a partner or equipment, such as a towel, pole, or rubber tubing, producing a safe stretch through a range of motion that could otherwise not be achieved.

Q. What is meant by PNF stretching?
A. Stretches that use the neuromuscular patterns of each muscle group to improve flexibility. See FM 21-20 for examples and proper techniques.

Q. Describe the recommended 5-step sequence for warm-up activities.
A. Step 1: Slow jogging in place or walking for two minutes.
Step 2: Slow joint rotation exercises (work each major joint for 5-10 seconds).
Step 3: Slow, static stretching of the muscles to be used during the upcoming conditioning period (hold each stretch 10-15 seconds).
Step 4: Perform calisthenic exercises to increase the intensity level prior to the conditioning period.
Step 5: If possible or applicable, mimic the activity to be performed (lift a lighter weight to warm up prior to lifting a heavier one, etc).

Q. Name some of the warm-up and cool-down stretches covered in FM 21-20.
A.
- neck and shoulder stretch
- chest stretch
- overhead arm pull
- hamstring stretch (standing)
- groin stretch (standing)
- groin stretch (seated straddle)
- calf stretch (variation: toe pull)
- abdominal stretch
- upper-back stretch
- thigh stretch
- hamstring stretch (seated)
- groin stretch (seated)
- calf stretch

- hip and back stretch (seated)
- hip and back stretch (lying down)

Q. Body composition, one of the five components of physical fitness, refers to the body's relative amounts of fat and lean body mass and is influenced by what four factors?
A. Age, diet, level of fitness, and genetic factors (gender/body type).

Q. What is considered to be the best way to lose unwanted body fat?
A. A combination of exercise and diet.

Q. What is the primary fuel source for muscles during short-term, high-intensity activities?
A. Carbohydrates, in the form of glycogen (a complex sugar).

Q. What are "calisthenics"?
A. Exercises that develop strength, endurance, coordination, and flexibility in all major muscle groups.

Q. What is meant by "normal cadence"?
A. It is the cadence prescribed for a particular exercise.

Q. All of the calisthenics covered in FM 21-20 are performed at either a slow or a moderate cadence. Explain the difference in terms of counts per minute.
A. Slow cadence = 50 counts per minute, unless directed otherwise
Moderate cadence = 80 counts per minute

Q. What are the three key points for ensuring safety during stretching and calisthenic exercises?
A. (1) Stretch slowly and without pain and unnatural stress to a joint. Use static (slow and sustained) stretching for warming up, cooling down, and increasing flexibility. Avoid ballistic (bouncy or jerky) stretching movements.
(2) Do not allow the angle formed by the upper and lower legs to become less than 90 degrees when the legs are bearing weight.
(3) A combination of spinal rotation and bending should generally be avoided. However, if done, use only slow, controlled movements with little or no extra weight.

Q. There are 17 calisthenic exercises recommended in FM 21-20. Name some of them and give the cadence for each.
A.
- side-straddle hop .... moderate
- mule kick .... moderate
- ski jump .... moderate
- flutter kick .... moderate
- bend and reach .... slow
- high jumper .... moderate
- squat bender .... moderate
- lunger .... moderate
- knee bender .... moderate
- swimmer .... moderate
- supine bicycle .... slow
- engine .... moderate
- cross-country skier .... moderate
- push-up .... cadence not specified
- sit-up .... cadence not specified
- chin-up (pull-up) .... cadence not specified

- parallel bar dip .... cadence not specified

Q. In addition to weight training and calisthenics, what are some of the other physical training exercises covered in FM 21-20?
A. Circuit training, grass drills, guerrilla drills, obstacle courses, rifle drills, log drills, aquatic exercise, road marching, and competitive fitness activities.

Q. Explain what a circuit drill is. What are the two types?
A. A group of stations or areas where specific tasks or exercises are performed.
The two types are free circuit (repetition-driven) and fixed circuit (time-driven).

Q. What are grass drills?
A. Drills consisting of movements that feature rapid changes in body position. They are vigorous drills that exercise all major muscle groups. Soldiers respond to commands as fast as possible and perform all movements at top speed. Though no cadence is counted, soldiers continue to do multiple repetitions of each exercise until the next command is given.

Q. What is the primary purpose of grass drills?
A. To decrease reaction time, develop muscular endurance, increase strength, and improve cardiorespiratory endurance.

Q. What are the four starting positions for grass drills?
A. Go, front, back, and stop.

Q. During the drills, the instructor only executes which positions for better supervision?
A. Go and stop.

Q. What command is used to halt the drill for instructional purpose or for rest?
A. "Up" (soldiers assume a relaxed standing position).

Q. How many types of grass drills are there and how many exercises are in each?
A. 2; 4.

Q. Which of the two grass drills is the more difficult?
A. Grass Drill Two.

Q. What four exercises are included in Grass Drill One?
A. Bouncing ball, supine bicycle, knee bender, and roll left/right.

Q. What four exercises are included in Grass Drill Two?
A. The swimmer, bounce and clap hands, leg spreader, and forward roll.

Q. Since grass drills are extremely strenuous, they should not last longer than how many seconds.
A. 30-45

Q. What are guerrilla exercises?
A. Exercises that combine individual and partner exercises and require rapid changing of positions and the execution of various basic skills while the soldiers move forward.

PHYSICAL FITNESS TRAINING
FM 21-20

Q. What PT formation is used for conducting guerrilla exercises?
A. The circular formation (use concentric circles if size exceeds 30 soldiers).

Q. Name the thirteen guerrilla exercises.
A.
- double time
- all fours run
- crab walk
- broad jump
- bottoms-up walk
- straddle run
- fireman's carry
- hobble hopping
- hand-kick walk
- the engine
- cross carry
- saddle-back (piggyback) carry
- single shoulder carry

Q. As a standard, each exercise in guerrilla drills should last how long?
A. 20 to 40 seconds.

Q. What are the two types of obstacle courses?
A. (1) Conditioning obstacle course: has low obstacles that must be negotiated quickly - against time.
(2) Confidence obstacle course: has higher, more difficult obstacles than those of the conditioning course; it is not run against time and soldiers are encouraged, not forced to negotiate the course.

Q. Rifle drill exercises develop the upper body and are most suitable for fitness training in the field. How many rifle drill exercises are there and what are they?
A. 4; fore-up, behind back; fore-up, back bend; up and forward; and fore-up, squat (all four-count exercises).

Q. What are the two prescribed formations for physical fitness training?
A. Extended rectangular and circular.

Q. Which of the above formations is the traditional formation for most physical training activities?
A. The extended rectangular formation.

Q. When forming a unit into the extended rectangular formation, the unit's final position should be centered and how far from the instructor or stand?
A. 5 paces.

Q. What eight commands are used to form the extended rectangular formation?
A.
- extend to the left, march
- arms downward, move
- left, face
- extend to the left, march
- arms downward, move
- right, face
- from front to rear, count off
- even numbers to the left, uncover.

Q. What command is used to reassemble the unit into the original formation?
A. Assemble to the right, march.

Q. On the command, "Extend to the left, March", what actions do the soldiers in the right flank file take?
A. Stand fast with both arms extended to the sides at shoulder level.

Q. While extended with the arms up, what should be the approximate distance

between soldiers' fingertips?
A. 12 inches.

Q. What is the advantage of the circular formation over the extended rectangular formation?
A. It affords better supervision of soldiers, especially for guerrilla exercises, the circuit interval course, grass drills, and some forms of running.

Q. When should separate circles be used?
A. When more than 60 soldiers must exercise.

NOTE: For guerrilla exercises, it is recommended that separate or concentric circles be used when more than 30 soldiers will be exercised.

Q. What commands are used to form the circular formation?
A. (1) "Circle Formation, Follow Me": the left flank squad of the column moves forward at double time. The unit gradually forms a circle in a counterclockwise direction.
(2) "Pick Up A 5-Yard Interval": ensures that the intervals between soldiers are uniform.

Q. Soldiers sometimes injure themselves during exercise, most often caused by too much exercise done too often with too rapid an increase in intensity (repetitions, weight, mileage, pace, etc). What word is used to remember how to treat most PT-related injuries and what does each letter stand for?
A. (R)est
(I)ce
(C)ompression
(E)levation

Q. What is a DA Form 705?
A. The Army Physical Readiness Test Scorecard.

Q. How many scorers should be supplied for an APRT?
A. A minimum of one for every 15 soldiers tested.

Q. The two-mile running course should be flat, with no more than a ___% grade, and a solid surface.
A. 3%

Q. If a road course is used how must it be marked?
A. The start and finish and one-mile (halfway) point must be clearly marked.

Q. What is the required test sequence for the three events of the APFT?
A. Push-ups, sit-ups, and then the 2-mile run.

Q. How long should soldiers be given to recover between events?
A. No less than 10, but ideally no more than 20 minutes.

Q. Under no circumstances is the APFT valid if a soldier cannot begin and end all three events in what time span?
A. 2 hours or less.

Q. When timing the push-up and sit-up events, how should the time be called out?
A. At each 30-second interval and on every second for the last ten seconds of

the 2 minutes.

Q. What is the correct positioning for a scorer of the push-up event?
A. Approximately 3 feet away from the participant's shoulder at a 45-degree angle. The scorer's head should be even with the participant's shoulder when the participant is in the front leaning rest position.

Q. What is the correct positioning for a scorer of the sit-up event?
A. Approximately 3 feet away from the participant's hips. The scorer's head should be even with the participant's shoulder when the latter is in the vertical position.

Q. Soldiers who start an event incorrectly must be stopped by the scorer before they complete ____ repetitions.
A. 10

Q. What is the proper way for a holder to hold an exerciser's feet?
A. Using <u>only</u> the hands.

Q. How long does a soldier have before he can be tested after a temporary profile expires?
A. Up to twice the length of the profile period - not to exceed 90 days.

Q. Who should receive an APFT with alternate test events?
A. Soldiers with permanent profiles and with temporary profiles greater than three month's duration.

Q. What are the four alternate APFT test events?
A. (1) 800-yard swim test.
(2) 6.2-mile stationary bicycle ergometer test with a resistance setting of 2 kilograms or 20 newtons.
(3) 6.2 mile conventional one-speed bicycle test.
(4) 2½ mile walk test (see ATSG-PFT MSG dtd 201500Z Mar 86).

Q. How is the score counted when an individual's run time falls between two point values?
A. The lower of the two point values is counted.

Q. What is a DA Form 3349 and what is its purpose?
A. Physical Profile form; informs soldiers and their commanders of not only their physical limitations but also the exercises they can perform (listed graphically on reverse of form).

Q. How do you prepare the unit for the last repetition of any exercise?
A. All numbers in the final repetition will be given with a raised inflection of the voice.

Q. How long does an appropriate physical training program last?
A. Year-round.

Q. How many points are required on the APFT to be awarded the Presidential Physical Fitness patch?
A. 290.

Q. Where is the Presidential Physical Fitness patch authorized to be worn?
A. Centered on the left side, above the breast, of the physical training t-shirt or sweatshirt (AR 670-1).

PHYSICAL FITNESS TRAINING
FM 21-20

Q. What must happen when a soldier fails the APFT for the first time or fails to take the APFT within the required period?
A. Must be flagged IAW AR 600-8-2.

Q. What may happen if a soldier fails the APFT twice?
A. The soldier may be processed for elimination from the service.

Q. A soldier that fails the APFT must be retested within how many months from the APFT failure?
A. 3 months (IAW AR 350-15, para 11).

NOTE: Commanders may allow soldiers to retake the test as soon as the soldiers and commanders feel they are ready.

Q. Are soldiers authorized to administer the APFT to themselves for the purpose of satisfying a unit's diagnostic or record APFT requirement?
A. No.

Q. Who is eligible to determine their score on an extended scale?
A. Only those soldiers who score 100 points in all three events.

Q. A normal daily exercise routine should consist of three periods. Recap these three periods and give the recommended actions and durations for each.

A. Period 1: Warm-up............ 1 minute walk/slow jog
2-3 minutes stretching
2-3 minutes calisthenics

5-7 minutes total time

Period 2: Conditioning....... 20-45 minutes
cardiorespiratory or strength activity

Period 3: Cool-down.......... 2-3 minutes low intensity exercises
3-4 minutes stretching

5-7 minutes total time

WEIGHT CONTROL
AR 600-9

Q. What Army regulation covers "The Army Weight Control Program"?
A. AR 600-9

Q. What is meant by the term "overweight"?
A. A soldier is considered overweight when his or her percent body fat exceeds the standard specified in paragraph 20c of AR 600-9.

NOTE: Keep in mind that a soldier may exceed the maximum screening table weight and **not** be considered overweight if they meet the body fat standard.

Q. What are the primary objectives of the Army Weight Control Program?
A. To insure that all personnel -
   (1) Are able to meet the physical demands of their duties under combat conditions.
   (2) Present a trim military appearance at all times.

Q. Give three reasons why the Army is so concerned about excess body fat.
A. (1) It connotes a lack of personal discipline.
   (2) It detracts from military appearance.
   (3) It is an indication that a poor state of health, physical fitness, or stamina may be present.

Q. Who is responsible for meeting the standards prescribed in AR 600-9?
A. Every soldier.

Q. To assist soldiers in meeting the requirements prescribed in AR 600-9, weight screening tables are used. The screening table weight is based on what two considerations?
A. Height and age (separate tables for male and female).

Q. What is the suggested maximum screening table weight to help soldiers in targeting their personal weight at a level which will minimize the probability of exceeding the screening table weight ceiling?
A. A weight that is 5% below your maximum table weight.

Q. It is a requirement that all TDY and PCS orders contain what statement in regards to weight control?
A. "You are responsible for reporting to your next duty station/school in satisfactory physical condition, able to pass the APFT and meet weight standards."

Q. What is the responsibility of health care personnel regarding weight control?
A. (1) Assist commanders and supervisors by providing weight reduction counseling to individuals who are overweight.
   (2) Identify those individuals who have a pathological condition requiring medical treatment.
   (3) Evaluate overweight soldiers when:
   - the soldier has a medical limitation (profile).
   - the soldier is pregnant.
   - requested by commander.
   - separation is being considered for failure to make satisfactory progress in a weight control program.
   - six months prior to ETS.

Q. How often should soldiers be weighed?
A. As a minimum, personnel will be weighed when they take the APFT or at least

every 6 months.

Q. If circumstances prevent the weighing of soldiers immediately following the APFT, when can they be weighed?
A. Any time within 30 days of the APFT.

Q. What is the maximum allowable percent body fat standard for your age?
A.

Age Group	Male	Female
17-20	20%	30%
21-27	22%	32%
28-39	24%	34%
40+	26%	36%

NOTE: These figures reflect interim change # IO1, dtd 4 Mar 94.

Q. Explain what is meant by "body composition".
A. The human body is composed of two major elements: lean body mass (which includes muscle, bone, and essential organ tissue) and body fat. Body fat is expressed as a percentage of total body weight that is fat. For example, an individual who weighs 200 pounds and 18% body fat has 36 pounds of fat. Women generally have a higher percentage of body fat than men because of genetic and hormonal differences; thus, body fat standards differ among men and women by age groups.

Q. In regards to percent body fat, all personnel are encouraged to achieve the more stringent Department of Defense-wide goal of what?
A. 20% for males; 26% for females.

Q. Name three limitations on personnel that are overweight.
A. (1) Nonpromotable.
(2) Will not be authorized to attend professional military or civilian schooling.
(3) Will not be assigned to command positions.

Q. When is a determination of percent body fat required to be made on personnel?
A. (1) When their body weight exceeds the screening table weight.
(2) When the unit commander or supervisor determines that the individual's appearance suggests that body fat is excessive.

Q. What is the determination of percent body fat on a soldier commonly called?
A. A "Tape" test.

Q. Who is authorized to "tape" a soldier?
A. Company or similar level commanders (or their designee) in accordance with standard methods prescribed in Appendix B of AR 600-9. Soldiers will be measured by individuals of the same gender. If this cannot be accomplished, a female soldier will be present when males measure females.

Q. How many people should be utilized in the taping of soldiers?
A. Two, one to place the tape measure and determine measurements, the other to assure proper placement and tension of the tape, as well as to record the measurement on the worksheet.

Q. How many times is each measurement required to be made?
A. Three times (if there is greater than 1/4" difference between the measurements, then continue measuring until you have three measurements within 1/4" of each other).

Q. Tape measures used for taping should be made of what?

WEIGHT CONTROL
AR 600-9

A. A non-stretchable material, preferably fiberglass. Cloth or steel tapes are unacceptable (cloth measuring tapes will stretch with usage and most steel tapes do not conform to body surfaces).

Q. Screening table weights and heights are measured to the nearest _______ while tape measurements are to the nearest _________.
A. pound/inch; 1/4-inch.

Q. What circumference sites are used for taping male and female soldiers?
A. Male - abdomen and neck.
Female - Neck, forearm, wrist, and hip.

Q. What three things **must** happen when a soldier is determined to be overweight?
A. (1) Weight reduction counseling by health care personnel.
(2) Entered into appropriate Weight Control Program by unit commanders.
(3) Flagged under the provisions of AR 600-31.

Q. When does enrollment in a Weight Control Program begin?
A. On the day that the soldier is informed by the unit commander that he/she has been entered in a weight control program.

Q. What is the required weight loss rate for soldiers in the Army Weight Control Program?
A. 3 to 8 pounds per month.

Q. How often should soldiers in the Weight Control Program weigh in?
A. Monthly - to measure progress.

Q. What happens if a soldier is unable to make satisfactory progress in the weight control program after any two consecutive weigh-ins or after a total period of dieting and/or exercise for 6 months?
A. The soldier will be referred by the commander or supervisor to health care personnel for evaluation or reevaluation. If health care personnel are unable to determine a medical reason for lack of weight loss - and if the individual is not in compliance with the body fat standards - the commander or supervisor will inform the individual in writing (formal counseling) that:

- Progress is unsatisfactory.
- Initiation of separation proceedings are being considered as per AR 635-200.

Q. When are soldiers removed from the Weight Control Program?
A. As soon as the body fat standard is achieved. **The screening table weight will not be used to remove soldiers from a Weight Control Program.** Removal of suspension of favorable personnel action will also be accomplished at this time.

Q. What must happen to a soldier that is determined to be overweight within 36 months of removal from a Weight Control Program?
A. (a) If it is within 12 months from the date of the previous removal from the program and no underlying or associated disease process is found as the cause of the condition, the individual will be subject to separation from the service as per AR 635-200.
(b) After the 12th month, but within 36 months from the date of the previous removal from the program, and no underlying or associated disease process is found as the cause of the condition, the individual will be allowed 90 days to meet the standards. Personnel who meet the standard within 90 days will be removed from the program. All others will be subject to separation from the service.

WEIGHT CONTROL
AR 600-9

Q. Can personnel that are overweight reenlist or extend their enlistment?
A. Not without an exception to policy approved by commander exercising GCM authority.

Q. What should a soldier be wearing when he/she is "taped"?
A. Standard PT uniform (shorts and T-shirt, without shoes).

MILITARY LEADERSHIP
FM 22-100/TC 22-6

Q. What is considered to be the Army's basic manual on leadership?
A. FM 22-100, Military Leadership.

Q. What are the two purposes of FM 22-100?
A. (1) To provide an overview of Army leadership doctrine.
(2) To prescribe the leadership necessary to be effective in peace and war.

Q. A trained and ready Army has as its foundation, competent and confident leaders. We develop such leaders through a dynamic process consisting of three equally important pillars designed to provide education, training, and experience that enable leaders to develop the necessary skills, knowledge, and attitudes. What are these three "Pillars of Leader Development"?
A. (1) Institutional training
(2) Operational assignments
(3) Self-development

Q. Army leaders must learn to fulfill the expectations of all soldiers, including other leaders. What are the "seven fundamental expectations" addressed by FM 22-100?
A. (1) Demonstrate tactical and technical competence.
(2) Teach subordinates.
(3) Be a good listener.
(4) Treat soldiers with dignity and respect.
(5) Stress basics.
(6) Set the example.
(7) Set and enforce standards.

Q. What is the fundamental mission of our Army?
A. To deter war and, if deterrence fails, to win in combat.

Q. The Army's leadership doctrine suggests that leaders must satisfy four leadership requirements. What are they?
A. (1) Lead in peace to be prepared for war.
(2) Develop individual leaders.
(3) Develop leadership teams.
(4) Decentralize.

Q. What does "decentralization" mean?
A. The release of authority for execution from senior to subordinate levels.

Q. What are the two leadership "modes"?
A. (1) Direct: junior level leadership (ie NCOs).
(2) Indirect: senior level leadership (ie Officers).

Q. Five manuals contain the Army's Leadership Doctrine. What are these manuals?
A. - FM 22-100, Military Leadership
- FM 22-101, Leadership Counseling
- FM 22-102, Soldier Team Development
- FM 22-103, Leadership and Command at Senior Levels
- FM 25-100, Training the Force

Q. What is meant by the term "leadership"?
A. The process of influencing others to accomplish the mission by providing purpose, direction, and motivation.

MILITARY LEADERSHIP
FM 22-100/TC 22-6

Q. What is the "Battlefield Challenge" for today's military leaders?
A. To inspire soldiers to do things against their natural will - to carry out missions for the greater good of the unit, the Army, and the country.

Q. The four major factors of leadership are always present and affect the actions you should take and when you should take them. What are the four leadership factors?
A. (1) The led
(2) The leader
(3) The situation
(4) Communications

Q. The 11 principles of Army leadership were developed in a 1948 leadership study and included in leadership doctrine in 1951. They are universal and represent fundamental truths that have stood the test of time. What are they?
A. (1) Know yourself and seek self-improvement.
(2) Be technically and tactically proficient.
(3) Seek responsibility and take responsibility for your actions.
(4) Make sound and timely decisions.
(5) Set the example.
(6) Know your soldiers and look out for their well-being.
(7) Keep your subordinates informed.
(8) Develop a sense of responsibility in your subordinates.
(9) Ensure the task is understood, supervised, and accomplished.
(10) Build the team.
(11) Employ your unit in accordance with its capabilities.

Q. What is a "leadership attribute"?
A. A quality, characteristic, knowledge, or skill seen as belonging to or representing someone or something.

Q. A soldier carries out the process of leadership by applying his/her leadership attributes. Name the six leadership attributes and give a brief definition of each.
A. (1) Beliefs: assumptions or convictions you hold as true about some thing, concept, or person.
(2) Values: attitudes about the worth or importance of people, concepts, or things.
(3) Ethics/Norms: Ethics are principles or standards that guide professionals to do the moral or right thing. Norms are the rules or laws normally based on agreed-upon beliefs and values that members of a group follow to live in harmony.
(4) Character: the sum total of your personality traits and the link between your values and your behavior.
(5) Knowledge: what you know about human nature and the technical and tactical elements of your job.
(6) Skills: the ability to do something well.

Q. What three attributes merge to form the basis of your character?
A. Beliefs, values, and ethics/norms.

Q. What are the four individual values that all soldiers (leaders and led) are expected to possess?
A. Courage, candor, commitment, and competence.

Q. "Candor" is being frank, open, honest, and sincere with your fellow soldiers, seniors, and peers. It is an expression of personal integrity. If

handled properly, disagreeing with others and presenting your point of view are not wrong. What three points should you always remember when "expressing your views"?
A. (1) Select the right time and place to offer your criticism or advice.
(2) Do not criticize a plan without giving a constructive alternative.
(3) Recognize that when your leader has made the final decision, you must end your discussion and support legal and proper orders even if you do not personally agree with them.

Q. Norms can be classified into what two categories?
A. Formal and informal.

Q. What is the key to building character?
A. Having the honesty to determine your own character weaknesses.

Q. What are the four steps to building a strong and honorable character?
A. (1) Assess the present strength of your values and character.
(2) Determine what values you want to promote.
(3) Seek out missions and situations that support developing such character.
(4) Select a role model who demonstrates the values and character you are trying to develop.

Q. What is "The Professional Army Ethic"?
A. It sets the moral context for service to the nation and inspires the sense of purpose necessary to preserve the nation, even by using military force.

Q. What FM contains the doctrinal statement of the professional Army ethic?
A. FM 100-1

Q. The four elements of the professional Army ethic contain the values that guide the way you must lead. What are they?
A. (1) Loyalty to the Nation, the Army, and the Unit
(2) Duty: a legal or moral obligation to do what should be done without being told to do it.
(3) Selfless service
(4) Integrity: being honest and upright, avoiding deception, and living the values you suggest for your subordinates.

Q. Every leader has three general ethical responsibilities. What are they?
A. (1) Be a role model.
(2) Develop subordinates ethically.
(3) Avoid creating ethical dilemmas for your subordinates.

Q. What is an "ethical dilemma"?
A. A situation that results when two or more deeply held values collide.

Q. What is the ethical decision-making process?
A. (1) Interpret the situation. What is the ethical dilemma?
(2) Analyze all the factors and forces that relate to the dilemma.
(3) Choose the course of action you believe will best serve the nation.
(4) Implement the course of action you have chosen.

Q. The factors and forces that will influence the ethical decision-making process depend on the dilemma. What are six principle influencing forces or factors that you should be concerned with?
A. - Legal standards
- Basic national values
- Unit operating values
- Individual values

MILITARY LEADERSHIP
FM 22-100/TC 22-6

- Traditional Army values - Institutional pressures

Q. Describe the BE-KNOW-DO characteristics of a good military leader.
A. (1) As a leader, you must BE:
- a person of strong and honorable character
- committed to the professional Army ethic
- an example of individual values
- able to resolve complex ethical dilemmas

(2) As a leader, you must KNOW:
- the four factors of leadership and how they affect each other
- standards
- yourself
- human nature
- your job (technical proficiency)
- your unit

(3) As a leader, you must DO:
- provide purpose
- provide direction
- provide motivation

Q. What are the nine principles of war?
A. (1) Objective: direct every military operation towards a clearly defined, decisive, and attainable objective.
(2) Offensive: seize, retain, and exploit the initiative.
(3) Mass: concentrate combat power at the decisive place and time.
(4) Economy of Force: allocate minimum essential combat power to secondary efforts.
(5) Maneuver: place the enemy in a position of disadvantage through the flexible application of combat power.
(6) Unity of Command: for every objective, ensure unity of effort under one responsible commander.
(7) Security: never permit the enemy to acquire an unexpected advantage.
(8) Surprise: strike the enemy at a time, at a place, or in a manner for which he is unprepared.
(9) Simplicity: prepare clear, uncomplicated plans and clear, concise orders to ensure thorough understanding.

Q. List seven ways that leaders provide direction.
A. - knowing and maintaining standards
- setting goals
- planning
- making decisions and solving problems
- supervising and evaluating
- teaching, coaching, and counseling
- training

Q. Goal setting is a critical part of leadership. What four key points should you remember when developing goals?
A. (1) Goals should be realistic and attainable.
(2) Goals should lead to improved combat readiness.
(3) Subordinates should be involved in the goal-setting process.
(4) You must develop a program to achieve each goal.

Q. What is meant by "backward planning" and what are the three steps?
A. (1) Determine the basics: what, how, and when.
(2) Identify tasks you want to accomplish and establish a sequence for them.
(3) Develop a schedule to accomplish the tasks you have identified. Start

with the last task to be accomplished and work back to the present time.

Q. What are the five steps in the problem-solving process?
A. (1) Recognize and define the problem.
   (2) Gather facts and make assumptions.
   (3) Develop possible solutions.
   (4) Analyze and compare the possible solutions.
   (5) Select the best solution.

Q. What is "stress"?
A. The body's response to a demand placed on it; may be physical or mental.

Q. What is "battle fatigue"?
A. A psychoneurotic reaction that can develop in an individual from stress in a combat environment.

Q. What are some of the indicators of battle fatigue?
A.
- tension: aches, pains, trembling, and fidgeting
- jumpiness at sudden sounds or movement
- cold sweat: dry mouth, pale skin, eyes hard to focus
- pounding heart: may feel dizzy or light-headed
- feeling out of breath
- upset stomach: may throw up
- diarrhea or constipation: frequent urination
- fatigue: feel tired, drained; takes an effort to move
- distant, haunted "1,000-yard" stare
- anxiety: keyed up, worrying, expecting the worst
- irritability: swearing, complaining, easily bothered
- difficulty paying attention, remembering details
- trouble sleeping, awakened by bad dreams
- grief: tearful, crying for dead or wounded buddies
- feeling bad about mistakes or what had to be done
- anger: feeling let down by leaders or others in unit
- beginning to lose confidence in self and unit

Q. What is perhaps the most powerful thing you can do for your soldiers in treating battle fatigue?
A. Look calm and remain in control. Also, when the tactical situation and safety permit, ensure that you and your soldiers-
- sleep
- drink plenty of fluids
- continue to eat normal portions of food
- continue to conduct training
- practice good personal hygiene
- talk about what happened
- share grief
- keep busy when not resting

Q. What are the six actions a leader must take to defeat battle stresses?
A. (1) Lead your unit
   (2) Build cohesion
   (3) Develop confidence
   (4) Train your unit
   (5) Develop a physically fit unit
   (6) Develop a winning attitude

Q. What is the best way to develop confidence in your soldiers?

A. Through realistic training and simulated combat experience.

Q. In 1989, the NCO Leader Development Task Force developed nine leadership competencies and the skills, knowledge, and attitudes NCOs should possess at each rank level. What are these nine "leadership competencies"?
A. (1) Communications
(2) Supervision
(3) Teaching and counseling
(4) Soldier team development
(5) technical and tactical proficiency
(6) decision making
(7) planning
(8) use of available systems
(9) professional ethics

Q. The 1989 NCO Leader Development Task Force found that though skills and knowledge are progressive and sequential throughout an NCOs career, the attitudes necessary to BE an effective leader remain the same, regardless of rank. This Task Force identified 14 attitudes common to all effective NCO leaders. What are they? (TC 22-6)
A. (1) Enforce standards
(2) Set the example
(3) Accomplish the mission
(4) Take care of soldiers
(5) Be dedicated and selfless
(6) Accept responsibilities for self and subordinates
(7) Obey lawful orders
(8) Be honest and courageous
(9) Maintain physical and mental toughness
(10) Show competence and self-confidence
(11) Act fairly and equitably with subordinates
(12) Be loyal to the nation and Constitution
(13) Be loyal to superiors and subordinates
(14) Show initiative and self-motivation

Q. What is meant by "effective communications"?
A. When others understand exactly what you are trying to tell them and when you understand exactly what they are trying to tell you.

Q. What is meant by "supervision"?
A. Controlling, directing, evaluating, coordinating, and planning the efforts of subordinates in the accomplishment of a task.

Q. What is the effect of <u>oversupervision</u>? Of <u>undersupervision</u>?
A. Resentment; frustration.

Q. How do you determine the amount of supervision needed to accomplish a task?
A. By considering your soldiers' competence, motivation, and commitment to perform the task.

Q. What is a "leadership style"?
A. It is the personal manner and approach a soldier uses when leading; it is the way leaders directly interact with their subordinates.

Q. What are the three basic styles of military leadership?
A. (1) Directing: tells subordinates what to do, how to do it, where to do it, and when it is to be done and then closely supervises to ensure that the

instructions were followed.

(2) Participating: involves subordinates in determining what to do and how to do it.

(3) Delegating: delegates problem-solving and decision-making authority to a subordinate or to a group of subordinates.

Q. What style of leadership should you use?
A. There is no "best" leadership style. The style you use should depend on your analysis of the four factors of leadership (leader, led, situation, and communications) at any given time. Also, ask yourself the following questions:
- How competent, motivated, and committed are my soldiers to accomplishing the task?
- Have they done this before?
- Were they successful?
- Will they need my supervision, direction, or encouragement to accomplish the mission to standards?

NOTE: You, as a leader, must develop the flexibility to use all three styles of leadership; further, you must develop the judgment to choose the style that best meets the situation and the needs of the subordinate.

Q. What steps should be taken when assuming a leadership position?
A. Plan every action, evaluate your unit, and establish your own policies and procedures.

Q. In the Army we have "commissioned" and "noncommissioned" officers. What exactly is meant by the term "commission"?
A. Commissions are legal instruments by which the President appoints and exercises direct control over qualified people to act as his legal agents and help him carry out his duties. The Army retains this "direct-agent" relationship with the President through its commissioned officers. NCOs do not derive authority from commissions. Rather, officers delegate the authority NCOs need to get the mission accomplished.

Q. Explain the relationship between the responsibilities of officers and noncommissioned officers.
A. **The OFFICER:**
- Commands, establishes policy, and manages the Army.
- Focuses on collective training leading to mission accomplishment.
- Is primarily involved with units and unit operations.
- Concentrates on unit effectiveness and readiness.
- Concentrates on the standards of performance, training, and professional development of officers and NCOs.

The NONCOMMISSIONED OFFICER:
- Conducts the daily business of the Army within established policy.
- Focuses on individual training that leads to mission capability.
- Is primarily involved with individual soldiers and team leading.
- Ensures subordinate NCOs and soldiers, with their personal equipment, are prepared to function as effective unit members.
- Concentrates on the standards of performance, training, and professional development of subordinate NCOs and soldiers.

Q. The Army has but one chain of command. What other channel of communication parallels and reinforces the chain of command?
A. The NCO support channel.

Q. The NCO Support Channel consists of whom?

MILITARY LEADERSHIP
FM 22-100/TC 22-6

A. Begins with the CSM and ends with section chiefs, squad leaders, or team leaders.

Q. What is the NCO support channel primarily used for?
A. Passing information, issuing orders, and accomplishing routine, but important, missions.

Q. There are three formal channels of communication in the Army. Two have already been mentioned. What is the third?
A. Staff and technical channels.

Q. What is meant by "authority"?
A. The legitimate power of leaders to direct subordinates or to take action within the scope of their responsibility.

Q. Where does an NCO derive his/her authority?
A. Legal authority begins with the Constitution which divides authority for the military between Congress and the President. Congress has the authority to make laws to govern the Army; the President has the authority to command the Army as Commander in Chief. The President exercises his authority through commissioned officers (as described previously) who, in turn, delegate the necessary authority to NCOs in order to accomplish the mission.

Q. What are the two types of authority?
A. (1) Command authority: can come from regulation or laws, but primarily originates with the President. Leaders have command authority when they fill positions requiring the direction and control of other members of the Army. It is restricted to the soldiers and facilities in their unit.
(2) General Military Authority: the authority extended to all soldiers to take action. It originates in oaths of office, law, rank structure, tradition, and regulation.

Q. When you are responsible for something, you are liable, or accountable, for the outcome. What are the two categories of responsibility?
A. (1) Individual responsibility: every soldier is held accountable for their own personal, individual conduct. It is assumed when you take the oath of enlistment.
(2) Command responsibility: refers to a commander's collective or organizational accountability of a unit. It encompasses being held accountable for how well a unit accomplished, or failed to accomplish, its organizational goals or missions.

Q. What is "developmental leadership assessment"?
A. A process used to improve a person's ability to lead.

Q. What are your two leadership assessment responsibilities?
A. (1) Assess your own leadership performance. Identify your strengths and weaknesses and work to improve yourself.
(2) Assess your subordinates' leadership performance, give them feedback, and help them overcome their weaknesses.

Q. A complete and accurate leadership assessment includes feedback from what six sources?
A. - the person himself
- leaders
- peers
- subordinates

- close friends and family members
- trained leadership assessors (ie, from service schools)

Q. What are the two basic responsibilities of a military leader? (NCO CREED)
A. Accomplish the mission and look out for the well-being of the soldiers.

NOTE: All of the information in TC 22-6, "The Army Noncommissioned Officer Guide", can be found in FM 22-100 with the exception of SKAs (Skills, Knowledge, and Attitudes). FM 22-100 touches on this subject in several instances but TC 22-6 breaks it down. The 14 attitudes common to all effective NCO leaders are covered in this section (Page 7). The skills and knowledge required of NCOs at different stages in their careers are covered in detail in TC 22-6 but will not be covered here. Keep in mind that the necessary skills and knowledge center around the nine competencies (see page 6).

THE FOLLOWING INFORMATION, ALTHOUGH NOT CONTAINED IN FM 22-100 OR TC 22-6, IS INCLUDED FOR YOUR REVIEW. THE MAJORITY OF THIS MATERIAL WAS OBTAINED THROUGH PUBLICATIONS OF THE SERGEANTS MAJOR ACADEMY.

Q. In what Army publications would you look for information about the "Duties, Responsibilities, and Authority of Noncommissioned Officers"?
A. AR 600-20, FM 22-100, TC 22-6.

Q. Who is the only person who performs as both a member of the Chain of Command and the NCO Support Channel?
A. The section, squad, or team leader.

Q. What are the three general categories of duties? Explain them.
A. (1) Specified duties: charged by ARs, DA General Orders, the UCMJ, and other publications.
(2) Directed duties: given verbally or in writing via LOIs, SOPs, memorandums, policy statements, etc (ie. CQ, guard duty, SDNCO, etc).
(3) Implied duties: neither specified nor directed but are all those other duties which we must perform in order to get the job done better and assist in keeping the unit functioning at an optimum level. In most cases it is dependent on individual initiative.

Q. What are the four SPECIFIC Noncommissioned Officer responsibilities?
A. (1) That each member of the unit is trained to proficiency in his or her MOS as prescribed in the appropriate Soldier's Manual.
(2) That all government property issued to members of their unit be properly maintained and accounted for at all times, and that discrepancies are reported promptly.
(3) That, while in a duty status, they be ready at all times to report the location and activity of all members of their unit.
(4) That the unit is trained to function in its primary mission role.

Q. What are "leadership traits"?
A. Personal qualities that will allow a leader to gain willing obedience, confidence, respect, and loyal cooperation in the accomplishment of the mission.

Q. What are the 19 leadership traits?
A. (1) Initiative: the ability to take actions, without waiting for orders or supervision, that you believe will accomplish unit goals.

(2) Will: the perseverance to accomplish a goal, regardless of seemingly insurmountable obstacles.
(3) Integrity: utter sincerity, honesty, and candor.
(4) Self-discipline: forcing yourself to do your duty regardless of how tired or unwilling you may be.
(5) Humility: the ability to honestly admit mistakes or imperfections in your character, knowledge, and skills.
(6) Tact: a keen sense of what to do or say that will allow positive interaction.
(7) Assertiveness: taking charge when necessary, making your ideas known, helping to define the problem, and getting others to do the right thing to solve the problem.
(8) Bearing: a person's posture, overall appearance, and manner of physical movement. It is an outward display of a person's inner feelings, fears, and overall inner confidence.
(9) Endurance: mental, spiritual, and physical stamina.
(10) Self-improvement: reading, studying, seeking challenging assignments, and working to strengthen beliefs, values, ethics, character, knowledge, and skills.
(11) Sense of Humor: not taking yourself too seriously; contributing to the laughter and morale of the people around you.
(12) Empathy or Compassion: being sensitive to the feelings, values, interests, and well-being of others.
(13) Decisiveness: the ability to make a good decision at the right time.
(14) Confidence: the assurance that you and your soldiers will be successful in whatever you do.
(15) Creativity: the ability to think of new ideas, programs, and solutions to problems - ingenuity.
(16) Coolness under stress: a confident calmness in looks and behavior.
(17) Maturity: the sense of responsibility a person develops.
(18) Flexibility: the capability to make timely and appropriate changes in thinking, plans, or methods when you see, or when others convince you, that there is a better way.
(19) Justice: the fair treatment of all people regardless of race, color, creed, gender, etc.

Q. What are the four fundamental steps in supervising subordinates in the accomplishment of a task?
A. (1) Assign the task
(2) Set standards
(3) Check progress
(4) Determine if standards have been met (follow-up).

Q. What is the definition of a "Combat Order"?
A. Written or oral communications that convey information and instruction that pertain to combat operations.

Q. What are the types of combat orders at the squad/section level?
A. Operation Orders, Warning Orders, Fragmentary Orders.

Q. What are the five elements of the 5-paragraph Operations Order (OPORD)?
A. Situation, Mission, Execution, Service Support (logistics), and Command & Signal.

Q. What is the purpose of a Fragmentary Order (FRAGO)?
A. It provides changes to existing operation orders.

MILITARY LEADERSHIP
FM 22-100/TC 22-6

Q. What are the eight troop-leading steps?
A. (1) Receive the mission
(2) Issue the warning order
(3) Make a tentative plan
(4) Start necessary movement
(5) Reconnaissance
(6) Complete the plan
(7) Issue the complete order
(8) Supervise

Q. What are the five basic rules of combat?
A. Move, shoot, communicate, secure, sustain.

Q. Can you delegate responsibility?
A. No, only authority can be delegated.

Q. List four indicators of unit effectiveness (unit leadership).
A. Morale, discipline, esprit de corps, and proficiency.

Q. List five things that affect a unit's morale.
A. Mess, military justice, mail, supply, and living conditions.

Q. What is a basic prerequisite to good leadership?
A. An understanding of human behavior (needs).

Q. What are the essential ingredients in a proper senior/subordinate relationship?
A. Mutual respect and restraint from undue familiarity.

Q. What are five roles of a leader?
A. Teacher, trainer, administrator, counselor, and commander.

LEADERSHIP COUNSELING
FM 22-101

Q. What FM covers "Leadership Counseling"?
A. FM 22-101

Q. What is "counseling"?
A. The process of communicating advice, instruction, or judgment with the intent of influencing a person's behavior or performance.

Q. What are the principal objectives of counseling?
A. Developing the counselee, improving well-being, and resolving problems.

Q. FM 22-101 contains suggestions and guidelines on military counseling. There is only one <u>absolute</u> requirement with respect to counseling. What is it?
A. That leaders regularly counsel their soldiers.

Q. The traditional leadership principles, a basis for the practice of good leadership, are also necessary for effective counseling. What are the 11 leadership principles?
A. (1) Know yourself and seek self-improvement.
(2) Be technically and tactically proficient.
(3) Seek responsibility and take responsibility for your actions.
(4) Make sound and timely decisions.
(5) Set the example.
(6) Know your soldiers and look out for their well-being.
(7) Keep your soldiers informed.
(8) Develop a sense of responsibility in your subordinates.
(9) Ensure that the task is understood, supervised, and accomplished.
(10) Train your soldiers as a team ("Build the team", FM 22-100).
(11) Employ your unit in accordance with its capabilities.

Q. In peacetime, all leaders are responsible for developing and preparing subordinates to assume higher positions in wartime. Counseling is one means of doing this. A good leader will counsel subordinates to do what six things?
A. (1) Praise and reward good performance.
(2) Develop teamwork.
(3) Inform soldiers on how well or how poorly they are performing.
(4) Assist soldiers to reach required standards.
(5) Cause soldiers to set personal and professional goals.
(6) Help soldiers resolve personal problems.

Q. A leader's efforts to develop soldiers should accomplish what four objectives?
A. (1) Cause the soldier to recognize the strengths or shortcomings and define any problems.
(2) Have the soldier determine possible courses of action based on facts, and then cause him to select one.
(3) Cause the soldier to actually take the appropriate action.
(4) Have the soldier assume full responsibility for his decisions and actions.

Q. How frequently a leader counsels or becomes involved in referring soldiers to seniors in the chain of command or to agencies outside the unit is determined by what four things?
A. Rank, leadership position, experience, and skill.

Q. Of the leader traits or characteristics promoting effective counseling, what is considered to be the most important?

LEADERSHIP COUNSELING
FM 22-101

A. A caring attitude.

Q. To be an effective counselor, leaders must set a proper ____________.
A. Example.

Q. In developing proper attitude and behavior, the leader should be aware of the characteristic aspects of effective counseling. What are the six characteristic aspects of effective counseling?
A. - Flexibility - Support
- Respect - Motivation
- Communication - Purpose

Q. What is "power"?
A. Power is the ability, either physical, mental, or moral, to have positive control over the actions of others.

Q. What are the five types of power?
A. (1) Legitimate power: based on the soldiers' perceptions that the leader's rank or position automatically gives him certain rights and authority.
(2) Reward power: based on the perception that the leader controls rewards that soldiers value and believe will be given for satisfactory performance.
(3) Coercive power: based upon the perception that the leader can and will punish soldiers who do not obey.
(4) Referent power: based on soldiers identifying with their leader.
(5) Expert power: based on the soldiers' perception that the leader has special knowledge, skills, or needed information that relates to the task to be performed.

Q. A leader often uses influence when directing subordinates. Influence may take many forms - depending on what is necessary to develop the subordinates and to meet the needs of the unit. List seven common "forms of influence".
A. Mapping alternatives, recommending, advising, persuading, urging, commanding, and punishing.

Q. What are the three approaches to counseling?
A. (1) Directive: counselor-centered; assumes the leader has the skills and knowledge to assess the situation and offer courses of action.
(2) Nondirective: soldier-centered; counselor causes the soldier to take responsibility for solving the problem.
(3) Combined: leader uses parts of the directive and nondirective approaches.

Q. Identify the following approaches to counseling:
(1) Allows both the leader and the soldier to participate in defining, analyzing, and solving the problem.
(2) Provides short-term solutions; counselor states the problem, identifies the cause, offers explanations, and lists the options available; counselor gives advice, offers solutions, and tells the soldier what must be done.
(3) Usually more relaxed and focuses on self-discovery; soldier has the opportunity to work out solutions to a problem through personal insight, judgment, and realization of facts.
(4) Quickest method; good for immature/insecure soldiers; tends to treat symptoms, not problems.
(5) Slowest method; requires greatest counselor skills.
(6) Blends leader's ability and personality to fit the situation; the most frequent approach to counseling.
A. (1) Combined; (2) Directive; (3) Nondirective; (4) Directive; (5)

Nondirective; (6) Combined.

Q. How do you determine which counseling approach to use?
A. The type of problem, personality of the soldier, physical surroundings, and time available will influence the selection of approach to be used. Leaders must be flexible; effective counselors use a uniquely different approach with each soldier.

Q. How are counseling skills developed/acquired?
A. Counseling skills are developed by studying human behavior, knowing the kinds of problems that affect soldiers, and becoming good at dealing with soldiers. They are acquired through study and through the practical application of counseling techniques.

Q. What are the three "groups" of basic counseling skills?
A. (1) Listening and watching skills: involve the counselor concentrating on what the soldier says and does.
(2) Responding skills: actions the leader takes to check his understanding of what the soldier is saying.
(3) Guiding skills: using problem-solving and decision-making skills to help a soldier reach a solution.

Q. Spoken words by themselves are only part of the message. What other "actions" should you be aware of when using proper "listening and watching" skills?
A. The tone of voice, the inflection, the pauses, the speed, and the look on the soldier's face, are all parts of the total message.

Q. Active listening is concentrating on what the soldier is saying. What are some elements of active listening that a counselor should consider?
A. Eye contact, posture, head nod, facial expressions, and verbal behavior.

Q. List four ways that responding skills can be used.
A. By questioning, summarizing, interpreting, and informing.

Q. What are the seven basic problem solving steps?
A. (1) Identify the problem.
(2) Gather information.
(3) Develop courses of action.
(4) Analyze and compare courses of action.
(5) Make a decision; select a course of action.
(6) Make a plan.
(7) Implement the plan.

Q. What are the five "reasons" for counseling (5 types of counseling)?
A. (1) Reception and integration: to foster soldier and team development by properly integrating new unit members or those returning after a long absence.
(2) Performance: to inform soldiers about their duties or appearance, explain how to meet required standards, and give honest feedback on actual performance.
(3) Personal: to help soldiers solve their own problems or to refer them to those who can and then to follow up to assure that soldiers are helped.
(4) Discipline: to improve soldier performance by correcting disruptive behavior and inappropriate actions.
(5) Professional growth and guidance: to guide subordinates' professional growth and inform them about opportunities for future service.

LEADERSHIP COUNSELING
FM 22-101

Q. Reception and integration counseling must accomplish two major transition objectives. What are they?
A. (1) Identify and resolve any problems or concerns that the soldier has before they reach a crisis.
(2) Set the standards.

Q. A complete reception and integration counseling program should do what 11 things?
A. (1) Resolve problems with personal affairs.
(2) Introduce the new soldier to peers and the leaders in the chain of command.
(3) Explain all of the procedures for in-processing and the schedule for accomplishing them.
(4) Explain the unit's history and traditions, missions, and activities.
(5) Explain how the new soldier's duty assignment is important to the unit and its mission.
(6) Explain the standards of conduct and the performance expected of the soldier in a new duty assignment.
(7) Explain the unit's policies on leaves and passes, duty rosters, promotions, and job performance evaluations.
(8) Explain opportunities and facilities for personal and professional improvement and development.
(9) Inform the new arrival of the facilities available for spiritual needs, conveniences, and off-duty recreation.
(10) Inform the new arrival of the functions and locations of assistance agencies.
(11) Explain the local customs and off-limits areas.

Q. How long after initial reception and integration counseling should you wait to perform a brief, informal follow-up to insure that the soldier has been completely integrated into the unit?
A. 30 days.

Q. Leaders should select soldiers for sponsorship that are experienced and knowledgeable and who will have a positive influence on new arrivals. What other criteria should be considered when choosing a sponsor?
A. Should have as much as possible in common with the new arrival, preferably of the same rank, MOS, and marital status.

Q. What are some conditions under a leader's control that stimulate learning and motivation?
A.
- Accurate evaluation of performance.
- Rapport between soldier and leader.
- Clear and understandable communication between leader and subordinate.
- Mutual agreement concerning performance areas where improvement is required.
- Specific actions for improving performance.
- Feedback on progress.
- Expectation of success.

Q. Successful personal counseling follows two basic guidelines. What are they?
A. (1) The leader must be committed to the principle that every soldier, regardless of rank or duty assignment, has the right to be heard.
(2) The leader should realize that relatively mature and healthy persons can look at their personal problems intelligently and reach satisfactory solutions.

LEADERSHIP COUNSELING
FM 22-101

Q. Although soldiers have the right to contact certain outside agencies on their own (such as the chaplain or inspector general), outside help should normally be obtained by using the chain of command. There are three reasons for this. What are they?
A. (1) The soldier must have permission to be absent from the unit.
(2) Many problems can be solved at company or battery level if they are known.
(3) The commander must be kept informed of problems or complaints in his unit.

Q. What is every leader's responsibility regarding the use of outside support agencies?
A. The leader, as counselor, must know the location and function of all available assistance agencies and know when to refer a subordinate to them through the chain of command.

Q. A variety of support agencies exist in and around most military communities. Describe some of them.
A. (1) Adjutant General (AG): provides personnel and administrative services support. These services include orders production, ID cards, retirement and survivor assistance, assignments, reassignments, deferments, and in/out processing. In overseas areas the Adjutant General provides postal services as well as additional services such as passport processing.
(2) Alcohol and Drug Control Officer (ADCO): strives to educate the entire military community, including family members and DA civilians, on alcohol and drug abuse and on personal roles in rehabilitation and prevention.
(3) American Red Cross (ARC): assists with communications between the soldier and his family in emergency and compassionate situations. It provides emergency financial assistance, discharge and review board counseling, and many volunteer service activities. Programs often include youth as well as adult courses in health, nursing, safety, first aid, and swimming.
(4) Army Community Services (ACS): provides assistance to military families through its information and referral services, budget and indebtedness counseling, household item loan closet, information on other military posts, and welcome packets to new arrivals.
(5) Army Education Center (AEC): provides services and programs for continuing education and individual learning. An MOS reference library is often operated to support individual soldier development.
(6) Army Emergency Relief (AER): gives financial assistance through interest-free loans or grants in situations involving medical expenses, family member funerals, required travel, basic living necessities, disaster assistance, or privation of family members.
(7) Career Counselors: provide current information on prerequisites for reenlistment and selective reenlistment bonuses and explain reenlistment options. Also a good source of information on service benefits and programs.
(8) Chaplains: are familiar with support activities in the local community. They provide enrichment programs, couples' communications seminars, religious retreats, parenting skills training, as well as other programs dealing with human issues, including sacramental rites and ordinances according to their denomination.
(9) Claims Section, Staff Judge Advocate (SJA): handles claims for and against the government, most often those for loss and damage to household goods. It processes claims involving medical expenses of the Army for treatment of soldiers and their families caused by the negligence of others.
(10) Community Counseling Center (CCC): provides alcohol and drug abuse prevention and control programs (ADAPCP) for the installation. These programs are directed and controlled by the ADCO (see above).

(11) Community Health Nurse: provides many preventive health care services including home and office visits, consultations, and group health instruction.

(12) Community Mental Health Service: provides assistance to soldiers and their family members through a professional staff of psychiatrists, social workers, psychologists, and behavioral science specialists. They conduct counseling treatment services, psychotherapy, crisis intervention, evaluations, and consultations.

(13) Equal Opportunity Staff Office (EO): is available to service members and their families for matters involving discrimination in race, color, national origin, sex, and religion. It provides information on procedures for initiating complaints, guidance on what constitutes an equal opportunity complaint, and assistance in resolving complaints informally.

(14) Family Advocacy Officer: conducts and coordinates programs in support of children and families including abuse and neglect investigations, counseling, special treatment, and educational programs.

(15) Finance and Accounting Office: often provides a Customer Service Branch to interface between the soldier and the pay system by handling inquiries for pay allowances and allotments.

(16) Housing Referral Officer (HRO): gives soldiers counseling, guidance, and up-to-date information on the local housing situation, both rental and sales. Responsible for receiving and processing any complaints for discrimination in off-post housing.

(17) Inspector General (IG): deals with rendering assistance, correcting injustices affecting individuals, and eliminating conditions determined to be detrimental to the efficiency, economy, morale, and reputation of the Army. Also investigates matters involving fraud, waste, and abuse.

(18) Legal Assistance, Staff Judge Advocate (JAG): employs a staff of lawyers and paraprofessionals. They may provide information or act as counsel in matters of contracts, debts, citizenship, adoption, marital problems, taxes, wills, or powers of attorney.

(19) Organizational Effectiveness Staff Officer: assists leaders, on request, to improve unit effectiveness and readiness of total organizational systems affecting people, processes, and structures.

(20) Social Work Service: provides services dealing with social problems to include crisis intervention, family therapy, marital counseling, abortion or adoption referral, financial counseling, and parent or child management assistance.

(21) Transportation Officer: is a source of information, advice, and counseling for service members and families regarding permanent change of station travel and shipment of household goods and privately owned vehicles.

(22) Unit Personnel NCO: is often located in the battalion Personnel and Administration Center (PAC). The soldier's first point of contact with the personnel support system, from assignments to welfare services for soldiers and family members.

Q. When should discipline counseling be used?
A. When soldiers have violated regulations, policies, or other set standards and when taking corrective steps that <u>will not</u> result in formal punitive action against the soldier under UCMJ (however, repetitious discipline counseling on a soldier may be an indication that they cannot benefit from non-punitive measures, in which case punishment under UCMJ would be more appropriate).

Q. If action by a commander under Article 15, UCMJ, or by a court-martial is likely, what is your responsibility as a leader and counselor?
A. Ensure that the accused soldier is advised of his Article 31, UCMJ, rights before discussing the incident.

LEADERSHIP COUNSELING
FM 22-101

Q. Performance counseling stresses success and uses praise to reinforce positive actions. How does this differ from discipline counseling?
A. Discipline counseling stresses failure to meet set standards of conduct. It is intended to be corrective, not punitive.

Q. Which "approach" to counseling is normally used during discipline counseling?
A. Directive.

Q. Like any other type of counseling, discipline counseling requires certain leader actions and preparation. List eight actions a counselor should take for discipline counseling.
A. (1) Tell the soldier why he is being counseled, what was expected, and how he failed to meet the standard.
(2) Address specific unacceptable behavior or action, not the character of the soldier.
(3) Tell the soldier of the impact of his behavior, actions, or performance on the rest of the unit.
(4) Actively listen to the soldier's response.
(5) Tell the soldier how to meet the standard.
(6) Determine the appropriate action such as reprimand, corrective training, administrative action, or referral to the commander.
(7) Explain to the soldier what will be done, and why.
(8) Take action and follow up.

Q. Various administrative actions (nonpunitive measures) can be initiated by the chain of command as corrective measures. Name some of these actions.
A.
- Deferment of discretionary benefits such as pass privileges, driving on post, or use of the PX or the EM club.
- Admonitions and reprimands.
- Corrective training.
- Administrative reduction.
- Revocation of security clearance.
- Bar to reenlistment.
- MOS reclassification.
- Transfer or reassignment.
- Alcohol and drug rehabilitation programs.

Q. Extra training led by an NCO on weekends or after normal duty hours is often more effective than formal punishment in improving soldier performance. What rule of thumb must be followed with regard to extra training?
A. It must be related to a specific deficiency, generally one involving inefficiency as opposed to misconduct. Its intent is to correct substandard performance in some area.

Q. An effective counseling program is essential to developing a cohesive unit capable of accomplishing its mission quickly and efficiently. Such a unit program should accomplish what 10 objectives?
A. (1) Strengthen the chain of command.
(2) Clarify policies and procedures.
(3) Reinforce standards.
(4) Prevent rumors.
(5) Praise success.
(6) Provide feedback on administrative actions.
(7) Clarify priorities.
(8) Avoid surprises.
(9) Provide needed information.

(10) Develop responsible subordinates.

Q. What is the key to a successful counseling session?
A. Preparation.

Q. In preparing for scheduled counseling sessions, what five points should a leader consider?
A. (1) Notify the soldier.
(2) Schedule the best time (selection of the time).
(3) Choose a suitable place (selection of the site).
(4) Decide the right atmosphere.
(5) Plan the discussion.

Q. Ideally, a counseling session should be shorter than _______, and always less than ________.
A. 30 minutes; 1 hour.

Q. What should you do if you expect a counseling session to last more than 30 minutes?
A. Schedule two separate counseling sessions.

Q. A complex problem that requires a counseling session or sessions more than one hour in duration may be an indication of what?
A. The need for additional expertise (chain of command or outside support agencies).

Q. A counseling session may be divided into three phases. What are they?
A. (1) Opening the session.
(2) Discussion.
(3) Closing the session.

Q. What are the two objectives of "opening the session"?
A. (1) Establish rapport.
(2) Explain the reason for and outline the conduct of the counseling session.

Q. What is the key to "closing the session"?
A. Summarize what has been discussed.

Q. What is the key to getting results from counseling?
A. Follow-up.

Q. What are some examples of good follow-up measures taken by a leader?
A.
- Letting the chain of command know the results of counseling regarding the soldier's reaction or decision.
- Taking action or making referrals to outside agencies as agreed upon during the session.
- Continuing to evaluate the situation to ensure that the problem is being resolved or that the proper action is being taken.
- Recognizing any positive results, even simple things. This can be done with a letter, a certificate, an award, a good efficiency report, or even with a pat on the back and simple praise.
- Taking corrective measures for poor results.

Q. What form is normally used to record most counseling?
A. DA Form 4856, General Counseling Form.

LEADERSHIP COUNSELING
FM 22-101

Q. When there is no locally required form or policy on records of counseling, what items are recommended to be included in written counseling?
A. - Date, time, and place of the counseling session.
- Reason for counseling.
- Individuals involved.
- Items or problems discussed.
- Soldier response.
- Recommendations made or actions to be taken.
- Required follow-up actions.
- Counselor's signature.

Q. Soldiers react to counseling in many ways - influenced by the reason for counseling and by the way it is initiated. Name some common soldier reactions to counseling.
A. - nervousness
- cooperation
- rational disagreement
- "too easy" agreement
- determination to argue
- attempts to shift blame
- loss of temper
- desire to quit

Q. A pitfall is a hidden or not easily recognized danger or difficulty. What are some examples of counseling pitfalls?
A. - personal bias
- rash judgments
- stereotyping
- loss of emotional control
- inflexible methods
- amateur character analysis
- improper follow-up
- reluctance to counsel

Q. Developing the ability to counsel results from practice. What three methods for training counselors are discussed in FM 22-101?
A. (1) Role modeling.
(2) Feedback (peer evaluation and leader evaluation).
(3) Role playing.

Q. Unit counseling training should be based on what two references?
A. FMs 22-100 and 22-101.

Q. Effective communication is essential to leadership and counseling. As mentioned earlier, this is done by active listening, responding, and guiding. Active listening comments include what three things?
A. (1) Reflective statements: leader paraphrases what the soldier says to bring out what the soldier means or feels.
- This is what you said...
- You say you feel...
- In essence, you've said this...
- In other words, what you are saying...

(2) General leads: statements used to encourage the soldier to continue.
- Tell me more about it.
- How's that?
- I see.
- I'd like to hear about it.

(3) Silence.

Q. To encourage feedback, a leader must avoid arguing his point, defending his position, explaining his rationale or reasons, or criticizing the giver. Proper feedback should be? (9 elements)
A. - requested
- appropriate
- clear
- specific
- descriptive
- useful

- accurate
- timely
- supportive

THE FOLLOWING INFORMATION, ALTHOUGH NOT CONTAINED IN FM 22-101, IS INCLUDED FOR YOUR REVIEW. THE MAJORITY OF THIS MATERIAL WAS OBTAINED THROUGH PUBLICATIONS OF THE SERGEANTS MAJOR ACADEMY.

Q. What are seven characteristics of a good counselor?
A. (1) Approachable.
(2) Experienced.
(3) Has unbiased approach to counselee's problem.
(4) Has good observation skills.
(5) Skilled communicator.
(6) Flexible.
(7) Aware of own limitations.

Q. What is the most crucial phase of the counseling session?
A. Your opening remarks.

Q. How often should soldiers be counseled?
A. As often as necessary (Army standard dictates that soldiers be counseled, as a minimum, every 90 days. It is recommended, and required in some commands, that soldiers receive counseling on a monthly basis).

Q. What is a good example of an "informal" form of counseling?
A. On-the-spot corrections.

Q. When making an "On-the-Spot" correction, what four items of information should be covered?
A. (1) Describe the behavior.
(2) Describe the policy.
(3) Describe the effect of not complying with the policy.
(4) Ensure the individual makes the correction.

Q. What are the two types of communication?
A. (1) Verbal communication: the spoken or written word.
(2) Non-verbal communication: gestures and facial expressions.

Q. Describe the three levels of listening.
A. (1) Level I listener: not hearing at all.
(2) Level II listener: selective or passive listening; receives only a part of the intended message, or hears only what he/she wants to hear.
(3) Level III listener: active listener, providing feedback to the speaker.

Q. Give some examples of barriers to effective communication.
A. - Physical barriers: noise, incorrect use of words or abbreviations, and failure to pronounce words correctly.
- Psychological barriers: rank, selective perception, and hidden assumptions.

Q. What are the six elements of essential communication?
A. Who, what, when, where, how, and why.

Q. Human needs are powerful forces in motivating soldiers. Human needs follow a natural progression upward from the simple needs of survival to the more

complex needs of high achievement. Human needs fall into five basic categories. What are they?
A. (1) Physical/survival
(2) Safety/security
(3) Social/belonging
(4) Ego/self-esteem
(5) Self-fulfillment/self-actualization

Q. What is meant by "self-actualization"?
A. Reaching the fullest possible integration of self, in which all talents, capacities, and potentials are being put to use.

Q. What Army motivational slogan emulates the concept of self-actualization?
A. "Be All You Can Be!"

Q. In order for a higher need to be the motivating cause of action, what must happen?
A. You must satisfy the lower needs that precede it.

Q. What are the essential ingredients in a proper senior/subordinate relationship?
A. Mutual respect and restraint from undue familiarity.

SOLDIER TEAM DEVELOPMENT
FM 22-102

Q. What FM covers the development of soldier teams to meet the challenges of combat on the air-land battlefield?
A. FM 22-102.

Q. Describe the characteristics of a combat-ready team.
A. (1) BE characteristics...
- A strong belief in the cause for which they are fighting - known as spirit.
- Professionalism.

(2) KNOW characteristics...
- Soldier knowledge.
- Battlefield knowledge.
- Ethical knowledge.
- People knowledge.

(3) DO characteristics...
- Assess.
- Communicate.
- Make decisions.
- Train.

Q. What is considered to be the cornerstone of the professional Army ethic?
A. Integrity.

Q. What are the four basic soldier values?
A. Courage, candor, commitment, and competence.

NOTE: The four basic soldier values (or Soldierly Values) are often referred to as the four individual values (FM 22-100), or the four Professional Character Traits.

Q. Regardless of how the unit is formed, it is important to remember that all units go through a fairly well-defined process of development that can be broken down into three stages. What are they?
A. (1) Formation stage: characterized by new soldiers' concern about fitting in and belonging.
(2) Development stage: characterized by soldiers' questioning and resistance to leadership.
(3) Sustainment stage: characterized by accomplishing the mission through teamwork and cohesion.

Q. What is the leader's primary role as a developer of soldier-teams?
A. To encourage acceptance, open communication, develop team members' reliance on one another, and promote team acceptance of shared standards and values.

Q. What are the two essential team formation activities covered in FM 22-102?
A. Well-developed reception and orientation activities.

Q. List some important areas to cover in an orientation.
A. - Unit values and standards.
- Unit missions and goals.
- Unit standing operating procedures (SOP).
- Unit heritage.

Q. Who is considered to be the key individual involved in successfully orienting a new soldier?
A. The squad leader.

SOLDIER TEAM DEVELOPMENT
FM 22-102

Q. What can a squad leader do to help with the integration of a new soldier in the midst of combat operations (when the squad leader will probably be extremely busy)?
A. Use the "buddy system" approach (buddy team selected should be a positive role model).

Q. What three leader actions are important during the development stage of soldier-team development?
A. (1) Listen.
(2) Establish clear lines of authority.
(3) Develop soldier and unit goals.

Q. Name four important principles of training that aid in developing cohesive units.
A. (1) Train as a unit.
(2) Train for combat.
(3) Build pride in accomplishment.
(4) Develop self-evaluation habits.

Q. Units which constructively deal with fear multiply combat power. What are three things a leader can do to deal with fear?
A. (1) Teach the soldiers about the physical effects of fear.
(2) Develop training tasks that require moral and physical courage.
(3) Tell the soldiers that extreme fear occurs in combat and they must prepare for it in advance.

Q. What variables will affect the development stage during combat?
A. The dimensions of time and space, the feelings of soldiers, the level of critical information, and the environment.

Q. What FM provides information on dealing with stress?
A. FM 26-2.

Q. Describe the leader actions that support the soldier-team sustainment process.
A. - Deal with change.
- Reassess goals and priorities.
- Focus on teamwork.
- Focus on training.
- Focus on maintaining.
- Ensure timely supply.
- Respond to soldier concerns.

Q. What unit activities support the soldier-team sustainment process?
A. - Military ceremonies.
- Sports activities.
- Social activities.
- Spiritual activities.

Q. Conditions in combat exert pressure on the leader's efforts to sustain his team. Identify some of the conditions that undermine teamwork.
A. - Continuous operations
- Enemy actions
- Casualties
- Boredom
- Rumors

Q. What are three actions a leader can take to help control rumors?

A. (1) Stress honesty.
(2) Keep soldiers informed.
(3) Identify and counsel those who spread rumors.

Q. Panic results when individual despairing behavior becomes group despairing behavior. Soldiers in panic have intense fear, are easily spooked, and tend to flee the battlefield. What are two battlefield conditions that are primary causes of panic?
A. (1) Belief by the group that all escape routes are rapidly closing.
(2) Group feelings of helplessness and anxiety caused by an unclear situation or by what the group perceives as an immediate threat.

Q. What is the best way to prevent panic?
A. Focus on and control what the soldiers believe to be true.

Q. If panic develops in spite of all the leader's efforts, he must take firm and decisive action to stop it as soon as possible. Why is this so very important?
A. *Panic is contagious!*

Q. What should a leader do once panic has been stopped?
A. Immediately restructure the situation and give the soldiers something constructive to do (this will distract them from their fears).

TRAINING THE FORCE
FM 25-100

Q. Why does the Army exist?
A. To deter war or, if deterrence fails, to reestablish peace through victory in combat wherever US interests are challenged.

Q. What are the nine principles of training?
A. (1) Train as a combined arms and services team.
(2) Train as you fight.
(3) Train using appropriate doctrine.
(4) Train using performance-oriented training.
(5) Train to challenge.
(6) Train to sustain proficiency.
(7) Train using multi-echelon techniques.
(8) Train to maintain.
(9) Make commanders and leaders the primary trainers.

Q. The full integration of the combined arms team is attained through the "slice" approach to training management. What is meant by a "slice"?
A. A slice is a term used to describe a grouping of combat, combat support, and combat service support units which are task organized for wartime missions or are habitually associated for peacetime training (ie, the divisional and nondivisional units that habitually train with the division are termed the "division slice").

Q. What is the goal of combat-level training?
A. Achieve combat-level standards.

Q. "Train as you fight" means integrating realistic combat conditions into peacetime training. What are some examples of such realistic conditions?
A. Use of smoke, noise, simulated NBC, battlefield debris, loss of key leaders, and cold weather, to name a few.

Q. Training must conform to Army doctrine. What are some sources of Army "doctrine"?
A. FM 100-5 (Operations) and supporting FMs and doctrinal manuals; mission training plans (MTPs); battle drill books; soldier's manuals; regulations; and training publications.

Q. What is meant by the "Band of Excellence"?
A. It represents a sustained level of wartime proficiency obtained through frequent training on critical tasks.

Q. What tools are used to help achieve and sustain collective and individual proficiency?
A. Mission training plans (MTPs) and the Individual Training and Evaluation Program (ITEP).

Q. Effective training requires the continuous personal time and energy of senior leaders to accomplish what 10 objectives?
A. (1) Develop and communicate a clear vision.
(2) Require subordinates to understand and perform their roles in training.
(3) Train all elements to be proficient on their mission essential tasks.
(4) Centralize training planning and decentralize training execution.
(5) Establish effective communications between command echelons.
(6) Develop subordinates.
(7) Get personally involved in planning, executing, and assessing training.
(8) Demand that training standards be achieved.

(9) Foster a command climate that is conducive to good training.
(10) Eliminate training distractions.

Q. What is meant by "Battle Focus"?
A. A concept used to derive peacetime training requirements from wartime missions.

Q. What are the steps of the Training Management Cycle?
A. Prepare (plan), execute, and assess.

Q. What is a "Mission Essential Task"?
A. A collective task in which an organization must be proficient to accomplish an appropriate portion of its wartime mission(s).

Q. What is a "METL"?
A. Mission Essential Task List. A compilation of collective mission essential tasks which must be successfully performed if an organization is to accomplish its wartime mission(s).

Q. What are the two primary inputs to METL development?
A. War plans and external directives.

Q. Which of the two primary inputs is the most critical?
A. War plans (wartime operations and contingency plans).

Q. What are external directives (give examples)?
A. Additional sources of training tasks that relate to an organization's wartime mission.
- Mission Training Plans (MTPs)
- Mobilization plans.
- Installation wartime transition and deployment plans.
- Force integration plans.

Q. What are the 5 fundamentals of METL development?
A. (1) The METL is derived from the organization's wartime missions and related tasks in external directives.
(2) Mission essential tasks must apply to the entire organization. METL does not include tasks assigned solely to subordinate organizations.
(3) Each organization's METL must support and complement higher headquarters' METL.
(4) The availability of resources does not affect METL development. The METL is an unconstrained statement of the tasks required to accomplish the wartime mission.
(5) Fully integrate the seven systems of the BOS.

Q. What does "BOS" stand for, explain it, and list the seven systems?
A. Battlefield Operating System; used to systematically ensure that all elements of the organization's combat power are directed toward accomplishing the overall mission. BOS are the major functions which occur on the battlefield and must be performed by the force to successfully execute operations.
- Maneuver
- Fire Support
- Command and Control (C^2)
- Intelligence
- Mobility/Countermobility/Survivability
- Combat Service Support

- Air Defense

Q. What information is contained in a "Battle Book"?
A. Detailed information concerning war plans, such as tactical routes to wartime areas of operation, ammunition upload procedures, execution of schemes of maneuver, and other support requirements.

Q. Who has the responsibility for developing a training strategy that will maintain unit proficiency for all tasks that have been designated as mission essential?
A. The commander.

Q. Which tasks within a METL should be given priority?
A. There should be **no** attempt to prioritize tasks within a METL. By definition, all tasks that have been placed on the METL are equally essential to ensure mission accomplishment.

Q. A supporting individual task list should be made for each mission essential task. What are two major source documents for the selection of appropriate individual tasks?
A. Soldier training publications and mission training plans (MTPs).

Q. How does the METL development process compare for Active and Reserve Component organizations?
A. They are the same - all training must be directed at wartime mission readiness.

Q. What is meant by a "Training Objective"?
A. A statement that describes the desired outcome of a training activity.

Q. A training objective consists of what three parts?
A. (1) Task: a clearly defined and measurable activity accomplished by individuals or organizations.
(2) Condition(s): the circumstances and environment in which a task is to be performed.
(3) Standard: the minimum acceptable proficiency required in the performance of a particular training task.

Q. What are some documents that will assist commanders and staffs in developing collective and individual training objectives?
A.
- Mission training plans (MTPs).
- Soldier's manuals.
- DA Pam 350-38, Standards in Weapons Training.
- Deployment or mobilization plans.
- General Defense Plans (GDPs).
- Army, MACOM, and local regulations.
- Local SOP.

Q. What is a "Battle Task"?
A. A command group, staff, or subordinate organization mission essential task that is so critical that its accomplishment will determine the success of the next higher organization's mission essential task.

Q. What is the goal of centralized planning?
A. To develop mutually supporting METL-based training at all levels within an organization.

TRAINING THE FORCE
FM 25-100

Q. At the start of the planning process the commander provides two principal inputs. What are they?
A. The METL and the training assessment.

Q. What is the "training assessment"?
A. A tool for comparing an organization's current level of training proficiency with the desired level of wartime proficiency.

Q. Where would a commander look to find the "desired" level of wartime proficiency for his organization?
A. This is defined in MTPs and in such publications as how to fight manuals and other doctrinal literature.

Q. When should the training assessment be updated?
A. At the beginning of each long-range and short-range planning cycle and after a major training event.

Q. What is meant by "training requirement"?
A. It is the training necessary to achieve and sustain desired levels of training proficiency for each mission essential task.

Q. How is task proficiency rated?
A. As one of the following:

- "T" (trained)
- "P" (needs practice)
- "U" (untrained)
- "?" (unknown)

Q. What is a commander's "training vision"?
A. The commander's broad concept for training the organization to achieve and sustain wartime proficiency.

Q. What are the three key elements which shape a commander's training vision?
A. The commander's understanding of training and operations doctrine, his assessment of METL proficiency levels, and knowledge of potential enemy capabilities.

Q. The commander's guidance, a product of the training planning process, is composed of what three things?
A. Training vision, goals, and priorities.

Q. Through the training planning process, the commander's guidance is melded together with the METL and the training assessment to make what?
A. Training plans.

Q. What are the three types of training plans?
A. Long-range, short-range, and near-term.

Q. Properly developed training plans will do what six things?
A. (1) Maintain a consistent battle focus.
(2) Be coordinated between associated combat, combat support, and combat service support organizations.
(3) Focus on the correct time horizon.
(4) Be concerned with future proficiency.
(5) Cause organizational stability.
(6) Make the most efficient use of resources.

TRAINING THE FORCE
FM 25-100

Q. What is the correct "time horizon" for each of the three types of training plans?
A. Long-range: should extend out at least a year.
Short-range: normally focus on upcoming quarter (3 months).
Near-term: starts approximately eight weeks prior to the execution of training.

Q. Identify the following types of training events.
A. JTX - Joint Training Exercise
CTX - Combined Training Exercise
FTX - Field Training Exercise
CALFEX - Combined Arms Live Fire Exercise
LFX - Live Fire Exercise
CFX - Command Field Exercise
DEPEX - Deployment Exercise
TEWT - Tactical Exercise Without Troops
CPX - Command Post Exercise
STX - Situational Training Exercise
MAPEX - Map Exercise
LOGEX - Logistics Exercise
FCX - Fire Coordination Exercise
EDRE - Emergency Deployment Readiness Exercise
BSX - Battle Simulation Exercise

Q. What is the purpose of time management systems?
A. To create prime time training periods for subordinate organizations on mission essential training.

Q. Describe the time management system mentioned in FM 25-100.
A. The Green-Amber-Red Time Management System; Organizations in Green periods conduct planned training without distraction and external taskings. Units in Red periods execute details and other administrative requirements and allow the maximum number of soldiers to take leaves. Organizations in Amber periods are assigned support taskings beyond the capability of those units in the Red period, but commanders strive for minimal disruption to Amber organizations' training programs.

Q. In recent years, the Army has increasingly emphasized externally supported training events. Give an example of an organization which provides combined arms and services battle-focused training that is externally supported.
A. Army Combat Training Centers (CTCs).

Q. There is a relationship between the number of miles or hours that an item of equipment, such as a tank, is operated and the dollars required to purchase the repair parts and POL for that piece of equipment. Funding authority to purchase the projected repair parts, fuel products, and other items necessary to support the training mission is allocated to units based on what?
A. Operating Tempo (OPTEMPO) - this is the average annual miles or hours of operation for a unit's major equipment systems.

Q. What is a "QTB"?
A. Quarterly Training Brief (a short-range training brief) - this is a conference conducted by senior commanders to review and approve the training plans of subordinate units.

Q. Are QTBs conducted before or after the time period addressed in the Quarterly Training Guidance?

A. Before.

Q. Near-term planning is primarily conducted at what levels?
A. Battalion and subordinate command levels.

Q. When does formal near-term planning culminate?
A. When the unit publishes the training schedule.

Q. Near-term planning and thus, training schedules, should cover a _____ week period prior to the conduct of training.
A. 6-8.

Q. Who must conduct training meetings?
A. Platoons, companies, and battalions.

Q. At battalion level, training meetings primarily cover training management issues; at company and platoon level, they are directly concerned with what?
A. The **specifics** of conducting training.

Q. Training schedule formats may vary among organizations, but they all must contain what six elements?
A. (1) Specify when training starts and where it takes place.
(2) Allocate the correct amount of time for scheduled training and also additional training as required to correct anticipated deficiencies.
(3) Specify individual, leader, and collective tasks to be trained.
(4) Provide concurrent training topics that will efficiently use available training time.
(5) Specify who conducts the training and who evaluates the results.
(6) Provide administrative information concerning uniform, weapons, equipment, references, and safety precautions.

Q. When is unit training officially considered to be "locked-in"?
A. When the training schedule is published (senior commanders normally have established policies that minimize changes to the training schedule, such as requiring that battalion commanders personally approve training schedule changes).

Q. What is command responsibility in regards to training schedules?
A.
- The company commander drafts the training schedule.
- The battalion commander approves the schedule and provides necessary administrative support.
- The brigade commander reviews each training schedule published in his command.
- The division commander reviews selected training schedules in detail and the complete list of organization-wide training highlights developed by division staff.

Q. What type of training inspections are normally the most beneficial to senior leaders and inspection teams?
A. Unannounced or short notice inspections.

Q. All good training, regardless of the specific collective and individual tasks being executed, must comply with certain common requirements. What are these requirements?
A. Adequate preparation, effective presentation and practice, and thorough evaluation.

TRAINING THE FORCE
FM 25-100

Q. What is the best way to describe properly presented and practical training?
A. It is accurate, well structured, efficient, realistic, safe, and effective.

Q. What are the different types of training evaluation?
A. Formal, informal, internal, external, or any combination of these.

Q. What is an "AAR"?
A. After Action Review; it is a structured review process that allows training participants to discover for themselves what happened, why it happened, and how it can be done better. It is a professional discussion that requires the active participation of those being trained.

Q. What are the four parts of an AAR?
A. (1) Establish what happened.
(2) Determine what was right or wrong with what happened.
(3) Determine how the task should be done differently the next time.
(4) Perform the task again.

Q. To keep the training system dynamic, senior leaders use _________ to determine the effectiveness of the planning, execution, and assessment portions of the training management cycle.
A. Feedback.

Q. Name some sources of training feedback that are available to senior leaders.
A.
- Training planning assessments.
- Senior, lateral, and subordinate headquarters training plans.
- Quarterly Training Briefs (QTBs).
- Resource allocation forums such as PBACs or range scheduling conferences.
- Personal observations.
- Leader development discussions.
- Staff visits.
- Evaluation data.

Q. What is the key feedback mechanism that maintains continuity among the many training systems?
A. Assessment.

Q. List some important sources of evaluation data.
A.
- Personal observations of training.
- Feedback from higher headquarters.
- Training briefings.
- ARTEP evaluations.
- SQT/CTT results.
- Maintenance and logistical evaluations and technical inspection results.
- IG
- Command inspections.
- APFT scores.
- Weapons qualification.

Q. What is a "T&EO"?
A. Training and Evaluation Outline - a summary document prepared for each training activity that provides information on collective training objectives, related individual training objectives, resource requirements, and applicable evaluation procedures.

TRAINING THE FORCE
FM 25-100

ALTHOUGH NOT CONTAINED IN FM 25-100, THE FOLLOWING TRAINING QUESTIONS ARE PRESENTED FOR YOUR REVIEW DUE TO THEIR POPULARITY IN USE.

Q. In addition to FM 25-100/101, what are some of the important publications that cover training in the Army?
A. FM 25-2........Unit Training Management
FM 25-3........Training in Units
FM 25-4........How to Conduct Training Exercises
FM 25-5........Training for Mobilization and War
AR 350-1.......The Army Training System

Q. What is the Army's training goal?
A. To develop a combat ready force which is physically and psychologically prepared to fight and win global war.

Q. Training is divided into what two categories?
A. (1) Individual training - training that soldiers receive to enable them to perform the specific tasks and duties related to the MOS and duty position to which assigned.
(2) Collective training - training which prepares a group of individuals to accomplish tasks that combine two or more individual tasks to complete a mission.

Q. What is the purpose of the Soldier's Manual?
A. It is designed to lay out what tasks you must know how to do, under what conditions to perform the specified tasks, and a step-by-step description of how to perform the tasks identified to standard.

Q. What is the NCOES? Describe the different levels of the NCOES System.
A. The Noncommissioned Officer Education System is a system of resident training (service schools and MACOM schools), supervised-on-the-job experience and self-study. It is designed to provide, as required in each MOS, progressive, continuous training from the primary through the senior level. The objectives of the NCOES are to train the NCO to be leaders and trainers of soldiers, provide technical and tactical training, and improve unit mission efficiency.

- **Primary Leadership Development Course (PLDC)**: a non-MOS specific leadership course. Its emphasis is on how to lead and train, and the duties, responsibilities, and authority of the NCO.
- **Basic Noncommissioned Officer Course (BNCOC)**: stresses performance-oriented techniques. Soldiers are trained in MOS critical job tasks to specified standards. Training in BNCOC compliments leadership training received in the primary level (PLDC).
- **Advanced Noncommissioned Officer Course (ANCOC)**: provides advanced levels of training which prepare career soldiers for duties at grade E-7 (Skill Level 4). Emphasis is placed on technical and advanced leadership skills and knowledge of military subjects required to train and lead other soldiers at the platoon level.
- **US Army Sergeants Major Course (USASMC)**: trains DA selected soldiers for positions of high responsibility throughout the Army. USASMC is the capstone of enlisted training. Master Sergeants and First Sergeants are prepared for both troop and staff assignments.

Q. You should always train using economical, technically correct, and safe procedures; your success as a trainer depends on your soldier's ability to

perform the tasks properly after you train them. There are five phases you should follow to ensure your success when presenting training. This is often referred to as the Five-P Model. Explain the five phases of the Five-P Model.
A. (1) PLANNING: Determine what tasks you need to train, who needs the training, how you are going to conduct the training, and if you have everything that you need to properly train your soldiers. The last step during this phase is to construct the training outline.
(2) PREPARING: You must be able to perform the task to standard, not just KNOW how to perform it (you should be a "subject matter expert"). Prepare and gather the required resources that you'll need to train your soldiers. Make the training as realistic as possible. The best place to look for resources is the manual you are training from. Announce the training to your soldiers. And lastly, rehearse your training session.
(3) PRESENTING: Your goal here is to train your soldiers and have them perform the task to standard. Your presentation should supply the soldiers with the necessary knowledge so that they too can perform the task to standard.
(4) PRACTICING: This is the actual hands-on, skill development phase of training. The practice phase converts what the student has seen and heard into something that the soldier does. Use the step-by-step method of instruction. After your soldiers can complete each of the steps correctly, have them combine several steps until they can complete the task in one continuous action.
(5) PERFORMING: Formally evaluate your soldiers on their ability to perform the task as required by the standards for the task. No matter how many soldiers you have trained, you should evaluate their performance individually.

Q. What is the purpose of a Training Outline?
A. It consists of hints and reminders that the trainer uses to make sure he has put all the key steps and important points in the training.

Q. A training outline consists of eight elements. What are they?
A. (1) TRAINING STATEMENT: This is the Task, Conditions, and Standards of the task. State these guidelines in your own words to ensure that your soldiers understand what the task is, under what conditions they must perform the task, and how well they must perform the task.
(2) CAUTION STATEMENT: Informs the soldiers of any safety hazards and/or security classification during the training.
(3) PRETEST: You must always offer a pretest to the soldiers you are training. If a soldier desires a pretest, you must prepare the conditions, read the soldier the task, conditions, and standards and proceed using the performance measures as a guide.
(4) ORIENTATION STATEMENT: This is the reason your soldiers are receiving the training. Why is this task important for them to know? How is it related to the other tasks and missions that they must perform? Here is where you tell them why they need, or how they are going to benefit from the training.
(5) DEMONSTRATION: This should provide the soldier with the exact model of what you want the soldier to do. You must perform a demonstrated task at normal speed and meet all the performance standards.
(6) TASK STEPS: Explain the task step-by-step. Once you explain and perform a step, have the soldiers perform the same step before you move on to the next step.
(7) PRACTICE: During this phase the soldiers learn, hands on, how to perform the task to standard. With you coaching and critiquing them on-the-spot, soldiers first practice the individual steps. As the soldiers master the individual steps put several steps together, and finally, perform the whole task. Practice until the soldiers are confident enough in themselves to take the performance evaluation.
(8) PERFORMANCE EVALUATION: This is exactly the same as the pretest. You

must set up the required conditions, and read them the task, conditions, and standards. Use the performance measures as a guide when evaluating the soldier. The performance evaluation should be performed individually.

Q. What are the four steps involved in PREPARING for training?
A. - Announce the training to the soldiers
- gather and prepare resources
- rehearse your training session
- revise the training outline

Q. What are the three methods of teaching?
A. Lecture, conference, and demonstration.

Q. What is a "job book"?
A. The job book is intended primarily as a noncommissioned officer training management tool used to record demonstrated proficiency on Soldier's Manual tasks. It enables the supervisor to know what tasks his/her soldiers are proficient in.

Q. How many job books should you have?
A. One for each skill level 1/2 soldier that you supervise.

Q. When should a job book be started on a soldier?
A. In the soldier's first unit of assignment after completion of initial entry training (IET).

Q. What is written on the front of the job book?
A. Name (ink); Unit and Rank (pencil).

Q. HOW do you record information in the job book?
A. Once a task has been evaluated, enter your initials in the "GO" column if it was completed to standard or the "NO GO" column if the task was not completed to standard. Enter the date of the evaluation. Make all entries in pencil.

Q. What regulation covers the Individual Training and Evaluation Program (ITEP)?
A. AR 350-37.

Q. What are the goals of ITEP?
A. Improve combat readiness by providing diagnostic information to commanders and MOS proponents on the effectiveness of training programs and products and to provide soldier proficiency information to career managers.

Q. What are the ~~three~~ two components of ITEP?
A. ~~SQT/SDT,~~ CTT and Commander's Evaluation (CE).

BATTLE FOCUSED TRAINING
FM 25-101

Q. What FM covers Battle Focused Training?
A. FM 25-101.

Q. Explain the relationship between FMs 25-100 and 25-101.
A. FM 25-100, "Training the Force", establishes the new Army training doctrine. FM 25-101, "Battle Focused Training", is the implementation manual for applying this doctrine. It is designed to assist leaders in the development and execution of training programs.

Q. The specific emphasis of commanders with respect to training is to train _____ level(s) down and evaluate ______ level(s) down.
A. 1;2 (ie, Company commanders train platoon leaders with their platoons and evaluate section, squad, team, and crew leaders with their units).

Q. The commander assigns primary responsibility to officers for _________ training and to noncommissioned officers for _________ training.
A. Collective; soldier (individual).

Q. Guidance on wartime missions and priorities flows _______; soldier, leader, and collective training needs flow ______.
A. Down; up.

Q. What are the three primary forums for the exchange of training information among leaders?
A. Training meetings, briefings, and After Action Reviews (AARs).

Q. The greatest combat power results when leaders synchronize combat, combat support, and combat service support systems to complement and reinforce one another. What concept refers to CS and CSS units task-organized to support a particular maneuver or combined arms unit?
A. The "slice" concept.

Q. Once soldiers and units have trained to standard, they maintain proficiency through what form of training?
A. Sustainment training.

Q. What is "opportunity training"?
A. Training conducted by section, squad, team, or crew-level leaders which is preselected, planned, and rehearsed, but not executed until unexpected training time becomes available (ie, awaiting transportation, completing scheduled training early).

Q. What is meant by "multiechelon" training?
A. The simultaneous training of more than one echelon on different tasks.

Q. Why is it so important to "Train to Maintain"?
A. Because training cannot happen if essential equipment and systems are nonmission capable (NMC).

Q. All maintenance must be on the unit training schedule and should focus on the total unit, to include what three things?
A. (1) The soldier, and his uniforms.
(2) The soldier's equipment (TA-50, weapons, protective mask, etc).
(3) Major end items (tracked and wheeled vehicles, helicopters, shop vans).

Q. "TA-50" is a common term that refers to a soldiers equipment issue. Where

does this term originate?
A. It is short for "Common Table of Allowances (CTA) 50."

Q. What is meant by "leader development"?
A. The process the Army uses to develop competent, confident leaders.

Q. There are seven stages in the leader development process. What are they?
A. Assessment, feedback, additional training and reinforcement, education, training, experience, and selection for advancement.

Q. Leader development programs must address officers, warrant officers, and NCOs. It should be published throughout the unit and should include what three phases?
A. (1) Reception and integration phase.
(2) Basic skills development phase.
(3) Advanced development and sustainment phase.

Q. Training management involves planning, execution, and assessment. It is a continuous process that centers on __________.
A. Feedback.

Q. Who is the approving authority for a unit METL?
A. The next higher wartime commander.

Q. What is the lowest level unit that prepares a METL?
A. Company.

Q. What is a "Battle Staff"?
A. It consists of the organic battalion primary and special staff, plus task-organized slice (CS and CSS) unit leaders.

Q. What are "battle tasks"?
A. A task which must be accomplished by a subordinate organization if the next higher headquarters is to accomplish a mission essential task. Battle tasks are selected by the senior commander from the subordinate organization's METL.

Q. What is the lowest level that has battle tasks?
A. Battalion.

Q. What does "TADSS" stand for?
A. Training aids, devices, simulators and simulations.

Q. A Training Objective consists of the tasks, conditions, and standards for a particular training event. The "conditions" statement of a training objective should include what information?
A. One or more of the following:
- Status and capability of threat forces.
- Equipment, material, tools, or other resources allocated for use in performing the task.
- References, checklists, and other memory aids for use during actual task performance.
- Physical or environmental conditions (darkness, dense tropical forest, cold weather, NBC conditions, etc).

Q. What should be the starting point of any training-planning process?
A. Assessment (in-depth assessment determines a strategy to improve training proficiency on specific weaknesses and plan sustainment training on

demonstrated strengths; it links the evaluation of training executed to the planning of upcoming training).

Q. What is meant by "training strategy"?
A. A concept used to attain desired levels of training proficiency on mission essential tasks.

Q. Time management systems are designed to protect training time for subordinate units. Various types of time management systems are used throughout the Army. Some systems consist of three cycles: units involved in training, units on alert status (mission), and units providing support. This is known as what system? Name another time management system in use.
A. The green-amber-red time management system; a two-cycle system: prime time training, and support. This latter time management system is better suited for the majority of CS and CSS units.

Q. How would the following events be rated on the green-amber-red time management system?
A. - Post support: red.
- Gunnery: green.
- FTX - green.
- Holiday half-day work schedule: red.
- Weapons qualification: amber.
- CALFEX: green.
- NTC: green.

Q. What is a "battle roster"?
A. A listing of individuals, crews, or elements that reflects capabilities, proficiencies of critical tasks, and other information concerning warfighting abilities.

Q. What is meant by "risk assessment"?
A. It is the thought process of making operations safer without compromising the mission.

Q. Training meetings are *non-negotiable* at battalion and company level. **They will be held.** What should be the primary focus of training meetings at battalion level?
A. Training management issues for the next six weeks.

Q. Who should participate in a company-level training meeting?
A. - Company commander
- 1SG
- XO
- Platoon leaders and platoon sergeants
- Supply sergeant
- NBC NCO or specialist
- Motor sergeant (as applicable)
- Slice team leaders (as applicable)
- Other key leaders designated by the commander

Q. Once the battalion commander approves and the company commander signs the training schedule, it is locked in and constitutes an official order. It can only be changed by whom?
A. The approving authority.

Q. What are "precombat" checks?

BATTLE FOCUSED TRAINING
FM 25-101

A. Detailed final checks that all units conduct before and during execution of training and combat operations.

Q. Trainers primarily use what three methods to present training to soldiers?
A. Lecture, conference, and demonstration.

Q. Which of the above methods is the least preferred?
A. Lecture.

Q. Which of the above methods is the preferred method?
A. Demonstration.

Q. There are three stages of training. Each stage can occur separately or in combination. What are they?
A. (1) Initial training - little or no familiarity with a given task.
(2) Refresher training - requires training on certain subtasks.
(3) Sustainment training - meets the training objective, but will lose proficiency without practice.

Q. What is a "battle drill"?
A. A collective action rapidly executed without applying a deliberate decision-making process.

Q. What are the characteristics of a battle drill?
A. - They require minimal leader orders to accomplish and are standard throughout the Army.
- Sequential actions are vital to success in combat or critical to preserving life.
- They apply to platoon or smaller units.
- They are trained responses to enemy actions or leaders' orders.
- They represent mental steps followed for offensive and defensive actions in training and combat.

Q. Where can a listing of Battle Drills be found?
A. In the appropriate ARTEP "-DRILL" manual (ie, ARTEP 5-145-DRILL for Engineer Battle Drills and Crew Drills; ARTEP 7-8-DRILL for Infantry Rifle Platoon and Squad Battle Drills; etc).

Q. What are "crew drills"?
A. Similar to battle drills only it involves a collective action that the crew of a weapon or piece of equipment must perform to use the weapon or equipment.

Q. Appendix B of FM 25-101 addresses the use of a "Leader Book". What information should be contained in a leader book?
A. Information addressing administrative data, common tasks, skill qualification assessment, and specific collective tasks which support the unit's METL. Also, personal information that affects soldiers' training performance and other information that leaders need to know to provide training which meets the soldiers' personal needs. The information recorded should be tailored to meet specific needs.

Q. What should a Leader Book look like?
A. It can be in any format the leader chooses. A small, pocket-sized memo book or a full-sized multipage notebook can be used. The bottom line is that leaders should have a way of recording information.

Q. How should leaders track the training status of their soldiers?

BATTLE FOCUSED TRAINING
FM 25-101

A. Leaders list in the leader's book the common tasks found in the Soldier's Manual of Common Tasks that support the unit METL. Track soldiers proficiency on these tasks.
Also record MOS-specific tasks which support the METL (or use job books) and annotate evaluation results.

NOTE: As a minimum, the leader book should contain the collective tasks and drills required to support the METL.

Q. The combat training center (CTC) program provides the most realistic environment available for corps and subordinate units during peacetime. What are the four centers of the CTC?
A. (1) Combat Maneuver Training Center (CMTC).
(2) National Training Center (NTC).
(3) Joint Readiness Training Center (JRTC).
(4) Battle Command Training Program (BCTP).

Q. What are the two types of AARs?
A. Formal and informal.

UNIFORMS AND INSIGNIA
AR 670-1

Q. What regulation covers "Wear and Appearance of Army Uniforms and Insignia"?
A. AR 670-1

Q. To whom does AR 670-1 not apply (disregarding civilians and members of other armed services)?
A. It does not apply to Generals of the Army or the Chief of Staff of the Army or former Chiefs of Staff of the Army, each of whom may prescribe his or her own uniform. Further, it does not apply to ROTC or West Point Cadets.

Q. What is the stated policy regarding alterations and changes to the basic design of uniforms or insignia?
A. "No item governed by this regulation (AR 670-1) will be altered in any way that changes the basic design or the intended concept of fit."

Q. What are the three classifications of service and utility or field uniforms?
A. (1) Class A: Army green coat and trousers (skirt or slacks), short or long sleeve AG 415 shirt, black four-in-hand necktie (male) or necktab (female), and authorized accessories.
(2) Class B: same as Class A except service coat is not worn.
(3) Class C: utility, field, and other organizational uniforms such as hospital duty and food service uniforms.

Q. What is the difference between the Class B uniform with the long sleeve and the short sleeve AG 415 shirt?
A. The black four-in-hand necktie (necktab) is required for wear with the long sleeve shirt; tie is optional with the short-sleeve shirt.

Q. What is the general personal appearance policy?
A. The Army is a uniformed service where discipline is judged, in part, by the manner in which the individual wears the uniform as prescribed. Therefore, a neat and well-groomed appearance by soldiers is fundamental to the Army and contributes to building the pride and esprit essential to an effective military force.

Q. What is the uniform appearance and fit policy for soldiers?
A. All personnel will maintain a high standard of dress and appearance. Uniforms will be properly fitted, clean, serviceable, and pressed as necessary. Personnel must project a military image that leaves no doubt that they live by a common military standard and are responsible to military order and discipline.

Q. Who is responsible for ensuring that military personnel present a neat and soldierly appearance?
A. Commanders and leaders (however, it is the duty of all soldiers to take pride in their appearance at all times).

Q. What are two important factors contributing to personal appearance?
A. Physical fitness and acceptable weight standards.

Q. AR 670-1 explains that soldiers may wear "religious apparel", articles, and jewelry so long as they are not visible or apparent, are considered "neat and conservative", and do not interfere with the performance of the soldier's duties. How is "religious apparel" defined?
A. Articles of clothing worn as part of the observance of the religious faith practiced by the soldier.

UNIFORMS AND INSIGNIA
AR 670-1

Q. When a soldier is wearing an Army uniform outside of worship services or other rites and rituals, "neat and conservative" items of religious apparel are those that meet what three criteria?
A. - Are discreet in style and design, and subdued in brightness or color;
- Do not replace or interfere with the proper wearing of any prescribed article of the uniform;
- Are not temporarily or permanently affixed or appended to any prescribed article of the uniform.

Q. What are the hair style standards for male and female soldiers?
A. - Male: the hair on top of the head will be neatly groomed. The length and bulk will not be excessive or present a ragged, unkempt, or extreme appearance. Hair will present a tapered appearance and when combed will not fall over the ears or eyebrows or touch the collar except for the closely cut hair at the back of the neck.
- Female: Hair will be neatly groomed. The length and bulk of the hair will not be excessive or present a ragged, unkempt, or extreme appearance. Hair will not fall over the eyebrows or extend below the bottom edge of the collar.

Q. In all cases, the bulk and length of hair should not do what?
A. Interfere with the normal wear of headgear or protective masks.

Q. Extreme or fad hair styles are not authorized (this includes lines or designs cut into the hair or scalp). If dyes, tints, or bleaches are used, what color should they be?
A. A color that is natural to human hair.

Q. Are block cuts for males permitted?
A. Yes, in moderate degree, as long as a tapered look is maintained.

Q. What is the grooming policy for mustaches?
A. It will be kept neatly trimmed, tapered, and tidy and will not present a chopped-off appearance. No portion of the mustache will cover the upper lip line or extend sideways beyond a vertical line drawn upward from the corners of the mouth.

Q. What is the grooming policy for sideburns?
A. They will be neatly trimmed. The base will not be flared and will be a clean-shaven, horizontal line. Sideburns will not extend below the lowest part of the exterior ear opening.

Q. If beard growth is prescribed by appropriate medical authority, what must also be specified (on the shaving profile)?
A. The maximum length required for medical treatment (ie, "A neatly trimmed beard is authorized. The length will not exceed 1/4 inch."). TB MED 287.

Q. Is the wear of a wig or hairpiece by male personnel in uniform or on duty authorized?
A. Yes, but only to cover natural baldness or physical disfiguration caused by accident or medical procedure (must conform to standard haircut criteria).

Q. May wigs be worn by female soldiers in uniform or on duty?
A. Yes, as long as it is a natural hair color and the style and length conforms to appearance standards.

Q. Are hairnets authorized to be worn by female soldiers?

A. No (unless required for health or safety reasons).

Q. What is the criteria for the wear of hair holding ornaments (barrettes, pins, clips) by female soldiers?
A. If used, they must be transparent or similar in color to the hair, and will be inconspicuously placed. Beads or similar ornamental items are not authorized.

Q. Are female soldiers authorized to wear cosmetics?
A. Yes, if applied conservatively (as determined by the commander) and in good taste.

Q. Female soldiers may wear lipstick and nail polish with all uniforms so long as what criteria is met?
A. As long as the color is conservative and complements the uniform. Extreme shades such as purple, gold, blue or white will not be worn.

Q. What is Army policy on the length of fingernails?
A. Fingernails should be kept clean and neatly trimmed so as not to interfere with performance of duty, detract from the military image, or present a safety hazard.

Q. What is the hygiene and body grooming policy outlined in AR 670-1?
A. Soldiers are expected to maintain good daily hygiene and wear their uniforms so as not to detract from the overall military appearance.

Q. Are tattoos authorized?
A. While not expressly prohibited, tattooing in areas of the body (ie, face, legs) that would cause the tattoo to be exposed while in Class A uniform is discouraged since it detracts from a soldierly appearance.

Q. How should items such as wallets, checkbooks, combs, and keys be carried in uniform pockets?
A. In such a way that they do not protrude from the pocket or present a bulky appearance.

Q. May items such as keys or key chains be attached to the belt loops or belts of the uniform?
A. Yes, if they are required for the performance of duties (ie, CQ, armorer).

NOTE: Local policy may dictate that NO items be attached to belts or belt loops.

Q. What is the policy regarding the placing of hands in the pockets?
A. While in uniform, personnel will not place their hands in their pockets except momentarily to retrieve objects.

Q. The BDU is made of wash and wear material. Does this mean that you can get away with not pressing the uniform?
A. No. AR 670-1 states, "Although some uniform items are made of wash and wear materials or treated with a permanent press finish, some pressing may be required to maintain a neat military appearance."

NOTE: Always comply with care instruction labels attached to uniform items.

Q. What are the fitting guidelines for the following articles of clothing?
A. (1) Long sleeve shirts: the sleeve length will extend to the center of the

wristbone.

(2) Uniform coats and jackets: the sleeve length will be 1 inch below the bottom of the wristbone.

(3) Black all-weather coat: the sleeve length will be 1/2 inch longer than the service coat when worn under the black all-weather coat. The bottom of the coat will reach to a point 1(1/2) inches below the midpoint of the knee (males); or 1 inch below the skirt hem but not less than 1(1/2) inches below the crease in the back of the knee (females).

(4) Knee-length skirts and dresses: lengths will not be more than 1 inch above or 2 inches below the crease in the back of the knee.

(5) Trousers: the lower edge of the waistband should be at the top of the hipbone, plus or minus 1/2 inch. The front crease of the trousers will reach the top of the instep and be cut on a diagonal line to reach a point approximately midway between the top of the heel and the top of the standard shoe in the back. The trousers may have a slight break in the front.

(6) Slacks: same as trousers except that the center of the waistband should be at the natural waistline.

(7) BDU shirt: the coat will not extend below the top of the cargo pocket on the pants and will not be any higher than the bottom of the side pocket on the pants.

Q. What section of AR 670-1 covers when the wearing of the Army uniform is required or prohibited?
A. Paragraph 1-10.

Q. What are some examples of when the wear of the Army uniform is **prohibited**?
A. - In connection with the promotion of any political or commercial interests.
- When engaged in off-duty civilian employment.
- When participating in public speeches, interviews, picket lines, marches, rallies, or public demonstrations, except as authorized by competent authority.
- **When wearing the uniform would bring discredit upon the Army.**

Q. The Class A or B service uniform is required to be worn on military airlift and DOD contract flights. What are two exceptions to this rule?
A. - When civilian clothing is mandatory at ports of embarkation or debarkation (this information should be entered on the individual's travel orders).
- The BDU may be worn when soldiers are deploying as part of a unit move and the mode of transportation is for the exclusive use of the military.

Q. Can commercial rucksacks, gymbags or like articles be worn while in uniform?
A. Yes, but only while riding a motorcycle or bicycle (once dismounted you must carry, not wear, these items).

Q. When is headgear not required to be worn with the Army uniform?
A. - When it would present a safety hazard (such as in the operation of certain military vehicles or around aircraft).
- While in a privately owned or commercial vehicle or public conveyance.
- When indoors unless under arms in an official capacity or directed by the commander (ie, indoor formation).

Q. In additional to the above circumstances, female personnel are not required to wear headgear with what uniforms?
A. The mess uniform or the Army blue, white, or enlisted green dress uniforms to an evening social event.

UNIFORMS AND INSIGNIA
AR 670-1

Q. What is meant by "uniformity of material"?
A. All outer garments are made of the same material.

Q. Can the hot weather and temperate BDU uniforms be worn intermixed (ie, hot weather top and cold weather bottom)?
A. No.

Q. No jewelry, watch chains, or similar items, to include pens and pencils, may appear exposed on uniforms. What are the two exceptions to this rule?
A. - A conservative tie tack or tie clasp may be worn with the black four-in-hand necktie.
- A pen or pencil may appear exposed on the hospital duty, food service, CVC, and flight uniforms.

Q. What are two exceptions to the "uniformity of material" policy?
A. - Garrison caps of polyester wool blend (enlisted issue) or the all polyester may be worn interchangeably with service uniforms of either shade;
- The woodland camouflage cold weather coat (field jacket) may be worn with all utility uniforms.

Q. Can commanders restrict the wear of civilian clothes by soldiers who have had their pass privileges revoked under the provisions of AR 630-5?
A. Yes.

Q. What jewelry is authorized for wear with Army uniforms?
A. - Wrist watch
- Wrist identification bracelet
- Not more than two rings (wedding band is considered one ring).
- Earrings (females): one pair, one earring per ear lobe.
- Religious articles and jewelry that are **not visible or apparent**.

Q. Female soldiers may not wear earrings with what class uniforms?
A. Class C.

Q. What are the limitations for the wear of earrings by female soldiers?
A. Earrings must be screw-on, clip-on, or post-type and may be worn with the service, dress, and mess uniforms only. They will not exceed 6-mm or 1/4 inch in diameter. They will be of gold, silver, or white pearl; unadorned and spherical. When worn, they will fit snugly against the ear and will be worn as a matched pair with only one earring per ear lobe.

Q. When are male soldiers **not** authorized to wear earrings?
A. When in uniform or when wearing civilian clothing on duty.

Q. Are fad devices, medallions, personal talismans, or amulets authorized for wear with the uniform or on duty?
A. No.

Q. What type eyeglasses are authorized for wear with the uniform?
A. Army issue or civilian prescription glasses (so long as they are conservative and do not have lenses or frames with initials).

Q. What are the limitations for the wear of sunglasses with the uniform?
A. Conservative prescription and nonprescription sunglasses are authorized when in a garrison environment - except in formation and while indoors.

UNIFORMS AND INSIGNIA
AR 670-1

NOTE: Individuals who are required by medical authority to wear sunglasses for medical reasons other than refractive error, may wear them except when safety considerations apply.

Q. How and when are identification tags required to be worn?
A. Identification tags will be worn around the neck, except when safety considerations apply, when engaged in field training, when traveling in aircraft, and when in uniform outside the United States.

Q. What is the only time that commercially designed protective headgear is authorized for wear with the uniform?
A. When operating motorcycles or bicycles and like vehicles (protective headgear will be removed and authorized Army headgear donned when travel is complete).

Q. What is "The Institute of Heraldry"?
A. The organization which, among other things, is responsible for authorizing the manufacture of heraldic items (according to Government specifications) and approving designs for distinctive unit insignia (DUI) and shoulder sleeve insignia (SSI).

Q. What does "AMCSS" stand for?
A. Army Military Clothing Sales Store.

Q. What is the responsibility of soldiers regarding the purchase of uniforms, uniform items, or heraldic items from a source other than the MCSS?
A. You must ensure that the items conform to appropriate military specifications. Items should contain a label, stamp, hallmark or certificate certifying that the item was produced in accordance with the appropriate military specification by a manufacturer certified by The Institute of Heraldry, US Army.

Q. What AR covers the "Issue and Sale of Personal Clothing"?
A. AR 700-84.

Q. What publication is titled "Clothing and Individual Equipment"?
A. CTA-50-900.

Q. Are <u>enlisted</u> soldiers required to maintain their initial clothing allowances and supplemental clothing allowances when issued?
A. Yes, IAW AR 700-84 and CTA 50-900.

NOTE: All officers are required to procure and maintain the uniforms and accessories appropriate to their assigned duties.

Q. When are the temperate and hot weather BDUs authorized for on duty wear?
A. Both styles are authorized for year-round wear. Commanders may prescribe a specific uniform for formations or ceremonial occasions, such as parades, when uniformity in appearance is required. When a specific uniform is not prescribed, soldiers may wear either style uniform.

Q. Are alterations to make the BDUs form fitting authorized?
A. No, they are designed to be loose fitting.

Q. How should the BDU trousers be bloused?
A. Using the draw cords or blousing rubbers if the trousers are not tucked into

the boots. Trouser legs will not be wrapped around the leg so tight as to present a pegged appearance.

Q. Should the Battle Dress Uniform be starched?
A. No, but some pressing may be required to maintain a neat military appearance.
NOTE: Commanders may require that these uniforms be pressed for those special occasions when appearance should be especially sharp such as parades, reviews, inspections, or other ceremonial occasions.

Q. When the sleeves of the BDU are worn rolled up, how should they look?
A. The sleeves should be rolled neatly above the elbow with the camouflage portion exposed. The roll will not be more than 3 inches above the elbow.

Q. What is the proper position of the BDU cap when worn on the head?
A. It should be worn straight on the head so that the cap band creates a straight line around the head parallel to the ground. No hair will be visible on the forehead.

Q. When may the earflaps of the BDU cap be worn down?
A. At the discretion of the individual during cold weather - except when in formation.

Q. Are you authorized to "block" the BDU cap?
A. No.

Q. What type insignia of grade must be worn on all headgear in a field environment?
A. Subdued.

Q. Who is authorized to wear insignia of branch on the BDU cap?
A. Chaplains.

Q. Can the black all-weather coat be worn as a raincoat when wearing BDUs?
A. Yes, but only in a garrison environment when organizational rain gear has not been issued.

Q. The hood of the field jacket may be worn at the soldier's option. What should be done with the hood when it is not worn?
A. It must be tucked into the jacket and the zipper zipped.

Q. When are female personnel authorized to carry handbags while wearing the BDU?
A. Only while in a garrison environment.

Q. Who is authorized to wear the field jacket or black all-weather coat unzipped/unbuttoned?
A. Female soldiers, if necessary, when wearing the maternity uniform.

Q. What are the two patterns of the Desert Battle Dress Uniform (DBDU)?
A. - Daytime pattern: three or six color desert camouflage pattern fabric.
- Night pattern: light green with dark green grid print.

NOTE: The six color DBDU has been replaced by a three color pattern.

Q. What does "ECWCS" stand for?
A. Extended Cold Weather Clothing System.

UNIFORMS AND INSIGNIA
AR 670-1

Q. When is the only time food service uniforms are authorized to be worn?
A. When in garrison.

Q. What is the standard headgear for wear with the food service uniform?
A. The green garrison cap.

Q. What coats are authorized to be worn with the food service uniform?
A. The black all-weather coat and the field jacket. The black windbreaker may also be worn except in formation.

Q. When may flight uniforms (flight suits) be worn?
A. On duty when flying or on standby awaiting flight or as directed by the commander.

Q. What does "ABDU" stand for?
A. Aircrew Battle Dress Uniform (new two-piece flight suit).

Q. What footwear is authorized with the flight suit?
A. The black leather combat boot and the black leather insulated boot.

Q. What is a CVC uniform?
A. A Combat Vehicle Crewman's uniform (tanker's suit).

Q. What is a "PFU" and what are its components?
A. Physical Fitness Uniform; gray T-shirt, trunks, sweat shirt (hooded with zipper), and sweat pants.

Q. What are the Army service uniforms?
A. - Male: Army green service uniform ("Greens"); Class A/B.
- Female: Army green service uniform ("Greens"); Class A/B.
  Green maternity service uniform.

Q. What are the Army dress uniforms?
A. - Male:
  - -- Army green service uniform with white shirt, black bow tie or black four-in-hand necktie, and trousers (commonly called "Dress Greens").
  - -- Army White Uniform ("Dress Whites").
  - -- Army Blue Uniform ("Dress Blues").
  - -- Army White Mess Uniform.
  - -- Army White Evening Mess Uniform.
  - -- Army Blue Mess Uniform.
  - -- Army Blue Evening Mess Uniform.
- Female:
  - - Army green service uniform with white shirt, black neck tab and skirt ("Dress Greens").
  - -- Army White Uniform ("Dress Whites").
  - -- Army Blue Uniform ("Dress Blues").
  - -- Army White Mess Uniform.
  - -- Army All White Mess Uniform.
  - -- Army White Evening Mess Uniform.
  - -- Army Blue Mess Uniform.
  - -- Army Blue Evening Mess Uniform.
  - -- Army Black Mess Uniform.
  - -- Army Black Evening Mess Uniform.

Q. "Dress Greens" may only be worn by whom?
A. Enlisted personnel.

UNIFORMS AND INSIGNIA
AR 670-1

Q. When can the black four-in-hand necktie be worn with dress greens?
A. Before retreat (black bow tie should be worn after retreat).

Q. Can combat boots and/or berets be worn with Dress Greens?
A. No

Q. Describe the coat sleeve ornamentation on the Class A coat.
A. - Generals officers: black braid 1(1/2) inches wide sewn on each sleeve with the lower edge parallel to and 3 inches above the bottom edge of the sleeve.
- Other officers: black braid 3/4 inches wide sewn on each sleeve as above.
- Enlisted personnel: sleeve is plain.

Q. Describe the trousers ornamentation on the service uniform trousers.
A. - General officers: two 1/2-inch wide black braids sewn 1/2 inch apart.
- Other officers: each leg will have one 1/2-inch black braid.
- Enlisted personnel: trouser leg is plain.

Q. What shirt is authorized to be worn with Class A or B uniforms?
A. The AG 415 short or long sleeve shirt.

Q. When the black sweater is worn over the AG 415 short sleeve shirt, how is the collar positioned?
A. Inside the sweater when wearing the black four-in-hand necktie; outside the sweater when not wearing the tie.

NOTE: The long-sleeve shirt will always be worn with the black necktie or necktab.

Q. Should the AG415 shirt be starched or bleached?
A. No.

Q. What headgear is authorized to be worn with the service uniform?
A. - Males: The garrison cap or the service cap (wheel cap).
- Females: The garrison cap, or the green service hat.

Q. Describe the ornamental braid on garrison caps.
A. - General officers: gold braid.
- Other commissioned officers: gold braid intertwined with black polyester.
- Warrant officers: silver braid intertwined with black polyester.
- Enlisted personnel: braid will be same material as cap, AG 344.

Q. Describe the proper wear of the garrison cap for male soldiers.
A. Will be worn with the front vertical crease of the cap centered on the forehead, in a straight line with the nose. The cap will be tilted slightly to the right, but in no case will the side of the cap rest on the top of the ear.

Q. Describe the proper wear of the garrison cap for female soldiers.
A. Will be worn with the front vertical crease of the cap centered on the forehead, with the front lower portion of the cap approximately 1 inch above the eyebrows (approximately the width of the first two fingers).

Q. Can commanders require the wear of optional items such as windbreakers or sweaters?
A. Only if they are provided to the soldier without cost.

UNIFORMS AND INSIGNIA
AR 670-1

Q. What is a "gig line"?
A. The alignment of the shirt edge with the front fly opening and the outside edge of the belt buckle.

Q. What insignia, awards, badges, and accouterments, if any, may be worn on the AG415 short or long-sleeve shirt?
A. All items normally worn with the Army green uniform except DUI, branch and U.S. insignia, sew-on insignia and combat leader's identification tabs.

Q. Describe the proper wear of the green service hat for women.
A. Will be worn straight on the head so that the hatband creates a straight line around the head parallel to the floor. Hair will not be visible on the forehead below the front brim of the hat. The brim of the hat should rest 1/2 to 1 inch above the eyebrows.

Q. What footgear is authorized for wear with the service uniform?
A. - Male: Black oxford shoes or the combat boot (authorized airborne personnel).
- Female: Black oxford shoes, black pumps, or the combat boot (as above).

Q. How is the AG 415 long or short sleeve shirt worn with the service uniform?
A. Tucked into the trousers for males (with "gig line" straight); either tucked in or left out of the skirt or slacks for females.

Q. What are the only socks authorized for wear with the black oxford or black pump footgear?
A. Black socks.

Q. What is the authorized footwear for the female Army white uniform?
A. White pumps and sheer stockings.

Q. Who is required to own a set of Dress Blues?
A. All active duty officers.

Q. When are Dress Blues considered to be an informal uniform?
A. When worn with the black four-in-hand necktie.

Q. Who is authorized to wear the blue cape with the Dress Blue uniform?
A. Only officers (as an individual option).

Q. When can full size or miniature medals be worn on Dress Blues in lieu of ribbons?
A. Only after retreat.

Q. When can dress miniature combat and special skill badges be worn on Dress Blues?
A. Only when dress miniature medals are worn.

Q. What footwear is authorized for female soldiers wearing Dress Blues?
A. Black pumps and sheer stockings. The black fabric pumps may also be worn with this uniform after duty hours.

Q. Are female soldiers authorized to wear slacks with dress blues?
A. Only if, in the performance of their duties (ie, band, honor guard, and female chaplains), wearing the slacks would be more appropriate than the blue skirt. Slacks will not be worn for social functions.

UNIFORMS AND INSIGNIA
AR 670-1

Q. What dress uniforms may be worn to a formal (Black Tie) affair?
A. The Army blue or white dress uniforms with black bow tie; blue, white, or black mess uniforms. Enlisted personnel may wear the Army green uniform (female with skirt) with white shirt and black bow tie or neck tab.

Q. What civilian attire is appropriate for a "Black Tie" affair?
A. Tuxedo.

Q. What uniform is considered to be the most formal uniform worn by Army personnel and corresponds to a civilian "white tie and tails"?
A. The Blue Evening Mess Uniform (the female black mess and evening mess uniforms are being replaced by the blue mess and evening mess uniform).

Q. Who is authorized to wear the blue mess or blue evening mess uniform?
A. All personnel.

Q. Who is authorized to wear the black mess or black evening mess uniform?
A. Only female officers.

Q. There are two types of belts that may be worn with the uniform. What are they and when is each worn?
A. (1) Brass tip belt - will only be worn with the brass buckle.
(2) Black tip belt - may be worn with the brass buckle and is required for wear with the black open-faced buckle.

Q. When either the brass tip or black tip belt is worn with the brass buckle, how far to the wearer's left may the tip extend?
A. It will not extend beyond the end of the buckle so that the fabric portion of the belt is visible.

Q. When the black tip belt is worn with the black open-faced buckle, how far to the wearer's left may the tip extend?
A. No more than 2 inches.

Q. Organizational berets come in three colors. What are they and who wears them?
A. Black (Rangers), green (Special Forces), and maroon (airborne personnel).

Q. Describe the proper way to wear an organizational beret.
A. The headband is worn straight across the forehead, 1 inch above the eyebrow with the top of the beret draped over the right ear with the stiffener positioned over the left eye.

Q. When may authorized personnel wear the beret?
A. Only with service uniforms and with utility uniforms in a garrison environment.

Q. What is the minimum possession policy for combat boots?
A. Combat boots are a clothing bag item, therefore all soldiers are required to possess two pairs of issue (specification) boots. Either the old style issue boots or the new style with closed-loop lace and padded collar are authorized. All other boots are optional purchase.

Q. How are combat boots required to be worn?
A. Diagonally laced with black laces, with the excess lace tucked into the top of the boot or under the bloused trousers or slacks or wrapped around the top of the boot.

UNIFORMS AND INSIGNIA
AR 670-1

Q. Are zipper inserts for combat boots authorized?
A. No.

Q. When are jungle boots not authorized for wear?
A. In formation when uniformity in appearance is required (formal formations, ceremonies, parades, etc).

Q. Where on the service uniform will you find the US Coat of Arms?
A. On the buttons.

Q. The cold weather cap (with black synthetic fur visor and side flaps) is authorized for wear with what uniforms?
A. The black windbreaker (when worn with the green uniform) and with the black all-weather coat (when worn with service, dress, mess, hospital duty, and food service uniforms).

Q. The black all-weather coat is authorized to be worn with what other uniforms?
A. The service, dress, mess, hospital duty and food service uniforms. Also may be worn with BDUs in a garrison environment when organizational raingear has not been issued.

Q. The new design black all-weather coat (male and female) has a mandatory possession date of 1 October 1997. What is the difference between the new one and the old one?
A. The old style all-weather coat is a single-breasted design while the new style is a six-button double-breasted model with a belt. Male and female coats are buttoned and belted from opposite directions.

Q. What type of rank is worn on the black all-weather coat?
A. Only nonsubdued pin-on rank.

Q. Are the black leather glove green inserts authorized to be worn without the black leather shells?
A. No.

Q. Are soldiers authorized to wear the black leather shell gloves with utility uniforms without cold weather outer garments?
A. Yes, as long as the sleeves are rolled down and are over the tops of the gloves.

Q. Are the black leather shell gloves required to be worn when cold weather outer garments are worn (ie, field jacket)?
A. No, they may be worn but are not required.

Q. When are the black leather dress gloves authorized to be worn?
A. With the Class A service, Army green dress, and Army maternity dress uniforms, and when wearing the black all-weather coat, windbreaker, or capes.

Q. What four types of handbags are authorized for female soldiers?
A. Black clutch-type, fabric or leather black dress, fabric or leather white dress, and the black service handbag.

Q. When may female soldiers carry the black clutch-type handbag?
A. When wearing the service uniforms and the utility uniforms (in garrison only). The leather version is authorized to be carried with the female Army

blue uniform during and after duty hours.

Q. When may female soldiers carry the black service handbag?
A. When wearing the service, utility (garrison only), and Army dress blue uniforms.

Q. The black bow tie should be black silk or satin without stripe or figure, of commercial design, and having square ends that do not exceed ______ inches in width.
A. 2(1/2)

Q. What is the authorized option to the black four-in-hand necktie?
A. A pretied snap-on necktie.

Q. What two knots are authorized for the black four-in-hand necktie?
A. Windsor or half-Windsor.

Q. When the necktie is properly tied, what should be the position of the bottom of the tie?
A. Not shorter than 2 inches above the top of the belt buckle and should not extend below the bottom of the belt buckle.

Q. When is the black scarf authorized to be worn?
A. When wearing the black all-weather coat and windbreaker.

Q. What is the proper way to wear scarves with the uniform?
A. Folded in half, lengthwise, and crossed left over right at the neck. The ends will be tucked neatly into the neckline of the outer garment.

Q. When is the green scarf authorized to be worn?
A. Only with cold weather utility coats (field jacket or parka).

Q. What is the maximum allowable height for the heels of the female black oxford shoe?
A. 2 inches.

Q. Are patent leather shoes authorized for wear?
A. No.

Q. What are the height limitations for the heels of female black pumps?
A. The heel may be from a minimum of 1/2-inch to a maximum of 3 inches.

Q. What type socks (color) are required to be worn when wearing combat boots or organizationally issued boots?
A. The olive green or black socks.

NOTE: The OG 408 green socks are being replaced by the black cushion sole socks. At this time there is no published wearout date for the green socks so they may continue to be worn.

Q. The black pullover sweater is authorized as an outer garment with what uniform?
A. Class B and food service supervisor's uniform.

Q. Where is insignia of grade worn on the black sweater?
A. Officers and enlisted personnel in the grade of corporal or higher will wear shoulder marks.

UNIFORMS AND INSIGNIA
AR 670-1

Q. What is the proper positioning for a nameplate and DUI on the black sweater?
A. The nameplate will be worn centered on the patch. If a DUI or regimental DUI is also worn, the nameplate will be centered 1/2 inch above the bottom of the patch, and the DUI will be centered from left to right, top to bottom above the nameplate.

Q. Who may carry an umbrella while in uniform?
A. Female personnel only, while wearing the service, dress, and mess uniforms.

Q. The black windbreaker is authorized to be worn with what uniforms?
A. The Class B service uniform, hospital duty, and food service uniforms.

Q. When the windbreaker is worn, how far up must it be zipped?
A. At least to the top of the second button from the top of the shirt.

Q. The old style windbreaker (no longer authorized for wear) has been replaced by a new windbreaker. Describe it.
A. The officer windbreaker has a knit collar, cuffs, and waist. The enlisted windbreaker has a standard collar, knit cuffs, and waist. Female windbreakers have bust darts.

Q. AR 670-1 specifically points out three uniform items that may be worn with civilian clothing if all insignia is removed. What are they?
A. The black all-weather coat, sweater, and windbreaker.

Q. Are male soldiers required to wear only the brown issue brief or boxer style drawers?
A. No, optional purchase white drawers of a commercial brief or boxer style may also be worn.

Q. What are "accouterments"?
A. Items such as medals, ribbons, insignia, badges, emblems, tabs, and tapes authorized for wear on uniforms.

Q. What are "appurtenances"?
A. Devices such as stars, letters, numerals, or clasps worn on the suspension ribbon of the medal, or on the ribbon bar, which indicate additional awards, participation in specific events, or other distinguishing characteristics of the award.

Q. How should embroidered cloth insignia be sewn on the uniform?
A. So that the stitching blends inconspicuously with the background material.

Q. Explain the positioning of insignia on the garrison cap.
A. Officers will wear nonsubdued insignia of grade, centered on the left curtain 1 inch from the front crease. Enlisted personnel will wear the DUI in the same location.

Q. What may the Sergeant Major of the Army (SMA) wear on the garrison cap in place of the DUI?
A. The SMA insignia.

Q. Explain the positioning of insignia of grade on the kevlar camouflage cover.
A. Centered on the front of the camouflage approximately 2(1/2) inches up from the bottom rim.

UNIFORMS AND INSIGNIA
AR 670-1

Q. Can soldiers be required to have embroidered rank sewn on the kevlar camouflage cover?
A. Only if it is issued and attached at no cost to the soldier.

Q. How should insignia of grade (insignia of branch for chaplains) be positioned on the BDU cap?
A. Centered on the front of the headgear left to right, top to bottom.

Q. Officers must wear _________ rank on their BDU caps when in garrison and ________ rank when in a field environment.
A. Nonsubdued; subdued.

Q. What is the correct placement of the "U.S." insignia on the male enlisted service uniform?
A. The bottom of the insignia will be placed approximately 1 inch above the notch, centered on the right collar with the center line of the insignia parallel to the inside edge of the lapel.

Q. What is the correct placement of the "U.S." insignia on the female enlisted service uniform?
A. The bottom of the insignia will be placed approximately 5/8-inch up from the notch, centered on the right collar with the center line of the insignia parallel to the inside edge of the lapel.

Q. What phrase can be used to easily remember which side of the collar the US Insignia is placed on?
A. "The U.S. is always RIGHT!"

Q. When is the "U.S." insignia worn on both collars of male and female service uniforms?
A. When in basic training (prior to award of basic MOS).

Q. When the insignia of grade for Colonel is worn on the uniform coat, how are the eagles positioned?
A. With the heads of the eagles facing the front.

Q. When the insignia of grade for colonel is worn on the headgear, how is the eagle positioned?
A. With the head of the eagle facing the wearer's right.

Q. When Lieutenant Colonel or Major insignia is worn on the uniform coat, how is the oak leaf positioned?
A. With the stem facing the outside shoulder seam.

Q. What is the correct placement for nonsubdued cloth insignia of grade for enlisted personnel on the Army green, blue, and white uniform coats?
A. Centered between the shoulder seam and the elbow.

Q. Who is required to wear nonsubdued pin-on insignia of grade on the AG 415 shirt?
A. Specialist and below.

Q. What is the correct placement of rank on the AG 415 shirt for Specialist and below?
A. Centered on both collars with the center line of the insignia bisecting the points of the collar and 1 inch up from the collar point.

UNIFORMS AND INSIGNIA
AR 670-1

Q. Who is required to wear shoulder marks on the AG 415 shirt?
A. Corporal and above.

Q. What is the difference between the shoulder marks of officers and that of enlisted personnel?
A. Shoulder marks for officers have a 1/8" yellow stripe sewn below the embroidered insignia of grade (outside edge). Officers are no longer authorized to wear green shoulder marks.

Q. How many sizes do shoulder marks come in?
A. Two (to accommodate differences in manufacturing of shoulder loops on shirts and sweaters).

Q. Describe the Insignia of Branch for a Command Sergeant Major.
A. The Coat of Arms of the United States on a 1-inch disk of gold color metal.

Q. Describe the correct placement of Branch Insignia on the male enlisted green, blue, or white uniforms.
A. The bottom of the insignia of branch disk will be placed approximately 1 inch above the notch and centered on the left collar with the center line of the insignia parallel to the inside edge of the lapel.

Q. How does the placement of the Branch Insignia differ for the female enlisted uniforms (see above question)?
A. There is no change for placement of Branch Insignia on the Army white and blue uniform coats; however, for the Army green uniform coat the bottom of the disk should be 5/8-inch up from the notch instead of 1 inch.

Q. When placing the Insignia of Branch or "US" Insignia on the uniform, how do you distinguish between the "collar" and the "lapel"?
A. The "collar" refers to that part of the coat or shirt around the neck, which forms a neckband and turnover piece. The "lapel" refers to the fold of the front of the coat that is a continuation of the collar and usually separated by a notch in the collar.

Q. Shoulder Sleeve Insignia (SSI) is most commonly called what?
A. The Organizational Patch ("organization" normally being a MACOM).

Q. What is the correct placement of SSI on the uniform?
A. Centered on the left sleeve 1/2-inch below the top of the shoulder seam.

Q. When a special skill or marksmanship tab is worn, how does the positioning of the SSI differ from above?
A. The tab is placed 1/2-inch below the top of the shoulder seam and the SSI 1/4-inch below the tab.

Q. Tabs that are an integral part of an SSI (such as airborne or mountain) are worn how?
A. Directly above the SSI with no space between insignia and tab.

Q. What is an SSI-FWS and what is it most commonly called? What is its correct placement on the uniform?
A. Shoulder Sleeve Insignia - Former Wartime Service: a US Army organizational SSI of a wartime unit that has been approved by HQDA; it is most commonly called the "Combat Patch"; it is worn centered, 1/2-inch below the top of the right shoulder seam.

UNIFORMS AND INSIGNIA
AR 670-1

Q. Is the SSI-FWS required to be worn on the uniform?
A. No, it is an individual option.

Q. When may Branch of Service Scarves be worn with service and utility uniforms?
A. When issued and prescribed for wear by the local commander for ceremonial occasions only.

Q. Who is authorized to wear the green cloth Combat Leader's Identification Tabs
and how are they worn?
A. Leaders of Category I organizations (specified by TOE: Armor, Infantry, Combat Engineer, Field Artillery, Air Defense Artillery, and Aviation units) and category II assault helicopter units. More specifically, the following leaders in the above organizations:

- Commanders
- Deputy Commanders
- Platoon Leaders
- Command Sergeants Major
- First Sergeants
- Platoon Sergeants
- Section Leaders (when designated by TOE)
- Squad Leaders and Tank Commanders
- Rifle Squad Fire Team Leaders

The green cloth loops are worn in the middle of both shoulder loops of the Army green service coats and the cold weather coat (field jacket) and on the center tab of the Gortex^{tm} parka.

Q. What does "DUI" stand for?
A. Distinctive Unit Insignia.

Q. When a DUI is authorized, the insignia will be worn by all assigned personnel of the organization, except whom?
A. General officers and the Sergeant Major of the Army.

Q. A complete set of DUI for the enlisted soldier consists of how many pieces?
A. 3; one for each shoulder loop of the service coat and one for the headgear.

Q. Describe the proper positioning of the DUI on the following: service coat, garrison cap, black sweater.
A. Service coat: centered on the shoulder loops, and equidistant from the outside shoulder seam to the outside edge of the button, with the base of the insignia toward the outside shoulder seam (not on the Army dress green).
Garrison cap: centered on the left curtain of the garrison cap, 1 inch from the front crease.
Black sweater: centered above the nameplate.

Q. What is an RDI?
A. Regimental Distinctive Insignia (regimental crest), formerly known as Regimental Distinctive Unit Insignia.

Q. Who is authorized to wear an RDI and how is it worn on the male service uniform?
A. All soldiers affiliated with a regiment; it is worn centered and 1/8-inch above the top of the pocket flap or 1/4-inch above unit awards or foreign badges.

Q. How does the positioning of the regimental crest on the female service uniform differ from the male uniform?
A. The crest is centered and 1/2-inch above the nameplate or 1/4-inch above unit awards or foreign badges.

UNIFORMS AND INSIGNIA
AR 670-1

Q. How long should the "U.S. ARMY" tape be?
A. 4(1/2) inches long or will extend to the edges of the pocket flaps.

Q. How long should the nametape for BDUs be?
A. Same as "U.S. ARMY" tape - 4(1/2) inches or extended to the edges of the pocket. Nametape and "U.S. ARMY" tape must be same length.

Q. Normally, names are printed in 3/4-inch black block letters. How are names printed that consist of 11 letters or more?
A. Franklin Gothic extra condensed print, 1/2-inch high.

Q. Describe the nameplate.
A. A black laminated plastic plate, 1 inch by 3 inches by 1/16-inch thick, with a white border not to exceed 1/32-inch in width. Lettering is block type, indented white lettering, 3/8-inch in height and centered on the plate. Finish may be gloss or non-gloss. Only last names will be used.

Q. Describe the proper positioning of the nameplate on the male service coat, AG 415 shirt, and black sweater.
A. Service coat: worn centered from left to right, top to bottom on the right breast pocket between the top of the button and the top of the pocket.
AG 415 shirt: same as above.
Sweater: centered on black patch when no DUI is worn; 1/2 inch above the bottom seam of the black patch when DUI is worn (with DUI centered above nameplate).

Q. Describe the proper positioning of the nameplate on the female service coat, AG 415 shirt, and black sweater.
A. Service coat: worn between 1-2 inches above the top of the top button centered horizontally on the wearer's right side.
AG 415 shirt: comparable position as above.
Sweater: same as male, above.

Q. Who is authorized to wear service aiguillettes?
A. Army attaches, assistant Army attaches, and aides.

Q. Describe the wear of service stripes on the uniform.
A. Centered on the outside bottom half of the left sleeve at a 45-degree angle with the lower end toward the inside seam of the sleeve and placed 4 inches from the bottom of the sleeve.

Q. How are service stripes awarded?
A. One stripe is authorized for each 3 years of active Federal service, active Reserve service, or a combination. Service need not have been continuous and the 10th stripe is authorized after 29(1/2) years.

Q. Describe the positioning of overseas service bars on the service uniform.
A. Will be worn centered on the outside bottom half of the right sleeve, 4 inches above and parallel to the bottom of the sleeve (enlisted personnel).

Q. How much space is there between multiple service stripes and overseas service bars?
A. 1/16-inch.

Q. What are "brassards" and where are they worn?
A. Cloth shoulder bands used to identify designated personnel who may be

required to perform a special task or to deal with the public; brassards are worn on the left sleeve of the outer garment with the bottom edge approximately two inches above the elbow.

Q. There are currently 18 different brassards (arm bands) authorized for wear. Name five of them.
A. - Acting NCO
- Acting officers
- Armed Forces Police
- Army Community Service
- Explosive Ordnance Disposal
- GAS
- Geneva Convention
- Mourning
- Military Police
- Movement Control
- Officer of the Day
- Officer of the Guard
- Photographer
- Port
- Trainees in Leadership Courses
- Unit Police
- Veterinary Corps
- CID

Q. What two distinctive items are authorized for wear on the service uniform by infantry personnel?
A. The blue shoulder cord and the blue Branch & US Insignia disks.

Q. Who is authorized to wear background trimming on the Parachutist or Air Assault badge?
A. Personnel of an airborne designated organization who have been awarded one of the parachutist badges or by personnel in an organization designated air assault who have been awarded the air assault badge. Only ONE background trimming will be worn.

Q. What is an "award"?
A. Any decoration, medal, badge, ribbon, or appurtenance bestowed on an individual or unit.

Q. What Army regulation provides the authorization and qualifying criteria for the US decorations, service medals, badges, unit awards, and appurtenances worn on the Army uniform?
A. AR 672-5-1.

Q. What is meant by the term "ribbon"?
A. That portion of the suspension ribbon of a service medal or decoration worn instead of the service medal or decoration and made in the form of a ribbon bar, 1(3/8) inches long by 3/8-inch wide.

Q. Are awards required to be worn on the service uniform?
A. It is normally an individual option. However, individuals are encouraged to wear authorized awards on the class A service, dress, and mess uniforms. Commanders may require the wear of awards for parades, reviews, inspections, funerals, and ceremonial and social occasions.

Q. When is the wearing of awards prohibited?
A. - On any uniform other than authorized by AR 670-1.
- By enlisted personnel while serving a sentence of confinement.
- When wearing civilian clothing, except for civilian awards, lapel buttons, or rosettes intended for wear with civilian clothing.
- By officers when suspended from rank or command.

NOTE: Soldiers may wear miniature medals on formal civilian attire at formal social functions when wearing the Army uniform would be inappropriate or not authorized.

UNIFORMS AND INSIGNIA
AR 670-1

Q. What is a "decoration"?
A. An award to an individual for an act of gallantry or meritorious service.

Q. What is the highest US Military decoration?
A. The Medal of Honor (Army, Navy, Air Force).

Q. What is the highest US nonmilitary decoration?
A. The Presidential Medal of Freedom.

Q. Can foreign decorations be worn on the uniform?
A. Yes, as long as at least one US decoration or service medal is worn at the same time (worn in order of receipt after all US decorations, GCM, campaign and service medals, and service and training ribbons).

Q. What three fourrageres are authorized to be worn with the uniform by qualified individuals?
A. The French and Belgian Fourrageres and the Netherlands Orange Lanyard.

Q. Describe the wear of ribbons on the service uniform.
A. Worn in order of precedence from the wearer's right to left in one or more rows. The first and second rows will contain the same number of ribbons (three or four) before starting a third row. The third and succeeding rows will contain the same or fewer ribbons than the first two rows. The top row will be centered on the row beneath or aligned to the left, whichever presents the best appearance. For male soldiers, the ribbons will be centered and 1/8-inch above the left breast pocket. Female soldiers will have the bottom row positioned parallel to the bottom edge of the nameplate (may be adjusted to conform to individual figure differences).

Q. How much space should there be between rows of ribbons?
A. Either no space or 1/8-inch space (but must be uniform).

Q. What is the maximum number of ribbons that may be worn in one row?
A. Four.

Q. Is the commercial mounting of ribbons on a cloth background authorized?
A. Yes, on an optional basis. The cloth background should be black, or of matching fabric of the uniform worn, and the border trim should not exceed 1/8-inch.

Q. When lapel buttons are worn on civilian clothing, what is their proper location?
A. The left lapel.

Q. When are full-size decorations and service medals authorized to be worn?
A. Only on Army blue and white uniforms, and the Army green dress uniform by enlisted personnel when worn for social functions.

Q. What is not authorized to be worn with full-size decorations and service medals?
A. Service and training ribbons and the Drivers and Mechanic Badge. In addition, special skill and marksmanship badges will not be worn on the pocket flap below the medals.

Q. Can full-size decorations and service medals be overlapped within a row?
A. No.

UNIFORMS AND INSIGNIA
AR 670-1

Q. How is the Medal of Honor worn?
A. With the neckband ribbon around the neck, outside the shirt collar and inside the coat collar, with the medal hanging over the necktie. Authorized foreign neck decorations are worn beneath the MOH.

Q. On what uniforms may miniature decorations and service medals be worn?
A. Male personnel: Army white and blue dress, white and blue mess, and white and blue evening mess uniforms; and on the left lapel of formal civilian attire when wearing of Army uniforms would be inappropriate or not authorized.
Female personnel: same as above except the all-white and black mess, and black evening mess uniforms are included.

NOTE: Miniature medals may only be worn on the Army blue and white dress uniforms when these uniforms are worn as formal dress uniforms (bow tie).

Q. What is the rule regarding the wear (placement) of miniature medals?
A. Miniature medals will be worn side by side when four or less are worn in the same row. They may be overlapped, so that each medal partially covers the medal at its left with the right medal showing in full when five, six, or seven medals are worn in the same row. The overlap will not exceed 50% and will be equal for all medals. Second and subsequent rows will be positioned so that the medal pendants on the row below are visible. The top row will be centered on the row below.

Q. What is the rule regarding the placement of Unit awards that have frames?
A. Will be worn with the laurel leaves of the frame pointing (growing) upward.

Q. Describe the proper placement of unit awards on the uniform.
A. All unit award emblems with and without frames will be worn in the order of precedence from the wearer's right to left in rows of not more than three emblems per row, with no space between emblems and with up to 1/8-inch space between rows. Male personnel will wear the emblems centered and 1/8-inch above the right breast pocket flap. Female soldiers will wear the emblems centered on the right side of the uniform with the bottom edge 1/2-inch above the top edge of the nameplate.

Q. How many fourrageres/aiguillettes/lanyards/cords may be worn on one shoulder?
A. Only one fourragere, lanyard, aiguillette, or cord will be on each shoulder.

Q. What US decoration cannot be worn as a miniature?
A. The Medal of Honor.

Q. Describe the "oak leaf cluster".
A. It is a bronze twig of four oak leaves with three acorns on each stem; it is worn to denote award of second and succeeding awards of decorations (other than the Air Medal).

Q. A silver OLC is worn in lieu of _____ bronze OLCs.
A. 5

Q. How should OLCs be positioned on the ribbon?
A. Centered with the stems of the leaves pointing to the wearer's right.

Q. How many OLCs may be worn side by side on service ribbons?
A. Four.

UNIFORMS AND INSIGNIA
AR 670-1

Q. What is a 'V' device?
A. A bronze block letter "V", 1/4 inch high, that is worn to denote participation in acts of heroism involving conflict with an armed enemy.

Q. How many 'V' devices may be worn on one ribbon?
A. One (when worn with an oak leaf cluster or numerals, the 'V' device will be worn on the wearer's right).

Q. What is the Arrowhead and how is it worn?
A. A bronze replica of an Indian arrowhead 1/4-inch high and used to denote participation in a combat parachute jump, combat glider landing, or amphibious assault landing; it is worn with the point facing upward and is placed to the wearer's right of all service stars.

Q. How many Arrowheads may be worn on one ribbon?
A. One.

Q. Are marksmanship badges from other US Services authorized for wear on the Army uniform?
A. No.

Q. What three tabs are authorized for wear on the Army uniform (does not include tabs that are an integral part of an SSI such as "AIRBORNE", "MOUNTAIN", "HONOR GUARD", or "PERSHING")?
A. The President's Hundred, Ranger, and Special Forces Tabs are the only tabs authorized for wear.

Q. How many of the above badges may be worn at one time if all three are authorized?
A. Either the President's Hundred or the Ranger and Special Forces (both of which may be worn together) but not all three.

Q. What is the correct placement of these three tabs on the Army uniform?
A. The full color tabs are worn 1/2-inch below the shoulder seam on the left sleeve of service uniforms and 1/8-inch below the shoulder seam on the left sleeve of the utility uniforms and field jackets.

Q. When the Ranger and Special Forces tabs are authorized and worn together which one goes on top and what is the correct spacing?
A. The Special Forces tab is on top and should be centered on the left shoulder sleeve 1/2-inch from the shoulder seam. The Ranger tab will be centered 1/8-inch below the Special Forces tab.

Q. What are the four categories of badges worn on the Army uniform?
A. (1) Marksmanship badges and tab.
(2) Combat and special skill badges and tabs.
(3) Identification badges.
(4) Foreign badges.

Q. List, in order, the eight marksmanship badges authorized for wear on the Army uniform.
A. (1) Distinguished International Shooter badge.
(2) Distinguished Rifleman badge.
(3) Distinguished Pistol Shot badge.
(4) National Trophy Match badges.
(5) Interservice Competition badges.

(6) US Army Excellence in Competition Rifleman badge.
(7) US Army Excellence in Competition Pistol Shot badge.
(8) Marksmanship Qualification badges (Expert, Sharpshooter, and Marksman).

Q. What is the maximum number of marksmanship badges that may be worn at one time?
A. Three.

Q. How many clasps may be attached to any one marksmanship badge?
A. No more than three.

Q. The total number of marksmanship **and** special skill badges worn on the pocket flap or below the ribbons will not exceed ______.
A. Three.

Q. Are marksmanship badges worn to the wearer's right or left of special skill badges worn in the same row?
A. Left.

Q. Describe the appropriate placement of marksmanship badges for the following conditions:
A. One marksmanship badge - centered from left to right with the upper portion of the badge 1/8-inch below the top of the pocket (1/4-inch below ribbons for females).

Two marksmanship badges - equally spaced from left to right with at least one inch space between badges. Vertical placement is same as above.

Three marksmanship badges - equally spaced on the pocket flap or similar location below ribbons for females. Vertical placement same as above.

Q. What are the combat and special skill badges authorized for wear on the Army uniform (in group precedence)?
A. (1) Group 1: Combat Infantry badges; Expert Infantry badge.
(2) Group 2: Combat Medical badges; Expert Field Medical badge.
(3) Group 3: Army Astronaut badges; Army Aviator badges; Flight Surgeon badges; Aircraft Crewman badges.
(4) Group 4: Glider badge; Combat Parachutist badges; Parachutist badges; Pathfinder badge; Air Assault badge.
(5) Group 5: Diver badges; Driver and Mechanic badges; Explosive Ordnance Disposal badges; Nuclear Reactor Operator badges; Parachute Rigger badge.
(6) Physical Fitness Training badge.

Q. How many combat and special skill badges may be worn at one time? What are the rules regarding the wear of combat and special skill badges?
A. Four (does not include special skill tabs such as Ranger and Special Forces); only one badge from groups 1, 2, 3, and 5 may be worn. Two badges from group 4 may be worn if no badge from group 5 is worn. Combat badges have precedence over special skill badges within the same group.

Q. Where is the Physical Fitness Badge authorized to be worn?
A. Centered on the left side, above the breast, of the physical training T-shirt or sweatshirt.

Q. Describe the placement of combat and special skill badges above the ribbons.
A. Will be worn one above the other 1/4-inch above the ribbons, or the top of the pocket, and spaced 1/2-inch apart (may be worn aligned with the left edge of the ribbons or medals when obscured by the coat lapel).

UNIFORMS AND INSIGNIA
AR 670-1

Q. Describe the placement of special skill badges below the ribbons (on pocket flap).
A. Same as for marksmanship badges above.

Q. Describe the placement of subdued combat and special skill badges on the BDU.
A. One badge: centered, 1/4-inch above the US Army tape.
Two badges: centered, in a vertical line above US Army tape, with 1/2-inch space between badges.
Three badges: two centered above US Army tape and one centered on pocket flap.
Four badges: three centered above US Army tape and one centered on pocket flap.

NOTE: Badges must be arranged in order of group preference (see above).

Q. There are eleven identification badges authorized for wear on the Army uniform. Name three of them.
A. (1) Presidential Service
(2) Vice-Presidential Service
(3) Secretary of Defense
(4) Joint Chiefs of Staff
(5) Army Staff
(6) Guard, Tomb of the Unknown Soldier
(7) Drill Sergeant
(8) U.S. Army Recruiter
(9) Career Counselor
(10) Military Police
(11) Army Medical Department Recruiter

NOTE: The last three ID badges listed above are not authorized for permanent wear.

Q. Which of the above identification badges are worn on the left side of the uniform?
A. Secretary of Defense, JCS, Recruiter, and MP.

Q. What is the maximum number of identification badges that may be worn on one side of the jacket or coat?
A. Two.

Q. Which of the above badges are authorized as a subdued embroidered cloth badge?
A. Drill Sergeant and Recruiter.

Q. What is the maximum number of foreign badges that may be worn at one time?
A. One.

Q. What is the correct placement of foreign badges on the service uniform?
A. 1/8-inch above the right pocket flap (1/2-inch above nameplate for females) and 1/2 inch above any unit awards if worn. Foreign badges that are only awarded as cloth badges will not be worn on the Army uniform.

Q. What is the German marksmanship award called and how is it worn?
A. Schuetzenschur; worn only by enlisted personnel, on the right side of the uniform coat with the upper portion attached under the center of the shoulder

loop, and the bottom portion attached under the lapel.

Q. Describe the policy on the wearing of the uniform by former members of the Army.
A. Former members of the Army who served honorably during a declared or undeclared war and whose most recent service was terminated under honorable conditions, may wear the Army uniform in the highest grade held during such war service. The uniform may be worn only for the following ceremonies and when traveling to and from the ceremony:

- Military funerals, memorial services, weddings, and inaugurals.
- Parades on National or State holidays, or other parades or ceremonies of a patriotic nature in which any active or reserve US military unit is taking part.

NOTE: Wearing the uniform at any other time is prohibited.

Q. What former members of the Army may wear the Army uniform at their pleasure except under circumstances outlined in paragraph 1-10 of AR 670-1?
A. Personnel who have been awarded the Medal of Honor.

Q. When may former members of the Army wear medals on civilian clothing?
A. On Veterans Day, Memorial Day, and Armed Forces Day as well as at formal occasions of ceremony and social functions of a military nature.

Q. Can the Distinctive Unit Insignia (DUI) be worn on civilian clothing?
A. Yes, on the breast pocket or the lapel by former members of a unit.

AWARDS & DECORATIONS
AR 672-5-1

Q. What Army regulation provides the authorization and qualifying criteria for US decorations, service medals, badges, unit awards, and appurtenances worn on the Army uniform?
A. AR 672-5-1.

Q. What is the objective of the DA Military Awards Program?
A. To provide tangible recognition for acts of valor, exceptional service or achievement, special skills or qualifications, and acts of heroism not involving actual combat.

Q. Individual awards are grouped into what six categories?
A. (1) Decorations
(2) Good Conduct Medal
(3) Service Medals
(4) Service Ribbons
(5) Badges and Tabs
(6) Certificates and Letters

Q. What are the two categories of Decorations?
A. Awards for heroism and awards for achievement.

Q. List the order of precedence for the wearing of individual awards.
A. (1) US military decorations
(2) US nonmilitary decorations
(3) Prisoner of War Medal
(4) Good Conduct Medal
(5) US Army Reserve Components Achievement Medal
(6) US service medals and service ribbons
(7) US Merchant Marine decorations
(8) Foreign decorations (excluding service medals and ribbons)
(9) Non-US service medals and ribbons

NOTE: The order of precedence for wear within the various classes of medals and service ribbons is further described in paragraph 28-6, AR 670-1.

Q. Who may recommend someone for an award?
A. It is the responsibility of any individual having personal knowledge of an act, achievement, or service believed to warrant the award of a decoration, to submit a formal recommendation into military command channels for consideration.

Q. Can you recommend yourself for an award of a military decoration?
A. No, the Army does not condone self-recognition.

Q. Is there a time limitation for the recommendation of an award?
A. Yes, each recommendation for an award of a military decoration must be entered administratively into military channels within 2 years of the act, achievement, or service to be honored.

Q. What is the required character of service for an individual to receive a decoration?
A. A medal will not be awarded or presented to any individual whose entire service subsequent to the time of the distinguished act, achievement, or service has not been honorable.

Q. What is the status of "flagged" soldiers with respect to awards?

AWARDS & DECORATIONS
AR 672-5-1

A. Individuals on whom favorable personnel actions have been suspended neither are recommended for nor receive awards during the period of suspension.

Q. Not more than one of the same decoration will be awarded to one person. What is awarded in lieu of decorations for each succeeding act or period of service that justifies the award of a decoration?
A. An oak leaf cluster (or numeral device for Air Medals).

Q. Can more than one decoration be awarded to an individual for the same act, achievement, or period of meritorious service.
A. No.

Q. How should the following awards be presented?
A. **Medal of Honor**: presented to living awardees by the President of the United States at the White House.
Other US military decorations: presented with an appropriate air of formality and with fitting ceremony.
Service medals and ribbons: usually are not presented with formal ceremony.
Badges: whenever practicable, presented to military personnel in a formal ceremony as provided in FM 22-5.
Good Conduct Medal: may be made at troop formations.

Q. With reference to posthumous awards, what are the eligible classes of next of kin?
A. In order of precedence, surviving spouse, eldest child, father or mother, eldest sibling, or eldest grandchild.

Q. Can the award of personal decorations be revoked?
A. Yes, it may be revoked by the awarding authority if facts subsequently determined would have prevented original approval of the award had they known at the time.

Q. When can the Parachutist Badge be revoked?
A. When the awardee is punished under the UCMJ for refusal to participate in a parachute jump.

Q. What is engraved on the reverse side of the Medal of Honor?
A. The grade, name, and organization of the awardee.

Q. What is engraved on the reverse side of all other decorations and the Good Conduct Medal?
A. The name only of the awardee.

Q. What special entitlements are authorized for Medal of Honor recipients?
A.
- Name may be entered on Medal of Honor Roll. This entitles awardee to special pension of $200.00 per month.
- Enlisted recipients of the MOH are entitled to a supplemental uniform allowance.
- MOH awardees are entitled to special Air Transportation rights (see DOD Reg 4515.13-R).
- Commissary privileges for MOH recipients and eligible dependents.
- Identification cards for MOH recipients and eligible dependents.
- Exchange privileges for MOH recipients and eligible dependents.
- Children of MOH recipients, otherwise qualified, are not subject to quota requirements for admission to any of the US Service Academies.
- 10 percent increase in retirement pay for enlisted MOH recipients.
- Special burial honors (AR 600-25).

AWARDS & DECORATIONS
AR 672-5-1

Q. Any enlisted soldier who is credited with extraordinary heroism in the line of duty and who retires after 20 or more years active Federal service, is entitled to a 10 percent increase in retired pay, subject to the 75 percent limit on total retired pay. Who, besides MOH recipients, satisfies the requirement for extraordinary heroism?
A. Any awardee of the Distinguished Service Cross, Navy Cross, or Air Force Cross.

Q. The recipients of what badges are entitled to an increase in pay (hazardous and special duty pay), contingent on certain restrictions?
A. Parachutist badges, aviator badges, diver badges, and explosive ordnance disposal badges.

Q. All US Army medals are presented without cost to an awardee. Can replacement medals be obtained without cost?
A. Yes, to an awardee in active Federal military service when his/her written request includes a statement that the original medal was lost, destroyed, or rendered unfit for use without fault or neglect on his/her part.

Q. Should awards for meritorious achievement or service be based upon the grade of the intended recipient?
A. No, the award should reflect both the individual's level of responsibility and his or her manner of performance.

Q. What should be the predominant factor in the decision to award an individual a decoration?
A. The degree to which an individual's achievement or service enhanced the readiness or effectiveness of his or her organization.

Q. Is an individual automatically entitled to an award upon departure from an assignment?
A. **No,** awards presented in conjunction with a PCS will be limited to exceptional cases.

Q. Can units set quotas on the number of awards that can be presented?
A. No, limiting awards to a specific number per unit is not authorized.

Q. There are 18 individual decorations listed in AR 672-5-1 (Army decorations). Name as many as you can, in order of precedence.
A. (1) Congressional Medal of Honor
(2) Distinguished Service Cross
(3) Defense Distinguished Service Medal
(4) Distinguished Service Medal
(5) Silver Star
(6) Defense Superior Service Medal
(7) Legion of Merit
(8) Distinguished Flying Cross
(9) Soldier's Medal
(10) Bronze Star Medal
(11) Purple Heart
(12) Defense Meritorious Service Medal
(13) Meritorious Service Medal
(14) Air Medal
(15) Joint Service Commendation Medal
(16) Army Commendation Medal
(17) Joint Service Achievement Medal
(18) Army Achievement Medal

Q. The Legion of Merit is awarded in four different degrees, each degree of award based on relative rank or position of the recipient. What are these four degrees in order of precedence from highest to lowest?
A. Chief Commander, Commander, Officer, and Legionnaire.

Q. How are subsequent awards of the Air Medal indicated?
A. Numerals, starting with 2 will be used to denote second and subsequent awards of the Air Medal.

AWARDS & DECORATIONS
AR 672-5-1

Q. Who should be awarded the Good Conduct Medal?
A. It is awarded on a selective basis to each soldier who distinguishes himself/herself from among his/her fellow soldiers by their exemplary conduct, efficiency, and fidelity throughout a specific period of continuous enlisted active Federal military service. There is no right or entitlement to the medal.

Q. What are the qualifying periods of service for award of the GCM?
A. (1) Each 3 years completed.
   (2) For first award only, upon termination of service of less than 3 years but more than 1 year.
   (3) For first award only, upon termination of service of less than 1 year when final separation was by reason of physical disability incurred in the line of duty.

Q. What is the minimum period of service required for the first award of the GCMDL?
A. 12 months (except as noted in "c" above).

Q. When are two successive enlistments not considered to be continuous and therefore not creditable toward an award?
A. When an interval in excess of 24 hours occurs between enlistments.

Q. What are the character of service requirements for the award of the GCMDL?
A.
- The immediate commander must evaluate the soldier's character as above reproach.
- The record of service must indicate that the soldier has willingly complied with the demands of the military environment, has been loyal and obedient to superiors, has faithfully supported the goals of the organization and the Army, and has conducted himself/herself in such an exemplary manner as to distinguish him/her from fellow soldiers.
- In terms of job performance, the soldier's efficiency must be evaluated as meeting all requirements and expectations for one of that soldier's grade, MOS, and experience.

Q. Can a soldier who has received nonjudicial punishment receive a GCMDL?
A. While any record of nonjudicial punishment could be in conflict with recognizing the soldier's service as exemplary, such record should not be viewed as automatically disqualifying. Commanders must analyze the record, giving consideration to the nature of the infraction, the circumstances under which it occurred, and when. So, conceivably, a soldier could be awarded the GCMDL even if he/she has received nonjudicial punishment.

Q. How does conviction by court-martial effect a soldiers qualification for the GCMDL?
A. Conviction by court-martial terminates a period of qualifying service; a new period of service begins following the completion of sentence imposed by court-martial.

Q. When is the DA Form 4950 (Good Conduct Medal Certificate) presented to enlisted soldiers?
A. Only on the following occasions:
- Concurrent with the first award of the GCMDL.
- Concurrent with retirement.

Q. Service medals and ribbons awarded by other US Services are authorized for

AWARDS & DECORATIONS
AR 672-5-1

wear on the Army uniform with what three exceptions?
A. Air Force Longevity Service Ribbon, Air Force Marksmanship Ribbon, and Navy Marksmanship Ribbon.

Q. The following abbreviations refer to what medals/ribbons?
A. CMOH: Congressional Medal of Honor (often referred to as simply, Medal of Honor).
DSC: Distinguished Service Cross.
DDSM: Defense Distinguished Service Medal.
DSM: Distinguished Service Medal.
SS: Silver Star
LM: Legion of Merit.
DFC: Distinguished Flying Cross.
SM: Soldier's Medal.
BSM: Bronze Star Medal.
MSM: Meritorious Service Medal.
AM: Air Medal.
ARCOM: Army Commendation Medal.
AAM: Army Achievement Medal.
GCMDL (or GCM): Good Conduct Medal.
NDSM: National Defense Service Medal.
HSM: Humanitarian Service Medal.
NCOPD: NCO Professional Development Ribbon.
ASR: Army Service Ribbon.
OSR: Overseas Service Ribbon.
MFO: Multinational Force and Observer's Medal.

NOTE: The above medals/ribbons are listed in order of precedence.

Q. What is a "PUC"? A "VUA"? A "MUC"?
A. A Presidential Unit Citation; a Valorous Unit Award; a Meritorious Unit Commendation.

Q. What signifies receipt of a second or subsequent award of the National Defense Service Medal?
A. A service star.

Q. What indicates the successful completion of the respective levels of the NCO Professional development courses?
A. The numeral devices 2, 3, and 4 as follows:
- Bar Ribbon Device = Primary Level (PLDC)
- 2 = Basic Level (BNCOC)
- 3 = Advanced Level (ANCOC)
- 4 = Senior Level (US Army Sergeants Major Academy (USASMA))

Q. What ribbon is awarded to members of the US Army for successful completion of initial entry training?
A. The Army Service Ribbon.

Q. What is used to denote second and subsequent awards of the Overseas Service Ribbon?
A. Numerals.

Q. Who qualifies for an MFO? How are subsequent awards of the MFO indicated?
A. Personnel serving 6 months (170 days minimum) with the multinational force in the Sinai Desert; by the appropriate numeral starting with 2.

AWARDS & DECORATIONS
AR 672-5-1

Q. What is the purpose of awarding badges?
A. To provide for public recognition by tangible evidence of the attainment of a high degree of skill, proficiency, and excellence in tests and competition, as well as in the performance of duties.

Q. What are the four categories or types of badges worn on the Army uniform?
A. (1) Combat and special skill badges.
(2) Marksmanship badges and tabs.
(3) Identification badges.
(4) Foreign badges.

NOTE: AR 672-5-1 does not reference foreign badges (see AR 670-1). Also, AR 672-5-1 indicates "Badges awarded by other US Services" as a type of badge. Authority for the wear of these badges must be obtained from Commander, PERSCOM.

Q. What badge is awarded to denote the attainment of a high degree of skill in the operation of motor vehicles?
A. The Driver and Mechanic Badge.

Q. What do the following component bars for the Driver and Mechanic Badge indicate?
A. Driver - W: for wheeled vehicles.
Driver - T: for tracked vehicles.
Driver - M: for motorcycles.
Driver - A: for amphibious vehicles.
Mechanic: for automotive or allied vehicles.
Operator - S: for special mechanical equipment.

Q. What are the three basic marksmanship qualification badges?
A. Expert, Sharpshooter, and Marksman.

Q. What component bar is authorized to be worn with marksmanship qualification badges?
A. Each bar will be attached to the basic badge which indicates the qualification last attained with the respective weapon.

Q. How many different weapons are authorized component bars?
A. 19.

Q. Who is awarded the President's Hundred Tab?
A. Each person who qualifies among the top 100 successful contestants in the President's Match held annually at the National Rifle Matches.

Q. Who may be awarded the Physical Fitness Badge?
A. Soldiers who obtain a minimum score of 290 on the Army Physical Readiness Test and meet weight control requirements in AR 600-9.

Q. How long can the Physical Fitness Badge be retained?
A. As long as a minimum passing score is achieved on subsequent APRTs and the weight control requirements are met.

Q. Are permanent orders required for the award of the Physical Fitness Badge?
A. No.

Q. Describe the service ribbon for the Medal of Honor.
A. It is the same color as the neck band (blue) showing five white stars in the

form of an "M".

Q. Miniature medals are authorized to be worn for all but what two decorations?
A. The Medal of Honor and the Legion of Merit in the Degrees of Chief Commander and Commander.

Q. Arabic numerals 3/16-inch in height are issued in lieu of a medal or ribbon for second and succeeding awards of what medals/ribbons?
A. The Air Medal, MFO, OSR, Army Reserve Components Overseas Training Ribbon, and the NCO Professional Development Ribbon (denoting successive levels).

Q. The "V" device is a bronze block letter, "V", 1/4-inch high. What does the "V" stand for and what does it denote?
A. Valor; denotes participation in acts of heroism involving conflict with an armed enemy.

Q. For what decorations is the "V" device authorized?
A. Bronze Star Medal, Air Medal, ARCOM, Joint Service Commendation Medal.

Q. How many "V" devices may be worn on a ribbon?
A. Not more than one.

Q. Clasps are authorized for wear on what medals?
A. GCMDL, WWI Victory Medal, American Defense Service Medal, Army of Occupation Medal, and the Antarctica Service Medal.

Q. All clasps are worn only on the suspension ribbon of the medal, with one exception. What is it?
A. The GCMDL (worn on the suspension bar of the medal or on the ribbon itself).

Q. Clasps indicating second or subsequent awards of the GCMDL are often called what?
A. "Knots"

Q. Explain the clasps or knots authorized for second and successive awards of the GCMDL.
A.

Award	Clasp
2nd	Bronze, 2 loops
3rd	Bronze, 3 loops
4th	Bronze, 4 loops
5th	Bronze, 5 loops
6th	Silver, 1 loop
7th	Silver, 2 loops
8th	Silver, 3 loops
9th	Silver, 4 loops
10th	Silver, 5 loops
11th	Gold, 1 loop
12th	Gold, 2 loops
13th	Gold, 3 loops
14th	Gold, 4 loops
15th	Gold, 5 loops

Q. The Army of Occupation Medal clasp is inscribed with what word(s)?
A. "Germany" or "Japan".

Q. The American Defense Service Medal clasp is inscribed with what words?
A. "Foreign Service", with a star at each end of the inscription.

AWARDS & DECORATIONS
AR 672-5-1

Q. The Antarctic Service Medal clasp is inscribed with what words?
A. "Wintered Over".

Q. What is an "Arrowhead" and what does it indicate?
A. The arrowhead is a bronze replica of an Indian arrowhead, 1/4-inch high. It denotes participation in a combat jump, helicopter assault landing, combat glider landing, or amphibious assault landing, while assigned or attached as a member of an organized force carrying out an assigned tactical mission.

Q. What device is a metal miniature replica of a C-54 type aircraft?
A. The Berlin Airlift Device.

Q. What device is a bronze hourglass with the roman numeral "X" superimposed and is worn on the service and suspension ribbon of the Armed Forces Reserve Medal?
A. The Ten-Year Device.

Q. Lapel buttons for military decorations are issued in what two forms?
A. (1) A rosette, 1/2-inch in diameter, for the Medal of Honor.
(2) A colored enamel replica (1/8-inch by 21/32-inch) of the service ribbon for other decorations.

Q. Describe the Army lapel button.
A. A gratuitous issue item comprised of a minute man in gold color on a red enamel disk surrounded by 16 pointed gold rays with an outside diameter of 9/16-inch. Normally issued at ETS.

Q. Are soldiers that are not airborne qualified by the US Army permitted to attend foreign military airborne courses or participate in foreign airborne operations?
A. No.

Q. Identify the following DA Forms:
A. DA Form 87: Certificate of Training
DA Form 638: Recommendation for Award
DA Form 2442: Certificate of Achievement
DA Form 3931: Certificate of Appreciation
DA Form 4950: Good Conduct Medal Certificate

Q. The degree of heroism required for the award of the Presidential Unit Citation is that which would warrant the award of what decoration to an individual?
A. Distinguished Service Cross

Q. When, by whom, and to whom is the French Fourragere awarded?
A. May be awarded only by the French Government when a unit has been cited twice for the Croix de Guerre (Cross of War). The colors are that of the Croix de Guerre (green and red). When a unit has been cited four times for the Croix de Guerre, the Fourragere is awarded in the colors of the Medaille Militaire (yellow and green). The Fourragere in the colors of the Medaille Militaire is the ranking decoration. The award of the Fourragere is not automatic, but requires a specific decree of the French Government.

Q. When, by whom, and to whom is the Belgian Fourragere awarded?
A. May be awarded only by the Belgian Government when a unit has been cited twice in the Order of the Day of the Belgian Army. The award of the Fourragere

is not automatic, but requires a specific decree of the Belgian Government.

Q. When, by whom, and to whom is the Netherlands Orange Lanyard (also considered a Fourragere) awarded?
A. May be awarded only by the Netherlands Government when a unit has been cited and awarded the Netherlands Military Order of William. It may also be awarded independently. Requires specific decree from Netherlands Government.

Q. Explain the "Ten Outstanding Young Americans" awards program.
A. Each year the Department of the Army nominates one or more members of the Army to include Department of the Army civilian personnel for the Ten Outstanding Young Americans award. The award is given annually by the United States Junior Chamber of Commerce to the ten men and women of the Nation selected for exceptional achievements that have been significant to their professions, communities, States, or the Nation.

Q. Who has final approval authority for the following decorations:
A. AAM: Lt Colonel and above.
ARCOM: Colonel and above.
MSM: Major General and above.
LM: Lt General and above.
DSM: Chief of Staff, US Army.

Q. Who is the approval authority for a Soldier's Medal during peacetime?
A. HQDA.

Q. What decorations cannot be awarded to general officers?
A. Army Commendation Medal, Joint Service Achievement Medal, and Army Achievement Medal.

Q. Who may be awarded an HSM?
A. Service members who directly participate in a DOD approved military act or operation of a humanitarian nature.

Q. What is meant by the phrase "above and beyond the call of duty"?
A. The acceptance of existing danger or extraordinary responsibility with praiseworthy fortitude; courage which is not, as a rule, expected.

Q. Name the US Unit Decorations that could be awarded to an Army unit.
A. (1) Presidential Unit Citation
(2) Valorous Unit Award
(3) Joint Meritorious Unit Award
(4) Meritorious Unit Commendation

Q. How many stars are on the blue silk shield from which the Army Medal of Honor is suspended?
A. 13

Q. What is the word inscribed on the suspension bar of the Army Medal of Honor?
A. "Valor"

Q. Whose profile is on the Army Medal of Honor?
A. Minerva, the Roman goddess of wisdom and righteous war.

Q. Whose profile is on the Purple Heart?
A. George Washington.

AWARDS & DECORATIONS
AR 672-5-1

Q. Name the three newest ribbons authorized for enlisted personnel.
A. ASR, OSR, NCO Professional Development Ribbon.

Q. What is the Army's newest decoration?
A. The Army Achievement Medal.

Q. What is the newest U.S. service medal?
A. Southwest Asia Service Medal.

Q. What is the newest non-U.S. service medal?
A. The Saudi Arabia Kuwait Liberation Medal.

Q. A Certificate of Achievement is worth how many promotion points?
A. Five.

Q. The Medal of Honor is the highest military award. What is the name of the highest civilian award (also presented by the President)?
A. The Medal of Freedom.

Q. What three words are inscribed on the front of the Good Conduct Medal?
A. Honor, Efficiency, and Fidelity.

Q. What words are inscribed on the reverse side of an AAM? An ARCOM?
A. "For Military Achievement"; "For Military Merit".

MILITARY JUSTICE (UCMJ)
AR 27-10

NOTE: See Appendix I for a list of UCMJ actions.

Q. What AR covers Military Justice?
A. AR 27-10

Q. What are some other publications of interest that deal with the Military Legal System?
A. FM 27-1: Legal Guide for Commanders
FM 27-14: Legal Guide for Soldiers

Q. What is the "UCMJ"?
A. The Uniform Code of Military Justice; the statute that prescribes criminal law for soldiers.

Q. How did the UCMJ come about?
A. In 1951 Congress enacted the Uniform Code of Military Justice which replaced, and was based upon, the Articles of War which had been in existence in various forms since 1775.

Q. What does the UCMJ establish?
A. The UCMJ declares what conduct is a crime, establishes the various types of courts and sets forth the basic procedure to be followed in the administration of military justice.

Q. The UCMJ is comprised of how many articles?
A. ~~140~~. 154.

NOTE: Recent changes to the Manual for Courts-Martial added articles 141-146. It can therefore be said that there are 146 articles to the UCMJ; however, there are eight separate articles that are subcategorized alphabetically (i.e. 6a, 50a, 58a, 67a, etc). In light of this, the more accurate answer would be 154 articles.

Q. Military Justice is administered at two levels. What are they?
A. (1) Nonjudicial punishment - Article 15 procedures used by commanding officers for relatively minor offenses.
(2) Judicial punishment - also known as courts-martial, the equivalent to trial by judge and jury.

Q. What is the purpose of nonjudicial punishment?
A. To educate and reform offenders; to correct misconduct in violation of the UCMJ.

Q. Who may impose an Article 15?
A. Any commanding officer, including a warrant officer exercising command.

Q. When might a commander choose to use Article 15 punishment?
A. When the offender has shown that they cannot benefit by less stringent methods.

Q. What are the three classifications of Article 15s?
A. Summarized, Company Grade, and Field Grade.

Q. What is a "Field Grade" Article 15?
A. An Article 15 imposed by an O-4 or above.

MILITARY JUSTICE (UCMJ)
AR 27-10

Q. Does a person have to accept an Article 15?
A. No, he/she has the right to demand a trial by court martial, unless assigned to or embarked on a vessel.

Q. What are the advantages of disposing of cases by Article 15?
A.
- The offender benefits in that there is no trial by court-martial.
- An Article 15 is not a federal conviction and, unlike a court-martial, will not follow the offender for life.
- Preserves an offender's record from unnecessary stigmatization.

Q. Can an individual appeal an Article 15?
A. Yes. Any person punished under Article 15 proceedings who considers his/her punishment unjust or disproportionate to the offense for which punished may, through proper channels, appeal to the next highest commander.

Q. What is the length of time one has to appeal an Article 15?
A. A reasonable time will vary according to the situation; however, an appeal submitted more than 5 calendar days after the punishment is imposed may be rejected as untimely.

Q. Does the offender have the right to counsel when offered an Article 15?
A. Yes. He/she must be informed of his/her right to see the Judge Advocate.

Q. Does an individual under Article 15 proceedings have the right to call witnesses in his/her behalf?
A. Yes, at any time.

Q. Punishments may be announced at unit formations or posted on the unit bulletin board. What is the purpose for this?
A. To preclude perceptions of unfairness of punishment and to deter similar misconduct by other service members.

Q. Can an NCO be given extra duty by an Article 15?
A. Yes, but only in a supervisory capacity.

Q. What six things should be considered when deciding whether or not to announce punishment of soldiers in the rank of SGT or above?
A. (1) The nature of the offense.
(2) The individual's military record and duty position.
(3) The deterrent effect.
(4) The impact on unit morale or mission.
(5) The impact on the victim.
(6) The impact on the leadership effectiveness of the individual concerned.

Q. The maximum punishment a Company Commander may impose is what?
A. 14 days extra duty
14 days restriction
7 days correctional custody (if E-3 and below)
7 days forfeiture of pay
1 grade reduction, grade E-4 and below (if commander can promote to present grade)
Oral or written Letter of Reprimand

Q. What is the maximum number of days of extra duty that may be given by a field grade commander?
A. 45 days.

MILITARY JUSTICE (UCMJ)
AR 27-10

Q. Who may be placed in correctional custody?
A. Soldiers with the rank Private First Class and below (soldiers in higher grades must first be reduced to the rank of PFC or below).

Q. Who may be reduced for misconduct under Article 15, UCMJ?
A. Soldiers in pay grade E2 - E6.

Q. How many pay grades can a soldier be reduced for inefficiency/ misconduct?
A. According to AR 600-200, Chpt 6, "enlisted soldiers may be reduced in rank by one pay grade for inefficiency and one or more pay grades for misconduct".

Q. What form is designed for the purpose of notifying a soldier of Article 15 proceedings against him/her?
A. DA Form 2627.

Q. What form is used to record summarized Article 15 proceedings?
A. DA Form 2627-1.

Q. What is the disposition of DA Form 2627-1?
A. These forms will be maintained locally in nonjudicial punishment files. They will be destroyed at the end of 2 years from the date of imposition of punishment or on the soldier's transfer from the unit, whichever occurs first.

Q. What is the disposition of DA Form 2627?
A. For soldiers E4 and below, the original will be filed locally in unit nonjudicial punishment files. For all other soldiers, the original will be filed in the OMPF. The decision to file the original DA Form 2627 on the performance fiche or the restricted fiche in the OMPF will be determined by the imposing commander at the time the punishment is imposed. Additional copies of the DA Form 2627 will be transmitted through the MILPO serving the soldier's MPRJ to the Finance and Accounting office as necessary (for reduction in rank, forfeiture of pay, etc).

Q. What article of the UCMJ is designed to protect the rights of the soldier?
A. Article 31.

Q. What does Article 31 specify?
A. No one may question a soldier suspected of having committed a crime without first determining that he understands the nature of the offense under investigation, his right to remain silent, and his right to counsel.

Q. What rights does the accused have in addition to Article 31?
A. - The right to remain silent.
- The right to have counsel present during questioning.
- The right to due process by law.
- The right under search and seizure.
- Protection against double-jeopardy.
- The right to sentence review.
- The right to a speedy public trial.
- The right to call witnesses favorable to you.
- The right to trial by court-martial.

Q. What are Articles 77 through 134 of the UCMJ known as?
A. Punitive Articles.

Q. When should punitive articles of the UCMJ be explained to the enlisted members?

MILITARY JUSTICE (UCMJ)
AR 27-10

A. When the individual enters the active service, or within six days thereafter; after completion of six months of active duty, and at the time of reenlistment.

Q. What is the purpose of an Article 32 investigation?
A. To investigate and determine the validity of the matter in the charges, and to determine what disposition should be made of the case in the interest of justice and discipline.

Q. What are the three types of Courts Martial?
A. Summary, Special, and General.

Q. If a service member has a court martial conviction, does his record follow him after he leaves the service?
A. Yes, a court martial conviction is a Federal conviction that a person carries for life.

Q. Can a court martial be appealed?
A. Yes, conviction by a general or special court martial in which a Bad Conduct Discharge was adjudged can be appealed to the Court of ~~Military Review~~ Criminal Appeals or the Court of ~~Military Appeals~~ Appeals for the Armed Forces. All other cases will be appealed to the Judge Advocate General.

Q. Can you refuse a Court Martial?
A. Yes, Summary but not Special or General.

Q. How many members are on a court martial board?
A. As a minimum: Summary - 1
Special - 3
General - 5

Q. Who may be tried by Summary court-martial?
A. Any person who is subject to the UCMJ, except officers, warrant officers, cadets, and midshipmen.

Q. A Summary Court may confine you to how many days at hard labor?
A. 1 to 30 days if E-4 and below. None for grades E-5 and above.

Q. What is the maximum punishment imposed by a Special Court martial?
A. Confinement at hard labor for 6 months.
Forfeiture of two-thirds pay per month for 6 months.
Reduction to lowest enlisted grade.

Q. What is the maximum sentence you can be judged by a General court martial?
A. Death.

Q. What is the major difference between a General and a Special court martial?
A. A General Court has a military judge who serves on it and may impose the death penalty.

Q. Is a military judge considered a member of the court?
A. No.

Q. What is the purpose of a military judge?
A. Insure the accused's rights are protected, and insure correct legal procedures are used.

MILITARY JUSTICE (UCMJ)
AR 27-10

Q. How is voting done on a special court martial?
A. By secret written ballot.

Q. May an enlisted person serve on a court martial?
A. Yes, when not a member of the unit of the accused, when the accused has requested enlisted members to serve on the board, and when the enlisted members on the board are higher in rank than the accused.

Q. What action can you take if you are being tried by a Special court-martial and you don't approve of one member of the Board?
A. You may have the member removed from the Board.

Q. In a Special or General court-martial does the accused have the right to be represented by a civilian counsel?
A. Yes, at his/her own expense.

Q. Who is the President of a court-martial?
A. The senior officer present.

Q. Who is the Law Officer on a Special court-martial?
A. The President of the court-martial.

Q. Who must review the case in a Summary or Special court-martial before the sentence is considered final?
A. The Staff Judge Advocate.

Q. May a plea of "no contest" be entered in military courts?
A. No.

Q. What are the five types of discharges?
A. Honorable, General, Other than Honorable, Bad Conduct, Dishonorable.

Q. What is the purpose of a "flagging" action?
A. To suspend all favorable personnel action on an individual while he/she is under investigation, or processing for disciplinary action or elimination proceedings.

Q. When may a commander initiate flagging action on a member of his/her command?
A. When it appears that action may be initiated which could result in court martial, disciplinary action or elimination proceedings.

Q. Can the First Sergeant give you company punishment?
A. No, but he can recommend it.

Q. What is the difference between arrest and confinement?
A. Arrest is the restraint of a person by an order directing him/her to remain within certain specified limits. Confinement is the physical restraint of a person.

Q. Pretending to be sick or injured is punishable under UCMJ and is known as what?
A. Malingering.

Q. At what time of day are extra duties required to be performed by offenders?
A. At any time.

MILITARY JUSTICE (UCMJ)
AR 27-10

Q. Which Amendment to our national Constitution provides us freedom from unreasonable searches and seizures?
A. The Fourth Amendment.

Q. What Amendment to the Constitution of the United States provides that no person shall be compelled to be a witness against himself in a criminal case?
A. The Fifth Amendment.

Q. The "right to a speedy trial" is guaranteed by what U.S. Amendment?
A. The Sixth Amendment (and also Article 10 of the UCMJ).

Q. Under the UCMJ, a suspect must not be questioned until he/she has been informed that he/she has the right to counsel with a lawyer. This is pursuant to the United States Supreme Court's decision in what famous case?
A. Miranda vs. Arizona, 384 U.S. 436 (1966).

Q. What is the difference between a "confession" and an "admission"?
A. A confession is an acknowledgment of guilt while an admission is an incriminating statement falling short of a confession.

Q. In the Army, who may issue search authorizations and when?
A. A commanding officer, military judge, or military magistrate when probable cause exists. A search authorization issued by competent military authority may be either written or oral.

Q. What is "probable cause"?
A. A reasonable belief that items related to criminal activity are in the place to be searched.

Q. If enlisted members serve on a court, what percentage can be enlisted?
A. One-third.

Q. What does "double-jeopardy" mean?
A. Being tried for the same offense twice.

Q. What do the letters "MCM" stand for?
A. Manual for courts-martial.

Q. What does the MCM do?
A. - The MCM explains what conduct is a violation of the UCMJ, Chapter XXVIII.
- MCM sets forth the rules of evidence, Chapter XXVII.
- Contains a list of maximum punishments for each offense.

Q. What is the role of the Staff Judge Advocate (SJA)?
A. The SJA is charged with insuring that criminal justice in the command is administered properly and fairly.

Q. In what areas can the SJA (JAG) assist the service member?
A. - Courts-martial and other disciplinary hearings.
- State or federal income tax returns.
- Personal property damage while on duty.
- Drafting of legal documents such as wills, powers-of-attorney, etc.
- Explanation of legal rights.

Q. Administrative discharges are separate and distinct from discharges given by court-martial, how are they classified?
A. Involuntary or Voluntary.

MILITARY JUSTICE (UCMJ)
AR 27-10

Q. What does a promulgating order do?
A. Such orders publish the result of a trial and the initial action of the convening authority.

Q. In conducting an investigation, what three questions must be answered?
A. - Was an offense committed?
- Was the SM involved in the offense?
- What is the character and military record of the suspected SM?

Q. What is "real" evidence?
A. Any tangible item other than that which is in writing (documentary evidence).

Q. What is "testimonial" evidence?
A. Verbal statements which have been reduced to writing.

Q. The Army refers to nonjudicial punishment as an Article 15. What do the Navy and Marines call this form of punishment?
A. Navy - Office Hours
Marines - Captain's Mast

Q. A Captain or below can make a service member forfeit how many days pay?
A. Seven days.

Q. A Captain or below can detain how many days pay?
A. 14 days.

Q. A Captain and below can make a service member work how many days extra duty, and how many hours per day?
A. 14 days and as many hours as necessary, as long as it does not impair the service member's health.

Q. A Major or higher can make a service member forfeit how many days pay?
A. One half of one month's pay for two months.

Q. A Major or above can detain pay for how long?
A. One half of one month's pay per month for three months. May be retained up to one year.

Q. A field grade commander can restrict for how long?
A. 60 days.

Q. Can a captain demote an E-5?
A. No, the next higher command must do this.

Q. If an Article 15 is appealed, what actions may the appealing authority take?
A. Suspend, vacate, mitigate, remit, or set aside punishment.

Q. Explain the following terms:
A. - Clemency power: the power that commanders imposing punishment under Article 15 have to suspend, mitigate, remit, or set aside that punishment if they conclude that this action is warranted by the circumstances of the case.
- Suspension: punishment is held in abeyance, or not put into effect, for a specified period of time.
- Vacation: the process of reinstating a suspended sentence for misconduct

during a suspension period.
- Mitigation: serves to reduce the severity of the punishment.
- Remission: cancellation of the unserved portion of the punishment.
- Setting aside: action whereby the commander "sets aside" an Article 15 when they are convinced that an injustice has occurred (such as in a case where new evidence or information indicates that a soldier is innocent). All rights, privileges, and property are returned.

Q. Does the failure to notify a soldier of his rights mean an automatic acquittal of the charges?
A. No.

Q. What four ways may restoration to former grade be made?
A. - Setting aside, mitigation, or suspension of nonjudicial punishment.
- Action under Article 58a(b) or 75, UCMJ.
- Reversal of conviction by a civil court.
- Other officer appellate reversal.

Q. Can a SM be tried by summary court martial over their objection?
A. No.

Q. Can a soldier be place on diminished rations?
A. Yes. Soldiers in pay grade E-3 or below may be place in confinement on bread and water or diminished rations.

Q. Can a punishment be administered under the provisions of Article 15 if the service member refuses to sign the DA Form 2627?
A. Yes, after being afforded a reasonable opportunity in which to make a decision.

Q. What steps are involved in the imposition of nonjudicial punishment?
A. (1) Preliminary inquiry.
(2) Notification and explanation of rights.
(3) Decision period.
(4) Hearing.
(5) Appeal.
(6) Recording and filing of DA Form 2627/2627-1.

Q. When nonjudicial punishment is imposed on an NCO, what are the three types of punishment it may not include?
A. - Correctional custody.
- Confinement on bread and water or diminished rations.
- Any form of extra duty not customarily performed by an NCO in his grade or rank.

Q. Where can a commander find a suggested guide for conducting the proceedings of a Formal or Summarized Article 15?
A. Appendix B of AR 27-10.

Q. What are nonpunitive disciplinary measures?
A. Nonpunitive measures deal with simple misconduct and do not warrant UCMJ. Examples:
- denial of pass privileges
- counseling
- administration reduction in grade
- reprimands and admonitions
- extra training (corrective actions)

- bar to reenlistment
- MOS reclassification
- administrative reduction
- revocation of security clearance

Q. What are the three primary objectives of punishment, punitive or nonpunitive?
A. (1) Protect society against the repetition of the offense.
(2) Reform the offender so he/she will not repeat the offense.
(3) Deter others from considering and committing such an offense.

Q. What is the highest court in the Army?
A. The Court of ~~Military Appeals~~. Appeals for the Armed Forces.

NOTE: Cases may still be reviewed by the Supreme Court when conditions warrant.

Q. Upon whom may nonjudicial punishment be imposed?
A. Any member of that commander's unit who has committed a minor offense and has not demanded trial by court martial.

Q. In formal proceedings, what must the commander or designated representative advise the offender of?
A.
- Intent to impose formal proceedings.
- Rights under Article 31 (b), UCMJ.
- Right to demand trial by court martial.
- Right to submit matters in defense, extenuation, and mitigation.
- Right to request an open hearing, have witnesses if available, and to have a spokesman present.
- Right to consult legal counsel.
- A period of time to respond to offenses made against him/her.

Q. When is it permitted for soldiers to "moonlight" a second job?
A. When the job does not interfere with official duties, does not bring discredit upon the Army, or does not violate basic ethical considerations.

Q. What article of the UCMJ authorizes commanders to delegate their authority to NCO's to order enlisted personnel into arrest or confinement?
A. Article 9.

Q. What article of the UCMJ gives NCOs the authority to apprehend?
A. Article 7.

Q. What article of the UCMJ protects soldiers from former jeopardy (double jeopardy)?
A. Article 44.

Q. What article of the UCMJ prohibits punishment of a soldier before trial, thereby protecting them from double jeopardy?
A. Article 13.

Q. What article of the UCMJ protects soldiers from cruel and unusual punishment?
A. Article 55.

Q. What article of the UCMJ covers investigations and dispositions of charges?
A. Article 32.

MILITARY JUSTICE (UCMJ)
AR 27-10

Q. What article of the UCMJ sets forth a soldier's specific counsel rights?
A. Article 27.

Q. What article of the UCMJ prohibits compulsory self-incrimination?
A. Article 31 (soldier's rights).

Q. What article of the UCMJ covers Commanding Officer's Nonjudicial punishment?
A. Article 15.

Q. What article of the UCMJ gives soldiers guidance if they believe they have been wronged by a commanding officer?
A. Article 138.

Q. What article of the UCMJ covers AWOL offenses?
A. Article 86.

Q. What article of the UCMJ covers disrespect or insubordinate conduct toward a superior commissioned officer? To warrant officers and NCOs?
A. Article 89; Article 91.

Q. What article of the UCMJ covers assault or willful disobeyance of a superior commissioned officer?
A. Article 90.

Q. What article of the UCMJ covers failure to obey an order or regulation from a warrant officer or NCO?
A. Article 92.

Q. What article of the UCMJ covers the improper use of countersign?
A. Article 101.

Q. What article of the UCMJ covers the sale, loss, damage, destruction, or wrongful disposition of military property?
A. Article 108.

Q. What article of the UCMJ covers drunken or reckless driving?
A. Article 111.

Q. What article of the UCMJ covers being intoxicated while on duty? Use of other controlled substances?
A. Article 112; Article 112a.

Q. What articles of the UCMJ cover fighting? Malingering?
A. Article 114; Article 115.

Q. What article of the UCMJ covers provoking speech and/or gestures?
A. Article 117.

Q. What article of the UCMJ covers writing bad checks?
A. Article 123a.

Q. What article of the UCMJ covers conduct unbecoming an officer and a gentleman?
A. Article 133.

Q. What is the General Article of the UCMJ?

MILITARY JUSTICE (UCMJ)
AR 27-10

A. Article 134.

NOTE: See additional Articles in Appendix I.

Punishments	Company Grade Commanders	Field Grade Commanders
Restriction	14 days	60 days
Extra duty	14 days	45 days
Correctional custody (E-3 and below)	7 days	30 days
Confinement on bread and water or diminished rations (E-3 or below attached to or embarked on a vessel)	3 days	3 days
Forfeiture of pay	7 days	1/2 of one month pay per month for 2 months
Reduction in grade	E-4 or below, 1 grade	E-4 or below, one or more grades; E-5 or E-6, one grade
Oral or written Letter of Reprimand	Yes	Yes

(SUMMARIZED PROCEEDING) Punishment	(ENLISTED PERSONNEL ONLY) All Commanders
Restriction	14 days
Extra duty	14 days
Oral admonition or reprimand	Yes

DRILL & CEREMONIES
FM 22-5

Q. What FM covers Drill and Ceremonies?
A. FM 22-5

Q. What is the primary purpose of drill in the Army?
A. It enables leaders to move an individual or a unit from one place to another in an orderly manner; it also aids in disciplinary training by instilling habits of precision and response to a leader's orders.

Q. What is the primary value of ceremonies?
A. To render honors, preserve tradition, and to stimulate esprit de corps.

Q. What is the origin of US ceremonies?
A. The first manual by which ceremonies were conducted in America was written in 1779 by former Prussian Officer - Baron Friedrich von Steuben, who also became the Continental Army's first Inspector General. This book was known as "The Regulations for the Order and Discipline of the Troops of the United States," and was commonly referred to as "The Blue Book." This book was the first Army Field Manual.

Q. What is an element?
A. An individual, squad, section, platoon, company or larger unit forming part of the next higher unit.

Q. What is a formation?
A. The arrangement of elements of a unit in a prescribed manner.

Q. What is a rank?
A. A line which is only one element in depth.

Q. What is a file?
A. A column which has a front of only one element.

Q. What is alignment?
A. The arrangement of several elements on the same line.

Q. What is cover?
A. Aligning yourself directly behind the man to your immediate front, while maintaining correct distance.

Q. What is the head?
A. The leading element of a column.

Q. What is depth?
A. The space from front to rear of a formation including front and rear elements.

Q. What is the post?
A. The correct place for an Officer or Non-Commissioned Officer to stand in a prescribed formation.

Q. Most drill commands have two parts. What are they?
A. (1) Preparatory command: indicates movement.
(2) Command of execution: indicates when a movement is to be executed.

Q. What is quick time cadence?
A. 120 steps per minute.

DRILL & CEREMONIES
FM 22-5

Q. How fast is the double-time cadence?
A. 180 steps per minute.

Q. What is a step?
A. The prescribed distance measured from heel to heel of a marching man.

Q. What command is given to revoke a preparatory command that has been given?
A. "As you were".

Q. What is the interval between the preparatory command and the command of execution?
A. One step or count.

Q. What are the five types of commands in drill?
A. Two part, combined, supplementing, directive, and mass.

Q. What commands are given without inflection and at a uniformly high pitch and loudness comparable to that for a normal command of execution?
A. Combined Commands.

Q. Give a few examples of a Combined Command.
A. At Ease, Fall In, Rest.

Q. What is a Supplementary Command?
A. Oral orders given by the subordinate leader reinforcing and complimenting the command's order which insures proper understanding and execution of movement ("echo" commands).

Q. What are Directives?
A. Oral orders by the commander that direct or cause a subordinate leader to take action. They are used when it is more appropriate for subordinate elements to execute a movement or perform a task as independent elements of the same formation. They are given in sentence form and are normally prefixed by the terms "HAVE YOUR UNITS" OR "BRING YOUR UNITS" (ie, "BRING YOUR UNITS TO PRESENT ARMS").

Q. What is the only directive on which a commander relinquishes his command and on which salutes are exchanged?
A. "Take charge of your units"

Q. When in formation at present arms, what should a subordinate leader do before echoing the supplementary command for order arms?
A. The subordinate leader should terminate the salute on the preparatory command and before giving the supplementary command (ie, On the preparatory command "Order" of "Order Arms", the platoon leader should terminate his/her salute before echoing the command "order").

Q. When a company commander gives the preparatory command "Company" of "Company, Attention", what supplementary command should be given by the platoon leader(s)?
A. "Platoon"

Q. What is a Mass Command?
A. Mass commands are used to develop confidence and promote enthusiasm. Mass commands are given simultaneously by each individual of a unit.

DRILL & CEREMONIES
FM 22-5

Q. What command is used to initiate mass commands?
A. "AT YOUR COMMAND"

Q. What are the two parts of a mass command?
A. **preparatory command**: <description of movement> (ie, "face the platoon to the right").
command of execution: "COMMAND" (On the command of execution "Command" all personnel of the platoon give the command "Right, FACE", in unison, and simultaneously execute the movement.

Q. What command is used to stop the use of mass commands?
A. "AT MY COMMAND"

Q. From what position are all stationary movements given?
A. ATTENTION

Q. What is the normal length of step in marching?
A. 30 inches.

Q. What foot is your leading foot?
A. Your left foot.

Q. What is your trailing foot?
A. Your right foot.

Q. What is the command given to get a formation to march with a 15 inch step?
A. Half Step, March.

Q. On the command "Dress Right, Dress", who is the only one that does not turn his/her eyes to the right?
A. The right flank soldier(s).

Q. When the command "Open Ranks, March" is given, which rank does not move?
A. The third rank.

Q. When is it proper to break ranks by yourself?
A. When your name is called in a platoon formation.

Q. What is a "Review"?
A. A military ceremony.

NOTE: See section 30, "Customs and Courtesies," for more information on Reviews.

Q. When passing uncased Colors, what do you do?
A. Salute six paces from the Colors and hold the salute six paces beyond the Colors.

Q. What is Reveille?
A. The raising of the Flag.

Q. What do you do when the National Anthem, To the Colors, Reveille, or Taps is played and you are outdoors?
A. Assume the position of attention and render the hand salute.

Q. What safety precaution is taken when forming or dismissing a unit under arms?

DRILL & CEREMONIES
FM 22-5

A. Inspection Arms

Q. What is normal interval?
A. The lateral space between personnel measured from right to left with extended arms (left arm extended).

Q. What is the purpose of a Retreat Formation?
A. To pay honors to the National Flag when it is lowered in the evening.

Q. What is the difference between reveille/retreat and command reveille/retreat?
A. During a command reveille/retreat, all members of the command are present.

Q. What is the normal distance between individuals?
A. Arms length plus six inches between personnel from front to rear.

Q. Describe the position of Attention.
A. Your weight should be distributed equally on the heels and balls of your feet. Heels should be together with the toes forming a 45° angle. Keep the legs straight without locking the knees. Hold body erect with hips level, chest lifted, and shoulders squared and even. Arms should hang straight but not stiff with the backs of the hand outward. Fingers curled so that thumb tips are alongside and touching the first joint of forefingers. Thumbs straight and along seams of trousers or skirt with the first joint of the forefingers touching the trousers or skirt. Head erect, eyes straight to the front.

Q. Describe the position of Stand-At-Ease.
A. On the command of execution "EASE", execute Parade Rest and turn your head and eyes directly toward the commander or person speaking. If that person is out of your field-of-view keep your head and eyes straight to the front (as in the position of Parade Rest).

Q. What is the difference between "rest" and "at ease"?
A. When "at ease", silence must be maintained and the right foot must remain in place. When at "rest", the right foot must still remain in place but you may talk.

Q. What is the difference between the commands "FALL OUT" and "DISMISSED"?
A. The command "FALL OUT" only gives a greater degree of relaxation than the rest positions and requires that soldiers remain in the immediate area. The command "DISMISSED" terminates the formation (but not necessarily the duty day).

Q. What are the commands to dismiss armed troops?
A. "Inspection, Arms....Ready, Port, Arms....Dismissed".

Q. In verbal commands, what is inflection?
A. The rise and fall in the pitch and tone of the voice.

Q. Explain the movement of each squad in platoon formation on the command "Open Ranks, March".
A. First rank takes two 30-inch steps forward.
Second rank takes one 30-inch step forward.
Third rank stands fast.
Fourth rank takes two 15-inch steps backward.

Q. Explain the movement of each squad in platoon formation on the command

"Close Ranks, March".
A. First rank takes four 15-inch steps backward.
Second rank takes two 15-inch steps backward.
Third rank stands fast.
Fourth rank takes one 30-inch step forward.

Q. What two commands may be given to call a unit or individuals to attention?
A. "FALL IN" and "ATTENTION".

Q. Who on the Battalion Commander's staff is responsible for the formation of troops?
A. The Adjutant

Q. How many types of intervals are there? What are they?
A. 3 -- normal interval
close interval
double interval

Q. What is a flank?
A. The extreme right or left side of any formation.

Q. When you are marching at a LEFT STEP or RIGHT STEP, the distance of each step is how many inches?
A. 15 inches.

Q. What is the proper procedure for reporting when in formation?
A. (1) When a report is appropriate, the platoon sergeant commands "REPORT." The squad leaders, in succession from front to rear, turn their heads and eyes toward the platoon sergeant and salute (holding the salute until returned) and report.

(a) When all squad members are in formation, the report is "All present."

(b) When squad members are absent, the soldiers are reported by name along with the reason for their absence (ie, "Pvt Smith - CQ runner; Pvt Jones - sick call"). **At no time should a squad leader render an "All present and accounted for" reply.**

(2) After receiving the report from the squad leaders, the platoon sergeant faces about and awaits the arrival of the platoon leader. When the platoon leader has halted at his post, the platoon sergeant salutes and reports, "Sir, all present"; or "Sir, all accounted for"; or "Sir, (so many) men absent." The platoon leader returns the salute. After the salute has been returned, the platoon sergeant positions himself at his post.

(3) If the platoon leader is not present for the formation, the platoon sergeant steps forward three steps (after receiving the squad leader's report) and assumes the duties of the platoon leader. Remember, appropriate replies to the Commander/XO/First Sergeant are, "Sir (1SG), all present"; or "Sir (1SG), all accounted for"; or "Sir (1SG), (so many) men absent." **At no time should a platoon sergeant or platoon leader render an "All present and accounted for" reply.**

Q. How should a soldier leave a formation?
A. The soldier should come to attention, take one 15 inch step backward, face to the right or left, march to the nearest flank, and when clear of the formation, double time to his post or assigned position. If the soldier is called by name, he should reply with "Here, Sir (Sergeant, First Sergeant)" after assuming the position of attention.

Q. You may talk in formation only after what command is given?

DRILL & CEREMONIES
FM 22-5

A. REST

Q. What are the five rest positions which may be given at halt?
A. Parade Rest, Stand At Ease, At Ease, Rest, and Fall Out.

Q. What is the length of the following steps?
A. Forward ------------ 30 inches
Half Step ---------- 15 inches
Left or Right Step - 15 inches
Backward ----------- 15 inches
Doubletime --------- 30 inches

Q. What is the position of the Platoon Leader when the platoon is in a line formation?
A. Six steps in front of the platoon and centered.

Q. What do you do if an Officer steps in front of you when you are standing in ranks at ease?
A. Come to attention.

Q. What three commands are given to line a platoon?
A. "Platoon, Attention", "Dress Right, Dress", and "Ready Front".

Q. What are the four types of foot marches?
A. Day, night, forced, and shuttle.

Q. What are the two classifications of foot marches?
A. Tactical and Administrative.

Q. When pallbearers carry a casket, how must it be moved at all times?
A. Feet first.

Q. How many personnel normally comprise a funeral detail for deceased Army personnel?
A. 15 -- 1 NCOIC
6 pallbearers
7 in firing squad
1 bugler

Q. What should the leader of a formation (not engaged in PT) do when his formation passes an officer while marching at Double Time?
A. The leader of the formation only, should slow down to quick time, salute, and return to double time.

Q. What is the purpose of a "muster" formation?
A. To determine if all personnel are present.

Q. What is the purpose of drill?
A. To develop an attitude in an individual to respond to commands instinctively, and to instill in his/her mind that he/she must perform as part of a team.

Q. What four marching commands can be given while at half step?
A. Forward march, mark time march, halt, and extend march.

Q. On what foot is the command "Rear March" given?
A. The right foot.

DRILL & CEREMONIES
FM 22-5

Q. When executed from a Halt, all steps in marching begin with the left foot except one, what is that exception?
A. Right Step March.

Q. What is "cadence"?
A. The uniform rhythm/number of steps or counts per minute; also, the uniform and rhythmic flow of words.

Q. The command "Change Step, March" is given as what foot strikes the ground?
A. The right foot.

Q. On what foot do you give the command "Halt"?
A. Either foot.

Q. When executing a "Left Step" or "Right Step", on which foot would you give the command "Halt"?
A. Give the command when the heels are together.

Q. Which foot do you pivot on when executing a "Rear March" command?
A. The balls of both feet.

Q. When marching, what is the proper measure of the arm swing?
A. Approximately 9 inches forward and 6 inches to the rear of the seam of the trousers.

Q. While marching in place (Mark Time), to resume marching with a 30 inch step, on what foot is the command "Forward, March" given?
A. Either foot.

Q. What is the only command given from Inspection Arms?
A. "Ready, Port, Arms"

Q. What are the two prescribed formations for a platoon?
A. (1) Column formation: elements one behind the other.
   (2) Line formation: elements side by side or abreast of each other.

Q. What are the three methods of instruction used to teach drill to soldiers?
A. (1) Step-by-Step method.
   (2) By the Numbers method.
   (3) Talk-through method.

Q. What is a drill command?
A. An oral order of a commander or leader. The precision with which a movement is executed is affected by the manner in which the command is given.

Q. How should you be positioned when giving commands to troops?
A. When at the halt, you should be facing the troops. When in motion, you should move simultaneously with the unit and turn your head in the direction of the troops to give commands.

Q. Most drill commands have two parts: the preparatory command and the command of execution. Are the commands "Ready, port, ARMS" and "Ready, aim, FIRE" considered to be two-part commands?
A. Yes, even though they both contain two preparatory commands.

Q. How are commands given for movements that change the direction of a unit

(ie, right flank, column left)?
A. The preparatory command and the command of execution are given so they begin and end on the foot in the direction of the turn (ie, "Right Flank, March" is given as the right foot strikes the marching surface, and so on).

Q. A platoon is in column formation, and the platoon leader commands "Column of files from the left (pause), MARCH". What action(s) should the squad leaders take during the pause between the preparatory command and the command of execution? What action(s) should the squad leaders take after the command of execution "MARCH"?
A. The first squad leader commands "Forward"; the second, third, and fourth squad leaders command "Stand Fast". On the command of execution "MARCH", the first squad marches forward. At the appropriate times, the squad leaders of each individual squad command "Forward, March" to complete the "column of files".

Q. At the position of "REST", "AT EASE", or "STAND AT EASE", what position is immediately assumed on the preparatory command for attention?
A. Parade Rest.

Q. Describe the proper hand salute.
A.
- Headgear with a visor: raise the right hand sharply, fingers and thumb extended and joined, palm facing down, and place the tip of the right forefinger on the rim of the visor slightly to the right of the right eye. The outer edge of the hand is barely canted downward so that neither the back of the hand nor the palm is clearly visible from the front. The hand and wrist are straight, the elbow inclined slightly forward, and the upper arm horizontal.
- Headgear without a visor or uncovered (not wearing glasses): as previously described except touch the tip of the right forefinger to the forehead near and slightly to the right of the right eyebrow.
- Headgear without a visor or uncovered (wearing glasses): same manner as described in first paragraph above except touch the tip of the right forefinger to that point on the glasses where the temple piece of the frame meets the right edge of the right brow.

Q. When double timing, what must you do before saluting?
A. Go to quick time.

Q. What is meant by "marching at attention"?
A. The combination of the position of attention and the procedures for the prescribed step executed simultaneously.

Q. What are the two 30-inch step rest movements?
A. At Ease March and Route Step March.

Q. What is the difference between At Ease March and Route Step March?
A. **At Ease March** - soldier is no longer required to retain cadence; however, silence and the approximate interval and distance are maintained.
Route Step March - Soldier may drink from canteen and talk.

Q. What are the only two commands that may be given while marching at ease?
A. "Quick time, March" and "Route Step, March".

Q. How do you change the direction of march while marching at route step or at ease march?
A. By informally directing the lead element to turn in the desired direction.

DRILL & CEREMONIES
FM 22-5

Q. When marching at route step or at ease march, the unit must resume marching in cadence before precision movements may be executed. What command is used to do this?
A. "Quick time, MARCH".

Q. When marking time as in "Mark time, March", you should raise each foot alternately how many inches off the marching surface?
A. 2 inches.

Q. From what two positions can the command "Double time, MARCH" be given?
A. From the halt and at Quick Time.

Q. When armed, soldiers should place their weapons in what position after receiving the preparatory command "Double time"?
A. Port Arms.

Q. What are the proper commands for halting a unit while double timing?
A. First give the command "Quick time, MARCH", then give the halt command.

Q. What is meant by the "Manual of Arms" for a particular weapon?
A. It is a series of authorized movements that are a combination of the position of attention and the procedures for the prescribed movement. Most manual of arms movements are executed with the head, eyes, and body as in the position of attention.

Q. The manual of arms for the M16 is comprised of what movements?
A. Order arms, sling/unsling arms, port arms, present arms, rest positions (parade rest, stand at ease, at ease, and rest), right shoulder arms, left shoulder arms, inspection arms, ready-port-arms, fix/unfix bayonets, and carry.

Q. What are the two positions of attention with the rifle?
A. Order arms and sling arms.

Q. Describe the carry position.
A. The rifle is carried horizontal to the ground by the carrying handle. This position allows soldiers to transport the rifle in a convenient manner when not in formation. The command "Assume the right (left) carry" is given only when teaching the procedures for executing present arms from the carry position. Carrying the rifle at sling arms, even when not in formation, is the traditional means of transport.

Q. All individual and unit drill movements for the M16 can be executed at sling arms except what three movements?
A. Stack arms, fix, and unfix bayonets (these are executed only at order arms).

Q. Unless otherwise specified, armed elements of a formation fall in at what manual of arms position?
A. Order arms (with slings loose).

Q. For drill purposes, the magazine is not carried in the rifle. When performing duty requiring the use of a magazine, the rifle should be carried at what position?
A. Sling arms.

Q. What is the procedure for executing stationary or short-distance marching movements with the M16 rifle while at order arms?

DRILL & CEREMONIES
FM 22-5

A. Automatically raise the rifle about 1 inch off the marching surface on the command of execution. When the movement has been completed, automatically return the rifle to order arms.

Q. What is the key position assumed in most manual of arms movements from one position to another?
A. Port arms.

Q. When the bayonet scabbard is worn, it should be on the left side with the tip of the scabbard on line with the trouser seam and the barrel ring where?
A. To the front.

Q. The command to fix or unfix bayonets is given from what position?
A. Order arms.

Q. How do you execute a salute at sling arms?
A. On the command of execution "ARMS" of "Present, ARMS", reach across the body with the left hand and grasp the sling just above the right hand. Release the right hand and execute the hand salute.

Q. Inspection Arms from Order Arms is a _________-count movement.
A. Seven.

Q. What is the proper procedure for executing inspection arms from sling arms?
A. Execute port arms and then execute counts three through seven in the same manner as for inspection arms from order arms.

Q. What is the procedure for executing inspection arms when a magazine is inserted in the rifle?
A. Remove the magazine (just prior to step three) with the left hand and place it between the waist (left front) and the clothing. Return the magazine immediately after pulling the trigger and before resuming port arms.

Q. When in an inspection formation with the rifle, at what time do you automatically execute inspection arms?
A. When the inspecting officer stops in front of you.

Q. After you have been inspected (see above question), when do you execute ready-port-arms?
A. (1) If the inspecting officer physically inspects your weapon (takes it from you), then you must execute ready-port-arms immediately after it is returned.
(2) If the inspecting officer does not physically inspect the weapon (does not take it from you), then you must remain at inspection arms until he/she has halted in front of and is facing the next soldier. Then execute ready-port-arms.

Q. If you are at inspection arms and the inspecting officer takes your rifle from you, what should you do?
A. Immediately assume the position of attention. Reach for the weapon only when the officer offers it back to you. Proceed as in (1) above.

Q. If you are a member of a color guard that is being inspected and you are a rifle bearer, do you execute inspection arms when the inspector stops in front of you?
A. No.

Q. Explain the correct method for manipulating the M16 rifle for inspection.

A. (1) When receiving the rifle from the inspected individual, reach forward and grasp the rifle at the upper portion of the handguard with the right hand. Lower the rifle diagonally to the left, insert the thumb into the receiver and look into the barrel (the finger reflects sufficient light for the inspection of the barrel).

(2) Grasp the small of the stock with the left hand and raise the rifle to a horizontal position (sights up) with the muzzle to the right. The rifle is centered on the body with the forearms horizontal and the palms up. Move the rifle horizontally to the left and inspect the upper portion of the rifle beginning with the flash suppressor/compensator. Move the rifle slowly to the right inspecting the butt. Return the rifle to the center of the body.

(3) Keeping the rifle horizontal, rotate it 180° (sights toward the body) so that the sights point toward the marching surface. Move the rifle horizontally to the left and inspect the muzzle. Move the rifle slowly to the right and inspect the butt. When moving the rifle across the body, twist the rifle as necessary and inspect the movable parts on the sides of the receiver. Having completed the inspection of the lower parts of the rifle, return it to the center of the body.

(4) Keeping the rifle horizontal, rotate the rifle 180° (sights away from the body) so that the sights are up. Release the left hand and return the rifle in the same manner as received.

Q. What are the only manual of arms movements that may be executed with the M203 weapon?
A. Sling/unsling arms, present arms (hand salute from sling arms), port arms, inspection arms, ready-port-arms.

Q. How does inspection arms with the M203 differ from that of the M16?
A. (1) Inspection arms with the M203 is only executed from sling arms. After completing the normal inspection arms movements (as with M16), press the barrel release latch with the left thumb, slide the barrel to the left, and visually inspect the chamber.

(2) Ready port arms is executed the same as for the M16 with one exception: on the command "Ready", the first action is to close the barrel and pull the trigger of the grenade launcher.

Q. What commands are used to align a squad at normal interval?
A. "Dress right, DRESS" and "Ready, FRONT".

Q. What action should be taken on the command "COVER"?
A. Each member (except the number one man) raises his left arm to a horizontal position, elbow locked, fingers and thumb extended and joined, palm facing down, and obtain an arm's length plus about 6 inches (from the fingertips) to the back of the man to his front. At the same time, each man aligns himself directly behind the man to his front.

Q. What action should be taken on the command "RECOVER"?
A. Resume the position of attention.

Q. When marching long distances, which of the two prescribed formations must be used?
A. Column.

Q. What command(s) may be used to change the direction of march 45°?
A. "Column half left (right), MARCH".

DRILL & CEREMONIES
FM 22-5

Q. What command is used to change the direction of march 180°?
A. "Rear, MARCH".

Q. What command(s) may be used to change the direction of march 90°?
A. "Column left (right), MARCH".

Q. What command(s) may be used to march the entire unit to the flank?
A. "Right (left) flank, MARCH".

Q. The platoon renders courtesy during ceremonies or when marching past the Colors by executing "eyes right". What are the two commands for this movement?
A. "Eyes, RIGHT" and "Ready, FRONT"

Q. On the command "Eyes, RIGHT", what does the platoon leader do?
A. Renders the hand salute.

Q. What actions are taken by the guidon bearer at the command "Eyes, RIGHT"?
A. On the preparatory command "Eyes", the guidon bearer lifts the guidon to the "raised guidon" position, and on the command of execution "RIGHT", the guidon bearer presents the guidon (horizontal to the ground).

Q. What is the difference between eyes right while marching and when stationary?
A. When stationary, **all** soldiers turn head and eyes to the right at a 45° angle. Focus on and follow the person passing to the front until the head is again straight, at which time the head and eyes remain fixed to the front as in the position of attention.
When marching, all men except the right file, turn head and eyes to the right. Continue looking to the right at a 45° angle until the command "Ready, FRONT" is given.

Q. On what two commands is the guidon presented?
A. "Present, arms" and "Eyes, right"

Q. On what four commands is the guidon raised?
A. Present arms, order arms, eyes right, and ready front.

Q. On what foot is the command "Eyes, Right" given?
A. The right foot.

Q. On what foot is the command "Ready, FRONT" given?
A. The left foot.

Q. When should the platoon leader terminate his hand salute when at "eyes right"?
A. On the command of execution "FRONT" of "Ready, FRONT".

Q. To avoid an obstacle in the path of the march without making precise movements, a platoon leader may use what command?
A. "INCLINE AROUND LEFT (RIGHT)"

Q. What command is used to march a unit in the opposite direction (reverse), with the squad leaders at the head of their squads?
A. "Counter column, MARCH".

Q. When executing a counter column march from the halt, what should each squad

do?
A. 1st squad: march forward THREE steps, execute a column right, march across the front of the platoon, and execute another column right just beyond the fourth squad.
2nd squad: march forward TWO steps, execute a column right, march forward, execute another column right between the third and fourth squads.
3rd squad: execute TWO short column lefts from the halt.
4th squad: march forward TWO steps, execute a column left, march across the front of the platoon, execute another column left between the first and second squads.

NOTE: Add one step when executing this movement while marching.

Q. What is the correct position for the guidon bearer?
A. Two 15-inch steps to the rear and two 15-inch steps to the left of the company commander.

Q. What are the correct posting positions for the following key personnel in the prescribed formations?
A. Company Commander: line - 12 steps to the front and centered on the company. When part of a larger unit, 6 steps to the front and centered.
column-12 steps from and centered on left flank.
Executive Officer: line - 2 steps to the rear of the First Sergeant.
column-3 steps to the rear of the last rank and off-center (one 15-inch step to the right) of the company.
First Sergeant: line - 3 steps to the rear of the last rank and centered on the company.
column-3 steps to the rear of the last rank and off-center (one 15-inch step to the left) of the company.

Q. What is the simplest way to form a squad at normal interval?
A. Command "Fall in".

Q. What is the "U" formation?
A. It is the formation that is best used for instruction and practical work in stationary movements and marching movements.

Q. What are the elements of a correct command?
A. Tone, cadence, and snap.

Q. What command is given from the halt to change a line formation to a column formation?
A. "Right, FACE".

Q. When marching troops at close march, what command is given to get the troops back to normal interval?
A. "Extend, MARCH".

Q. Where is the honor position in a military review?
A. Regardless of rank it is the reviewing officer's post.

Q. What are the primary characteristics of a parade?
A. The appearance and movement of troops in formation.

DRILL & CEREMONIES
FM 22-5

Q. What does an honor guard consist of?
A. A band, Colors, salute battery, and a formation of troops.

Q. When an In-Ranks inspection is conducted, who does the commander inspect first?
A. The guidon bearer.

Q. When an inspecting officer enters a room for inspection, is "Attention" automatically called when he enters?
A. No, the individuals in the room automatically assume the position of attention when the inspector enters the room. The inspector then commands "AT EASE". As the inspector approaches each soldier, the soldier assumes the position of attention and resumes at ease after he/she has been inspected.

Q. Can you be given the command "At Ease" from the position of parade rest?
A. Yes.

Q. In what publication will you find the "Manual of the Guidon"?
A. FM 22-5, Appendix C.

Q. When is a soldier authorized to salute with the left hand?
A. A guidon bearer, while carrying the guidon (not in formation), salutes by moving the left hand sharply across the chest to a position so that the first joint of the forefinger is touching the staff. The fingers and thumb are extended and joined, palm down, wrist straight, and forearm horizontal to the ground.

Q. Can the guidon bearer carry a weapon?
A. Yes. When armed with a rifle, the guidon bearer slings the weapon behind his back with the sling diagonally across his chest and the muzzle end up and to the left.

Q. How is the guidon carried at double time?
A. It is carried diagonally across the body in a "port arms" position.

Q. What is meant by the command "Face to the right (left) in marching, MARCH"?
A. Facings in marchings from a halt are important parts of the following movements: alignments, column movements, inspecting soldiers in ranks, and changing from normal interval to double interval and vice-versa. When this movement is executed, the entire body is pivoted 90° (to the right or left as appropriate) after which, you step off in the indicated direction. Execute the pivot and step in one count, and continue marching in the new direction. The command itself is only used for instructional purposes.

FLAGS & GUIDONS
AR 840-10/FM 22-5

Q. What Army regulation prescribes the design, acquisition, display, and use of flags, guidons, streamers, automobile and aircraft plates, and tabards?
A. AR 840-10

Q. What other Army publication is a good source of information on Flags and Guidons?
A. FM 22-5, Guidons...............Appendix C
Flags and Colors......Appendix E

Q. To what regulation would you refer for occasions when the flag of the United States is raised, lowered, or flown at half-staff?
A. AR 600-25, "Salutes, Honors, and Visits of Courtesy."

Q. What is a "flag"?
A. Any type of cloth device used to convey information.

Q. When a flag is no longer suitable for display, how should it be disposed of?
A. If not preserved, it will be destroyed privately, preferably by burning or by some other method that does not show irreverence or disrespect to the flag.

Q. What is meant by the term "Color"?
A. A specific flag symbolic of the spirit and tradition of either the United States, or the position, individual, or organization represented. The flag of the United States when displayed as indicated in AR 840-10 is known as the "National Color." The term "color" when used alone refers to the national color. The term "colors" means the national and positional or organizational colors.

Q. Describe the flag of the United States.
A. The US flag is a symbol of our nation. It represents a living country, and as such, is considered a living thing. The union, the white stars on a field of blue, is the honor point of the flag. There are 50 stars within the union representing each of the 50 states. They are arranged in four rows of five and five rows of six. Thirteen stripes, seven red and six white, represent each of the original thirteen colonies. The first and last stripes are red. Red can be said to represent "hardiness" and "valor"; white - "purity" and "innocence"; and blue - "justice" and "vigilance".

Q. When was the current 50-star flag adopted?
A. July 4, 1960.

Q. How many US flags are authorized to be flown at one time at any CONUS Army installation?
A. One.

Q. The flag of the United States is the only flag that may be flown from a _________ over a CONUS Army installation.
A. Flagpole.

Q. As an exception to the above rule, what three flags may be flown immediately below the US flag on a flagpole?
A. The Minuteman flag, the Prisoner of War/Missing in Action flag, or the Commander in Chief's Installation Excellence Award flag (when authorized).

Q. Not more than one flag (see above question) will be displayed below the flag of the United States and, if displayed, will be approximately how far below the

flag of the United States?
A. 6 inches.

Q. MACOM commanders may authorize the permanent or semipermanent (more than one week at a time) 24-hour display of the flag provided what happens?
A. The flag must be properly illuminated with its own power source during hours of darkness.

NOTE: Nighttime display of the US flag may be authorized by local or installation commanders during special events or on special occasions provided the same provisions as above are made.

Q. Name some places where the US flag is flown night and day.
A. - Fort McHenry National Monument
- The White House
- The Moon
- Arlington National Cemetery
- The Tomb of the Unknowns
- Battleship USS Arizona, Pearl Harbor
- US Capitol, Washington D.C.
- Francis Scott Key's grave
- Flag House Square, Baltimore MD
- Hospital Ship Hope

Q. What are the 10 types of National flags?
A. (1) Garrison flag - flown on holidays and special occasions. Material is nylon-wool.
(2) Post flag - flown daily except when the garrison and storm flags are flown. Material is nylon.
(3) Field flag - may be displayed from a flagpole only when distinguished visitors are present and only with the positional field flag. It is 6'8" in hoist by 12' in fly and is made of nylon-wool.
(4) Storm flag - flown during inclement weather. Material is nylon.
(5) Interment flag - authorized for deceased military personnel and for deceased veterans. It is 5' in hoist by 9'6" in fly and is made of cotton bunting.
(6) Boat flag - displayed only with positional boat flag colors and general officers flags. It is 3' in hoist by 4' in fly and is made of nylon-wool.
(7) Ensign - displayed on vessels when required to indicate nationality. It is 2'4(7/16)" in hoist by 4'6" in fly and is made of nylon.
(8) Union jack - consists of a blue base with white stars similar in all respects to the union of the flag of the United States. It is flown on ships at anchor or tied up at pier. When flown with the US flag, the union jack will be the same size as the union of the national color being flown.
(9) Grave decoration flag - this flag has a 7" hoist and 11" fly and is made of cotton muslin.
(10) Automobile flags.

NOTE: FM 22-5 lists the "Standard" as a military flag type - it is a name formerly used for flags of mounted units.

Q. Which of the above three types of National flags are normally flown over Army installations (only one at any given time) and what are their dimensions?
A. (1) Storm - 5' x 9'6"
(2) Post - 8'11(3/8)" x 17'
(3) Garrison - 20' x 38'

FLAGS & GUIDONS
AR 840-10/FM 22-5

Q. What flag may be substituted for the Garrison flag on National Holidays?
A. The Post flag.

Q. What is meant by the "hoist" of the flag?
A. The width from top to bottom of the vertical edge of the flag.

Q. What is meant by the "fly" of the flag?
A. The length from left to right of the horizontal edge of the flag.

Q. What is the "heading" of a flag?
A. That section of a flag which attaches to the flagstaff, flagpole, or mast.

Q. The rules and customs for displaying the US flag, adopted by an act of Congress in 1942 and amended in 1976, can be found where?
A. Title 36 of the United States Code.

Q. What are the only two acceptable ways for displaying the US flag?
A. It should always be free, either hung flat against a wall or flown free from a staff (it is never stretched flat or carried horizontally; it is never used as a drapery; it is never festooned over doorways or arches, tied in a bow, or fashioned into a rosette).

Q. Describe the position and manner of display of the US flag in the following situations.
A. - Ceremonies and parades: It is always displayed in the position of honor. When carried in a procession with other flags, it will be on the marching right; or, if there is a line of other flags, in front of the center of that line. It should never be carried flat or horizontally but always aloft and free. When displayed from a vehicle, the staff of the flag will be clamped firmly to the right front fender.
- With foreign national flags: All flags must be comparable in size. The flagstaffs or flagpoles on which they are flown will be of equal height. The tops of all flags should be of equal distance from the ground.
- From staffs: When a number of flags are grouped and displayed from staffs radiating from a central point, and no foreign flags are involved, the flags are arranged alternatively on each side of the US flag in order of precedence to the right and left (US flag will be at the highest point in the group). When a number of flags are displayed from staffs set in a line, the flag of the United States will be at the flag's own right (observer's left). If no foreign flags are involved, the flag may be placed at the center of the line providing it is displayed at a higher level.
- With state flags: All flags will be of comparable size. They will be displayed from separate flagstaffs of equal height set on the same level.
- Against a wall: When displayed with another flag against a wall with crossed staffs, should be on the flag's own right with its staff in front of the staff of the other flag. When displayed either horizontally or vertically against a wall, thc union will be uppermost and to the flaq's own right.
- In auditorium, meeting hall, or chapel: Should be in the position of honor at the speaker's right (audience left). Other flags should be on the speaker's left.
- Halfstaff: The flag is considered to be in a halfstaff position anytime the flag is below the top of the pole. Generally, the position of the flag is at halfstaff when the middle point of the hoist of the flag is halfway between the top of the staff and the foot.

Q. Traditionally, there is one permissible departure from the rules for display of the flag of the United States. What is it?

FLAGS & GUIDONS
AR 840-10/FM 22-5

A. In a dire emergency, the flag may be flown upside down as a distress signal.

Q. The US flag is flown at halfstaff to signify what?
A. Mourning.

Q. How are flags carried by troops placed in mourning?
A. A streamer of black crepe 7' long and 1' wide is attached to the staff at the center of the streamer immediately below the spearhead of the US flag and the organizational flag.

Q. The US flag is folded in the triangular shape of a cocked hat. Why is this?
A. It symbolizes the three-pointed hats worn by soldiers of the Revolutionary War.

Q. How is an interment flag placed on a casket?
A. Closed casket - the flag is placed lengthwise, with the union at the head and over the left shoulder of the deceased.
Full-couch casket (open) - flag is removed, folded into the shape of a cocked hat and placed in the lid at the head end of the casket and just above the decedent's left shoulder.
Half-couch (open) - flag is folded on the lower half of the casket in the same relative position as when displayed full length on a closed casket.

Q. What are the disposition instructions for an interment flag?
A. It **will not** be lowered into the grave or allowed to touch the ground. It will be given to the nearest of kin at the conclusion of the interment.

Q. What is the order of precedence of flags?
A. - The flag of the United States.
- Foreign national flags.
- Flag of the President of the United States.
- State flags.
- Military organizational flags of the Services in order of precedence.
- Military organizational flags within a service by echelon.
- Individual flags in order of rank.

Q. What is the "golden rule" regarding the placement of the US flag in relation to other flags or pennants?
A. "No other flag or pennant should be placed above or, if on the same level, to the right of the flag of the United States of America except during church services conducted by naval chaplains at sea, when the church pennant may be flown above the flag during church services for Navy personnel, and except as required by multinational agreements to which the United States is a signatory."

Q. Is the flag of the United States, when flown at a military post or when carried by troops, ever dipped in salute?
A. No.

Q. The US flag cannot be used to drape over the front of a speaker's platform. What should be used for this purpose?
A. Bunting - a skirt of colors arranged with the blue of the bunting in the place of honor at the top of the arrangement followed by white in the middle and red below.

Q. Are cords and tassels authorized to be placed on the US flag?
A. Yes, when it is displayed with a flag also equipped with a cord and tassel.

FLAGS & GUIDONS
AR 840-10/FM 22-5

The cord is 8'6" in length with a tassel at each end and is attached at the center of the cord below the finial on the staff. The colors are red, white, and blue.

Q. What is meant by "positional" colors?
A. Colors authorized to indicate official status or rank of certain civilian and military officials of the Federal Government.

Q. Positional colors are authorized in what two sizes?
A. (1) 4'4" x 5'6"
(2) 3' x 4'

Q. Describe the positional colors for the Office of the President of the United States.
A. It is national flag blue. A Presidential coat of arms is centered on the flag in proper colors and encircled by white stars, the same number as in the union of the US flag. The fringe is silver and gold bullion. Cord and tassels are red, white, and blue.

Q. Describe the individual flag for a General officer.
A. The flag is scarlet, 3-foot hoist by 4-foot fly, with a horizontal line of white five-pointed stars, the number indicating the grade. Fringe is yellow.

NOTE: General of the Army flag has a circular pattern of white, five-pointed stars.

Q. An automobile plate indicates the official status or rank of the individual occupying the vehicle. What should be done when the individual for whom the plate is issued is not in the vehicle?
A. The plate should be removed or covered.

Q. On what date was the present US Army flag approved?
A. June 12, 1956 by Executive Order 10670.

Q. What is Flag Day?
A. June 14; on this date in 1956 the newly approved US Army flag was unfurled at Independence Hall, Philadelphia, Pennsylvania, by the Honorable Wilbur M. Brucker, Secretary of the Army. June 14, 1956 was the 181st anniversary of the United States Army.

Q. Describe the US Army flag.
A. It is 4' 4" in hoist by 5' 6" in fly and is trimmed on three sides with yellow fringe 2½" in width. It is made of white silk and bears an embroidered replica of the official seal of the Department of the Army (w/out the roman numerals) in ultramarine blue. A scarlet roll inscribed, "United States Army" in white is centered between the device and the ultramarine blue numerals "1775". Streamers represent the campaigns since its inception.

Q. Under what conditions are streamers authorized to be awarded?
A. In recognition of a display of heroism or meritorious service or achievement which is the result of a group effort.

Q. What is a guidon?
A. It is a swallow-tailed unit identification marker, 20" x 27", with a fork 10" long. It is approved by HQDA and authorized for units with an authorized strength of 20 or more military personnel.

FLAGS & GUIDONS
AR 840-10/FM 22-5

Q. What is a "flagstaff"?
A. The staff on which a color, distinguishing flag, or guidon is carried or displayed.

Q. What are the authorized flagstaff lengths for the following flags?
A. (1) National flag - same length as flagstaffs of accompanying flags in 2, 3, and 4 below.
(2) US Presidential flag - either 10'3" or 7'9"
(3) General officers' flags - 8 feet.
(4) Guidons - 8 feet.
(5) Markers and marking pennants - 7 feet.
(6) Automobile flags - sufficient height that, when mounted, the lower edge of the flag will fly about one inch higher than the crest of the automobile's hood.

Q. What is a "finial"?
A. A flagstaff head - the decorative ornament at the top of a flagstaff.

Q. Only four finials are authorized to be used on flagstaffs. What are they?
A. (1) Eagle - Presidential flagstaffs.
(2) Spearhead (arrowhead) - Army flagstaffs.
(3) Acorn - Markers and marking pennant flagstaffs.
(4) Ball - Outdoor wall mounted for advertising or recruiting.

Q. What is the only finial device used with Army flags?
A. The spearhead.

Q. What is a "canton"?
A. A square or rectangle in the upper left-hand corner of a flag.

Q. What is a "dexter"?
A. The side of the shield or design element appearing to the viewer's left.

Q. What is a "sinister"?
A. The side of the shield or design element appearing to the viewer's right.

Q. What is a "halyard"?
A. The rope or cable that raises a flag up and down the flagpole.

Q. How many soldiers normally comprise a flag detail?
A. One NCOIC, two halyard pullers, and two to eight flag handlers as outlined below:

	NCOIC	HALYARD PULLERS	FLAG HANDLERS	TOTAL
Storm Flag (small)	1	2	2	5
Post Flag (medium)	1	2	6	9
Garrison Flag (large)	1	2	8	11

Q. What is the purpose of the flag handlers in a flag detail?
A. To ensure correct folding (unfolding) of the flag and to ensure that the flag does not touch the ground.

Q. How should commands or directives to ensure the proper performance of the flag detail be given by the NCOIC?
A. Inconspicuously.

FLAGS & GUIDONS
AR 840-10/FM 22-5

Q. Is the NCOIC permitted to assist the flag handlers?
A. Yes, as necessary (ie, windy days).

Q. The ceremonial raising of the flag is known as what?
A. Reveille.

Q. The ceremonial lowering of the flag is known as what?
A. Retreat.

Q. When do the flag handlers salute the flag during reveille or retreat?
A. Anytime they are not physically holding or reaching for the flag.

Q. What is a TRK (pronounced "truck")?
A. Customarily refers to the finial of a flagpole.

NOTE: AR 840-10 makes no reference to a "truck" or "TRK". It is given here because of its common usage.

Q. What is a "tabard"?
A. A rayon banner cloth with two rayon (or nylon) cords having an acorn at each end, for attachment to the tubing of band instruments.

Q. What are the five authorized categories of streamers and silver bands?
A. (1) Unit Decoration streamers.
(2) Infantry and Medical streamers.
(3) Campaign streamers.
(4) Campaign silver bands.
(5) War Service streamers.

Q. If the National flag touches the ground or becomes soiled, must it be destroyed?
A. It is disrespectful to deliberately allow the US flag to touch anything beneath it. However, if it should become soiled by accidentally touching the ground or by other means, it is necessary only to have it cleaned.

Q. How do you clean a serviceable flag?
A. In the manner best suited for the material.

Q. What is the height of the flagpole on which the National flag is flown?
A. 50, 60, or 70 feet.

Q. Describe the proper procedure for folding the US flag.
A. (1) Fold the lower striped section of the flag over the blue field.
(2) Fold the folded edge over to meet the open edge.
(3) Start a triangular fold by bringing the striped corner of the folded edge to the open edge.
(4) Fold the outer point inward parallel with the open edge to form a second triangle.
(5) Continue folding until the entire length of the flag is folded into a triangle with only the blue field and margin showing.
(6) Tuck the remaining margin into the pocket formed by the folds at the blue edge of the flag.
(7) The properly folded flag should resemble a cocked hat.

MILITARY CUSTOMS AND COURTESIES
FM 22-5/AR 600-25

Q. What Army regulation covers "Salutes, Honors, and Visits of Courtesy"?
A. AR 600-25.

Q. What other Army publication is a good source of information regarding Military Customs and Courtesies?
A. FM 22-5, Appendix A.

Q. What are "customs"?
A. Commonly practiced or observed events that have become tradition and make up the unwritten "common law" of the Army.

Q. What is meant by "Military Courtesy"?
A. The respect and consideration shown by military personnel to others.

Q. What is considered to be the most important of all military courtesies?
A. The hand salute.

Q. Why do we salute?
A. It is an act of courtesy and recognition between military members.

Q. What is the origin of the hand salute?
A. Although uncertain, some historians believe that it began in late Roman times when assassinations were common. A citizen who wanted to see a public official had to approach with his right hand raised to show that he did not hold a weapon. Knights in armor raised visors with the right hand when meeting a comrade. This practice gradually became a way of showing respect and, in early American history, sometimes involved removing the hat. By 1820, the motion was modified to touching the hat, and since then it has become the hand salute used today.

Q. At what position are salutes always given?
A. The position of ATTENTION (includes "walking" at attention but never running).

Q. Army personnel in uniform are required to salute when they meet and recognize persons entitled (by grade) to a salute except for what circumstances?
A. When it is inappropriate or impractical (in public conveyances such as planes and buses, in public places such as outside athletic facilities, inside theaters, or when driving a vehicle).

Q. Name some other times when a soldier is required to salute.
A.
- When the United States National Anthem, "To the Color", "Reveille", "Hail to the Chief", or foreign national anthems are played.
- To uncased National Color outdoors.
- On ceremonial occasions (as directed).
- At reveille and retreat ceremonies, during the raising or lowering of the flag.
- When pledging allegiance to the US Flag outdoors.
- When turning over control of formations.
- When rendering reports or when reporting to an official board or officer indoors.
- To officers of friendly foreign countries.

Q. When are salutes **not** required?
A.
- Indoors, except when reporting to an officer or when on duty as a guard.

- When a prisoner.
- Whenever saluting would be inappropriate (ie, when carrying articles with both hands, or being otherwise so occupied as to make saluting impracticable).
- Either the senior or subordinate is wearing civilian clothes.
- When actively participating in physical training or games.
- When a member of a work detail (unless you are the individual in charge and you are not actively engaged - in which case you would salute for the entire detail).
- When maneuvering against a hostile armed force or participating in field training exercises.

Q. When meeting an officer outdoors at what distance should you salute?
A. At approximately six paces (hold the salute until returned by the officer and give the greeting of the day).

Q. What is meant by "the greeting of the day"?
A. The appropriate greeting may be "Good morning <afternoon><evening>, Sir!", or it may be an approved, brief expression such as, "AIRBORNE", "AIR ASSAULT", "STEEL", "CHARLIE ROCK, Sir", etc.

Q. Is an officer required to return the salute of an enlisted member?
A. Yes.

Q. Is it customary for warrant officers of the same branch of service to salute one another?
A. No.

Q. What is the rule of thumb to remember when doubt exists as to whether or not you should salute?
A. "When in doubt, salute!"

Q. What is the proper procedure for reporting indoors?
A. Remove the headgear (except when under arms), approach to within two paces of the desk, halt, salute, and report, "<Sir><Ma'am><SGM>, Private Jones reports." The salute is held until the report is completed and the salute has been returned. When the business is completed, the soldier salutes, holds the salute until it has been returned, executes the appropriate facing movement, and departs.

Q. What is meant by the term "under arms"?
A. Carrying a weapon in your hands or having the weapon attached to you by a sling or holster.

Q. How should military personnel that are under arms render the salute?
A. The salute for the prescribed weapon with which they are armed will be given, whether or not that weapon is ordinarily prescribed as part of their equipment.

Q. What is the proper procedure for reporting outdoors?
A. Halt approximately three steps from the officer, salute, and report (as when indoors). Exchange salutes again when dismissed.

Q. Is the practice of saluting officers in official vehicles (recognized individually by grade or identifying vehicle plates and/or flags) considered an appropriate courtesy?
A. Yes.

MILITARY CUSTOMS AND COURTESIES
FM 22-5/AR 600-25

Q. Salutes are not required to be rendered by or to personnel who are driving or riding in privately owned vehicles except by whom?
A. Gate guards, who render salutes to recognized officers in all vehicles unless their duties make the salute impractical.

Q. When is the only time individuals in formation are required to salute?
A. When given the command PRESENT, ARMS.

Q. What is the proper procedure for a leader of a squad or larger element to salute?
A. The leader brings the unit to attention and then salutes for the entire formation.

Q. What should you do if you are in formation and you are addressed by an officer?
A. Assume the position of attention (if not already at this position).

Q. An officer approaches a group of individuals **not in formation.** What is the appropriate courtesy?
A. The first person to see the officer calls the group to attention and all salute.

Q. An officer approaches a group of individuals **resting** alongside a road. What is the appropriate courtesy?
A. If the officer is merely passing by and does not address the group then no action is required. However, if the officer addresses an individual (or the group), then the individual (or the group) comes to attention and remains at attention (unless otherwise ordered) until the termination of the conversation, at which time the individual (or group) salutes the officer.

Q. You are outdoors, **not in formation**, when you hear the National Anthem, "To the Color", "Reveille", or "Hail to the Chief". What should be your actions?
A. At the first note all dismounted personnel face the flag (or the music, if the flag is not in view), stand at ATTENTION and render the prescribed salute. The salute is held until the last note of the music is sounded. Military personnel not in uniform will stand at attention (remove headdress, if any, with the right hand) and place the right hand over the heart.

Q. What would be the proper procedure for the above question if you were in or on a privately owned vehicle?
A. Vehicles in motion are brought to a halt. Persons riding in a passenger car or on a motorcycle dismount, face the flag (or music, if flag is not in view), and salute.

Q. If you were in a military vehicle, what would you do differently from the above question?
A. Occupants of military vehicles and buses remain in the vehicle; the individual in charge of each vehicle dismounts and renders the hand salute. Tank and armored car commanders salute from the vehicle.

Q. Are women (military or civilian) required to remove their headdress during ceremonies?
A. No.

Q. What is the appropriate courtesy when rendering honors to the National Anthem while indoors?

MILITARY CUSTOMS AND COURTESIES
FM 22-5/AR 600-25

A. Officers and enlisted personnel stand at attention and face the music, or the flag if one is present.

Q. What should you do when passing uncased National Colors?
A. Salute at six steps distance and hold the salute until you have passed six steps beyond the flag.

Q. What should you do if uncased National Colors passes your position?
A. Assume the position of attention. Salute when the flag is six paces away, holding the salute until the flag has passed six paces beyond you.

Q. At what times would it be appropriate for a soldier **under arms** to uncover (remove headgear)?
A. - When seated as a member of (or in attendance on) a court or board.
- When entering a place of divine worship.
- When in attendance at an official reception.

Q. When is headgear not required **outdoors**?
A. Only when the wearing of headgear poses a safety hazard (ie, around operating aircraft).

Q. What is the proper courtesy rendered by Army personnel when boarding a US Naval ship?
A. Upon reaching the top of the gangway, face and salute the national ensign. After completing this salute, salute the officer of the deck who will be standing on the quarter deck at the head of the gangway. When saluting the officer of the deck, request permission to board, "Sir, Request permission to come aboard." The officer of the deck will return the salute. When leaving the ship, render the same salutes in reverse order, and request permission to leave, "Sir, Request permission to go ashore."

Q. What is a "review"?
A. A military ceremony used to:
(1) Honor a visiting, high-ranking commander, official, or dignitary, and/or permit them to observe the state of training of a command.
(2) Present decorations and awards.
(3) Honor or recognize unit or individual achievements.
(4) Commemorate events.

Q. What is the primary purpose of ceremonies?
A. To render honors, preserve tradition, and stimulate esprit de corps.

Q. What are military "ruffles and flourishes"?
A. Drum and trumpet honors.

Q. Reviews were originally practiced by revolutionary soldiers and were outlined in what document?
A. Baron Friedreich von Steuben's "Blue Book".

Q. What are the seven parts of a military review?
A. (1) Formation of troops.
(2) Presentation of Command and honors.
(3) Inspection.
(4) Honors to the Nation.
(5) Remarks.
(6) March in review.
(7) Conclusion.

MILITARY CUSTOMS AND COURTESIES
FM 22-5/AR 600-25

Q. What other ceremonial activities may be incorporated within the framework of a review?
A. Decorations, awards, and individual retirement; change of command; the activation or deactivation of units; and retreat.

Q. In order that a commander may review his own command or accompany a visiting reviewing officer or new commander, the commander normally designates an officer of his command to be responsible for the preparation of the troops for the review. What is the officer called?
A. Commander of Troops (COT).

Q. What are the nine parts of a parade?
A. (1) Formation of troops.
(2) Sound off by a band.
(3) Honors to the nation.
(4) Presentation.
(5) Manual of arms.
(6) Report.
(7) Orders published.
(8) Officers center.
(9) Pass in review.

Q. What are the two primary characteristics of a parade?
A. The appearance and movement of troops in formation.

Q. An Honor Guard consists of what four elements?
A. Band, Colors, salute battery (when available and appropriate), and a formation of troops.

Q. What is an Honor Cordon?
A. A trimmed-down version of the Honor Guard designated to honor and provide security at the immediate arrival or departure site of distinguished visitors.

Q. An Honor Cordon is normally made up of what elements?
A. Two 10-man squads, a senior sergeant, a cordon commander, and a host.

Q. What is a "ramp guard"?
A. This is another name for a Cordon Guard or an Honor Cordon.

Q. What is "Retreat"?
A. A ceremony in which the unit honors the US flag when it is lowered in the evening.

Q. Who normally sets the time for the sounding of retreat?
A. The installation commander.

Q. Explain the origin of Retreat.
A. The term "Retreat" is taken from the French word "Retraite" and refers to the evening ceremony. The bugle call sounded at retreat was first used in the French army and dates back to the Crusades. Retreat was sounded at sunset to notify sentries to start challenging until sunrise, and to tell the rank and file to go to their quarters. The ceremony remains as a tradition.

Q. What two bugle calls are normally heard at "Retreat"?
A. "Retreat" and "To the Colors".

MILITARY CUSTOMS AND COURTESIES
FM 22-5/AR 600-25

Q. When is the cannon fired during a retreat ceremony?
A. At the last note of retreat (just prior to "To the Colors").

Q. How long is the call "To the Colors"?
A. 40 seconds.

Q. What may be substituted for "To the Colors" during a Retreat ceremony?
A. The National Anthem.

Q. The present bugle call "To the Color" was originally known as what?
A. "To the Standard".

Q. What is "Reveille"?
A. A ceremony in which the unit honors the US flag as it is raised in the morning.

Q. Who normally sets the time for the sounding of reveille?
A. The installation commander.

Q. Explain the origin of reveille.
A. Reveille was not originally intended as honors to the flag. In 1812, it was a drum call to signify that soldiers should rise for day duty and sentries should leave off night challenging. As time passed, reveille came to denote when the flag was raised in the morning and honors paid to it.

Q. How long is "Reveille"?
A. 20 seconds.

Q. How does the raising of the US flag differ from the lowering of the flag?
A. During reveille, the flag is raised quickly to the top of the flag pole. During retreat, the flag is lowered slowly and ceremoniously. It should reach the bottom at the last note of "To the Colors".

Q. A flag detail passes you carrying the US flag, folded in the shape of a "cocked hat". What should be your actions.
A. Nothing. Once the flag has been folded it is treated as a cased color and not saluted by persons meeting the flag detail.

Q. What are the two classes of funerals?
A. (1) Chapel service, followed by movement to the grave or place of local disposition with the prescribed escort.
(2) With graveside service only.

Q. When does the National Color dip in salute?
A. The National Color renders no salute (dip). An exception to this rule is followed by naval vessels when, upon receiving a salute of this type from a vessel registered by a nation formally recognized by the United States, the compliment must be returned.

Q. When are organizational colors required to be dipped in salute?
A. In all military ceremonies while the National Anthem, "To the Color", or a foreign national anthem is being played, and when rendering honors to the organizational commander, an individual of higher grade including foreign dignitaries of higher grade, but in no other case.

Q. Is the United States Army flag considered to be an organizational color?
A. Yes.

MILITARY CUSTOMS AND COURTESIES
FM 22-5/AR 600-25

Q. The US Army flag is dipped in salute for what individuals?
A. The Army Chief of Staff, his direct representative, or an individual of equivalent or higher grade, but in no other case.

Q. A Color Guard consists of how many soldiers?
A. Two or three sergeants and two specialists or privates (the senior NCO is the Color guard commander and carries the National Color).

Q. What is the procedure for saluting while under arms?
A. Military personnel under arms give the salute prescribed for the weapon with which they are armed.

Q. What is the tile of address of an officer or civilian?
A. "Sir" or "Ma'am".

Q. When walking outdoors, where should the junior ranking soldier always walk in relation to a senior?
A. Always on the left.

Q. What is the customary order (by rank) for soldiers to enter and exit a vehicle or small boat?
A. The junior soldier enters first, followed by others in inverse order of rank. When exiting, the senior person gets out first and the junior last.

Q. What is the 50-gun (cannon) salute called and when is it used?
A. Salute to the Union; on the 4th of July.

Q. The national salute and the salute to a national flag are both _____ guns each.
A. 21

Q. On what holiday is the National Flag displayed at half staff from reveille until noon?
A. Memorial Day - the last Monday in May. At 1200 hours, the national salute (21 guns) will be fired and the flag hoisted to the top of the pole where it remains until retreat.

Q. National Holidays, established by law, will be observed by the Army except when military operations prevent. List these Holidays and give the dates for each.
A. (1) New Year's Day .... 1 January
(2) President's Day ...... third Monday in February
(3) Memorial Day .... last Monday in May
(4) Independence Day ..... 4 July
(5) Labor Day .... first Monday in September
(6) Columbus Day .... second Monday in October
(7) Veteran's Day .... 11 November
(8) Thanksgiving Day ..... fourth Thursday in November
(9) Christmas Day .... 25 December

NOTE: When these holidays fall on a Saturday, the preceding Friday also will be considered a holiday. When holidays fall on Sunday, the succeeding Monday also will be considered a holiday.

Q. What is the significance of Memorial Day? Independence Day?
A. Memorial Day: also known as Decoration Day, it is a day of remembrance for

those who have died in the nation's service. It was first widely observed on May 30, 1868, when flowers were placed on the graves of Union and Confederate soldiers.

Independence Day: celebrates the adoption of the Declaration of Independence by the Second Continental Congress on July 4, 1776.

Q. Although not considered a National Holiday, this day is the anniversary of the adoption of the American Flag on June 14, 1777. What day is it?
A. Flag Day

Q. What day has been set aside to commemorate the Armed Forces of the United States?
A. Armed Forces Day, the 3rd Saturday in May.

Q. Give the number of cannon salutes on arrival and departure for the following individuals.

A.	Arrival	Departure
President	21	21
Ex-President	21	21
Vice President	19	none
Secretary of Defense	19	19
Secretary of the Army	19	19
Chairman, JCS	19	19
Army Chief of Staff	19	19
Generals	17	17
Lieutenant General	15	none
Major General	13	none
Brigadier General	11	none

Q. When should cannon salutes **not** be fired?
A. Between retreat and reveille, on Sundays, or on National Holidays (excluding Memorial and Independence Days) unless, in the discretion of the officer directing the honors, international courtesy or the occasion requires an exception. NOTE: They will be fired at the first available opportunity thereafter, if still appropriate.

Q. High ranking officials and dignitaries customarily receive how many "ruffles and flourishes"?
A. Generals (and civilian equivalent) receive one set of ruffles and flourishes for each star (ie, BG=1, MG=2, etc). 4-star generals and higher, to include the President, receive four ruffles and flourishes.

Q. Should the Pledge of Allegiance be recited in military formations or in military ceremonies?
A. No.

Q. What should be your response anytime you hear or recite the Pledge of Allegiance?
A. - Civilian clothes: face the flag, assume the position of attention, and recite the pledge with the right hand over the heart. Men remove headdress with right hand and hold over left shoulder, with the hand over the heart.

- Uniform, outdoors: stand at attention, remain silent, face the flag, and give the hand salute.

- Uniform, indoors: stand at attention, remain **silent**, and face the flag. Reciting the pledge is optional for personnel in uniform when the majority of participants are civilians or in civilian attire.

Q. What should be done when an officer enters a dining facility?

MILITARY CUSTOMS AND COURTESIES
FM 22-5/AR 600-25

A. The first soldier to see the officer calls "At Ease!"(unless a higher ranking officer is known to be present).

Q. When are you required to salute a Noncommissioned Officer?
A. When reporting before an NCO Board, when reporting in formation and when turning over a formation.

Q. What is the purpose of Unit or Organizational Day?
A. Originally a celebration of the Unit's Birthday in which the traditions of the organization were kept in the spotlight all day. It is more currently recognized as an annual unit holiday in which soldiers participate in a variety of competitive games and sports while enjoying a festive, picnic-type atmosphere. It is intended to build morale and esprit de corps.

Q. What is the proper title of address of an E-9?
A. "Sergeant Major" or "Top" (although the latter title is most often reserved for a First Sergeant).

Q. What is the proper title of address of a SSG, SFC, or MSG?
A. "Sergeant"

Q. How should a member of the Army be addressed if the name and rank are not known?
A. Simply as "soldier".

Q. What is the proper title of address of a PV1, PV2, or PFC?
A. "Private"

Q. What is the proper title of address of an E-4?
A. "Specialist" or "Corporal" as appropriate.

Q. A US flag flown at halfstaff symbolizes what?
A. Mourning.

Q. How is the flag placed at half-staff?
A. It is first raised quickly to full-staff and then slowly and ceremoniously lowered to half-staff.

Q. What is the proper procedure for lowering a flag from half-staff?
A. The Flag must first be raised quickly to full-staff and then ceremoniously lowered in the traditional manner.

Q. When would the US Flag be flown upside down?
A. Only as a distress signal (dire emergency).

Q. What is the name of our National Anthem and when was it adopted?
A. "The Star-Spangled Banner" officially became the National Anthem by law on March 3, 1931, in title 36, United States Code 170.

Q. Who wrote our National Anthem?
A. Francis Scott Key, on September 14, 1814, at Ft McHenry (Baltimore, MD), during a British bombardment.

Q. What bugle call is traditionally played at military funerals?
A. "Taps".

Q. A ceremonial firing party consists of how many men?

A. 8; 1 NCOIC and a 7-man firing squad.

Q. Who is traditionally responsible for the care of the unit colors?
A. The Command Sergeant Major.

Q. What is the name of the Official Army Song? When was it written and by whom?
A. "The Army goes Rolling Along"; it was dedicated on Veterans Day, 11 November 1956, by the Secretary of the Army but was not officially announced until 12 December 1957 (AR 28-76). It was originally known as the "Caisson Song" and was composed by Lt Edmund L. Gruber in 1908.

Q. Is it necessary to stand at attention when the Army Song is played?
A. There is no DA directive in this regard; however FM 22-5 encourages personnel to stand at attention when it is played to pay tribute to the Army.

Q. When foreign troops are invited by U.S. Forces to participate in parades where should they be positioned in the line of march?
A. They will be assigned a position of honor ahead of United States troops.

Q. An announcement of death of a President, ex-President, or President-elect will be made how?
A. Announcement will be made by the Secretary or Acting Secretary of the Army and will be published in Headquarters, Department of the Army orders.

Q. What honors are required for the death of a President, ex-President, or President-elect?
A. Commanders of military installations will ensure that:
(1) One gun is fired every half-hour, beginning at reveille and ending at retreat.
(2) All troops are assembled at 1000 hours and the official notification of death will be read.
(3) On the day of internment, a 21-gun salute, fired at one-minute intervals, will be fired at noon. Personnel will not salute.
(4) Also on the day of internment, a salute of a number of guns equal to the number of States of the Union will be fired at retreat. The salute will be fired at 5-second intervals immediately following the lowering of the flag. Personnel will not salute.
(5) The National Flag will be flown at halfstaff for 30 days from the day of death from reveille until retreat.

Q. In the event of the death of the Vice-President, how long is the National Flag required to be flown at half-staff?
A. 10 days from the day of death from reveille until retreat.

ENLISTED PERSONNEL MANAGEMENT SYSTEM/PROMOTIONS
AR 600-200

Q. What does "EPMS" stand for?
A. Enlisted Personnel Management System.

Q. What Army regulation covers the EPMS?
A. AR 600-200.

Q. What are the five personnel classification measuring devices mentioned in AR 600-200?
A. (1) Army personnel tests (aptitude and selection, including Armed Services Vocational Aptitude Battery (ASVAB) or Defense Language Aptitude Battery (DLAB)).
(2) Physical Profile Serial (PULHES).
(3) Personnel interviews.
(4) Skill Qualification Test (SQT)/Self Development Test (SDT).
(5) Performance appraisal and rating documents.

Q. PULHES is a numerical physical profile serial code. Each letter represents an evaluated medical (physical or mental) condition. What does each letter represent?
A. P - physical capacity or stamina.
U - upper extremities.
L - lower extremities.
H - head and hearing.
E - eyes.
S - psychiatric rating.

Q. The use of PULHES for MOS classification, reclassification, and assignment are limited to what?
A. Initial selection of basic combat trainees for advanced individual training.

Q. What personnel may be awarded an MOS without attending AIT?
A. Personnel with civilian-acquired skills.

Q. What does "MOS" stand for? PMOS? CPMOS? AMOS? SMOS?
A. Military Occupational Specialty; Primary MOS; Career Progression MOS; Additional MOS; Secondary MOS.

Q. What does "CMF" stand for?
A. Career Management Field - a manageable grouping of related MOSs that provide visible progression to grade E9.

Q. When is a PMOS first awarded?
A. Upon successful completion of AIT (unless awarded as a result of civilian acquired skills).

Q. When can a new MOS be awarded?
A. (1) Upon successful completion of MOS training offered by an Army service school or training activity.
(2) Upon HQDA directed, successful completion of on-the-job training for not less than 60 days.
(3) Upon identification of civilian acquired skills having a direct MOS counterpart.
(4) Upon withdrawal of PMOS.

Q. What is an "MOSC"?
A. MOS Code - it represents not only the 3-character MOS, but additional

characters that include skill level and special skill identifiers.

Q. What is represented by the fourth character of an MOSC?
A. Skill level.

Q. How many skill levels are there and when are they awarded?
A. 6;
Skill level 0 - Used to identify soldiers being trained for a PMOS (BCT, AIT).
Skill level 1 - Awarded upon successful completion of training that leads to a PMOS. Commensurate with grade of PVT through CPL/SPC.
Skill level 2 - Upon promotion/reduction to the grade of SGT.
Skill level 3 - Upon promotion/reduction to the grade of SSG.
Skill level 4 - Upon promotion/reduction to the grade of SFC.
Skill level 5 - Upon promotion/reduction to the grade of MSG and higher.

Q. How are skill levels for SMOS computed?
A. Same as for a PMOS (determined by rank). Skill level 0 is not used.

Q. What is represented by the fifth character in an MOSC?
A. The Special Qualification Identifier (SQI) - it identifies special qualifications that a soldier has.

Q. Name some special qualifications that warrant a Special Qualification Identifier.
A. Ranger/Parachutist, Parachutist, Ranger, First Sergeant, Drill Sergeant, Instructor, EO Advisor, Special Forces, Linguist, Flight Medic Aidman.

Q. When a prior-awarded SQI is removed from PMOS due to award of an SQI with higher precedence, what is done with the lower precedence SQI?
A. It will be recorded in the fifth position of the SMOS (if there is one).

Q. What is inserted as the fifth character of the MOSC when an individual is not qualified for award of an SQI?
A. The letter "O".

Q. What is contained in the sixth and seventh characters of the MOSC?
A. The Additional Skill Identifier (ASI) - it identifies skills acquired through functional training or OJT in maintenance and operation of weapon or equipment systems or subsystems, and other training not identified by MOS or SQI.

Q. When a soldier is qualified in more than one ASI that may be used with the PMOS, which is assigned?
A. The latest ASI.

Q. What is inserted in the sixth and seventh characters of an MOSC when a soldier is not qualified for award of an ASI?
A. Two zeros (00).

Q. What is contained in the eighth and ninth characters of the MOSC?
A. Language identifier.

Q. What is inserted in these spaces when an individual is not qualified as a linguist?
A. The letters "OO".

ENLISTED PERSONNEL MANAGEMENT SYSTEM/PROMOTIONS
AR 600-200

Q. What is "TAPDB" and how does it relate to SQI, ASI, and language codes?
A. Total Army Personnel Data Base; it is a database that will be used to record and retain all SQIs, ASIs, and Language Identifiers awarded to a soldier during their career.

Q. What is a "lateral" appointment?
A. A change from one rank to another within the same pay grade (ie, Specialist to Corporal or Master Sergeant to First Sergeant).

Q. What is the sole criteria for a lateral appointment of Specialists to the rank of Corporal?
A. Unit Commanders or higher may laterally appoint Specialist to Corporal without local selection board action provided they are assigned to an authorized NCO position.

Q. Maximum effort should be made to utilize soldiers in properly authorized TOE or TDA positions, consistent with their PMOS or CPMOS qualifications. A soldier is determined to be properly utilized when any of what conditions apply?
A.
- Assigned to authorized position in PMOS at the same rank or two ranks higher.
- Assigned and utilized in PMOS in a one-grade lower position (only when surplus). Exception to this is rank of SGM/CSM.
- In a shortage or balanced MOS in which he/she is being trained, provided current PMOS is listed as overstrength in DA Circular 611 series.
- The sole purpose of the assignment is to qualify the soldier for a shortage MOS.
- Assignment is under special instructions from HQDA.

Q. What is "SDAP"?
A. Special Duty Assignment Pay. It is a monthly monetary incentive that is paid to enlisted personnel who qualify for and serve in designated special duty assignments. It is used for designated personnel who have extremely demanding duties that require an extraordinary effort for satisfactory performance or an unusual degree of responsibilities.

Q. Who is the approval authority for determining which special duties are eligible to receive SDAP?
A. The Secretary of the Army.

Q. In order to be eligible for SDAP you must be a ___(rank)___ or higher.
A. Private First Class.

Q. The amount of SDAP a service member receives is based on the special duty (SD) level assigned to the soldier. How many SD levels are there and how much does each pay?
A. 5; SD-1=$55.00, SD-2=$110.00, SD-3=$165.00, SD-4=$220.00, SD-5=$275.00.

Q. List some duties that are authorized SDAP.
A. Recruiters, Career Counselors, Retention NCOs, and Drill Sergeants.

Q. Who has the authority to administratively reduce soldiers in the grades E-2 through E-9?
A. E2 - E4...........Company Commander or higher
E5 - E6...........Battalion Commander (O-5 or higher)
E7 - E9...........Brigade Commander (O-6 or higher)

ENLISTED PERSONNEL MANAGEMENT SYSTEM/PROMOTIONS AR 600-200

Q. Name five reasons that a soldier may be administratively reduced.
A. (1) Erroneous enlistment grade.
(2) Misconduct.
(3) Inefficiency.
(4) Approved for discharge from service under other than honorable conditions.
(5) Failure to complete training (ie, OCS, Flight School).

Q. There are three different ways that a soldier may be reduced for misconduct. What are they?
A. By Article 15, Court Martial, or conviction by a civil court.

Q. What is meant by "inefficiency"?
A. A demonstration of characteristics that shows that a person cannot perform duties and responsibilities of the grade and MOS. It also may include any act or conduct that clearly shows that the soldier lacks those abilities required and expected of a person of that grade and experience (ie, long-standing unpaid personal debts).

Q. How many days must a soldier be assigned to a unit before he can be reduced for inefficiency?
A. 90 days.

Q. A soldier that is to appear before a reduction board will be given at least how many working days written notice before the date of the hearing?
A. 15

Q. Final action on appeals for reduction due to misconduct will be taken by whom?
A. (1) Next higher authority above reduction authority for rank of SSG and below.
(2) First general officer in the chain of command above the reduction authority for ranks of SFC and above.

NOTE: Appeals for reduction by reason of Article 15 or Court Martial are governed by article 15, UCMJ; paragraph 135, MCM; and AR 27-10. See section 27, "Military Justice" for more information.

Q. When the separation authority determines that a soldier is to be discharged from the service under other than honorable conditions, he or she will be reduced to what grade?
A. The lowest enlisted grade - PV1.

Q. As a minimum, reduction orders must cite what two things?
A. Reason for reduction and authority.

Q. A soldier that attends fixed-wing or rotary wing aviation training is automatically promoted to SGT (if a lower rank is held prior to attending school). What happens if this soldier fails to complete the training?
A. He/she will be reduced to the grade held on entry, or to a grade considered appropriate, or released altogether from active duty.

Q. What chapter of AR 600-200 contains information on promotions?
A. Chapter 7.

Q. When should soldiers be recommended for promotion?
A. Only after they develop the skills and abilities necessary to perform the

duties and responsibilities of the next higher grade.

Q. What should you look for when recommending an individual for promotion?
A. Overall performance, attitude, leadership ability, and development potential.

Q. What must be done for soldiers (SGT and below) who meet advancement or promotion eligibility, without waiver, but are not recommended for promotion?
A. The soldier should be counseled. This counseling should be directed towards those areas in which the soldier needs to improve in order to qualify for the next higher grade.

Q. What are the objectives of the Army Promotion System?
A. (1) Fill authorized enlisted spaces with qualified soldiers.
(2) Provide for career progression and rank which is in line with potential.
(3) Recognize the best qualified soldier which will attract and retain the highest caliber soldier for a career in the Army.
(4) Preclude promoting the soldier who is not productive or not best qualified.
(5) Provide an equitable system for all soldiers.

Q. Who has the authority to promote soldiers in the grades E2 through E9?
A. E4 & below.........Unit Commander
E5 - E6............Battalion Commander (O-5 or higher)
E7 - E9............Brigade Commander (O-6 or higher)

NOTE: Authority to promote has the same authority to reduce.

Q. How are promotions to E4 and below announced?
A. By DA Form 4187.

Q. How are promotions to E5 through E9 announced?
A. This is announced on orders.

Q. What actions can cause soldiers (E1 - E8) to be in a nonpromotable status?
A.
- AWOL, in confinement, in desertion, confined by civil authorities, under arrest, or ill or injured not in the line of duty.
- Under court-martial charges.
- Serving a court-martial sentence, including suspended sentence.
- In proceedings that may result in other than honorable discharge.
- Flagged on DA Form 268 IAW AR 600-31.
- A written recommendation has been sent to the promotion authority to reclassify a soldier for inefficiency or disciplinary reasons.
- Being punished under Article 15, UCMJ, including suspended punishment (summarized article 15 alone will not result in nonpromotable status).
- Ineligible for reenlistment.
- Inability to obtain security clearance necessary to perform duties in PMOS at next grade.
- A written recommendation has been sent to the promotion authority (E5 & below) for possible board action, which may result in removal from a recommended list, or reduction to a lower grade.
- Fail to take SQT due to own fault.
- Receive second SQT failure in current PMOS (unless waiver is obtained).
- Failure to qualify for reenlistment or extension of current enlistment to meet the current service remaining obligation for promotion to SSG.
- DA or locally imposed bar to reenlistment.
- Selected for assignment and removed for declining reenlistment or

extension.
- Voluntary retirement application has been approved.
- Exceed body fat standard or maximum allowable weight established in AR 600-9.
- Failed APRT or have not taken the APRT within the last 9 months.
- When enrolled in the Army Drug and Alcohol Prevention and Control Program (ADAPCP).

Q. What are the three levels of promotion?
A. Unit level, semi-centralized, and DA centralized.

Q. When is a soldier promoted to PV2?
A. When he completes 6 months of active Federal Service, **unless** it is stopped by the commander.

Q. Promotion to PV2 is automatic unless stopped by the commander. How is this done?
A. By submitting a DA Form 4187 prior to the effective date.

Q. Is time spent in the delayed entry program counted towards promotion?
A. No.

Q. To recognize outstanding soldiers, local commanders may advance soldiers to PV2 with less than 6 months time in service (TIS). What is the minimum TIS requirement and how many can the commander promote in this manner?
A. 4 months minimum TIS; only 20% of assigned and attached PV2 soldiers may have less than 6 months TIS.

Q. As an exception to the above rule, when can a soldier be promoted to PV2 without regard to TIS?
A. Commanders at BCT/OSUT are authorized to advance up to 3% of each company to PV2.

Q. Is the advancement of a soldier to PFC automatic or mandatory?
A. No.

Q. What are the normal Time in Service (TIS)/Time in Grade (TIG) requirements for promotion to Private First Class?
A. TIS: 12 months; TIG: 4 months (waiver of 2 months TIG is authorized).

Q. To recognize outstanding soldiers, local commanders may advance soldiers to PFC with less than 12 months TIS. What is the minimum TIS requirement and how many can the commander promote in this manner?
A. 6 months minimum TIS; only 20% of assigned and attached PFC soldiers may have less than 12 months TIS.

Q. What are the normal requirements for promotion to Specialist?
A. TIS: 26 months; TIG: 6 months (waiver of 3 months TIG is authorized); security clearance appropriate for MOS.

Q. To recognize outstanding soldiers, local commanders may advance soldiers to Specialist with less than 26 months TIS. What is the minimum TIS requirement and how many can the commander promote in this manner?
A. 12 months; not more than 20% of the total number of assigned E4 strength can have less than 26 months TIS.

Q. What are two exceptions to the above 20%-rule for promoting soldiers to

Specialist?
A. (1) Local commanders may advance one soldier per quarter to the grade of Specialist without regard to percentage requirements.
(2) Commanders with zero waiver authorizations may promote any soldier with 18 or more months time in grade.

Q. How many "zones" are there for promotion to grades E5 and E6? Name them.
A. 2; primary zone and secondary zone (sometimes referred to as "below the zone").

Q. The promotion authority may waive no more than _________ of the three requirements of TIS, TIG, and SQT for soldiers who are otherwise highly qualified.
A. Two.

Q. What is the purpose of the secondary zone?
A. It provides incentives to those who strive for excellence and whose accomplishments, demonstrated capacity for leadership, and marked potential warrant promotion ahead of their peers.

Q. Promotion to SGT/SSG represents what level of promotion?
A. Semi-centralized.

Q. What are the requirements for promotion to Sergeant?
A.

	Primary Zone (without waiver)	Secondary Zone (with waiver)
Time in service	36 months	18 months
Time in grade	8 months	4 months
Completion of PLDC		
Passing score on promotion board		
Meet or exceed the required promotion point cutoff score.		

Q. What are the requirements for promotion to Staff Sergeant?
A.

	Primary Zone (without waiver)	Secondary Zone (with waiver)
Time in service	84 months	48 months
Time in grade	10 months	5 months
Passing score on promotion board		
Meet or exceed the required promotion point cutoff score.		

NOTE: In all promotion cases, ½ the time in grade may be waived.

Q. What is the earliest that a soldier may be boarded for promotion to sergeant? Staff sergeant?
A. Sergeant - 18 months; staff sergeant - 45 months.

Q. What is the remaining service obligation for promotion to staff sergeant?
A. 12 months.

Q. Can a soldier be promoted to SGT or SSG if there are not any local vacancies?
A. Yes, soldiers eligible for promotion and on a current promotion standing list will be promoted in their CPMOS, provided they equal or exceed the promotion point cutoff for their MOS, regardless of local vacancies.

ENLISTED PERSONNEL MANAGEMENT SYSTEM/PROMOTIONS
AR 600-200

~~Q. What is an "SQT"? What is its replacement?~~
~~A. Skill Qualification Test - it is a test of a soldier's understanding of the critical tasks required by his/her MOS; the Self Development Test (SDT).~~

~~NOTE: SQT is covered here because it will continue to have an administrative impact on soldiers for the next several years.~~

~~Q. What is considered a passing score on the SQT?~~
~~A. 60 or above.~~

~~Q. Can a soldier be promoted with an SQT score of less than 60?~~
~~A. Yes, but only if the soldier has an approved waiver (counts as one of the two allowable waivers).~~

~~Q. How often is a soldier tested in his/her PMOS?~~
~~A. Once per year.~~

~~Q. How often is a soldier tested in a SMOS?~~
~~A. Once during career.~~

Q. Recommendations for promotion are prepared on what form?
A. DA Form 3355.

Q. How often are promotion boards convened?
A. Once a month, except when no soldier is recommended for board action. Boards must be conducted before the 15th of the month.

Q. Who sits on a promotion board?
A. The board may be composed of commissioned officers, warrant officers, enlisted personnel or any combination.

NOTE: Promotion boards are traditionally considered to be an NCO function and thus are almost always composed of all enlisted personnel.

Q. Who is the President of a promotion board?
A. The senior member of the board. For an all enlisted board, the President will be a command sergeant major, a frocked CSM, or a SGM if no CSM is present or assigned.

Q. Can a specialist sit on a promotion board?
A. Yes, if senior in grade to those being considered for promotion.

Q. What special consideration should be made when boarding soldiers of different gender?
A. At least one voting member of the board must be the same sex as those being considered. If this cannot be accomplished due to cogent reasons, the board recorder will record the reason in the board proceedings.

Q. A soldier's promotion packet for SGT/SSG should consist of what items?
A. (1) DA Form 3355 used for initial board appearance.
(2) Latest two DA Forms 3355 used for recomputation or reevaluation (if applicable).
(3) A copy of any document(s) used to confirm the award of promotion points on DA Form 3355 that is not filed in the MPRJ.

Q. After being boarded, when are soldiers eligible for promotion?
A. On the first day of the third month following date of board (ie, soldier

boarded in January will be eligible for promotion on 1 April).

Q. Soldiers are required to have their promotion points recomputed (recomp) at least how often?
A. Once per year.

Q. In addition to recomp (see above question), when may a soldier add points?
A. When they have increased their administrative promotion points by 35 or more points.

Q. Can a soldier request to be boarded again in order to try for a better score?
A. Yes (however, a lower score could be the result, or worse, you may not be recommended - in which case your name would be removed from the promotion list).

Q. What are the only two types of promotion point adjustments authorized?
A. (1) Correction of an error.
(2) Adding of additional administrative points.

Q. What is the maximum number of points possible on the Promotion Point Worksheet (DA Form 3355)?
A. 800 points ~~for promotion to SGT; 1000 for SSG.~~

Q. What is the minimum number of points required for promotion to SGT? To SSG?
A. 450; 550.

Q. How many promotion points are required to be "guaranteed" a promotion after the 90-day waiting period?
A. 798.

Q. Explain the various categories of the Promotion Point Worksheet and tell what the maximum number of points is for each area.

A.

		maximum points
Part 1	Duty Performance (awarded by commander)	200
Part 2	SQT/SDT x 2 (SSG only)	rescinded
Part 3	Awards and Decorations	50
Part 4	Military Education	150
Part 5	Civilian Education	100
Part 6	Military Training	100
	A. Marksmanship....50	
	B. Physical Readiness Test....50	
Part 7	Total Administrative Points	600 possible
Part 8	Total Board Points	200 possible
Part 9	Total Promotion Points	800 possible

NOTE: Part 2 is no longer used for promotional consideration.

Q. Promotion to SFC and above represents what level of promotion?
A. DA centralized.

Q. Eligibility for promotion consideration to SFC or higher is based on what?
A. Date of Rank (DOR).

Q. What is the minimum TIS requirements for promotion to grades E7 - E9?
A. 6, 8, and 10 years, respectively.

Q. What is the NCOES requirement for promotion to SFC?

ENLISTED PERSONNEL MANAGEMENT SYSTEM/PROMOTIONS
AR 600-200

A. Must be a graduate of ANCOC.

Q. Soldiers promoted to grades E7-E9 will incur a _______-year service obligation.
A. Two.

Q. What are some instances when a soldier may be promoted to the grades E5-E9 and NOT be on a promotion list issued by DA?
A. - Frocking: SFC assigned to authorized 1SG position may wear the rank of 1SG.
- Promotions of students, officer candidates, and trainees.
- Appointments of acting NCOs.
- Lateral appointments.
- Promotions of hospitalized or missing personnel.

Q. A specialist or below entering Officer Candidate School or the Warrant Officer Entry Course will automatically be promoted to the rank of sergeant. When does this promotion take place?
A. One day prior to departure from the losing organization.

Q. Can a soldier be promoted to SFC with only 3 years of active service?
A. Yes, if they are bandpersons assigned to the Fife and Drum Corps, 3d Infantry (Old Guard), or the three designated special bands. These are the US Army Band, the US Army Field Band, and the US Military Academy Band.

Q. Certificates of promotion will be issued to soldiers at the promotion ceremony. This is DA Form ______ for Specialists and DA Form ______ for the NCO ranks (corporal through CSM).
A. 4874; 4872.

Q. What does "MPRJ" stand for? "OMPF"?
A. Military Personnel Records Jacket; Ongoing Military Personnel File.

Q. The MPRJ is commonly called what?
A. "201" File.

Q. What are DA Forms 2A and 2-1 and where are they placed in the MPRJ?
A. Personnel Qualification Records; in the middle of the MPRJ between the Action Pending and Temporary sections.

Q. Where are your ongoing military records kept?
A. At Fort Benjamin Harrison, Indiana.

Q. Where is your MPRJ kept?
A. At your Personnel Service Center (PSC).

NOTE: The Personnel Service Centers are replacing the bulky 201-files with microfiche.

NCOERs/SEPARATIONS
DA Cir 623-88-1/AR 635-200

NCOERs

Q. What Army publications cover the new NCOER system?
A. DA Cir 623-88-1 and AR 623-205.

Q. What does the abbreviation "EER" stand for?
A. "Enlisted Evaluation Report" - it is the old evaluation system for noncommissioned officers in the Army. It was replaced by the NCOER system.

Q. What does NCOER stand for?
A. Noncommissioned Officer Evaluation Report.

Q. What is the major reason why the EER was replaced by the NCOER?
A. The EER became so inflated it was of little use to selection boards and career managers.

Q. What is the purpose of the NCOER?
A. The NCOER is designed to identify specific skills, knowledge, and attitudes, called "SKAs", of an NCO at various points in their career. Its primary purpose is to point out immediate/potential weak areas and to strengthen strong areas, thereby improving performance and professionally developing the rated NCO.

Q. SKAs (see above question) are linked closely to nine competencies the Army says are key to effective leadership. What are these nine competencies?
A.
- communications
- supervision
- teaching and counseling
- soldier-team development
- technical and tactical proficiency
- decision-making
- planning
- use of available systems
- professional ethics

NOTE: Together, the competencies define what the Army calls the "Be-Know-Do" concept of leadership.

Q. What is the major difference between the NCOER and the EER?
A. Numerical scores in the EER were eliminated in favor of box checks and short, concise comments that make a specific point.

Q. What is a "bullet" in reference to an NCOER?
A. A "bullet" is a short, concise comment that makes a specific point. An ideal bullet is one, no more than two, typed lines that justify a rating official's evaluation of "excellence", "success", or "needs improvement" in the Values and NCO Responsibilities section of the report.

Q. What ratings require a bullet comment?
A. "Excellence" and "Needs Improvement".

Q. On what DA Form was the EER recorded?
A. DA Form 2166-6.

Q. On what DA Form is the NCOER recorded?

NCOERs/SEPARATIONS
DA Cir 623-88-1/AR 635-200

A. DA Form 2166-7.

Q. What four signatures are required in Part II - Authentication, of the NCOER?
A. Rated NCO, Rater, Senior Rater, and Reviewer.

Q. Explain the rating chain for the NCOER.
A. Rater - primary evaluation focuses on performance; responsible for counseling.
Senior Rater - primary evaluation focuses on the potential; responsible for overwatching performance evaluation.
Reviewer - responsible for rating safeguard, oversees program, and comments only when he/she disagrees with rater/senior rater.

Q. Is the identity of the soldier's Rater and Sr Rater made known to the SM?
A. Yes, through publication and posting of an official rating chain within the unit or activity of assignment.

Q. What is this rating chain (see above question) normally called?
A. The Rating Scheme.

Q. What are the five parts (sections) of the NCOER?
A. Part I - Administrative Data
Part II - Authentication
Part III - Duty Description (Rater)
Part IV - Values/NCO Responsibilities (Rater)
Part V - Overall Performance and Potential

Q. Where in the NCOER will you find information on areas of special emphasis, appointed duties, and counseling dates?
A. Part III.

Q. Who should receive an NCOER?
A. Mandatory for NCOs, CPL thru SFC, optional for other senior NCOs.

NOTE: NCOERs on CPLs are kept at the unit level (not forwarded).

Q. Part IV of the NCOER rates an NCOs "VALUES". What are the two types of values and the subdivisions of each?
A. - PERSONAL VALUES
- -- courage
- -- candor
- -- commitment
- -- competence

- ARMY ETHIC VALUES
- -- loyalty
- -- duty
- -- selfless service
- -- integrity

Q. What are the four choices the rater has to select from when rating an NCOs values/responsibilities on the NCOER?
A. Excellence (exceeds standards), Success (meets standards), Needs Improvement (some), Needs Improvement (much).

Q. What three performance selections does the rater have to choose from when deciding on overall performance and potential? How would you define these?
A. Among the Best - NCOs who have demonstrated a very good, solid performance,

and a strong recommendation for promotion and/or service in positions of greater responsibility.

Fully Capable - NCOs who have demonstrated a good performance and, should sufficient allocations be available, a promotion recommendation.

Marginal - NCOs who have demonstrated poor performance and should not be promoted at this time.

Q. Explain the rating criteria that apply to senior raters.
A. Successful/Superior - A "1" or "2" rating represents a very good, solid performance and is a strong recommendation for promotion; however, a "2" is not as good as a "1". A "3" rating also represents a good performance and, should sufficient allocations be available, is a recommendation for promotion; however, it is not as good as a "2".

Fair - Represents NCOs who may require additional training/observation and should not be promoted at this time.

Poor - Represents NCOs who are weak or deficient and, in the opinion of the senior rater, needs significant improvement in one or more areas. Do not promote.

Q. What are the different types of NCOERs that a soldier may receive?
A. (According to DA CIR 623-88-1) First Report, Annual, Change-of-Rater, Complete-the-Record, and Relief-for-Cause.

NOTE: The "Special" and "Directed" reports have been deleted.

Q. What is the minimum period in which a "Relief for Cause" report can be given, and can this minimum period be waived?
A. 30 days; yes, by a General Officer of GCM authority.

Q. What is a DA Form 2166-7-1?
A. The NCO Counseling Checklist/Record.

Q. When should the NCO Counseling Checklist be used?
A. Initial counseling must be conducted within the first 30 days of each rating period, and at least quarterly thereafter.

Q. What information is recorded on the NCO Counseling Checklist/Record?
A. Only key points for each quarter (they are short comments as to what the soldier has done or will do and will greatly help you in writing the NCOER).

Q. On DA Form 2166-7-1, what are the titles of the counseling blocks?
A. Initial, Later, Later, Later.

Q. How does a soldier verify the information on DA Form 2166-7-1?
A. He/she initials and dates the checklist.

Q. The best counseling is always "looking forward". What does this mean?
A. It does not dwell on the past and on what was done, rather on the future and what can be done better.

Q. How long must a rater be the First Line Supervisor of the rated soldier before an NCOER can be given?
A. 3 rated months.

Q. Can a civilian be a rater of a soldier? When?
A. Yes, when the military supervisor is not available and the civilian supervisor is in the best position to evaluate the soldier. Must be a GS-6 or

above.

SEPARATIONS

Q. In what Army regulation will you find information regarding separations, discharges, and characterizations of service?
A. AR 635-200, "ENLISTED PERSONNEL"

Q. The law requires that each lawfully inducted or enlisted member of the Army be furnished a discharge certificate on separation from the service except under what circumstances?
A. When separated for other than honorable conditions.

Q. Discharges can be the result of administrative action (ETS/retirement, convenience of the government, hardship, etc) or judicial action (misconduct, fraudulent entry, security reasons, etc) and may be divided into what five types?
A. (1) Honorable
(2) General (under honorable conditions)
(3) Under Other Than Honorable
(4) Bad-Conduct
(5) Dishonorable

Q. Which of the five types of discharges (see above question) are issued as a result of administrative action?
A. Honorable, General, and Under Other Than Honorable.

NOTE: An "Under Other Than Honorable conditions" discharge may be issued as a result of court-martial proceedings.

Q. Which types of discharges may only be issued as a result of approved sentence to such a discharge by a court-martial?
A. Bad Conduct discharge - special or general court-martial.
Dishonorable discharge - general court-martial.

Q. A servicemember can be assured of full rights and benefits only under which types of discharges?
A. Honorable or General.

Q. There are many ways that a soldier may be separated or "chaptered" out of the Army. How many such "chapters" are covered in AR 635-200? What are they?
A. 14;
Chapter 4 - Separation for expiration of service obligation.
Chapter 5 - Separation for convenience of the government.
Chapter 6 - Separation because of dependency or hardship.
Chapter 7 - Defective enlistment/reenlistment and extensions.
Chapter 8 - Separation of enlisted women (pregnancy).
Chapter 9 - Alcohol or other drug use rehabilitation failure.
Chapter 10 - Discharge in lieu of trial by courts-martial.
Chapter 11 - Entry level performance and conduct.
Chapter 12 - Retirement for length of service.
Chapter 13 - Separation for unsatisfactory performance.
Chapter 14 - Separation for misconduct.
Chapter 15 - Separation for homosexuality.
Chapter 16 - Selected changes in service obligations.

NCOERs/SEPARATIONS
DA Cir 623-88-1/AR 635-200

Chapter 18 - Failure to meet body fat standards.

Q. Which "Chapter" used to be referred to as "Discharge for the Good of the Service"?
A. Chapter 10 - Discharge in Lieu of Trial by Courts-Martial.

Q. What characterization of service is normally appropriate for a soldier who is discharged in lieu of trial by courts-martial?
A. Under other than honorable conditions.

Q. What is the characterization of service for soldiers separated under the provisions of Chapter 11, or for soldiers separated under any of the other Chapters while in Entry Level Status?
A. Service will be uncharacterized.

Q. When is a soldier considered to be in Entry Level Status?
A. For Regular Army soldiers, entry level status is defined as the first 180 days of continuous active duty or the first 180 days of continuous active duty following a break of more than 92 days of active military service.

Q. What is the lowest character of discharge a person may receive that is separated for misconduct?
A. Under Other Than Honorable conditions.

Q. What is the newest "Chapter" to AR 635-200?
A. Chapter 18 - Failure to Meet Body Fat Standards.

Q. Prior to the introduction of Chapter 18, soldiers who failed to meet Army body composition/weight control standards were separated under what Chapter?
A. Chapter 5 - Separation for Convenience of the Government.

Q. Who should be separated under the provisions of Chapter 18, AR 635-200?
A. Soldiers that have been given a reasonable opportunity to comply with and meet the body fat standards set forth in AR 600-9, but fail to do so.

Q. Provided no medical condition exists that would preclude a soldier from participating in the Army body fat reduction program, when would initiation of separation proceedings under the provisions of Chapter 18 be required?
A. If satisfactory progress in the program is not shown after a period of 6 months, unless the responsible commander chooses to impose a bar to reenlistment. Also, soldiers that fail to meet screening table weight and body fat standards during the 12-month period following removal from the weight control program.

MAINTENANCE PROCEDURES
DA PAM 738-750

NOTE: This chapter is divided into three sections: **TAMMS**, **ULLS**, and **VEHICLES**. ULLS is the automated system that replaces much of TAMMS and is provided here for units using the system. It should be remembered that ULLS does not completely replace TAMMS. For this reason, and because there are many similarities between the two systems, it is recommended that both sections be reviewed. The VEHICLES section provides some questions about selected Army motor vehicles - taken from the applicable -10. No attempt has been made to include questions about every Army vehicle since this would make the section more in-depth than necessary.

TAMMS

Q. What does "TAMMS" stand for and what is its purpose?
A. The Army Maintenance Management System; its purpose is to create, maintain, and properly dispose of operational, maintenance, and equipment historical records.

Q. What are the two ways of operating the TAMMS system?
A. Manually or using the automated Unit Level Logistics System (ULLS).

Q. What is the functional user's manual for TAMMS?
A. DA Pam 738-750

Q. What is the difference between TAMMS and TAMMS-A and what is the functional user's manual for TAMMS-A?
A. TAMMS-A contains information specific to the Aviation aspects of maintenance management; DA Pam 738-751.

Q. What publication is titled, "Leader's Unit Level Maintenance Handbook"?
A. DA Pam 750-1.

Q. When filling out maintenance forms and records, what should you do with "blanks" that do not apply?
A. Leave them blank (do not put "N/A").

Q. What should be used to complete forms and records, pen or pencil?
A. Unless specific instructions tell you to use ink, all entries on forms should be filled out in pencil.

Q. If ink is specified for a particular form (see above question), what color must be used?
A. Blue or black pen (repeated information may be entered by blue or black rubber stamp).

NOTE: Certain entries in TAMMS-A use red ink.

Q. Can abbreviations be used on Army forms and records?
A. Yes, considerable time and effort may be saved by using abbreviations; however, only **authorized** abbreviations may be used.

Q. Where can a list of "authorized" abbreviations (see above question) be found?
A. AR 310-50, AR 700-138 (appendix B), and the consolidated glossary.

MAINTENANCE PROCEDURES
DA PAM 738-750

Q. Are ditto symbols authorized to be used on Army forms and records?
A. Yes, so long as they cannot be misunderstood (ie, as the number 11).

Q. If you are filling out a form and there is a conflict between the example/illustration you are looking at and the printed text, which should you use?
A. The printed instructions - use the examples/illustrations as a guide only.

Q. Status symbols are used on forms and records to show the seriousness of equipment faults or problems. How many status symbols are there and what are they?
A. 5;
(1) X - indicates an equipment deficiency (places equipment in inoperable status).
(2) Circled X - indicates that the equipment has a deficiency, but may be operated under set limitations.
(3) Horizontal dash (-) - indicates that an inspection or component replacement has not been done.
(4) Diagonal slash (/) - indicates an equipment fault, other than a deficiency.
(5) Last name initial - indicates a completely satisfactory condition or a corrected fault.

Q. Explain the following abbreviations: FMC, NMC, NMCM, NMCS, PMC.
A. FMC - Fully Mission Capable: no deficiencies exist.
NMC - Not Mission Capable: deficiencies exist (equipment is deadlined).
NMCM - Not Mission Capable, Maintenance: equipment is NMC due to maintenance.
NMCS - Not Mission Capable, Supply: equipment is NMC due to supply (awaiting parts).
PMC - Partially Mission Capable.

Q. Can equipment be operated with a deficiency (X condition)?
A. No, no one may authorize or order equipment operated until the X condition is repaired or changed for a specific operation (circled X).

Q. Who may authorized limited operation of equipment with a deficiency (circled X)?
A. Only the commander, maintenance/motor officer or higher authority.

Q. What status symbol would be used to show that an overdue normal MWO has not been applied?
A. Horizontal dash (-).

Q. Can an individual be ordered to change a status symbol?
A. No, but the commander or maintenance officer may disagree with a status symbol if, in their opinion, the wrong status symbol was selected. They then have the authority to change (downgrade or upgrade) the status symbol.

Q. Unit level maintenance is considered to be the foundation of the Army's maintenance system. What is considered to be the foundation of unit level maintenance?
A. The PMCS.

Q. What does "PMCS" stand for and what is its purpose?
A. Preventive Maintenance Checks and Services; PMCS as a system includes all checks and services performed by the operator, crew and the unit maintenance

section to identify and correct faults and perform required services on all assigned equipment.

Q. What inspections or checks are involved in the PMCS?
A. Before, During, After, Weekly, and Monthly.

Q. What is the purpose of performing "Before" operation checks?
A. To identify faults in equipment before the use of the equipment causes damage/injury to the individual or equipment.

Q. BEFORE operations checks should not take over ______ minutes for completion by the operator/crew.
A. 20

Q. Under what two circumstances should you perform WEEKLY as well as BEFORE Preventive Maintenance Checks and Services on a vehicle?
A. (1) You are the operator of the equipment but have not operated it since the last weekly.
(2) You are operating the equipment for the first time.

Q. What is the definition of TM -10/-20 PMCS standard?
A. The status of the equipment when:
- The equipment is fully mission capable (FMC).
- All faults are identified using the "items to be checked" column of the applicable -10 and -20 TM's PMCS Table and:
  - -- Corrective actions, authorized to be accomplished at unit level with the required parts available, are completed.
  - -- Faults, requiring parts to complete the corrective actions have the required parts on valid funded request.
  - -- Corrective actions, authorized to be accomplished at a maintenance level above the unit, are on a valid direct support maintenance request.
- Equipment services are performed within the scheduled service interval.
- All urgent and limited urgent Modification Work Orders are applied.
- All authorized Basic Issue Items (BII) and components of the end item (COEI) are present and serviceable or on a valid funded request.

Q. Explain what the following forms are used for.
A. DA FORM 348 ...... Equipment Operator's Qualification Record
DA FORM 2401 ..... Organizational Control Record for Equipment
DA FORM 2402 ..... Exchange Tag
DA FORM 2404 ..... Equipment Inspection and Maintenance Worksheet
DA FORM 2405 ..... Maintenance Request Register
DA FORM 2407 ..... Maintenance Request
DA FORM 2407-1 ... Maintenance Request Continuation Sheet
DA FORM 2408-14 .. Uncorrected Fault Record
DA FORM 2410 ..... Component Removal and Repair/Overhaul Record
DA FORM 5823 ..... Equipment Identification Card
DA LABEL 80 ...... Calibrated Instrument Label
DD 518 .... Accident Identification Card
DD FORM 314 ..... Preventive Maintenance Schedule and Record
DD FORM 1970 ..... Motor Equipment Utilization Record (dispatch)
DD FORM 2026 ..... Oil Analysis Request
OF 346 .... U.S. Government Motor Vehicle Operator's Identification Card (replaces SF 346)
SF 91 .... Operator Report on Motor Vehicle Accidents

MAINTENANCE PROCEDURES
DA PAM 738-750

Q. The method by which a commander controls the use of equipment is known as what?
A. Dispatching.

Q. The Dispatch Loop describes the procedures that must be followed when dispatching equipment. Describe the steps in the Dispatch Loop.
A. (1) Operator reports to dispatcher. For equipment requiring licensed operators, military license must list or cover the item being dispatched.
(2) Dispatcher issues operator the Equipment Record Folder with all the forms that will be needed for the mission (see question below). Both the dispatcher and operator should check the Equipment Identification Card on the front of the folder for services due on the equipment.
(3) The operator uses the equipment TM for before-operation PMCS. Any faults the operator can fix will be fixed. Other faults, not already on the 2408-14, should be annotated on the 2404.
(4) If possible, the operator and/or mechanic fix any new faults. The commander or designated representative will decide if any remaining faults go on the 2408-14 or keep the equipment from being dispatched.
(5) If the equipment is ready for dispatch, the dispatcher makes needed entries on the 2401 and validates the 1970 with signature and date.
(6) The operator leaves with the equipment and Equipment Record Folder with all needed forms. During-operation checks are noted during the dispatch.
(7) When the mission is completed, the operator performs the after-operation PMCS on the equipment and annotates new faults on the 2404. The operator and/or mechanic will fix any faults they can and secure the equipment.
(8) The operator turns in the Equipment Record Folder and all forms to the dispatcher. The dispatcher checks the forms for any open faults or needed actions. If the 1970 has been completely filled, the dispatcher transfers needed information to a new 1970. The dispatcher then closes out the 2401 entry for that item.

Q. For routine dispatches, the Equipment Record Folder (log book) is required to have what forms?
A. DA Form 2404, DA Form 2408-14 (for any deferred maintenance), DD Form 1970, SF 91, and DD 518.

NOTE: Local SOP may require additional items such as Vehicle Commander Responsibilities, etc, to be carried in the Equipment Record Folder.

Q. Equipment Record Folders should be assigned to a specific piece of equipment. What form ties the Equipment Record Folder to the equipment?
A. DA Form 5823 (Equipment Identification Card).

Q. Are vehicles the only Military Equipment that require a Log Book?
A. No, log books are required on all equipment and/or arms that have a power source, and/or are used for multi-area operations (ie, radios, generators, trailers, cannons, etc).

Q. What information is contained on the Equipment Identification Card?
A. Identification of equipment assigned to log book, services due, and assigned operator and leader.

Q. The operator's and supervisor's or leader's names are listed on the Equipment Identification Card primarily for what two reasons?
A. (1) If the folder is lost or misplaced, the finder will have names to track down.
(2) More important, those names show who is responsible for the equipment,

the forms in the folder and the information on the equipment's condition.

Q. The DD Form 1970, or "dispatch" as it is often called, can accommodate how many different operators?
A. There are designated spaces on the form for up to four (4) operators. However, if additional operators are needed before a new dispatch can be obtained, enter the operator name(s), time, and miles/hours in the Remarks block.

Q. When a vehicle is on dispatch and the driver adds oil or fuel, what must he/she do to the DD Form 1970?
A. The driver must enter in the remarks column the amount and type of additive that was required.

Q. After the driver is finished with the vehicle, what must be done before turning in the dispatch?
A. - Record the miles and/or hours in the "IN" column of DD Form 1970.
- Refuel ("top off") the vehicle and enter on DD Form 1970.
- Clean the equipment.
- Perform all "After" operation checks and maintenance.

Q. How should times be entered in the IN/OUT TIME blocks on the dispatch?
A. Show time on the 24-hour clock to the nearest 5 minutes (times should not be separated by colons (:)).

Q. How should time be entered in the TOTAL TIME blocks on the dispatch?
A. Separate hours and minutes by putting a colon (:) between them.

Q. If the odometer/hourmeter on the equipment is broken the operator should still enter an estimated mileage/hours in the appropriate MILES or HOURS column. In this instance, what should be entered before the estimated mileage/hours?
A. The letters "EST".

Q. Whose name should be printed in the REPORT TO block for each operator?
A. The name of the person that is responsible for the equipment while in use and to whom the operator is to report when completed.

Q. Who should sign in the RELEASED BY column on the dispatch?
A. The person responsible for the equipment on dispatch (name in REPORT TO block) or senior person present when individual in REPORT TO block is not available. This shows the place where the equipment was released to another location or for return to the motor pool.

Q. What should be reported in the REMARKS column of the dispatch?
A. Any unusual or abnormal situations encountered during the dispatch (ie, accidents, breakdowns, unplanned stops or changes in location, etc), and any fuel or oil added during operation.

Q. How long should a DD Form 1970 be used for **regular** dispatches?
A. Until all the spaces in either the operator or **action** section have been filled.

Q. How long should a DD Form 1970 be used for **extended** dispatches?
A. Until all the spaces in either the operator or **destination** sections have been filled.

MAINTENANCE PROCEDURES
DA PAM 738-750

Q. When should an extended dispatch be used in lieu of a regular dispatch?
A. Whenever the equipment being dispatched will not return to the motor pool within the dispatch day.

Q. What should be entered on the first line of the REMARKS section for all extended dispatches?
A. The words "EXTENDED DISPATCH" and the expected date of return.

Q. What form is used as a record of operators and location of equipment on dispatch or in use?
A. DA Form 2401.

Q. The DD Form 314 has two sides. Under TAMMS, what should each side be used for?
A. The front side should be used to schedule services. The reverse side should be used to track NMCM/NMCS time.

Q. Can a DD Form 314 be used to track more than one piece of equipment?
A. Yes, if the services are scheduled and pulled on the same date (when using a DD Form 314 to track more than one item of equipment they should be "like items." Examples of "like items" are small arms, telephone sets, trailers, and M11 decons).

Q. How far in advance should services be scheduled?
A. AT LEAST one month in advance or one service in advance, whichever is greater.

Q. Since services cannot always be pulled exactly when they are scheduled an allowance or variance is authorized. If you stay within the plus or minus variance, the service is treated as if you did it on the day/miles/hours it was scheduled. What are the allowed variances?
A. (1) +/- 10 days of the scheduled day
(2) +/- 10 hours of the scheduled hours
(3) +/- 100 miles of the scheduled miles
(4) +/- 160 kilometers of the scheduled kilometers
(5) +/- 10% of scheduled date or hours/miles for oil samples only.

Q. Different symbols are used on the DD Form 314 to show the type of service scheduled. Explain the following service symbols: L, W, M, Q, S, A, Z.
A. "L" .... lubrication
"W" .... weekly service
"M" .... monthly (1 month) service
"Q" .... quarterly (3 months) service
"S" .... semiannual (6 months) service
"A" .... annual (1 year)(12 months) service
"Z" .... oil sampling

Q. Can additional symbols or subsymbols not covered in DA Pam 738-750 be used on the DD Form 314?
A. Yes, so long as they do not conflict with the symbols required by the pamphlet.

Q. What symbols should be used on the reverse side of DD Form 314 to track equipment NMC time?
A. - Show unit NMCM days with the symbol "O". Place the letter "S" inside the "O" to track unit NMCS days.
- Show support NMCM days with the symbol "X". Place the letter "S" over

the "X" to track support NMCS days.

Q. What entry should be made in the TYPE INSPECTION block on the DA Form 2404?
A. The type of inspection or service to be done (lubrication, PMCS, monthly, quarterly, semiannual, BDAR, etc). Enter whichever is greater. When doing more than one inspection or service at the same time, put the service symbols in this block (ie, L/S, etc).

Q. If the TM for an item of equipment has changes, how should this be annotated on the 2404?
A. Enter the number and date of the equipment TM in the TM NUMBER and TM DATE blocks respectively, then print "W/C" and the latest change number after the TM number (only the date of the basic TM should be entered in the TM DATE block).

Q. When should the MILES and HOURS blocks be filled in on the 2404?
A. Only after a shortcoming or deficiency is found or, in the case of a service, the hours and/or miles when the service is performed.

Q. Either miles or kilometers may be entered in the MILES block of the 2404. How do you distinguish between the two?
A. Prefix the distance with an "M" for miles or a "K" for kilometers.

Q. When should the date be entered in the DATE block of the 2404?
A. Only after a shortcoming or deficiency is found or, in the case of a service, the date the service is performed.

Q. When should a signature be entered on the 2404? What is the purpose of the signature?
A. (1) When a service is performed, the person performing the service should enter his/her signature in the first SIGNATURE block. A signature in this block keeps the form from being used past the current service.
(2) When used for PMCS, a signature is entered in the first SIGNATURE block only after a shortcoming or deficiency is found. A signature in this block keeps the form from being used past the current dispatch.

Q. Who is authorized to place their signature in the second SIGNATURE block of the 2404?
A. The CO, maintenance/motor officer or designated representative.

Q. What should be placed in the TM ITEM NO block of the 2404?
A. The TM item number that applies to the fault in the DEFICIENCIES AND SHORTCOMINGS column.

Q. What should be placed in the TM ITEM NO block of the 2404 if the fault does not have an item number in the PMCS manual?
A. List the page, paragraph, or sequence number.

Q. What should be done to the TM item number (see above question) if the fault makes the equipment NMC?
A. The TM item number should be circled.

Q. What is the easiest way to tell is a fault makes the equipment NMC?
A. If the fault is listed in the "Equipment not ready/available if" column of the appropriate PMCS manual (TM).

Q. How many lines should be skipped between faults on the 2404?
A. You may skip from one to three lines.

MAINTENANCE PROCEDURES
DA PAM 738-750

Q. What should be entered in the CORRECTIVE ACTION column of the 2404?
A. Any of the following are considered acceptable entries:
(1) Explain the action you took to correct or take care of the fault. Note any parts replaced or ordered and work done in this column.
(2) If parts are needed have the PLL clerk order them and enter the document number(s) in this column.
(3) Faults that need support maintenance should be entered on DA Form 2407. Print "DA Form 2407 (SPT)" in this column for those items.
(4) Faults the CO or designated representative decides to defer should be entered on DA Form 2408-14. Print "DA Form 2408-14" in this column for those items.

Q. When should initials be entered in the INITIAL WHEN CORRECTED column of the 2404? What is the correct location for the initials?
A. After the CORRECTIVE ACTION column has been completed, the person taking the corrective action must place his/hers initials in this column. In addition, the mechanic must place his/her last name initial on any dash or diagonal status symbols that have been fixed. The correct placement of the initials is on the last line for the entry.

Q. Who is authorized to place their last name initial over condition "X" or Circled "X" deficiencies?
A. Only a technical inspector (TI) or designated representative.

Q. On a 2404 that is being used for PMCS what should be entered on the form if no shortcomings or deficiencies are noted?
A. If you do not find any faults during the BEFORE operation checks in the PMCS, enter the date of the inspection in the DEFICIENCIES AND SHORTCOMINGS column. At the end of the dispatch, do the AFTER operation checks. If no faults are found DURING or AFTER operation enter your initials in the INITIAL WHEN CORRECTED column. If the PMCS is a weekly, the letter "W" should be entered in the CORRECTIVE ACTION column. If the PMCS is a monthly, the letters "W/M" should be entered in this column.

Q. Can a 2404 be used for more than one piece of equipment?
A. Yes, simply enter the serial or administration number for the item with the fault and enter fault information on the line below the serial number.

Q. What are the disposition instructions for the DA Form 2404?
A. All DA Forms 2404 carrying a status symbol "X" must be kept until the "X" is cleared. All other forms used for periodic service may be destroyed after all uncorrected faults have been moved to a DA Form 2408-14 or DA Form 2407 and the service has been recorded on the DA Form 314.

Q. What status symbol faults cannot be entered onto DA Form 2408-14?
A. Any "X" faults.

Q. Operators should review the 2408-14 each time the vehicle is dispatched. How often, as a minimum, are maintenance supervisors and leaders required to review the 2408-14 and what should they look for?
A. Every two weeks; should look for the following:
- status of parts on order
- faults that have been fixed but not closed out
- any faults that are overdue to be fixed

Q. What does "AOAP" stand for and what is its purpose?

MAINTENANCE PROCEDURES
DA PAM 738-750

A. Army Oil Analysis Program; used as a diagnostic tool to determine the physical condition of used lubricants and the internal conditions of engines, transmissions, hydraulic systems, and other fluid-wetted components.

Q. What form is used to track equipment ownership, location, usage, transfers, gains, losses, selected repair actions, and overhaul/rebuild?
A. DA Form 2408-9 (Equipment Control Record).

Q. What does "SMART" stand for and what is its purpose?
A. Supply and Maintenance Assessment and Review Team; established to examine, streamline, and improve unit level logistics support, particularly within the division, and at direct support levels and below.

Q. What is a DA Form 5533?
A. SMART suggestion form.

Q. Selected ideas adopted through SMART will be announced to the field by a sequentially numbered system known as what?
A. SMART messages

Q. What is a "QDR" and what form is used to report it?
A. Quality Deficiency Report; SF 368.

Q. What is an "EIR" and what form is used to report it?
A. Equipment Improvement Report; also SF 368.

Q. What are some examples of when a QDR should be used?
A.
- A condition in or with equipment that is dangerous to people, other equipment or missions.
- An item or equipment that does not work right or last as long as it should because of bad design or materials.
- Low quality workmanship.
- Dangerous situations due to incorrect or missing data.
- Maintenance problems.
- Conditions that keep you from using the equipment.
- Repeated problems that take a lot of your time and a solution is not in sight.
- Corrosion problems in or on parts, components, assemblies, weapon systems, and equipment.

Q. What are the two categories of QDR reports?
A. Category I - A defect that may cause death, injury, or severe job illness; would cause loss or major damage to a weapon system; or critically restricts the combat readiness capabilities of the unit. Also improvement recommendations that would prevent the above conditions.
Category II - A defect or recommendation that does not meet the criteria of Category I.

Q. Category I deficiency reports should be prepared and forwarded how soon after the defect or problem is found?
A. Within 48 hours.

Q. Category II deficiency reports should be prepared and forwarded how soon after the defect or problem is found?
A. Within 5 work days.

MAINTENANCE PROCEDURES
DA PAM 738-750

ULLS

Q. What does "ULLS" stand for and what is its purpose?
A. Unit Level Logistics System; it is an automated program designed to collect maintenance and supply data and provide management information at the unit level (it replaces portions of TAMMS).

Q. Unlike TAMMS, which has eleven categories of maintenance records, ULLS has only three. What are they?
A. Operational, maintenance, and historical records.

Q. Under ULLS, DA Form 5987-E (Motor Equipment Dispatch) replaces the requirement for what two TAMMS forms?
A. DD Form 1970 and DA Form 2401.

Q. What form is normally generated with DA Form 5987-E and replaces the need to manually prepare a DA Form 2404 and DA Form 2408-14?
A. DA Form 5988-E (Equipment Inspection and Maintenance Worksheet).

Q. Under ULLS, what form is used to dispatch all vehicles on alerts?
A. DA Form 5987-1-E (Motor Equipment Dispatch - Alert).

Q. What ULLS form replaces the manual DA Form 348?
A. DA Form 5983-E (Equipment Operator Qualification Record).

Q. What ULLS form can be used in lieu of OF 346 (military license)?
A. DA Form 5984-E (Operator's Permit Report, U.S. Army Motor Vehicle Operator's Identification Card).

Q. Is a manual DD Form 314 required to be maintained under ULLS?
A. Yes. The ULLS DA Form 5986-E (Preventive Maintenance Schedule and Record) replaces the **front side only** of DD Form 314. There is still a requirement to manually track equipment NMCM/NMCS time, and this is accomplished on the DD Form 314.

Q. As part of the Dispatch Loop under TAMMS, all operators are required to show the dispatcher that they possess a valid military license listing or covering the item being dispatched. How does this differ from the ULLS system?
A. Under ULLS all licensed operators, and the equipment that they are authorized to operate, should be registered within the computer system. Only in the event that an operator is not registered should the dispatcher check the operator's OF 346.

Q. Except for the above case, how does the Dispatch Loop under ULLS differ from that under TAMMS?
A. The dispatch process is the same - except ULLS generated forms are used in lieu of TAMMS manual forms as stated above).

Q. For routine dispatches under ULLS, the Equipment Record Folder (log book) is required to have what forms?
A. The current ULLS generated DA Form 5988-E, DA Form 5987-E, SF 91, and DD Form 518.

Q. Is a manual DA Form 5823, Equipment Identification Card, required to be

maintained even if you are operating under ULLS?
A. Yes.

Q. If you have a CUCV that is going to support maintenance and the support maintenance activity is located within your motor pool area, are you required to dispatch the vehicle on DA Form 5987-E?
A. No, all you need is a DA Form 5990-E (Maintenance Request) to accompany the equipment.

Q. Are units operating under ULLS required to maintain the DA Form 2401 (Organizational Control Record for Equipment)?
A. No, it is automated within ULLS.

Q. What are the disposition instructions for a DA Form 5988-E?
A.
- Used for PMCS, no faults listed: will be kept in the log book until no longer needed (ie, upon updating the ULLS system and generating a new listing).
- Used for PMCS, faults listed: will be reviewed by maintenance section leaders prior to destruction to ensure that all actions have been recorded within ULLS.
- Used for Technical Inspections: will stay with the item until all maintenance is performed or the item is destroyed.

Q. What are the following abbreviations in the PARTS REQUESTED section of the DA Form 5988-E (Equipment Inspection/Maintenance Worksheet): DCN, NIIN, DI QTY, DLC?
A. DCN - Document Control Number
NIIN - National Item Identification Number
DI QTY - Due-In Quantity
DLC - Deadline Code

Q. What might you expect to see in the DLC column of a DA Form 5988-E?
A. A "D" if the equipment is deadlined, a blank if the equipment is not deadlined.

Q. What does "SAMS" stand for and what is its purpose?
A. Standard Army Maintenance System; it is an automated maintenance and management information network that allows for the collection and dissemination of ULLS information from the individual unit to division or corps, wholesale, and DA levels.

Q. SAMS is divided into two levels. What are they?
A. SAMS 1 - operates at the GS/DS maintenance company.
SAMS 2 - operates at command levels above the maintenance company.

Q. Unit level activities with ULLS are required to report maintenance information to SAMS. Is this true for units without ULLS?
A. Unit level activities without ULLS are not required to report maintenance information to ULLS unless local or higher commands desire.

Q. What is a "UND" and what are the three priorities?
A. Urgency of Need Designator;
UND A - Unit is unable to perform its assigned operational or training mission.
UND B - Unit's ability to perform assigned operational mission is impaired.
UND C - Used for assignment of maintenance priorities for all conditions not covered under UND A/B.

MAINTENANCE PROCEDURES
DA PAM 738-750

Q. The Army maintenance system consists of how many levels?
A. 4 for ground ==> unit, direct support (DS), general support (GS), and depot.
3 for air ==> unit (AVUM), intermediate (AVIM), and Depot.

Q. Who is responsible for first echelon maintenance on Military Vehicles and Equipment?
A. The Vehicle or Equipment Operator.

Q. TMs are broken down for use by different levels of maintenance. What level of maintenance would be authorized to use the TM -20 level?
A. The second echelon or Organizational Maintenance, and the third echelon or Direct Support Maintenance.

Q. What is an "MEL"?
A. Maintenance Expenditure Limit; the total allowable one-time cost to restore an end-item, major component, or reparable component to a fully serviceable condition as prescribed in the appropriate TM.

Q. What is the difference between "controlled exchange" and "cannibalization"?
A. Cannibalization is the authorized removal of components from material that has been designated for disposal. Controlled exchange is the removal of a serviceable component from an unserviceable economically reparable end item for immediate reuse in restoring a like item to a FMC condition. The unserviceable component must then replace the removed serviceable component and remain with the unserviceable end item.

Q. What is an "MWO"?
A. Modification Work Order.

Q. Modifications to Army material are either mandatory or nonmandatory. What are the three classifications of mandatory modifications (MWOs)?
A. Urgent, limited urgent, or normal.

Q. What is the status of equipment waiting the application of an urgent MWO?
A. The equipment is deadlined.

Q. What is the status of equipment waiting the application of a limited urgent MWO?
A. The equipment is deadlined if the MWO is not applied in the time frame specified in the MWO.

Q. What is a "WOLF"?
A. Work Order Logistics File - the Army central file for selected data from DA Form 2407 generated at DS and GS levels and transmitted through SAMS.

Q. What does "MAIT" stand for and what is its primary purpose?
A. Maintenance Assistance and Instruction Team; ensure that commanders at all levels are provided assistance in identifying and resolving maintenance, supply, and maintenance management problems within their units.

Q. What AR covers MAIT policies and procedures?
A. AR 750-1.

Q. What is a "maintenance float"?
A. A selected end item authorized for stockage and used as a replacement of

like items turned in by using units requiring immediate replacement.

Q. What are the two types of floats?
A. Repair Cycle Float (RCF) and Operational Readiness Float (ORF).

Q. What does "BDAR" stand for and what is its purpose?
A. Battle Damage Assessment and Repair; its purpose is to rapidly return disabled equipment to combat or to enable the equipment to self-recover.

Q. Explain what "PLL" stands for and its purpose.
A. Prescribed Load List; it consists of unit maintenance repair parts (either demand supported or non-demand supported) and specified initial stockage repair parts for newly introduced end items. Most, but not all, of the repair parts stocked on PLL will be demand supported.

Q. A PLL is required to carry a _____-day supply of essential repair parts determined by Department of the Army and the unit's demand history.
A. 15 days.

Q. How many demands for a part within a 180 day period qualify the item to be stocked on PLL?
A. Three (essentiality code must be "C" and maintenance code "O" on AMDF).

Q. What is a unit's "MPL"?
A. Mandatory Parts List.

Q. What do the following abbreviations stand for: SSA, DSSA, AMSA?
A. Supply Support Activity; Direct Supply Support Activity; Area Maintenance Support Activity.

Q. What does "AMDF" stand for?
A. Army Master Data File.

Q. What is a "USR" and what security classification is it?
A. Unit Status Report; at least "CONFIDENTIAL".

Q. What form is used to order publications against the unit account and keep the Publications Center updated on the quantity and types of publications that the unit will have to keep current?
A. The DA Form 12 series.

Q. What are the **minimum** publications required for a unit maintenance operation?
A. One operator's manual and lube order (LO) for each piece of equipment, one set of TMs and LOs for each company maintenance team (CMT) and one complete set of TMs, LOs, FMs, TBs, SCs, and ARs for the unit maintenance platoon/section headquarters.

Q. What is a "Lube Order"?
A. Lubrication Order (LO); graphically displays all lubrication points on the equipment, the type of lubricant to be used, lubrication intervals, and approximate man-hours.

Q. What does the term "motor stables" mean?
A. An organized period of vehicle maintenance.

Q. What two forms will a vehicle operator need if involved in an accident?
A. DD Form 518 and SF 91.

MAINTENANCE PROCEDURES
DA PAM 738-750

Q. What is a "risk assessment"?
A. It is a safety precaution required by commanders that assesses the level of risk to personnel and equipment - thereby providing a tool to improve efficiency, effectiveness, and safety in all operations.

Q. What are the seven functional areas of the risk assessment?
A.
- Leader rest & time for preparation
- First line supervision
- Soldier selection
- Nature of operation
- Equipment status
- Soldier alertness and operation
- Environmental/weather conditions

Q. List five risk-reduction options.
A.
- eliminate the hazard
- control the hazard
- change operational procedures
- educate
- motivate

Q. What are some of the symptoms of exhaust poisoning (carbon-monoxide poisoning)?
A. Headache, dizziness, sleepiness, and/or loss of muscular control.

Q. What is the best defense against exhaust poisoning in an operating vehicle?
A. Adequate ventilation.

Q. What does "BII" stand for and where will you find the BII List?
A. Basic Issue Items/Inventory; in the back of the -10.

VEHICLES

Q. What are some of the features and characteristics that are standard on military vehicles?
A.
- 24-volt, fully waterproof, fungus-proof electrical systems that are fully suppressed to prevent interference to electronic equipment.
- Engines capable of operating while fully submerged in either freshwater or seawater.
- Oversized air, oil, and fuel filtering capacities.
- Oversized generator capacity.
- Oversized engine oil and cooling capacities.
- Engines that are less critical of the fuel they require and have a lower specific weight (pound per horsepower).
- Reliability over an extremely wide temperature range.
- Provisions for operating during blackout conditions.
- All-wheel drive on wheeled vehicles.
- Improved ease of servicing and maintenance.

Q. What are the three categories of military vehicles?
A. Administrative, tactical, and combat.

Q. What TM would you check for servicing a vehicle?
A. The -10 manual on that vehicle.

MAINTENANCE PROCEDURES
DA PAM 738-750

Q. When removing a battery from a vehicle, what lead do you disconnect first?
A. Negative.

Q. When installing a battery, what lead is connected first?
A. Positive.

Q. What gauges on a panel can automatically deadline a vehicle?
A. Oil pressure, engine temperature, and air pressure (select vehicles).

Q. What might happen if you overfill an engine with oil?
A. You may blow the seals.

Q. Give the numerical designation for the following types of vehicles.
A. Truck, Cargo, Tactical, 1¼-T, 4x4, CUCV M-1008
Truck, Utility, Tactical, 3/4T, 4x4, CUCV Blazer M-1009
Truck, Ambulance, Tactical, 3/4T, 4x4 .... M-1010
Truck, Cargo, Tactical, 2½-T M-35A2
Tractor, 5-ton M-931
Truck, Cargo, Tactical, 1¼-T, HMMWV M-998

NOTE: The above vehicles may have varying configurations with different numerical designations (ie, HMMWV with winch .... M-1038, etc).

Q. How many classes of leaks are there for operator PMCS? Describe them.
A. 3; Class I: Seepage of fluid (as indicated by wetness or discoloration) not great enough to form drops.
Class II: Leakage of fluid great enough to form drops but not enough to cause drops to drip from item being checked/inspected.
Class III: Leakage of fluid great enough to form drops that fall from item being checked/inspected.

Q. Can equipment be operated with minor leaks?
A. Yes, equipment may be operated with Class I or II leaks provided consideration is given to the fluid capacity in the item/system being checked and that you continue to check fluid levels as required in PMCS.

Q. What leaks, no matter how bad, will deadline a vehicle?
A. Brake fluid or MOGAS leaks. Class I or II diesel fuel leaks are generally considered acceptable.

Q. The Army's 2½-ton truck, commonly referred to as a "Deuce & ½" or just "deuce", uses what type of fuel?
A. The primary fuel for the deuce is diesel, but it will run on practically any fuel.

Q. The Deuce & ½ has a multi-fuel engine that will operate on a variety of fuels. What part of the engine gives it this capability?
A. The Fuel Density Compensator.

Q. How many spark plugs does an M-35A2 (Deuce & ½) have?
A. None, it uses glow plugs.

Q. What type of fuel is used in the CUCV Series of trucks?
A. Diesel (DS-2). NOTE: Will also run on JP-4/-8.

Q. Will pumping the accelerator pedal before or during cranking help start a

diesel engine (CUCV/Deuce/HMMWV)?
A. No.

Q. Every attempt should be made to maintain <u>at least</u> _______-tank of fuel in freezing or sub-freezing temperatures.
A. ¼ tank.

Q. All CUCV trucks have an automatic transmission with _____ forward and _____ reverse speeds.
A. 3; 1.

Q. What are the four transfer case control lever positions on a CUCV?
A. (1) "N" (neutral) - front and rear axles are not engaged.
(2) "2H" (two-wheel-drive high range) - normal driving.
(3) "4L" (four-wheel-drive low range) - used for driving under unusual conditions in LOW speed ranges.
(4) "4H" (four-wheel-drive high range) - used for driving under unusual conditions in HIGH speed ranges.

Q. What will happen if you place the transmission gearshift lever of a CUCV in "P" (park) with the transfer case lever in "N" (neutral)?
A. Injury to personnel or equipment damage may result since this WILL NOT stop the truck from moving.

Q. When parking a CUCV on a hill, what should you do before shifting the transmission gearshift lever to "P" (park)?
A. Set the parking brake to avoid putting unnecessary force on the transmission.

Q. When switching to four-wheel-drive in a CUCV, what must you do before completing transfer case shift?
A. Make sure that both locking hubs are in the same position - "locked".

Q. Under what conditions should transmission fluid level of a CUCV be checked?
A. With engine running, parking brake set, transmission gearshift lever in "P" (park), and truck on level ground, if possible.

Q. What does "mogas" stand for?
A. It is short for Motor Gasoline.

Q. The Army's HUMMV, or "hummer" as it is often called, is actually abbreviated "HMMWV." What does this stand for?
A. High Mobility Multi-purpose Wheeled Vehicle.

Q. The HMMWV in the cargo configuration is capable of transporting a payload of ________ pounds. The troop carrier is capable of transporting a two-man crew and ______ passengers.
A. 2,500; 8.

Q. The HUMMWV will climb road grades as steep as _____% and traverse a side slope of up to _____%.
A. 60%; 40%.

Q. The HUMMWV will ford hard bottom water crossings up to _____ inches without a deep-water fording kit and _____ inches with the kit.
A. 30; 60.

MAINTENANCE PROCEDURES
DA PAM 738-750

Q. The transfer case of a HUMMWV has four shift lever positions. Which position should be used for normal operation on all primary, secondary, and off-road surfaces where little or no wheel slippage exists?
A. "H" (high range)

Q. Which transfer case drive range should be selected only when continuous wheel slippage is evident?
A. "H/L" (high lock range)

Q. A problem that many people encounter with the HMMWV is the unusual width. Exactly how wide is the HMMWV?
A. 85" (just over 7 feet)

Q. How do you get maximum load capacity from the vehicle winch (HUMMWV)?
A. Spool out the cable until only the first layer is visible. Capacity is then 6,000 lbs.

Q. What protective measure should be taken when handling the winch cable?
A. Wear leather gloves when handling winch cable.

Q. For winch operations, how much slack should be allowed in order for the winch motor to gain maximum pulling power?
A. 1 ft

Q. If the winch stops repeatedly during operation and restarts within approximately five seconds, what is the most likely cause?
A. The electronic current limiter is being activated, indicating an overload condition.

Q. What is the proper procedure for checking the transmission fluid level in a HUMMWV?
A. Start engine, apply brakes, and move transmission shift lever through all operating ranges, then check fluid level with shift lever in "N" (neutral) position. Fluid level should be at crosshatch marks. Add fluid as necessary.

Q. When checking for contaminated fuel during a PMCS, approximately how much fuel should be drained from the draincock?
A. 1 pt

Q. What step(s) must be accomplished in order for the horn or turn signals to be operational?
A. The light switch must be set to "stop light" or "service drive."

Q. When starting a diesel engine, what must you wait for prior to engaging the starter?
A. Wait until the "wait-to-start" lamp is out.

Q. The HUMMWV will not start with the drive train selector lever in any position except ________.
A. Neutral "N".

Q. Smoking is not permitted in Army motor vehicles or within how many feet of the vehicle?
A. 50 feet

MILITARY PROGRAMS

QOLP

Q. What is the Army QOLP?
A. Quality of Life Program

Q. The Army's QOLP is dedicated to the precept that the Army's number one operational resource must be taken care of. What is this resource?
A. The soldier.

Q. Quality of Life needs, and the programs and actions to address them, are categorized under two general headings. What are they?
A. Living conditions and duty environment.

Q. The Community Life System, a major component of the QOLP, consists of 6 sub-systems. What are they?
A. (1) Army Community Services (ACS)
(2) Army Morale Support Activities (AMSA)
(3) Army Continuing Education System (ACES)
(4) Army Club Management System (ACMS)
(5) Army Postal System (APS)
(6) Army and Air Force Exchange Service (AAFES)

Q. What are some examples of the Quality of Life Program in use for soldiers today?
A.
- Postal Services
- PX/Commissary privileges
- Clubs
- Physical Fitness Centers
- Recreation facilities
- Banking services
- ACS/AER/ARC/EO
- Community Sports Programs
- MWR
- Education services
- AFN radio and television
- etc, etc, etc.

ACS

Q. What does "ACS" stand for?
A. Army Community Services.

Q. What is the mission of ACS?
A. To improve readiness and increase retention by providing services to assist soldiers and their families in solving problems beyond their ability to solve alone through the provisions of the ~~seven~~ eight essential services outlined in AR 608-1.

Q. What is the ACS program policy?
A. It is a community-oriented, social service program.

Q. What does the ACS symbol represent?
A. - The heart (giving).
- The cross (help).
- The gyroscope (equilibrium and stability).

Q. What is the theme of ACS?
A. "Self-help, Service, and Stability"

MILITARY PROGRAMS

Q. List the ~~seven~~ eight essential services of ACS.
A. (1) The Relocation Assistance Program (includes Loan Closet).
(2) The Family Member Employment Assistance Program.
(3) The Exceptional Family Member Program.
(4) The Family Advocacy Program.
(5) The Information, Referral, and Follow-up Program.
(6) The Consumer Affairs and Financial Assistance Program.
(7) The Outreach Program.
(8) Foster Care

NOTE: The above services, or subprograms, are considered essential to the life support of soldiers and their family members. However, ACS services are not limited to these eight services.

Q. Name some additional services (see above NOTE) that may be provided by ACS.
A. (1) Army Family Team Building
(2) Mayoral programs
(3) Volunteer Services
(4) The Army Career and Alumni Program (ACAP)

Q. What are the four primary objectives of the Family Advocacy Program?
A. (1) Prevent spouse and child abuse.
(2) Prevent physical neglect.
(3) Prevent sexual abuse.
(4) Prevent emotional maltreatment.

Q. What is the outreach mode of service delivery?
A. It is where the provider seeks out the client instead of the reverse.

Q. What is the purpose of financial planning and assistance services?
A. - To help service members improve their credit, reliability, and reputation.
- To reduce indebtedness.
- To promote consumer awareness.
- To enhance local community relations.

Q. What are the essential services of financial planning assistance?
A. - Financial Planning Education.
- Consumer education.
- Budget development and planning.
- Debt liquidation.

Q. What is the purpose of ACS relocation services?
A. Provides timely and useful information, guidance, and assistance to individuals planning for their move from one military community to another and settling into a new community.

Q. Relocation services include computerized information through the "SITES" and welcome packets from installations world-wide. What does "SITES" stand for?
A. Standard Installation Topic Exchange Service.

Q. What does the ACS Loan Closet do for the service member?
A. Loans them household items when establishing new households.

Q. What is the ACS support role of handicapped dependents (Exceptional Family Member Program)?
A. To assist assignment authorities in the reassignment of service members who have handicapped adult or minor dependents.

MILITARY PROGRAMS

Q. What does "ACAP" stand for?
A. Army Career and Alumni Program.

Q. What is the purpose of ACAP and what are its two primary concerns?
A. Provides transition/employment service and information, including Job Fairs.
(1) Employment Assistance;
(2) Transition Assistance.

Q. In coordination with ACAP, Job Fairs are normally conducted how often?
A. As a minimum, twice per year.

Q. How is the ACS primarily staffed?
A. By volunteers.

ACES

Q. What does "ACES" stand for?
A. Army Continuing Education System.

Q. What is the primary purpose of ACES?
A. ACES exists to fulfill the Army responsibility of developing and conserving its human resources by providing on-duty, job-related educational programs and off-duty educational opportunities for professional and personal development.

Q. List some of the basic services provided by the Army Continuing Education Center.
A.
- Basic Skills Education Program (BSEP)
- Advanced Skills Education Program (ASEP)
- Armed Forces Classification Test Preparation Course
- English-as-a-second-language (ESL)
- High School Completion Program (HSCP)
- MOS related Development Courses
- Typing
- Defense Activity for Non-Traditional Education Support Activities (DANTES)
- Servicemembers Opportunity Colleges Associates Degree Program (SOCAD)
- Bachelor Degrees for Soldiers (BDFS) Program
- Skill Recognition Programs (Army Apprenticeship Program (AAP))
- Command Language Programs (Headstart/Gateway)
- Learning Resources Center (LRC - incl MOS Library)
- Education Counseling Services
- Transition Management (Soldier-to-Civilian)
- Tuition Assistance
- VEAP/GI Bill

Q. If a soldier under your supervision had a GT score of less than 110, what program would you refer him/her to?
A. BSEP (normally, soldiers having a GT score below 100 will automatically be eligible for BSEP attendance. However, soldiers having a GT between 100 and 110 may attend BSEP if command referred).

Q. Explain the BSEP program.
A. BSEP is a program designed to improve educational deficiencies in the basic skills of reading, math, and language. A diagnostic test (TABE) is administered to determine the areas needing improvement. The program is conducted for 60 hours, on duty time, and participation is voluntary and free.

MILITARY PROGRAMS

Q. What does "TABE" stand for?
A. Test of Adult Basic Education.

Q. Explain the ASEP program.
A. ASEP is the primary command-on-duty program intended to help the NCOs meet their training responsibilities as supervisors, managers, and communicators. It is designed to improve MOS performance and help career growth for soldiers E-5 and above. Each class is 20 hours long and usually runs 4 hours per day for 5 days. There are 6 management and 6 communications ASEP classes.

Q. Which of the ACES programs take precedence over all others?
A. ESL (English as a Second Language).

Q. Explain the purpose of ESL.
A. English as a second language (ESL) is a program designed for soldiers whose primary language is not English and who are experiencing difficulty in reading, speaking, or understanding English. Eligibility and placement is determined by diagnostic testing and/or command referral. Soldiers are sent on TDY to the 60 hour course. It is free of charge.

Q. Can family members attend the High School Completion Program (HSCP)?
A. Yes, on a space available basis.

Q. What does "DANTES" stand for and what is its purpose?
A. Defense Activity for Non-Traditional Educational Support; it is an educational agency providing free, standardized testing services to military personnel.

Q. What are some of the tests administered under the auspices of the DANTES program?
A. - General Education Development Equivalency Diploma (GED - overseas only).
- College Level Examination Program (CLEP)
- American College Test (ACT)
- Scholastic Aptitude Test (SAT)
- Graduate Record Examination (GRE)

Q. Are DANTES examinations available to family members/civilians?
A. Yes, on a cost per test basis.

Q. What is a GED?
A. The General Education Development tests are developed by the American Council on Education to enable persons who have not graduated from high school to demonstrate the attainment of abilities normally acquired through completion of a high school program of study. The GED test battery consists of five major education skills - writing, social studies, science, reading, and mathematics.

Q. What is the purpose of the Skill Recognition Programs offered by ACES?
A. To provide soldiers opportunities to document military skills and training in a form meaningful to potential civilian employers - to assist the servicemember in obtaining recognition and credit for the knowledge and experience acquired while in the service.

Q. Completion of the requirements of the Army Apprenticeship Program (AAP) leads to what?
A. Certification as a Journeyman.

Q. What do the letters "SOC" stand for?
A. Service Members Opportunity Colleges.

MILITARY PROGRAMS

Q. What does "SOCAD" stand for? Explain it.
A. Servicemembers Opportunity College Associates Degree (program); it is a voluntary, off-duty associate degree program network relating college directly to military job specialties. These programs are provided in an organized worldwide system which will allow service members to complete associate degrees regardless of mobility. SOCAD consists of more than 350 colleges and universities.

Q. How are associate degrees awarded under SOCAD?
A. Associate degrees are offered in 21 military job areas, called networks, which are directly related to CMFs and MOSs. Normally, the degree is awarded by the first SOCAD college the soldier attended.

Q. List some of the colleges participating in the SOCAD Program?
A.
- City Colleges of Chicago
- Central Texas College
- Embry-Riddle Aeronautical University
- University of Maryland
- Big-Bend Community College
- Boston University
- University of Southern California

Q. What is the "BDFS" Program?
A. Bachelors Degrees for Soldiers - a new SOC program similar to the established SOCAD Network. Curriculum areas include accounting, computer studies, and management.

Q. Explain HEADSTART and GATEWAY TO GERMAN.
A. HEADSTART is a mandatory German language and culture program which is provided during duty hours to newly arrived military personnel (E1 - E6) who do not have measurable German language proficiency. The course is designed to ease the "culture shock" experienced by personnel transferring from a familiar, stateside environment to the unfamiliar, German environment. The course consists of 40 hours of instruction, usually four hours per day for ten consecutive work days. It is open to family members and DOD civilian personnel on a space-available basis.

GATEWAY TO GERMAN is a mandatory command language program course which provides military service personnel with the opportunity to learn the basics of the language, as well as the customs. The program usually is conducted four hours per day for ten consecutive work days. Attendance is required for all newly arrived USAREUR personnel, E7-E9, Warrant Officers and Officers, who do not have measurable German language proficiency.

Q. The typical Learning Resources Center (LRC) consists of three separate facilities. What are they?
A. A language lab, a technical or "MOS" library, and a Training Extension Course (TEC) classroom facility.

Q. Transition Management is yet another program offered by the Education Center. What is its purpose?
A. It is designed to help the ETSing soldier further his/her education after leaving active duty. The soldier learns about education benefits, applies for financial aid, applies for admission to school of choice, etc. By using the Transition Management Program, it is possible for a soldier to be admitted to a school for the term immediately following his/her ETS date.

Q. When should a soldier be sent to Transition Management?
A. About 6 months prior to the ETS date.

MILITARY PROGRAMS

Q. What is "TA"?
A. Tuition Assistance - financial assistance used to defray the cost of tuition for active duty military personnel.

Q. Tuition Assistance is a grant that pays how much of tuition?
A. 75%.

Q. What is the requirement for the use of tuition assistance?
A. The course to be taken must be job-related.

Q. The New GI Bill is for soldiers who began their active service on or after what date?
A. July 1985.

Q. What is the required contribution to the GI Bill? How much will you receive back from the GI Bill?
A. $100.00 per month for 12 months; $300.00 per month for up to 3 years or $10,800.

Q. Name three of the Federal Financial Aid Programs available to the soldier through ACES.
A. Pell Grant, Perkins Loans (NDSL), Guaranteed Student Loans (GSL).

AER

Q. What is the AER?
A. Army Emergency Relief - it was chartered in 1942 as a private non-profit organization to provide Army soldiers, their dependents, widows/widowers and orphans with financial assistance in time of emergency need. In addition, it provides educational assistance for spouses and dependent children of soldiers.

Q. What Army publication states programs and policies for AER assistance to eligible Army members and their dependents?
A. AR 930-4.

Q. Why does AER exist?
A. Solely for the purpose of "helping the Army take care of its own".

Q. The AER coordinates closely with what other organization in order to avoid duplication and assure coverage of all areas of aid?
A. The American Red Cross (ARC).

Q. Describe the types and forms of assistance that AER provides.
A. LOANS with interest for immediate conditions.
GRANTS if repayment would cause hardships or if the ability to repay could be at a later date.
LOAN and GRANTS for partial repayment.

Q. Describe loan repayments to AER.
A. Repayment starts the 1st day of the second month following the initiation of the loan, normally does not extend more than 12 months and is made by allotment for active duty personnel.

Q. When is an AER loan considered delinquent?
A. When repayment has not been received one month after the due date.

Q. When is an AER loan considered uncollectible?

MILITARY PROGRAMS

A. - When the borrower is deceased, dishonorably discharged, discharged under other than honorable circumstances, or is dropped from the rolls as a deserter.
- When repayment will cause undue hardship.
- When reasonable efforts to obtain repayment from the borrower fail.
- When the delinquent loan balance is less than $5.00.

Q. What is the basic guideline for emergency financial assistance?
A. Any member of the Army faced with a real emergency, within the framework of policy, should be given AER assistance.

Q. What are some of the categories of authorized emergency financial assistance?
A. - nonreceipt of pay
- loss of funds
- medical, dental, or hospital expense
- funeral expenses
- emergency travel
- rent
- food
- utilities (other than phone)
- essential transportation (POV)
- clothing
- fire or other disaster
- lack of necessities (privation)

Q. What is the purpose of the AER Annual Fund Campaign?
A. To raise funds to help cover the financial assistance program, increase awareness about AER assistance, publicize procedures, and help the Army take care of it's own.

Q. How are contributions made to AER?
A. Allotment, cash, or check.

Q. The AER Annual Fund Campaign is held Army-wide during what dates?
A. 1 March - 1 July.

Q. What is the minimum contribution by allotment?
A. $1.00 per month for 3 months.

Q. Who is the Educational Assistance Program for?
A. For unmarried dependent children of Army personnel.

Q. What is the interest rate on AER loans?
A. AER loans are interest-free.

Q. Is there a dollar limit on AER loans?
A. No.

Q. Are you required to contribute to AER in order to receive help?
A. No.

MILITARY PROGRAMS

ARC

Q. What Army publication provides information concerning the mission, operation, and Army utilization of the American Red Cross (ARC)?
A. AR 930-5.

Q. Briefly describe what the American Red Cross (ARC) is.
A. It is a voluntary health and welfare organization established in 1881. Its primary purpose is to improve the quality of human life; to enhance self-reliance and concern for others; and to help people avoid, prepare for, and cope with emergencies.

Q. What American was responsible for pioneering the Red Cross movement in the United States and who, with a group of friends, founded the American Association of the Red Cross?
A. Clara Barton.

Q. What does "ICRC" stand for?
A. International Committee for the Red Cross.

Q. Describe the symbol used for the Red Cross.
A. It is simply a Greek red cross on a white background (which, incidentally, are the reverse of the colors of the Swiss flag).

Q. The red cross symbol is sometimes referred to as what?
A. The Geneva Cross.

Q. The Geneva Convention limits the use of the Red Cross emblem and the words "Red Cross" and "Geneva Cross" to what activities during both peacetime and wartime?
A. - Facilities for the care of the wounded and sick members of the military;
- armed forces medical personnel and equipment;
- military chaplains;
- the International Committees of the Red Cross;
- the League of Red Cross Societies;
- the various Red Cross societies (including the American Red Cross).

Q. Why are Red Cross personnel considered and given neutrality status?
A. They are considered to be exclusively engaged in the search for, or collection, transport, or treatment of the wounded or sick, or in the prevention of diseases, or are exclusively engaged in the administration of medical units and establishments.

Q. What are ~~five~~ some of the primary services of the ARC?
A. (1) Communication services (by wire).
(2) Financial assistance.
(3) Counseling and referral services.
(4) Health and safety services.
(5) Volunteer services.
(6) Disaster services.
(7) Blood services.
(8) Transplantation services.
(9) AIDS education.
(10) Military/Social services.
(11) International services.

(12) Youth services.

Q. What is the interest rates on ARC loans?
A. They are interest-free.

Q. How is the Red Cross primarily staffed?
A. By volunteers.

Q. What ARC services are provided relating to prisoners of war?
A. - Handles inquiries concerning prisoner of war welfare.
- Obtains names of prisoners of war.
- Aids in the processing and packaging of items for distribution.

ADAPCP

Q. What is the primary drug of abuse in the military?
A. Alcohol.

Q. What does "ADAPCP" stand for?
A. Alcohol and Drug Abuse Prevention and Control Program.

Q. What publication defines Army policy on alcohol and other drug abuse as well as defining responsibilities for implementation of the program?
A. AR 600-85.

Q. Who is authorized ADAPCP services?
A. Personnel entitled to military medical services as well as personnel covered by the Federal Civilian Employees Occupational Health Services Program.

Q. What law, passed in Sept 1971, mandated a program for the identification and treatment of drug and alcohol dependent persons in the Armed Forces?
A. Public Law 92-129.

Q. What are the seven functional areas of the ADAPCP?
A. Prevention, education, identification, rehabilitation, treatment, program evaluation, and research.

Q. The current focus of the ADAPCP places major emphasis on what?
A. The prevention aspects of substance abuse.

Q. What identification tool does the Commander have to detect drug abuse?
A. An active and aggressive urinalysis program.

Q. Describe the urine specimen policy.
A. Specimens will be collected under the direct observation of responsible personnel (E5 or above of the same sex) to insure that no substitutions are made.

Q. What is DA's policy on alcohol?
A. Abuse or excessive use of alcohol will not be condoned or accepted as part of any military tradition, ceremony or event.

Q. What does the acronym "CCC" stand for?
A. Community Counseling Center.

Q. What are the five methods of ADA identification?
A. (1) Voluntary (self) identification.

(2) Command identification.
(3) Biochemical (urinalysis or alcohol breath testing).
(4) Medical (blood).
(5) Investigation/apprehension.

Q. What is the most desirable method of discovering alcohol or drug abuse?
A. Voluntary (self) identification.

Q. When command referred, a service member must do what?
A. Participate in one or more of the three ADAPCP tracks.

Q. Describe the three tracks of the ADAPCP (see NOTE below).
A. Track I : Awareness education and group counseling, as required. Enrollment will not exceed 30 days; 12 hours of counseling.

Track II : Rehabilitation (nonresidential); intensive individual or group counseling (may include awareness education). Consists of 12 hours of counseling usually once per week for a minimum of 30 days, not to exceed ~~360~~ 364 days.

Track III : Rehabilitation (residential); medical treatment with nonresidential follow-up. Enrollment in this track is limited to those clients who have been evaluated by a physician as requiring residential treatment. Generally, residential care will be reserved for those individuals with long standing problems of abuse, but for whom prognosis for recovery is favorable with proper treatment. Enrollment is for 360 days (3 - 6 wks residential care).

NOTE: The ADAPCP program is steering away from the "Track" terminology. Change 2 to AR 600-85 drops Track III altogether and refers only to Tracks I and II. This has to do more with terminology than it does to sweeping program changes. The regulations are being re-written to reflect that there are three "Levels" of treatment instead of three "Tracks". Track I is being replaced by "Level I - Drug and Alcohol Education"; Track II is being replaced by "Level II - Outpatient"; and Track III is being replaced by "Level III - Inpatient". In all other respects the programs remain basically the same.

Q. What does "ADAPT" stand for?
A. Alcohol and Drug Abuse Prevention Training.

Q. What is the purpose of ADAPT?
A. To provide alcohol and other drug awareness education designed to focus the patient's attention on the adverse effects and consequences of alcohol and other drug abuse. A 6-month follow-up is an integral part of this education and referral to rehabilitation is a viable option at any point.

Q. Another drug and alcohol education program is called "STOP". What does this stand for?
A. Short-Term Outpatient treatment Program.

Q. Military personnel enrolled in the ADAPCP (Track I and II) are not eligible for reassignment to another unit until at least how many days of rehabilitation have been completed?
A. 30 days.

Q. What is one of the most critical and difficult aspects of the rehabilitation process?
A. The reinvolvement of the service member in his or her role and responsibilities in the unit.

Q. Describe the ADAPCP rehabilitation and treatment process.
A. The first stage is at the unit level where counseling, referral, and

administrative actions or a combination of these actions may take place. Then the individual is referred to the community counseling center for screening and evaluation. This is followed by ADAPCP enrollment where the individual will be placed in one or more of the tracks for education/rehabilitation for a maximum of 30 days/minimum of 30 days, or a maximum of one year for TRACK I, II, and III
respectively.

Q. What does "ATF" stand for? "RTF"?
A. Alcohol Treatment Facility; Residential Treatment Facility.

Q. What does "SUUTCO" stand for?
A. Selective Unit Urine Testing of Company-sized Organizations.

Q. General Army policy mandates that military personnel on duty will NOT have a blood alcohol level of what percent?
A. .05% or above

Q. Basic Army policy mandates what actions for a DWI?
A. - Referral to ADAPCP.
- General Officer letter of reprimand.
- Suspension of post driving privileges.
- Possible bar to reenlistment.

NOTE: Additional repercussions from local and unit policy may also result.

Q. What is the NCA?
A. The National Council on Alcoholism.

Q. What is the NIAAA?
A. The National Institute on Alcohol Abuse and Alcoholism.

Q. What are the three levels of alcohol prevention?
A. (1) Primary: prevention of the occurrence of the illness (alcoholism) (ie. education)
(2) Secondary: prevention of the further development of the illness after the occurrence (ie. crisis monitoring/referral)
(3) Tertiary: prevention of the reoccurrence of the illness during the later stages of treatment (ie. residential treatment & detoxification).

Q. What is one of the most frequently cited reasons for drug abuse and other health problems in the work environment?
A. Stress related to job conditions.

Q. Is an order from a competent authority to submit to a urinalysis a lawful order?
A. Yes.

Q. Army Forensic Toxicology Drug Testing Laboratories (FTDTLs) currently test every specimen for what drug?
A. THC (the drug found in marijuana) and cocaine. In addition, they are licensed for and capable of testing for amphetamines, barbiturates, and opiates, and will do so at the request of commanders.

Q. What is the only drug testing technique that is fully supportable for UCMJ action?
A. FTDTL tests.

Q. What is the degree of accuracy of FTDTL testing?

A. There has never been a reported false positive result in an Army FTDTL.

Q. What is a UADC and what is his/her function?
A. Unit Alcohol and Drug Coordinator; the UADC is responsible to the unit commander for ensuring that drug testing is conducted in accordance with existing regulations.

Q. What is a "BAT"?
A. Blood Alcohol Test.

Q. What does "BTC" stand for? "ADCO"?
A. Biochemical Testing Center; Alcohol and Drug Control Office.

Q. What is the preferred method of analysis for blood alcohol determinations?
A. Blood testing (vs. breath analysis).

Q. What are some things a leader can watch for to recognize and identify the problem drinker/drug abuser?
A. - attendance pattern
- job performance
- accidents
- personality changes

SAFETY

Q. The word "Safety" is often associated with what terminology?
A. Risk Management (or Risk Assessment).

Q. What AR covers Safety?
A. AR 385-10.

Q. What are the goals of the Army Safety Program?
A. (1) Reduce and keep to a minimum accidental manpower and monetary losses, thus providing more efficient use of resources and advancing the combat effectiveness of the Army.
(2) Provide a safe and healthful environment at all times for all Army personnel and others exposed to Army operations.

Q. Safety is the primary responsibility of whom?
A. It can be said that every soldier is a "Safety Officer" and this is true to some extent; however, safety has been designated as an NCOs responsibility. Therefore, the senior NCO in any unit/organization is the Safety Officer.

Q. Who is the Safety officer for your company?
A. Name him/her.

Q. Accidents are reported IAW which regulation?
A. AR 385-40.

Q. Name at least three safety features commonly found in Army barracks.
A. - lights in stairwells
- fire extinguishers and alarms
- CQ
- fire lights (emergency lighting)
- safety posters
- storage of dangerous tools
- hand rails

MILITARY PROGRAMS

EO

Q. What Army publication covers the Army Equal Opportunity Program?
A. AR 600-21 was superseded by Chapter 6, AR 600-20.

NOTE: Chapter 6 of AR 600-20 is printed in the form of an Interim Change.

Q. What is meant by "equal opportunity" in the Army?
A. Consideration and treatment based on merit, fitness, and capability irrespective of race, color, religion, gender, or national origin ("Everyone has the same opportunity to excel!").

Q. What is the Army's written policy on EO?
A. Provide equal opportunity and ensure fair treatment for military personnel, civilian employees, and their family members without regard to race, color, sex, religion, age, or national origin. This applies both on and off post and within the limits of the laws of localities, states, and host nations.

Q. Who is responsible for Army-wide policies, doctrines, plans, and initiatives pertaining to the Army EO Program?
A. The Deputy Chief of Staff for Personnel (DCSPER).

Q. What are the only two exceptions to a totally nonbiased personnel management process?
A. (1) The assignment and utilization of female soldiers in selected combat arms positions;
(2) Support for established equal opportunity goals (affirmative action plans).

Q. Who is the EO officer and NCO for your company?
A. Name them.

Q. What is the primary channel for correcting discriminatory practices?
A. The processing of EO complaints through the chain of command is strongly encouraged; however, it does not serve as the only channel available to soldiers and family members.

Q. If a complainant feels uncomfortable in filing a complaint with his/her chain of command, a number of alternative agencies exist through which a complaint may be processed. Name some of these agencies.
A. - Higher echelon in chain of command
- Equal Opportunity Advisor
- Inspector General
- Chaplain
- Provost Marshal/Criminal Investigation Command (CID)
- Medical agencies
- Staff Judge Advocate
- Housing Referral Office (HRO)

Q. The comlaints processing system consists of two types of complaints - formal and informal. What is the major difference between these?
A. An informal complaint is used when a soldier or family member does not wish to file the complaint in writing.

Q. What form is used for formal complaints?
A. DA Form 7279-R.

MILITARY PROGRAMS

Q. A time limit on equal opportunity complaints is established in order to set reasonable parameters for the investigation and resolution of complaints, to include ensuring the availability of witnesses, accurate recollection of events, and timely remedial action. What is this time limit?
A. Soldiers and family members have 60 calendar days from the date of the alleged incident in which to file a formal complaint.

Q. How do complaints filed through the Inspector General (IG) differ from those filed with other agencies?
A. Complaints filed through the Inspector General will be processed as Inspector General Assistance Requests (IGARs) in accordance with AR 20-1 rather than under the procedures outlined in AR 600-20. As such, no timelines will be imposed on the conduct of the investigation and/or on feedback to the complainant, and DA Form 7279-R will not be used.

Q. Rapid resolution of EO complaints is in the best interest of both the person filing the complaint and of the command. After receipt of a complaint, a commander has how long to conduct an investigation or refer the case to a higher echelon commander?
A. 14 calendar days.

NOTE: The commander may obtain an extension, not to exceed 30 calendar days, in writing from the next higher echelon commander.

Q. In addition, a complainant must receive written feedback from the commander on DA Form 7279-R, Parts II and III, within ______ calendar days after acknowledgment of the complaint.
A. 14

Q. If an appeal is made to a complaint case, it should be made through the next higher commander within the chain of command. How long do you have to make such an appeal?
A. 7 calendar days following notification of the results of investigation and acknowledgment of the actions of the command to resolve the complaint or issue. This appeal should be made in writing on DA Form 7279-R, Part IV.

Q. What actions may be taken against a soldier who knowingly submits a false equal opportunity complaint (to include a complaint containing information or allegations known to be false)?
A. This is punishable under UCMJ.

Q. Complaints of housing discrimination involving unequal treatment because of race, color, religion, gender, or national origin should be forwarded to whom?
A. The local Housing Referral Office (HRO).

Q. What are the two components of the EO program?
A. (1) Affirmative action component (to identify and correct existing inequities in an organization).
(2) Education and training component (to promote EO, harmonious relations amongst all Army personnel and provide positive motivation of those personnel).

Q. What is an "affirmative action plan"?
A. It is a comprehensive public document which requires good faith and time tables for achieving EO for all DOD personnel. Race is a factor in devising the AAP but is not a sole factor. AAPs must consist of planned, achievable steps that eliminate practices denying equal opportunity to soldiers and their families and that monitor progress toward these goals.

MILITARY PROGRAMS

Q. Define the term "ethnic group".
A. A group of individuals distinguished from the general population, based on actual or perceived criteria.

Q. Define the term "minority group".
A. Any group distinguished from the general population in terms of race, religion, sex, age, or national origin.

Q. Define "racism" or "sexism".
A. The acting out of prejudices by individuals against other individuals or groups because of race or gender.

Q. What is meant by sexual harassment?
A. It is a form of gender discrimination that involves unwelcome sexual advances, requests for sexual favors, and other verbal or physical conduct of a sexual nature.

Q. In order for an "incident" to be considered sexual harassment, one or more of three conditions must be met. What are they?
A. (1) Submission to, or rejection of, such conduct (see above definition) is made either explicitly or implicitly a term or condition of a person's job, pay, or career; or
(2) Submission to, or rejection of, such conduct by a person is used as a basis for career or employment decisions affecting that person; or
(3) Such conduct interferes with an individual's performance or creates an intimidating, hostile, or offensive environment.

Q. One enlisted soldier with the primary duty as Equal Opportunity Advisor (EOA) will be available full-time as the advisor for each brigade-level or equivalent and higher unit commander. This soldier should be what rank?
A. SFC or higher.

Q. What is an "EOR"?
A. Equal Opportunity Representative, this soldier has been designated to assist their commander at the battalion-level and below in carrying out the EO program within their respective units.

Q. EORs should normally be what rank?
A. SSG - SFC.

Q. Mandatory unit EO training must be conducted at least how often?
A. Twice per year.

NOTE: Listed below are the special/ethnic observances listed in AR 600-20, Chapter 6 (Interim Change I04):

January (3rd Monday) - Martin Luther King, Jr's Birthday (Federal Holiday)
February - African-American/Black History Month
March - Women's History Month
April/May - "Days of Remembrance" for victims of the Holocaust (celebrated Sunday to Sunday for week incorporating *Yom Hashoah*).
May - Asian Pacific Heritage Month
August 26th - Women's Equality Day
September 15th through October 15th - National Hispanic Heritage Month
November - National Native American Indian Heritage Month

MILITARY PROGRAMS

SPONSORSHIP

Q. What regulation covers the Total Army Sponsorship Program?
A. ~~AR 612-10~~ AR 600-8-8

Q. Should there be a sponsorship program for a soldier departing the unit?
A. Yes.

Q. What form is used to transmit sponsorship requirements to gaining commands?
A. DA Form 5434.

Q. What is a DA Form 5434-E?
A. An electronically generated DA Form 5434.

Q. As a minimum, how many welcome letters should a new arrival receive?
A. Unless sponsorship is declined a soldier should receive a minimum of two letters; one from the battalion commander (officers) or command sergeant major (enlisted) and one from the designated sponsor. If sponsorship is declined, a welcome letter should still be received from the command activity.

Q. Sponsors should be appointed within ________ calendar days after battalion or higher activity receives the DA Form 5434.
A. 10 (unless sponsorship is declined).

Q. What is a "reactionary" sponsor?
A. A person assigned to an individual that has declined sponsorship - in the event that questions arise.

Q. What are the general rules for appointing a sponsor?
A. The sponsor selected will be:
(1) In a grade equal to or higher than the incoming soldier, when practical;
(2) Of the same gender, marital status, and military career field or occupational series as the incoming soldier, when practical;
(3) Familiar with the unit or activity and community.

NOTE: The sponsor normally should not be the person being replaced by the incoming soldier and should not be within 60 days of PCS.

Q. Explain the sponsorship program in your unit.
A. Explain it.

REENLISTMENT

Q. What regulation covers reenlistment?
A. AR 601-280.

Q. What are the basic eligibility requirements for reenlistment?
A. - Must be over 18 years of age, but under 55 years of age.
- Must be a U.S. citizen.
- Must possess a high school diploma or GED.
- Must pass the APFT and meet height and weight standards.
- Must meet the years per grade requirement:
  -- E-4 8 yrs, 29 days
  -- E-5 13 yrs, 29 days

-- E-6 20 yrs, 29 days
-- E-7 24 yrs
-- E-8 27 yrs
-- E-9 30 yrs

Q. What is the maximum number of years that a soldier may reenlist for?
A. 4 years.

NOTE: Soldiers reenlisting in an MOS identified as critical by PERSCOM may reenlist for up to 6 years with authorization.

Q. How many months out can a soldier reenlist?
A. 8 months (max).

NOTE: Reenlistment window opens 8 months prior to ETS and closes one day after 3 months prior to ETS.

Q. What are some reasons that a soldier would be ineligible for reenlistment?
A. - Soldier barred/flagged.
- Soldier enrolled in ADAPCP.
- Soldier failed SQT.

Q. What is a bar to reenlistment?
A. It is an administrative action initiated by an immediate commander to prevent a substandard individual from reenlisting or reentering the service.

Q. What criteria governs a bar to reenlistment?
A. A soldier may be barred from reenlistment if his/her character, conduct, attitude, proficiency, motivation or general desirability for retention are not consistent with the high qualities demanded by the United States Army.

Q. What are some examples of deficiencies that may result in a Bar to Reenlistment?
A. - Tardiness for formation or duties.
- AWOL for 1 to 24 hour periods.
- Losses of clothing and equipment.
- Substandard personal appearance & hygiene.
- Persistent indebtedness.
- Frequent traffic violations.
- Recurrent punishments under Article 15, UCMJ.
- Use of sick call without medical justification.
- Unwillingness to follow orders.
- Untrainability.
- Unadaptability to the military.
- Failure to manage personal affairs.
- Frequent difficulties with fellow soldiers.

Q. How often is a bar to reenlistment reviewed?
A. Every 3 months or 30 days prior to PCS/ETS.

Q. Who may lift a bar?
A. With written recommendation from the unit commander, the same authority that approved the bar may lift it.

Q. Who can initiate a bar to reenlistment?
A. Any commander in the soldiers chain of command.

Q. What is an "SRB"?
A. Selective Reenlistment Bonus.

MILITARY PROGRAMS

Q. How are SRBs computed?
A. Amount of newly obligated service (# years reenlistment) (x) base pay (x) SRB multiplier.

Q. What is the maximum SRB amount that a soldier may receive?
A. $20,000.

Q. When are reenlistment interviews due?
A. - 90 days after assignment to unit.
- 12 months before ETS.
- 8 months before ETS.
- 3 to 4 months before ETS.

Q. Who does the reenlistment interview?
A. The commander and Re-up NCO.

Q. What is the BEAR Program and who can request it?
A. The Bonus Extension and Retraining program - the BEAR program allows a soldier to extend for training in a new MOS and then reenlist for the bonus that the new MOS pays. It is available for E-5s and below and E-6s in an overage PMOS.

Q. Can a soldier reenlist if they are overweight?
A. Only with an exception to policy.

Q. Soldiers in the rank of ___________ and below (as a result of a reduction in rank under any UCMJ actions) are not authorized to extend.
A. PFC

Q. Soldiers are no longer authorized to extend or reenlist if they are within ______ months of their scheduled ETS (without an exception to policy approved by HQDA).
A. 3 months.

NCODP

Q. What does "NCODP" stand for?
A. Noncommissioned Officer Development Program.

Q. What Army regulation covers NCODP?
A. AR 350-17.

Q. Explain what NCODP is.
A. The NCODP is the commander's formal program for developing the leadership skills and professional attributes of the unit's enlisted leaders. It encompasses all forms of leader training from individual coaching and counseling to formal instruction for groups of NCOs. It is tailored to the unique requirements of the unit and its NCOs. In short, it is the process of continuing the education of NCOs and focuses on warfighting requirements and preparation of NCOs at all levels to teach their soldiers the battlefield skills needed to fight, win, and survive. NCODP subjects are 75% war-related and driven by the METL and STXs.

Q. NCODP is the responsibility of whom?
A. NCODP is the commander's responsibility, but implementation is delegated to the NCO Support Channel. The senior NCO at each level of the Support Channel

has primary responsibility for training the next subordinate level of NCOs.

Q. What are the goals of NCODP?
A. - Develop and strengthen leadership skills and professional attributes.
- Provide guidance.
- Increase confidence.
- Improve unit effectiveness.
- Identify substandard NCOs and rehabilitate, reduce, reclassify, or eliminate as appropriate.
- Realize the potential of the NCO Support Channel.

Q. NCODP supports the commander's training objective and guidance and compliments, reinforces, and supports what three areas?
A. - ARTEP training.
- Special training events.
- Physical readiness.

Q. What are the key ingredients to a successful NCODP program?
A. - NCO sponsorship.
- NCO rites of passage ceremony.
- Train to train.
- Daily training through counseling, correcting, and other routine activities.
- Formal and informal discussions.
- Professional reading.
- Correspondence courses (individual and group).

Q. NCODP builds upon the contributions of what two other programs?
A. The EPMS and the NCOES.

MISC

Q. What does "DEERS" stand for?
A. Defense Enrollment Eligibility Reporting Systems.

Q. How do you enroll your family members in DEERS?
A. At your servicing Personnel Administration Center (PAC) when applying for their ID cards.

Q. What does "CHAMPUS" stand for?
A. Civilian Health and Medical Program of the Uniformed Services.

Q. What is CHAMPUS designed for?
A. To supplement the military care available to dependents of active duty service members, retired service members and dependents of retired or deceased members.

Q. List some Military Entitlements a soldier may receive while on active duty.
A. - Separate Rations (if not assigned a meal card)
- Variable Housing Allowance (VHA)
- Cost of Living Allowance (COLA)
- Basic Allowance for Quarters (BAQ)
- Clothing Allowance
- Overseas Housing Allowance (OHA)
- Leave

Q. When does a service member receive his/her clothing allowance in their

paycheck?
A. Enlisted personnel only - once per year, during their anniversary month (month they entered the service).

Q. What are the different types of leave that a soldier is entitled to?
A. Convalescent, Emergency, Administrative, Terminal, and Advance Leave.

Q. List some of the major Benefits available to service members.
A.
- Medical
- Dental
- Educational
- Legal Services
- SGLI

Q. What are some of the Military Privileges available to service members?
A.
- PX
- Commissary
- Morale Support Activities
- Family Housing
- Passes

Q. What does "BOSS" stand for?
A. Better Opportunities for Single Soldiers. Targets single and unaccompanied soldiers and is designed to give them greater input into the MWR activities in their respective communities.

PRE-BOARD REVIEW
QUESTIONS

ABOUT THIS SECTION

This section of the study guide is a good starting point for beginners and, when used together with the "STUDY TEMPLATES" (section 36), is an excellent way for anyone to review for upcoming boards. "PRE-BOARD REVIEW" is essentially a mini study guide and contains what I feel are the "basics" for each subject covered.

I recommend that you start here, in this section. The material covered here will give you an excellent foundation on which to build your military knowledge. If time permits, progress to each individual section in this study manual for more in-depth study/review.

"PRE-BOARD REVIEW" is divided into two sections, "Questions" and "Answers". You can quickly tell which section you are in by looking at either the page header or the page number. The page number will be prefixed by a "Q" for questions and an "A" for answers. If you want to find a particular section in "PRE-BOARD REVIEW", look in the index at the beginning of each section. The index will tell you two things:

(1) The location of the desired subject in the section;
(2) The location of the desired subject in the study manual.

If you cannot recall the answer to a particular question, refer to the same number under the same topic in the "Answers" section. For your convenience, each subject/topic "marker" has the location of the related answers/questions.

PRE-BOARD REVIEW QUESTIONS

QUESTIONS INDEX

PRE-BOARD REVIEW QUESTIONS

CODE OF CONDUCT

ANSWERS PAGE A:35.2

1. What AR covers the Code of Conduct?
2. Who authorized the publishing of the Code of Conduct in 1955?
3. What is the Code of Conduct and what is it's purpose?
4. What are the six Articles of the Code of Conduct?
5. A good way to remember what you should do if you capture a prisoner is to use the 5-"S" Rule. What are the 5 S's?
6. Prisoners should be separated into what groups?

GUARD DUTY

ANSWERS PAGE A:35.2

1. What Field Manual covers Guard Duty?
2. What are the two types of guard duty?
3. A guard on post is governed by two types of orders. What are they?
4. What are the three General Orders?
5. What is meant by "countersign"?
6. What is meant by "challenge"?
7. How are the challenge and password (countersign) given?
8. What is a "parole word"?
9. What are the two main qualifications for performing guard duty?

PHYSICAL SECURITY

ANSWERS PAGE A:35.3

1. What FM covers Physical Security and what AR deals with the Army Physical Security Program?
2. What is the purpose of physical security?
3. What are considered physical security measures?
4. What is considered a "security threat"?
5. Security threats are classified into two categories. Name these categories and give some examples of each.
6. Of the two categories of security threats, which is not normally preventable by physical security measures?
7. What is considered to be the standard identification media for military personnel?
8. Explain the "two-man rule".
9. What are the four designations of restricted areas?
10. What are the three levels of security classifications and what cover sheets are used for each?
11. What is the highest classification of material that may be discussed over the phone?
12. What four types of fencing are authorized for the protection of restricted areas?
13. J-SIIDS is the functional intruder detection system used in most arms rooms. What does "J-SIIDS" stand for?
14. What is considered to be the most accepted and widely used security device of the basic safeguards in protecting installations and activities, personnel, classified material, and government and personal property?
15. What words should be imprinted on all master and higher level control keys?
16. What is DA Form 4986 used for?

PRE-BOARD REVIEW QUESTIONS

FIRST AID

ANSWERS PAGE A:35.3

1. What FM covers "First Aid for Soldiers"?
2. What is meant by "first aid"?
3. What is the first thing you should do if you come upon a sick or injured soldier?
4. What are the eight steps in properly evaluating a casualty?
5. What are the two vital body functions?
6. What are the three *basic measures* (life-saving steps) of first aid?
7. What are the two prescribed methods for opening an airway?
8. What are the two prescribed methods of rescue breathing? Which is preferred?
9. What are the steps in performing artificial respiration?
10. What are the five prescribed methods (in order of precedence) for controlling bleeding?
11. What should you do after applying a tourniquet to a casualty?
12. What are the seven steps in treating/preventing shock?
13. What is the first aid measure for chemical burns to the eyes?
14. How do you treat a chest wound?
15. What are the first aid measures for an abdominal wound?
16. What is a "fracture"?
17. What are the two kinds of fractures?
18. What is the *Basic Splinting Principle*?
19. What is the first and last thing you should do when splinting a fracture?
20. What are the three types of heat injuries?
21. Name the cold weather injuries.
22. What are the eight MILD symptoms of nerve agent poisoning?
23. What are the nine SEVERE symptoms of nerve agent poisoning?
24. What is contained in the Mark I, Nerve Agent Antidote Kit?
25. Where is the injection site for the Mark I, Nerve Agent Antidote Kit?
26. How long should the autoinjectors be held in place once activated?
27. How many sets of the nerve agent antidote are you authorized to administer to yourself?
28. There may be some instances when a manual carry is essential to saving a casualty's life. Although manual carries are accomplished by one or two bearers, the two-man carries are used whenever possible. The distance a casualty can be carried depends on what four factors?
29. Name some of the one-man carries?
30. Name some of the two-man carries?

FIELD SANITATION

ANSWERS PAGE A:35.5

1. What FM covers "Field Hygiene and Sanitation"?
2. What is "hygiene"?
3. What is "sanitation"?
4. What is meant by "military sanitation"?
5. How do you define "communicable diseases"?
6. What are the five communicable disease groups classified by the Army?
7. Which of the five communicable disease groups accounts for the highest incidence of disease in the Army?
8. What is the chain of disease transmission?
9. What are the three basic control measures for communicable diseases?
10. What are the five Fs of field sanitation?
11. What is meant by "potable" water?

12. Good water discipline involves filling your canteen with treated water at every chance. When treated water is not available, you must disinfect the water in your canteen using one of five approved methods. What are they? Which is the preferred method?
13. Iodine tablets used to purify individual water supplies should be what color?
14. A mess kit laundry (wash line) should contain how many cans? What is contained in each can and how many personnel will such a wash line support?
15. What are the four types of field waste?
16. What is a "cat-hole"?
17. How far should field latrines be located from food operations and sources of water?
18. What three things must you consider when determining the TYPE of latrine(s) to be constructed?
19. What two things, in order of precedence, must be considered when determining the LOCATION within the camp area for construction of latrines?
20. When should latrines and garbage pits be closed?
21. What is the proper procedure for closing a latrine or garbage pit?
22. Name five diseases commonly carried by mosquitos.
23. What are some commonly used control measures for mosquitos?
24. Name three diseases commonly carried by flies.
25. Name some diseases commonly carried by rodents.
26. Why is it so important that **ALL** members of a team or unit practice good personal hygiene?

MAP READING

ANSWERS PAGE A:35.6

1. What FM covers "MAP READING AND LAND NAVIGATION"?
2. What is a "map"?
3. Military maps are categorized by what two things?
4. What is meant by the "scale" of a map?
5. What are the three different scales of military maps?
6. What is the standard "small scale" map and what is it used for?
7. What is the standard "medium scale" map and what is it used for?
8. What is the standard "large scale" map and what is it used for?
9. What are some examples of different TYPES of maps?
10. Where does a map get its name?
11. Identify the colors used to facilitate the identification of features on a military map.
12. What is meant by the "military grid reference system"?
13. What is the distance between grid lines on a military map?
14. What is the military principle for reading maps?
15. How many digits are required to locate a point to within 100 meters? To within 10 meters?
16. The graphic scale is divided into two parts. What are they?
17. What is an "azimuth"?
18. Name three common units of angular measure used by military personnel to express direction.
19. Describe the three norths on a military map.
20. What is a "back azimuth" and how is it obtained?
21. What is the back azimuth of 20 degrees?
22. What is the "declination diagram" and where is it located?
23. What is the Grid-Magnetic (G-M) Angle used for and where is it found?
24. What is meant by "intersection"?
25. What is meant by "resection"?

PRE-BOARD REVIEW QUESTIONS

26. What are the four types of compasses described in FM 21-26?
27. What are the three major parts of the lensatic compass?
28. There are two scales on a lensatic compass; the outer scale, normally in _______ (color) denotes ________ and the inner scale, normally in ______ denotes __________.
29. The bezel ring on the base of a lensatic compass is a ratchet device that clicks when turned. It contains ______ clicks when rotated fully; each click is equal to ____ degrees. What is its primary purpose?
30. What are the two approved techniques for holding the compass when sighting?
31. Name three field expedient methods for determining the four cardinal directions.
32. What is "elevation"?
33. What is "relief"?
34. What are the five methods of depicting relief?
35. Which of the above methods is the most common on standard topographic maps?
36. What are "contour lines"?
37. What are the three types of contour lines?
38. What are the five **MAJOR** terrain features?
39. What are the three **MINOR** terrain features?
40. What are the two **SUPPLEMENTAL** terrain features?
41. What is the best way to orient a map without a compass?
42. In military symbols (not topographic symbols), what colors are often used and what are their meanings?
43. From questions 11 and 42 it can be said that there are 7 colors used on a military map. What are they?
44. What four units of measure are most commonly used on military maps and can be found in the Graphic (Bar) Scales?

M16A1/A2 AND MARKSMANSHIP

ANSWERS PAGE A:35.8

1. What Army publication covers the M16A1/A2 rifles and the fundamentals of rifle marksmanship?
2. Describe the M16A1 Rifle.
3. Describe the M16A2 Rifle.
4. What are the firing weights of the M16A1 and M16A2 Rifle with 20- and 30-round magazines?
5. It follows then, from the above question, that the difference in firing weight between the M16A1 and M16A2 rifles is what?
6. What is the overall length of the M16A1 rifle with flash suppressor?
7. What is the overall length of the M16A2 rifle with compensator?
8. What types of ammunition are used in the M16 rifle?
9. What is the recommended basic load for the M16 rifle (30-round magazine)?
10. Describe the differences in the maximum effective rates of fire of the two weapons. M16A1 M16A2
11. What are the **maximum** ranges of the two weapons?
12. What are the **maximum effective** ranges of the M16A1/A2 rifles?
13. Name some of the basic differences between the two rifles.
14. What is the purpose of the compensator on the M16A2?
15. What are the eight steps in the cycle of functioning of the M16 rifle?
16. What is meant by the "stoppage" of a weapon?
17. What is meant by "immediate action"?
18. What word is commonly used to remember the procedure for applying immediate action?
19. How many times should immediate action be applied to a weapon?
20. What is meant by "remedial action"?

PRE-BOARD REVIEW QUESTIONS

21. What is considered a "malfunction"?
22. What are the three primary categories of malfunctions?
23. What are the four basic fundamentals of rifle marksmanship?
24. What are the two basic firing positions?
25. What is the larger aperture, marked 0-2, on the M16A2 used for? The unmarked aperture?
26. Explain how to place the initial sight setting on the M16A2 rifle for 25 meters.
27. Explain how to set an M16A1 to mechanical zero.
28. Which sight aperture is used for zeroing on an M16A1?
29. What are the standards for zeroing an M16A2 rifle?
30. What are the qualification standards for a Record Fire (RF) range (pop-up targets)?
31. What are the qualification standards for the Known Distance Alternate Course (KDAC) or the scaled 25-meter Alternate Course (AC)?
32. When the M16A2 (w/magazine)is properly field stripped, how many parts are there (not including bipod)?
33. Are the M16A1 and M16A2 zeroing targets the same?
34. Proper maintenance of the M16A2 rifle includes what five steps?
35. What does "CLP" stand for and how does it work?
36. Explain the proper procedure for performing a function check on an M16A2 rifle.
37. The first consideration when handling any weapon is to do what?

NBC

ANSWERS PAGE A:35.10

1. What does "NBC" stand for?
2. What are some of the major Army Field Manuals that cover Nuclear, Chemical, and Biological warfare, its effects on battle doctrine, and how to train and prepare for NBC operations?
3. What Army regulation covers "Nuclear, Biological and Chemical Defense and Chemical Warfare".
4. What are the three fundamentals of NBC defense?
5. NBC hazards can be classified into two types. What are they?
6. NBC protection is divided into what two broad areas?
7. What is current US policy regarding the use of nuclear, chemical, and biological assets?
8. What forms do NBC contaminants come in?
9. What are the ~~four~~ five contamination hazards?
10. When emplacing NBC markers, how far apart should they be?
11. What is meant by "persistency"?
12. What ~~seven~~ eight factors affect persistency?
13. What are the three classifications of NBC markers? Describe them.
14. For biological contamination and for persistent or nonpersistent agents, what other information is required to be entered on the appropriate NBC marker?
15. How many NBC Reports are there and what is the purpose of each?
16. What are the four **principles** of decontamination?
17. Which of the above principles is considered to be the most important?
18. What are the ~~two~~ three **levels** of decontamination?
19. What seven decontamination **techniques** are used to support the three levels of decontamination?
20. What are the four portals of entry that toxic agents may use when entering the body?
21. What is "MOPP"?
22. The MOPP suit protective overgarment is known as what? Describe it.

PRE-BOARD REVIEW QUESTIONS

23. When the BDO is removed from the package and donned, how long will it retain its protective qualities?
24. Once the BDO is contaminated with a liquid chemical agent, how long will it provide protection?
25. Once the CPOG is contaminated with a liquid chemical agent, how long will it provide protection?
26. What is the standard time allowed for a soldier (at MOPP level 0) to achieve MOPP levels 1 through 4 in sequence?
27. When properly fitted and worn, the protective mask will protect the wearer against what?
28. The protective mask will not protect against what two types of gases?
29. What is the standard time allowed for the donning of the protective mask?
30. What is the last step in donning the protective mask?
31. There are ~~two~~ three approved methods for wearing the protective mask carrier. What are they?
32. How many levels of MOPP are there? Describe them.
33. Soldiers in MOPP 4 may lose how much water per hour through perspiration?
34. By what means can soldiers be identified while wearing MOPP 4?
35. What does "MGX" stand for?
36. What are the three types of procedures for MOPP gear exchange?
37. When would the "triple buddy" system be used for MPX (see above question)?
38. When would the individual procedure be used for MPX?
39. Explain the ~~eight~~ nine steps of MOPP Gear Exchange.
40. What is the approximate amount of time that should be allotted for MGX?
41. What are the **four** principal effects of any nuclear explosion?
42. What is the cause of most of the material destruction accompanying a nuclear explosion?
43. Thermal radiation, which accounts for approximately 35% of the burst energy of a nuclear explosion, has two dangerous components. What are they?
44. Nuclear radiation from a blast can be further divided into two major types. What are they?
45. What is "EMP"?
46. What is "TREE"?
47. What are the three types of nuclear bursts?
48. What is ~~"NUCWARN"~~ "STRIKWARN"?
49. The indicators of a nuclear attack are unmistakable. What is normally the first indication that a nuclear explosion has occurred? Name three other indicators of a nuclear explosion.
50. What should you do if you are in the open and see a brilliant flash you recognize as a nuclear explosion?
51. What actions should be taken after a nuclear strike?
52. What equipment is available for monitoring radiological contamination?
53. What are the two **types** of area monitoring?
54. In addition to the two types of monitoring there are two techniques. What are the two **techniques**?
55. What are the two types of radiation surveys?
56. What dose rate requires that a radiological contamination marker be emplaced?
57. Biological agents can be placed into two ~~classes~~ broad categories. What are they?
58. How are ~~germs~~ pathogens delivered?
59. The body possesses several defenses against biological agents. What are they?
60. What are the most effective protective measures against biological agents?
61. Name four indicators of a possible biological or chemical attack.
62. What is the preferred decontaminate for biological contamination?
63. Chemical agents are classified by the U.S. into three categories. What are

they?
64. Threat forces classify chemical agents according to their effect on the body. What are the six major types of chemical agents as classified by threat forces?
65. By what six means may chemical or biological agents be delivered?
66. What is "CHEMWARN"?
67. What is a "CDM" and how often is it issued?
68. What **decontamination** equipment is available for chemical agents?
69. What detection equipment is available for chemical agents?
70. What is meant by VGH agents? L-agents?
71. Where can you find a color comparison bar chart for use with the M8 detector paper? What are the colors and what do they represent?
72. What is the proper method for using M8 detector paper?
73. When attaching M9 Chemical Agent Detector Paper to clothing, where should it be placed?
74. Describe proper unmasking procedures with and without the M256 Kit.
75. What is the inspection interval for the protective mask?
76. What does "CARC" stand for?

PHYSICAL FITNESS

ANSWERS PAGE A:35.15

1. What Army publications cover the Army Physical Fitness Program?
2. There are many things one must consider when developing an effective physical fitness program. How many "considerations" are there and what are they?
3. Physical fitness is composed of factors (components) that allow soldiers to function effectively in physical and mental work, training, and recreation and still have energy to handle emergencies. What are the five COMPONENTS of fitness?
4. What are the seven PRINCIPLES of exercise?
5. What is the primary objective of a physical training program?
6. The acronym "FITT" makes it easier to remember the key factors in a training program. What do the letters stand for?
7. What is the Army's policy concerning the length and duration of exercise periods?
8. What are the three PHASES of fitness?
9. As an active duty soldier, what "phase" of fitness should you be in?
10. What are the three TYPES of Army fitness programs?
11. Who is evaluated during an APFT?
12. How often is the APFT administered?
13. What are APFT standards based on?
14. What is the Army standard (including AIT) for passing the APFT?
15. What is meant by "cool-down" and how long should it last?
16. Name the different conditioning activities recommended by FM 21-20.
17. What are the two prescribed formations for physical fitness training?
18. Which of the above formations is the traditional formation for most physical training activities?
19. What eight commands are used to form the extended rectangular formation?
20. What command is used to reassemble the unit into the original formation?
21. What is a DA Form 705?
22. What is the required test sequence for the three events of the APFT?
23. How long does a soldier have before he can be tested after a temporary profile expires?
24. How many points are required on the APFT to be awarded the Presidential Physical Fitness patch?

PRE-BOARD REVIEW QUESTIONS

WEIGHT CONTROL

ANSWERS PAGE A:35.16

1. What Army regulation covers "The Army Weight Control Program"?
2. What is meant by the term "overweight"?
3. What are the primary objectives of the Army Weight Control Program?
4. To assist soldiers in meeting the requirements prescribed in AR 600-9, weight screening tables are used. The screening table weight is based on what two considerations?
5. How often should soldiers be weighed?
6. What is the maximum allowable percent body fat standard for your age?
7. What three things **must** happen when a soldier is determined to be overweight?
8. What is the required weight loss rate for soldiers in the Army Weight Control Program?
9. How often should soldiers in the Weight Control Program weigh in?
10. What should a soldier be wearing when he/she is weighed?

LEADERSHIP

ANSWERS PAGE A:35.16

1. What is considered to be the Army's basic manual on leadership?
2. What are the two leadership "modes"?
3. What is meant by the term "leadership"?
4. The four major factors of leadership are always present and affect the actions you should take and when you should take them. What are the four leadership factors?
5. What are the 11 principles of leadership?
6. What are the four individual values that all soldiers (leaders and led) are expected to possess?
7. Describe the BE-KNOW-DO characteristics of a good military leader.
8. What are the five steps in the problem-solving process?
9. What are the three basic styles of military leadership?
10. What style of leadership should you use?
11. What are the three formal channels of communication in the Army?
12. Where does an NCO derive his/her authority?
13. What are the two types of authority?
14. What are the two basic responsibilities of a military leader?
15. In what Army publications would you look for information about the "Duties, Responsibilities, and Authority of Noncommissioned Officers"?
16. Who is the only person who performs as both a member of the Chain of Command and the NCO Support Channel?
17. What are the four SPECIFIC Noncommissioned Officer responsibilities?
18. What are the four fundamental steps in supervising subordinates in the accomplishment of a task?
19. Who can delegate responsibility?
20. List four indicators of unit effectiveness (unit leadership).
21. What is a basic prerequisite to good leadership?
22. What are the essential ingredients in a proper senior/subordinate relationship?
23. What are five roles of a leader?

PRE-BOARD REVIEW QUESTIONS

COUNSELING

ANSWERS PAGE A:35.18

1. What FM covers "Leadership Counseling"?
2. What is "counseling"?
3. What are the principal objectives of counseling?
4. FM 22-101 contains suggestions and guidelines on military counseling. There is only one **absolute** requirement with respect to counseling. What is it?
5. Of the leader traits or characteristics promoting effective counseling, what is considered to be the most important?
6. A leader often uses influence when directing subordinates. Influence may take many forms - depending on what is necessary to develop the subordinates and to meet the needs of the unit. List seven common "forms of influence".
7. What are the three approaches to counseling?
8. How do you determine which counseling approach to use?
9. What are the three "groups" of basic counseling skills?
10. What are the five "reasons" for counseling (5 types of counseling)?
11. What is the **key** to a successful counseling session?
12. In **preparing** for scheduled counseling sessions, what five points should a leader consider?
13. Ideally, a counseling session should be shorter than _______, and always less than ________.
14. What should you do if you expect a counseling session to last more than 30 minutes?
15. A counseling session may be divided into three phases. What are they?
16. What are the two objectives of "opening the session"?
17. What is the key to "closing the session"?
18. What is the key to getting results from counseling?
19. What form is normally used to record most counseling?
20. Unit counseling training should be based on what two references?
21. What are seven characteristics of a good counselor?
22. How often should soldiers be counseled?
23. What is a good example of an "informal" form of counseling?
24. When making an "On-the-Spot" correction, what four items of information should be covered?

TRAINING

ANSWERS PAGE A:35.19

1. Name some of the important Army publications that cover training.
2. What is the Army's training goal?
3. Training is divided into what two categories?
4. What are the nine principles of training?
5. What is meant by the "Band of Excellence"?
6. What is meant by "Battle Focus"?
7. What are the steps of the Training Management Cycle?
8. What is a "Mission Essential Task"?
9. What is a "METL"?
10. What are the two primary inputs to METL development?
11. Which of the two primary inputs is the most critical?
12. What does "BOS" stand for, explain it, and list the seven systems?
13. What information is contained in a "Battle Book"?
14. Which tasks within a METL should be given priority?
15. What is meant by a "Training Objective"?
16. A training objective consists of what three parts?

PRE-BOARD REVIEW QUESTIONS

17. What is a "Battle Task"?
18. What are the three types of training plans?
19. Near-term planning and thus, training schedules, should cover a _____ week period prior to the conduct of training.
20. All good training, regardless of the specific collective and individual tasks being executed, must comply with certain common requirements. What are these requirements?
21. What is the best way to describe properly presented and practical training?
22. What is an "AAR"?
23. What are the four parts of an AAR?
24. What is the purpose of the Soldier's Manual?
25. What is the NCOES? What are the different levels of the NCOES System?
26. What are the five parts of the "5-P" training model?
27. What are the eight elements of a training outline?
28. What are the three methods of teaching?
29. What regulation covers the Individual Training and Evaluation Program (ITEP)?
30. What are the goals of ITEP?
31. What are the three components of ITEP?

UCMJ

ANSWERS PAGE A:35.20

1. What AR covers Military Justice?
2. What is the "UCMJ"?
3. Does a person have to accept an Article 15?
4. What article of the UCMJ is designed to protect the rights of the soldier?
5. What are Articles 77 through 134 of the UCMJ known as?
6. Can a court martial be appealed?
7. Who may be placed in correctional custody?
8. What are the three classifications of Article 15s?
9. What is the length of time one has to appeal an Article 15?
10. What is the purpose of a "flagging" action?
11. Who may impose an Article 15?
12. How is voting done on a special court martial?
13. May an enlisted person serve on a court martial?
14. Can you refuse a Court Martial?
15. How many members are on a court martial board?
16. Pretending to be sick or injured is punishable under UCMJ and is known as what?
17. What is the maximum sentence you can be judged by a General court martial?
18. The UCMJ is comprised of how many articles?
19. What are the three types of Courts Martial?
20. Military Justice is administered at two levels. What are they?
21. When might a commander choose to use Article 15 punishment?
22. What form is designed for the purpose of notifying a soldier of Article 15 proceedings against him/her?
23. What form is used to record summarized Article 15 proceedings?
24. What is the disposition of DA Form 2627-1?
25. What is the disposition of DA Form 2627?
26. What is a "Field Grade" Article 15?
27. What is "probable cause"?
28. If enlisted members serve on a court, what percentage can be enlisted?
29. What does "double-jeopardy" mean?
30. What do the letters "MCM" stand for?
31. Who may be reduced for misconduct under Article 15, UCMJ?

32. What does a promulgating order do?
33. If an Article 15 is appealed, what actions may the appealing authority take?
34. What is the highest court in the Army?
35. What is the maximum punishment allowed under Article 15 of the UCMJ?

DRILL & CEREMONIES

ANSWERS PAGE A:35.22

1. What FM covers Drill and Ceremonies?
2. What is the primary purpose of drill in the Army?
3. Most drill commands have two parts. What are they?
4. What is quick time cadence?
5. How fast is the double-time cadence?
6. What are the five types of commands in drill?
7. What is the normal length of step in marching?
8. What foot is your leading foot?
9. What is your trailing foot?
10. What are the commands to dismiss armed troops?
11. Explain the movement of each squad in platoon formation on the command "Open Ranks, March".
12. Explain the movement of each squad in platoon formation on the command "Close Ranks, March".
13. How many types of intervals are there? What are they?
14. What are the five rest positions which may be given at halt?
15. You may talk in formation only after what command is given?
16. What is the length of the following steps? Forward, Half-step, Left/Right step, Backward, and Doubletime.
17. What three commands are given to line a platoon?
18. What are the four types of foot marches?
19. What are the two classifications of foot marches?
20. When executed from a Halt, all steps in marching begin with the left foot except one, what is that exception?
21. When marching, what is the proper measure of the arm swing?
22. What are the two prescribed formations for a platoon?
23. What are the two 30-inch step rest movements?
24. What is the difference between At Ease March and Route Step March?
25. When marking time as in "Mark time, March", you should raise each foot alternately how many inches off the marching surface?
26. What are the proper commands for halting a unit while double timing?
27. Inspection Arms from Order Arms is a _________-count movement.
28. When in an inspection formation with the rifle, at what time do you automatically execute inspection arms?
29. After you have been inspected (see above question), when do you execute ready-port-arms?
30. What commands are used to align a squad at normal interval?
31. What is the simplest way to form a squad at normal interval?
32. In what publication will you find the "Manual of the Guidon"?
33. When is a soldier authorized to salute with the left hand?
34. Can the guidon bearer carry a weapon?
35. How is the guidon carried at double time?

PRE-BOARD REVIEW QUESTIONS

FLAGS

ANSWERS PAGE A:35.23

1. What Army regulation prescribes the design, acquisition, display, and use of flags, guidons, streamers, automobile and aircraft plates, and tabards?
2. What other Army publication is a good source of information on Flags and Guidons?
3. What is a "flag"?
4. When a flag is no longer suitable for display, how should it be disposed of?
5. What is meant by the term "Color"?
6. Describe the flag of the United States.
7. When was the current 50-star flag adopted?
8. How many US flags are authorized to be flown at one time at any CONUS Army installation?
9. Name some places where the US flag is flown night and day.
10. There are 10 types of National Flags. What are the only three that are flown over US Army installations?
11. What flag may be substituted for the Garrison flag on National Holidays?
12. What is meant by the "hoist" of the flag?
13. What is meant by the "fly" of the flag?
14. What is the "heading" of a flag?
15. The US flag is flown at halfstaff to signify what?
16. The US flag is folded in the triangular shape of a cocked hat. Why is this?
17. On what date was the present US Army flag approved?
18. What is Flag Day?
19. Describe the US Army flag.
20. What is a guidon?
21. What is a "finial"?
22. Only four finials are authorized to be used on flagstaffs. What are they?
23. What is the only finial device used with Army flags?
24. What is a "canton"?
25. What is a "dexter"?
26. What is a "sinister"?
27. What is a "halyard"?
28. The ceremonial raising of the flag is known as what?
29. The ceremonial lowering of the flag is known as what?
30. If the National flag touches the ground or becomes soiled, must it be destroyed?
31. How do you clean a serviceable flag?
32. What is the height of the flagpole on which the National flag is flown?

CUSTOMS & COURTESIES

ANSWERS PAGE A:35.25

1. What Army regulation covers "Salutes, Honors, and Visits of Courtesy"?
2. What other Army publication is a good source of information regarding Military Customs and Courtesies?
3. What are "customs"?
4. What is meant by "Military Courtesy"?
5. What is considered to be the most important of all military courtesies?
6. What is the origin of the hand salute?
7. What is the proper procedure for reporting indoors?
8. When is the only time individuals in formation are required to salute?
9. What is the proper procedure for a leader of a squad or larger element to

salute?
10. What should you do when passing uncased National Colors?
11. What is the primary purpose of ceremonies?
12. What are the two primary characteristics of a parade?
13. What two bugle calls are normally heard at "Retreat"?
14. How long is the call "To the Colors"?
15. What may be substituted for "To the Colors" during a Retreat ceremony?
16. What is the name of our National Anthem?
17. How long is "Reveille"?
18. How does the raising of the US flag differ from the lowering of the flag?
19. A flag detail passes you carrying the US flag, folded in the shape of a "cocked hat". What should be your actions.
20. The US Army flag is dipped in salute for what individuals?
21. A Color Guard consists of how many soldiers?
22. When walking outdoors, where should the junior ranking soldier always walk in relation to a senior?
23. What is the customary order (by rank) for soldiers to enter and exit a vehicle or small boat?
24. What is the 50-gun (cannon) salute called and when is it used?
25. The national salute and the salute to the flag are both _____ guns each.
26. On what holiday is the National Flag displayed at half staff from reveille until noon?
27. Give the number of cannon salutes on arrival and departure for the following individuals: President, Ex-President, Vice-President, Secretary of Defense, Secretary of the Army, Chairman (JCS), Army Chief of Staff, Generals, LTG, MG, BG.
28. What should be done when an officer enters a dining facility?
29. How is the flag placed at half-staff?
30. What is the proper procedure for lowering a flag from half-staff?
31. When would the US Flag be flown upside down?
32. What bugle call is traditionally played at military funerals?
33. A ceremonial firing party consists of how many men?
34. Who is traditionally responsible for the care of the unit colors?
35. What is the name of the Official Army Song? When was it written and by whom?
36. Is it necessary to stand at attention when the Army Song is played?

MILITARY PROGRAMS

ANSWERS PAGE A:35.26

1. What is the Army QOLP?
2. The Community Life System, a major component of the QOLP, consists of 6 sub-systems. What are they?
3. What does "ACS" stand for?
4. What is the mission of ACS?
5. List the ~~seven~~ eight essential services of ACS.
6. What does "ACES" stand for?
7. What is the primary purpose of ACES?
8. List some of the basic services provided by the Army Continuing Education Center.
9. Explain the BSEP program.
10. Explain the ASEP program.
11. Which of the ACES programs take precedence over all others?
12. Explain the purpose of ESL.
13. Tuition Assistance is a grant that pays how much of tuition?
14. What is the requirement for the use of tuition assistance?

PRE-BOARD REVIEW
QUESTIONS

15. What is the AER?
16. What is the basic guideline for emergency financial assistance?
17. What are some of the categories of authorized emergency financial assistance?
18. What are ~~the five~~ some of the primary services of the ARC?
19. What is the primary drug of abuse in the military?
20. What does "ADAPCP" stand for? "ADAPT"? "STOP"?
21. What publication defines Army policy on alcohol and other drug abuse as well as defining responsibilities for implementation of the program?
22. What are the seven functional areas of the ADAPCP?
23. The current focus of the ADAPCP places major emphasis on what?
24. What identification tool does the Commander have to detect drug abuse?
25. Describe the urine specimen policy.
26. What is DA's policy on alcohol?
27. What does the acronym "CCC" stand for?
28. What are the five methods of ADA identification?
29. What is the most desirable method of discovering alcohol or drug abuse?
30. Describe the three tracks or levels of the ADAPCP.
31. What is one of the most critical and difficult aspects of the rehabilitation process?
32. What is a UADC and what is his/her function?
33. What AR covers Safety?
34. The word "Safety" is often associated with what terminology?
35. What are the goals of the Army Safety Program?
36. What Army publication covers the Army Equal Opportunity Program?
37. What is "equal opportunity"?
38. What is the Army's written policy on EO?
39. Who is the EO officer and NCO for your company?
40. What is the primary channel for correcting discriminatory practices?
41. What are the two components of the EO program?
42. What regulation covers the Total Army Sponsorship Program?
43. Explain the sponsorship program in your unit.
44. As a minimum, how many welcome letters should a new arrival receive?
45. Sponsors should be appointed within ________ calendar days after battalion or higher activity receives the DA Form 5434.
46. What is a "reactionary" sponsor?
47. What are the general rules for appointing a sponsor?
48. What regulation covers reenlistment?
49. What are the basic eligibility requirements for reenlistment?
50. What is the maximum number of years that a soldier may reenlist for?
51. How many months out can a soldier reenlist?
52. Soldiers are no longer authorized to extend or reenlist if they are within ______ months of their scheduled ETS (without an exception to policy approved by HQDA).
53. What does "NCODP" stand for?
54. What Army regulation covers NCODP?
55. What does "BOSS" stand for?
56. What does "ACAP" stand for and what is its purpose?

PRE-BOARD REVIEW
ANSWERS

ANSWERS INDEX

PRE-BOARD REVIEW
ANSWERS

CODE OF CONDUCT

QUESTIONS PAGE Q:35.3

1. AR 350-30.
2. President Dwight D. Eisenhower.
3. It is a set of rules that outline the basic responsibilities and obligations of all members of the Armed Forces of the United States during times of conflict. It is designed to give the U.S. Soldier strength and guidance should they fall into the hands of the enemy.
4. (1) I am an American, fighting in the forces which guard my country and our way of life. I am prepared to give my life in their defense.
   (2) I will never surrender of my own free will. If in command, I will never surrender the members of my command while they still have the means to resist.
   (3) If I am captured, I will continue to resist by all means available. I will make every effort to escape and aid others to escape. I will accept neither parole nor special favors from the enemy.
   (4) If I become a prisoner of war, I will keep faith with my fellow prisoners. I will give no information or take part in any action which might be harmful to my comrades. If I am senior, I will take command. If not, I will obey the lawful orders of those appointed over me and will back them up in every way.
   (5) When questioned, should I become a prisoner of war, I am required to give only my name, rank, service number and date of birth. I will evade answering further questions to the utmost of my ability. I will make no oral or written statement disloyal to my country and its allies or harmful to their cause.
   (6) I will never forget that I am an American, fighting for freedom, responsible for my actions, and dedicated to the principles which made my country free. I will trust in my God and in the United States of America.
5. Search, segregate, silence, speed, and safeguard.
6. Officers, NCOs, enlisted personnel, civilians and females.

GUARD DUTY

QUESTIONS PAGE Q:35.3

1. FM 22-6
2. Interior guard and exterior guard.
3. General orders and special orders.
4. Number 1: I will guard everything within the limits of my post and quit my post only when properly relieved.
   Number 2: I will obey my special orders and perform all my duties in a military manner.
   Number 3: I will report violations of my special orders, emergencies, and anything not covered in my instructions to the Commander of the Relief.
5. The combination of a secret challenge and its reply, or password.
6. Any process carried out by one unit or person with the objective of ascertaining the friendly or hostile character or identity of another. It is the first part of the countersign and requires an appropriate reply.
7. In a low tone to prevent them from being overheard by others.
8. A secret word imparted only to those persons entitled to inspect the guard and to commanders and members of the guard.
9. (1) Guards must have completed range firing (qualification or familiarization) or training with the weapon they use on guard duty.
   (2) Guards must know the three general orders.

PRE-BOARD REVIEW
ANSWERS

PHYSICAL SECURITY — QUESTIONS PAGE Q:35.3

1. FM 19-30; AR 190-13.
2. To identify, reduce, eliminate, or neutralize conditions favorable to criminal activity; or, in other words, to make access so difficult that an intruder will hesitate to attempt penetration, or to provide for his apprehension should he be successful.
3. Physical systems or devices used to protect security interests.
4. Acts or conditions that may result in the compromise of information; loss of life; damage, loss, or destruction of property; or disruption of the mission of the installation or facility.
5. (1) Natural threats: floods, storms, earthquakes, winds, snow and ice, fires, fog.
   (2) Human threats: pilferage, sabotage, espionage, attacks on key persons, carelessness, human intelligence (HUMINT) threat.
6. Natural threats.
7. The DD Form 2A (Military ID Card).
8. At least two authorized persons, each capable of detecting incorrect or unauthorized procedures with respect to the task being performed and who are familiar with applicable safety and security requirements, will be present during any operation that affords access to sensitive weapons. It is designed to prohibit access to sensitive weapons by a lone individual.
9. Restricted Area, Controlled Area, Limited Area, and Exclusion Area.
10. Confidential......DA Label 22.....Blue
    Secret............DA Label 23.....Red
    Top Secret........DA Label 24.....Yellow
11. Unclassified.
12. Chain-link, barbed wire, barbed tape, and concertina.
13. Joint Service Interior Intrusion Detection System.
14. The lock.
15. "US Government - DO NOT REPRODUCE".
16. It is the Personal Property Record, commonly referred to as the "high value item sheets" or "high dollar item sheets" and is a list by name, brand/model, serial number, and value of all personal property in excess of $50.00 in value.

FIRST AID — QUESTIONS PAGE Q:35.4

1. FM 21-11.
2. The emergency care given to the sick or injured before medical treatment can be administered by medical personnel.
3. Properly evaluate the casualty as to the nature and extent of the injuries.
4. (1) Check the casualty for responsiveness.
   (2) Check for breathing.
   (3) Check for pulse.
   (4) Check for bleeding.
   (5) Check for shock.
   (6) Check for fractures.
   (7) Check for burns.
   (8) Check for possible head injury.
5. Respiration and blood circulation.
6. (1) Open the airway and restore breathing.
   (2) Stop the bleeding and protect the wound.
   (3) Check and treat for shock.

PRE-BOARD REVIEW
ANSWERS

7. The jaw thrust or head tilt/chin lift methods.
8. Mouth-to-mouth and mouth-to-nose resuscitation; mouth-to-mouth.
9. (1) Open the airway.
(2) Take a deep breath and place your mouth (in an airtight seal) around the casualty's mouth.
(3) Blow two full breaths into the casualty's mouth. Watch the casualty's chest out of the corner of your eye to determine if sufficient air is getting to the casualty's lungs.
(4) After giving two breaths which cause the chest to rise, attempt to locate a pulse on the casualty. Allow 5 to 10 seconds to determine if there is a pulse. If no pulse, immediately seek medical attention. If pulse is found, continue rescue breathing at the rate of one breath every five seconds (approximately 12 breaths per minute).
10. Field dressing, manual pressure, elevation, pressure dressing, and tourniquet.
11. Mark the casualty's head with a "T" to indicate that a tourniquet has been applied. If necessary, use the casualty's blood to make this mark.
12. (1) Move the casualty to cover, if cover is available and the situation permits.
(2) Position the casualty on their back.
(3) Elevate the casualty's feet higher than the level of their heart.
(4) Loosen constricting clothing (at the neck, waist, boots, or wherever it may be binding).
(5) Prevent chilling or overheating.
(6) Calm the casualty.
(7) Seek medical aid.
13. Flush with large amounts of water for 5 to 20 minutes (5-10 minutes for acids; 20 minutes for alkalis), or as long as necessary to flush out the chemical. Apply a bandage over the eyes and evacuate.
14. When the casualty exhales, seal the wound and make it airtight by covering it with plastic, cellophane, foil, the casualty's poncho, or similar material (the inside of the field dressing packet or an MRE packet will work). Secure in place with a pressure dressing. Apply manual pressure for 5 to 10 minutes to help control the bleeding.
15. - Position casualty's knees in an upright (flexed) position.
- Remove the casualty's clothing to expose the wound but do not attempt to remove clothing that is stuck to the wound.
- Apply a field dressing to the wound and loosely secure with a nonslip knot at the casualty's side. The dressing should be tied firmly enough to prevent slipping without applying pressure to the wound site.
16. A break in the bone.
17. (1) Closed fracture: a broken bone that does not break the overlying skin.
(2) Open fracture: A break in the bone with a corresponding break in the overlying skin. The bone may protrude through the skin or, as in the case of an open fracture produced by a missile, a bullet or shell fragment may go through the flesh and break the bone.
18. *Immobilize the joints above and below any fracture.*
19. Check the circulation below the sight of the injury.
20. Heat cramps, heat exhaustion, and heatstroke (sunstroke).
21. Chilblain, immersion syndrome (immersion foot/trench foot), frostbite, snow blindness, dehydration, and hypothermia.
22. - unexplained runny nose
- unexplained sudden headache
- sudden drooling
- difficulty seeing (blurred vision)
- tightness in chest or difficulty in breathing
- localized sweating and twitching (as a result of small amount of nerve agent on skin)

- stomach cramps
- nausea

23. - strange or confused behavior
- wheezing, difficulty in breathing, and coughing
- severely pinpointed pupils
- red eyes with tearing (if agent gets into the eyes)
- vomiting
- severe muscular twitching and general weakness
- loss of bladder/bowel control
- convulsions
- unconsciousness
- stoppage of breathing

24. One atropine autoinjector and one pralidoxime chloride (2 PAM CL) autoinjector.
25. Normally the outer thigh muscle. It is important that the injections be given into a large muscle area. If the individual is thinly built, then the injections must be administered into the upper outer quarter (quadrant) of the buttocks.
26. At least 10 seconds.
27. Three.
28. (1) Strength and endurance of the bearer(s).
(2) Weight of the casualty.
(3) Nature of the casualty's injuries.
(4) Obstacles encountered during transport.
29. - fireman's carry
- support carry
- arms carry
- saddleback carry
- pack-strap carry
- pistol-belt carry
- pistol-belt drag
- neck drag
- cradle drop drag
30. - two-man support carry
- two-man arms carry
- two-man fore-and-aft carry
- two-hand seat carry
- four-hand seat carry

FIELD SANITATION

QUESTIONS PAGE Q:35.4

1. FM 21-10.
2. The self-employment of practices which will keep one healthy.
3. The effective use of measures which will create and maintain healthful environmental conditions.
4. Includes the practice of both environmental sanitation and personal hygiene, particularly within the framework of situations and experiences associated with Army life.
5. Those illnesses that can be transmitted from man to man, from animal to man, and from insect to man. They are often called "contagious" or "infectious" diseases.
6. Respiratory, intestinal, insect-borne, venereal, and miscellaneous.
7. Respiratory infections.
8. Reservoir (source) --> vehicle (means of transmission) --> susceptible person.
9. Control the source, stop the transmission, and protect the susceptible person.
10. Feces, flies, fingers, food, and fluids.
11. Water that is safely drinkable.
12. Iodine tablets, chlorine (calcium hypochlorite) ampules, tincture of iodine, household/common bleach, or boiling; Iodine tablets for individual canteens of water; calcium hypochlorite (chlorine) for disinfecting large

quantities of water such as a Lyster bags or water buffalos.
13. Steel-gray.
14. 4; (1) Scrap can: for food waste.
(2) Wash can: hot soapy water (120-150 degrees F) for scrubbing mess kit; use long handle brush.
(3) Rinse: clear boiling water.
(4) Disinfect: clear boiling water - immerse mess kit for at least 10 seconds, shake off excess water and allow to air dry.
Each hot water setup of four cans will support 80 personnel.
15. Garbage, rubbish, liquid kitchen or bathing waste, and human waste.
16. A field expedient human waste hole used primarily when on the move. It is dug approximately 12 inches wide, 6-12 inches deep and covered up when finished.
17. At least 100 yards from food operations - downwind and on down slope if possible; and at least 100 feet down slope of any unit ground water sources.
18. The length of stay, the water level, and the soil conditions.
19. (1) Protection from food preparation areas and water sources.
(2) Accessibility to the users.
20. When filled to within 1 foot of the ground surface.
21. (1) Spray with residual insecticide.
(2) Pack dirt in successive 3-inch layers until mounded 1 foot above ground level. Spray again with residual insecticide.
(3) Post a sign with the date and the words "closed latrine" or "closed garbage pit" (except in combat).
22. Malaria, yellow fever, dengue fever, encephalitis (sleeping sickness), and filariasis (elephantiasis).
23. Screens, residual sprays such as Malathion, insecticides such as pyrethrum, individual issue insect repellents such as DEET, and in some cases, chemoprophylactic medication.
24. Cholera, typhoid fever, and dysentery.
25. Plague and salmonella.
26. Because one careless member of the team can cause disease that may incapacitate the entire unit.

MAP READING

QUESTIONS PAGE Q:35.5

1. FM 21-26.
2. A map is a graphic representation of a portion of the earth's surface drawn to scale, as seen from above.
3. Scale and Type.
4. The scale is expressed as a fraction and gives the ratio of map distance to ground distance.
5. Small scale --------- 1:1,000,000 and smaller
Medium scale -------- 1:75,000 to 1:1,000,000
Large scale --------- 1:75,000 and larger
6. 1:1,000,000; it is used for general planning and for strategical studies.
7. 1:250,000; it is used for planning operations, including the movement and concentration of troops and supplies.
8. 1:50,000; it is used to meet the tactical, administrative, and logistical needs of field units.
9. TOPOGRAPHIC, planimetric, photomap, Joint Operations Graphics (JOG), photomosaic, terrain model, military city, and special.
10. A map is named after the most prominent cultural or geographical feature.
11. Black - indicates cultural (man-made) features, ~~such as buildings and roads~~ other than roads.
Blue - identifies hydrography or water features such as lakes, swamps,

rivers, and drainage.

Brown - identifies all relief features and elevation, such as contours on older edition maps, and cultivated land on red-light readable maps.

Green - identifies vegetation with military significance, such as woods, orchards, and vineyards.

Red - classifies cultural features, such as populated areas, main roads, and boundaries, on older maps.

Red-Brown - the colors red and brown are combined to identify cultural features, all relief features, non-surveyed spot elevations, and elevation such as contour lines on red-light readable maps.

12. A network of squares formed by north-south, east-west lines on a military map.
13. 1,000 meters (1 km).
14. Read RIGHT and UP.
15. 6; 8.
16. Primary Scale and Extension Scale.
17. A horizontal angle measured in a clockwise manner from a north base line.
18. Degree (360 deg in circle); Mil (6400 mils in circle); Grad (400 grads in circle).
19. True North - a line from any point on the earth's surface to the north pole. True north is usually represented by a line with a star at the apex.

Magnetic North - the direction to the north magnetic pole, as indicated by the north-seeking needle of a magnetic instrument. Magnetic north is usually symbolized by a line ending with a half-arrowhead.

Grid North - the north that is established by using the vertical grid lines on the map. Grid north is symbolized by the letters "GN" or the letter "y" at the apex.

20. A back azimuth is the opposite direction of an azimuth. To obtain a back azimuth from an azimuth: if the azimuth is less than 180 deg - add 180 deg; if more than 180 deg - subtract 180 deg.
21. 200 degrees.
22. It is located in the lower central portion of the margin and shows the angular relationship between true north, grid north, and magnetic north.
23. It is used for converting from grid north to magnetic north and vice-versa; it is found in the declination diagram.
24. Intersection is the location of an unknown point by successively occupying at least two (preferably three) known positions on the ground and then map sighting on the unknown locations.
25. Resection is the method of locating one's position on a map by determining the grid azimuth to at least two well-defined locations that can be pinpointed on the map. For greater accuracy, the desired method of resection would be to use three well-defined locations.
26. Lensatic, artillery, wrist/pocket, and protractor.
27. Cover, base, and lens.
28. Black - mils; red - degrees.
29. 120; 3; for use at night (if you need to make a 30 degree turn, rotate the bezel ring 10 "clicks" in the desired direction).
30. Centerhold and Compass-to-cheek.
31. Shadow-Tip method, Watch method, and Star method.
32. The vertical distance above or below the datum plane.
33. The representation of the shapes of hills, valleys, streams, or landforms on the earth's surface.
34. Layer tinting, form lines, shaded relief, hachures, and contour lines.
35. Contour lines.
36. Imaginary straight lines on the ground that connect points of equal elevation.
37. Index, intermediate, and supplementary.
38. Hill, ridge, valley, saddle, depression.

PRE-BOARD REVIEW
ANSWERS

39. Draw, spur, and cliff.
40. Cuts and fills.
41. By aligning the features on the map with the same features on the ground (terrain association).
42. Blue or Black------------- friendly forces
    Red----------------------- enemy forces
    Green--------------------- engineering obstacles both friendly and enemy
    Yellow-------------------- contaminated areas both friendly and enemy
43. Red, green, blue, brown, black, red-brown, and yellow (note that the colors may represent different things - topographic or symbolic).
44. Statute miles, nautical miles, yards, and meters.

| M16A1/A2 AND MARKSMANSHIP |

QUESTIONS PAGE Q:35.6

1. FM 23-9
2. It is a 5.56-mm, magazine-fed, gas-operated, shoulder-fired weapon capable of firing in either the semiautomatic or automatic modes through the use of a selector lever (SAFE, SEMI, and AUTO).
3. It is a 5.56-mm, magazine-fed, gas-operated, shoulder-fired weapon capable of firing in either the automatic three-round burst or semiautomatic single-shot modes (SAFE, SEMI, and BURST).
4.

	M16A1	M16A2
20-round mag..................	7.6 lbs	8.5 lbs
30-round mag..................	7.9 lbs	8.8 lbs

5. Approx 1 pound (15 oz).
6. 39 inches
7. 39(5/8) inches
8. Ball, tracer, blank, dummy, and plastic.
9. 210 rounds (one mag in weapon and six in ammo pouches).
10. semiautomatic..........45-65 rpm.................45 rpm
    automatic..............150-200 rpm...............90 rpm (3-rnd burst)
    sustained..............12-15 rpm.................same
11. M16A1 - 2,653 meters; M16A2 - 3,600 meters.

NOTE: Some references give maximum range of M16A2 as 3,534 meters. In this instance the maximum range has been rounded off. In all instances, the maximum range would depend on a variety of factors and is never absolute.

12. M16A1 - 460 meters; M16A2 - 550 meters (point target), 800 meters (area target).
13. The M16A2 is 5/8" longer; the A1 has a flash suppressor - the A2 a compensator; the barrel on the A2 has a larger outside diameter; A2 handguards are interchangeable; A2 has brass deflector molded into receiver; sight system is different; A2 fires on 3-round burst; A2 is more accurate at longer distances and recommended ammunition is different.
14. Helps keep the muzzle down during firing.
15. Feeding, chambering, locking, firing, unlocking, extracting, ejecting, and cocking.
16. The failure to complete the cycle of functioning of a weapon.
17. The unhesitating application of a probable remedy to reduce a stoppage without investigating the cause.
18. SPORTS;
    (S)lap upward on the magazine;
    (P)ull the charging handle to the rear;
    (O)bserve the chamber;
    (R)elease the charging handle;
    (T)ap the forward assist;
    (S)hoot.

PRE-BOARD REVIEW
ANSWERS

19. Only once, if the rifle still fails to fire, inspect it to determine the cause of the stoppage or malfunction and take appropriate remedial action.
20. The continuing effort, through inspection, to return a weapon to operation.
21. A procedural or mechanical failure of the rifle, magazine, or ammunition.
22. (1) Failure to feed, chamber, or lock.
    (2) Failure to fire cartridge.
    (3) Failure to extract and eject.
23. Steady position, Aiming, Breath Control, and Trigger Squeeze.
24. Individual supported and prone unsupported.
25. For engaging moving targets and for engaging targets in limited visibility; for normal firing situations, zeroing, and with the elevation knob for target distances up to 800 meters.
26. Adjust the front sight post up or down until the base of the sight post is flush with the sight post well. Turn the rear windage knob until the index mark on the 0-2 sight is aligned with the rear sight base index. Turn the elevation knob all the way down and then up, one click past the 8/3 mark (8/3 + 1).
27. Adjust the front sight post up or down until the base of the sight post is flush with the sight post well. Then adjust the front sight post 11 clicks in the "UP" direction (marked on weapon). This moves the post down into the well 11 clicks. Turn the rear windage drum until the rear sights are all the way to the left side. Then turn the windage drum back (right) 17 clicks so the rear sight is approximately centered.
28. The "L" sight ("L"ong range).
29. Using 18 rounds or less, fire five out of six rounds in two consecutive shot groups within a 4-cm circle (STP 21-1-SMCT, P. 167).
30. Expert........36 - 40
    Sharpshooter..30 - 35
    Marksman......23 - 29
    Unqualified...22 - below
31. Expert........38 - 40
    Sharpshooter..33 - 37
    Marksman......26 - 32
    Unqualified...25 - below
32. 14
33. No, they are different.
34. Clear, disassemble, Inspect, Clean & lubricate, Assemble.
35. Cleaner, Lubricant, and Preservative.
36. (1) Place the selector lever on SAFE. If the selector lever will not go on SAFE, pull the charging handle to the rear and release. Place the selector lever on SAFE. Pull the trigger to the rear. The hammer should not fall.

    (2) Place the selector lever on SEMI. Pull the trigger to the rear and hold. The hammer should fall. While holding the trigger to the rear, pull the charging handle to the rear and release. Release the trigger and pull it to the rear again. The hammer should fall.

    (3) Place the selector lever on BURST. Pull the charging handle to the rear and release. Pull the trigger to the rear and hold. The hammer should fall. While holding the trigger to the rear, pull the charging handle to the rear three times and release. Release the trigger and pull it to the rear again. The hammer should fall.
37. CLEAR IT!

PRE-BOARD REVIEW
ANSWERS

NBC — QUESTIONS PAGE Q:35.7

1. Nuclear, Biological, and Chemical.
2. FM 3-3....Chemical and Biological Contamination Avoidance
   FM 3-3-1..Nuclear Contamination Avoidance
   FM 3-4....NBC Protection
   FM 3-5....NBC Decontamination
   FM 3-7....NBC Handbook
   FM 3-100..NBC Operations
3. AR 350-41
4. Contamination avoidance, protection, and decontamination.
5. Immediate and residual.
6. Individual and collective protection.
7. Biological....No use.
   Chemical......No first use.
   Nuclear.......Last resort (will use first only if necessary).
8. Solids, liquids, and gases.
9. Transfer, spread, vapor, desorption, and radiation.
10. Adjacent signs should be within sight of each other - normally 25-100 meters apart depending on terrain.
11. The length of time that a hazard remains.
12. (1) Type of contamination.
    (2) Concentration and droplet size.
    (3) Temperature.
    (4) Wind speed.
    (5) Sunlight.
    (6) Humidity and rain.
    (7) Composition of the contaminated surface.
    (8) Type of soil and terrain.
13. Chemical: Red letters "GAS" on a yellow background.
    Biological: Red letters "BIO" on a blue background.
    Radiological: Black letters "ATOM" on a white background.
14. Type of agent (if known), date and time of detection.
15. Six;
    NBC 1 - Observers' Initial Report.
    NBC 2 - Evaluated Data Report.
    NBC 3 - Warning of Predicted Contamination Report.
    NBC 4 - Monitoring and Survey Report.
    NBC 5 - Actual Contaminated Areas Report.
    NBC 6 - Detailed Information on Chemical/Biological Attack Report.

NOTE: Only the first five NBC reports are used in support of radiological defense.

16. (1) Speed: decontaminate as soon as possible.
    (2) Need: decontaminate only what is necessary to continue the mission.
    (3) Limit: decontaminate as far forward as possible (limit spread).
    (4) Priority: decontaminate the most important things first and the least important things last.
17. Decontaminate as soon as possible.
18. (1) Immediate - purpose is to minimize casualties, save lives, and limit the spread of contamination. Carried out by individuals immediately after becoming contaminated.
    (2) Operational - purpose is to sustain operations, reduce the contact hazard and limit the spread of contamination to eliminate the necessity or reduce the duration of wearing MOPP gear.
    (3) Thorough - purpose is to reduce or eliminate the need for individual protective clothing.

PRE-BOARD REVIEW
ANSWERS

19. IMMEDIATE
    (1) Skin Decon
    (2) Personal Wipedown
    (3) Operator's Spraydown
  OPERATIONAL
    (4) MOPP Gear Exchange
    (5) Vehicle Washdown
  THOROUGH
    (6) Detailed Equipment/Aircraft Decon (DED/DAD)
    (7) Detailed Troop Decon (DTD)

20. Nose, eyes, mouth, and skin.

21. Mission Oriented Protective Posture; a flexible system of protection against chemical and biological agents.

22. Battledress Overgarment (BDO). It is a two-piece suit in a camouflage pattern. The material consists of an outer layer of nylon-cotton and an inner layer of charcoal-impregnated polyurethane foam. It comes sealed in a vapor-barrier bag that protects against rain, moisture, and sunlight. The BDO protects the wearer against contact with chemical agent vapors, aerosols, and droplets of liquids; live biological agents; toxins; and radioactive alpha and beta particles. The BDO is water repellent and should be worn as an outer garment. The BDO is not designed to be decontaminated or reimpregnated for reuse and should, therefore, be discarded when unserviceable or contaminated.

23. 14 days, so long as it remains serviceable and uncontaminated.

24. About ~~6 hours~~ 24 hours.

25. About 6 hours.

26. 8 minutes.

27. Field concentrations of all known chemical and biological agents in vapor or aerosol form.

28. Ammonia vapors or carbon monoxide.

29. **M17-series**: 9 seconds, plus an additional 6 seconds for the hood; total time - 15 seconds (mask must be cleared and sealed within first 9 seconds).
  M24-series: 10 seconds to remove the flight helmet and 9 seconds to put on, clear and seal the mask for a total of 19 seconds.
  M25-series: 6 seconds to remove the CVC helmet, 9 seconds to put on, clear and seal the mask, plus an additional 6 seconds for the hood. Total = 21 seconds.
  M40-series: 9 seconds to put on, clear and seal the mask. This is the only portion that is timed. The hood should then be "donned so that it lies smoothly on the head."
  M42-series: 6 seconds to remove the CVC helmet plus 9 seconds to put on, clear and seal the mask, for a total of 15 seconds. Donning of the hood is not timed.
NOTE: For aviators using the M42-series protective mask, 10 seconds should be allowed for the removal of the flight helmet instead of 6. Total time should then be 19 seconds, as with the M24.

30. Snap the mask carrier closed.

31. The shoulder carry, the hip leg carry, and the pistol belt carry.

32. Five;
    MOPP 0 - Mask carried; MOPP gear readily available.
    MOPP 1 - Protective overgarment worn.
    MOPP 2 - Add protective overboots.
    MOPP 3 - Add mask/hood.
    MOPP 4 - Add protective gloves.

33. One quart or more.

34. Use tape showing the soldier's name and rank placed on the protective mask carrier and overgarment pocket.

35. MOPP Gear Exchange.

36. Buddy team, triple buddy, and individual.

PRE-BOARD REVIEW
ANSWERS

NOTE: MOPP gear exchange can be described for the Battle Dress Overgarment (BDO) and the Chemical Protective Undergarment (CPU). The procedures are roughly the same and only the BDO will be discussed here.

37. This method is used by soldiers equipped with the tankers or aviators masks. A third soldier is needed to hold the filter canister and hose to prevent the transference of contamination to the soldier undergoing the procedure.

38. Only in extreme emergencies, when no one can assist, since there is a high risk of transferring contamination from the overgarment to skin or undergarments.

39. Pair into "buddy teams". Perform Step 1 simultaneously or in succession. Perform Steps 2-7 before alternating;

(1) Decon gear;
(2) Prepare for decon;
(3) Decon hood;
(4) Remove overgarment/overshoes;
(5) Remove gloves;
(6) Put on new overgarment;
(7) Put on new overboots and gloves;
(8) Secure hood;
(9) Secure gear.

40. 45 minutes.

41. Thermal radiation, nuclear radiation, blast, and EMP.

42. The blast (accounts for approximately 50% of the burst energy).

43. Heat and light.

44. Initial radiation (approx 4% of the burst energy)
Residual radiation (approx 10% of the burst energy)

45. Electromagnetic Pulse - represents approximately 1% of the total energy produced by a nuclear burst and can destroy or cause serious damage to electronic equipment through current surges.

46. Transient Radiation Effects on Electronics - has similar effects to EMP, except that TREE is caused by gamma and neutron (initial) radiation. Gamma radiation causes temporary ionization of electronic components, which can lead to permanent damage to other components. Fast neutrons can also cause permanent damage by emplacing (or dislodging) atoms in crystals.

47. Air, surface, and subsurface.

48. Notification of a friendly nuclear strike.

49. A flash of intense light (brighter than the sun) and heat; enormous explosion, high winds, and mushroom-shaped cloud.

50. (1) Immediately drop to the ground facedown, with head toward blast if possible. A log, large rock, or any depression in the earth's surface provides some protection.

(2) Close eyes.

(3) Protect exposed skin from heat and debris by putting hands and arms under or near the body and keeping the helmet on.

(4) Remain facedown until both the initial and return blast waves have passed and debris stops falling.

(5) Stay calm, check for injury, check weapons and equipment for damage, and prepare to continue the mission.

51. Assess the situation, put out fires before they can spread, assist casualties, secure and organize equipment/check weapons systems, improve or reinforce fighting positions/shelters, and prepare for possible fallout.

52. IM-93/UD Dosimeter - it is a tubular device, about the size of a fountain pen, which allows the user to read the accumulated gamma total dose simply by looking through the lens while pointing the instrument toward the sun or another bright-light source.

IM-174B/PD Radiacmeter - standard ion-chamber gamma survey meter.

AN/PDR-27 Radiac Set - contains a low-range dose-rate Geiger-Mueller type instrument and is used for measuring food, personnel, and equipment.

AN/VDR-2 - used to locate and measure radioactivity in the form of gamma rays and beta particles. It displays dose rates and total accumulated dose resulting from fallout.

DT 236 - a "watch-like" device worn on the wrist and issued to soldiers. It is designed to measure the accumulated neutron and gamma dose rate.

CP696/PDR75 - computer indicator and radiacmeter used to "read" the accumulated dose rate from DT236 dosimeters.

53. Periodic and continuous.
54. Direct and indirect.
55. Aerial and ground.
56. 1 or more cGyph at a height of 1 meter.
57. ~~Germs~~ Pathogens and toxins.
58. Either directly by aerosol (artillery or aircraft spray) or indirectly through vectors.
59. Physical barriers (skin), natural immunity, and acquired immunity (chemoprophylaxis).
60. Up-to-date immunizations, good field sanitation and personal hygiene, a properly fitted and readily available protective mask, and good physical condition.
61. (1) Artillery shells with less powerful explosions than HE rounds.
    (2) Aerial bombs that pop rather than explode.
    (3) Mist or fog sprayed from low flying aircraft.
    (4) Ground generators spraying a fog or mist.
62. Hot, soapy water. An alternate decontaminant is a 0.5% sodium hypochlorite (household bleach) solution. (DS2 or STB are also effective against most known biological contamination, but because of their caustic nature are not preferred).
63. Persistent, nonpersistent, and dusty.
64. Nerve, blood, blister, choking, psychochemical and irritants.
65. Mines, artillery, rockets, bombs, aircraft spray, and covert/sabotage.
66. Notification of a friendly chemical strike.
67. Chemical Downwind Message; issued every six hours and is valid for three consecutive two-hour periods.
68. M258A1 - Individual Decontamination Kit; comes in a hard plastic case containing three sets of foil-packaged decontaminating wipes (each set containing one Decon 1 and one Decon 2 wipe packet). The Decon wipe 1 works better against G-type nerve agents but can burn skin. Decon wipe 2 works better against VX-type nerve agents and blister agents. It is not as caustic to skin and helps to neutralize some of the caustic compounds in wipe 1. Each soldier carries a kit in his or her mask carrier (unless an M291 has been issued).

M291 - Individual Decontamination Kit; designed as a replacement for the M258A1. The M258A1 IDK will be used until depleted or expired. Soldiers issued M291 IDKs should store them in the right cargo pocket of the BDU trousers or BDO trousers. Basis of issue is two M291s (12 packages) per soldier.

ABC-M11 - Portable Decontaminating Apparatus; a steel container with an aluminum spray-head assembly and a nitrogen-gas cylinder that provides pressure. It resembles a fire extinguisher (but should **never** be used as one) and is filled with 1(1/3) quarts of DS2, which is sufficient for covering 135 square feet. It is used primarily for decontaminating small areas, such as the steering wheel or other equipment that soldiers must touch. Effective spray range is 6-8 feet.

M13 - Portable Decontaminating Apparatus; about the size of a 5-gallon gas can, it comes prefilled with 14 liters of DS2 decon agent. Decon capability is 1,200 square feet and is normally used to decontaminate vehicles and crew-served weapons larger than .50 caliber.

PRE-BOARD REVIEW
ANSWERS

M12A1 - Power Driven Decontaminating Apparatus (PDDA); a 500-gal tank and pump unit (TPU) used to mix and spray decontaminating agent slurries and solutions, and hot, soapy water rinses during field decon operations. Also may be used for showering personnel in the field.

M17 - Lightweight Decon System (LDS); portable pump and water heating unit for producing hot water and steam. The system incorporates a 1,580-gal collapsible water tank, two wand assemblies, connecting hoses, and a shower rail. Also used during vehicle operational and thorough decon operations.

69. ABC-M8 VGH Chemical Agent Detector Paper - consists of a book of 25 sheets of perforated, chemically treated, dye impregnated paper that turns either dark green, yellow or red upon contact with liquid VGH agents.

M9 Chemical Agent Detector Paper - consists of a 7-oz dispenser containing a 30-foot roll of 2" wide detector paper and a resealable plastic storage bag. It has an adhesive backing for attaching to equipment and clothing and it is used to detect the presence of liquid chemical agents. The paper indicates the presence of liquid V, G, H, and L agents by turning a red or reddish color.

M256/M256A1 Chemical Agent Detector Kit - provides a squad-level ability to identify field concentrations of nerve-, blister-, and blood-agent vapors. It consists of 12 individually packaged samplers/detectors, a set of instruction cards, and a packet of ABC-M8 VGH chemical agent detector papers. A new improved kit is capable of detecting T2 mycotoxin.

M8 Automatic Chemical Agent Alarm (ACAA) - portable, electrochemical, point-sampling chemical agent alarm that can either be hand-carried, backpacked, or vehicle mounted. It consists of the M43 detector unit and the M42 alarm unit. It detects low concentrations of toxic nerve, blood, and choking agent vapors or inhalable aerosols and automatically signals the presence of agent in the air.

Remote Sensing Chemical Agent Alarm (RSCAAL), XM21 - a passive infrared spectroradiometer that uses an onboard microprocessor to detect and identify agent clouds. It operates by viewing a background scene (sky, terrain, buildings, etc) and the airpath along its line of sight. A properly emplaced XM21 will detect significant G, HD, and L munitions events and resulting clouds at ranges of 5 km with a greater than 85% probability of detection.

Chemical Agent Monitor (CAM) - a portable, point-sampling vapor monitor used to search out "clean" areas, to search and locate contamination on personnel, equipment, buildings and terrain, structures, aircraft and land vehicles, and to monitor the effectiveness of decontamination. It responds to nerve and blister agent vapors down to the lowest concentrations that could affect personnel over short periods.

M272 Water Testing Kit, Chemical Agents - a lightweight, portable kit that will detect and identify harmful amounts of chemical warfare agents when present in raw and treated water. The kit will detect cyanide, mustard, lewisite, and nerve agents.

FOX, XM93, NBC Reconnaissance System (NBCRS) - six-wheel, amphibious armored cargo and tactical transport vehicle powered by a 320 hp V8 diesel engine. Its maximum speed is 65 mph with a cruising range of 500 miles. It weighs 18.7 tons combat loaded and 16.9 tons without the crew and ammunition. It is equipped with a collective protection system which keeps the crew's working area free from contamination.

70. V- and G-type agents are nerve agents; H- and L-type agents are blister agents.

71. Inside the front cover; dark green - V (nerve), yellow - G (nerve), and red -H (blister).

72. Blot the paper on the suspected contaminated surface. Do not rub the paper against a suspected surface because false positive (red) streaks are produced.

73. On opposite sides of the body. If you are right-handed, place a strip of M9 paper around your right upper arm, left wrist, and right ankle. If you are left-handed, place the M9 paper around your left upper arm, right wrist, and

left ankle.

74. With M256: Procedure takes approximately 15 minutes. After all tests with the kit, including a check for liquid contamination, have been performed and the results are negative, the senior person should select one or two soldiers to start the unmasking procedures. If possible, move to a shady place. Bright, direct sunlight can cause pupils in the eyes to constrict, giving a false symptom. The selected soldiers unmask for 5 minutes, reseal, and clear their masks. Observe for 10 minutes. If no symptoms appear, it is safe to give the all-clear signal and unmask.

Without M256: Procedure takes approximately 35 minutes. Find a shady area. Use M8 paper to check the area for possible liquid contamination. When a reasonable amount of time has passed after the attack, the senior person should select one or two soldiers. The selected soldiers take a deep breath and break the mask seals, keeping their eyes wide open, for about 15 seconds. They then clear and reseal their masks. Observe them for 10 minutes. If no symptoms develop, they again break the seals and take two or three breaths, clear, and reseal their masks. Again observe them for 10 minutes. If no symptoms appear, the selected soldiers unmask for 5 minutes and then remask. If no symptoms appear in 10 minutes after remasking, everyone can unmask.

75. - Every time the mask is used; or
- Every 6 months during peacetime; or
- Weekly during combat.

76. Chemical Agent Resistant Coating - a polyurethane base paint that resists the absorption of chemical agents.

PHYSICAL FITNESS

QUESTIONS PAGE Q:35.9

1. AR 350-15 and FM 21-20.
2. 5; components of fitness, principles of exercise, phases of fitness, types of programs, and evaluation.
3. Muscular strength, muscular endurance, cardiorespiratory endurance, flexibility, and body composition.
4. Regularity, progression, overload, balance, specificity, variety, and recovery.
5. To enhance soldiers' abilities to meet the physical demands of war.
6. Frequency, Intensity, Time, and Type.
7. They should be of sufficient intensity, frequency, and duration so as to produce a training effect (AR 350-15).
8. Preparatory, Conditioning, and Maintenance.
9. Maintenance (maintaining) phase.
10. Unit, Individual, and Special Fitness.
11. All soldiers, regardless of age, in all three events.
12. Four times per year - twice per year (once every six months) for record, and twice for diagnostic purposes (minimum of 4 months must separate record tests).
13. Age and physiological differences between men and women.
14. A minimum of 60 points per event and 180 points overall.
15. The cool-down serves to gradually slow the heart rate and helps prevent pooling of the blood in the legs and feet. Also, stretching during the cool-down period results in optimum improvement in flexibility. Soldiers should walk or stretch until their heart rates return to less than 100 beats per minute (BPM) and heavy sweating stops. Under normal conditions, five to seven minutes is considered a sufficient period of time for cool-down.
16. Weight training, calisthenics, circuit training, grass drills, guerrilla drills, obstacle courses, rifle drills, log drills, aquatic exercise, road marching, and competitive fitness activities.

PRE-BOARD REVIEW
ANSWERS

17. Extended rectangular and circular.
18. The extended rectangular formation.
19. - extend to the left, march
    - arms downward, move
    - left, face
    - extend to the left, march
    - arms downward, move
    - right, face
    - from front to rear, count off
    - even numbers to the left, uncover.
20. Assemble to the right, march.
21. The Army Physical Readiness Test Scorecard.
22. Push-ups, sit-ups, and then the 2-mile run.
23. Up to twice the length of the profile period - not to exceed 90 days.
24. 290.

WEIGHT CONTROL QUESTIONS PAGE Q:35.10

1. AR 600-9
2. A soldier is considered overweight when his or her percent body fat exceeds the standard specified in paragraph 20c of AR 600-9.
3. To insure that all personnel -

   (1) Are able to meet the physical demands of their duties under combat conditions.

   (2) Present a trim military appearance at all times.
4. Height and age (separate tables for male and female).
5. As a minimum, personnel will be weighed when they take the APFT or at least every 6 months.
6.

Age Group	Male	Female
17-20	20%	30%
21-27	22%	32%
28-39	24%	34%
40+	26%	36%

7. (1) Weight reduction counseling by health care personnel.

   (2) Entered into appropriate Weight Control Program by unit commanders.

   (3) Flagged under the provisions of AR 600-31.
8. 3 to 8 pounds per month.
9. Monthly - to measure progress.
10. Standard PT uniform (shorts and T-shirt, without shoes).

LEADERSHIP QUESTIONS PAGE Q:35.10

1. FM 22-100, Military Leadership.
2. (1) Direct: junior level leadership (ie NCOs).

   (2) Indirect: senior level leadership (ie Officers).
3. The process of influencing others to accomplish the mission by providing purpose, direction, and motivation.
4. (1) The led

   (2) The leader

   (3) The situation

   (4) Communications
5. (1) Know yourself and seek self-improvement.

   (2) Be technically and tactically proficient.

PRE-BOARD REVIEW
ANSWERS

(3) Seek responsibility and take responsibility for your actions.
(4) Make sound and timely decisions.
(5) Set the example.
(6) Know your soldiers and look out for their well-being.
(7) Keep your subordinates informed.
(8) Develop a sense of responsibility in your subordinates.
(9) Ensure the task is understood, supervised, and accomplished.
(10) Build the team.
(11) Employ your unit in accordance with its capabilities.

6. Courage, candor, commitment, and competence.
7. (1) As a leader, you must BE:
   - a person of strong and honorable character
   - committed to the professional Army ethic
   - an example of individual values
   - able to resolve complex ethical dilemmas

   (2) As a leader, you must KNOW:
   - the four factors of leadership and how they affect each other
   - standards
   - yourself
   - human nature
   - your job (technical proficiency)
   - your unit

   (3) As a leader, you must DO:
   - provide purpose
   - provide direction
   - provide motivation
8. (1) Recognize and define the problem.
   (2) Gather facts and make assumptions.
   (3) Develop possible solutions.
   (4) Analyze and compare the possible solutions.
   (5) Select the best solution.
9. Directing, participating, and delegating.
10. There is no "best" leadership style. The style you use should depend on your analysis of the four factors of leadership (leader, led, situation, and communications) at any given time.
11. Chain of Command, NCO Support Channel, and Staff and technical channels.
12. Legal authority begins with the Constitution which divides authority for the military between Congress and the President. Congress has the authority to make laws to govern the Army; the President has the authority to command the Army as Commander in Chief. The President exercises his authority through commissioned officers (as described previously) who, in turn, delegate the necessary authority to NCOs in order to accomplish the mission.
13. Command authority and General Military Authority.
14. Accomplish the mission and look out for the well-being of the soldiers.
15. AR 600-20, FM 22-100, TC 22-6.
16. The section, squad, or team leader.
17. (1) That each member of the unit is trained to proficiency in his or her MOS as prescribed in the appropriate Soldier's Manual.

    (2) That all government property issued to members of their unit be properly maintained and accounted for at all times, and that discrepancies are reported promptly.

    (3) That, while in a duty status, they be ready at all times to report the location and activity of all members of their unit.

    (4) That the unit is trained to function in its primary mission role.
18. (1) Assign the task
    (2) Set standards
    (3) Check progress
    (4) Determine if standards have been met (follow-up).

19. No one, only authority can be delegated.
20. Morale, discipline, esprit de corps, and proficiency.
21. An understanding of human behavior (needs).
22. Mutual respect and restraint from undue familiarity.
23. Teacher, trainer, administrator, counselor, and commander.

COUNSELING

QUESTIONS PAGE Q:35.11

1. FM 22-101
2. The process of communicating advice, instruction, or judgement with the intent of influencing a person's behavior or performance.
3. Developing the counselee, improving well-being, and resolving problems.
4. That leaders regularly counsel their soldiers.
5. A caring attitude.
6. Mapping alternatives, recommending, advising, persuading, urging, commanding, and punishing.
7. Directive, Nondirective, and Combined.
8. The type of problem, personality of the soldier, physical surroundings, and time available will influence the selection of approach to be used. Leaders must be flexible; effective counselors use a uniquely different approach with each soldier.
9. (1) Listening and watching skills: involve the counselor concentrating on what the soldier says and does.
   (2) Responding skills: actions the leader takes to check his understanding of what the soldier is saying.
   (3) Guiding skills: using problem-solving and decision-making skills to help a soldier reach a solution.
10. Reception and integration, Performance, Personal, Discipline, and Professional Growth and guidance.
11. Preparation.
12. (1) Notify the soldier.
    (2) Schedule the best time (selection of the time).
    (3) Choose a suitable place (selection of the site).
    (4) Decide the right atmosphere.
    (5) Plan the discussion.
13. 30 minutes; 1 hour.
14. Schedule two separate counseling sessions.
15. (1) Opening the session.
    (2) Discussion.
    (3) Closing the session.
16. (1) Establish rapport.
    (2) Explain the reason for and outline the conduct of the counseling session.
17. Summarize what has been discussed.
18. Follow-up.
19. DA Form 4856, General Counseling Form.
20. FMs 22-100 and 22-101.
21. (1) Approachable.
    (2) Experienced.
    (3) Has unbiased approach to counselee's problem.
    (4) Has good observation skills.
    (5) Skilled communicator.
    (6) Flexible.
    (7) Aware of own limitations.
22. As often as necessary (Army standard dictates that soldiers be counseled, as a minimum, every 90 days. It is recommended, and required in some commands,

that soldiers receive counseling on a monthly basis).
23. On-the-spot corrections.
24. (1) Describe the behavior.
    (2) Describe the policy.
    (3) Describe the effect of not complying with the policy.
    (4) Ensure the individual makes the correction.

TRAINING

QUESTIONS PAGE Q:35.11

1. FM 25-100......Training the Force
   FM 25-101......Battle Focused Training
   FM 25-2........Unit Training Management
   FM 25-3........Training in Units
   FM 25-4........How to Conduct Training Exercises
   FM 25-5........Training for Mobilization and War
   AR 350-1.......The Army Training System
2. To develop a combat ready force which is physically and psychologically prepared to fight and win global war.
3. Individual and Collective training.
4. (1) Train as a combined arms and services team.
   (2) Train as you fight.
   (3) Train using appropriate doctrine.
   (4) Train using performance-oriented training.
   (5) Train to challenge.
   (6) Train to sustain proficiency.
   (7) Train using multi-echelon techniques.
   (8) Train to maintain.
   (9) Make commanders and leaders the primary trainers.
5. It represents a sustained level of wartime proficiency obtained through frequent training on critical tasks.
6. A concept used to derive peacetime training requirements from wartime missions.
7. Prepare (plan), execute, and assess.
8. A collective task in which an organization must be proficient to accomplish an appropriate portion of its wartime mission(s).
9. Mission Essential Task List. A compilation of collective mission essential tasks which must be successfully performed if an organization is to accomplish its wartime mission(s).
10. War plans and external directives.
11. War plans (wartime operations and contingency plans).
12. Battlefield Operating System; used to systematically ensure that all elements of the organization's combat power are directed toward accomplishing the overall mission. BOS are the major functions which occur on the battlefield and must be performed by the force to successfully execute operations.
    - Maneuver
    - Fire Support
    - Command and Control (C^2)
    - Intelligence
    - Mobility/Countermobility/Survivability
    - Combat Service Support
    - Air Defense
13. Detailed information concerning war plans, such as tactical routes to wartime areas of operation, ammunition upload procedures, execution of schemes of maneuver, and other support requirements.
14. There should be **no** attempt to prioritize tasks within a METL. By

definition, all tasks that have been placed on the METL are equally essential to ensure mission accomplishment.
15. A statement that describes the desired outcome of a training activity.
16. Tasks, Condition, and Standard.
17. A command group, staff, or subordinate organization mission essential task that is so critical that its accomplishment will determine the success of the next higher organization's mission essential task.
18. Long-range, short-range, and near-term.
19. 6-8.
20. Adequate preparation, effective presentation and practice, and thorough evaluation.
21. It is accurate, well structured, efficient, realistic, safe, and effective.
22. After Action Review; it is a structured review process that allows training participants to discover for themselves what happened, why it happened, and how it can be done better. It is a professional discussion that requires the active participation of those being trained.
23. (1) Establish what happened.
(2) Determine what was right or wrong with what happened.
(3) Determine how the task should be done differently the next time.
(4) Perform the task again.
24. It is designed to lay out what tasks you must know how to do, under what conditions to perform the specified tasks, and a step-by-step description of how to perform the tasks identified to standard.
25. The Noncommissioned Officer Education System; PLDC, BNCOC, ANCOC, and USASMA (Sergeants Major Academy).
26. Plan, prepare, present, practice, and perform.
27. Training Statement, Caution Statement, Pretest, Orientation Statement, Demonstration, Task Steps, Practice, and Performance Evaluation.
28. Lecture, conference, and demonstration.
29. AR 350-37.
30. Improve combat readiness by providing diagnostic information to commanders and MOS proponents on the effectiveness of training programs and products and to provide soldier proficiency information to career managers.
31. SQT/SDT, CTT, and Commander's Evaluation (CE).

UCMJ

QUESTIONS PAGE Q:35.12

1. AR 27-10
2. The Uniform Code of Military Justice; the statute that prescribes criminal law for soldiers.
3. No, he/she has the right to demand a trial by court martial, unless assigned to or embarked on a vessel.
4. Article 31.
5. The Punitive Articles.
6. Yes, conviction by a general or special court martial in which a Bad Conduct Discharge was adjudged can be appealed to the Court of Military Review or the Court of Military Appeals. All other cases will be appealed to the Judge Advocate General.
7. Soldiers with the rank Private First Class and below.
8. Summarized, Company Grade, and Field Grade.
9. A reasonable time will vary according to the situation; however, an appeal submitted more than 5 calendar days after the punishment is imposed may be rejected as untimely.
10. To suspend all favorable personnel action on an individual while he/she is under investigation, or processing for disciplinary action or elimination proceedings.

PRE-BOARD REVIEW
ANSWERS

11. Any commanding officer, including a warrant officer exercising command.
12. By secret written ballot.
13. Yes, when not a member of the unit of the accused, when the accused has requested enlisted members to serve on the board, and when the enlisted members on the board are higher in rank than the accused.
14. Yes, Summary but not Special or General.
15. As a minimum: Summary - 1
Special - 3
General - 5
16. Malingering.
17. Death.
18. ~~140.~~ 154.

NOTE: Recent changes to the Manual for Courts-Martial added articles 141-146. It can therefore be said that there are 146 articles to the UCMJ; however, there are eight separate articles that are subcategorized alphabetically (i.e. 6a, 50a, 58a, 67a, etc). In light of this, the more accurate answer would be 154 articles.

19. Summary, Special, and General.
20. Nonjudicial punishment in the form of Article 15s, and Judicial punishment in the form of Courts Martial.
21. When the offender has shown that they cannot benefit by less stringent methods.
22. DA Form 2627.
23. DA Form 2627-1.
24. These forms will be maintained locally in nonjudicial punishment files. They will be destroyed at the end of 2 years from the date of imposition of punishment or on the soldier's transfer from the unit, whichever occurs first.
25. For soldiers E4 and below, the original will be filed locally in unit nonjudicial punishment files. For all other soldiers, the original will be filed in the OMPF. The decision to file the original DA Form 2627 on the performance fiche or the restricted fiche in the OMPF will be determined by the imposing commander at the time the punishment is imposed. Additional copies of the DA Form 2627 will be transmitted through the MILPO serving the soldier's MPRJ to the Finance and Accounting office as necessary (for reduction in rank, forfeiture of pay, etc).
26. An Article 15 imposed by an O-4 or above.
27. A reasonable belief that items related to criminal activity are in the place to be searched.
28. One-third.
29. Being tried for the same offense twice.
30. Manual for Courts-Martial.
31. Soldiers in pay grade E2 - E6.
32. Such orders publish the result of a trial and the initial action of the convening authority.
33. Suspend, vacate, mitigate, remit, or set aside punishment.
34. The Court of ~~Military Appeals~~. Appeals for the Armed Forces.

NOTE: Cases may still be reviewed by the Supreme Court when conditions warrant.

PRE-BOARD REVIEW
ANSWERS

35. See charts below:

Punishments	Company Grade Commanders	Field Grade Commanders
Restriction	14 days	60 days
Extra duty	14 days	45 days
Correctional custody (E-3 and below)	7 days	30 days
Confinement on bread and water or diminished rations (E-3 or below attached to or embarked on a vessel)	3 days	3 days
Forfeiture of pay	7 days	1/2 of one month pay per month for 2 months
Reduction in grade	E-4 or below, 1 grade	E-4 or below, one or more grades; E-5 or E-6, one grade

(SUMMARIZED PROCEEDING) Punishment	(ENLISTED PERSONNEL ONLY) All Commanders
Restriction	14 days
Extra duty	14 days

DRILL & CEREMONIES

QUESTIONS PAGE Q:35.13

1. FM 22-5
2. It enables leaders to move an individual or a unit from one place to another in an orderly manner.
3. Preparatory command and the command of execution.
4. 120 steps per minute.
5. 180 steps per minute.
6. Two part, combined, supplementing, directive, and mass.
7. 30 inches.
8. Your left foot.
9. Your right foot.
10. "Inspection, Arms....Ready, Port, Arms....Dismissed".
11. First rank takes two 30-inch steps forward.
    Second rank takes one 30-inch step forward.
    Third rank stands fast.
    Fourth rank takes two 15-inch steps backward.
12. First rank takes four 15-inch steps backward.
    Second rank takes two 15-inch steps backward.
    Third rank stands fast.
    Fourth rank takes one 30-inch step forward.
13. 3; normal interval, close interval, and double interval.
14. Parade Rest, Stand At Ease, At Ease, Rest, and Fall Out.

15. REST
16. Forward ------------ 30 inches
    Half Step ---------- 15 inches
    Left or Right Step - 15 inches
    Backward ----------- 15 inches
    Doubletime --------- 30 inches
17. "Platoon, Attention", "Dress Right, Dress", and "Ready Front".
18. Day, night, forced, and shuttle.
19. Tactical and Administrative.
20. Right Step March.
21. Approximately 9 inches forward and 6 inches to the rear of the seam of the trousers.
22. Column and Line formation.
23. At Ease March and Route Step March.
24. At Ease March - soldier is no longer required to retain cadence; however, silence and the approximate interval and distance are maintained.
    Route Step March - Soldier may drink from canteen and talk.
25. 2 inches.
26. First give the command "Quick time, MARCH", then give the halt command.
27. Seven.
28. When the inspecting officer stops in front of you.
29. (1) If the inspecting officer physically inspects your weapon (takes it from you), then you must execute ready-port-arms immediately after it is returned.
    (2) If the inspecting officer does not physically inspect the weapon (does not take it from you), then you must remain at inspection arms until he/she has halted in front of and is facing the next soldier. Then execute ready-port-arms.
30. "Dress right, DRESS" and "Ready, FRONT".
31. Command "Fall in".
32. FM 22-5, Appendix C.
33. A guidon bearer, while carrying the guidon (not in formation), salutes by moving the left hand sharply across the chest to a position so that the first joint of the forefinger is touching the staff. The fingers and thumb are extended and joined, palm down, wrist straight, and forearm horizontal to the ground.
34. Yes. When armed with a rifle, the guidon bearer slings the weapon behind his back with the sling diagonally across his chest and the muzzle end up and to the left.
35. It is carried diagonally across the body in a "port arms" position.

FLAGS

QUESTIONS PAGE Q:35.14

1. AR 840-10
2. FM 22-5, Guidons..............Appendix C
   Flags and Colors......Appendix E
3. Any type of cloth device used to convey information.
4. If not preserved, it will be destroyed privately, preferably by burning or by some other method that does not show irreverence or disrespect to the flag.
5. A specific flag symbolic of the spirit and tradition of either the United States, or the position, individual, or organization represented. The flag of the United States when displayed as indicated in AR 840-10 is known as the "National Color." The term "color" when used alone refers to the national color. The term "colors" means the national and positional or organizational colors.
6. The US flag is a symbol of our nation. It represents a living country, and

PRE-BOARD REVIEW
ANSWERS

as such, is considered a living thing. The union, the white stars on a field of blue, is the honor point of the flag. There are 50 stars within the union representing each of the 50 states. They are arranged in four rows of five and five rows of six. Thirteen stripes, seven red and six white, represent each of the original thirteen colonies. The first and last stripes are red. Red can be said to represent "hardiness" and "valor"; white - "purity" and "innocence"; and blue - "justice" and "vigilance".

7. July 4, 1960.
8. One.
9. - Fort McHenry National Monument
   - The White House
   - The Moon
   - Arlington National Cemetery
   - The Tomb of the Unknowns
   - Battleship USS Arizona, Pearl Harbor
   - US Capitol, Washington D.C.
   - Francis Scott Key's grave
   - Flag House Square, Baltimore MD
   - Hospital Ship Hope
10. Storm, post, and garrison.
11. The Post flag.
12. The width from top to bottom of the vertical edge of the flag.
13. The length from left to right of the horizontal edge of the flag.
14. That section of a flag which attaches to the flagstaff, flagpole, or mast.
15. Mourning.
16. It symbolizes the three-pointed hats worn by soldiers of the Revolutionary War.
17. June 12, 1956 by Executive Order 10670.
18. June 14; on this date in 1956 the newly approved US Army flag was unfurled at Independence Hall, Philadelphia, Pennsylvania, by the Honorable Wilbur M. Brucker, Secretary of the Army. June 14, 1956 was the 181st anniversary of the United States Army.
19. It is 4' 4" in hoist by 5' 6" in fly and is trimmed on three sides with yellow fringe 2½" in width. It is made of white silk and bears an embroidered replica of the official seal of the Department of the Army (w/out the roman numerals) in ultramarine blue. A scarlet roll inscribed, "United States Army" in white is centered between the device and the ultramarine blue numerals "1775". Streamers represent the campaigns since its inception.
20. It is a swallow-tailed unit identification marker, 20" x 27", with a fork 10" long. It is approved by HQDA and authorized for units with an authorized strength of 20 or more military personnel.
21. A flagstaff head - the decorative ornament at the top of a flagstaff.
22. (1) Eagle - Presidential flagstaffs.
    (2) Spearhead (arrowhead) - Army flagstaffs.
    (3) Acorn - Markers and marking pennant flagstaffs.
    (4) Ball - Outdoor wall mounted for advertising or recruiting.
23. The spearhead.
24. A square or rectangle in the upper left-hand corner of a flag.
25. The side of the shield or design element appearing to the viewer's left.
26. The side of the shield or design element appearing to the viewer's right.
27. The rope or cable that raises a flag up and down the flagpole.
28. Reveille.
29. Retreat.
30. It is disrespectful to deliberately allow the US flag to touch anything beneath it. However, if it should become soiled by accidentally touching the ground or by other means, it is necessary only to have it cleaned.
31. In the manner best suited for the material.
32. 50, 60, or 70 feet.

PRE-BOARD REVIEW
ANSWERS

CUSTOMS & COURTESIES

QUESTIONS PAGE Q:35.14

1. AR 600-25.
2. FM 22-5, Appendix A.
3. Commonly practiced or observed events that have become tradition and make up the unwritten "common law" of the Army.
4. The respect and consideration shown by military personnel to others.
5. The hand salute.
6. Although uncertain, some historians believe that it began in late Roman times when assassinations were common. A citizen who wanted to see a public official had to approach with his right hand raised to show that he did not hold a weapon. Knights in armor raised visors with the right hand when meeting a comrade. This practice gradually became a way of showing respect and, in early American history, sometimes involved removing the hat. By 1820, the motion was modified to touching the hat, and since then it has become the hand salute used today.
7. Remove the headgear (except when under arms), approach to within two paces of the desk, halt, salute, and report, "<Sir><Ma'am><SGM>, Private Jones reports." The salute is held until the report is completed and the salute has been returned. When the business is completed, the soldier salutes, holds the salute until it has been returned, executes the appropriate facing movement, and departs.
8. When given the command PRESENT, ARMS.
9. The leader brings the unit to attention and then salutes for the entire formation.
10. Salute at six steps distance and hold the salute until you have passed six steps beyond the flag.
11. To render honors, preserve tradition, and stimulate esprit de corps.
12. The appearance and movement of troops in formation.
13. "Retreat" and "To the Colors".
14. 40 seconds.
15. The National Anthem.
16. The Star-Bangled Banner.
17. 20 seconds.
18. During reveille, the flag is raised quickly to the top of the flag pole. During retreat, the flag is lowered slowly and ceremoniously. It should reach the bottom at the last note of "To the Colors".
19. Nothing. Once the flag has been folded it is treated as a cased color and not saluted by persons meeting the flag detail.
20. The Army Chief of Staff, his direct representative, or an individual of equivalent or higher grade, but in no other case.
21. Two or three sergeants and two specialists or privates (the senior NCO is the Color guard commander and carries the National Color).
22. Always on the left.
23. The junior soldier enters first, followed by others in inverse order of rank. When exiting, the senior person gets out first and the junior last.
24. Salute to the Union; on the 4th of July.
25. 21
26. Memorial Day - the last Monday in May. At 1200 hours, the national salute (21 guns) will be fired and the flag hoisted to the top of the pole where it remains until retreat.
27.

	Arrival	Departure
President	21	21
Ex-President	21	21
Vice President	19	none

Secretary of Defense..........19.............19
Secretary of the Army.........19.............19
Chairman, JCS.................19.............19
Army Chief of Staff...........19.............19
Generals......................17.............17
Lieutenant General............15...........none
Major General.................13...........none
Brigadier General.............11...........none

28. The first soldier to see the officer calls "At Ease!"(unless a higher ranking officer is known to be present).
29. It is first raised quickly to full-staff and then slowly and ceremoniously lowered to half-staff.
30. The Flag must first be raised quickly to full-staff and then ceremoniously lowered in the traditional manner.
31. Only as a distress signal (dire emergency).
32. "Taps".
33. 8; 1 NCOIC and a 7-man firing squad.
34. The Command Sergeant Major.
35. "The Army goes Rolling Along"; it was dedicated on Veterans Day, 11 November 1956, by the Secretary of the Army but was not officially announced until 12 December 1957 (AR 28-76). It was originally known as the "Caisson Song" and was composed by Lt Edmund L. Gruber in 1908.
36. There is no DA directive in this regard; however FM 22-5 encourages personnel to stand at attention when it is played to pay tribute to the Army.

MILITARY PROGRAMS

QUESTIONS PAGE Q:35.15

1. Quality of Life Program
2. (1) Army Community Services (ACS)
   (2) Army Morale Support Activities (AMSA)
   (3) Army Continuing Education System (ACES)
   (4) Army Club Management System (ACMS)
   (5) Army Postal System (APS)
   (6) Army and Air Force Exchange Service (AAFES)
3. Army Community Services.
4. To improve readiness and increase retention by providing services to assist soldiers and their families in solving problems beyond their ability to solve alone through the provisions of the ~~seven~~ eight essential services outlined in AR 608-1.
5. (1) The Relocation Assistance Program (includes Loan Closet).
   (2) The Family Member Employment Assistance Program.
   (3) The Exceptional Family Member Program.
   (4) The Family Advocacy Program.
   (5) The Information, Referral, and Follow-up Program.
   (6) The Consumer Affairs and Financial Assistance Program.
   (7) The Outreach Program.
   (8) Foster Care
6. Army Continuing Education System.
7. ACES exists to fulfill the Army responsibility of developing and conserving its human resources by providing on-duty, job-related educational programs and off-duty educational opportunities for professional and personal development.
8. - Basic Skills Education Program (BSEP)
   - Advanced Skills Education Program (ASEP)
   - Armed Forces Classification Test Preparation Course
   - English-as-a-second-language (ESL)
   - High School Completion Program (HSCP)

PRE-BOARD REVIEW
ANSWERS

- MOS related Development Courses
- Typing
- Defense Activity for Non-Traditional Education Support Activities (DANTES)
- Servicemembers Opportunity Colleges Associates Degree Program (SOCAD)
- Bachelor Degrees for Soldiers (BDFS) Program
- Skill Recognition Programs (Army Apprenticeship Program (AAP))
- Command Language Programs (Headstart/Gateway)
- Learning Resources Center (LRC - incl MOS Library)
- Education Counseling Services
- Transition Management (Soldier-to-Civilian)
- Tuition Assistance
- VEAP/GI Bill

9. BSEP is a program designed to improve educational deficiencies in the basic skills of reading, math, and language. A diagnostic test (TABE) is administered to determine the areas needing improvement. The program is conducted for 60 hours, on duty time, and participation is voluntary and free.
10. ASEP is the primary command-on-duty program intended to help the NCOs meet their training responsibilities as supervisors, managers, and communicators. It is designed to improve MOS performance and help career growth for soldiers E-5 and above. Each class is 20 hours long and usually runs 4 hours per day for 5 days. There are 6 management and 6 communications ASEP classes.
11. ESL (English as a Second Language).
12. English as a second language (ESL) is a program designed for soldiers whose primary language is not English and who are experiencing difficulty in reading, speaking, or understanding English. Eligibility and placement is determined by diagnostic testing and/or command referral. Soldiers are sent on TDY to the 60 hour course. It is free of charge.
13. 75%.
14. The course to be taken must be job-related.
15. Army Emergency Relief - it was chartered in 1942 as a private non-profit organization to provide Army soldiers, their dependents, widows/widowers and orphans with financial assistance in time of emergency need. In addition, it provides educational assistance for spouses and dependent children of soldiers.
16. Any member of the Army faced with a real emergency, within the framework of policy, should be given AER assistance.
17.
- nonreceipt of pay
- loss of funds
- medical, dental, or hospital expense
- funeral expenses
- emergency travel
- rent
- food
- utilities (other than phone)
- essential transportation (POV)
- clothing
- fire or other disaster
- lack of necessities

18.
(1) Communication services (by wire).
(2) Financial assistance.
(3) Counseling and referral services.
(4) Health and safety courses.
(5) Volunteer services.
(6) Disaster services.
(7) Blood services.
(8) Transplantation services.
(9) AIDS education.
(10) Military/social services.

PRE-BOARD REVIEW
ANSWERS

(11) International services.
(12) Youth services.
19. Alcohol.
20. Alcohol and Drug Abuse Prevention and Control Program; Alcohol and Drug Abuse Prevention Training; Short-Term Outpatient treatment Program.
21. AR 600-85.
22. Prevention, education, identification, rehabilitation, treatment, program evaluation, and research.
23. The prevention aspects of substance abuse.
24. An active and aggressive urinalysis program.
25. Specimens will be collected under the direct observation of responsible personnel (E5 or above of the same sex) to insure that no substitutions are made.
26. Abuse or excessive use of alcohol will not be condoned or accepted as part of any military tradition, ceremony or event.
27. Community Counseling Center.
28. Voluntary, Command, Biochemical (urinalysis), Medical, and Investigation/apprehension.
29. Voluntary (self) identification.
30. Track I : Awareness education and group counseling, as required. Enrollment will not exceed 30 days; 12 hours of counseling.

Track II : Rehabilitation (nonresidential); intensive individual or group counseling (may include awareness education). Consists of 12 hours of counseling usually once per week for a minimum of 30 days, not to exceed ~~360~~ 364 days.

Track III : Rehabilitation (residential); medical treatment with nonresidential follow-up. Enrollment in this track is limited to those clients who have been evaluated by a physician as requiring residential treatment. Generally, residential care will be reserved for those individuals with long standing problems of abuse, but for whom prognosis for recovery is favorable with proper treatment. Enrollment is for 360 days (3 - 6 wks residential care).
NOTE: The ADAPCP program is steering away from the "Track" terminology. Change 2 to AR 600-85 drops Track III altogether and refers only to Tracks I and II. This has to do more with terminology than it does to sweeping program changes. The regulations are being re-written to reflect that there are three "Levels" of treatment instead of three "Tracks". Track I is being replaced by "Level I - Drug and Alcohol Education"; Track II is being replaced by "Level II - Outpatient"; and Track III is being replaced by "Level III - Inpatient". In all other respects the programs remain basically the same.
31. The reinvolvement of the service member in his or her role and responsibilities in the unit.
32. Unit Alcohol and Drug Coordinator; the UADC is responsible to the unit commander for ensuring that drug testing is conducted in accordance with existing regulations.
33. AR 385-10.
34. Risk Management (or Risk Assessment).
35. (1) Reduce and keep to a minimum accidental manpower and monetary losses, thus providing more efficient use of resources and advancing the combat effectiveness of the Army.

(2) Provide a safe and healthful environment at all times for all Army personnel and others exposed to Army operations.
36. AR 600-21 was superseded by Chapter 6, AR 600-20. Chapter 6 of AR 600-20 is printed in the form of an Interim Change.
37. Consideration and treatment based on merit, fitness, and capability irrespective of race, color, religion, gender, or national origin ("Everyone has the same opportunity to excel!").
38. Provide equal opportunity and treatment for uniformed members without regard to race, color, sex, religion, age, or national origin.

PRE-BOARD REVIEW
ANSWERS

39. Name them.
40. The processing of EO complaints through the chain of command is strongly encouraged; however, it does not serve as the only channel available to soldiers and family members.
41. Affirmative action and Education/training.
42. ~~AR 612-10~~ AR 600-8-8.
43. Explain it.
44. Unless sponsorship is declined a soldier should receive a minimum of two letters; one from the battalion commander (officers) or command sergeant major (enlisted) and one from the designated sponsor. If sponsorship is declined, a welcome letter should still be received from the command activity.
45. 10 (unless sponsorship is declined).
46. A person assigned to an individual that has declined sponsorship - in the event that questions arise.
47. The sponsor selected will be:
    (1) In a grade equal to or higher than the incoming soldier, when practical;
    (2) Of the same gender, marital status, and military career field or occupational series as the incoming soldier, when practical;
    (3) Familiar with the unit or activity and community.
48. AR 601-280.
49. - Must be over 18 years of age, but under 55 years of age.
    - Must be a U.S. citizen.
    - Must possess a high school diploma or GED.
    - Must pass the APFT and meet height and weight standards.
    - Must meet the years per grade requirement:
        -- E-4 8 yrs, 29 days
        -- E-5 13 yrs, 29 days
        -- E-6 20 yrs, 29 days
        -- E-7 24 yrs
        -- E-8 27 yrs
        -- E-9 30 yrs
50. 4 years.
51. 8 months (max).
52. 3 months.
53. Noncommissioned Officer Development Program.
54. AR 350-17.
55. Better Opportunities for Single Soldiers - pilot program in USAREUR. Targets single and unaccompanied soldiers and is designed to give them greater input into the MWR activities in their respective communities.
56. Army Career and Alumni Program; provides transition/employment service and information, including Job Fairs.

STUDY TEMPLATES

ABOUT THIS SECTION

A lot of people have asked me how I manage to be so successful on Board appearances. I've been told that I must have a photographic memory. Unfortunately, that is not the case. But I do want to share with you a technique that I use - one that has proven to be very successful for me. This study technique is one of my own design and I call it "Study Templates." It's really sort of a modified outline for each subject area; a skeleton - with just enough meat added to trigger a response. The templates won't work by themselves, however. They won't make any sense to you unless you have done some studying before you get here. Used properly, they are indispensable for self-study and are an excellent "nut shell" review. Here is how they work. Let's say that you are studying for a Board and one of the subjects is Map Reading. You have already done some studying on this subject and you wish to review. You turn to page 36.9 of the Study Templates and this is part of what you see:

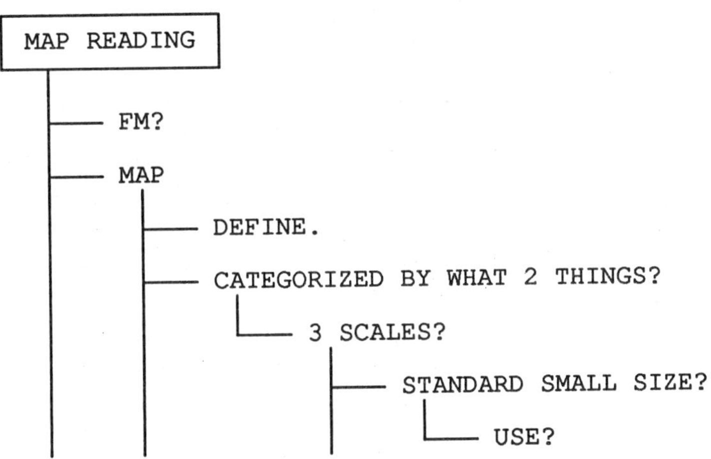

This portion of the template should "trigger" the following response (or something similar to it):

"FM 21-26 covers MAP READING. A map is a graphic representation of all or a portion of the earth's surface, drawn to scale, as seen from above. Maps are categorized by scale and type. The three scales are small, medium, and large. The standard small scale map is 1:1,000,000. It is used for general planning and for strategical studies at the higher echelons. Etc, etc, etc. If you run across something you can't recall - look it up. Its easy once you get used to it!

Use these templates, modify them to suit your needs, or design your own. Do whatever works best for you.

STUDY TEMPLATES

STUDY TEMPLATES INDEX

STUDY TEMPLATES

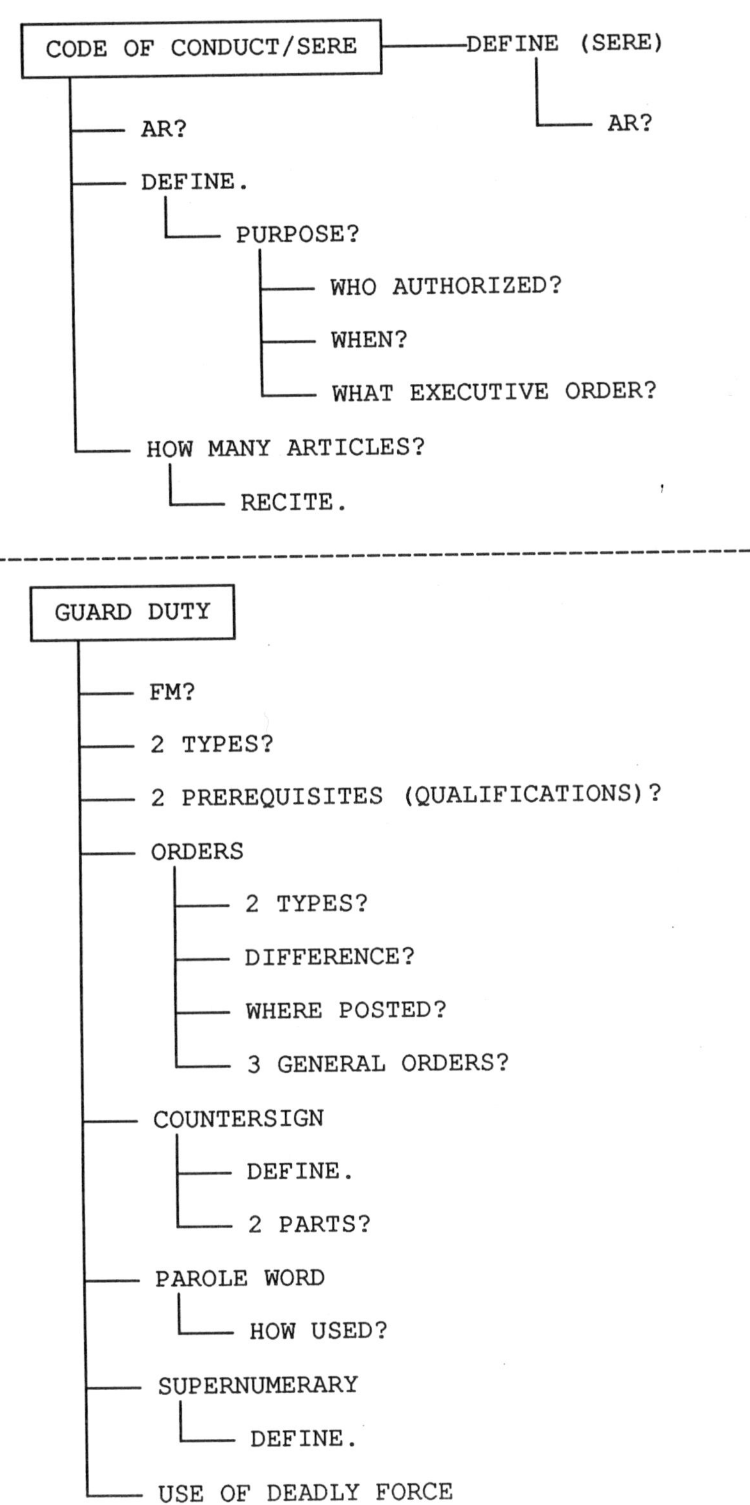
CODE OF CONDUCT/SERE
DEFINE (SERE)
AR?
AR?
DEFINE.
PURPOSE?
WHO AUTHORIZED?
WHEN?
WHAT EXECUTIVE ORDER?
HOW MANY ARTICLES?
RECITE.
GUARD DUTY
FM?
2 TYPES?
2 PREREQUISITES (QUALIFICATIONS)?
ORDERS
2 TYPES?
DIFFERENCE?
WHERE POSTED?
3 GENERAL ORDERS?
COUNTERSIGN
DEFINE.
2 PARTS?
PAROLE WORD
HOW USED?
SUPERNUMERARY
DEFINE.
USE OF DEADLY FORCE

- ARMY POLICY?

PHYSICAL SECURITY

- AR/FM?
- PURPOSE?
- WHO RESPONSIBLE?
  - EXERCISED THRU WHOM?
- PHYSICAL SECURITY MEASURES
  - DEFINE.
  - EXAMPLES?
- PHYSICAL SECURITY TRAINING/EDUCATION
  - PERTINENT SUBJECTS?
  - PURPOSE?
- SECURITY THREAT
  - DEFINE.
  - 2 CATEGORIES?
    - WHICH PREVENTABLE?
- 2-MAN RULE?
- RESTRICTED AREAS
  - DEFINE.
  - 4 DESIGNATIONS?
- SECURITY CLASSIFICATIONS
  - 3 LEVELS?
  - COLOR OF COVER FOR?
- FENCING
  - 4 TYPES?

FIRST AID

- FM?

STUDY TEMPLATES

- DEFINE.
- 3 "BASICS" OF FIRST AID?
- EVALUATING CASUALTY
  - 8 STEPS?
- 2 VITAL BODY FUNCTIONS?
  - 4 "ADVERSE" CONDITIONS?
- 3 "BASIC MEASURES" (LIFE-SAVING STEPS)?
  - 2 METHODS OF OPENING AIRWAY?
  - 2 METHODS OF RESCUE BREATHING?
    - PREFERRED?
  - CONTROLLING BLEEDING
    - 5 METHODS (IN ORDER)?
  - SHOCK
    - 7 STEPS IN TREATING/PREVENTING?
- HEAD INJURY
  - SIGNS/SYMPTOMS?
- CHEST WOUND/ABDOMINAL WOUND
  - HOW TREATED?
- FRACTURES
  - 2 TYPES?
    - DEFINE.
  - SIGNS/SYMPTOMS?
  - BASIC SPLINTING PRINCIPLE?
- BURNS
  - 4 TYPES?
  - 4 FIRST AID MEASURES?
  - 3 DEGREES?
    - DIFFERENCE?
- HEAT INJURIES

STUDY TEMPLATES

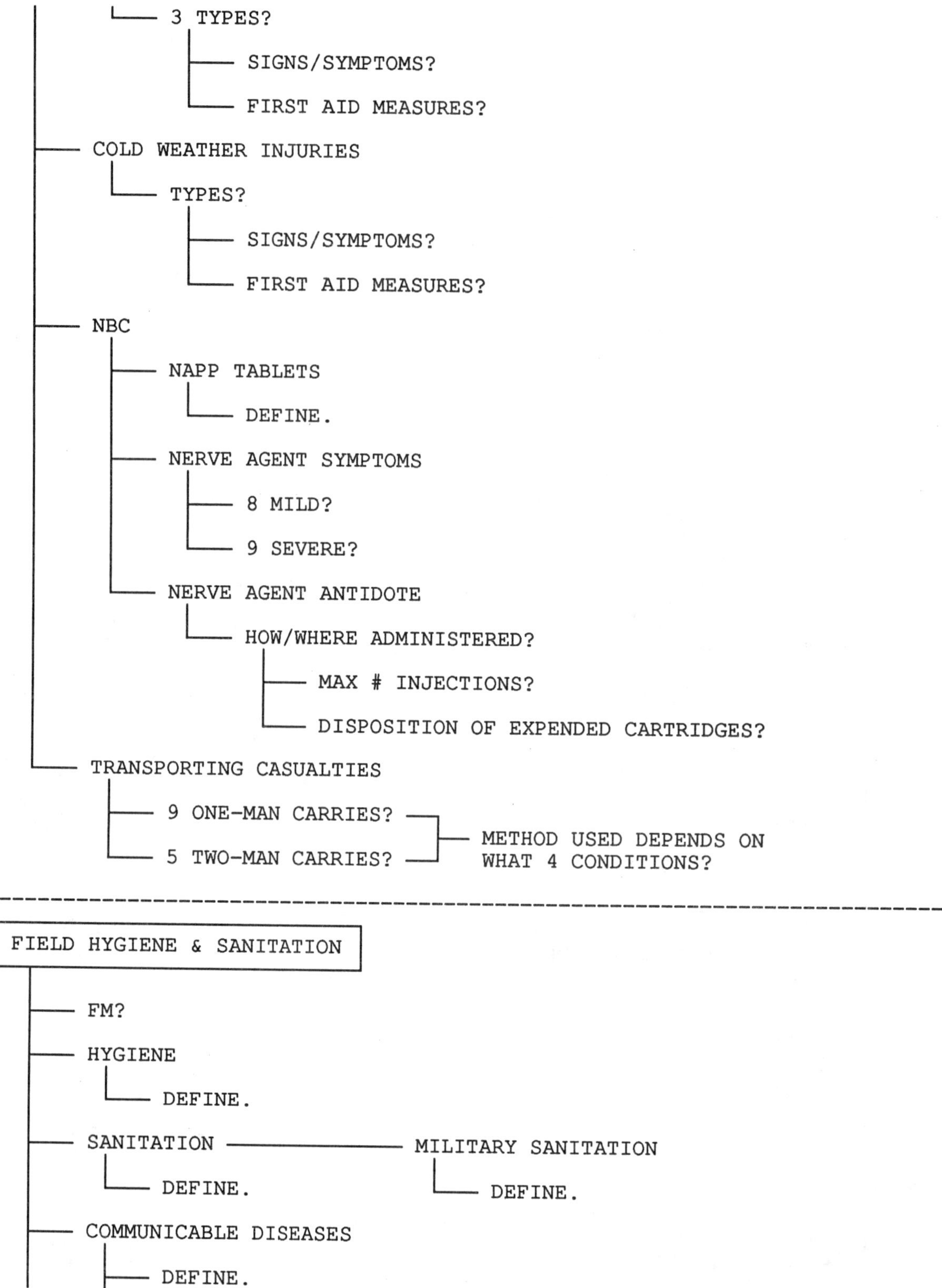

3 TYPES?
SIGNS/SYMPTOMS?
FIRST AID MEASURES?
COLD WEATHER INJURIES
TYPES?
SIGNS/SYMPTOMS?
FIRST AID MEASURES?
NBC
NAPP TABLETS
DEFINE.
NERVE AGENT SYMPTOMS
8 MILD?
9 SEVERE?
NERVE AGENT ANTIDOTE
HOW/WHERE ADMINISTERED?
MAX # INJECTIONS?
DISPOSITION OF EXPENDED CARTRIDGES?
TRANSPORTING CASUALTIES
9 ONE-MAN CARRIES?
5 TWO-MAN CARRIES?
METHOD USED DEPENDS ON WHAT 4 CONDITIONS?
FIELD HYGIENE & SANITATION
FM?
HYGIENE
DEFINE.
SANITATION
DEFINE.
MILITARY SANITATION
DEFINE.
COMMUNICABLE DISEASES
DEFINE.

STUDY TEMPLATES

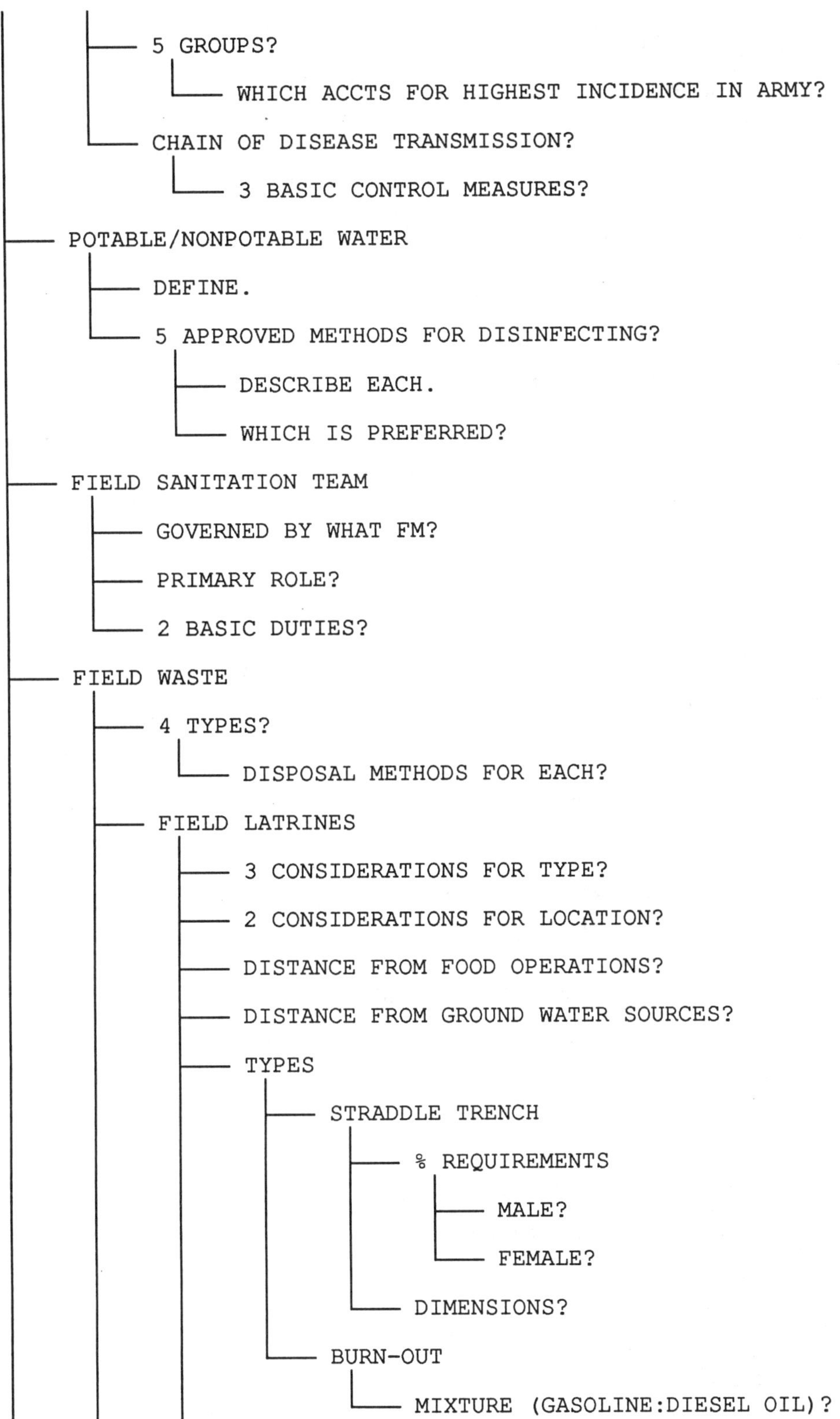

5 GROUPS?
WHICH ACCTS FOR HIGHEST INCIDENCE IN ARMY?
CHAIN OF DISEASE TRANSMISSION?
3 BASIC CONTROL MEASURES?
POTABLE/NONPOTABLE WATER
DEFINE.
5 APPROVED METHODS FOR DISINFECTING?
DESCRIBE EACH.
WHICH IS PREFERRED?
FIELD SANITATION TEAM
GOVERNED BY WHAT FM?
PRIMARY ROLE?
2 BASIC DUTIES?
FIELD WASTE
4 TYPES?
DISPOSAL METHODS FOR EACH?
FIELD LATRINES
3 CONSIDERATIONS FOR TYPE?
2 CONSIDERATIONS FOR LOCATION?
DISTANCE FROM FOOD OPERATIONS?
DISTANCE FROM GROUND WATER SOURCES?
TYPES
STRADDLE TRENCH
% REQUIREMENTS
MALE?
FEMALE?
DIMENSIONS?
BURN-OUT
MIXTURE (GASOLINE:DIESEL OIL)?

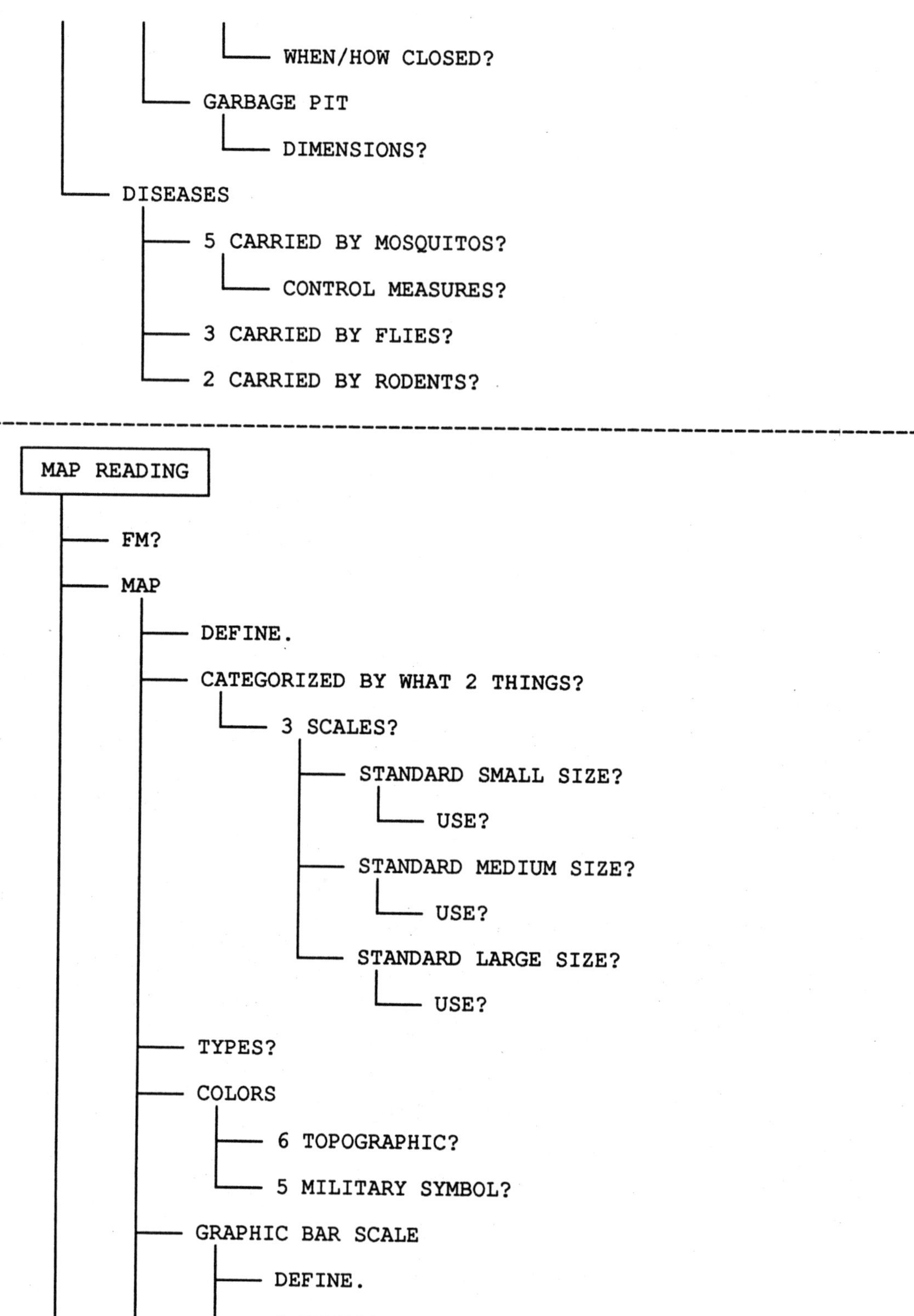
WHEN/HOW CLOSED?
GARBAGE PIT
DIMENSIONS?
DISEASES
5 CARRIED BY MOSQUITOS?
CONTROL MEASURES?
3 CARRIED BY FLIES?
2 CARRIED BY RODENTS?
MAP READING
FM?
MAP
DEFINE.
CATEGORIZED BY WHAT 2 THINGS?
3 SCALES?
STANDARD SMALL SIZE?
USE?
STANDARD MEDIUM SIZE?
USE?
STANDARD LARGE SIZE?
USE?
TYPES?
COLORS
6 TOPOGRAPHIC?
5 MILITARY SYMBOL?
GRAPHIC BAR SCALE
DEFINE.
2 PARTS?

STUDY TEMPLATES

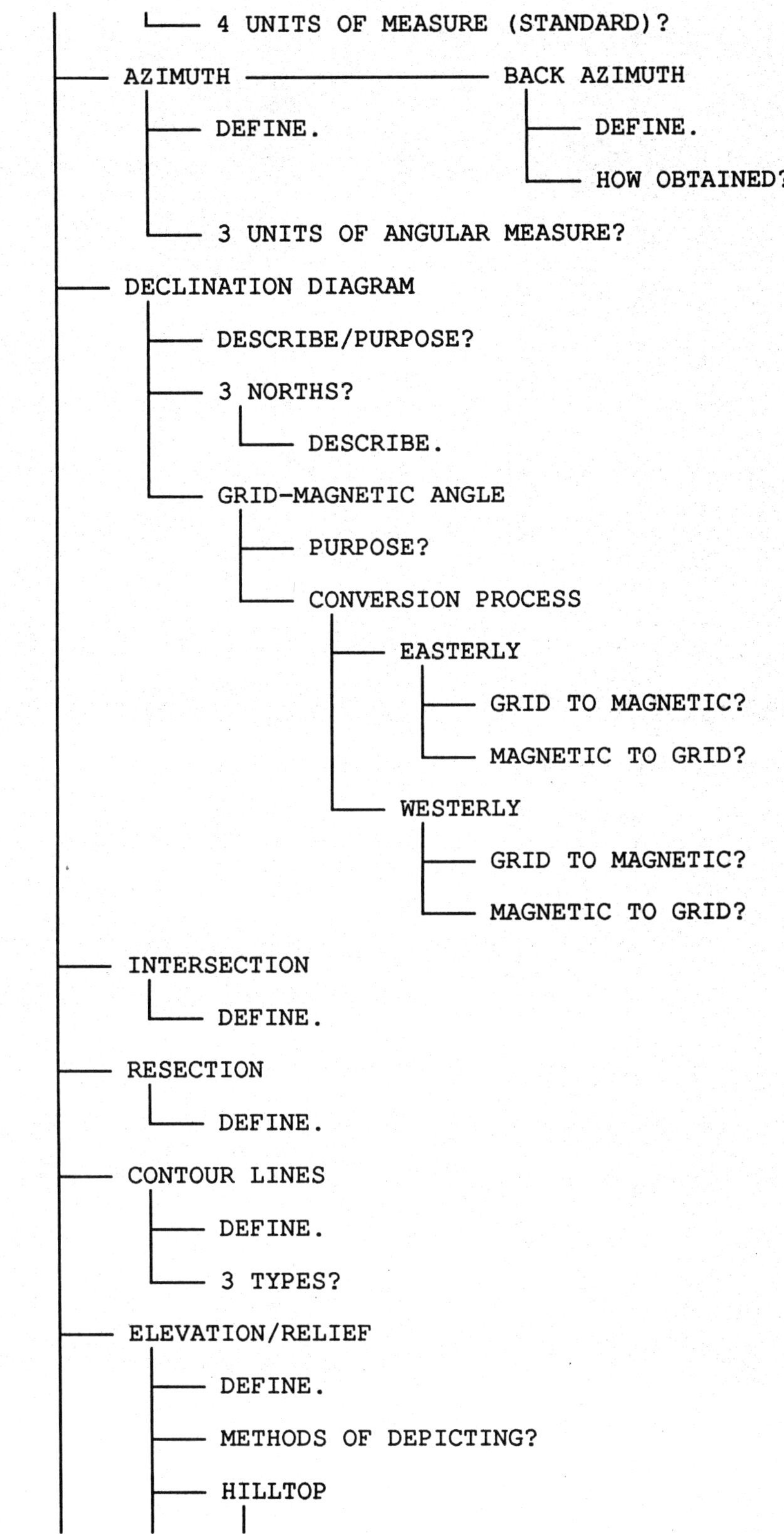

4 UNITS OF MEASURE (STANDARD)?
AZIMUTH
BACK AZIMUTH
DEFINE.
DEFINE.
HOW OBTAINED?
3 UNITS OF ANGULAR MEASURE?
DECLINATION DIAGRAM
DESCRIBE/PURPOSE?
3 NORTHS?
DESCRIBE.
GRID-MAGNETIC ANGLE
PURPOSE?
CONVERSION PROCESS
EASTERLY
GRID TO MAGNETIC?
MAGNETIC TO GRID?
WESTERLY
GRID TO MAGNETIC?
MAGNETIC TO GRID?
INTERSECTION
DEFINE.
RESECTION
DEFINE.
CONTOUR LINES
DEFINE.
3 TYPES?
ELEVATION/RELIEF
DEFINE.
METHODS OF DEPICTING?
HILLTOP

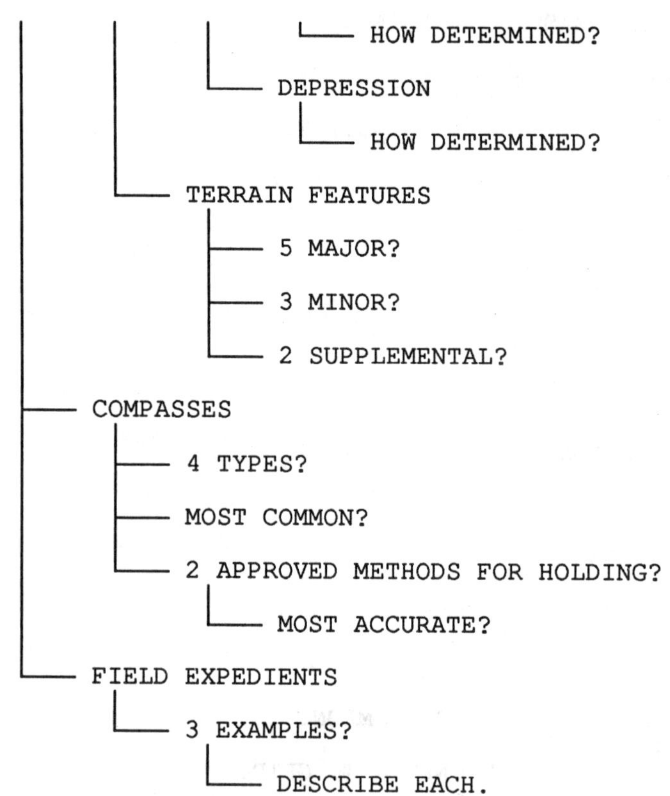
HOW DETERMINED?
DEPRESSION
HOW DETERMINED?
TERRAIN FEATURES
5 MAJOR?
3 MINOR?
2 SUPPLEMENTAL?
COMPASSES
4 TYPES?
MOST COMMON?
2 APPROVED METHODS FOR HOLDING?
MOST ACCURATE?
FIELD EXPEDIENTS
3 EXAMPLES?
DESCRIBE EACH.

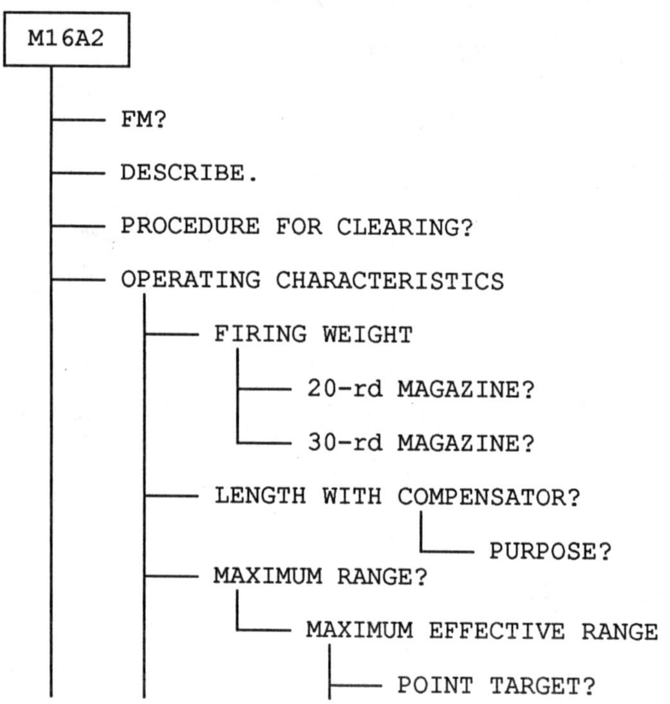
M16A2
FM?
DESCRIBE.
PROCEDURE FOR CLEARING?
OPERATING CHARACTERISTICS
FIRING WEIGHT
20-rd MAGAZINE?
30-rd MAGAZINE?
LENGTH WITH COMPENSATOR?
PURPOSE?
MAXIMUM RANGE?
MAXIMUM EFFECTIVE RANGE
POINT TARGET?

STUDY TEMPLATES

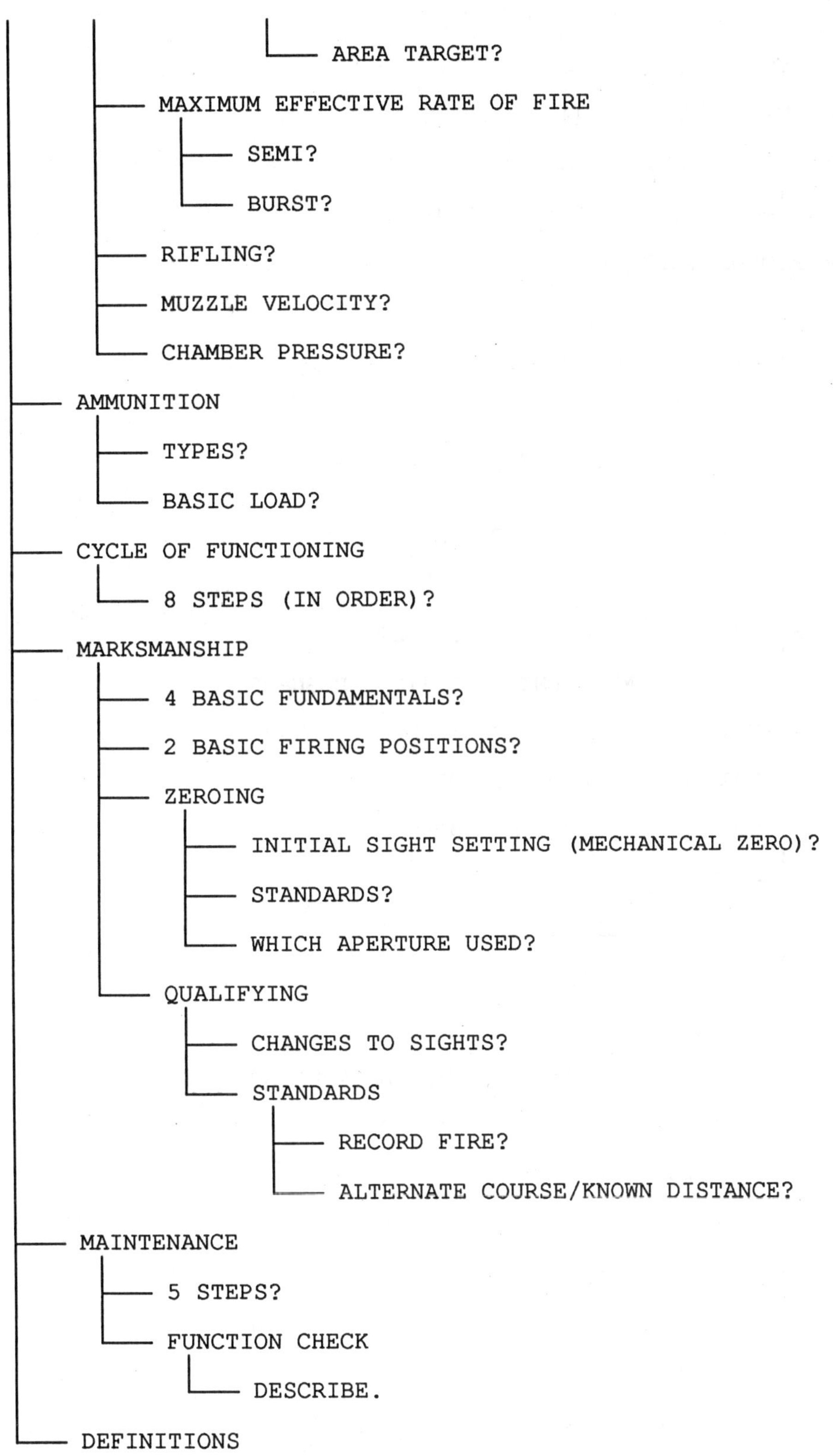
AREA TARGET?
MAXIMUM EFFECTIVE RATE OF FIRE
SEMI?
BURST?
RIFLING?
MUZZLE VELOCITY?
CHAMBER PRESSURE?
AMMUNITION
TYPES?
BASIC LOAD?
CYCLE OF FUNCTIONING
8 STEPS (IN ORDER)?
MARKSMANSHIP
4 BASIC FUNDAMENTALS?
2 BASIC FIRING POSITIONS?
ZEROING
INITIAL SIGHT SETTING (MECHANICAL ZERO)?
STANDARDS?
WHICH APERTURE USED?
QUALIFYING
CHANGES TO SIGHTS?
STANDARDS
RECORD FIRE?
ALTERNATE COURSE/KNOWN DISTANCE?
MAINTENANCE
5 STEPS?
FUNCTION CHECK
DESCRIBE.
DEFINITIONS

STUDY TEMPLATES

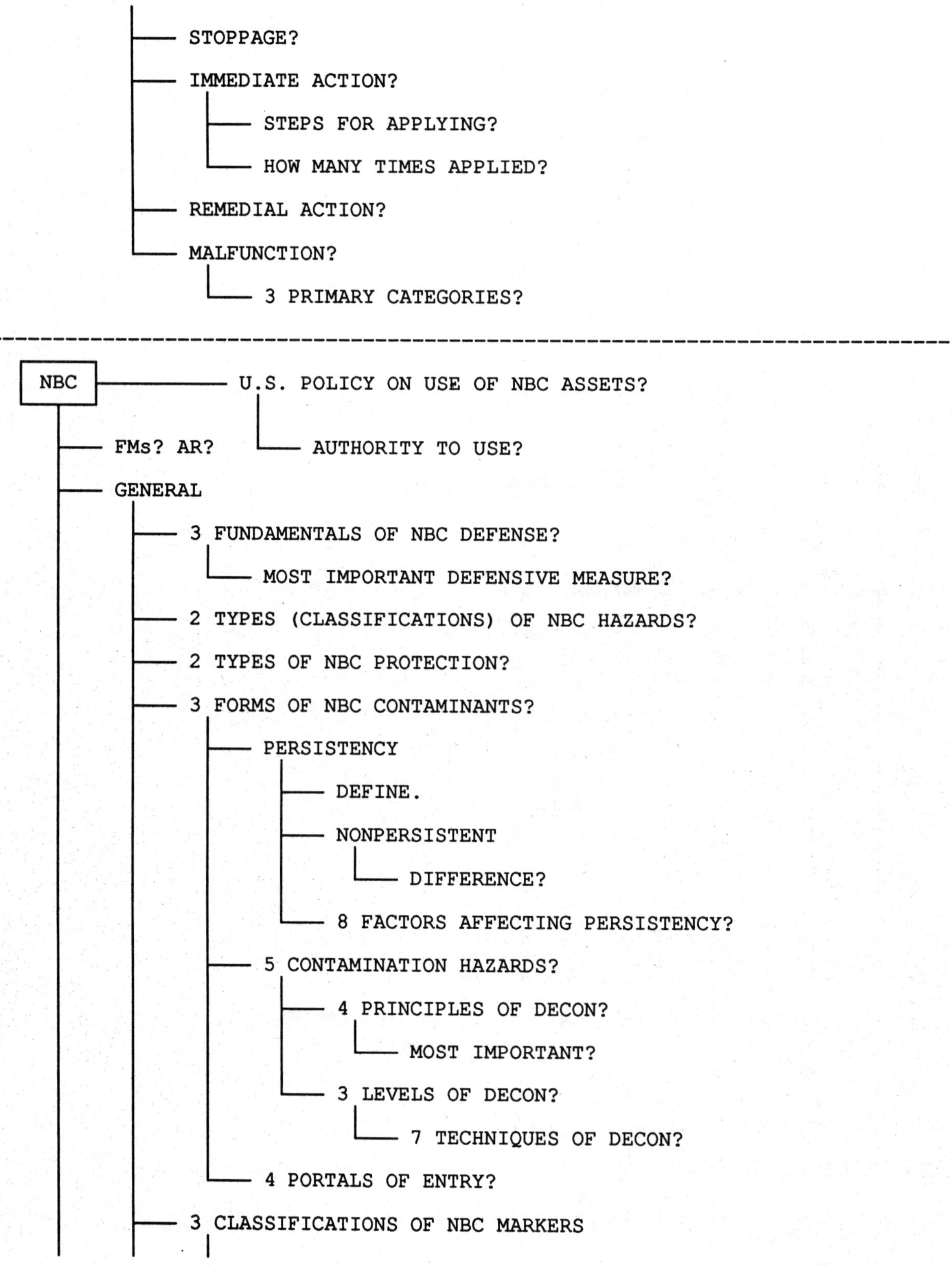

STOPPAGE?
IMMEDIATE ACTION?
STEPS FOR APPLYING?
HOW MANY TIMES APPLIED?
REMEDIAL ACTION?
MALFUNCTION?
3 PRIMARY CATEGORIES?
NBC
U.S. POLICY ON USE OF NBC ASSETS?
AUTHORITY TO USE?
FMs? AR?
GENERAL
3 FUNDAMENTALS OF NBC DEFENSE?
MOST IMPORTANT DEFENSIVE MEASURE?
2 TYPES (CLASSIFICATIONS) OF NBC HAZARDS?
2 TYPES OF NBC PROTECTION?
3 FORMS OF NBC CONTAMINANTS?
PERSISTENCY
DEFINE.
NONPERSISTENT
DIFFERENCE?
8 FACTORS AFFECTING PERSISTENCY?
5 CONTAMINATION HAZARDS?
4 PRINCIPLES OF DECON?
MOST IMPORTANT?
3 LEVELS OF DECON?
7 TECHNIQUES OF DECON?
4 PORTALS OF ENTRY?
3 CLASSIFICATIONS OF NBC MARKERS

STUDY TEMPLATES

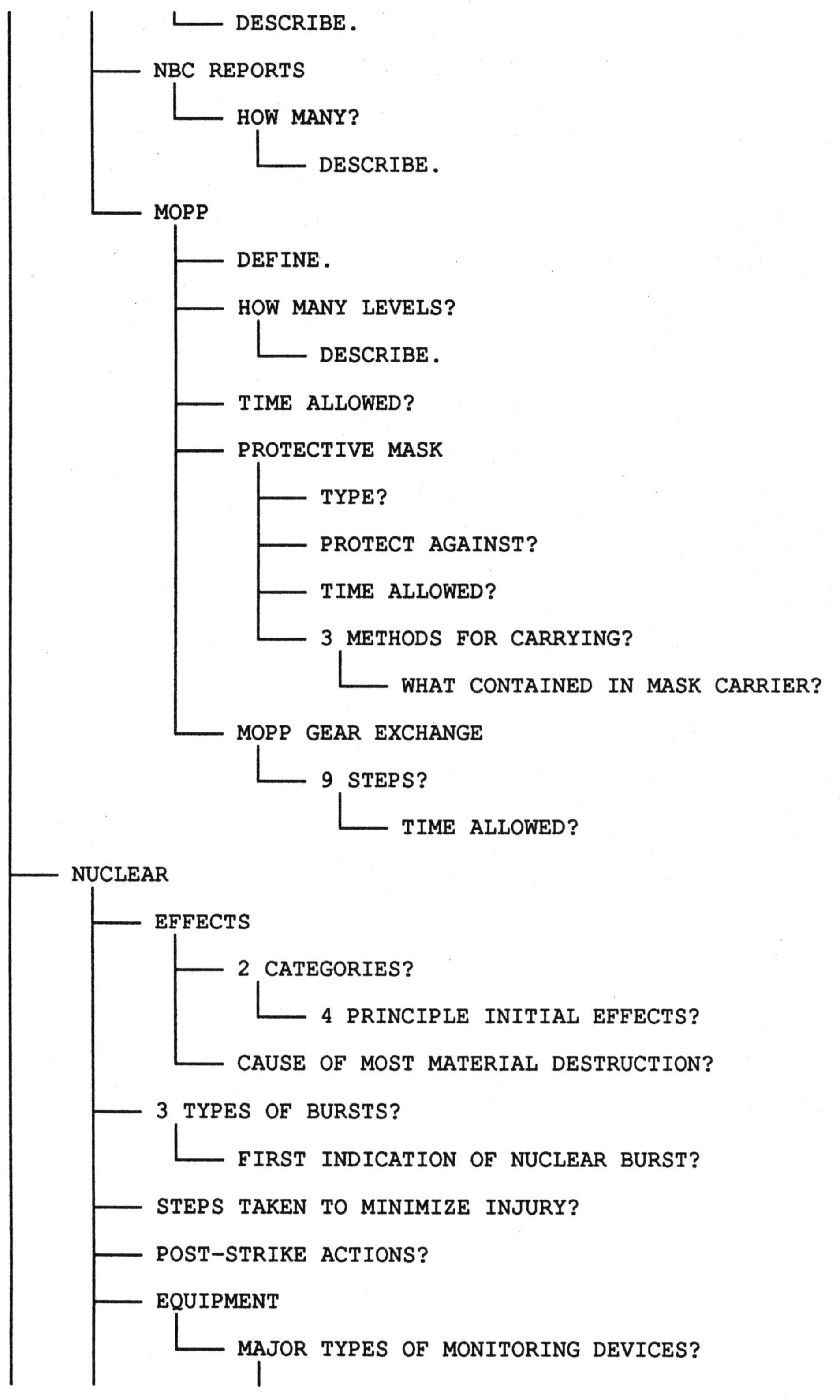
DESCRIBE.
NBC REPORTS
HOW MANY?
DESCRIBE.
MOPP
DEFINE.
HOW MANY LEVELS?
DESCRIBE.
TIME ALLOWED?
PROTECTIVE MASK
TYPE?
PROTECT AGAINST?
TIME ALLOWED?
3 METHODS FOR CARRYING?
WHAT CONTAINED IN MASK CARRIER?
MOPP GEAR EXCHANGE
9 STEPS?
TIME ALLOWED?
NUCLEAR
EFFECTS
2 CATEGORIES?
4 PRINCIPLE INITIAL EFFECTS?
CAUSE OF MOST MATERIAL DESTRUCTION?
3 TYPES OF BURSTS?
FIRST INDICATION OF NUCLEAR BURST?
STEPS TAKEN TO MINIMIZE INJURY?
POST-STRIKE ACTIONS?
EQUIPMENT
MAJOR TYPES OF MONITORING DEVICES?

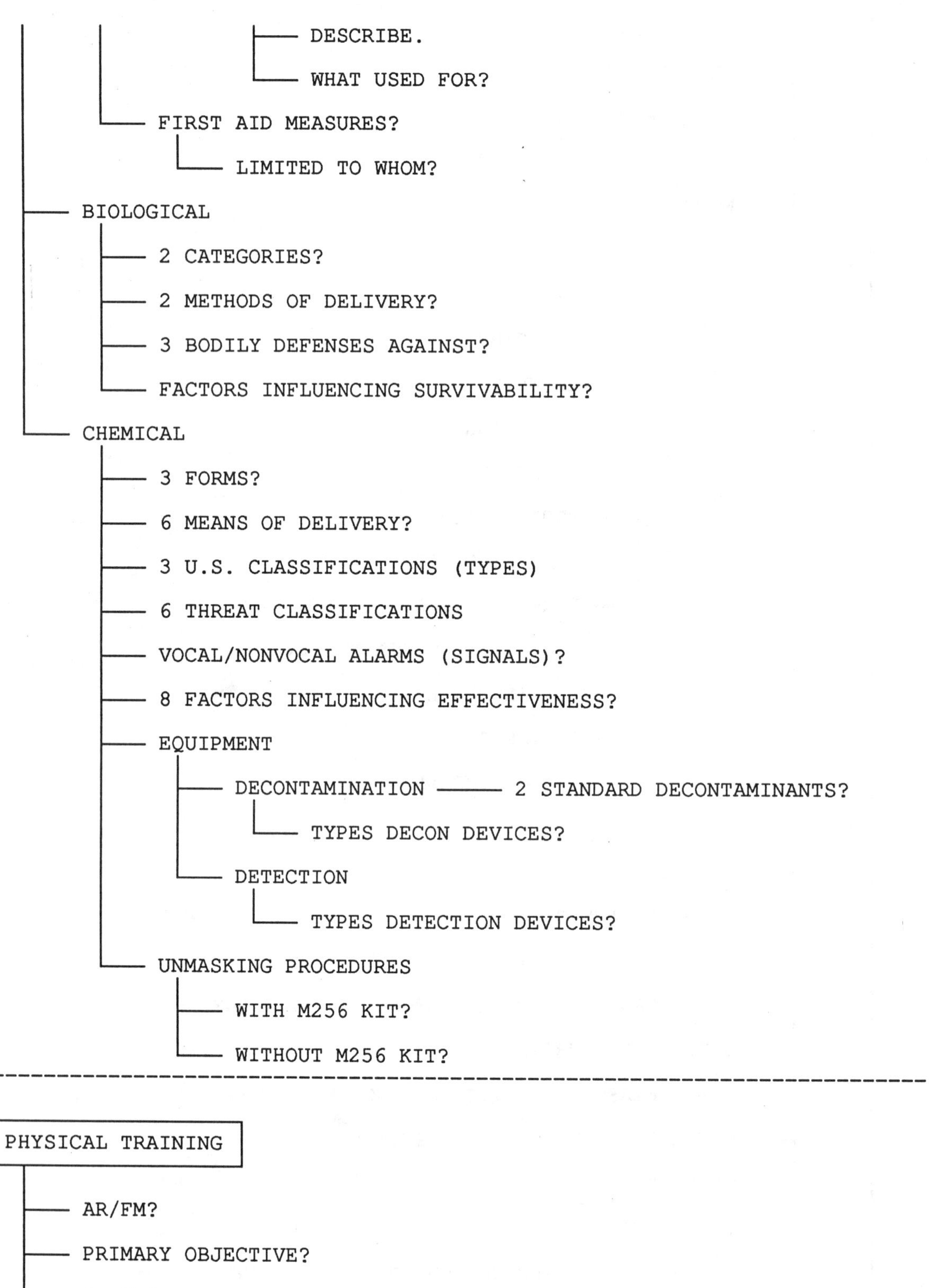

PHYSICAL TRAINING

- AR/FM?
- PRIMARY OBJECTIVE?
- 5 CONSIDERATIONS?

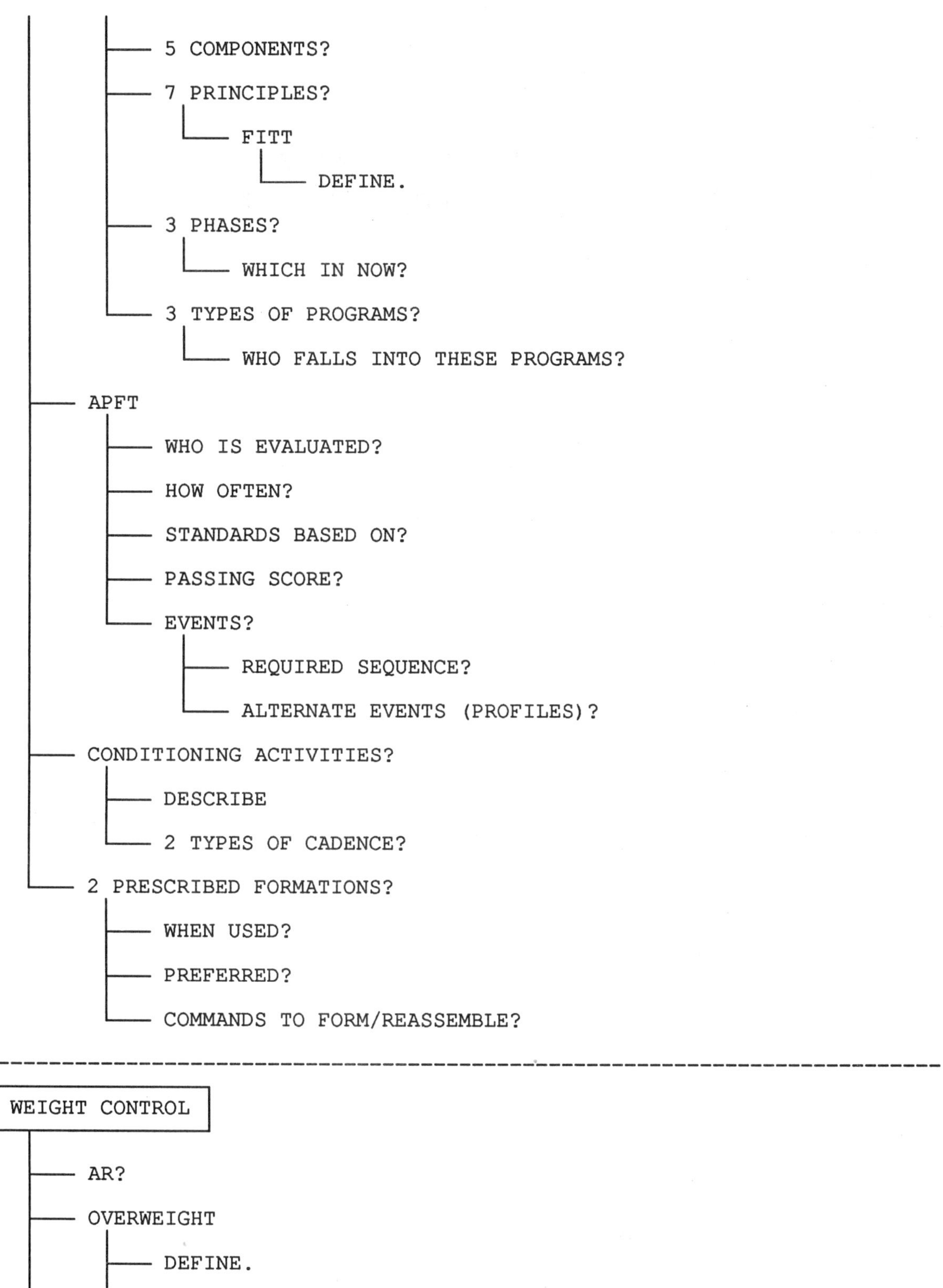
5 COMPONENTS?
7 PRINCIPLES?
FITT
DEFINE.
3 PHASES?
WHICH IN NOW?
3 TYPES OF PROGRAMS?
WHO FALLS INTO THESE PROGRAMS?
APFT
WHO IS EVALUATED?
HOW OFTEN?
STANDARDS BASED ON?
PASSING SCORE?
EVENTS?
REQUIRED SEQUENCE?
ALTERNATE EVENTS (PROFILES)?
CONDITIONING ACTIVITIES?
DESCRIBE
2 TYPES OF CADENCE?
2 PRESCRIBED FORMATIONS?
WHEN USED?
PREFERRED?
COMMANDS TO FORM/REASSEMBLE?

WEIGHT CONTROL

- AR?
- OVERWEIGHT
  - DEFINE.

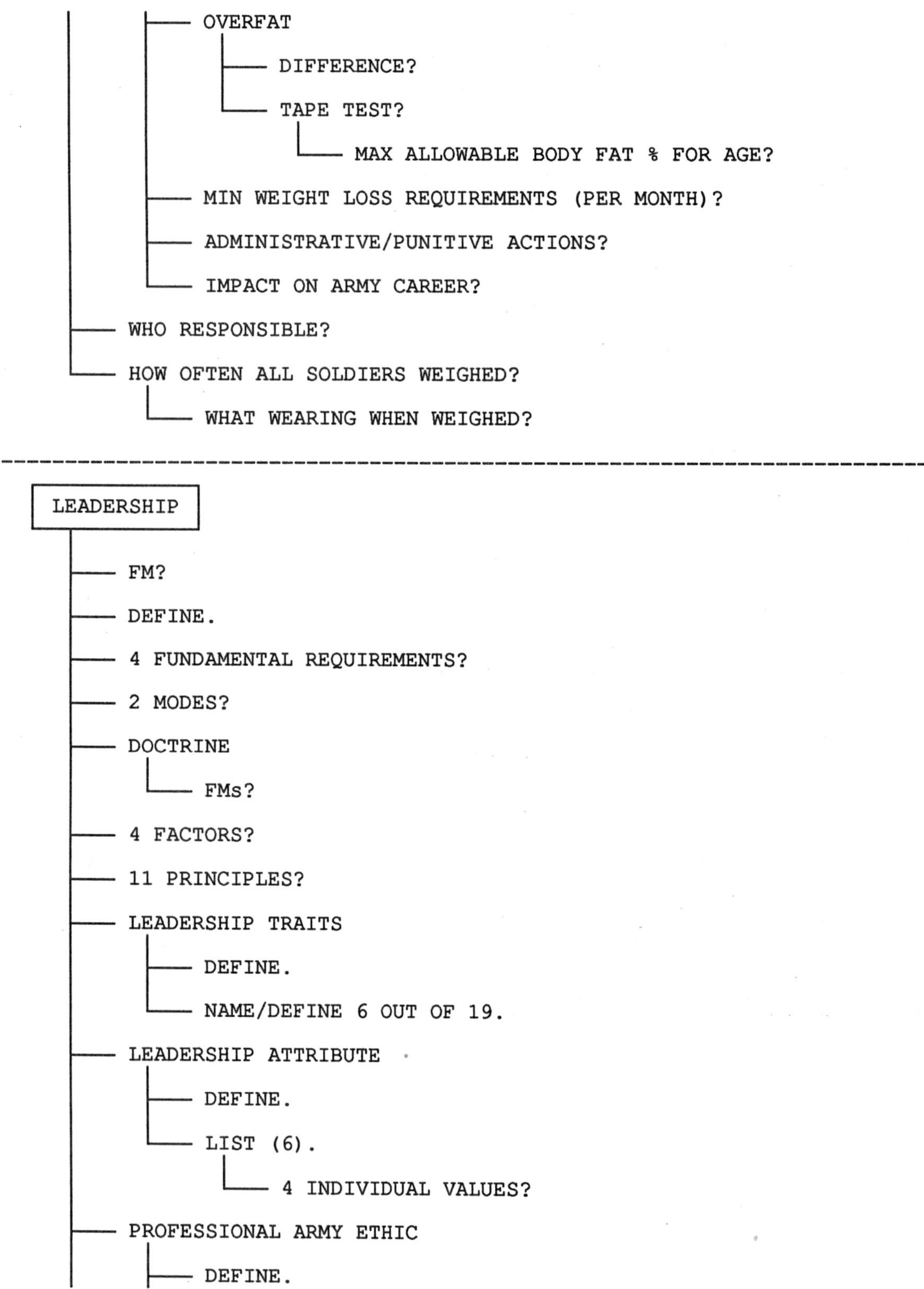
OVERFAT
DIFFERENCE?
TAPE TEST?
MAX ALLOWABLE BODY FAT % FOR AGE?
MIN WEIGHT LOSS REQUIREMENTS (PER MONTH)?
ADMINISTRATIVE/PUNITIVE ACTIONS?
IMPACT ON ARMY CAREER?
WHO RESPONSIBLE?
HOW OFTEN ALL SOLDIERS WEIGHED?
WHAT WEARING WHEN WEIGHED?
LEADERSHIP
FM?
DEFINE.
4 FUNDAMENTAL REQUIREMENTS?
2 MODES?
DOCTRINE
FMs?
4 FACTORS?
11 PRINCIPLES?
LEADERSHIP TRAITS
DEFINE.
NAME/DEFINE 6 OUT OF 19.
LEADERSHIP ATTRIBUTE
DEFINE.
LIST (6).
4 INDIVIDUAL VALUES?
PROFESSIONAL ARMY ETHIC
DEFINE.

STUDY TEMPLATES

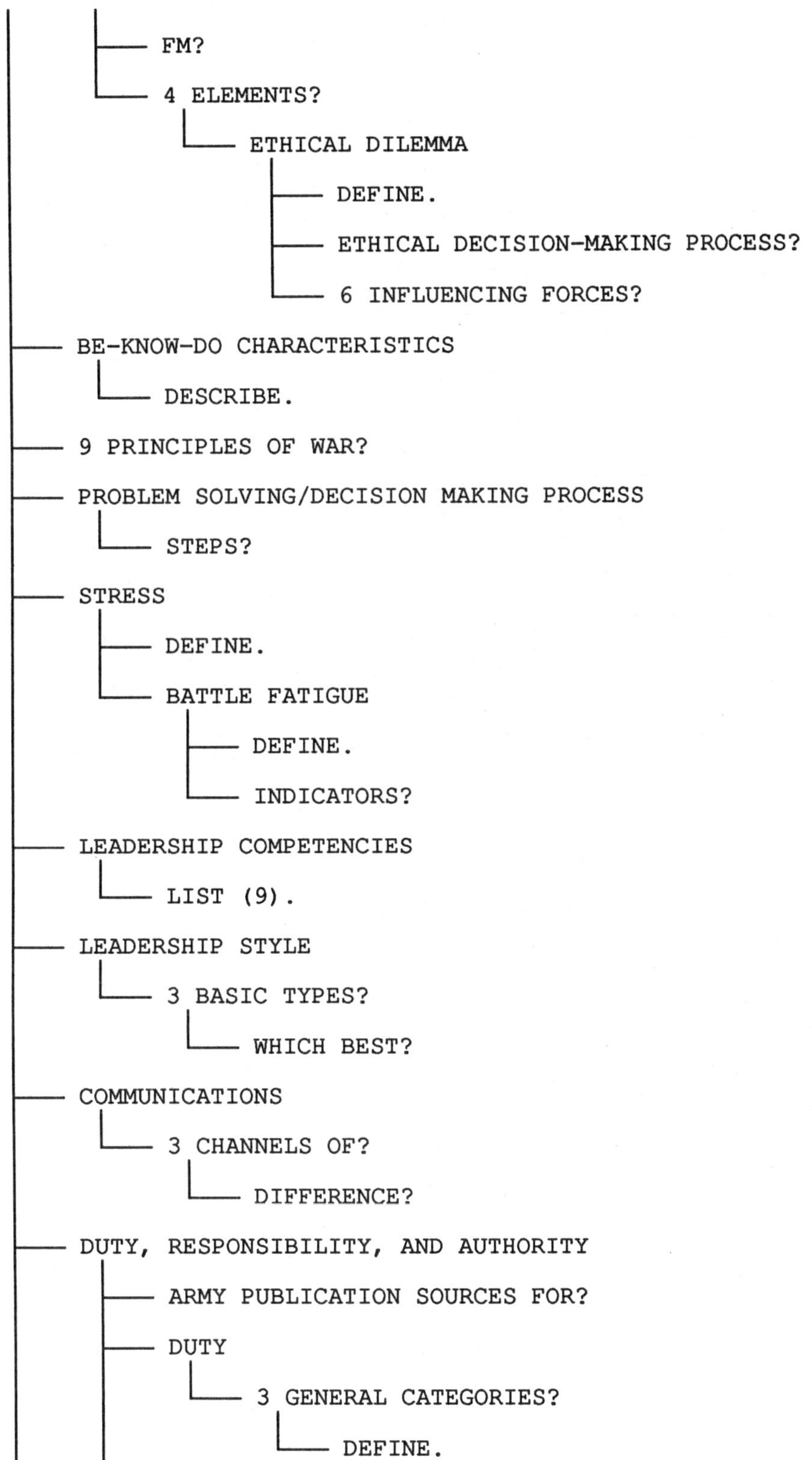
FM?
4 ELEMENTS?
ETHICAL DILEMMA
DEFINE.
ETHICAL DECISION-MAKING PROCESS?
6 INFLUENCING FORCES?
BE-KNOW-DO CHARACTERISTICS
DESCRIBE.
9 PRINCIPLES OF WAR?
PROBLEM SOLVING/DECISION MAKING PROCESS
STEPS?
STRESS
DEFINE.
BATTLE FATIGUE
DEFINE.
INDICATORS?
LEADERSHIP COMPETENCIES
LIST (9).
LEADERSHIP STYLE
3 BASIC TYPES?
WHICH BEST?
COMMUNICATIONS
3 CHANNELS OF?
DIFFERENCE?
DUTY, RESPONSIBILITY, AND AUTHORITY
ARMY PUBLICATION SOURCES FOR?
DUTY
3 GENERAL CATEGORIES?
DEFINE.

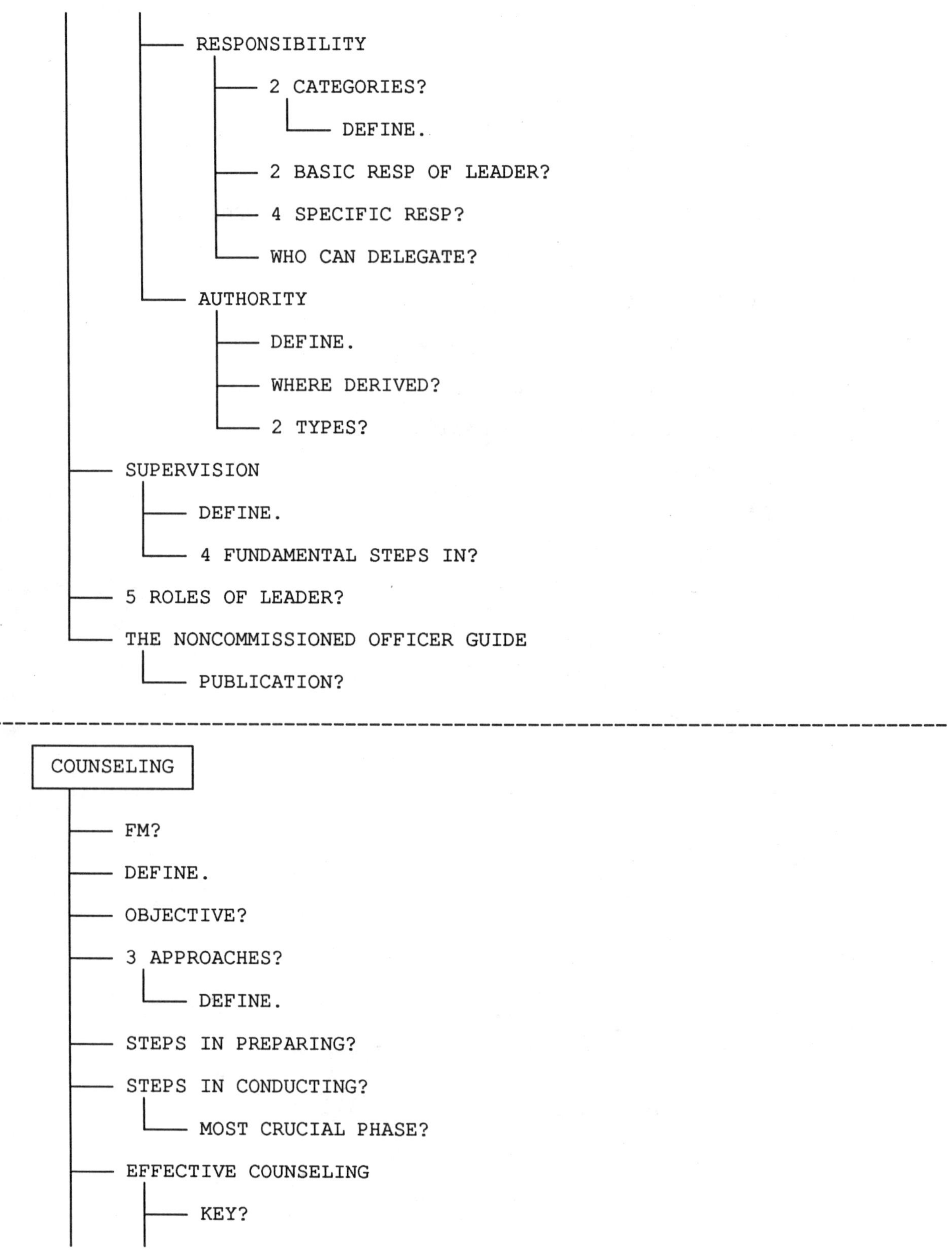
RESPONSIBILITY
2 CATEGORIES?
DEFINE.
2 BASIC RESP OF LEADER?
4 SPECIFIC RESP?
WHO CAN DELEGATE?
AUTHORITY
DEFINE.
WHERE DERIVED?
2 TYPES?
SUPERVISION
DEFINE.
4 FUNDAMENTAL STEPS IN?
5 ROLES OF LEADER?
THE NONCOMMISSIONED OFFICER GUIDE
PUBLICATION?
COUNSELING
FM?
DEFINE.
OBJECTIVE?
3 APPROACHES?
DEFINE.
STEPS IN PREPARING?
STEPS IN CONDUCTING?
MOST CRUCIAL PHASE?
EFFECTIVE COUNSELING
KEY?

STUDY TEMPLATES

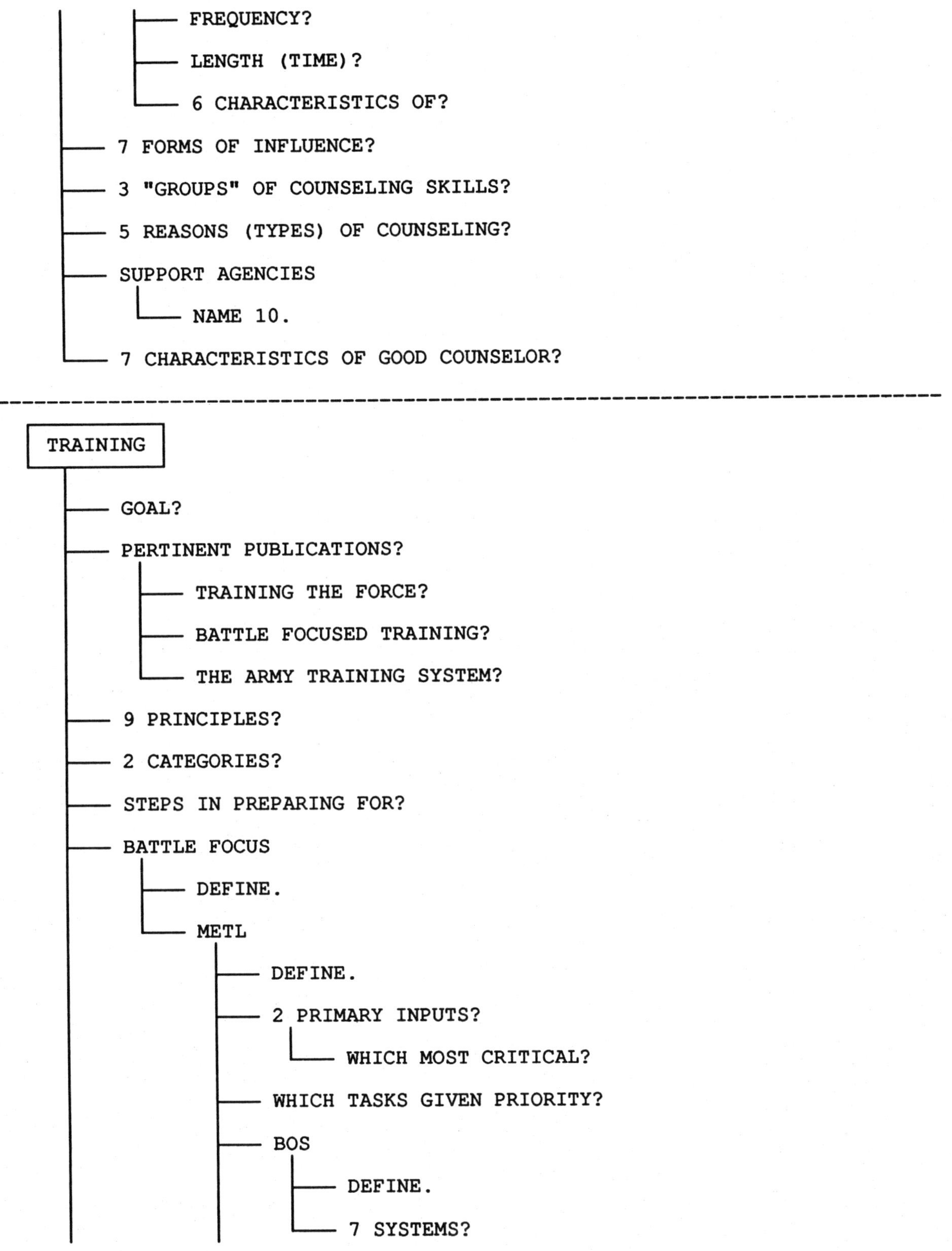

FREQUENCY?
LENGTH (TIME)?
6 CHARACTERISTICS OF?
7 FORMS OF INFLUENCE?
3 "GROUPS" OF COUNSELING SKILLS?
5 REASONS (TYPES) OF COUNSELING?
SUPPORT AGENCIES
NAME 10.
7 CHARACTERISTICS OF GOOD COUNSELOR?
TRAINING
GOAL?
PERTINENT PUBLICATIONS?
TRAINING THE FORCE?
BATTLE FOCUSED TRAINING?
THE ARMY TRAINING SYSTEM?
9 PRINCIPLES?
2 CATEGORIES?
STEPS IN PREPARING FOR?
BATTLE FOCUS
DEFINE.
METL
DEFINE.
2 PRIMARY INPUTS?
WHICH MOST CRITICAL?
WHICH TASKS GIVEN PRIORITY?
BOS
DEFINE.
7 SYSTEMS?

STUDY TEMPLATES

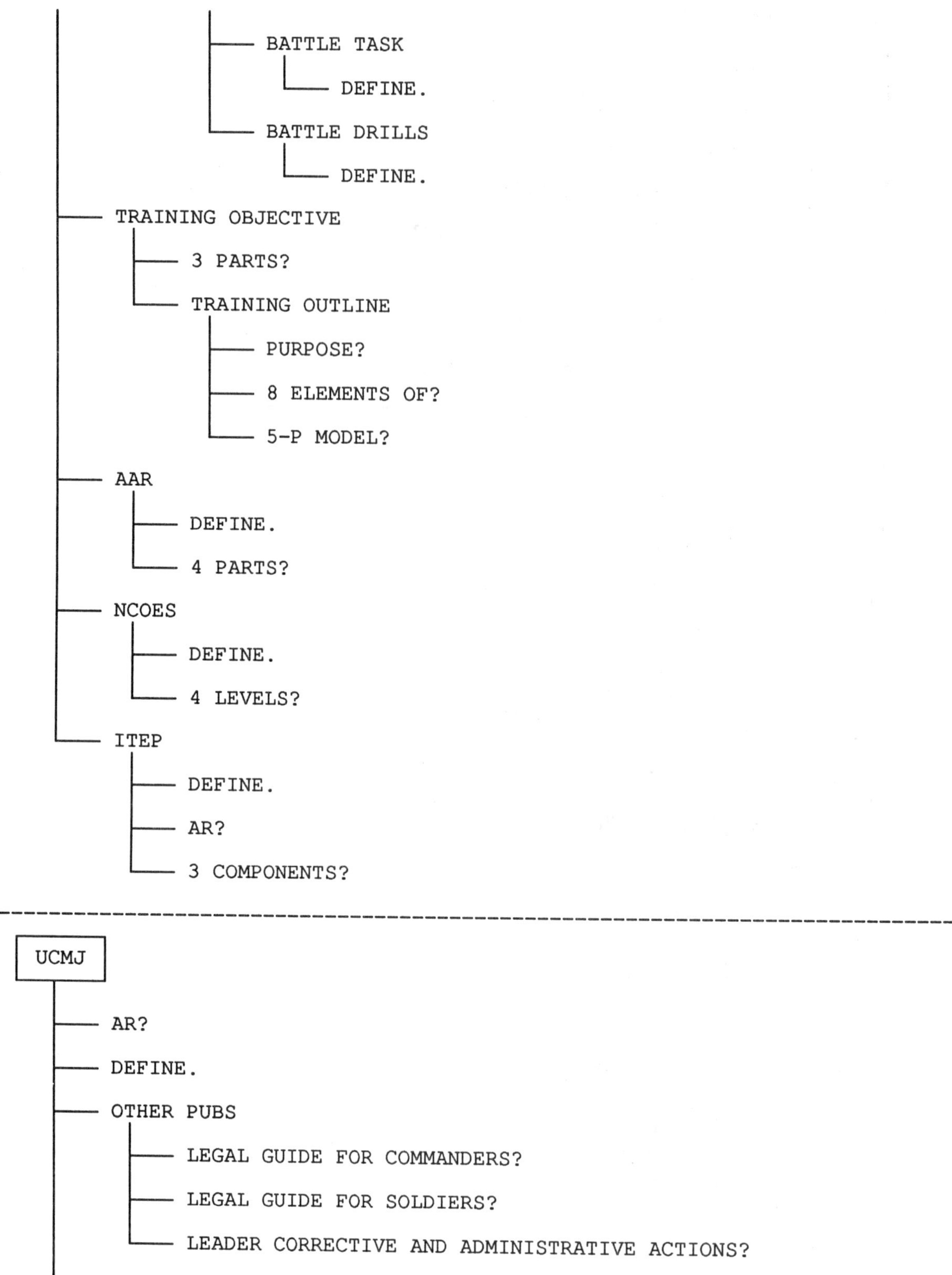
BATTLE TASK
DEFINE.
BATTLE DRILLS
DEFINE.
TRAINING OBJECTIVE
3 PARTS?
TRAINING OUTLINE
PURPOSE?
8 ELEMENTS OF?
5-P MODEL?
AAR
DEFINE.
4 PARTS?
NCOES
DEFINE.
4 LEVELS?
ITEP
DEFINE.
AR?
3 COMPONENTS?
UCMJ
AR?
DEFINE.
OTHER PUBS
LEGAL GUIDE FOR COMMANDERS?
LEGAL GUIDE FOR SOLDIERS?
LEADER CORRECTIVE AND ADMINISTRATIVE ACTIONS?

STUDY TEMPLATES

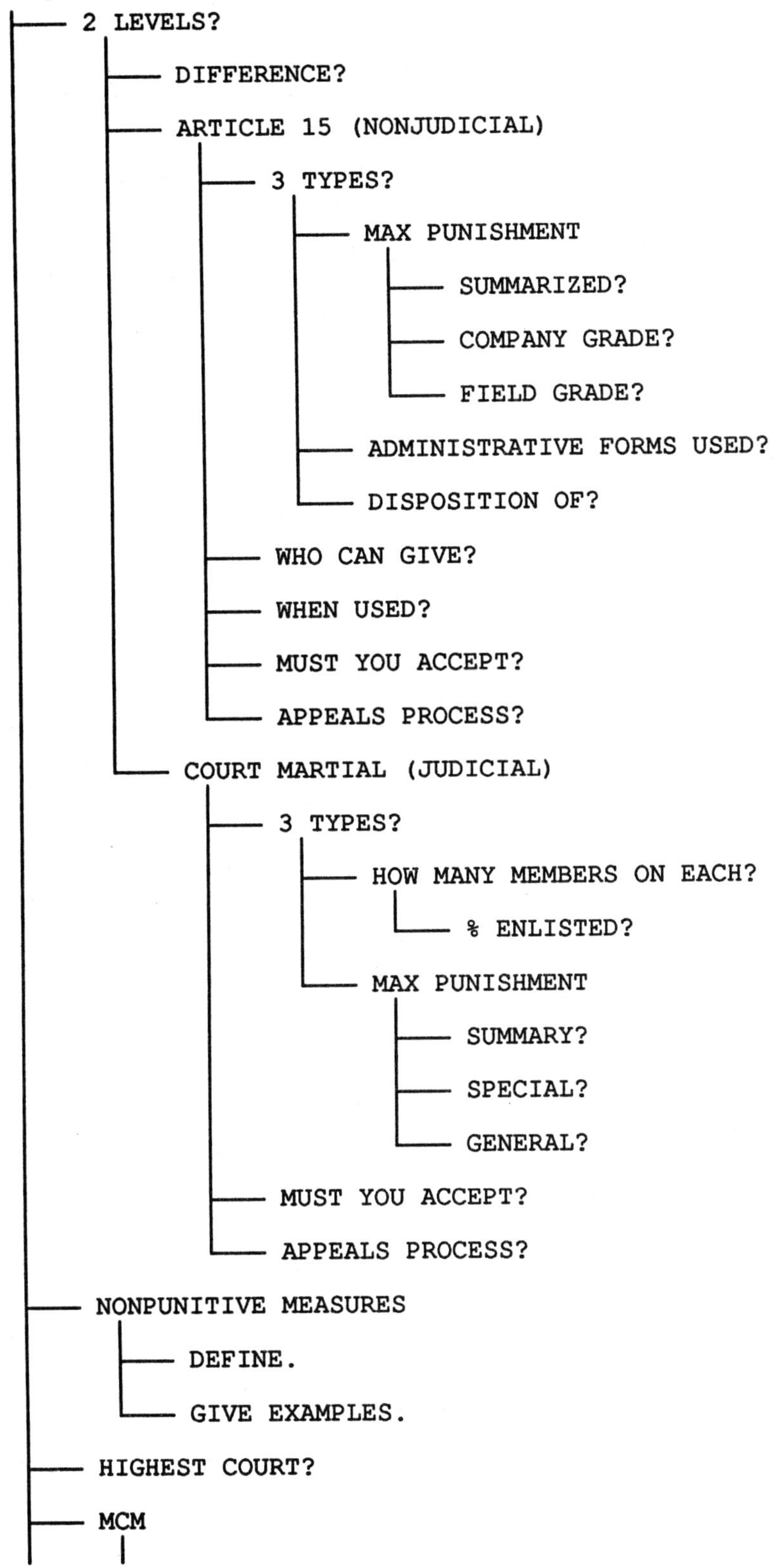
2 LEVELS?
DIFFERENCE?
ARTICLE 15 (NONJUDICIAL)
3 TYPES?
MAX PUNISHMENT
SUMMARIZED?
COMPANY GRADE?
FIELD GRADE?
ADMINISTRATIVE FORMS USED?
DISPOSITION OF?
WHO CAN GIVE?
WHEN USED?
MUST YOU ACCEPT?
APPEALS PROCESS?
COURT MARTIAL (JUDICIAL)
3 TYPES?
HOW MANY MEMBERS ON EACH?
% ENLISTED?
MAX PUNISHMENT
SUMMARY?
SPECIAL?
GENERAL?
MUST YOU ACCEPT?
APPEALS PROCESS?
NONPUNITIVE MEASURES
DEFINE.
GIVE EXAMPLES.
HIGHEST COURT?
MCM

STUDY TEMPLATES

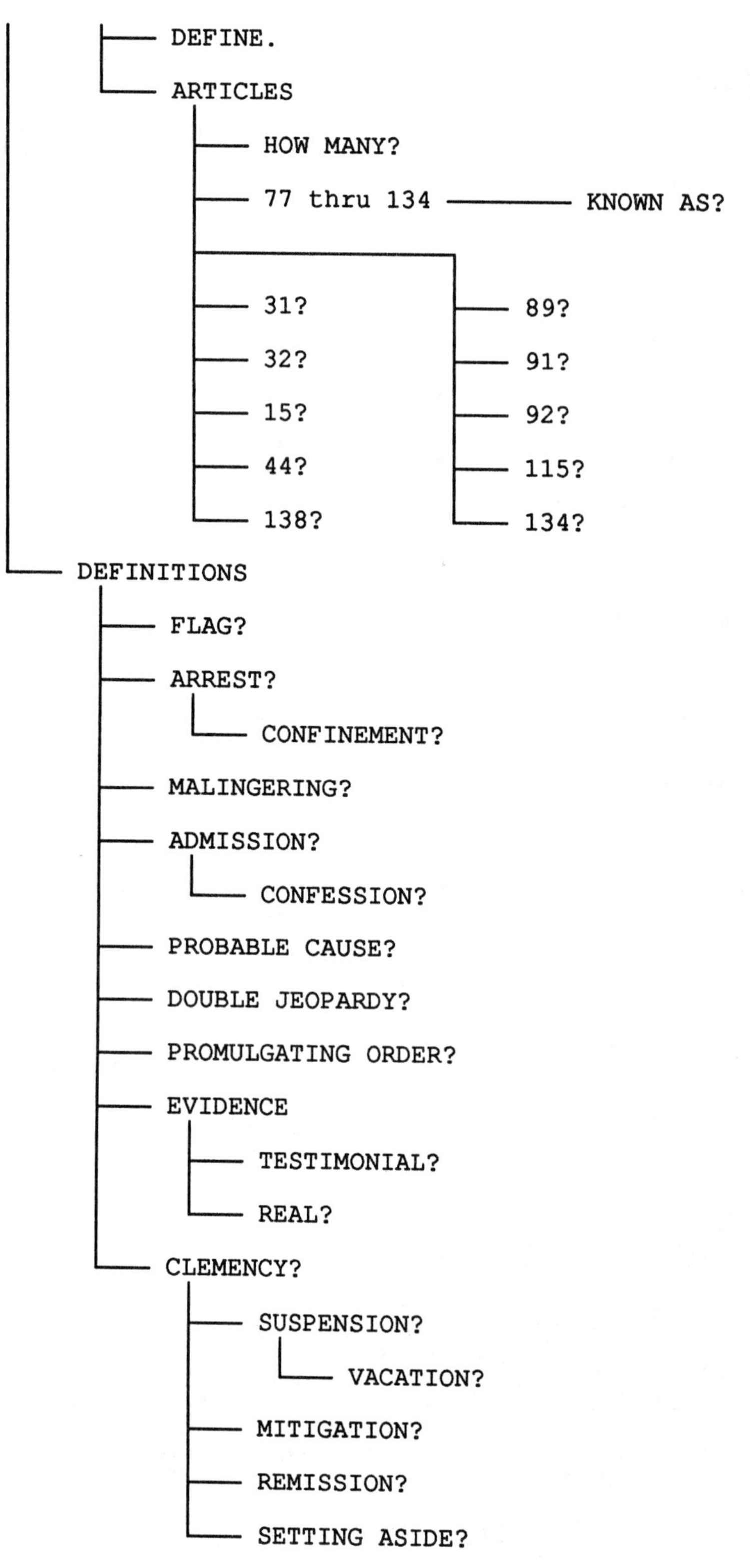
DEFINE.
ARTICLES
HOW MANY?
77 thru 134
KNOWN AS?
31?
32?
15?
44?
138?
89?
91?
92?
115?
134?
DEFINITIONS
FLAG?
ARREST?
CONFINEMENT?
MALINGERING?
ADMISSION?
CONFESSION?
PROBABLE CAUSE?
DOUBLE JEOPARDY?
PROMULGATING ORDER?
EVIDENCE
TESTIMONIAL?
REAL?
CLEMENCY?
SUSPENSION?
VACATION?
MITIGATION?
REMISSION?
SETTING ASIDE?

STUDY TEMPLATES

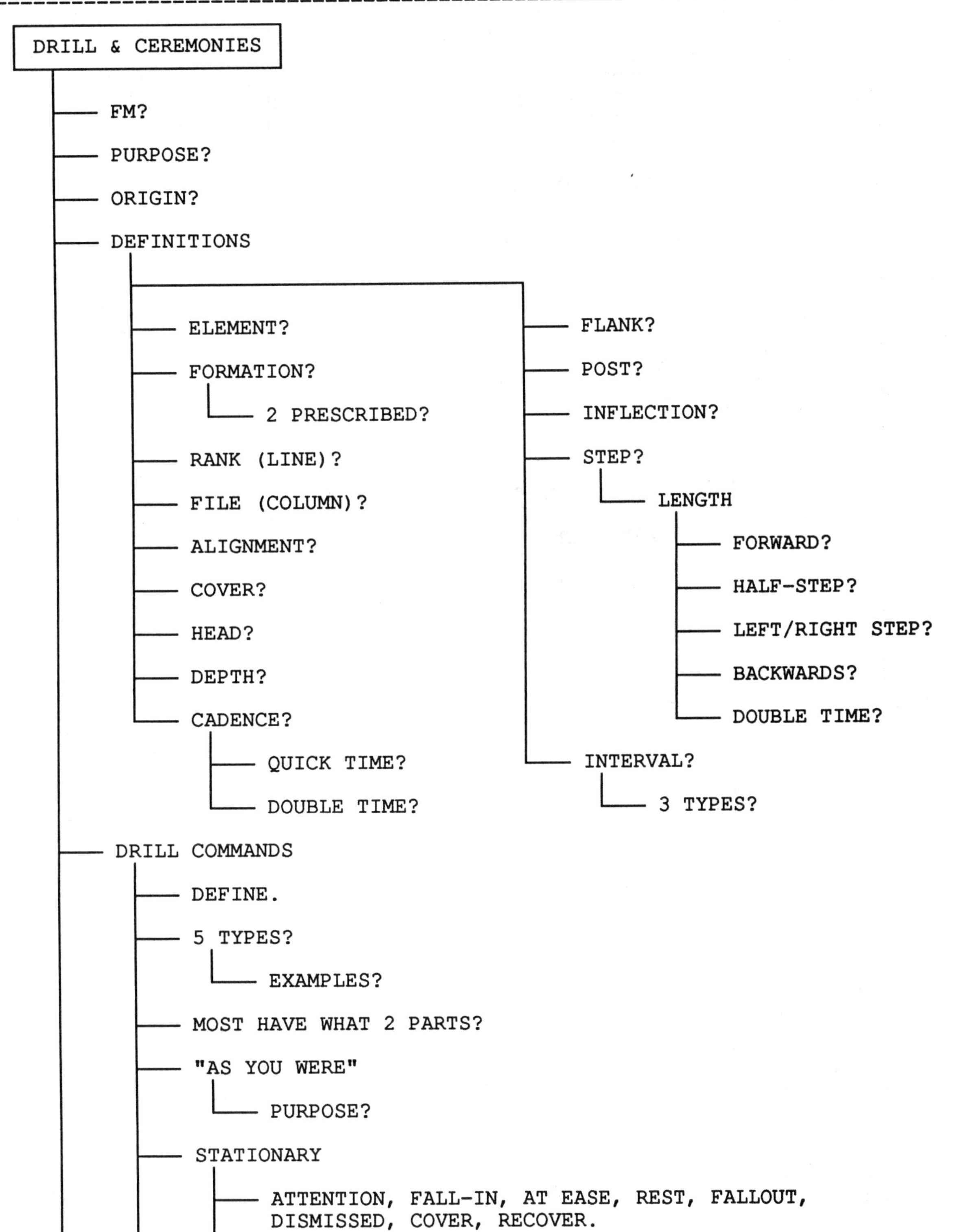
DRILL & CEREMONIES
FM?
PURPOSE?
ORIGIN?
DEFINITIONS
ELEMENT?
FORMATION?
2 PRESCRIBED?
RANK (LINE)?
FILE (COLUMN)?
ALIGNMENT?
COVER?
HEAD?
DEPTH?
CADENCE?
QUICK TIME?
DOUBLE TIME?
FLANK?
POST?
INFLECTION?
STEP?
LENGTH
FORWARD?
HALF-STEP?
LEFT/RIGHT STEP?
BACKWARDS?
DOUBLE TIME?
INTERVAL?
3 TYPES?
DRILL COMMANDS
DEFINE.
5 TYPES?
EXAMPLES?
MOST HAVE WHAT 2 PARTS?
"AS YOU WERE"
PURPOSE?
STATIONARY
ATTENTION, FALL-IN, AT EASE, REST, FALLOUT,
DISMISSED, COVER, RECOVER.

STUDY TEMPLATES

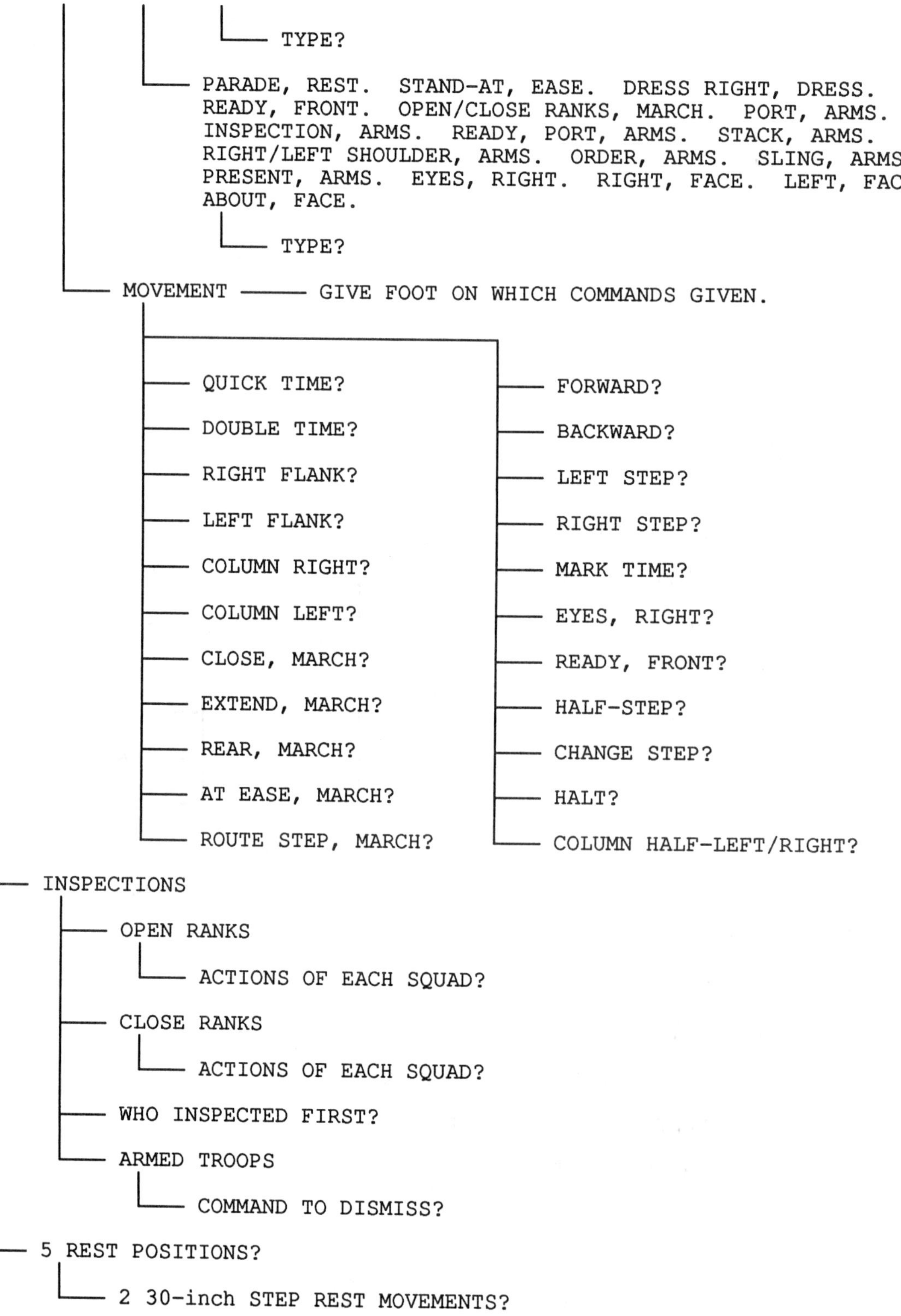

TYPE?
PARADE, REST. STAND-AT, EASE. DRESS RIGHT, DRESS. READY, FRONT. OPEN/CLOSE RANKS, MARCH. PORT, ARMS. INSPECTION, ARMS. READY, PORT, ARMS. STACK, ARMS. RIGHT/LEFT SHOULDER, ARMS. ORDER, ARMS. SLING, ARMS. PRESENT, ARMS. EYES, RIGHT. RIGHT, FACE. LEFT, FACE. ABOUT, FACE.
TYPE?
MOVEMENT
GIVE FOOT ON WHICH COMMANDS GIVEN.
QUICK TIME?
DOUBLE TIME?
RIGHT FLANK?
LEFT FLANK?
COLUMN RIGHT?
COLUMN LEFT?
CLOSE, MARCH?
EXTEND, MARCH?
REAR, MARCH?
AT EASE, MARCH?
ROUTE STEP, MARCH?
FORWARD?
BACKWARD?
LEFT STEP?
RIGHT STEP?
MARK TIME?
EYES, RIGHT?
READY, FRONT?
HALF-STEP?
CHANGE STEP?
HALT?
COLUMN HALF-LEFT/RIGHT?
INSPECTIONS
OPEN RANKS
ACTIONS OF EACH SQUAD?
CLOSE RANKS
ACTIONS OF EACH SQUAD?
WHO INSPECTED FIRST?
ARMED TROOPS
COMMAND TO DISMISS?
5 REST POSITIONS?
2 30-inch STEP REST MOVEMENTS?

STUDY TEMPLATES

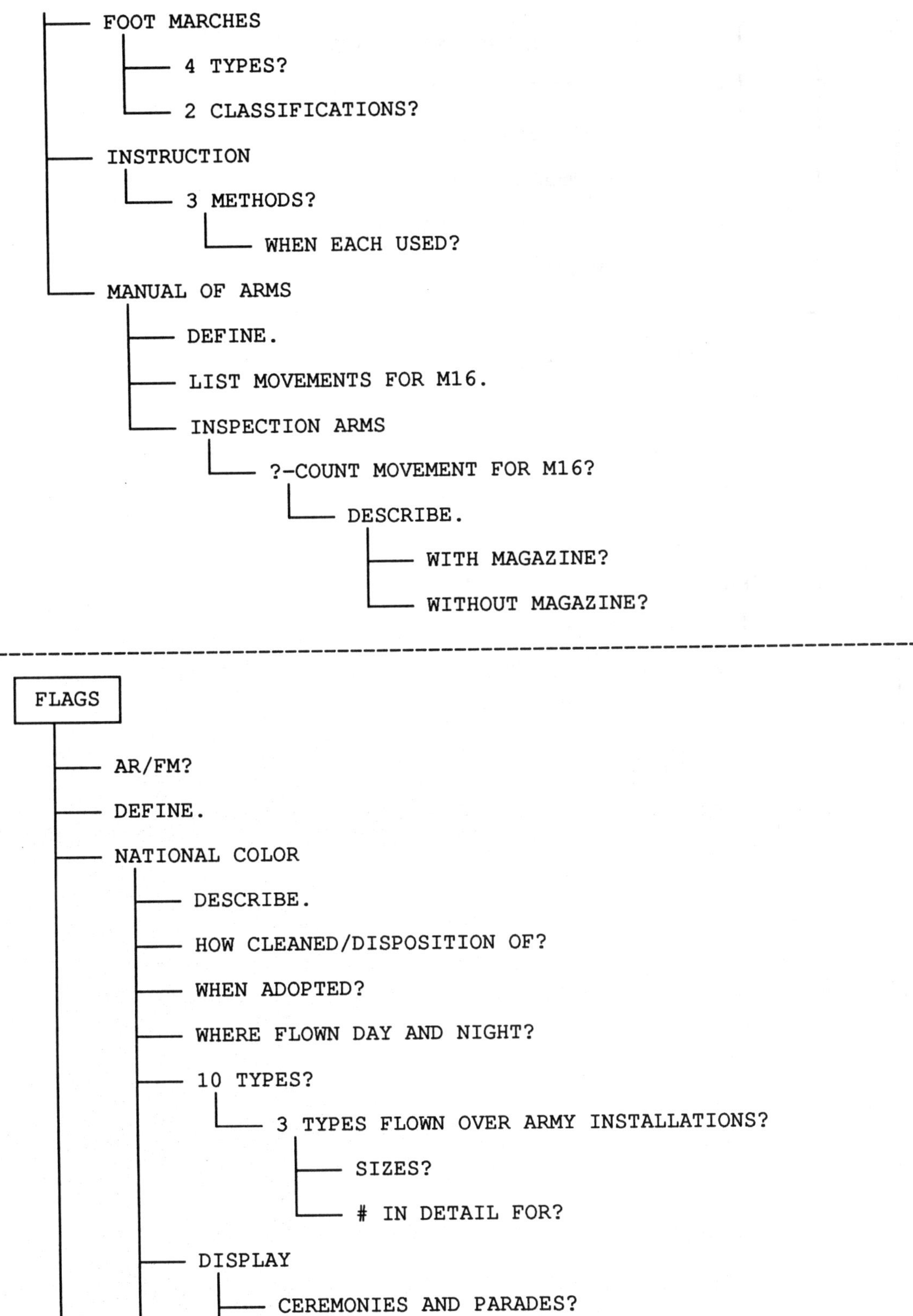
FOOT MARCHES
4 TYPES?
2 CLASSIFICATIONS?
INSTRUCTION
3 METHODS?
WHEN EACH USED?
MANUAL OF ARMS
DEFINE.
LIST MOVEMENTS FOR M16.
INSPECTION ARMS
?-COUNT MOVEMENT FOR M16?
DESCRIBE.
WITH MAGAZINE?
WITHOUT MAGAZINE?
FLAGS
AR/FM?
DEFINE.
NATIONAL COLOR
DESCRIBE.
HOW CLEANED/DISPOSITION OF?
WHEN ADOPTED?
WHERE FLOWN DAY AND NIGHT?
10 TYPES?
3 TYPES FLOWN OVER ARMY INSTALLATIONS?
SIZES?
IN DETAIL FOR?
DISPLAY
CEREMONIES AND PARADES?

STUDY TEMPLATES

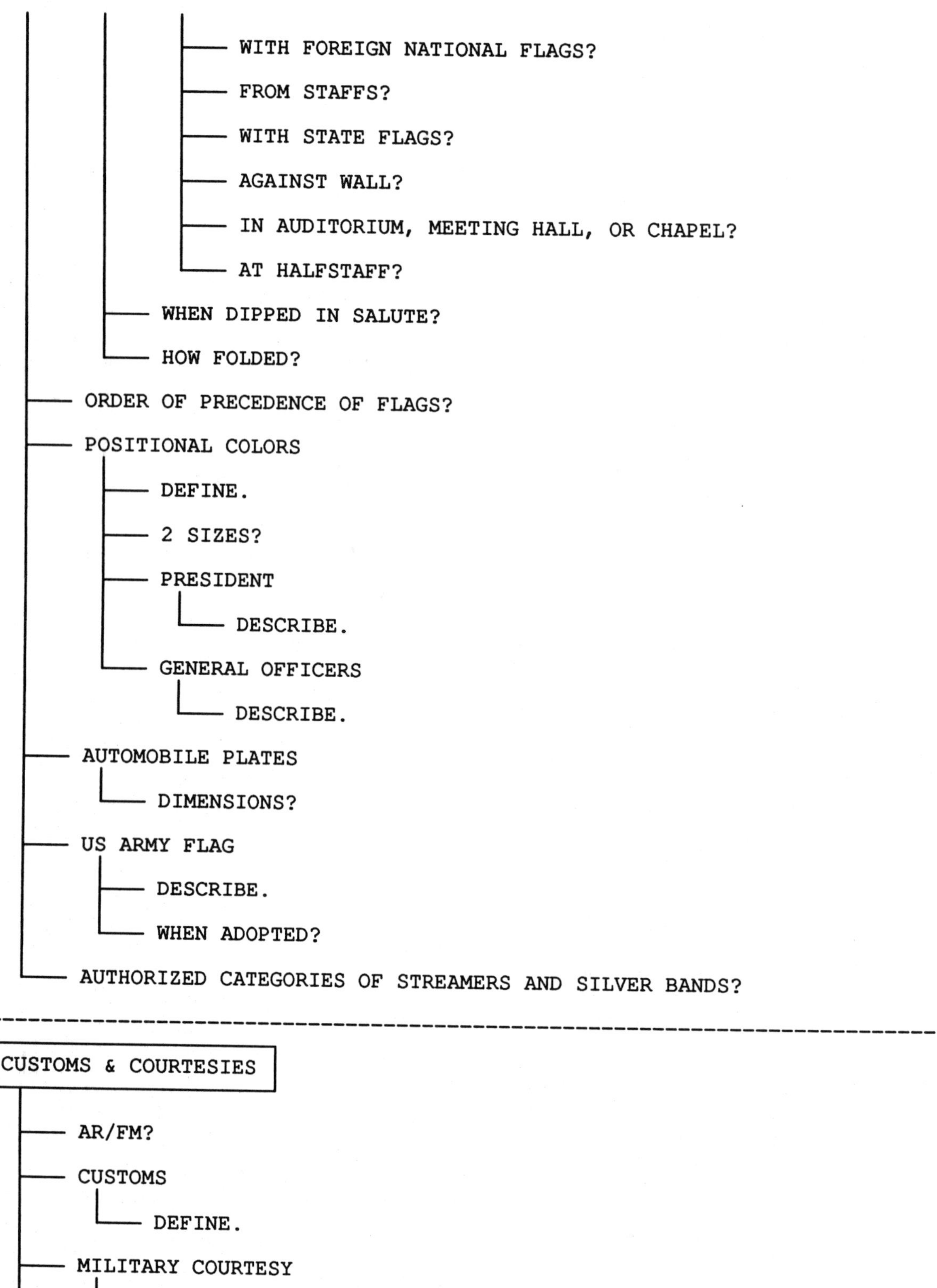
WITH FOREIGN NATIONAL FLAGS?
FROM STAFFS?
WITH STATE FLAGS?
AGAINST WALL?
IN AUDITORIUM, MEETING HALL, OR CHAPEL?
AT HALFSTAFF?
WHEN DIPPED IN SALUTE?
HOW FOLDED?
ORDER OF PRECEDENCE OF FLAGS?
POSITIONAL COLORS
DEFINE.
2 SIZES?
PRESIDENT
DESCRIBE.
GENERAL OFFICERS
DESCRIBE.
AUTOMOBILE PLATES
DIMENSIONS?
US ARMY FLAG
DESCRIBE.
WHEN ADOPTED?
AUTHORIZED CATEGORIES OF STREAMERS AND SILVER BANDS?
CUSTOMS & COURTESIES
AR/FM?
CUSTOMS
DEFINE.
MILITARY COURTESY

STUDY TEMPLATES

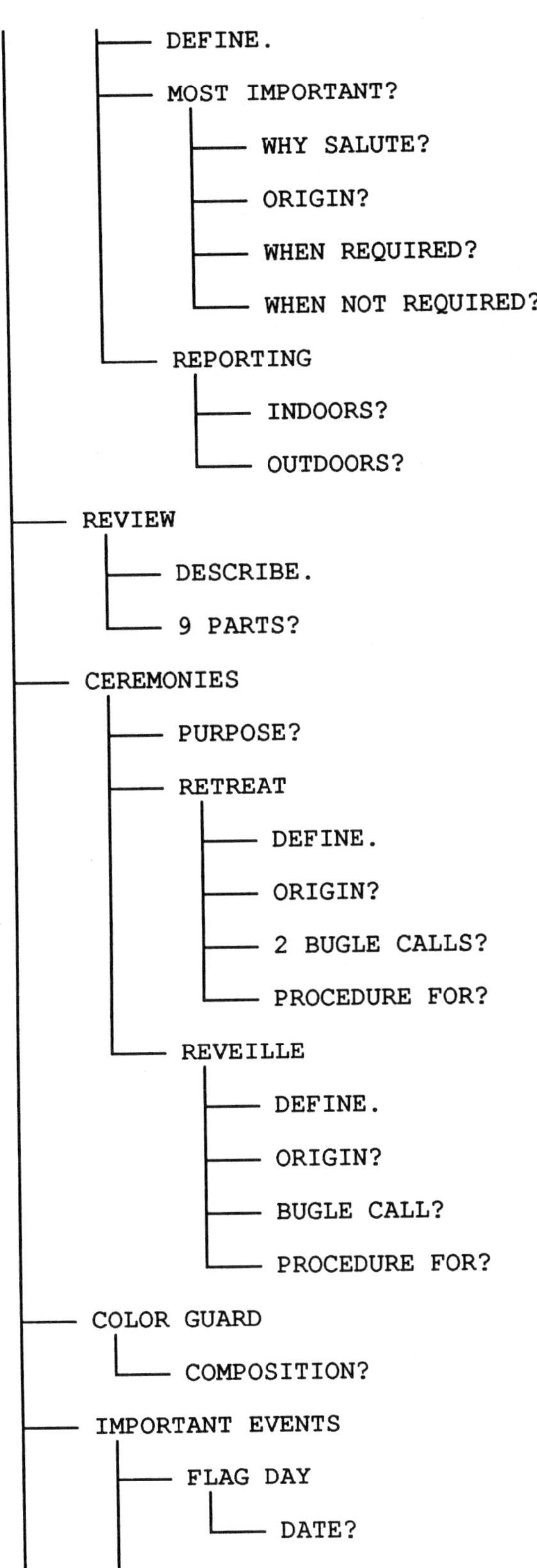
DEFINE.
MOST IMPORTANT?
WHY SALUTE?
ORIGIN?
WHEN REQUIRED?
WHEN NOT REQUIRED?
REPORTING
INDOORS?
OUTDOORS?
REVIEW
DESCRIBE.
9 PARTS?
CEREMONIES
PURPOSE?
RETREAT
DEFINE.
ORIGIN?
2 BUGLE CALLS?
PROCEDURE FOR?
REVEILLE
DEFINE.
ORIGIN?
BUGLE CALL?
PROCEDURE FOR?
COLOR GUARD
COMPOSITION?
IMPORTANT EVENTS
FLAG DAY
DATE?

STUDY TEMPLATES

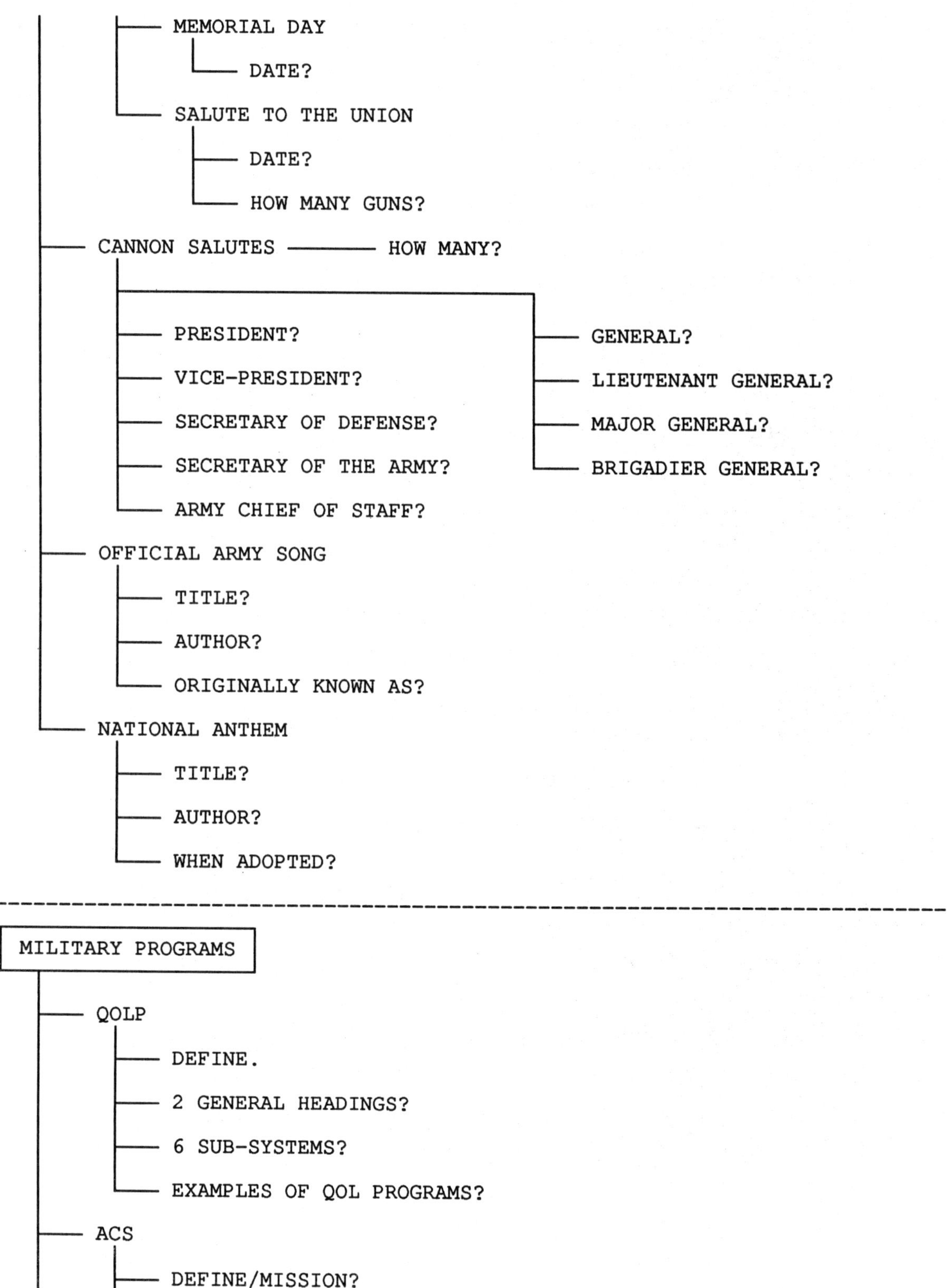

MEMORIAL DAY
DATE?
SALUTE TO THE UNION
DATE?
HOW MANY GUNS?
CANNON SALUTES
HOW MANY?
PRESIDENT?
VICE-PRESIDENT?
SECRETARY OF DEFENSE?
SECRETARY OF THE ARMY?
ARMY CHIEF OF STAFF?
GENERAL?
LIEUTENANT GENERAL?
MAJOR GENERAL?
BRIGADIER GENERAL?
OFFICIAL ARMY SONG
TITLE?
AUTHOR?
ORIGINALLY KNOWN AS?
NATIONAL ANTHEM
TITLE?
AUTHOR?
WHEN ADOPTED?
MILITARY PROGRAMS
QOLP
DEFINE.
2 GENERAL HEADINGS?
6 SUB-SYSTEMS?
EXAMPLES OF QOL PROGRAMS?
ACS
DEFINE/MISSION?

STUDY TEMPLATES

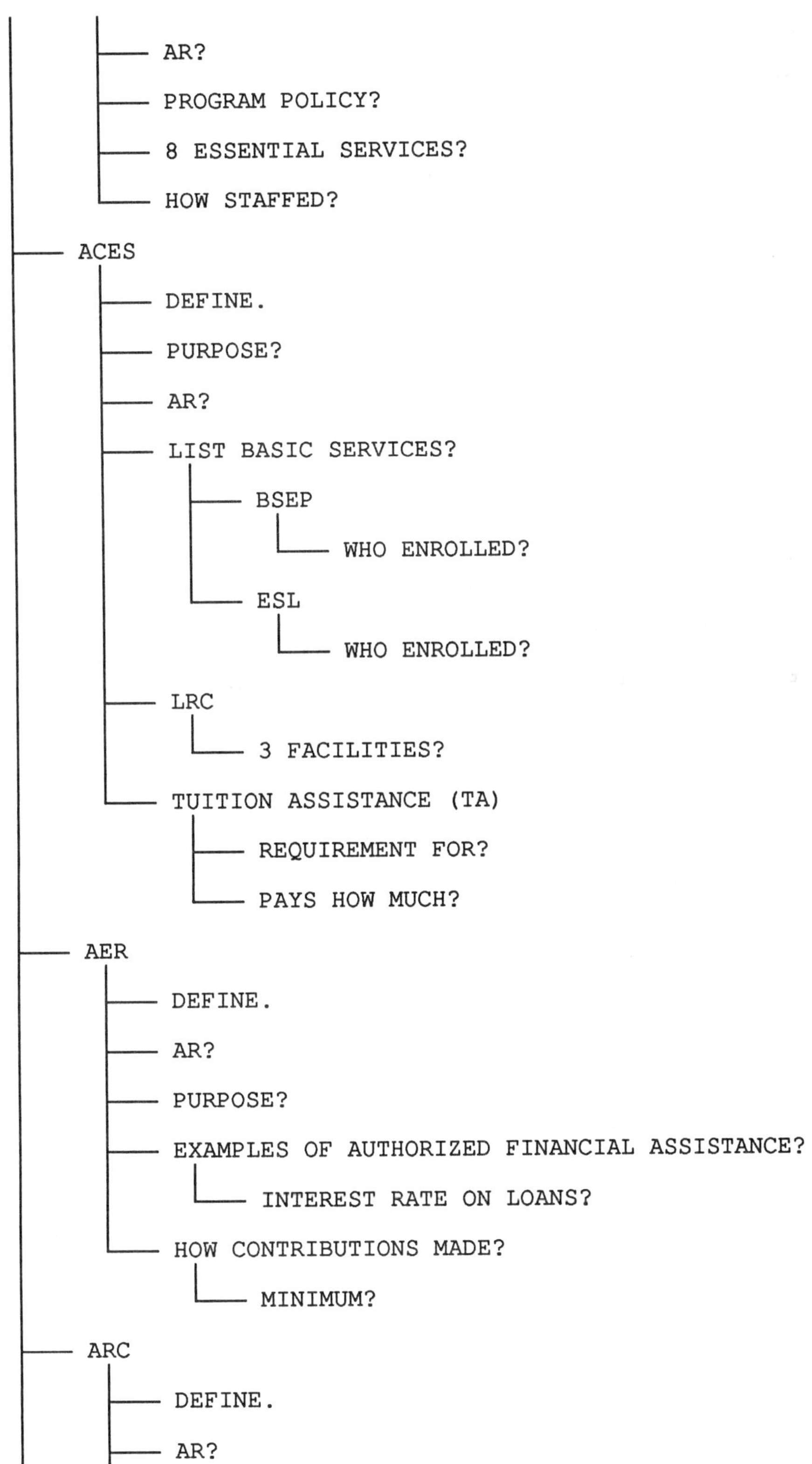
AR?
PROGRAM POLICY?
8 ESSENTIAL SERVICES?
HOW STAFFED?
ACES
DEFINE.
PURPOSE?
AR?
LIST BASIC SERVICES?
BSEP
WHO ENROLLED?
ESL
WHO ENROLLED?
LRC
3 FACILITIES?
TUITION ASSISTANCE (TA)
REQUIREMENT FOR?
PAYS HOW MUCH?
AER
DEFINE.
AR?
PURPOSE?
EXAMPLES OF AUTHORIZED FINANCIAL ASSISTANCE?
INTEREST RATE ON LOANS?
HOW CONTRIBUTIONS MADE?
MINIMUM?
ARC
DEFINE.
AR?

STUDY TEMPLATES

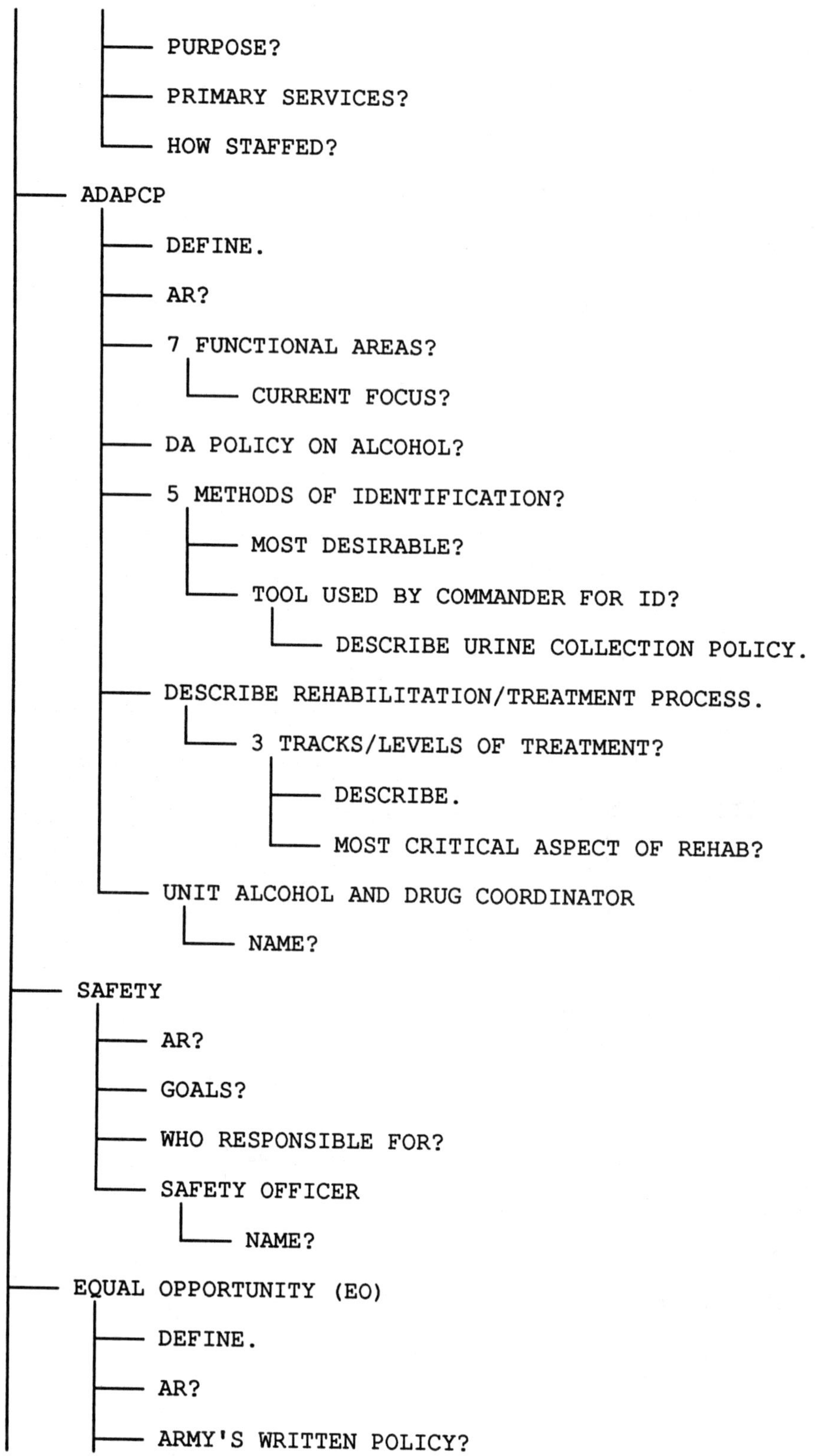
PURPOSE?
PRIMARY SERVICES?
HOW STAFFED?
ADAPCP
DEFINE.
AR?
7 FUNCTIONAL AREAS?
CURRENT FOCUS?
DA POLICY ON ALCOHOL?
5 METHODS OF IDENTIFICATION?
MOST DESIRABLE?
TOOL USED BY COMMANDER FOR ID?
DESCRIBE URINE COLLECTION POLICY.
DESCRIBE REHABILITATION/TREATMENT PROCESS.
3 TRACKS/LEVELS OF TREATMENT?
DESCRIBE.
MOST CRITICAL ASPECT OF REHAB?
UNIT ALCOHOL AND DRUG COORDINATOR
NAME?
SAFETY
AR?
GOALS?
WHO RESPONSIBLE FOR?
SAFETY OFFICER
NAME?
EQUAL OPPORTUNITY (EO)
DEFINE.
AR?
ARMY'S WRITTEN POLICY?

STUDY TEMPLATES

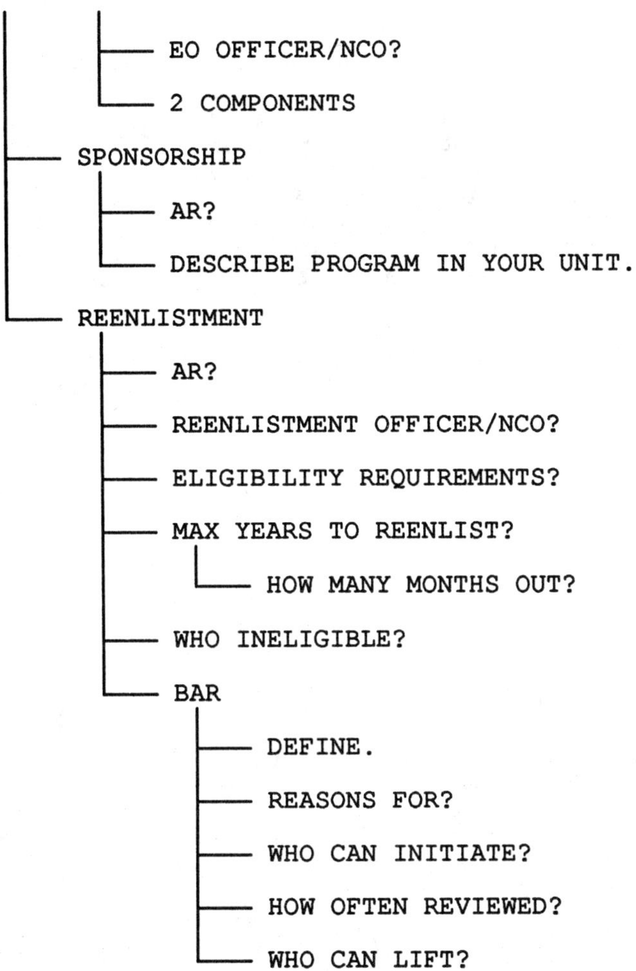
EO OFFICER/NCO?
2 COMPONENTS
SPONSORSHIP
AR?
DESCRIBE PROGRAM IN YOUR UNIT.
REENLISTMENT
AR?
REENLISTMENT OFFICER/NCO?
ELIGIBILITY REQUIREMENTS?
MAX YEARS TO REENLIST?
HOW MANY MONTHS OUT?
WHO INELIGIBLE?
BAR
DEFINE.
REASONS FOR?
WHO CAN INITIATE?
HOW OFTEN REVIEWED?
WHO CAN LIFT?

THE SERGEANT MORALES BOARD
USAREUR Reg 600-2

The Sergeant Morales Club (SMC) is an elite organization consisting of those noncommissioned officers whose demonstrated performance is characterized by that of Sergeant Morales. The SMC was started in 1973 by LTG George S. Blanchard, then VII Corps Commander (US Army, Europe), to recognize the non-commissioned officers who demonstrate the highest degree of leadership, professionalism, and regard for soldiers' welfare. The club's first selection board convened November 19, 1973. It was adopted by USAREUR throughout the command two years later.

"Sergeant Morales" is the fictitious name of a noncommissioned officer who, as a squad leader, consistently demonstrated the highest qualities of leadership, professionalism, and regard for the welfare of the soldier (see "The Sergeant Morales Story" below).

* Primary requirements for selection as a Sergeant Morales Club member are:

    a. Must be an NCO (CPL through SFC or PSG).
    b. Must directly supervise a minimum of two soldiers by TO&E or TDA position.
    c. Must be selected for membership by a final selection authority level board (Corps level Sergeant Morales Board).

* Selection into the Sergeant Morales Club requires a recommendation from the Sergeant Morales Board at each command level to include, but not limited to, Battalion, Brigade, Division, and the final selection authority at Corps level. The Board normally consists entirely of CSMs and requires a broad knowledge of general subject areas and family/soldier support agencies (see sample subject areas below). It may also include hands-on proficiency evaluations in certain areas (ie, weapons function checks, weapons zero procedures including shot-group analysis, weaponeer, call-for-fire computer simulation, drill movements/commands, etc). Quotas are not established. Selection boards will not select nominees if they do not meet the required standards of excellence.

* Selection into the Sergeant Morales Club is not only a very prestigious honor but an excellent career move as well. Such an achievement annotated on your records will only serve to highlight you as an exemplary NCO and will almost assuredly result in your promotion ahead of your peers.

* The Sergeant Morales Club and the Sergeant Audie Murphy Club (see Appendix B) are similar in many respects, the largest difference being the geographic location where membership is offered. The Sergeant Morales Club is exclusive to Europe while the Sergeant Audie Murphy Club is exclusive to CONUS. Membership in either of these organizations is an outstanding achievement; membership in both represents a truly stellar level of NCO performance.

THE SERGEANT MORALES STORY

"After completing a tour with a stateside division, Sergeant Morales was selected for an oversea tour in Germany. He was assigned to a unit that was part of the United States Army, Europe. Before coming to Germany, he had completed his high school education, continued to improve his command of the English language, and maintained himself in top physical condition. Arriving in his unit, Sergeant Morales immediately settled in and used his experience and leadership techniques. He began his duty day in the barracks when his squad awoke in the morning, participated with his soldiers in physical training, ate his meals in the unit's dining facility, organized and supervised the routine housekeeping and work details, and prepared the squad for the day's training requirements. During the course of his supervision, he was not reluctant to get his hands dirty.

Sergeant Morales made sure that the members of his squad were trained in their military occupational specialties (MOS). He frequently used the Soldier's Manual and designated tasks that were required during the hands-on portion of the skill qualification test (SQT). In addition, he stressed the tactical, technical know-how that makes a better soldier. Race relations and equal opportunity were not new to him: he lived them.

The M113 was new to Sergeant Morales, but maintenance was not. He readily applied his knowledge to the M113. He took a hard look at the accountability of his soldiers, as well as the accounting, cleanliness, and serviceability of individual and squad property.

Sergeant Morales kept a leader's notebook containing personal data for each soldier. In addition, the soldier's job book was based on the proficiency of each soldier. Sergeant Morales counseled his soldiers monthly in personal and job performance areas. The counseling records reflected complimentary as well as derogatory information. The information from the leader's notebook, soldier's job book, and counseling was used to guide his soldiers in promotion, proficiency, and career development, including their professional and academic education. He frequently held meetings with his squad, keeping members informed of what was going on. They discussed training, problems, and areas the squad performed well in, and sought recommendations for improvement. The soldiers in Sergeant Morales' squad knew exactly where they stood.

The squad was united, including family members and friends, through social gatherings in the unit and community. He took pride that no squad member had ever been absent without leave (AWOL). This was attributed to his personal concern for every member of his squad.

Sergeant Morales was proud of the personnel of his squad, their outward appearance, and the way they proudly wore their uniforms. Conduct and bearing were of the highest standards at all times. He ensured newly assigned members were properly oriented, sponsored, processed, and introduced to all other squad members at the first opportunity. Rehabilitation transfers to his squad were accepted and treated on the same level as newly assigned squad members. Sergeant Morales took additional steps in guidance counseling and training to help the rehabs become effective members of the team.

Results of his caring about his soldiers were reflected in the squad's achievements during SQT, ARTEP, MET, AGI, daily living standards, and many other measures of team performance.

Sergeant Morales led by example. He showed true concern for the soldier and family members. He took great pride in his soldiers, his unit, and his country. Sergeant Morales was a member of the NATO team. He was a leader."

MET -- Maintenance Evaluation Team
AGI -- Annual General Inspection
ARTEP -- Army Training and Evaluation Program
SQT -- Skill Qualification Test
Rehabs -- Rehabilitative Transfers

USAREUR NCODP - USAREUR Noncommissioned Officer Development Program; a command program in the United States Army - Europe, designed to increase combat readiness by strengthening the NCO corps through the continuing improvement of NCO quality, morale, performance, and potential.

PREPARING FOR THE SERGEANT MORALES BOARD

There is not any one study guide for a Sergeant Morales Club candidate - nor should there be. A candidate is expected to have a broad knowledge of general military subjects and family/soldier support agencies, to be an expert in his/her technical field (MOS), and to know the common tasks required of all soldiers.

A leadership notebook with current data on the soldiers you lead, including a short synopsis on performance counseling, should be carried with you when appearing before the board (see "LEADER's NOTEBOOK" below).

Sample subject areas:

< > Physical Fitness
< > First Aid
< > Military Customs & Courtesy
< > Weight Control
< > Current Events
< > Map Reading
< > Community Activities/Community Involvement
< > Community Programs (ACS, ACES, AER, ARC, etc)
< > UCMJ
< > Leader's Book
< > SOFA/SAEDA
< > Chain of Command/NCO Support Channel
< > Military Leadership
< > Caring for the Soldier
< > Code of Conduct/Geneva Convention
< > Education
< > Leadership Counseling
< > SQT(SDT)/CTT/ITEP/BTMS
< > Training the Force (FM 25-100)
< > Battle Focused Training (FM 25-101)
< > Equal Opportunity
< > NCOER
< > M16A2 Rifle & procedures (incl maint, zero, etc)

THE SERGEANT MORALES BOARD
USAREUR Reg 600-2

< > Weaponeer
< > Misc US Weapons
< > Drug and Alcohol Program
< > Sexual Harassment
< > Promotions
< > History of the 3ID
< > Awards and Decorations
< > Risk Management (Safety)
< > Job Books
< > Sponsorship
< > Reenlistment
< > Maintenance Procedures (TAMMS, PMCS)
< > NCODP

OTHER AREAS OF INTEREST/SAMPLE QUESTIONS

NOTE: These are sample questions only. Do not attempt to limit your study solely to these areas.

- Tell the board members about yourself.
- How many soldiers do you lead/supervise?
- What would you like for soldiers to say about you 10 years from now?
- Tell the board members the Sergeant Morales Story (know verbatim).
- Why are you a Sergeant Morales candidate?
- Why do you feel you should be inducted into the SMC?
- Compare yourself to Sergeant Morales.
- Identify each person in your chain of command starting from yourself and ending with the President? Do the same for NCO Support Channel.
- Be prepared to do drill and ceremonies movements/commands.
- How many soldiers do you have in the Weight Control Program and what are you doing for them?
- Have you ever recommended any soldiers for UCMJ action? For what reason? What did you recommend? Did you get it?
- How many of your soldiers are married? Where do they live? Have you ever been there?
- How many soldiers do you have on profiles? What are you doing for them?
- Explain the duties and responsibilities of your job.
- Explain your unit maintenance program. How do you get involved in this program? What is the status of your equipment?
- Where do you check for parts?
- How many weapons are assigned to your section? What kind are they? When were they fired last and when will you fire again?
- Describe the standards of the rooms/billets.
- How do you set the standard of the uniform/room?
- How many of your soldiers have POVs and when do you conduct inspections on them?
- How often and when do you inspect your soldiers?
- What is the purpose of AER, ACS, Red Cross, the Education Center, JAG, CHAMPUS, CCC and what can these agencies do for you and your soldiers?
- Without looking, explain everything on your uniform starting from your left sleeve and ending with your right sleeve.
- Explain all the MOPP levels.
- Explain CTT, SQT, and their purpose.
- What is an ISR?
- When was your last command inspection and how did your

section/squad/platoon do?
- Who has the highest APFT score in your section/squad/platoon?
- How far does your unit run during PT?
- Who leads the PT sessions in your unit?
- What exercises does your unit do? (explain PT program)
- How many soldiers do you rate on the NCOER?
- Name the last soldier you rated and state what type of report he/she received.
- Name the types of NCOERs.
- Does your section/squad/platoon eat in the dining facility?
- What is the most common complaint about the dining facility?
- When is the best meal of the day and why?
- How much does it cost for each meal in the dining facility (for non-meal card holders)?
- What would you do if a soldier came to formation with a deficiency?
- What is your training philosophy?
- What is ESL and do you have soldiers that need it?
- How many soldiers do you have that live in government/economy quarters?
- When was the last Health and Welfare inspection in your unit?
- How often does it seem that urinalysis tests are conducted?
- Explain how the sponsorship program works in your unit.
- What action would you take if one of your soldiers has financial problems?
- What conditions must exist in order to bar a soldier from reenlistment?
- When would you have a senior sergeant working for a junior sergeant?
- Do you contribute to AER, CFC, AUSA, NCOA?
- What does GDP (General Defense Plan) mean to you?
- Explain the purpose and the mission of the NCO Support Channel.
- What does the NCO guide cover?
- What are the four factors of leadership?
- What are the four soldierly values?
- What AR gives Officers and NCOs their authority?
- What is counseling? How often do you counsel your soldiers?
- Do you have a job book on the soldiers you supervise and what is the purpose of the job book?
- Do you have NCOs that work under you?
- How do you enroll a soldier in the overweight program and what must you do prior to enrollment?
- What AR covers the wear of the uniform?
- What AR covers decorations, awards, and honors?
- Do you visit your soldier's quarters in civilian or military clothing and does it make a difference?
- Do you ever invite soldiers to your quarters? If so, why and when was the last time?
- Do your soldiers ask you to come by their quarters or do you just pop in?
- Does your company have an Order of Merit list? What is it used for?
- What programs does the education center offer soldiers and family members?
- How much notice is a soldier given prior to the SQT/SDT?
- Should there be any practice test prior to the SQT/SDT?
- Which of the leadership traits do you favor the most and why?
- Which leadership principle do you favor the most and why?
- What AR covers haircuts/mustaches and describes the appearance?
- What AR covers Reenlistment and what are the criteria?
- What AR covers the Overweight Program? Explain it.
- What AR covers ADAPCP? How are you enrolled in the program? Explain the tracks/levels.
- What FM covers Physical Fitness training?
- What are the prescribed types of PT formations and where do you stand when

conducting PT?
- How often do you inventory your soldier's TA-50 and when was the last inventory?
- What can the next higher authority do under Article 15 procedures?
- What publication covers NCOERs?
- What AR covers NCODP?
- What AR covers separations and discharges?
- What is ITEP, METL, METT-T, ARTEP, MTP and explain them?
- What are the troop leading procedures?
- What is the five paragraph operations order?
- What regulation covers the Sergeant Morales Story?
- How do you brief a newly assigned soldier to the unit?
- What is AR 600-200 and what is covered in it?
- Explain the difference between nonpunitive and nonjudicial punishment?
- What are the maximum punishments a company and field grade officer may impose on a soldier?
- When was the last time the non-telephonic alert roster was used and did it work?
- What type of education do your soldiers have and what are you doing to help them improve?
- How does a summarized Article 15 work and what is the purpose of it?
- Where should a soldier's battlesight zero be stored?
- What does SOFA and SAEDA stand for? Do you have the proper cards on you?
- How do you prepare a soldier for promotion?
- What are the signals for an NBC attack?
- How do you protect yourself from an NBC attack?
- What do TAMMS and PMCS stand for?
- Who supervises the maintenance of your vehicles?
- What time do your soldiers get up in the morning?
- What time do you arrive at your unit in the morning and at what time do you leave in the evening?
- What is the proper length of the male trousers and female skirt?
- Do you have input to the training schedule and does it get recorded?
- How long can a soldier remain in a MOPP suit after contamination?
- How much time does a soldier have to put the entire MOPP suit on?
- What is M8/M9 paper used for and what is the difference between the two?
- What are the major groups of the M60 machine gun?
- What is the purpose of the range card and what information is put on it?
- Who is your newest soldier?
- How are you improving the PT program?
- What are the three types of courts-martial and how many members sit on each board?
- What would you do to improve the image of the NCO Corps?
- What one area would you change in the Army if given the opportunity?
- How well did your soldiers do on their SQT/CTT and why?
- Who may impose nonjudicial punishment?
- What duties do your other NCOs perform?
- Do you have any soldiers moon-lighting a second job and why?
- What do you think is expected of a SMC member?
- Are your soldiers counseled only when they are wrong?
- Name the three parts of ITEP and when do they apply?
- What are the levels of the NCOES?
- What FM covers leadership?
- What FM covers counseling?
- What FM covers Drill and Ceremonies?
- What is an STX and give an example?
- What is the difference between the M16A2 and the M16A1?

THE SERGEANT MORALES BOARD
USAREUR Reg 600-2

- Who gets your leader book when you are not present for duty?
- Did you ever have a soldier write a bad check? What did you do about it?
- How do you conduct a counseling session? What is the most important part of counseling?
- What is the problem-solving/decision-making process?
- What must you do prior to conducting a counseling session?
- What information is stored on the front of job books?
- What do you do with the job book as the soldier departs the unit?
- What are the promotion requirements for the grades E-2 through E-6?
- Do your soldiers have a will?
- What do you do when a soldier is known to be AWOL and how long do you have to do it?
- What should you do if a soldier comes and tells you that a relative just passed away?
- What is OPSEC, COMSEC?
- When was the last time you and your soldiers reviewed their 201 files?
- What does the SQT test notice tell you and your soldiers?
- What does AUSA do for you and the soldiers?
- What should happen if a soldier is a rehabilitated failure of the alcohol and drug program or the overweight program?
- What is the purpose of the Code of Conduct and who established it? How many articles are there and what are they?
- How did your soldiers do on their last SQT and what areas were they weak in?
- Have you had any discipline problems in the last six months? If yes, for what? What did you do about it?
- How many of your soldiers have received an award for a good job?
- How many of your soldiers are married? Where do they reside? How many children do they each have? What are their names/birth days? Do they have any special problems?
- Do any of your soldiers have allergies? If so, what are they?
- What is the three-step teaching process?
- How much leave do your soldiers have? When did they last take leave? Where did they go on leave?
- How do you refer a soldier to CCC?
- How many AWOL soldiers have you had?
- How many of your soldiers would you promote or reenlist and why?
- When is an NCOER due on a newly promoted sergeant?
- Can a sergeant rate a sergeant?
- What do you know about BTMS?
- What is your command's training philosophy?
- Do you document or ensure documentation of all of your soldiers' training?
- Where does your unit go on GDP? Have you been there?
- When does your unit exchange linen? How do you know all soldiers changed their linen? Do you allow soldiers to wash their linen in the barracks?
- How often do you check the serviceability of your soldiers' boots and shoes?
- When did you have your last show-down inspection for initial issue of clothing?
- How often do you inspect your soldiers in Class As?
- How many of your squad/platoon vehicles are deadlined today and for what reasons?
- What equipment are you signed for?
- What do your soldiers do on their time off?
- What is the purpose of NCODP for your unit, command, and Army? What was the subject of last week's NCODP class? What is scheduled this week? How does it work in your unit? Have you ever taught an NCODP class? If so,

what was the subject?
- Also know the following:
  - -- basic reenlistment eligibility criteria
  - -- Morale Support Activities
  - -- dining facility hours daily and on weekends
  - -- sponsorship and orientation program
  - -- enlisted personnel management and correlation with NCOES
- How many of your people are getting close to reenlistment? What are you doing about it?
- How many of your personnel have driver's licenses (POV/Military)? What are they authorized to operate? What are the procedures for obtaining a POV license in your unit?
- What is the purpose of a line of duty investigation?
- How do you insure that your personnel have all of their equipment? How do you insure that this equipment is accounted for and properly maintained?
- How does one obtain unit patches and name tapes in your unit?
- What do you do when your subordinates complain about food in the dining facility?
- Are your soldier's living conditions adequate in the barracks? If you have soldiers living in government quarters or on the economy, how much do they pay for rent, utilities, etc?
- Does your unit have adequate recreational programs for the troops? Do you plan events with your subordinates and their families? How often?
- How do you handle one of your soldiers who shows disrespect towards you? Another NCO?
- Explain "probable cause" as it relates to search and seizure. Do you have the authority to apprehend someone that is committing an offense?
- What actions would you take if you found a soldier using drugs?
- What does "SUUTCO" stand for? Does your unit test newly assigned personnel? If yes, how soon after arrival?
- Are soldiers returning from leave given a urinalysis test? If so, how soon after returning from leave?
- Who is the CCC counselor for your unit/post?
- What actions are you taking to educate your personnel on drug-related problems?
- What actions are required if a soldier receives a "DWI" or "DUI"? How do you determine if an individual has a drinking problem?

THE SMC SELECTION WORKSHEET

A selection worksheet will be used by the board members to rate your performance. A sample Selection Board Worksheet is shown below:

I. PERSONAL ATTRIBUTES:
   a. Uniform and Appearance
   b. Oral Communication
   c. Confidence/Composure
   d. History of organization (Military Customs & Courtesies)

II. PERFORMANCE/QUALIFICATIONS:
   a. Weapons Qualification
   b. Skill Qualification Test
   c. Crew/Squad/Platoon Efficiency
   d. APRT
   e. Self-Improvement

f. CTT

III. LEADERSHIP TECHNIQUES:
a. Daily Routine (Supervisory)
b. Counseling
c. Leadership Situations
d. Leader's Notebook
e. EER/NCOER

IV. TRAINING and MAINTAINING:
a. ITEP
b. ACES
c. TAMMS
d. PMCS
e. BTMS
f. NCODP
g. Supply economy

V. CARING and CONCERN:
a. After normal duty hours involvement
b. Daily living standards, on and off post
c. Sponsorship (in/out)
d. Social Functions
e. Equal Opportunity
f. Fraternization

VI. GENERAL SUBJECTS:
a. Problem solving agencies
b. Quality of Life programs
c. UCMJ
d. Alcohol and Drug Abuse program
e. Weight control program
f. Reenlistment program
g. Risk Management (Safety)

The above subject areas are individually rated as a "GO" or "NO-GO" with an overall evaluation of a "GO" or "NO-GO".

AWARDS

Commanders should consider NCOs selected for membership into the SMC for an appropriate military award which should include, but is not limited to, the following:

- ARCOM
- SMC framed certificate
- 3-day pass at the convenience of the unit
- SMC coin
- letter from the Commander

In addition, when a SMC member departs an installation the installation commander will send a Letter of Introduction to the gaining installation commander. This Letter of Introduction is similar to that used for the Audie Murphy Board (see Appendix B).

LEADER'S NOTEBOOK

The Leader's Notebook is an essential management tool for the Noncommissioned Officer. It contains personal data on each soldier supervised as well as soldier/squad performance data and all other material essential for the proper training, maintaining, and caring for the soldier.

There is not a set format for the Leader's Notebook. In fact, the notebook will vary widely from person to person depending on the mission, number of soldiers supervised, personal preference, etc. The primary consideration is that it be organized and fully functional for your leadership requirements.

I have included on the following pages extracts from my own Leader's Notebook to give you an idea on how to get started. Use them if you like or design your own. I use a black notebook with a 2-inch binder, encased in a camouflage cover that has a zipper enclosure around the outside edges. In addition, it has handles for carrying like a briefcase. My nametape is sewn on the outside for easy identification. I have found this type of leader's notebook to be not only functional, but practical and versatile as well. The zipper enclosure will allow you to retain important documents and keep out dust and dirt - both in the field and in garrison. These notebook covers are available in solid black or camouflage at most PXs and MCSSs. Use document protectors for the individual pages - this will allow you to mark on them with a permanent marker, which may be erased with tissue and alcohol (some erasers work great, too!).

Refer to Appendix B of FM 25-101 for more information concerning the Leader Book.

The following "examples" have been slightly modified. All names and related information are purely fictitious. If you see something here you like, feel free to copy it and use in your own Leader Book. Refer to the end of this section for additional information regarding these pages.

LEADER's NOTEBOOK

SGT DAVID W. CREECH

I Co, 3rd Avn Regt

KNOWLEDGE
LEADERSHIP
RESPONSIBILITY

IF FOUND PLEASE CALL XXX-XXXX

REWARD OFFERED

CREED OF THE NONCOMMISSIONED OFFICER

No one is more professional than I. I am a noncommissioned officer, a leader of soldiers. As a noncommissioned officer, I realize that I am a member of a time-honored corps, which is known as the "backbone" of the Army.

I am proud of the corps of noncommissioned officers and will at all times conduct myself so as to bring credit upon the corps, the military service, and my country. Regardless of the situation in which I find myself, I will not use my grade or position to attain pleasure, profit, or personal safety.

Competence is my watchword. My two basic responsibilities will always be uppermost in my mind -- accomplishment of my mission and the welfare of my soldiers. I will strive to remain tactically and technically proficient. I am aware of my role as a noncommissioned officer. I will fulfill my responsibilities inherent in that role. All soldiers are entitled to outstanding leadership; I will provide that leadership. I know my soldiers and will always place their needs above my own. I will communicate consistently with my soldiers and never leave them uninformed. I will be fair and impartial when recommending both rewards and punishment.

Officers of my unit will have maximum time to accomplish their duties; they will not have to accomplish mine. I will earn their respect and confidence as well as that of my soldiers. I will be loyal to those with whom I serve; seniors, peers, and subordinates alike. I will exercise initiative by taking appropriate action in the absence of orders. I will not compromise my integrity, nor my moral courage. I will not forget, nor will I allow my comrades to forget, that we are professionals, noncommissioned officers, leaders!

THE SERGEANT MORALES BOARD
USAREUR Reg 600-2

TABLE OF CONTENTS
LEADER BOOK

PRIVACY ACT STATEMENT

The personnel listed below authorize SGT CREECH, David W., 123-45-6789, to maintain their SSN and personal information in his Leader's Notebook with the understanding that this information will not be disclosed except in the line of his official duties.

NAME	SSN	SIGNATURE	DATE
SMITH, MARK S.	123-45-6789		
STEVENS, JOHN R.	123-45-6789		
JOHNSON, TIMOTHY A.	123-45-6789		
ROGERS, WAYNE T.	123-45-6789		
DOE, JOHN (NMI)	123-45-6789		
WILLIAMS, ROBERT C.	123-45-6789		

THE SERGEANT MORALES BOARD
USAREUR Reg 600-2

DATE: ____________

SQUAD MEMBER DUTY STATUS SHEET

NAME	RANK	DUTY STATUS
SMITH, MARK S.	SGT	______________
STEVENS, JOHN R.	SPC	______________
JOHNSON, TIMOTHY	PFC	______________
ROGERS, WAYNE T.	PFC	______________
DOE, JOHN	PV2	______________
WILLIAMS, ROBERT C.	PV2	______________

ASSIGNED............. _________

ATTACHED........... _________

OPCON.............. _________

DUTY............... _________

LEAVE/PASS......... _________

AWOL............... _________

OTHER.............. _________

PRESENT.............. _________

PERSONNEL DATA SHEET - Page I

NAME: ______________________ **SSN:** ______________________

ADMINISTRATIVE

RANK: **DOR:** **TIS:** months **TIG:** months

PROMOTABLE?: YES / NO **ZONE:**

 # POINTS: **LAST NCOES:**

PMOS: **SMOS:** **BASD:** **ETS:**

DOB: **AGE:** **PAY OPTION:** **LEAVE:** days

ASSIGNED TO UNIT (date): **DEROS:**

HOME ADDRESS: **PHONE:**

HOR ADDRESS: **PHONE:**

COMMAND SPONSORED?: **ACCOMPANIED?:**

SPOUSE NAME: **DOB:**

MEDICAL

HT: **WT:** lbs **BLOOD TYPE:**

KNOWN ALLERGIES:

PREV COLD/HOT WEATHER INJURIES?: **LAST FLU SHOT:**

CAN SWIM? **LAST DROWNPROOFING:** **AFRAID OF HT?:**

COMBAT LIFESAVER?: **ISSUED BAG?:** **OTHER:**

PULHES: **PROFILE:**

PERSONNEL DATA SHEET - Page II

QUALIFICATIONS

EDUCATION LEVEL: **GT:**

CTT SCORE: **DATE:**

APFT/DATE (diag): **APFT/DATE (record):**

WPN QUALIFICATION (indiv)/DATE/ZERO:

WPN QUALIFICATION (crew)/DATE/ZERO:

EQUIPMENT

WPN TYPE: **WPN RACK #:** **WPN SN:**

MASK TYPE: **MASK #:** **MASK SIZE:**

OTHER

RELIG PREF: **MIL LIC?:** **FOR:**

SCTY CLNCE:

DEP NAMES:

AWARDS/DECORATIONS:

ITEP CONSOLIDATION

NAME	CTT/DATE	APFT/DATE	MARKS/DATE
SMITH	________	________	________
STEVENS	________	________	________
JOHNSON	________	________	________
AVERAGE	________	________	________

SQUAD APRT: AT-A-GLANCE (RECORD)

DATE TESTED: COMPANY STANDARD: 230

NAME	PUSHUPS/PTS	SITUPS/PTS	RUN/PTS	TOTAL POINTS
SMITH	________	________	________	________
STEVENS	________	________	________	________
JOHNSON	________	________	________	________
AVERAGE	________	________	________	________

SQUAD APRT: AT-A-GLANCE (DIAGNOSTIC)

DATE TESTED: COMPANY STANDARD: 230

NAME	PUSHUPS/PTS	SITUPS/PTS	RUN/PTS	TOTAL POINTS
SMITH	________	________	________	________
STEVENS	________	________	________	________
JOHNSON	________	________	________	________
AVERAGE	________	________	________	________

NEAR-TERM PLANNING

WEEK: ____________________

MONDAY

TUESDAY

WEDNESDAY

THURSDAY

FRIDAY

SATURDAY

SUNDAY

SHORT-RANGE PLANNING

NOTE: Insert monthly calendars here. Should look out at least three months.

MESSAGES

SMITH										
STEVENS										
JOHNSON										
ROGERS										
DOE										
WILLIAMS										

POINTS OF CONTACT

TYPE OF PROGRAM	CONTACT	PHONE
EQUAL OPPORTUNITY		
OIC		
NCOIC		
SAFETY		
OIC		
NCOIC, GROUND		
NCOIC, AIR		
REENLISTMENT		
OIC		
NCOIC		
DRUG & ALCOHOL		
OIC		
NCOIC		
NEO		
OIC		
NCOIC		
TRAINING		
NCOIC		
COMMO/COMSEC		
OIC		
NCOIC		
PHYSICAL SECURITY		
OIC		
NCOIC		

ADDITIONAL NOTES

---

1. Most of the previous pages are self-explanatory. However, you may be wondering about page A-21, "Messages". This page is great for keeping track of important messages. With this it is easy to tell at a glance who has and has not received a particular message. For instance, say its a Monday afternoon just before COB when you receive notice that all soldiers are required to bring their MOPP gear to Tuesday morning's formation. You simply jot down "MOPP gear, Tue a.m." on the "message" sheet (or something similar so you'll remember it). When you put this information out to your soldiers, put a check mark next to the names of those present. This will let you know who you need to contact later and will prevent those annoying "Well I didn't know!" or "Nobody told **me**!" excuses.

2. It is a good idea to keep a running log of when your soldiers have duty. There are a number of creative ways to do this and the information can come in handy later.

3. The short-range planning calendar should look out at least 3 months so keep a minimum of three of these in your Leader Book.

4. I include with my notebook a listing of each of the following for reference:

- Articles of the UCMJ
- Selected Army Forms and Records
- Selected Army Publications

Why? Well, I don't have a photographic memory and it beats carrying around the MCM and a micro-fiche. By the way, these listings can be found in Appendices I, G, and F, respectively.

5. Also include a current copy of your organization METL, broken down into Battle Drills/Crew Drills, and some or all of the following:

- Platoon/Squad SOP
- Alert roster (incl nontelephonic)
- Pre-Combat Inspection Checklist
- Field Site Occupation Checklist
- Bivouac Area Orientation Checklist
- Stand-to Checklist
- Vehicle Operations Checklist
- Upload Priority Plan
- Contents for A & B bags
- etc, etc, etc.

Don't overload your Leader Book. This is easy to do when you start including a lot of the above material. I keep most of the checklists, load plans, etc in a separate notebook.

THE SERGEANT AUDIE MURPHY BOARD
FORSCOM Cir 215-91-10

The Sergeant Audie Murphy Club (SAMC) is an elite organization consisting of those noncommissioned officers whose leadership achievements merit special recognition - specifically, those NCOs who have contributed significantly to the development of a professional NCO Corps and a combat ready Army, and whose demonstrated performance is characterized by that of Sergeant Audie Murphy.

"Sergeant Audie Murphy" is the name of an NCO who, as a squad leader, consistently demonstrated the highest qualities of leadership, professionalism, and regard for the welfare of the soldier (see "The Autobiography of Audie Murphy" below).

* Primary requirements for selection as a Sergeant Audie Murphy Club member are:

a. Must be an NCO (CPL through SFC or PSG).
b. Must directly supervise a minimum of two soldiers.
c. Must be selected for membership by a final selection authority level board (MACOM).

* Selection into the Sergeant Audie Murphy Club requires successful completion of three phases:

a. Phase I - Commander's Evaluation:
  - -- Major unit commanders who recommend NCOs for membership in the SAMC must screen candidates and submit nominations for candidates to appear before the next level board. The CSM at each level will convene and chair selection boards.

b. Phase II - Performance Test:
  - -- The SAMC Performance Test is based on recorded accomplishments of both candidates and subordinate soldiers and must be attached to the commander's evaluation.
  - -- A numerical vote will determine if a candidate should continue in the selection process and be scheduled to appear before the final selection board.

c. Phase III - Final Selection Board:
  - -- Only those candidates successfully completing Phases 1 and 2 will appear before a final board. The board will determine through a question and answer system if the candidate has reached a level of knowledge in a range of subject matter to warrant induction into the SAMC (outlined in the SAMC Board Work Sheet).
  - -- Quotas are not established. Selection boards will not select nominees if they do not meet the required standards of excellence.

* Selection into the Sergeant Audie Murphy Club is not only a very prestigious honor but an excellent career move as well. Such an achievement annotated on your records will only serve to highlight you as an exemplary NCO and will almost assuredly result in your promotion ahead of your peers.

* The Sergeant Audie Murphy Club and the Sergeant Morales Club (see Appendix A) are similar in many respects, the largest difference being the geographic location where membership is offered. The Sergeant Morales Club is exclusive to Europe while the Sergeant Audie Murphy Club is exclusive to CONUS. Membership in either of these organizations is an outstanding achievement; membership in both represents a truly stellar level of NCO performance.

THE SERGEANT AUDIE MURPHY BOARD
FORSCOM Cir 215-91-10

THE AUTOBIOGRAPHY OF AUDIE MURPHY

"Audie Leon Murphy was a legend in his own time. A war hero, movie actor, writer of country and western songs, and poet. His biography reads more like fiction than fact. He lived only 46 years, but he made a lasting imprint on American history.

Audie was born on a sharecropper's farm in North Texas on June 20, 1924. As a boy, he chopped cotton for $1 a day and was noted for his feats of derange-do and his accuracy with a gun. He had only 5 years of schooling, and he was orphaned at age 16.

After being refused enlistment during World War II in both the Marines and Paratroopers for being too small (5'5") and underweight (110 lbs), he enlisted in the U.S. Army a few days after his 18th birthday. After basic training at Camp Wolters, Texas, and advanced training at Fort George G. Meade, Maryland, Audie was sent overseas. He was assigned to the famous 15th Infantry Regiment of the 3rd Infantry Division where he fought in North Africa, Sicily, Italy, France, and Germany. He earned a battlefield commission for his courage and leadership ability as well as citations and decorations including every medal for valor that America gives. He was also awarded three French and one Belgian medal. Lieutenant Audie Murphy was the highest decorated soldier in American history.

Discharged from the Army on September 21, 1945, Audie went to Hollywood at the invitation of movie star James Cagney. He remained in California for the rest of his life and was closely associated with the movie industry, both as an actor and a producer. He acted in 44 films, starring in 39 of them. His best known film was "To Hell and Back," adopted from the best-selling book of his war experiences by the same name. Most of his movies were westerns. In 1955, Audie Murphy was voted the Most Popular Western Actor in America by the Motion Picture Exhibitors.

Audie wrote the lyrics to 16 country and western songs, the most popular of which was "Shutters and Boards," written with Scott Turner in 1962. This song was recorded by over 30 pop singers, including Jerry Wallace, Dean Martin, and Porter Waggoner. He was an accomplished poet; unfortunately, only a few of his poems have survived.

In 1950 Audie joined the 36th Infantry Division ("T-Patchers") of the Texas National Guard and served with it until 1966. He was a Mason and a Shriner and belonged to several veterans organizations. Audie Murphy was killed in a plane crash on a mountain top near Roanoke, Virginia on May 28, 1971. Fittingly, his body was recovered 2 days later on Memorial Day.

Audie could very well be the last American war hero. He was the greatest combat soldier in the 200-year plus history of the United States."

THE SERGEANT AUDIE MURPHY BOARD
FORSCOM Cir 215-91-10

PREPARING FOR THE SERGEANT AUDIE MURPHY BOARD

Preparation for the SAMC is much the same as preparation for the SMC. See Appendix A for more information and an example of the leader book. See SAMC Board Work Sheet below for subject areas.

THE SAMC BOARD WORK SHEET

Subject:

1. Drill and Ceremonies
2. Leadership
3. NBC
4. First Aid (Combat Leader)
5. Preparing Defensive Positions:
   a. Use of Terrain
   b. Use of Weapons
   c. Use of Diagrams/Maps/Range Cards
   d. Standards for Fighting Positions
6. Maintenance Management Procedures
7. Training the Force (FM 25-100/FM 25-101)
8. NCOES Requirements and Procedures
9. Knowledge of Family/Soldier Support Agencies:
   a. Alcohol and Drug Abuse Prevention and Control
   b. Red Cross
   c. ACS
   d. Outreach
   e. Financial Support
   f. CHAMPUS
   g. EO/EEO
10. Safety Program
11. Military Bearing and Appearance

NOTE: The above subject areas are individually rated as a "GO" or "NO-GO" with an overall evaluation of a "GO" or "NO-GO." The PASS RATE is 80% for the first 10 areas.

AWARDS

Commanders should consider NCOs selected for membership into the SAMC for an appropriate military award which should include, but is not limited to, the following:

- ARCOM
- SAMC framed certificate
- 3-day pass at the convenience of the unit
- SAMC coin
- letter from the Commander

In addition, when a SAMC member departs an installation the installation commander will send a Letter of Introduction (see example below) to the gaining installation commander.

SAMPLE MEMORANDUM OF INTRODUCTION

FCJI-CFN (672)

MEMORANDUM FOR: (Commander Concerned)

SUBJECT: Memorandum of Introduction

1. This memorandum of Introduction is being forwarded for ________________ who has been assigned to your command. ________________ is a member of the Sergeant Audie Murphy Club and has earned the distinction of being the finest of the ______________ noncommissioned officers.

2. Membership in the ________________ Sergeant Audie Murphy Club is a primary indicator that __________________ has demonstrated ability to meet the challenges of leadership and caring for soldiers. This organization was established to recognize those noncommissioned officers who best exemplify that special kind of leadership that shows a personal concern for the needs, training, development, and welfare of the soldier - leadership that draws the very best from every individual. To attain membership in the elite Sergeant Audie Murphy Club, ______________ had to exhibit the highest standards of leadership and achievement and be selected by a board of senior Command Sergeants Major.

3. I am pleased to personally introduce ________________ to you. I am confident he/she will be an invaluable asset to your organization.

Lieutenant General
U.S. Army
Commanding

COMPARATIVE RANKS
AR 600-20

	ARMY	AIR FORCE	MARINE CORPS	NAVY
	- COMMISSIONED -			
Special (GA)*	General of the Army	General of the Air Force	--	Fleet Admiral
0-10 (GEN)	General	General	General	Admiral
0-9 (LTG)	Lieutenant General	Lieutenant General	Lieutenant General	Vice Admiral
0-8 (MG)	Major General	Major General	Major General	Rear Admiral (U)
0-7 (BG)	Brigadier General	Brigadier General	Brigadier General	Rear Admiral (L)
0-6 (COL)	Colonel	Colonel	Colonel	Captain
0-5 (LTC)	Lieutenant Colonel	Lieutenant Colonel	Lieutenant Colonel	Commander
0-4 (MAJ)	Major	Major	Major	Lieutenant Commander
0-3 (CPT)	Captain	Captain	Captain	Lieutenant
0-2 (1LT)	First Lieutenant	First Lieutenant	First Lieutenant	Lieutenant Junior Grade
0-1 (2LT)	Second Lieutenant	Second Lieutenant	Second Lieutenant	Ensign

COMPARATIVE RANKS
AR 600-20

	ARMY	AIR FORCE	MARINE CORPS	NAVY
	- WARRANT -			
W-5 (MW5)	Master Warrant Officer, Five		Master Warrant Officer, Five	
W-4 (CW4)	Chief Warrant Officer, Four		Chief Warrant Officer, Four	
W-3 (CW3)	Chief Warrant Officer, Three		Chief Warrant Officer, Three	
W-2 (CW2)	Chief Warrant Officer, Two		Chief Warrant Officer, Two	
W-1 (WO1)	Chief Warrant Officer, One		Chief Warrant Officer, One	
	- ENLISTED SOLDIERS -			
E-9 (SMA)	Sergeant Major of the Army	Chief Master Sgt of the Air Force	Sergeant Major of the MC	Master Chief Petty Officer of Navy
E-9 (CSM)	Command Master Sergeant	Chief Master Sgt	Sergeant Major	Command Master Chief Petty Off
E-9 (SGM)	Sergeant Major	--	Master Gunnery Sergeant	Master Chief Petty Officer

COMPARATIVE RANKS
AR 600-20

	ARMY	AIR FORCE	MARINE CORPS	NAVY
E-8 (1SG)	First Sergeant	Senior Master Sergeant	First Sergeant	Senior Chief Petty Officer
E-8 (MSG)	Master Sergeant	--	Master Sergeant	--
E-7 (SFC)	Sergeant First Class	Master Sergeant	Gunnery Sergeant	Chief Petty Officer
E-6 (SSG)	Staff Sergeant	Technical Sergeant	Staff Sergeant	Petty Officer First Class
E-5 (SGT)	Sergeant	Staff Sergeant	Sergeant	Petty Officer Second Class
E-4 (CPL)	Corporal	Sergeant	Corporal	Petty Officer Third Class
E-4 (SPC)	Specialist	--	--	--
E-3 (PFC)	Private First Class	Airman First Class	Lance Corporal	Seaman
E-2 (PV2)	Private	Airman	Private First Class	Seaman Apprentice
E-1 (PV1)	Private	Basic Airman	Private	Seaman Recruit

* -- Abbreviations for grades of rank are for U.S. Army only.

THE HISTORY OF THE SOLDIER'S HOME

The United States Soldier's Home was established by an act of Congress on March 3, 1851. The original funds to establish the Home came from a draft for $118,000 - part of the tribute levied on Mexico City by General Winfield Scott, and from about $50,000 from the unexpended portion of a fund set up for the return of wounded and disabled veterans of the war with Mexico to their home. Except for this reappropriation of $50,000, no money has ever been appropriated for the support of the Home. It has been and still is supported by deductions from the pay of enlisted men and women, and from warrant officers in the Regular Army and Air Force; by interest on the soldiers' and airmens' Home permanent trust fund in the US Treasury; by the collection of a monthly user fee since November 1, 1976 from the members of the Home; by the unclaimed estates of deceased enlisted and warrant officer personnel of those forces; and by the effects of deserters from these two services. As of October 1, 1981, the Home has received all Article 15 fines.

Those eligible for admission to the United States Soldier's Home are retired and/or discharged enlisted and warrant officer personnel, both men and women, of the Regular Army and Air Force who have served 20 or more years as warrant officers or enlisted or have a service or non-service connected disability rendering them unable to earn a livelihood and those who have served during a war.

Personnel are encouraged to visit the Home and grounds. The main entrance is located on the Rock Creek Church Road, N.E. Washington D.C.

CREED OF THE NONCOMMISSIONED OFFICER TC 22-6

No one is more professional than I. I am a Noncommissioned Officer, a leader of soldiers. As a Noncommissioned Officer, I realize that I am a member of a time honored corps, which is known as "The backbone of the Army."

I am proud of the Corps of Noncommissioned Officers and will at all times conduct myself so as to bring credit upon the Corps, the Military Service and my country. Regardless of the situation in which I find myself, I will not use my grade or position to attain pleasure, profit, or personal safety.

Competence is my watchword. My two basic responsibilities will always be uppermost in my mind - accomplishment of my mission and the welfare of my soldiers. I will strive to remain tactically and technically proficient. I am aware of my role as a Noncommissioned Officer. I will fulfill my responsibilities inherent in that role. All soldiers are entitled to outstanding leadership; I will provide that leadership. I know my soldiers and will always place their needs above my own. I will communicate consistently with my soldiers and never leave them uninformed. I will be fair and impartial when recommending both rewards and punishment.

Officers of my unit will have maximum time to accomplish their duties; they will not have to accomplish mine. I will earn their respect and confidence as well as that of my soldiers. I will be loyal to those with whom I serve; seniors, peers, and subordinates alike. I will exercise initiative by taking appropriate action in the absence of orders. I will not compromise my integrity, nor my moral courage. I will not forget, nor will I allow my comrades to forget that we are professionals, Noncommissioned Officers, leaders!

SELECTED ARMY PUBLICATIONS
DA PAM 25-30 (CD-ROM)

ARMY REGULATIONS (AR) ---

AR 1-32	DISCIPLINARY CONTROL OF US ARMY PERSONNEL
AR 10-5	DEPARTMENT OF THE ARMY
AR 10-6	BRANCHES OF THE ARMY
AR 20-1	INSPECTOR GENERAL ACTIVITIES AND PROCEDURES
AR 25-400-2	THE MODERN ARMY RECORD KEEPING SYSTEM (MARKS)
AR 27-10	MILITARY JUSTICE
AR 27-20	CLAIMS
AR 27-40	LITIGATION
AR 27-50	STATUS OF FORCES POLICIES, PROCEDURES, AND INFORMATION
AR 37-104-3	JUMPS-ARMY PAY AND ALLOWANCE PROCEDURES
AR 40-3	MEDICAL, DENTAL, AND VETERINARY CARE
AR 40-5	PREVENTIVE MEDICINE
AR 40-121	UNIFORMED SERVICES HEALTH BENEFITS PROGRAM
AR 40-501	STANDARDS OF MEDICAL FITNESS
AR 40-562	IMMUNIZATION REQUIREMENTS AND PROCEDURES
AR 50-5	NUCLEAR SURETY
AR 50-6	CHEMICAL SURETY
AR 55-29	MILITARY CONVOY OPERATIONS IN CONUS
AR 95-16	WEIGHT AND BALANCE - ARMY AIRCRAFT
AR 115-11	ARMY TOPOGRAPHY
AR 135-7	INCENTIVE PROGRAM
AR 135-91	SERVICE OBLIGATIONS
AR 135-100	APPOINTMENT OF COMMISSIONED AND WARRANT OFFICERS OF THE ARMY
AR 140-10	ASSIGNMENTS, ATTACHMENTS, DETAILS, AND TRANSFERS
AR 140-111	ENLISTMENT AND REENLISTMENT
AR 140-192	MILITARY INTELLIGENCE, SIGNAL INTELLIGENCE, LECTRONIC WARFARE, AND SIGNAL UNITS
AR 145-1	SROTC PROGRAM
AR 190-11	PHYSICAL SECURITY OF ARMS, AMMUNITION, AND EXPLOSIVES
AR 190-13	PHYSICAL SECURITY
AR 190-14	CARRYING OF FIREARMS
AR 190-22	SEARCH, SEIZURE, AND DISPOSITION OF PROPERTY
AR 190-28	USE OF FORCE BY PERSONNEL ENGAGED IN LAW ENFORCEMENT AND SECURITY DUTIES
AR 190-30	MILITARY POLICE INVESTIGATIONS
AR 190-40	SERIOUS INCIDENT REPORT (SIR)
AR 190-47	US ARMY CORRECTIONAL SYSTEM
AR 190-51	SECURITY OF ARMY PROPERTY AT UNIT AND INSTALLATION LEVEL
AR 195-2	CRIMINAL INVESTIGATION ACTIVITIES
AR 200-1	ENVIRONMENTAL PROTECTION AND ENHANCEMENT
AR 210-10	ADMINISTRATION
AR 215-series	MORALE, WELFARE, AND RECREATION
AR 220-1	UNIT STATUS REPORTING
AR 220-58	ORGANIZATION AND TRAINING FOR CHEMICAL, BIOLOGICAL, AND RADIOLOGICAL DEFENSE OPERATIONS
AR 310-10	MILITARY ORDERS
AR 310-25	DICTIONARY OF US ARMY TERMS
AR 310-31	MANAGEMENT SYSTEM FOR TABLES OF ORGANIZATION AND EQUIPMENT (The TOE System)
AR 310-50	AUTHORIZED ABBREVIATIONS, BREVITY CODES, AND ACRONYMS

SELECTED ARMY PUBLICATIONS
DA PAM 25-30 (CD-ROM)

AR 340-3	OFFICIAL MAIL
AR 340-15	PREPARING CORRESPONDENCE
AR 340-16	SAFEGUARDING "FOR OFFICIAL USE ONLY" INFORMATION
AR 340-18	THE ARMY FUNCTIONAL FILE SYSTEM
AR 340-21	THE ARMY PRIVACY PROGRAM
AR 350-1	THE ARMY TRAINING SYSTEM
AR 350-4	QUALIFICATION AND FAMILIARIZATION WITH WEAPONS AND WEAPONS SYSTEMS
AR 350-15	THE ARMY PHYSICAL FITNESS PROGRAM
AR 350-17	THE NONCOMMISSIONED OFFICER PROFESSIONAL DEVELOPMENT PROGRAM (NCODP)
AR 350-30	CODE OF CONDUCT, SURVIVAL, EVASION, RESISTANCE, AND ESCAPE (SERE)
AR 350-37	ARMY INDIVIDUAL TRAINING EVALUATION PROGRAM
AR 350-41	NUCLEAR, BIOLOGICAL AND CHEMICAL DEFENSE AND CHEMICAL WARFARE
AR 351-1	INDIVIDUAL MILITARY EDUCATION AND TRAINING
AR 351-5	ARMY OFFICER CANDIDATE SCHOOLS
AR 351-20	ARMY CORRESPONDENCE COURSE PROGRAM
AR 380-5	DEPARTMENT OF THE ARMY INFORMATION SECURITY PROGRAM
AR 380-20	RESTRICTED AREAS
AR 381-20	US ARMY COUNTERINTELLIGENCE ACTIVITIES
AR 385-10	ARMY SAFETY PROGRAM
AR 385-30	SAFETY COLOR CODE MARKINGS AND SIGNS
AR 385-40	ACCIDENT REPORTING AND RECORDS
AR 385-55	PREVENTION OF MOTOR VEHICLE ACCIDENTS
AR 385-63	POLICIES AND PROCEDURES FOR FIRING AMMUNITION FOR TRAINING, TARGET PRACTICE, AND COMBAT
AR 530-1	OPERATIONS SECURITY (OPSEC)
AR 600-8-2	SUSPENSION OF FAVORABLE PERSONNEL ACTIONS (FLAGS)
AR 600-9	THE ARMY WEIGHT CONTROL PROGRAM
AR 600-15	INDEBTEDNESS OF MILITARY PERSONNEL
AR 600-20	ARMY COMMAND POLICY AND PROCEDURES
AR 600-21	EQUAL OPPORTUNITY (superseded by Chpt 6, AR 600-20)
AR 600-25	SALUTES, HONORS, AND VISITS OF COURTESY
AR 600-31	SUSPENSION OF FAVORABLE PERSONNEL ACTIONS FOR MILITARY PERSONNEL
AR 600-43	CONSCIENTIOUS OBJECTION
AR 600-50	STANDARDS OF CONDUCT FOR DEPARTMENT OF THE ARMY PERSONNEL
AR 600-55	MOTOR VEHICLE DRIVER AND EQUIPMENT OPERATOR SELECTION, TRAINING, TESTING, AND LICENSING
AR 600-60	PHYSICAL PERFORMANCE EVALUATION SYSTEM
AR 600-85	ALCOHOL AND DRUG ABUSE PREVENTION AND CONTROL PROGRAM
AR 600-100	ARMY LEADERSHIP
AR 600-200	ENLISTED PERSONNEL MANAGEMENT SYSTEM/PROMOTIONS
AR 600-290	PASSPORTS AND VISAS
AR 601-210	REGULAR ARMY ENLISTMENT PROGRAM
AR 601-280	TOTAL ARMY RETENTION PROGRAM (REENLISTMENT)
AR 606-5	PERSONNEL IDENTIFICATION: ID CARDS, TAGS
AR 608-1	ARMY COMMUNITY SERVICES (ACS)
AR 608-50	LEGAL ASSISTANCE
AR 611-5	ARMY PERSONNEL TESTS
AR 611-201	ENLISTED CAREER MANAGEMENT FIELDS AND MOSs
AR 614-3	ASSIGNMENT OF MILITARY PERSONNEL TO PRESIDENTIAL SUPPORT ACTIVITIES
AR 614-6	PCS POLICY

SELECTED ARMY PUBLICATIONS
DA PAM 25-30 (CD-ROM)

AR 614-30	OVERSEA SERVICE
AR 614-100	OFFICER PERSONNEL
AR 614-200	ENLISTED PERSONNEL SELECTION, TRAINING, AND ASSIGNMENT SYSTEM
AR 621-5	ACES
AR 623-105	ARMY OER
AR 623-205	ARMY EER
AR 630-5	LEAVES, PASSES, PERMISSIVE TDY
AR 630-10	AWOL, DESERTION
AR 635-10	PROCESSING PERSONNEL FOR SEPARATION
AR 635-100	OFFICER PERSONNEL
AR 635-200	ENLISTED PERSONNEL/SEPARATIONS
AR 640-2-1	PERSONNEL QUALIFICATION RECORDS
AR 640-3	ID CARDS, TAGS AND BADGES
AR 640-10	INDIVIDUAL MILITARY PERSONNEL RECORDS
AR 670-1	WEAR AND APPEARANCE OF THE UNIFORM
AR 672-5-1	MILITARY AWARDS
AR 672-20	INCENTIVE AWARDS
AR 700-84	ISSUE AND SALE OF PERSONAL CLOTHING
AR 750-1	ARMY MATERIEL MAINTENANCE POLICIES
AR 840-10	FLAGS, GUIDONS, STREAMERS, TABARDS, AND AUTOMOBILE AND AIRCRAFT PLATES
AR 930-4	ARMY EMERGENCY RELIEF (AER)
AR 930-5	AMERICAN RED CROSS (ARC)

COMMON TABLE OF ALLOWANCES (CTA) ---

CTA-50-900	CLOTHING AND INDIVIDUAL EQUIPMENT
CTA 50-970	EXPENDABLE/DURABLE ITEMS

DEPARTMENT of the ARMY PAMPHLETS (DA PAM) ------------------------------------

DA PAM 1-1	STATE, OFFICIAL, AND SPECIAL MILITARY FUNERALS
DA PAM 20-203	RUSSIAN COMBAT METHODS IN WWII
DA PAM 20-231	COMBAT IN RUSSIAN FORESTS AND SWAMPS
DA PAM 20-236	NIGHT COMBAT
DA PAM 20-292	WARFARE IN THE FAR NORTH
DA PAM 25-30	LIST OF ARMY PUBLICATIONS AND BLANK FORMS
DA PAM 27-21	MILITARY ADMINISTRATIVE LAW HANDBOOK
DA PAM 28-6	INTRAMURAL SPORTS FOR THE ARMY
DA PAM 28-9	UNIT LEVEL RECREATIONAL SPORTS
DA PAM 30-60-1	KNOW YOUR ENEMY
DA PAM 310-1	CONSOLIDATED INDEX OF ADMINISTRATIVE PUBLICATIONS AND BLANK FORMS
DA PAM 310-50	AUTHORIZED ABBREVIATIONS AND ACRONYMS
DA PAM 350-2	DEVELOPING AND MAINTAINING COHESION
DA PAM 350-15	COMMANDER'S HANDBOOK ON PHYSICAL FITNESS
DA PAM 350-21	FAMILY FITNESS HANDBOOK
DA PAM 350-38	STANDARDS IN WEAPONS TRAINING
DA PAM 351-4	US ARMY FORMAL SCHOOLS CATALOG
DA PAM 351-20	CORRESPONDENCE COURSE CATALOG
DA PAM 360-501	OUR FLAG
DA PAM 621-15	A SOLDIER'S GUIDE TO EDUCATION
DA PAM 710-2-1	USING UNIT SUPPLY SYSTEM (MANUAL PROCEDURES)
DA PAM 738-750	THE ARMY MAINTENANCE MANAGEMENT SYSTEM (TAMMS)
DA PAM 738-751	THE ARMY MAINTENANCE MANAGEMENT SYSTEM - AVIATION (TAMMS-A)

SELECTED ARMY PUBLICATIONS
DA PAM 25-30 (CD-ROM)

DA PAM 750-35	FUNCTIONAL USER'S GUIDE FOR MOTOR POOL OPERATIONS

FIELD MANUALS (FM) --

FM 1-5	INSTRUMENT FLYING AND NAVIGATION FOR ARMY AVIATORS
FM 1-102	ARMY AVIATION IN AN NBC ENVIRONMENT
FM 1-400	AVIATOR'S HANDBOOK
FM 3-3	CHEMICAL AND BIOLOGICAL CONTAMINATION AVOIDANCE
FM 3-3-1	NUCLEAR CONTAMINATION AVOIDANCE
FM 3-4	NBC PROTECTION
FM 3-5	NBC DECONTAMINATION
FM 3-6	FIELD BEHAVIOR OF CHEMICAL AGENTS
FM 3-7	NBC HANDBOOK
FM 3-8	CHEMICAL REFERENCE HANDBOOK
FM 3-9	MILITARY CHEMISTRY AND CHEMICAL COMPOUNDS
FM 3-10	EMPLOYMENT OF CHEMICAL AGENTS
FM 3-10-1	CHEMICAL WEAPONS EMPLOYMENT
FM 3-12	OPERATIONAL ASPECTS OF RADIOLOGICAL DEFENSE
FM 3-15	NUCLEAR ACCIDENT CONTAMINATION CONTROL
FM 3-19	NBC RECONNAISSANCE
FM 3-21	CHEMICAL-BIOLOGICAL CONTAMINATION AND CONTROL
FM 3-50	DELIBERATE SMOKE OPERATIONS
FM 3-87	NBC RECONNAISSANCE AND DECONTAMINATION OPERATIONS
FM 3-100	NBC OPERATIONS
FM 3-101	CHEMICAL UNITS
FM 5-15	FIELD FORTIFICATION
FM 5-20	CAMOUFLAGE
FM 5-25	EXPLOSIVES AND DEMOLITIONS
FM 5-100	ENGINEER COMBAT OPERATIONS (HOW TO FIGHT)
FM 5-103	SURVIVABILITY
FM 5-250	EXPLOSIVES AND DEMOLITIONS
FM 6-15	FIELD ARTILLERY METEOROLOGY
FM 6-20	FIRE SUPPORT IN COMBINED ARMS OPERATIONS (HOW TO FIGHT)
FM 7-7	THE MECHANIZED INFANTRY PLATOON AND SQUAD (APC)
FM 7-7J	THE MECHANIZED INFANTRY PLATOON AND SQUAD (BRADLEY)
FM 7-8	INFANTRY PLATOON AND SQUAD (INFANTRY, AIRBORNE, AIR ASSAULT, RANGER)
FM 7-10	THE RIFLE COMPANY, PLATOON, AND SQUADS
FM 8-9	NATO HANDBOOK ON THE MEDICAL ASPECTS OF NBC DEFENSIVE OPERATIONS
FM 8-33	CONTROL OF COMMUNICABLE DISEASES IN MAN
FM 8-34	FOOD SANITATION FOR THE SUPERVISOR
FM 8-35	EVACUATION OF THE SICK AND WOUNDED
FM 8-230	MEDICAL SPECIALIST
FM 8-250	PREVENTIVE MEDICINE SPECIALIST
FM 8-285	TREATMENT OF CHEMICAL AGENT CASUALTIES AND CONVENTIONAL MILITARY CHEMICAL INJURIES
FM 9-13	AMMUNITION HANDBOOK
FM 10-23	ARMY FOOD SERVICE OPERATIONS
FM 10-52	FIELD WATER SUPPLY
FM 10-52-1	COMMANDER'S HANDBOOK FOR WATER USAGE IN DESERT OPERATIONS
FM 10-63	HANDLING OF DECEASED PERSONNEL IN THEATERS OF OPERATIONS
FM 10-63-1	GRAVES REGISTRATION HANDBOOK
FM 11-50	COMBAT COMMUNICATIONS WITHIN THE DIVISION (HOW TO

	FIGHT)
FM 17-12	TANK GUNNERY
FM 17-50	ATTACK HELICOPTER OPERATIONS
FM 17-95	CAVALRY (HOW TO FIGHT)
FM 19-5	THE MILITARY POLICE HANDBOOK
FM 19-30	THE ARMY PHYSICAL SECURITY PROGRAM
FM 20-3	CAMOUFLAGE
FM 20-22	VEHICLE RECOVERY
FM 20-30	BATTLEFIELD DAMAGE ASSESSMENT AND REPAIR
FM 20-32	MINE/COUNTERMINE OPERATIONS
FM 20-33	COMBAT FLAME OPERATIONS
FM 21-6	HOW TO PROGRAM AND CONDUCT MILITARY TRAINING
FM 21-10	FIELD HYGIENE AND SANITATION
FM 21-10-1	UNIT FIELD SANITATION TEAM
FM 21-11	FIRST AID FOR SOLDIERS
FM 21-15	CARE AND USE OF INDIVIDUAL CLOTHING AND EQUIPMENT
FM 21-18	FOOT MARCHES
FM 21-20	PHYSICAL FITNESS TRAINING
FM 21-26	MAP READING AND LAND NAVIGATION
FM 21-30	MILITARY SYMBOLS
FM 21-31	TOPOGRAPHIC SYMBOLS
FM 21-33	TERRAIN ANALYSIS
FM 21-40	NBC DEFENSE (superseded by FM 3-3/-4/-5)
FM 21-60	VISUAL SIGNALS
FM 21-75	COMBAT SKILLS OF THE SOLDIER
FM 21-76	SURVIVAL
FM 21-150	COMBATIVES
FM 21-305	MANUAL FOR THE WHEELED VEHICLE DRIVER
FM 21-306	MANUAL FOR THE TRACK COMBAT VEHICLE DRIVER
FM 22-5	DRILL AND CEREMONIES
FM 22-6	GUARD DUTY
FM 22-8	UNIT COHESION
FM 22-9	SOLDIER PERFORMANCE IN CONTINUOUS OPERATIONS
FM 22-100	MILITARY LEADERSHIP
FM 22-101	LEADERSHIP COUNSELING
FM 22-102	SOLDIER TEAM DEVELOPMENT
FM 22-103	LEADERSHIP AND COMMAND AT SENIOR LEVELS
FM 22-600-20	THE ARMY NCO GUIDE (superseded by TC 22-6)
FM 23-8	M14 AND M14A1 RIFLES AND RIFLE MARKSMANSHIP
FM 23-9	M16A1 AND M16A2 RIFLE MARKMANSHIP
FM 23-11	90-mm RECOILLESS RIFLE, M67
FM 23-14	M249 SQUAD AUTOMATIC WEAPON (SAW)
FM 23-23	ANTI-PERSONNEL MINE M18A1 (CLAYMORE)
FM 23-30	GRENADES AND PYROTECHNIC SIGNALS
FM 23-31	40 mm GRENADE LAUNCHERS M203 and M79
FM 23-33	M72A2 LIGHT ANTI-TANK WEAPON (LAW)
FM 23-35	PISTOLS AND REVOLVERS
FM 23-65	BROWNING MACHINEGUN, CALIBER .50 HB, M2
FM 23-67	MACHINEGUN, 7.62-mm, M60
FM 24-1	COMBAT COMMUNICATIONS
FM 24-18	TACTICAL SINGLE-CHANNEL RADIO COMMUNICATIONS TECHNIQUES
FM 25-1	TRAINING
FM 25-2	UNIT TRAINING MANAGEMENT
FM 25-3	HOW TO CONDUCT TRAINING IN UNITS
FM 25-4	HOW TO CONDUCT TRAINING EXERCISES
FM 25-100	TRAINING THE FORCE

SELECTED ARMY PUBLICATIONS
DA PAM 25-30 (CD-ROM)

FM 25-101	BATTLE FOCUSED TRAINING
FM 26-2	MANAGEMENT OF STRESS IN ARMY OPERATIONS
FM 27-2	YOUR CONDUCT IN COMBAT UNDER THE LAW OF WAR
FM 27-10	THE LAW OF LAND WARFARE
FM 30-5	COMBAT INTELLIGENCE
FM 30-10	MILITARY GEOGRAPHIC INTELLIGENCE (TERRAIN)
FM 30-15	INTELLIGENCE INTERROGATION
FM 30-16	TECHNICAL INTELLIGENCE
FM 31-36	NIGHT OPERATIONS
FM 31-70	BASIC COLD WEATHER MANUAL
FM 31-71	NORTHERN OPERATIONS
FM 33-1	PSYCHOLOGICAL OPERATIONS: US ARMY DOCTRINE
FM 34-1	INTELLIGENCE AND ELECTRONIC WARFARE OPERATIONS
FM 34-3	INTELLIGENCE ANALYSIS
FM 43-5	UNIT MAINTENANCE OPERATIONS
FM 44-8	SMALL UNIT SELF-DEFENSE AGAINST AIR ATTACK
FM 44-30	VISUAL AIRCRAFT RECOGNITION
FM 57-38	PATHFINDER OPERATIONS
FM 71-1	TANK AND MECHANIZED INFANTRY COMPANY TEAM (HOW TO FIGHT)
FM 90-2	TACTICAL DECEPTION (HOW TO FIGHT)
FM 90-3	DESERT OPERATIONS (HOW TO FIGHT)
FM 90-4	AIRMOBILE OPERATIONS (HOW TO FIGHT)
FM 90-5	JUNGLE OPERATIONS (HOW TO FIGHT)
FM 90-6	MOUNTAIN OPERATIONS (HOW TO FIGHT)
FM 90-10	MILITARY OPERATIONS ON URBANIZED TERRAIN (MOUT)
FM 90-10-1	AN INFANTRYMAN'S GUIDE TO URBAN COMBAT
FM 90-13	RIVER CROSSING OPERATIONS (HOW TO FIGHT)
FM 100-1	THE ARMY
FM 100-2-3	THE SOVIET ARMY: TROOPS, ORGANIZATION AND EQUIPMENT
FM 100-5	OPERATIONS (HOW TO FIGHT)
FM 100-10	COMBAT SERVICE SUPPORT
FM 101-5	STAFF ORGANIZATION AND OPERATIONS
FM 101-5-1	OPERATIONAL TERMS AND GRAPHICS

GRAPHIC TRAINING AIDS (GTA) ---

GTA 3-6-3	NBC
GTA 5-2-12	MAP READING COORDINATE SCALES AND PROTRACTORS
GTA 5-10-24	MINEFIELD CLEARING AND BREACHING OPERATION
GTA 5-10-27	MINE CARD
GTA 8-5-45	HEAT INJURY PREVENTION AND FIRST AID
GTA 8-6-12	ADVERSE EFFECTS OF COLD, CAUSE AND SYMPTOMS
GTA 17-2-9	COMBAT VEHICLE RECOGNITION
GTA 17-2-11	COMBAT VEHICLE IDENTIFICATION
GTA 17-2-13	ARMORED VEHICLE RECOGNITION
GTA 21-1-3	M16 RIFLE MAINTENANCE CARD
GTA 21-1-4	RIFLE SHOT GROUP ANALYSIS CARD
GTA 44-2-10	PLAY CARDS, AIRCRAFT RECOGNITION

JOINT CHIEFS OF STAFF PUBLICATION (JSC PUB) ---------------------------------

JCS PUB 1	DICTIONARY OF MILITARY AND ASSOCIATED TERMS

STANDARDIZATION AGREEMENTS (STANAG) --

STANAG 2041	OPERATIONAL ROAD MOVEMENT ORDERS

SELECTED ARMY PUBLICATIONS
DA PAM 25-30 (CD-ROM)

STANAG 2042	METHOD OF CHALLENGING BY GUARDS AND SENTRIES
STANAG 2047	EMERGENCY ALARMS OF HAZARD OF ATTACK
STANAG 2079	REAR AREA SECURITY
STANAG 2129	RECOGNITION AND IDENTIFICATION OF FORCES
STANAG 3117	AIRCRAFT MARSHALLING SIGNALS
STANAG 3379	INFLIGHT VISUAL SIGNALS
STANAG 3570	DROP ZONES: VISUAL SIGNALS

SOLDIER'S TRAINING PUBLICATIONS (STP) --

STP-7-11BCHM14-SM-TG	SOLDIER'S MANUAL AND TRAINER'S GUIDE, MOS 11B, 11C, 11H, AND 11M, SKILL LEVELS 1, 2, 3, 4
STP-21-1-SMCT	SOLDIER'S MANUAL OF COMMON TASKS

MEDICAL TRAINING BULLETINS (TB MED) --

TB MED 81	COLD INJURY
TB MED 507	OCCUPATIONAL AND ENVIRONMENTAL HEALTH PREVENTION, TREATMENT, AND CONTROL OF HEAT INJURY
TB MED 577	SANITARY CONTROL AND SURVEILLANCE OF FIELD WATER SUPPLIES
TB MED 290	DRUG ABUSE

TRAINING CIRCULARS (TC) --

TC 3-3	HOW TO USE THE AUTOMATIC CHEMICAL AGENT ALARM
TC 5-200	CAMOUFLAGE PATTERN PAINTING
TC 7-1	THE RIFLE SQUAD (HOW TO FIGHT)
TC 7-3	THE RIFLE PLATOON
TC 21-3	SOLDIER'S HANDBOOK FOR INDIVIDUAL OPERATIONS AND SURVIVAL IN COLD-WEATHER AREAS
TC 22-6	THE ARMY NONCOMMISSIONED OFFICER GUIDE
TC 23-44	AIR DEFENSE
TC 27-10-1	SELECTED PROBLEMS IN THE LAW OF WAR
TC 27-10-2	PRISONERS OF WAR
TC 30-3	SOVIET EQUIPMENT RECOGNITION GUIDE
TC 90-1	MOUT TRAINING
TC 90-11-1	MILITARY SKIING

TECHNICAL MANUALS (TM) --

TM 3-366	FLAME FUELS
TM 3-4230-204-12&P	DECONTAMINATING APPARATUS: PORTABLE DS-2/ABC-M11
TM 3-4230-214-12&P	DECONTAMINATING APPARATUS: PORTABLE 14-liter, M13
TM 3-4230-216-10	M258A1 AND M58A1 SKIN DECON KITS
TM 3-4240-279-10	MASK, CHEMICAL-BIOLOGICAL: FIELD, M17-series
TM 3-4240-280-10	MASK, CHEMICAL-BIOLOGICAL: ACFT, M24 and TANK, M25/M25A1
TM 3-6665-307-10	DETECTOR KIT, CHEMICAL AGENT, M256/M256A1
TM 9-1005-224-10	MACHINEGUN, 7.62mm, M60
TM 9-1005-249-10	M16A1 RIFLE
TM 9-1005-319-10	M16A2 RIFLE
TM 9-1010-221-10	M203 GRENADE LAUNCHER, 40-mm
TM 9-1300-214	MILITARY EXPLOSIVES
TM 9-1315-886-12	OPERATOR'S AND UNIT MAINTENANCE MANUAL FOR M136 (AT4)
TM 9-1330-200-12	GRENADES
TM 9-1340-241-10	66mm, M72A2 LIGHT ANTI-TANK WEAPON (LAW)

SELECTED ARMY PUBLICATIONS
DA PAM 25-30 (CD-ROM)

TM 9-1340-886-14	LAUNCHER AND CARTRIDGE, 84mm, M136 (AT4)
TM 9-1345-203-128&P	LAND MINES
TM 9-1900	AMMUNITION, GENERAL
TM 10-227	FITTING OF ARMY UNIFORMS AND FOOTWEAR
TM 11-5805-201-12	TELEPHONE SET: TA-312/PT
TM 11-5820-667-12	RADIO SET: AN/PRC-77
TM 11-6665-209-15	RADIAC SET: AN/PDR-27
TM 11-6665-213-12	RADIACMETER: IM-174/PD
TM 11-6665-214-10	RADIACMETER: IM-93/UD
TM 55-1520-236-CL	OPERATORS AND CREWMEMBERS CHECKLIST (AH-1)

MISC ---

MCM	MANUAL FOR COURTS-MARTIAL

SELECTED ARMY FORMS AND RECORDS
DA PAM 25-30 (CD-ROM)

Form	Title
AE FORM 133-17-R	COMMAND REFERRAL FOR FINANCIAL COUNSELING
AE FORM 190-IN	APPLICATION FOR MOTOR VEHICLE REGISTRATION AND ALLIED TRANSACTIONS
AE FORM 3231	SMLM SIGHTING/DETENTION INSTRUCTIONS (SMLM CARD)
AE FORM 3398	APPLICATION FOR USAREUR POV OPERATOR'S LICENSE AND ALLIED TRANSACTIONS
AE FORM 600-702A	USAREUR/USAFE RATION CARD
AE LABEL 83	MANEUVER DAMAGE CARD
DA FORM 1045	ARMY IDEAS FOR EXCELLENCE PROGRAM (AIEP) PROPOSAL (formerly ARMY SUGGESTION PROGRAM)
DA FORM 1059	SERVICE SCHOOL ACADEMIC EVALUATION REPORT
DA FORM 1059-1	CIVILIAN INSTITUTION ACADEMIC EVALUATION REPORT
DA FORM 1222-R	ROUTING SLIP
DA FORM 1256	INCENTIVE AWARD NOMINATION AND APPROVAL
DA FORM 1307	INDIVIDUAL JUMP RECORD
DA FORM 1315	REENLISTMENT DATA CARD
DA FORM 1341	JUMPS - ALLOTMENT AUTHORIZATION
DA FORM 1352	ARMY AIRCRAFT INVENTORY, STATUS & FLYING TIME
DA FORM 137-R	INSTALLATION CLEARANCE RECORD
DA FORM 145	ARMY CORRESPONDENCE COURSE ENROLLMENT APPLICATION
DA FORM 1563	CERTIFICATE OF HONORABLE SERVICE
DA FORM 1594	DAILY STAFF JOURNAL OR DUTY OFFICER'S LOG
DA FORM 160	APPLICATION FOR ACTIVE DUTY
DA FORM 1659	REPORT OF SURVEY REGISTER
DA FORM 1687	NOTICE OF DELEGATION OF AUTHORITY - RECEIPT FOR SUPPLIES (SIGNATURE CARD)
DA FORM 1695	OATH OF EXTENSION OF ENLISTMENT
DA FORM 17	REQUISITION FOR PUBLICATIONS AND BLANK FORMS
DA FORM 1971-2-R	CHEMICAL DATA SHEET - MONITORING OR SURVEY
DA FORM 2A	PERSONNEL QUALIFICATION RECORD -- PART I
DA FORM 2-1	PERSONNEL QUALIFICATION RECORD -- PART II
DA FORM 200	TRANSMITTAL RECORD
DA FORM 201	MILITARY PERSONNEL RECORDS JACKET (MPRJ)
DA FORM 2012	COMSEC ACCOUNT DATA
DA FORM 2028	RECOMMENDED CHANGES TO PUBLICATIONS & BLANK FORMS
DA FORM 2062	HAND RECEIPT/ANNEX NUMBER
DA FORM 2142	PAY INQUIRY
DA FORM 2166-6	ENLISTED EVALUATION REPORT
DA FORM 2166-7	NCO EVALUATION REPORT
DA FORM 2166-7-1	NCO COUNSELING CHECKLIST/RECORD
DA FORM 2339	APPLICATION FOR VOLUNTARY RETIREMENT
DA FORM 2397-AB-R	ABBREVIATED AVIATION ACCIDENT REPORT (replaces PRAM)
DA FORM 2401	ORGANIZATIONAL CONTROL RECORD FOR EQUIPMENT
DA FORM 2402	EXCHANGE TAG
DA FORM 2404	EQUIPMENT INSPECTION AND MAINTENANCE WORKSHEET
DA FORM 2405	MAINTENANCE REQUEST REGISTER
DA FORM 2406	MATERIAL CONDITION STATUS REPORT
DA FORM 2407	MAINTENANCE REQUEST
DA FORM 2407-1	MAINTENANCE REQUEST CONTINUATION SHEET
DA FORM 2408	EQUIPMENT LOG
DA FORM 2408-4	WEAPON RECORD DATA
DA FORM 2408-5	EQUIPMENT MODIFICATION RECORD
DA FORM 2408-9	EQUIPMENT CONTROL RECORD
DA FORM 2408-12	ARMY AVIATOR'S FLIGHT RECORD

SELECTED ARMY FORMS AND RECORDS
DA PAM 25-30 (CD-ROM)

Form	Title
DA FORM 2408-13	AIRCRAFT INSPECTION AND MAINTENANCE RECORD
DA FORM 2408-14	UNCORRECTED FAULT RECORD
DA FORM 2408-15	HISTORICAL RECORD
DA FORM 2408-16	COMPONENT HISTORICAL RECORD
DA FORM 2408-17	AIRCRAFT INVENTORY RECORD
DA FORM 2408-18	EQUIPMENT INSPECTION LIST
DA FORM 2408-20	OIL ANALYSIS LOG
DA FORM 2409	EQUIPMENT MAINTENANCE LOG
DA FORM 2410	COMPONENT REMOVAL AND REPAIR/OVERHAUL RECORD
DA FORM 2415	AMMUNITION CONDITION REPORT
DA FORM 2442	CERTIFICATE OF ACHIEVEMENT
DA FORM 2446	REQUEST FOR ORDERS (RFO)
DA FORM 2496	DISPOSITION FORM (DF) - no longer used
DA FORM 2627	RECORD OF PROCEEDINGS UNDER ARTICLE 15, UCMJ
DA FORM 2627-1	SUMMARIZED RECORD OF PROCEEDINGS UNDER ARTICLE 15, UCMJ
DA FORM 268	REPORT FOR SUSPENSION OF FAVORABLE PERSONNEL ACTIONS (FLAG)
DA FORM 2765-1	REQUEST FOR ISSUE/TURN-IN
DA FORM 285	U.S. ARMY ACCIDENT INVESTIGATION REPORT
DA FORM 285-AB-R	ABBREVIATED GROUND ACCIDENT REPORT
DA FORM 3078	PERSONAL CLOTHING REQUEST
DA FORM 31	REQUEST AND AUTHORITY FOR LEAVE
DA FORM 3161	REQUEST FOR ISSUE OR TURN-IN
DA FORM 3286	STATEMENTS FOR ENLISTMENT
DA FORM 3349	PHYSICAL PROFILE
DA FORM 3355	PROMOTION POINT WORKSHEET
DA FORM 3356	BOARD MEMBER APPRAISAL WORKSHEET
DA FORM 3357	BOARD RECOMMENDATION
DA FORM 3444 series	TREATMENT RECORDS
DA FORM 348	EQUIPMENT OPERATOR'S QUALIFICATION RECORD
DA FORM 348-E	OPERATOR QUALIFICATION RECORD
DA FORM 3513	INDIVIDUAL FLIGHT RECORDS FOLDER, US ARMY
DA FORM 3645-1	INDIVIDUAL CLOTHING AND EQUIPMENT RECORD
DA FORM 3685	JUMPS - JSS PAY ELECTIONS
DA FORM 3686-1	LEAVE AND EARNINGS STATEMENT (LES)
DA FORM 3716	PERSONAL FINANCIAL RECORD, US ARMY
DA FORM 3749	EQUIPMENT RECEIPT (WEAPONS CARD)
DA FORM 3918-R	FACSIMMILE TRANSMITTAL HEADER SHEET
DA FORM 3975	MILITARY POLICE REPORT
DA FORM 3997	MILITARY POLICE DESK BLOTTER
DA FORM 4187	PERSONNEL ACTION
DA FORM 428	APPLICATION FOR IDENTIFICATION CARD
DA FORM 453-1	TRAVEL ORDERS
DA FORM 481	MILITARY LEAVE RECORD
DA FORM 4833	COMMANDER'S REPORT OF DISCIPLINARY ACTION OR ADMINISTRATIVE ACTION
DA FORM 4856	GENERAL COUNSELING FORM
DA FORM 4886	PERSONAL CLOTHING RECORD
DA FORM 4986	PERSONAL PROPERTY RECORD
DA FORM 5180-R	URINALYSIS CUSTODY AND REPORT RECORD
DA FORM 5409	INOPERATIVE EQUIPMENT REPORT
DA FORM 5429-R	CONDUCT OF FIRE
DA FORM 5504	MAINTENANCE REQUEST
DA FORM 5513	KEY CONTROL REGISTER AND INVENTORY
DA FORM 5519-R	TOOL SIGN OUT LOG/REGISTER
DA FORM 5533	SMART SUGGESTION FORM
DA FORM 5823	EQUIPMENT IDENTIFICATION CARD

SELECTED ARMY FORMS AND RECORDS
DA PAM 25-30 (CD-ROM)

DA FORM 5960	AUTH TO START, STOP, OR CHANGE BAQ OR VHA
DA FORM 5982-E	CONTROL LOG DISPATCH (ULLS)
DA FORM 5983	EQUIPMENT OPERATOR QUALIFICATION RECORD (ULLS)
DA FORM 5983-1-E	OPERATOR'S QUALIFICATION RECORD (ULLS)
DA FORM 5984-E	OPERATOR'S PERMIT RECORD (ULLS)
DA FORM 5986-E	PREVENTIVE MAINTENANCE SCHEDULE/RECORD (ULLS)
DA FORM 5987-E	MOTOR EQUIPMENT DISPATCH (ULLS)
DA FORM 5987-1-E	MOTOR EQUIPMENT DISPATCH/ALERT (ULLS)
DA FORM 5988-E	EQUIPMENT MAINTENANCE AND INSPECTION WORKSHEET (ULLS)
DA FORM 5989-E	MAINTENANCE REQUEST REGISTER (ULLS)
DA FORM 5990-E	MAINTENANCE REQUEST (ULLS)
DA FORM 5991-E	OIL ANALYSIS REQUEST (ULLS)
DA FORM 5992-E	EQUIPMENT USAGE REPORT (ULLS)
DA FORM 6	DUTY ROSTER
DA FORM 638	RECOMMENDATION FOR AWARD
DA FORM 638-1	RECOMMENDATION FOR AWARD OF AAM, ARCOM, OR MSM
DA FORM 647	PERSONNEL REGISTER
DA FORM 67-8	OFFICER EVALUATION REPORT
DA FORM 67-8-1	OFFICER EVALUATION REPORT SUPPORT FORM
DA FORM 705	APFT SCORECARD
DA FORM 71	OATH OF OFFICE - MILITARY PERSONNEL
DA FORM 727	ACCESS ROSTER
DA FORM 7279-R	EQUAL OPPORTUNITY COMPLAINT FORM
DA FORM 7323-R	M72-SERIES LAW SCORECARD
DA FORM 7324-R	M136 AT4 SCORECARD
DA FORM 83	FIRING RECORD
DA FORM 87	CERTIFICATE OF TRAINING
DA FORM 873	CERTIFICATE OF CLEARANCE AND/OR SECURITY DETERMINATION
DA FORM 904	GUARD REPORT
DD FORM 1131	CASH COLLECTION VOUCHER
DD FORM 1173	DEPENDENT'S IDENTIFICATION CARD
DD FORM 1351	TRAVEL VOUCHER
DD FORM 1351-2	TRAVEL VOUCHER OR SUBVOUCHER
DD FORM 1475	BASIC ALLOWANCE FOR SUBSISTENCE - CERTIFICATION
DD FORM 1577	UNSERVICEABLE (CONDEMNED) TAG - MATERIEL
DD FORM 1577-2	UNSERVICEABLE (REPARABLE) TAG - MATERIEL
DD FORM 1610	REQUEST AND AUTHORIZATION FOR TDY TRAVEL
DD FORM 1970	MOTOR EQUIPMENT UTILIZATION RECORD (DISPATCH)
DD FORM 2A	US ARMED FORCES IDENTIFICATION CARD
DD FORM 2026	OIL ANALYSIS REQUEST
DD FORM 214	CERTIFICATE OF RELEASE OR DISCHARGE FROM ACTIVE DUTY
DD FORM 2266	HOMETOWN NEWS RELEASE
DD FORM 256A	HONORABLE DISCHARGE CERTIFICATE
DD FORM 257A	GENERAL DISCHARGE CERTIFICATE
DD FORM 258A	UNDESIREABLE DISCHARGE CERTIFICATE - REPLACED
DD FORM 259A	BAD-CONDUCT DISCHARGE CERTIFICATE
DD FORM 260A	DISNONORABLE DISCHARGE CERTIFICATE
DD FORM 314	PREVENTIVE MAINTENANCE SCHEDULE AND RECORD
DD FORM 362	STATEMENT OF CHARGES/CASH COLLECTION VOUCHER
DD FORM 363A	CERTIFICATE OF RETIREMENT
DD FORM 398-2	PERSONNEL SECURITY QUESTIONNAIRE
DD FORM 47	RECORD OF INDUCTION
DD FORM 518	ACCIDENT IDENTIFICATION CARD
DD FORM 669	EDUCATIONAL DEVELOPMENT RECORD
DD FORM 689	SICK CALL SLIP
DD FORM 788	POV SHIPPING DOCUMENT

SELECTED ARMY FORMS AND RECORDS
DA PAM 25-30 (CD-ROM)

DD FORM 794A	UNDER OTHER THAN HONORABLE CONDITIONS DISCHARGE CERTIFICATE
DD FORM 93	RECORD OF EMERGENCY DATA
OF 346	MOTOR VEHICLE IDENTIFICATION CARD (LICENSE)
SF 364	REPORT OF DISCREPANCY (ROD)
SF 368	PRODUCT QUALITY DEFICIENCY REPORT (QDR)
SF 46	MILITARY VEHICLE OPERATOR'S PERMIT (MIL LICENSE)
SF 91	OPERATOR'S REPORT ON MOTOR VEHICLE ACCIDENTS
VA FORM 29-8286	SGLI ELECTION
____________	______________________________
____________	______________________________
____________	______________________________
____________	______________________________
____________	______________________________
____________	______________________________
____________	______________________________
____________	______________________________
____________	______________________________

ABBREVIATIONS, BREVITY CODES, AND ACRONYMS
AR 310-50

Abbreviation - a shortened form of a word (ie, appt=appointment).

Brevity Code - the shortened form of a frequently used unclassified phrase, sentence, or group of sentences (ie, SQT=Skill Qualification Test).

Acronym - a word formed from the initial letters of a name or parts of a series of words (ie, MARKS=Modern Army Record Keeping System).

A ---

AA - Active Army; Anti-Aircraft; Assembly Area
AAA - Anti-Aircraft Artillery
AAAA - Army Aviation Association of America
AAAR - Abbreviated Aviation Accident Report (replaces PRAM)
AADCOM - Army Air Defense Command(er)
AADS - AntiAircraft Defense System
AAF - Army Airfield
AAFES - Army and Air Force Exchange Service
AAH - Advanced Attack Helicopter
AAHA - Awaiting Action Higher Authority
AAM - Army Achievement Medal; Air-to-Air Missile
AAP - Affirmative Action Plan
AAR - After Action Review
AB - Air Base
ABCA - America, Britain, Canada, Australia
ABDU - Aircrew Battle Dress Uniform
ABM - Anti-Ballistic Missile
AC - Hydrogen Cyanide (blood agent)
ACAP - Army Child Advocacy Program; Army Career and Alumni Program
ACC - Area Coordination Center
ACCMB - AirCraft Crewmember Badge
ACCNET - Army Command and Control Network
ACCP - Army Correspondence Course Program
ACES - Army Continuing Education System
ACFT - Aircraft
ACK - Acknowledge
ACOE - Army Communities of Excellence
ACofS - Army Chief of Staff
ACR - Armored Cavalry Regiment
ACRV - Artillery Command and Reconnaissance Vehicle
ACS - Army Community Service
ACT - American College Test
AD - Active Duty; Air Defense
ADA - Air Defense Artillery
ADAM - Area Denial Artillery Munition
ADAPCP - Alcohol and Drug Abuse Prevention and Control Program
ADAPT - Alcohol and Drug Abuse Prevention Training
ADC - Aerospace Defense Command; Area Damage Control
ADF - Automatic Direction Finder
ADM - Admiral; Atomic Demolition Munitions
ADMC - Air Defense Missile Command
ADX - Advanced Development eXperimental
AEF - American Expeditionary Force
AER - Army Emergency Relief
AET - Army Extension Training
AEW - Airborne Early Warning
AF - Air Force; Armed Forces; Audio Frequency; Adjust Fire

ABBREVIATIONS, BREVITY CODES, AND ACRONYMS
AR 310-50

AFB - Air Force Base
AFDCB - Armed Forces Disciplinary Review Board
AFEES - Armed Forces Examining and Entrance Station
AFFS - Army Field Feeding System
AFN - American Forces Network
AFQT - Armed Forces Qualification Test
AFRC - Armed Forces Recreation Center
AFRTS - American Forces Radio and Television Service
AG - Adjutant General; Army Green (shade)
AGAR - Abbreviated Ground Accident Report
AGL - Above Ground Level
AGPU - Auxiliary Ground Power Unit
AGR - Ability Group Run
AGZ - Actual Ground Zero
AH - Attack Helicopter
AHB - Attack Helicopter Battalion
AHC - Attack Helicopter Company
AHIP - Attack Helicopter Improvement Program
AIDS - Acquired Immune Deficiency Syndrome
AIEP - Army Ideas for Excellence Program
AIPD - Army Institute for Professional Development
AIT - Advanced Individual Training
A/L - Administrative and Logistics
ALARACT - All Army Activities
ALBM - Air Launched Ballistic Missile
ALF - Auxiliary Landing Field
ALGOL - Algebraic Oriented Language
ALICE - All-purpose Lightweight Individual Carrying Equipment
ALO - Air Liaison Officer
ALOC - Air Lines Of Communication
ALSE - Aviation Life Support Equipment
AM - Amplitude Modulation
AMC - Army Materiel Command
AMCSS - Army Military Clothing Sales Store
AMDF - Army Master Data File
AMEDD - Army Medical Department
AMMC - US Army Aviation Material Management Center
AMO - Automation Management Office(r)
AMTP - Army Mission Training Plan
AMTRAC - Amphibious Tractor
ANC - Army Nurse Corps
ANCOC - Advanced Noncommissioned Officer's Course
ANG - Air National Guard
ANGUS - Air National Guard of the United States
AN/PVS - Army Navy Passive Vision Sight
AO - Area of Operations; Aerial Observer
AOAP - Army Oil Analysis Program
AP - Anti-Personnel
APC - Armored Personnel Carrier
APFT - Army Physical Fitness Test
APG - Aberdeen Proving Ground
API - Armor-Piercing Incendiary
APO - Army Post Office
APOC - Army Point of Contact
APOD - Aerial Port of Debarkation
APOE - Aerial Port Of Embarkation
APP - Air Parcel Post
APRT - Army Physical Readiness Test

ABBREVIATIONS, BREVITY CODES, AND ACRONYMS
AR 310-50

APU - Auxiliary Power Unit; Army Postal Unit
AR - Army Regulation; Automatic Rifle
ARC - American Red Cross
ARCOM - Army Commendation Medal; Army Reserve Command
ARNG - Army National Guard
ARR - Aerial Radiological Recon
ART - Assessment and Recovery Team
ARTBASS - Army Training Battle Simulation System
ARTEP - Army Training and Evaluation Program
ARTY - Artillery
ARV - Armored Recovery Vehicle
AS - Army Shade
ASAP - As Soon As Possible
ASCII - American Standard Code for Information Interchange
ASEP - Advanced Skills Education Program
ASG - Area Support Group
ASI - Additional Skill Identifier
ASL - Above Sea Level
ASM - Air-to-Surface Missile
ASP - Ammunition Supply Point
AST - Area Support Team
ASVAB - Armed Services Vocational Aptitude Battery
ASW - Anti-Submarine Warfare
AT - Annual Training
ATA - Actual Time of Arrival
ATC - Air Traffic Control; Air Training Command
ATD - Actual Time of Departure
ATF - Alcohol Treatment Facility
ATGM - Anti-Tank Guided Missile
ATLS - Advanced Trauma Life Support
ATP - Allied Tactical Publication; Army Training Program; Ammunition Transfer Point; Adenosine TriPhosphate
ATR - Annual Training Requirement
AUS - Army of the United States
AUSA - Association of the United States Army
AUT - Advanced Unit Training
AUTODIN - Automatic Digital Network
AUTOVON - Automatic Voice Network
AV - Aviation; Autovon
AVIM - Aviation Intermediate Maintenance
AVIONICS - Aviation Electronics
AVLB - Armored Vehicle Launched Bridge
AVN - Aviation
AVSCOM - U.S. Army Aviation Systems Command
AVUM - Aviation Unit Maintenance
AWACS - Airborne Warning And Control System
AWOL - Absent Without Leave
AWS - Air Weather Service
AXP - Ambulance Exchange Point
AZ - Azimuth

B --

BAI - Battlefield Air Interdiction
BAMO - Battalion Aircraft Maintenance Office
BAQ - Basic Allowance for Quarters
BAS - Battalion Aid Station
BASD - Basic Active Service Date

ABBREVIATIONS, BREVITY CODES, AND ACRONYMS
AR 310-50

BC - Battery/Battalion Commander
BCD - Bad Conduct Discharge; Binary Coded Decimal
BCPC - Bradley Crew Proficiency Test
BCT - Basic Combat Training
BCTP - Battle Command Training Program
BDA - Battle Damage Assessment
BDAR - Battle Damage Assessment and Repair
BDE - Brigade
BDO - Battle Dress Overgarment
BDU - Battle Dress Uniform
BEAR - Bonus Extension And Reenlistment/Retraining
BENELUX - Belgium, Netherlands, Luxembourg
BESD - Basic Enlisted Service Date
BFA - Blank Firing Adapter
BFV - Bradley Fighting Vehicle
BGST - Bradley Gunners' Skills Test
BI - Branch Immaterial
BII - Basic Issue Item
BIIL - Basic Issue Items List
BITE - Built-In Test Equipment
BLSA - Basic Loading and Storage Area
BM - Boundary Marker
BMNT - Beginning (of) Morning Nautical Twilight
BMP - Enemy APC
BMW - Bavarian Motor Works
BN - Battalion
BNCOC - Basic Noncommissioned Officer's Course
BOB - Beginning Of Business
BOC - Battalion Operations Center
BOQ - Bachelor Officer's Quarters
BOS - Battlefield Operating System
BOSS - Better Opportunities for Single Soldiers
BP - Battle Position
BPED - Basic Pay Entry Date
BPM - Beats Per Minute (heartrate)
BSA - BDE/BN Support Area
BSB - Base Support Battalion
BSEP - Basic Skills Education Program
BSX - Battle Simulation Exercise
BT - Basic Training; Bradley Table
BTMS - Battalion Training Management System
BTR - Enemy APC
BTU - British Thermal Unit

C ---

C - Celsius or Centigrade
C2 - Command & Control
C3 - Command, Control, and Communications
C3I - Command, Control, Communications, and Intelligence
C4 - Composition 4 (plastic explosive)
CA - Combined Arms; Combat Arms; Civil Affairs
CAAS - Combined Arms and Support
CAB - Combat Aviation Brigade
CAL - Caliber
CALFEX - Combined Arms Live Fire EXercise
CAM - Chemical Agent Monitor
CANE - Combined Arms in the Nuclear/Chemical Environment

CARC - Chemical Agent Resistant Coating
CARS - Combat Arms Regimental System
CAS - Close Air Support
CAS3 - (pron "CAS-CUE") Close Air Support, Command, Control, & Communications
CASP - Civilian Acquired Skills Program; Chemical Ammunition Supply Point
CATC - Combined Arms Training Center
CATD - Combined Arms Training Division
CATV - Community Antenna Television
CAV - Cavalry
CB - Chemical-Biological (agents)
CBR - Chemical, Biological and Radiological (now NBC)
CBS - Corps Battle Simulation (previously known as JESS)
CBU - Cluster Bomb Unit
CC - Company Commander
CCC - Community Counseling Center
CCF - Communist-Chinese Forces
CDM - Chemical Downwind Message
CE - Commander's Evaluation
C-E - Communications-Electronics
CEEB - College Entrance Examination Board
CEI - Communication Electronic Instructions
CENTCOM - Central Command
CENTO - Central Treaty Organization
CEOI - Communications-Electronics Operation Instructions
CEP - Commander's Evaluation Program
CEV - Combat Engineer Vehicle
CEWI - Combat Electronic Warfare Intelligence
CF - Correlation Factor
CFA - Covering Force Area
CFF - Call For Fire
CFL - Coordinated Fire Line
CFMB - Combat Field Medical Badge
CFSC - Corps Finance Support Center
CFV - Cavalry Fighting Vehicle
CFX - Command Field EXercise
CG - Commanding General; Center of Gravity; Phosgene (choking agent)
cGy - Centigray (abbrev)
cGyph - Centigrays per hour
CHAMPUS - Civilian Health And Medical Program of the Uniformed Services
CHOP - Change of Operational Control
CHOT - Comprehensive Hands-On Test
CI - Commander's Inspection; Counterintelligence
CIA - Central Intelligence Agency
CIB - Combat Infantry Badge
CID - Criminal Investigation Division
CIDCON - Civil Disturbance Readiness Condition
CIE - Combat and Individual Equipment
CIF - Central Issue Facility
CINC - Commander In Chief
CIP - Command Information Program; Command Inspection Program
CK - Cyanogen Chloride (blood agent)
CLP - Cleaner, Lubricant and Preservative
CLS - Contractor Logistics Support; Closed Loop Support; Combat Lifesaver
CM - Court-Martial
CMB - Combat Medical Badge
CMD - Command
CMF - Career Management Field
CMH - Congressional Medal of Honor

ABBREVIATIONS, BREVITY CODES, AND ACRONYMS
AR 310-50

CMOH - Congressional Medal Of Honor
CMT - Comment; Common Military Training
CMTC - Combat Maneuver Training Center
CO - Commanding Officer; Company
COB - Close Of Business
COBOL - Common Business-Oriented Language
COFT - Conduct-Of-Fire Trainer
COHORT - Cohesion, Operational Readiness Training
COLA - Cost Of Living Allowance
COLT - Combat Observation/Lasing Team
COMEX - Communications Exercise
COMINT - Communications Intelligence
COMMZ - Communications Zone
COMSEC - Communications Security
CON - Control
CONAD - Continental Air Defense Command
CONEX - Container, Express
CONUS - Continental United States
CONUSA - the numbered armies in the continental United States
COR - Commander-Of-the-Relief
CORBAN - Corps Battle Analyzer
COSCOM - Corps Support Command
CP - Command Post; Chemical Protective
CPE - Collective Protection Equipment
CPL - Corporal
CPMOS - Career Progression MOS
CPO - Civilian Personnel Office
CPOG - Chemical Protective Overgarment
CPQC - Combat Pistol Qualification Course
CPR - Cardio-Pulmonary Resuscitation
CPU - Central Processing Unit; Chemical Protective Undergarment
CPX - Command Post Exercise
CQ - Charge of Quarters
CR - CardioRespiratory (endurance)
CRE - Combat Readiness Evaluation
CRT - Combat Readiness Training; Cathode Ray Tube
CS - Combat Support; a chemical agent (tear gas)
CS1 - Critically Sensitive - level 1
CS2 - Critically Sensitive - level 2
CS3 - Critically Sensitive - level 3
CSA - Chief of Staff, U.S. Army; Corps Support Area
CSC - Command & Staff College
CSM - Command Sergeant Major
CSR - Combat Stress Reaction
CSS - Combat Service Support
CTA - Common Table of Allowances
CTC - Combat Training Center
CTG - Command Training Guidance
CTO - Control Tower Operator
CTT - Common Task Training/Test
CTX - Combined Training EXercise
CUCV - Commercial Utility Cargo Vehicle
CVC - Combat Vehicle Crew/Crewman
CVSP - Cardiovascular Screening Program
CW - Chief Warrant (Officer); Chemical Warfare
CX - Phosgene Oxime (blister agent)
CZ - Combat Zone

D --

DA - Department of the Army
DAC - Department of the Army Civilian
DAG - Division Artillery Group
DAP - Decontaminating Apparatus
DARE - Drug Abuse Resistance Education
DBDU - Desert Battle Dress Uniform
DBF - Data Base File
DCS - Division Clearing Station
DD - Dishonorable Discharge; Department of Defense
DED - Detailed Equipment Decon
DEERS - Defense Enrollment Eligibility Reporting System
DEFCON - Defense Readiness Condition
DEMOD - Deployment Model
DENTAC - Dental Activity
DEPEX - Deployment EXercise
DEROS - Date Eligible to Return from Overseas
DEW - Distant Early Warning
DF - Disposition Form; Defensive Fire
DGZ - Desired Ground Zero
DIC - Document Identifier Code
DICC - Deputy Installation Community Commander
DISCOM - Division Support Command
DIV - Division
DIVAD - Division Air Defense
DIVARTY - Division Artillery
DKIE - Decontaminating Kit, Individual Equipment
DLAB - Defense Language Aptitude Battery
DMA - Defense Mapping Agency
DMATC - Defense Mapping Agency Topographic Center
DME - Distance Measuring Equipment
DMZ - Demilitarized Zone
DNBI - Diseases and NonBattle Injuries
DOA - Dead On Arrival
DOB - Date Of Birth
DOCE - Date Of Current Enlistment
DOD - Department Of Defense (or DD)
DODAAC - DOD Activity Address Code
DODAC - DOD Ammunition Code
DOI - Date Of Issue
DOR - Date Of Rank
DOS - Date Of Separation; Digital Operating System
DOT - Department of Transportation
DOW - Died Of Wounds
DP - by Direction of the President; Diphosgene (choking agent); Displaced Persons; Dual Purpose
DPP - Delayed Payment Program
DPTM - Directorate of plans, training, and mobilization
DPU - Data Processing Unit
DS - Direct Support
DSA - Division Support Area
DS-2 - Decontaminating Solution #2
DSCC - Deputy Sub-Community Commander
DSP - Distribution Points
DSSA - Direct Supply Support Activity
DTD - Detailed Troop Decon
DTG - Date-Time Group

DTOC - Division Tactical Operations Center
DUI - Driving Under the Influence (of alcohol); Distinctive Unit Insignia
DWI - Driving While Intoxicated
DX - Direct eXchange
DZ - Drop Zone

E ---

E - East
E&E - Escape and Evasion
EAD - Entry on Active Duty; Earliest Arrival Date
EAO - Enlisted Aerial Observer
EAP - Emergency Action Procedures
EASI - Expanded Additional Skill Identifier
EASY - Early Acquisition System
ECCM - Electronic Counter-Countermeasures
ECM - Electronic Countermeasures
ECMF - Enlisted Career Management Field
ECWCS - Extended Cold-Weather Clothing System
EDRE - Emergency Deployment Readiness Exercise
EEC - Emergency Essential Civilian
EEFI - Essential Elements of Friendly Information
EEI - Essential Elements of Information
EENT - Eye, Ear, Nose, and Throat; End (of) Evening Nautical Twilight
EEO - Equal Employment Opportunity
EER - Enlisted Evaluation Report
EFMB - Expert Field Medical Badge
EGT - Exhaust Gas Temperature
EIB - Expert Infantry Badge
EIR - Equipment Improvement Recommendation
ELINT - Electronic Intelligence
ELSEC - Electronic Security
ELT - Emergency Locator Transmitter
EM - Enlisted Member
EMF - Electro-Motive Force
EMP - Electro-Magnetic Pulse
EMR - Electro-Magnetic Radiation
EMT - Emergency Medical Treatment; Emergency Medical Technician
ENDEX - End of Exercise
ENGR - Engineer
ENTNAC - Entrance National Agency Check
EO - Executive Order; Equal Opportunity
EOB - Electronic Order of Battle
EOD - Explosive Ordnance Disposal
EOM - End of Mission; End of Message
EPMS - Enlisted Personnel Management System
EPW - Enemy Prisoner of War
ERB - Enlisted Record Brief
ERBS - Extended Range Ballistic Missile
ESI - Extremely Sensitive Information
ESL - English as a Second Language
ETA - Estimated Time of Arrival
ETC - Estimated Time of Completion
ETD - Estimated Time of Departure
ETM - Extension Training Materials
ETR - Estimated Time of Return
ETS - Expiration Term of Service
ETT - Estimated Travel Time

EUCOM - European Command
EW - Electronic Warfare
EXEVAL - External Evaluation

F ---

F - Fahrenheit
FA - Field Artillery
FAA - Federal Aviation Administration
FAAR - Forward Area Alerting Radar
FAC - Forward Air Controller
FAO - Finance and Accounting Officer
FARP - Forward Arming & Refueling Point
FARRP - Forward Area Rearm/Refuel Point
FASCAM - Family of Scatterable Mines
FAT - Free Air Temperature
FBI - Federal Bureau of Investigation
FBR - Fireball Radius
FC - Field Circular
FCC - Federal Communications Commission; Flight Communications Center; Fire Control Center
FCL - Final Coordination Line
FCU - Field Communication Unit
FCX - Fire Coordination EXercise
FDC - Fire Direction Center
FDO - Fire Direction Officer
FDS - Fire Direction System
FEBA - Forward Edge of the Battle Area
FFA - Free Fire Area
FFAR - Folding Fin Aerial Rocket; Free-Flight Aerial Rocket
FFE - Fire for Effect
FHT - Field Handling Trainer
FIFO - First In/First Out
FIST - Fire Support Team
FISTV - Fire Support Team Vehicle
FITT - Frequency, Intensity, Time, and Type
FLIR - Forward Looking Infrared
FLOT - Forward Line of Own Troops
FLPP - Foreign Language Proficiency Pay
FM - Field Manual; Frequency Modulation
FMC - Fully Mission Capable; Field Medical Card
FO - Forward Observer
FOC - Flight Operations Center
FOD - Foreign Object Damage; Field Officer of the Day
FofF - Field of Fire
FOMET - Fallout Meteorological Message
FORSCOM - U.S. Army Forces Command
FORTRAN - Formula Transition
FOUO - For Official Use Only
FOV - Field Of View
FPF - Final Protective Fire
FPL - Final Protective Line
FPO - Fleet Post Office
FPS - Feet Per Second
FRAGO - Fragmentary Order
FRG - Federal Republic of Germany
FROG - Free Rocket Over Ground
FSA - Family Separation Allowance

FSB - Forward Support Battalion
FSCL - Fire Support Coordination Line
FSCOORD - Fire Support Coordinator
FSD - Fuel Supply Depot
FSE - Fire Support Element
FSN - Federal Stock Number
FSO - Fire Support Officer
FSOP - Field Standing Operating Procedures
FSS - Fire Support Sections
FST - Field Sanitation Team
FT - Fort; Feet
FTDTL - Forensic Toxicology Drug Testing Laboratory
FTX - Field Training eXercise
FW - Fixed Wing
FY - Fiscal Year
FYI - For Your Information

G ---

G-M - Grid-Magnetic
G/VLLD - Ground/Vehicular Laser Locator Designator
G1 - Asst Chief of Staff (Personnel)
G2 - Asst Chief of Staff (Intelligence)
G3 - Asst Chief of Staff (Operations and Plans)
G4 - Asst Chief of Staff (Logistics)
G5 - Asst Chief of Staff (Civil Affairs)
GA - General of the Army
GB - Sarin (nerve agent)
GCA - Ground Controlled Approach
GD - General Discharge
GDP - General Defense Plan
GDR - German Democratic Republic
GE - Germany
GEBA - Government Excess Baggage Authorization
GED - General Equivalency Diploma (high school)
GFA - Gun Fire Area
GHE - Ground Handling Equipment
GI - Government Issue
GL - Grenade Launcher
GM - Guided Missile
GMT - Greenwich Mean Time
GN - Grid North
GP - General Purpose; Group
GPFU - Gas-Particulate Filter Unit
GPM - Gallons Per Minute
GPS - Global Positioning System; Gunner's Primary Sight
GRR - Ground Radiological Recon
GRREG - Graves Registration
GS - General Support
GSE - Ground Servicing/Support Equipment
GSR - Ground Surveillance Radar
GT - General Technical
GTA - Graphic Training Aid; Grafenwoehr Training Area
GVO - Green Vinyl Overboots
GZ - Ground Zero

H ---

HB - Heavy Barrel; High Burst
HD - Mustard gas (blister agent)
HE - High Explosive
HEAP - High-Explosive, Armor-Piercing
HEAT - High-Explosive, Anti-Tank
HEDP - High-Explosive, Dual-Purpose
HEI - High-Explosive Incendiary
HELLFIRE - Heliborne Laser Fire and Forget
HEMATT - Heavy Expanded Mobility Tactical Truck
HEP - High-Explosive Plastic
HET - Heavy-Equipment Transporter
HF - High Frequency
HHC - Headquarters and Headquarters Company
HHD - Headquarters and Headquarters Detachment
HIMAD - High-to-Medium-altitude Air Defense
HIT - Health Indicator Test
HIV - Human Immunodeficiency Virus
HMMWV - High-Mobility Multi-purpose Wheeled Vehicle
HN - Host Nation
HNS - Host Nation Support
HOB - Height of Burst
HOR - Home Of Record
HQ - Headquarters
HQDA - Headquarters, Department of the Army
HR - Hour
HRO - Housing Referral Office
HRR - Heart Rate Reserve
HSC - U.S. Army Health Services Command
HSC - U.S.Army Health Services Command
HT - Height
HTA - Hohenfels Training Area
HTF - How To Fight (manuals)
HTH - High Test Hypochlorite (calcium hypochlorite)
HUMINT - HUMan INTelligence
HVAP - High-Velocity, Armor-Piercing
HVY - Heavy

I --

IADT - Initial Active Duty for Training
IAW - In Accordance With
ICBM - Intercontinental Ballistic Missile
ICD - Imitative Communication Deception
ICM -Improved Conventional Munitions
ICRC - International Committee for the Red Cross
ID - Identification
IDK - Individual Decon Kit
IDT - Inactive Duty Training
IEDK - Individual Equipment Decon Kit (also see DKIE)
IERW - Initial Entry Rotary Wing (training)
IET - Initial Entry Training
IEW - Intelligence and Electronic Warfare
IFF - Identification, Friend or Foe (radar)
IFR - Instrument Flight Rules
IFV - Infantry Fighting Vehicle
IG - Inspector General
IGAR - Inspector General Action Request
IMETP - International Military Education and Training Program

ABBREVIATIONS, BREVITY CODES, AND ACRONYMS
AR 310-50

IMINT - Imagery Intelligence
IN - Inch
INSCOM - U.S. Army Intelligence and Securities Command
INSEC - Internal Security
INTSUM - Intelligence Summary
IOAC - Infantry Officer Advanced Course
IOBC - Infantry Officer Basic Course
IP - Instructor Pilot; Intelligence Preparation; Initial Point
IPB - Intelligence Preparation of the Battlefield
IPE - Individual Protective Equipment
IPS - Inches Per Second
IR - Infrared
IRBM - Intermediate-Range Ballistic Missile
IRR - Individual Ready Reserve
IS - Immediate Suppression
ISR - Individual Soldier's Report
ITEP - Individual Training and Evaluation Program
ITL - Individual Task List
ITO - Individual Travel Orders
ITV - Improved TOW Vehicle
IV - Intravenous Infusion

J ---

J1 - Personnel Directorate
J3 - Operations Directorate
J4 - Logistics Directorate
J5 - Plans and Policy Directorate
J6 - Communications-Electronics Directorate
JA - Judge Advocate
JAAT - Joint Air Attack Team
JAG - Judge Advocate General
JATO - Jet Assisted Take-Off
JCS - Joint Chiefs of Staff
JD - Julian Date
JESS - Joint Exercise Support System
JOPS - Joint Operations Planning System
JSS - Joint Service Software (replaces JUMPS)
JTF - Joint Task Force
JTIDS - Joint Tactical Information Distribution System
JTX - Joint Training eXercise
JUMPS - Joint Uniform Military Pay System

K ---

K - Kelvin
KAWOL - Knowledgeable AWOL
KD - Known Distance
KG - Kilogram
KIA - Killed In Action
KM - Kilometer
KPH - Kilometers Per Hour
KPS - Kilometers Per Second
KT - Kiloton; Knots

L ---

L - Lewisite (blister agent)

ABBREVIATIONS, BREVITY CODES, AND ACRONYMS
AR 310-50

LAC - Local Agency Check
LANTIRN - Low Altitude Navigation and Targeting Infrared System
LARC - Lighter Amphibious Resupply Cargo
LASER - Light Amplification by Stimulated Emission of Radiation
LAW - Light Anti-tank Weapon; Lubricating oil, Arctic Weapons
LB - Local Battery
LBE - Load Bearing Equipment
LCE - Load Carrying Equipment
LD - Line of Departure
LDA - Local Deployment Area
LD/R - Laser Designator/Range finder
LDS - Lightweight Decontaminating System
LE - Low Explosive
LERTCON - aLert Condition
LET - Launch Effects Trainer
LES - Leave And Earnings Statement
LFX - Live Fire eXercise
LGB - Laser Guided Bomb
LGM - Laser Guided Missile
LID - Light Infantry Division
LLLGB - Low-Level Laser Guided Bomb
LLLSS - Low Light Level Sight System
LN - Local National(s)
LNO - Liaison Officer
LO - Liaison Officer
LOAL - Lock On After Launch
LOBL - Lock On Before Launch
LOC - Lines Of Communication (logistic routes)
LOGEX - Logistical eXercise
LOGMIS - Logistics Management Information System
LOGPAC - Logistical Package
LOI - Letter Of Instruction
LOMAH - Location of Miss and Hit
LORAD - Long-Range Air Defense
LORAN - Long-Range Navigation
LP - Listening Post
LRC - Leadership Reaction Course; Learning Resources Center
LRP - Long-Range Patrol
LRRP - Long-Range Reconnaissance Patrol
LRSU - Long-Range Surveillance Unit
LSA - Lubricating oil, Weapons, Semi-fluid
LTA - Local Training Area
LTD - Laser Target Designator
LUF - Lowest Usable Frequency
LWOP - Leave Without Pay
LZ - Landing Zone

M ---

M - Meter
MAAG - Military Assistance Advisory Group
MAC - Military Airlift Command; Maintenance Allocation Chart
MACOM - Major Army Command
MACS - Multiarcade Combat System
MAIT - Maintenance Assistance and Instruction Team
MANPAD - Man Portable Air Defense
MANPRINT - Manpower Personnel Integration Center
MAG - Military Advisory Group

ABBREVIATIONS, BREVITY CODES, AND ACRONYMS
AR 310-50

MAP - Military Assistance Program
MAPEX - Map eXercise
MARKS - Modern Army Record-Keeping System
MARS - Military Affiliate Radio Station
MASCAL - Mass Casualty
MASER - Microwave Amplification by Stimulated Emission of Radiation
MASH - Mobile Army Surgical Hospital
MAW -Medium Anti-tank Weapon
MBA - Main Battle Area
MCI - Meal, Combat, Individual
MCM - Manual for Courts-Martial
M/CM/S - Mobility, Countermobility, and Survivability
MCOFT - Mobile Conduct-Of-Fire Trainer
MCSS - Military Clothing Sales Store
MDC - Movement Designator Code
MDS - Model, Design, Series
MEDDAC - Medical Department Activity
MEDEVAC - Medical Evacuation
MEPCOM - Military Enlistment Processing Command
MEPS - Military Entrance Processing Station
METL - Mission Essential Task List
METT-T - Mission, Enemy, Terrain, Troops, and Time available
MFO - Multinational Force
MFR - Memorandum for Record
MFT - Mechanized Flamethrower; Master Fitness Trainer
MG - Major General; MachineGun
MGX - MOPP Gear eXchange
MHR - Maximum Heart Rate
MI - Middle Initial; Military Intelligence
MIA - Missing In Action
MICLIC - Mine Clearing Line Charge
MIJI - Meaconing, Intrusion, Jamming, and Interference (report)
MILES - Multiple Integrated Laser Engagement System
MILPERCEN - Military Personnel Center
MILPO - Military Personnel Office(s)
MILVAN - Military owned demountable container (van)
Min - Minute
MkI - Mark I (nerve agent antidote kit)
MKT - Mobile Kitchen Trailer
MLRS - Multiple Launch Rocket System
mm - millimeter
MMC - Material Management Center
MMS - Mast Mounted Sight
MMT - Miniature Moving Target
MOB - Military Operating Base
MOBEX - Mobilization Exercise
MOC - Maintenance Operational Check
MOGAS - Motor Gasoline
MOH - Medal Of Honor
MOI - Memorandum of Instruction
MOM - Military Official Mail
MOP - Military Operations
MOPP - Mission Oriented Protective Posture
MOS - Military Occupational Specialty
MOUT - Military Operations on Urbanized Terrain
MOV - Military-Owned Vehicle
MP - Military Police
MPH - Miles Per Hour

ABBREVIATIONS, BREVITY CODES, AND ACRONYMS
AR 310-50

MPRJ - Military Personnel Records Jacket
MPS - Military Postal System; Meters Per Second
MQS - Military Qualification Standards
MRA - Maneuver Rights Area
MRB - Motorized Rifle Battalion
MRC - Motorized Rifle Company
MRD - Motorized Rifle Division
MRDA - Military Recommended Daily Allowance
MRE - Meal, Ready to Eat
MRR - Motorized Rifle Regiment
MSB - Main Support Battalion
MSD - Minimum Safe Distance
MSE - Mobile Subscriber Equipment
MSG - Master Sergeant
MSR - Main Supply Route
MST - Maintenance Support Team
MTA - Major Training Area
MTC - Maneuver Training Command
MTEP - Mission Training Evaluation Plan
MTF - Maintenance Test Flight
MTMC - Military Traffic Management Command
MTOE - Modified Table of Organization and Equipment
MTP - Mission Training Plan
MTR - Missile Tracking Radar
MUST - Medical Unit, Self-contained, Transportable
MUTA - Multiple Unit Training Assembly
MVA - Modern Volunteer Army
MVR - Maneuver
MWO - Modification Work Order; Master Warrant Officer
MWR - Morale, Welfare and Recreation

N --

N - North
N1 - Avn, Gas Turbine Speed
N2 - Avn, Power Turbine Speed
NA - Not Applicable
NAAK - Nerve Agent Antidote Kit
NAC - National Agency Check
NAF - Non-Appropriated Funds
NAIAD - Nerve Agent Immobilized enzyme Alarm & Detection
NAPP - Nerve Agent Pyridostigmine Pretreatment (tablets)
NAR - No Answer (action) required
NASA - National Aeronautics and Space Administration
NATO - North Atlantic Treaty Organization
NBC - Nuclear, Biological and Chemical (Warfare)
NBCC - NBC Center
NBCWRS - NBC Warning and Reporting System
NCE - Nuclear Chemical Environment
NCMC - NORAD Cheyenne Mountain Complex
NCO - Non-Commissioned Officer
NCOA - Non-Commissioned Officer Academy
NCODP - NCO Development Program
NCOER - NCO Evaluation Report
NCOES - Non-Commissioned Officer Education System
NCOIC - Non-Commissioned Officer In Charge
NCOPD - NCO Professional Development (ribbon)
NCS - Net Control Station

NET - New Equipment Training
NF - Normalizing Factor
NFL - No Fire Line
NHA - Next Higher Assembly
NIGA - Neutron-Induced Gamma Radiation
NLT - Not Later Than
NM - Nautical Mile
NMC - Nonmission Capable
NMCM - Nonmission Capable, Maintenance
NMCS - Nonmission Capable, Supply; National Military Command System
NOD - Night Observation Device
NOE - Nap-Of-the-Earth
NOK - Next Of Kin
NORAD - North American Air Defense
NORS - Not Operationally Ready Supply
NPRC - National Personnel Records Center
NSA - National Security Agency
NSI - Nuclear Surety Inspection
NSN - National Stock Number
NTC - National Training Center
NTE - Not To Exceed
NTSB - National Transportation Safety Board, DOT
NVD - Night Vision Device
NVG - Night Vision Goggles; Navigate/Navigation
NWC - National War College

O --

OA - On or About
OAC - Officer Advanced Course
OAT - Outside Air Temperature
OBC - Officer Basic Course
OBJ - Objective
OCIE - Organizational Clothing and Equipment
OCF - Overall Correlation Factor
OCONUS - Outside the Continental United States
OCS - Officer Candidate School
OCT - Officer Candidate Test
OD - Officer of the Day; Olive Drab (shade)
ODCSPER - Office of the Deputy Chief of Staff for Personnel
ODT - Overseas Deployment for Training
ODTS - Optical Discrimination and Tracking System
OER - Officer Evaluation Report
OF - Observed Fire
OG - Olive Green (shade)
OGE - Out of Ground Effect
OH - Observation Helicopter
OHR - Occupational Hazard Report
OIC - Officer In Charge (of)
OIR - Other Intelligence Requirements
OJE - On the Job Experience
OJT - On the Job Training
OLC - Oak Leaf Cluster
OML - Order of Merit List
OMPF - Official Military Personnel File
OO - On Order
OP - Observation Post
OPCON - Operational Control

ABBREVIATIONS, BREVITY CODES, AND ACRONYMS
AR 310-50

OPFOR - Opposing Forces
OPLAN - Operational Plan
OPMS - Official Personnel Management System
OPORD - Operational Order
OPSEC - Operations Security
OR - Operational Readiness
ORB - Officer Record Brief
ORD - Objective Rally Point
ORP - Objective Rally Point
OSHA - Occupational Safety and Health Act
OSUT - One Station Unit Training
OTRA - Other Than Regular Army

P ---

PAC - Personnel and Administration Center
PACOM - Pacific Command
PADS - Position and Azimuth Determining System
PAL - Parcel Air Lift
PAO - Public Affairs Officer
PASGT - Personnel Armor System, Ground Troops
PC - Production Control
PCL - Prescribed Chemical Load
PCS - Permanent Change of Station
PD - Point of Departure; Point Detonating
PDAS - Primary Date of Active Service
PDDA - Power Driven Decon Apparatus
PDDE - Power Driven Decon Equipment
PDF - Principle Direction of Fire
PDS - Personnel Decontamination Station
PDW - Personal Defense Weapon
PEARL - Personal Equipment And Rescue/Survival Lowdown
PEBD - Pay Entry Basic Date
PED - Promotion Eligibility Date
PERINTREP - Periodic Intelligence Report
PERINTSUM - Periodic Intelligence Summary
PERSCOM - Personnel Command
PERSTATREP - Personnel Status Report
PEWS - Platoon Early Warning System
PF - Performance Factor
PFC - Private First Class
PFU - Physical Fitness Uniform
PGE - Preliminary Gunners Examination
PGM - Precision Guided Missile
PIC - Pilot In Command
PIP - Product Improvement Program/Proposal
PIR - Priority Information Requirement
PL - Phase Line
PLC - Primary Leadership Course (now PLDC)
PLD - Probable Line of Deployment
PLDC - Primary Leadership Development Course
PLL - Prescribed Load List
PLRS - Position Location Reporting System
PLT - Platoon
PM - Provost Martial; Phased Maintenance
PMC - Partial Mission Capable
PMCS - Preventive Maintenance Checks and Services
PMD - Preventive Maintenance Daily

ABBREVIATIONS, BREVITY CODES, AND ACRONYMS
AR 310-50

PMI - Preliminary Marksmanship Instruction; Preventive Maintenance Inspection
PMM - Preventive Medicine Measures
PMOS - Primary Military Occupational Specialty
PMS - Professor of Military Science
PMT - Preparatory Marksmanship Training
PNF - Proprioceptive Neuromuscular Facilitation
PNL - Prescribed Nuclear Load
POC - Point Of Contact
POE - Point of Embarkation
POI - Program of Instruction
POL - Petroleum, Oil, and Lubricants
POM - Preparation for Overseas Movement
POPGUN - Policy and Procedure Governing the Use of Nicknames
POV - Privately Owned Vehicle
POW - Prisoner of War
PP - Parcel Post; Permanent Party; Physical Profile; Passage Point
PRAM - Preliminary Report of Aircraft Mishap (replaced by AAAR)
PRC - Portable Radio Communicator
PRE - Partner Resisted Exercise
PROWORD - Procedural Word
PRR - Portable Radio Receiver
PRT - Portable Radio Transmitter; Physical Readiness Training
PSC - Personnel Service Center
PSI - Pounds per Square Inch
PSP - Prestock Point
PSYOP - Psychological Operations
PT - Physical Training; Point
PTL - Primary Target Line
PUC - Presidential Unit Citation
PULHES - physical profile serial code (numerical) = Physical capacity, Upper extremities, Lower extremities, Hearing, Eyes, pSychiatric
PV1&2 - Private E1 and E2
PVT - Private
PW - See POW/EPW
PX - Post eXchange
PZ - Pickup Zone

Q --

% Q - Percent Torque
QC - Quality Control
QDR - Quality Deficiency Report
QM - Quartermaster
QMP - Qualitative Management Program
QOL - Quality Of Life
QOLP - Quality of Life Program
QSTAG - Quadripartite Standardization Agreement
QT - Quart
QTB - Quarterly Training Brief
QTC - Quarterly Training Calendar
QTR - Quarter

R --

R - Rifleman
R/C - Rate of Climb
R/D - Rate of Descent
R&D - Research and Development

ABBREVIATIONS, BREVITY CODES, AND ACRONYMS
AR 310-50

RA - Regular Army
RAC - Regular Army Careerist
RACO - Rear Area Combat Operations
RACES - Radio Amateur Civil Emergency Service
RADAR - Radio Detection And Ranging
RADIAC - Radiation Detection, Identification, And Computation
RAF - Royal Air Force
RAG - Regimental Artillery Group (OPFOR)
RAM - Reliability, Availability, and Maintainability
RAOC - Rear Area Operations Center
RAP - Rocket Assisted Projectile; Rear Area Protection
RATELO - Radio Telephone Operator
RC - Riot Control (agents); Reserve Component
RCVR - Receiver
RD - Round
RDI - Regimental Distinctive Insignia (regimental crest)
REC - Radioelectronic Combat
RECONDO - Reconnaissance Commando Doughboy
REDCON - Readiness Condition
REENLB - Reenlistment Bonus
REFORGER - Return of Forces to Germany
REGT - Regiment
REM - Roentgen Equivalent Man (mammal); Rapid Eye Movement (sleep)
REMBASS - Remotely Monitored Battlefield Sensor System
REMS - Remotely Employed Sensor
RES - Radiation Exposure Status
RETS - Remoted Target System
RF - Radio Frequency; Representative Fraction
RFL - Restrictive Fire Line
RFO - Request for Orders
RHIP - Rank Has It's Privileges
RHR - Resting Heart Rate
RICE - Rest, Ice, Compression, and Elevation
RIF - Reduction In Force
RM - Repetition Maximum
RMI - Radio Magnetic Indicator
ROD - Report of Discrepancy
ROE - Rules Of Engagement
ROK - Republic Of Korea
ROTC - Reserve Officer Training Corps
RP - Release Point
RPC - Regional Personnel Center
RPG - Rocket Propelled Grenade (enemy)
RPM - Revolutions Per Minute
RPV - Remotely Piloted Vehicle
RSOP - Readiness Standing Operating Procedures
RSSK - Rigid Seat Survival Kit
RTB - Return To Base
RTCL - Reticle
RTD - Return To Duty
RTF - Regional Treatment Facility
RTO - Radio Telephone Operator
RTOC - Rear Tactical Operation Center
RW - Rotary Wing
RWBH - Records Will Be Hand carried
RWNBH - Records Will Not Be Hand carried
RX - Repairable Exchange

S

S - South
S&D - Search and Destroy
S1 - Adjutant (U.S.Army)
S2 - Intelligence Officer
S3 - Operations and Training Officer
S4 - Supply Officer
S5 - Civil Affairs Officer
SA - Secretary of the Army
SAC - Strategic Air Command
SAD - Safety and Arming Device
SADARM - Search And Destroy Armor
SAEDA - Subversion And Espionage Directed against the Army
SALT - Strategic Arms Limitations Treaty
SALUTE - Size, Activity, Location, Unit, Time, and Equipment
SAM - Surface-to-Air Missile; Space-Available Mail
SAS - Stability Augmentation System
SAT - Scholastic Aptitude Test
SATS - Standard Army Training System
SAW - Squad Automatic Weapon
SCAITS - Simulent Chemical Agent Identification Training Set
SCAS - Stability and Control Augmentation System
SCUBA - Self-contained Underwater Breathing Apparatus
SDA - Special Duty Assignment
SDAP - Special Duty Assignment Pay
SDK - Skin Decon Kit
SDNCO - Staff Duty Non-Commissioned Officer
SDT - Self Development Test
SEAD - Suppression of Enemy Air Defense
SEAL - Sea-Air-Land team (Navy)
SEATO - South East Asia Treaty Organization
SEAVAN - commercial or Government-owned shipping container
SEE - Small Emplacement Excavator
SEER - Senior Enlisted Evaluation Report
SERE - Survival, Evasion, Resistance and Escape
SF - Standard Form; Special Forces
SFC - Sergeant First Class
SFTS - Synthetic Flight Training System
SG - Sergeant of the Guard
SGLI - Servicemen's Group Life Insurance
SGM - Sergeant Major
SGT - Sergeant
SHA - Station Housing Allowance
SHAPE - Supreme Headquarters Allied Powers Europe
SHC - Surveillance Helicopter Company
SHF - Super High Frequency
SHORAD - Short-Range Air Defense
SIDPERS - Standard Installation/Division Personnel System
SIF - Selective Identification Features
SIGINT - Signals Intelligence
SIGSEC - Signals Security
SIMNET - Simulations Networking
SIR - Serious Incident Report
SITMAP - Situation Map
SITREP - Situation Report
SJA - Staff Judge Advocate
SKAs - Skills, Knowledge, and Attitudes

ABBREVIATIONS, BREVITY CODES, AND ACRONYMS
AR 310-50

SL - Skill Level; Squad Leader
SLAM - Supersonic Low-Altitude Missile
SLAR - Side-Looking Airborne Radar
SLBM - Sea-Launched Ballistic Missile
SLCM - Sea-Launched Cruise Missile
SM - Service Member; Soldier's Manual
SMA - Sergeant Major of the Army
SMCT - Soldier's Manual of Common Tasks
SMLM - Soviet Military Liaison Mission
SMOS - Secondary Military Occupational Specialty
SMR - Source, Maintenance, and Recoverability
SN - Serial Number; Service Number
SNAFU - System Normal: All Fouled Up
SNAP - Short Notice Annual Practice
SOC - Servicemember's Opportunity Colleges; Special Operations Command
SOCAD - Servicemember's Opportunity College Associates Degree
SOE - Status Of Equipment
SOF - Safety Of Flight
SOFA - Status of Forces Agreement
SOI - Signal Operation Instructions
SOP - Standard/Standing Operating Procedure(s)
SORNG - Sound Ranging
SOU - Safety Of Use
SP - Start Point
SPACON - Space Control
SPAM - Shop, Portable, Air-Mobile
SPC - Specialist
SPH - Statement of Personal History
SPOD - Sea Point of Debarkation
SPOE - Sea Point of Embarkation
SPORTS - Slap, Pull, Observe, Release, Tap, Shoot (immediate action drill)
SQ FT - Square Feet
SQDN - Squadron
SQI - Special Qualification Identifier
SQS - Skill Qualification Score
SQT - Skill Qualification Test
SRAM - Short-Range Attack Missile
SRB - Selective Reenlistment Bonus
SRO - Standing Route Order
SSAN - Social Security Administration Number (see SSN)
SSB - Single Side Band
SSG - Staff Sergeant
SSI - Shoulder Sleeve Insignia; Special Skill Identifier
SSI-FWS - Shoulder Sleeve Insignia - Former Wartime Service (combat patch)
SSM - Surface-to-Surface Missile
SSN - Social Security Number
SSSC - Self-Service Supply Center
SSVC - Selective Service
ST - Skill Technical
STA - Staff Training Assistant; Station
STANAG - Standardization Agreement
STANO - Surveillance, Target Acquisition, and Night Observation
STARC - State Area Command
STARPUBS - Standard Army Publication System
STARTEX - Start of Exercise
STB - SuperTropical Bleach
STBY - Standby
STD - Sexually Transmitted Disease(s)

STINFO - Scientific and Technical Information
STON - Short Ton
STOP - Short-Term Outpatient treatment Program
STP - Soldier Training Publication
STRAC - Standards in Training Commission
STX - Situational Training eXercise
SUM - Surface-to-Underwater Missile
SUPCOM - Support Command
SUPPT - Supply Point
SUSV - Small Unit Support Vehicle
SUUTCO - Selective Unit Urine Testing of Company-sized Organizations
SVC - Service
SWO - Staff Weather Officer
SWOTC - Senior Warrant Officer Training Course
SYSCON - Systems Control

T ---

TA - Telephone Apparatus; Table of Allowance
TAABS - The Automated Army Budget System
TAACOM - Theatre Army Area Command
TAADS - The Army Authorization Documents System
TAB - Target Acquisition Battery
TAC - Tactical Air Command
TADS - Target Acquisition and Designation System
TADSS - Training Aids, Devices, Simulators, and Simulations
TAG - The Adjutant General
TAMMS - The Army Maintenance Management System
TAMMS-A - The Army Maintenance Management System - Aviation
TAOC - The Army Operations Center
TAOR - Tactical Area Of Responsibility
TARR - Time of ARRival
TAS - True Airspeed
TASC - Training and Audiovisual Support Center
TASO - Training Aides Service Center
TB - Technical Bulletin
TBA - To Be Announced
TBD - To Be Determined
TBO - Time Between Overhaul
TBP - To Be Published
TC - Training Circular; Tank Commander
TCF - Tactical Combat Forces
TDA - Tables of Distribution and Allowances
TDY - Temporary Duty
TEAC - Turbine Engine Analysis Check
TEC - Training Extension Course
TECOM - United States Army Test and Evaluation Command
TEWT - Tactical Exercise Without Troops
TF - Task Force; Transmission Factor
TGT - Turbine Gas Temperature
THR - Training Heart Rate
TI - Technical Inspector/Inspection
TIG - Time In Grade
TIS - Time In Service; Thermal Imagery System
TIT - Turbine Inlet Temperature
TL - Team Leader
TLA - Temporary Lodging Allowance
TM - Technical Manual

TMDE - Test, Measurement, and Diagnostic Equipment
TML - TOW Missile Launcher
TMP - Transportation Motor Pool
TMT - Transportation Motor Transport
TNT - Tri-Nitro Toluene (composition similar to dynamite)
TO - Technical Order; Travel Order; Take Off; Training Objective
TOA - Terms Of Agreement
TOB - Time of Burst
TOC - Tactical Operations Center
TOD - Time Of Detonation
TOE - Table(s) of Organization and Equipment
TOF - Time Of Flight
TOPS - Take Off Pounds Sensibly
TOT - Time Of Transmission; Time On Target
TOW - Tube-launched, Optically-sighted, Wire-guided
TP - Technical Publication; Training Practice
TPU - Tank and Pump Unit
TR - Transportation Request
TRADOC - U.S. Army Training and Doctrine Command
TREE - Transient Radiation Effects on Electronics
TRP - Target Reference Point
TRV - Tank Recovery Vehicle
TSC - Training Support Center
TSE - Tactical Support Equipment
TSFO - Training Set, Fire Observation (old); Tactical Simulations Forward Observer (new)
TSN - Time Since New
TSO - Time Since Overhaul
TSOP - Tactical Standing Operating Procedure
TSU - Telescopic Sight Unit
TTP - Tactics, Techniques, and Procedures
TTR - Target Tracking Radar
TVI - Technical Validation Inspection
TZ - Tactical Zone

U --

UA - Uniform Allowance
UAM - Underwater-to-Air Missile
UCMJ - Uniform Code of Military Justice
UCOFT - Unit Conduct-Of-Fire Trainer
UD - Undesirable Discharge
UDT - Underwater Demolition Team
UFA - Until Further Advised
UH - Utility Helicopter
UHF - Ultra-High Frequency
UIC - Unit Identification Code
ULLS - Unit Level Logistics System
UN - United Nations
UPS - United Parcel Service; Universal Polar Stereographic (map)
URMSG - Your Message
US - United States
USA - United States of America; United States Army
USAF - United States Air Force
USAPFS - United States Army Physical Fitness School
USAR - United States Army Reserve
USAREUR - U.S. Army in Europe
USARPAC - U.S. Army Pacific

USASMA - U. S. Army Sergeants-Major Academy
USC - United States Code
USCG - United States Coast Guard
USM - Underwater-to-Surface Missile
USMA - United States Military Academy
USMC - United States Marine Corps
USMTF - US Message Text Format
USN - United States Navy
UTA - Unit Training Assembly
UTM - Universal Transverse Mercator (grid map)
UUM - Underwater-to-Underwater Missile (torpedo)
UW - Unconventional Warfare
UXB - Unexploded Bomb(s)

V --

VA - Veterans Administration
VAC - Volts, Alternating Current
VB - Vapor Barrier
VDC - Volts, Direct Current
VCF - Vehicle Correlation Factor
VFR - Visual Flight Rules
VGT - Viewgraph Transparency
VHF - Very High Frequency
VIP - Very Important Person
VISMOD - Visual Modification
VLF - Very Low Frequency
VNAS - Vehicular Navigating Aids System
VO_2max - maximum oxygen consumption per minute
VOA - Voice Of America
VOCO - Verbal Order of Commanding Officer
VOLAR - Volunteer Army (see MVA)
VOQ - Visiting Officers Quarters
VOR - VHF Omnidirectional Range
VRB - Variable Reenlistment Bonus
VSTOL - Vertical and Short Take-Off/Landing
VTOL - Vertical Take-Off/Landing
VTR - Video Tape Recorder

W --

W - West
WBGT - Wet Bulb Globe Temperature
WC - With Change
WCF - Wind Chill Factor
WESTCOM - Western Command
WIA - Wounded in Action
WO - Warrant Officer; Warning Order
WOC - Warrant Officer Candidate
WOCC - Warrant Officer Candidate Course
WOCS - Warrant Officer Candidate School
WON - Work Order Number
WP - White Phosphorus
WPN - Weapon
WT - Weight
WUC - Work Unit Code

X --

XMIT - Transmit
XMSN - Transmission
XMTR - Transmitter
XO - eXecutive Officer
XSTR - Transistor
XTAL - Crystal

Y ---

YTB - Yearly Training Brief
YTC - Yearly Training Calendar
YTG - Yearly Training Guidance

Z ---

ZF - Zone of Fire
ZOE - Zone Of Entry

ARTICLES OF THE UCMJ
MANUAL FOR COURTS-MARTIAL (MCM)

ARTICLE	SUBJECT
GENERAL PROVISIONS	
1	DEFINITIONS
2	PERSONS SUBJECT TO UCMJ
3	JURISDICTION TO TRY CERTAIN PERSONNEL
4	DISMISSED OFFICER'S RIGHT TO TRIAL BY COURT MARTIAL
5	TERRITORIAL APPLICABILITY OF UCMJ
6	JUDGE ADVOCATES & LEGAL OFFICERS
6a	INVESTIGATION & DISPOSITION OF MATTERS PERTAINING TO THE FITNESS OF MILITARY JUDGES
APPREHENSION AND RESTRAINT	
7	APPREHENSION
8	APPREHENSION OF DESERTERS
9	IMPOSITION OF RESTRAINT
10	RESTRAINT OF PERSONS CHARGED WITH OFFENSES
11	REPORTS AND RECEIVING OF PRISONERS
12	CONFINEMENT WITH ENEMY PRISONERS PROHIBITED
13	PUNISHMENT PROHIBITED BEFORE TRIAL
14	DELIVERY OF OFFENDERS TO CIVIL AUTHORITIES
NON-JUDICIAL PUNISHMENT	
15	COMMANDING OFFICER'S NONJUDICIAL PUNISHMENT
COURT-MARTIAL JURISDICTION	
16	COURTS-MARTIAL CLASSIFIED
17	JURISDICTION OF COURTS-MARTIAL IN GENERAL
18	JURISDICTION OF GENERAL C-M
19	JURISDICTION OF SPECIAL C-M
20	JURISDICTION OF SUMMARY C-M
21	JURISDICTION OF C-M NOT EXCLUSIVE
COMPOSITION OF COURTS-MARTIAL	
22	WHO MAY CONVENE GENERAL C-M
23	WHO MAY CONVENE SPECIAL C-M
24	WHO MAY CONVENE SUMMARY C-M
25	WHO MAY SERVE ON A C-M
26	MILITARY JUDGE OF A GENERAL OR SPECIAL C-M
27	DETAIL OF TRIAL COUNSEL AND DEFENSE COUNSEL
28	DETAIL OR EMPLOYMENT OF REPORTERS & INTERPRETERS
29	ABSENT AND ADDITIONAL MEMBERS
PRE-TRIAL PROCEDURE	
30	CHARGES AND SPECIFICATIONS
31	COMPULSORY SELF-INCRIMINATION PROHIBITED
32	INVESTIGATION
33	FORWARDING OF CHARGES
34	ADVICE OF STAFF JUDGE ADVOCATE & REFERENCE FOR

ARTICLES OF THE UCMJ
MANUAL FOR COURTS-MARTIAL (MCM)

ARTICLE	SUBJECT
	TRIAL
35	SERVICE OF CHARGES

TRIAL PROCEDURE

ARTICLE	SUBJECT
36	PRESIDENT MAY PRESCRIBE RULES
37	UNLAWFULLY INFLUENCING ACTION OF COURT
38	DUTIES OF TRIAL COUNSEL AND DEFENSE COUNSEL
39	SESSIONS
40	CONTINUENCES
41	CHALLENGES
42	OATHS
43	STATUTE OF LIMITATIONS
44	FORMER JEOPARDY
45	PLEAS OF THE ACCUSED
46	OPPORTUNITY TO OBTAIN WITNESSES & OTHER EVIDENCE
47	REFUSAL TO APPEAR OR TESTIFY
48	CONTEMPTS
49	DEPOSITIONS
50	ADMISSABILITY OF RECORDS OF COURTS OF INQUIRY
50a	DEFENSE OF LACK OF MENTAL RESPONSIBILITY
51	VOTING & RULINGS
52	NUMBER OF VOTES REQUIRED
53	COURT TO ANNOUNCE ACTION
54	RECORD OF TRIAL

SENTENCES

ARTICLE	SUBJECT
55	CRUEL AND UNUSUAL PUNISHMENTS PROHIBITED
56	MAXIMUM LIMITS
57	EFFECTIVE DATE OF SENTENCES
58	EXECUTION OF CONFINEMENT
58a	SENTENCES: reduction in enlisted grade upon approval

POST-TRIAL PROCEDURE AND REVIEW OF COURTS-MARTIAL

ARTICLE	SUBJECT
59	ERROR OF LAW; lesser included offense
60	ACTION BY THE CONVENING AUTHORITY
61	WAIVER OR WITHDRAWAL OF APPEAL
62	APPEAL BY THE UNITED STATES
63	REHEARINGS
64	REVIEW BY A JUDGE ADVOCATE
65	DISPOSITION OF RECORDS
66	REVIEW BY COURT OF ~~MILITARY REVIEW~~ CRIMINAL APPEALS
67	REVIEW BY COURT OF ~~MILITARY~~ APPEALS FOR THE ARMED FORCES
67a	REVIEW BY THE SUPREME COURT
68	BRANCH OFFICES
69	REVIEW IN THE OFFICE OF THE JUDGE ADVOCATE GENERAL (JAG)
70	APPELLATE COUNSEL
71	EXECUTION OF SENTENCE; SUSPENSION OF SENTENCE
72	VACATION OF SUSPENSION

ARTICLES OF THE UCMJ
MANUAL FOR COURTS-MARTIAL (MCM)

ARTICLE	SUBJECT
73	PETITION FOR A NEW TRIAL
74	REMISSION & SUSPENSION
75	RESTORATION
76	FINALITY OF PROCEEDINGS, FINDINGS, AND SENTENCES
76a	LEAVE REQUIRED TO BE TAKEN PENDING REVIEW OF CERTAIN COURT-MARTIAL CONVICTIONS

PUNITIVE ~~PROVISIONS~~ ARTICLES

ARTICLE	SUBJECT
77	PRINCIPALS
78	ACCESSORY AFTER THE FACT
79	CONVICTION OF LESSER INCLUDED OFFENSE
80	ATTEMPTS
81	CONSPIRACY
82	SOLICITATION
83	FRAUDULENT ENLISTMENT, APPOINTMENT OR SEPARATION
84	UNLAWFUL ENLISTMENT, APPOINTMENT, OR SEPARATION
85	DESERTION
86	AWOL
87	MISSING MOVEMENT
88	CONTEMPT TOWARD OFFICIALS
89	DISRESPECT TOWARD A SUPERIOR COMMISSIONED OFFICER
90	ASSAULTING OR WILLFULLY DISOBEYING SUPERIOR COMMISSIONED OFFICER
91	INSUBORDINATE CONDUCT TOWARD WARRANT OFFICER, NONCOMMISSIONED OFFICER, OR PETTY OFFICER
92	FAILURE TO OBEY ORDER OR REGULATION
93	CRUELTY AND MALTREATMENT
94	MUTINY AND SEDITION
95	RESISTANCE, BREACH OF ARREST, AND ESCAPE
96	RELEASING PRISONER WITHOUT PROPER AUTHORITY
97	UNLAWFUL DETENTION
98	NONCOMPLIANCE WITH PROCEDURAL RULES
99	MISBEHAVIOR BEFORE THE ENEMY
100	SUBORDINATE COMPELLING SURRENDER
101	IMPROPER USE OF COUNTERSIGN
102	FORCING A SAFEGUARD
103	CAPTURED OR ABANDONED PROPERTY
104	AIDING THE ENEMY
105	MISCONDUCT AS A PRISONER
106	SPIES
106a	ESPIONAGE
107	FALSE OFFICIAL STATEMENTS
108	MILITARY PROPERTY OF THE UNITED STATES - loss, damage, destruction, or wrongful disposition
109	PROPERTY OTHER THAN MILITARY PROPERTY OF THE UNITED STATES - waste, spoilage, or destruction
110	IMPROPER HAZARDING OF VESSEL
111	DRUNKEN OR RECKLESS OPERATION OF A VEHICLE, ACFT, OR VESSEL
112	DRUNK ON DUTY
112a	WRONGFUL USE, POSSESSION, etc, OF CONTROLLED

ARTICLES OF THE UCMJ
MANUAL FOR COURTS-MARTIAL (MCM)

ARTICLE	SUBJECT
	SUBSTANCES
113	MISBEHAVIOR OF SENTINEL
114	DUELING
115	MALINGERING
116	RIOT OR BREACH OF PEACE
117	PROVOKING SPEECHES OR GESTURES
118	MURDER
119	MANSLAUGHTER
120	RAPE AND CARNAL KNOWLEDGE
121	LARCENY AND WRONGFUL APPROPRIATION
122	ROBBERY
123	FORGERY
123a	MAKING, DRAWING, OR UTTERING CHECK, DRAFT, OR ORDER WITHOUT SUFFICIENT FUNDS
124	MAIMING
125	SODOMY
126	ARSON
127	EXTORTION
128	ASSAULT
129	BURGLARY
130	HOUSEBREAKING
131	PERJURY
132	FRAUDS AGAINST THE UNITED STATES
133	CONDUCT UNBECOMING AN OFFICER AND A GENTLEMAN
134	GENERAL ARTICLE

MISC PROVISIONS

ARTICLE	SUBJECT
135	COURTS OF INQUIRY
136	AUTHORITY TO ADMINISTER OATHS AND TO ACT AS NOTARY
137	ARTICLES TO BE EXPLAINED
138	COMPLAINTS OF WRONGS
139	REDRESS OF ~~INQUIRIES~~ INJURIES TO PROPERTY
140	DELEGATION BY THE PRESIDENT

COURT OF APPEALS FOR THE ARMED FORCES

ARTICLE	SUBJECT
141	STATUS
142	JUDGES
143	ORGANIZATION AND EMPLOYEES
144	PROCEDURE
145	ANNUITIES FOR JUDGES AND SURVIVORS
146	CODE COMMITTEE

ARTICLES OF THE UCMJ
MANUAL FOR COURTS-MARTIAL (MCM)

ARTICLE	SUBJECT

Article 134 of the UCMJ may include the following:

- abusing public animal
- adultery
- assault (indecent)
- assault (with intent to commit murder, voluntary manslaughter, rape, robbery, sodomy, burglary, or housebreaking)
- bigamy
- bribery and graft
- burning with intent to defraud
- offenses against correctional custody
- worthless checks
- wrongful cohabitation
- failing to pay debts
- disloyal statements
- disorderly conduct
- drunkenness
- false or unauthorized pass offenses
- false pretenses
- false swearing
- discharging firearm through negligence
- willfully discharging firearm (under such circumstances as to endanger human life)
- fleeing scene of an accident
- fraternization
- gambling with subordinate
- negligent homicide
- impersonating officers, NCO
- indecent acts or liberties with child
- indecent exposure
- indecent language
- indecent acts with another
- abuses of mail system
- obstructing justice
- pandering/prostitution
- breaking restriction
- knowingly receiving, buying, or concealing stolen property
- straggling
- threat or hoax
- communicating a threat
- unlawful entry
- carrying concealed weapon
- wearing unauthorized insignia, decoration, badge, ribbon, device, or lapel button
- jumping from a vessel into the water
- kidnapping
- wrongful interference with an adverse administrative proceeding
- perjury
- breaking quarantine (knowingly)
- requesting or soliciting another to commit an offense
- self-injury (without intent to avoid service)

REFERENCES

Chain of Command

AR 600-20.."ARMY COMMAND POLICY", 30 MAR 88 (w/interim change #I04, dtd 17 SEP 93), HQDA

Code of Conduct/Geneva Convention/Law of Land Warfare

AR 350-30.."CODE OF CONDUCT/SERE", 10 DEC 85, HQDA
FM 27-2...."YOUR CONDUCT IN COMBAT UNDER THE LAW OF WAR", 23 NOV 84, HQDA
FM 27-10..."THE LAW OF LAND WARFARE", 18 JUL 56 (w/change 1, 15 JUL 76), HQDA
STP 21-1-SMCT..."SOLDIER'S MANUAL OF COMMON TASKS," 1 OCT 94, HQDA

Guard Duty

FM 22-6...."GUARD DUTY", 17 SEP 71 (w/change 1, 15 JAN 75), HQDA

Physical Security

FM 19-30..."PHYSICAL SECURITY", 01 MAR 79, HQDA
AR 190-13.."THE ARMY PHYSICAL SECURITY PROGRAM", 30 SEP 93, HQDA

First Aid

FM 21-11..."FIRST AID FOR SOLDIERS", 27 OCT 88 (change 1, 28 AUG 89; change 2, 4 DEC 91), HQDA
STP 21-1-SMCT..."SOLDIER'S MANUAL OF COMMON TASKS," 1 OCT 94, HQDA

Field Sanitation

FM 21-10..."FIELD HYGIENE AND SANITATION", 22 NOV 88, HQDA
FM 21-10-1."UNIT FIELD SANITATION TEAM", 11 OCT 89, HQDA

Map Reading and Land Navigation

FM 21-26..."MAP READING AND LAND NAVIGATION", 7 MAY 93, HQDA

M16A1 and M16A2 Rifle Marksmanship

FM 23-9...."M16A1 AND M16A2 RIFLE MARKSMANSHIP", 03 JUL 89, HQDA
TM 9-1005-249-10, 11 FEB 85 (change 1, 9 DEC 87; change 2, 11 MAY 90), HQDA
TM 9-1005-319-10 (w/ch 1-3), AUG 86, HQDA
STP 21-1-SMCT..."SOLDIER'S MANUAL OF COMMON TASKS," 1 OCT 94, HQDA

M203 Grenade Launcher

FM 23-31..."40-MM GRENADE LAUNCHER, M-203", 20 SEP 94 (incl change 1), HQDA

M60 Machinegun, 7.62-mm

FM 23-67..."MACHINEGUN, 7.62-mm, M60", 29 FEB 84 (w/change 1, 17 MAR 87), HQDA
TM 9-1005-224-10, 30 JUL 85 (change 1, 9 DEC 87), HQDA
STP 21-1-SMCT..."SOLDIER'S MANUAL OF COMMON TASKS," 1 OCT 94, HQDA

Grenades

FM 23-30..."GRENADES AND PYROTECHNIC SIGNALS", 27 DEC 88, HQDA
STP 21-1-SMCT..."SOLDIER'S MANUAL OF COMMON TASKS," 1 OCT 94, HQDA

M18A1 Antipersonnel mine, Claymore

FM 23-23..."ANTIPERSONNEL MINE, M18A1 CLAYMORE", 6 JAN 66 (change 1, 17 DEC 68; change 2 - 30 MAR 73), HQDA
STP 21-1-SMCT..."SOLDIER'S MANUAL OF COMMON TASKS," 1 OCT 94, HQDA

REFERENCES

Light Antiarmor Weapons (M72-series LAW/M136 AT-4)

FM 23-25..."LIGHT ANTIARMOR WEAPONS", 17 AUG 94, HQDA

NBC

FM 3-3....."CHEMICAL AND BIOLOGICAL CONTAMINATION AVOIDANCE", 16 NOV 92 (change 1, 29 SEP 94), HQDA
FM 3-3-1..."NUCLEAR CONTAMINATION AVOIDANCE", 9 SEP 94, HQDA
FM 3-4....."NBC PROTECTION", 29 MAY 92 (w/change 1, 28 OCT 92), HQDA
FM 3-5....."NBC DECONTAMINATION", 17 NOV 93, HQDA
FM 3-7....."NBC HANDBOOK", 29 SEP 94, HQDA
FM 3-100..."NBC OPERATIONS", 23 MAY 91, HQDA
STP 21-1-SMCT..."SOLDIER'S MANUAL OF COMMON TASKS," 1 OCT 94, HQDA

Communications

FM 24-1...."COMBAT COMMUNICATIONS", 15 OCT 90, HQDA
FM 24-18..."TACTICAL SINGLE-CHANNEL RADIO COMMUNICATIONS TECHNIQUES", 30 SEP 87, HQDA
STP 21-1-SMCT..."SOLDIER'S MANUAL OF COMMON TASKS," 1 OCT 94, HQDA
Student Handout for SINCGARS, FEB 93, USAAVNC/DOTD (reviewed for OPSEC considerations)

Physical Fitness Training

FM 21-20..."PHYSICAL FITNESS TRAINING", 30 SEP 92, HQDA
AR 350-15.."THE ARMY PHYSICAL FITNESS PROGRAM", 3 NOV 89, HQDA

Weight Control

AR 600-9..."THE ARMY WEIGHT CONTROL PROGRAM", 1 SEP 86 (change 1, 13 FEB 87; change 2, 10 JUN 87), ALL RANKS UPDATE 15, and Interim Change #I01, dtd 4 MAR 94, HQDA

Military Leadership

FM 22-100.."MILITARY LEADERSHIP", 31 JUL 90, HQDA

Leadership Counseling

FM 22-101.."LEADERSHIP COUNSELING", 03 JUN 85, HQDA

Soldier Team Development

FM 22-102.."SOLDIER-TEAM DEVELOPMENT", 02 MAR 87, HQDA

Training the Force

FM 25-100.."TRAINING THE FORCE", 15 NOV 88, HQDA

Battle Focused Training

FM 25-101.."BATTLE FOCUSED TRAINING", 30 SEP 90, HQDA

Uniforms and Insignia

AR 670-1..."WEAR AND APPEARANCE OF ARMY UNIFORMS AND INSIGNIA", 1 SEP 92, HQDA

Awards and Decorations

AR 672-5-1."MILITARY AWARDS", 12 APR 84 (w/changes 1-15), ALL RANKS UPDATE 15, 01 OCT 90, HQDA

Military Justice, UCMJ

AR 27-10..."MILITARY JUSTICE", 08 AUG 94, UPDATE 16 DEC 94, HQDA

REFERENCES

Drill and Ceremonies

FM 22-5...."DRILL AND CEREMONIES", 08 DEC 86, HQDA

Flags and Guidons

AR 840-10.."FLAGS, GUIDONS, STREAMERS, TABARDS, AND AUTOMOBILE AND AIRCRAFT PLATES", 29 OCT 90, HQDA

Military Customs and Courtesies

FM 22-5...."DRILL AND CEREMONIES", 08 DEC 86, HQDA
AR 600-25.."SALUTES, HONORS, AND VISITS OF COURTESY", 16 MAY 70 (w/changes 1-9), 01 OCT 83, HQDA

Enlisted Personnel Management System

AR 600-200."ENLISTED PERSONNEL MANAGEMENT SYSTEM", 05 JUL 84 (w/changes 1-15), ENLISTED RANKS UPDATE 16, 10 OCT 90, HQDA

NCOERs/Separations

DA Cir 623-88-1, HQDA
AR 635-200."ENLISTED PERSONNEL", 05 JUL 84 (w/changes 1-14), ENLISTED RANKS UPDATE 16, 10 OCT 90; interim changes dtd 11 JUN 93 and 30 NOV 94, HQDA

Maintenance Procedures

DA PAM 738-750."THE ARMY MAINTENANCE MANAGEMENT SYSTEM (TAMMS)", 21 SEP 91, MM UPDATE 13, 27 SEP 91, HQDA
AR 750-1......."ARMY MATERIEL MAINTENANCE POLICIES", 01 AUG 94, MM UPDATE 13, 27 SEP 91, HQDA
DA PAM 750-35.."FUNCTIONAL USER'S GUIDE FOR MOTOR POOL OPERATIONS", 27 SEP 91 (w/ch 1), MM UPDATE 13, 27 SEP 91, HQDA
TM 9-2320-289-10, 04 JUL 86 (w/changes 1-5), 01 MAY 92, HQDA
TM 9-2320-280-10, 18 JUN 91 (w/change 3), (changes 4/5, 16 FEB 94), HQDA

Military Programs

AR 608-1..."ARMY COMMUNITY SERVICES", 30 OCT 90, (w/interim changes dtd 11 JUN 93 and 17 FEB 95), HQDA
AR 621-5..."THE ARMY CONTINUING EDUCATION SYSTEM", UPDATE - 17 NOV 93, HQDA
AR 930-4..."ARMY EMERGENCY RELIEF", 04 SEP 92 (chg 1, 30 AUG 94), HQDA
AR 930-5..."AMERICAN RED CROSS", 16 NOV 69, (chg 1, 15 DEC 70; chg 2, 23 APR 71; chg 3, 24 MAY 73), HQDA
AR 600-85.."ALCOHOL AND DRUG ABUSE PREVENTION AND CONTROL PROGRAM", 03 NOV 86 (w/ch 1, 21 OCT 88; UPDATE - 01 OCT 903), HQDA
AR 385-10.."THE ARMY SAFETY PROGRAM", 23 MAY 88, HQDA
AR 600-20.."ARMY COMMAND POLICY (Army Equal Opportunity Program)", 30 MAR 88 (w/interim change #IO4 dtd 17 SEP 93), HQDA
AR 612-10.."REASSIGNMENT PROCESSING AND ARMY SPONSORSHIP AND ORIENTATION PROGRAM", 01 AUG 81 (w/chg 1, 15 JUN 84), HQDA
AR 601-280."TOTAL ARMY RETENTION PROGRAM", 05 JUL 84 (w/changes 1-15); ENLISTED RANKS UPDATE 16, 10 OCT 90, HQDA
AR 350-17.."THE NONCOMMISSIONED OFFICER DEVELOPMENT PROGRAM", 31 MAY 91, HQDA

The Sergeant Morales Board

USAREUR Reg 600-2.."LEADERSHIP - USAREUR SERGEANT MORALES CLUB", 13 NOV 86 (w/ch 1-3 and supplements), HQUSAREUR

REFERENCES

The Sergeant Audie Murphy Board
FORSCOM Cir 215-91-10

Comparative Ranks
AR 600-20.."ARMY COMMAND POLICY", 30 MAR 88 (w/interim change #IO4 dtd 17 SEP 93), HQDA

Creed of the Noncommissioned Officer
TC 22-6...."THE ARMY NONCOMMISSIONED OFFICER'S GUIDE", 23 NOV 90, HQDA

Army Publications
DA Pam 25-30 (CD-ROM), 01 JUL 95, HQDA

Forms & Records
DA Pam 25-30 (CD-ROM), 01 JUL 95, HQDA

Abbreviations
AR 310-50.."AUTHORIZED ABBREVIATIONS, BREVITY CODES, AND ACRONYMS", 15 NOV 85, HQDA

Articles of the UCMJ
"MANUAL FOR COURTS-MARTIAL, UNITED STATES", 1995 Edition, HQDA

COMMENTS/CORRECTIONS

It is my intention that "The Soldier's Comprehensive Study Manual" be as complete and up-to-date as possible. I realize however that in compiling a book with such a diversity of subject areas mistakes can and will be made. Although this edition has been revised considerably since the previous edition, there may still be information that has changed without my knowledge.

I believe this study manual to be one of the most comprehensive, as well as one of the most current, available. I welcome professional comments and/or suggestions for a better study guide. If you would like to recommend changes/corrections, please use the following format:

(1) Name

(2) Unit/Address

(3) Subject area concerned/page (in study manual)

(4) Question/Answer as it appears in this study manual

(5) Question/Answer as it should appear

(6) Reference source for correction (incl page & paragraph)

(7) Additional comments

Send correspondence in care of the following:

Bagwell & Associates
329 N. Dogwood Rd
Powell, TN 37849

All correspondence will receive a reply.

Thank You!

BAGWELL & ASSOCIATES
329 NORTH DOGWOOD ROAD
POWELL, TN 37849

Please send me __________ copies of:
The Soldier's Comprehensive Study Manual, 6th Edition
by D.W. Creech

Enclosed is a check or money order in the amount of
$29.95 per copy
(Price includes tax, shipping, and handling)

Address to be shipped to:

____

____

____

____

Amount Enclosed: $______________
Make payable to: Bagwell & Associates

** Please allow 4-6 weeks for delivery **

BAGWELL & ASSOCIATES
329 NORTH DOGWOOD ROAD
POWELL, TN 37849

Please send me __________ copies of:
The Soldier's Comprehensive Study Manual, 6th Edition
by D.W. Creech

Enclosed is a check or money order in the amount of
$29.95 per copy
(Price includes tax, shipping, and handling)

Address to be shipped to:

____

____

____

____

Amount Enclosed: $______________
Make payable to: Bagwell & Associates

** Please allow 4-6 weeks for delivery **